·Possible Lives·

·Possible Lives·

Authors and Saints in Renaissance Italy

ALISON KNOWLES FRAZIER

Columbia University Press • New York

Columbia University Press
Publishers Since 1893
New York   Chichester, West Sussex
Copyright © 2005 Columbia University Press
All rights reserved

Columbia University Press expresses appreciation for
a University Cooperative Society Subvention Grant
awarded by the University of Texas at Austin that
helped with publication.

Columbia University Press also expresses appreciation
for a grant from the Gladys Krieble Delmas Foundation
to assist with the production of this book.

Library of Congress Cataloging-in-Publication Data
Frazier, Alison Knowles
    Possible lives : authors and saints in Renaissance Italy /
Alison Knowles Frazier.
        p. cm.
    Includes bibliographical references and index.
    ISBN 0-231-12976-9 (cloth : alk. paper)
        1. Christian hagiography—history—To 1500.
        2. Christian literature, Latin (Medieval and
    modern)—Italy—History and criticism. 3. Renaissance—
Italy. I. Title.

BX4662.F74   2004
235'.2'094509024—dc22   2004050215

∞
Columbia University Press books are printed
on permanent and durable acid-free paper.
Printed in the United States of America
c 10 9 8 7 6 5 4 3 2 1

for
Dorothy and Ray,
and
Rufus and Helen,
with love

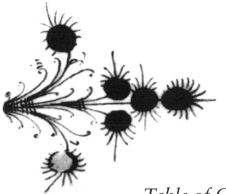

Table of Contents

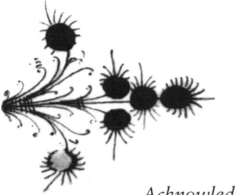

Acknowledgments

Possible Lives began with a visit, more than a decade ago, to the Manhattan apartment of Paul Oskar Kristeller. As we sat at a small table, surrounded by books and papers and card files, Kristeller described from memory more than a dozen manuscripts and *fonds* that I should examine and suggested connections between certain authors. Keep a card file, he urged, and cross-reference everything. Kristeller then dropped the bombshell: he had recorded writings about saints in the course of assembling the *Iter Italicum* but had not been consistent in his attention to this literature. In consequence, he explained, I should repeat his *dépouillement* of catalogs. My heart sank; anyone who has consulted Kristeller's *Latin Manuscript Books* will know why. It seemed to me that I could write a dissertation or I could undertake to repeat his life's work for hagiography in manuscript and early printed sources, but—even supported by the Bollandists' catalogs—I could not do both. To calm my anxiety, I focused on taking notes. Kristeller's eyebrows rose as I began: the writing implement to hand in my bag was a pen with green ink.

Those mortifyingly green notes traveled with me for years, a practical reminder of tasks and a conceptual map. I'd long since transferred their contents to index cards and then to computer files, but a talismanic quality now attached to them. They reminded me of the elderly scholar, of his enthusiasm for the project of collecting and analyzing the fifteenth-century humanists' lives of the saints. By virtue of his attention to the *vitae sanctorum* by these authors, Kristeller was unusual. But he was almost unique in his attention to their engagement with a chronological range of saints and in his refusal to dispense with even the most derivative of their contributions. All would be evidence for the reassembly of a forgotten moment in the cult of the saints and in the history of the *studia humanitatis*.

That visit was the only time Kristeller and I talked face to face about the topic of humanist hagiography. It was easy to convince myself not to bother him: he had the magnum opus of the *Iter Italicum* under way and was helping many scholars around the world with their projects. Years later, when Kristeller published his article on humanist sources for the supposed child martyr Simon of Trent—surely a model of what he expected from me—he sent a copy. I was surprised and gratified and chastened. We had not been in touch. But the gift of the offprint and the little note that accompanied it showed that he had greater confidence in the significance of the undertaking than I.

This study falls far from what Kristeller would have wished. It incorporates conceptual positions for which he had little patience and does not—could not possibly—represent the thorough *dépouillement* he suggested. But it does attempt to answer wholeheartedly his faith in the multifarious reality of the intellectual moment of humanist hagiography.

If Kristeller is the distant deity of this study, John Monfasani, Eugene F. Rice Jr., and Caroline Walker Bynum are its godparents. To John I owe my first steps in the technical training that lies behind *Possible Lives*; I hope that the book does not embarrass him. John has read more shaky first and second drafts than anyone, and I thank him for his early encouragement and reliable support.

Gene was still collecting accolades for *Saint Jerome in the Renaissance* when I arrived at Columbia University. In the wake of that elegant study, of Donald Weinstein and Rudolph Bell's innovative *Saints and Society*, and of André Vauchez's magisterial *La Sainteté en Occident*, it was not surprising that he sent me off to investigate humanist participation in the cult of the saints. *Saint Jerome*, however, set me a problem, for it forced me to confront the *bivia*: how could I answer, on one hand, Kristeller's desire for compendiousness and breadth and, on the other, Gene's exemplary close study of humanists' responses to one saint?

Caroline Bynum began to shape this study in the course of a year-long seminar on hagiography; I am grateful for her insightful and enthusiastic responses to dissertation chapters and then to book drafts. In a series of conversations, she encouraged me to face the problem of structuring *Possible Lives*. The answer, I gradually decided, was to embrace the contrast of historiographical styles represented by the work of my two constant mentors, Caroline and John. As a result, the chapters that follow might be described as a social history of intellectuals: they are designed to capture the sheer inventiveness with which humans make and respond to their religious environments and to document in detail the contribution of the *studia humanitatis*. Such an encounter between what is usually treated as elite history and what is usually treated as popular history is relatively unusual. If it succeeds here, that is in large part due to what I have learned from Caroline.

My third great debt is to librarians. At my home institution, the University of Texas at Austin, the interlibrary loan department headed by Wendy Nesmith, the bibliographers for history and religion, Gera Draaijer and Shiela Winchester, and the rare book librarians of the Harry Ransom Research Center have helped with innumerable requests. The Vatican Microfilm Archive at St. Louis University has been an indispensable support for a scholar so far from Italy. Abroad, I was received kindly by librarians and archivists who arranged lighting, described archival organization and bureaucratic procedures, sorted out confusing shelf marks, and made time and space for me when seats were full. I especially thank the staffs at the American Academy in Rome, directed by Christina Huemer; the Biblioteca Apostolica Vaticana; the Bibliothèque nationale and the library of Ste. Geneviève in Paris; the British Library and the John Rylands Library; and the staffs of *archivi, biblioteche nazionale, comunali, episcopali,* and *del seminario* in Belluno, Bergamo, Bologna, Brescia, Florence, Mantua, Milan, Naples, Padua, Palermo, Rome, Udine, Venice, Vicenza, and Volterra.

The cheeriest part of book writing is the sustaining goodwill and interest of colleagues and friends. Here in Austin I have been especially fortunate to share ideas and drafts with Susan Boettcher, Caroline Castiglione, Jennifer Ebbeler, Julie Hardwick, David Hunter, Lisa Kallett, Ernie Kaulbach, Janet Meisel, Chela Metzger, Howard Miller, Timothy Moore, Martha Newman, Guy Raffa, Jeffrey Chipps Smith, Denise Spellberg, Cynthia Talbot, Mauricio Tenorio, Louis Waldman, Michael Winship, and Dolora Wojciehowski, as well as former colleagues Zilla Goodman, Anne MacNeil, and Ann Ramsey. At the American Academy in Rome, conversations with a formidable and diverse group of classicists shaped the dissertation revisions: I warmly thank Shane Butler, Nicholas Horsfall, G. N. Knauer, and acknowledge with warm regret the late Steven Lowenstam. Ray Clemens, Arnaldo Ganda, and Paul Gehl read early versions of chapter 3, making exceptionally helpful observations. Paul Needham's close attention to that chapter saved me from many errors. Martin Camargo and Marjorie Curry Woods helped me learn what I needed to know for chapter 4, as did Andrea Tilatti for chapter 5. I also thank scholars and friends who generously lent microfilm or helped with photocopying, above all Nelson Minnich. The misapprehensions and errors that remain are the result of my own stubbornness or inattention.

Several institutions funded this project at crucial stages. While I was a graduate student, Columbia University underwrote preliminary research. The completion of the dissertation was made possible by a grant from the Newcombe Foundation, and then the American Academy in Rome provided a precious year of postdoctoral research. Opportune grants for travel and research came from the American Bibliographical Association, the Delmas Foundation, and the Newberry Library. The University of Texas at Austin funded summer travel and supplemented my year at the American Academy. For their decision to risk limited resources on an untried scholar, I am deeply grateful to all these institutions.

The past months of book production have also taught me the gratitude that authors owe editors. Wendy Lochner and especially Anne McCoy have been patient and impatient, scolding and encouraging, in doses appropriate to the nervous author of a complicated production that has taxed two copyeditors. My deep thanks to both of them and to the regents of Columbia University Press, for supporting a project that was about saints but not the vernacular, about humanists but not the classics.

My family and close friends offered their love, patience, and humor through the many years of research and writing. This possible life I owe to them.

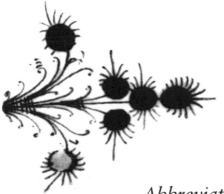

Abbreviations

AA	*Analecta Augustiniana*
AASS	*Acta sanctorum quotquot tota orbe coluntur.* 1st ed., Antwerp and Brussels, 1643–1748; 2d ed., Venice, 1734–1770; 3d ed. Paris and Rome, 1863– .
AB	*Analecta bollandiana*
AFH	*Archivum franciscanum historicum*
AFP	*Archivum fratrum praedicatorum*
AS	Archivio di Stato
ASI	*Archivio storico italiano*
ASM	Archivio di Stato, Milan
BAV	Biblioteca apostolica vaticana
BBU	Bologna, Biblioteca universitaria
BC	Biblioteca communale
BEFR	Bibliothèque de l'École française de Rome
BHG	*Bibliotheca hagiographica graeca antiquae et mediae aetatis.* 3d ed. Rev. and updated, ed. François Halkin, Brussels, 1957. Repr. 1986.
BHL	*Bibliotheca hagiographica latina antiquae et mediae aetatis.* Ed. Bollandist Society. Orig. 2 vols., Brussels, 1898 and 1899. Repr., Brussels, 1949 and 1992. New supp., ed. Henri Fros, Brussels: Société des Bollandistes, 1986.

BMC	*Catalogue of Books Printed in the Fifteenth Century, Now in the British Museum.* 12 vols. London, 1908–1985.
BN/NB	Biblioteca nazionale; Bibliothèque nationale; Nationalbibliothek
BS	*Bibliotheca sanctorum.* 14 vols. Rome: Istituto Giovanni XXIII, 1961–1970. With appendix, 1986.
BU	Biblioteca universitaria
C	Copinger, W. A. *Supplement to Hain's Repertorium Bibliographicum.* 2 vols. London, 1895–1902.
c.d.	canonization date
Cochrane, Historians	Cochrane, Eric. *Historians and Historiography in the Italian Renaissance.* Chicago: University of Chicago Press, 1981.
Cosenza, Dictionary	Cosenza, Mario. *Biographical and Bibliographical Dictionary of the Italian Humanists.* 2d ed., 6 vols., Boston, 1962–1967.
DBI	*Dizionario biografico degli Italiani.* Rome, 1960– .
Degli Agostini, Notizie	Degli Agostini, Giovanni. *Notizie istorico-critiche intorno la vita e le opere degli scrittori viniziani.* 2 vols. 1752. Repr., Bologna: Forni, 1975.
DHGE	*Dictionnaire d'histoire et de géographie ecclésiastiques.* Paris, 1912–1995.
DIP	*Dizionario degli istituti di perfezione.* Rome: Edizione Paoline, 1974–1997.
DS	*Dictionnaire de spiritualité.* Paris, 1937– .
FBNC	Florence, Biblioteca nazionale centrale
f.d.	feast date
Fonctions	*Les fonctions des saints dans le monde occidental (IIIe–XIIIe siècle). Actes du colloque organisé par l' École française de Rome avec le concours de l'Université de Rome "La Sapienza." Rome, 27–29 octobre 1988.* Rome: École française de Rome, 1991.
Frati, "Indice"	Ludovico Frati, "Indice dei codici latini conservati nella R. Biblioteca Universitaria di Bologna." *Studi italiani di filologia classica* 16–17 (1908–1909).
Ganda, I primordi	Ganda, A. *I primordi della tipografia milanese.* Florence: Olschki, 1984.
GLS	*Il Grande Libro dei Santi.* Ed. C. Leonardi, G. Zarri, Elio Guerriero, Tonino Toniz, Claudio Leonardi,

Andrea Riccardi, Gabriella Zarri. 3 vols. Turin: San
Paolo, 1998.

Goff Goff, F. R. *Incunabula in American Libraries: A
Third Census.* New York, 1964.

GSLI *Giornale storico della letteratura italiana*

GW *Gesamtkatalog der Wiegendrucke.* Vols. 1–7, Leipzig
1925–1940. Vols. 7–9, Stuttgart, 1972–1985.

H Hain, Ludwig. *Repertorium bibliographicum.* 4 vols.
Stuttgart, 1826–1838.

HC Copinger, W. A. *Supplement to Hain's* Repertorium
Bibliographicum. 2 vols. London, 1895–1902.

IERS *Indice delle edizioni romane a stampa (1467–1500).*
Ed. P. Casciano, G. Castoldi, M. P. Criteli, G. Curcio,
P. Farenga, A. Modigliani. In C. Bianca, P. Casciano,
Scuola vaticana di paleografia, diplomatica e archivis-
tica, eds., *Scrittura, biblioteche e stampa a Roma nel
Quattrocento: Aspetti e problemi. Atti del seminario
1–2 giugno 1979.* Vatican City, 1980, vol. II.

IGI *Indice generale degli incunaboli delle Biblioteche d'I-
talia.* 6 vols. Rome, 1943–1981.

IMH *Italia medioevale et humanistica*

JMRS *Journal of Medieval and Renaissance Studies*

Kaeppeli,
Scriptores Kaeppeli, Tommaso. *Scriptores Ordinis Praedicatorum Medii Aevi.* Rome, 1970–1993.

Kelly, *ODP* Kelly, J. N. D. *Oxford Dictionary of the Popes.* New
York: Oxford University Press, 1986.

Kristeller,
"Contribution" Kristeller, P. O. "The Contribution of the Religious
Orders to Renaissance Thought and Learning."
American Benedictine Review 21 (1970): 1–55.
Reprinted in P. O. Kristeller, *Medieval Aspects of
Renaissance Learning,* 95–163. Durham N.C., 1974;
reprint, New York, 1992.

Kristeller, *Iter* Kristeller, P. O. *Iter Italicum: A Finding List of
Uncatalogued or Incompletely Catalogued Humanis-
tic Manuscripts of the Renaissance in Italian and
Other Libraries.* 6 vols. London: Warburg Institute,
1963–1992.

LA Jacobus de Voragine. *Legenda Aurea.* Ed. G. P. Maggioni. 2d ed. Milan, 1998.

Lind, *Letters* Lind, Levi R. *The Letters of Giovanni Garzoni,
Bolognese Humanist and Physician (1419
[sic]–1505).* Atlanta: Scholar's, 1992.

LTK	*Lexikon für Theologie und Kirche.* Freiburg, 1937– .
Mazzatinti, *Inventari*	Mazzatinti, Giuseppe, et alii. *Inventari dei mano-scritti delle biblioteche d'Italia.* Multiple volumes. Florence, 1890– .
Mazzucchelli, *Scrittori*	Mazzucchelli, Giammaria. *Gli scrittori d'Italia cioè notizie storiche e critiche intorno alle vite e agli scritti dei letterati italiani.* 2 vols. Brescia, 1753.
MBA	Milan, Biblioteca Ambrosiana
MD	*Memorie domenicane*
MEFR	*Mélanges de l'École française de Rome*
MGH	*Monumenta Germaniae Historica*
MOSSM	*Monumenta ordinis servorum Mariae*
MRTS	Medieval and Renaissance Text Society
O'Malley, *Praise*	O'Malley, John W. *Praise and Blame in Renaissance Rome: Rhetoric, Doctrine, and Reform in the Sacred Orators of the Papal Court, c. 1450–1521.* Durham, N.C.: Duke University Press, 1979.
Pastor, *History*	Pastor, Ludwig. *The History of the Popes from the Close of the Middle Ages.* Ed. F. I. Antrobus and R. F. Kerr. St. Louis, Mo., 1898–1953.
Pellechet Polain	M. L. C. Pellechet and M-L Polain. *Catalogue général des incunables des bibliothèques publiques de France.* 3 vols. Paris, Picard et fils, 1897–1907.
PL, PG	Migne, Jacques Paul. *Patrologia cursus completus. Series latina,* 221 vols. Paris, 1844–1864. *Series graeca,* 161 vols. Paris, 1857–1864.
Polain, *Catalogue*	M-L Polain. *Catalogue des livres imprimées au quinzième siècle des bibliothèques de Belgique.* 5 vols. Brussels: 1932–1978.
Poncelet 1909	Poncelet, A. *Catalogus codicum hagiographicorum latinorum bibliothecarum romanarum praeter quam Vaticanae.* Brussels: Société des Bollandistes, 1909.
Poncelet 1910	Poncelet, A. *Catalogus codicum hagiographicorum latinorum Bibliothecae Vaticanae.* Brussels: Société des Bollandistes, 1910.
Poncelet 1924	Poncelet, A. "Catalogus Codicum Hagiographicorum Latinorum Bibliothecae Universitatis Bononiensis." *AB* 42 (1924): 321–370.
QFIAB	*Quellen und Forschungen aus italienischen Archiven und Bibliotheken*

R   Reichling, D. *Appendices ad Hainii-Copingeri reper-*
                           torium bibliographicum: Additiones et emendationes.
                           6 vols. 1905–1911. Supp., 1914.

Rogledi Manni,
Tipografia   Rogledi Manni, Teresa. *La tipografia a Milano nel*
                           XV secolo. Florence: Olschki, 1980.

RQ   *Renaissance Quarterly*

RRIISS   *Rerum italicarum scriptores*

RSCI   *Rivista di storia della chiesa in Italia*

Sabbadini,
Epistolario   Sabbadini, Remigio. *Epistolario di Guarino*
                           Veronese. 3 vols. Venice, 1915, 1916, 1919.

Schutte, *PIVRB*   Schutte, A. J. *Printed Italian Vernacular Religious*
                           Books, 1465–1550. Geneva: Droz, 1983.

SH   Vincent of Beauvais. *Bibliotheca mundi seu speculi*
                           maioris. Vol. 4, *Speculum historiale.* Douai: Baltazar
                           Bellerus, 1624. Anastatic reprint, Graz, 1965. (N.B.:
                           The book and chapter divisions of this edition do not
                           correspond to those given in the *BHL*.)

SIFC   *Studi italiani di filologia classica*

SMHM   Dubois, Jacques and Jean-Loup Lemaitre. *Sources et*
                           méthodes de l'hagiographie médiévale. Paris: Cerf,
                           1993.

Ughelli,
Italia Sacra   Ughelli, Ferdinano. *Italia sacra.* 10 vols. Venice,
                           1717–1722. Repr., Sala Bolognese: Forni,
                           1973–1987.

Vauchez,
La sainteté   Vauchez, André. *La sainteté en occident aux derniers*
                           siècles du Moyen Age d'après les procès de canonisa-
                           tion et les documents hagiographiques. Rome, 1981.

VBG   Volterra, Biblioteca Guarnacciana

VBM   Venice, Biblioteca Marciana

Webb, *Patrons*   Webb, Diana. *Patrons and Defenders: The Saints in*
                           the Italian City-States. London: Tauris, 1996

Zeno,
Dissertazioni   Zeno, Apostolo. *Dissertazioni Vossiane, ossia Giunte*
                           e Osservazioni intorno agli storici italiani che hanno
                           scritto latinamente, rammentati dal Vossio nel III
                           libro de "Historicis Latinis." 2 vols. Venice: Alerizzi,
                           1752–1773.

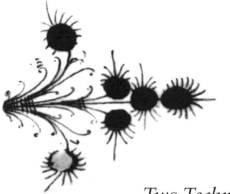

Two Technical Notes

Names of authors and the titles of their writings about saints recur throughout this study. To control the length of footnotes, information about all the humanists' *vitae et passiones sanctorum* (lives and passions of saints) mentioned in the text is placed in a hand list. The list is ordered alphabetically by author's name. Under the author's name, writings are ordered alphabetically by the name of the saint. Insofar as possible, the compositions are dated, dedicatees and circumstances of composition are recorded, the incipit and explicit are given, and manuscripts and early printed editions are listed.

The hand list also identifies texts by the number assigned them by the Bollandists in their hagiographical catalogs, the *Bibliotheca hagiographica latina* and *graeca*. In these reference works, the Bollandists list narratives in alphabetical order by saint, and, under each saint, the narratives are roughly in chronological order: for example, Jerome's life of Hilarion is *BHL* 3879; Flodoard's metric retelling of that account is *BHL* 3880. The *BHL* and *BHG* reference works are indispensable, but they do not catalog everything. Sermons, for example, are not often recorded: Agostino Dati's fifteenth-century sermon/life of Jerome has no number. The *BHL* and *BHG* also do not catalog narratives composed after 1500. Since this study extends into the 1520s, that silence represents a considerable deficit. Texts that have not been assigned numbers by the Bollandists are represented with a dash, as *BHL* —.

EDITORIAL PRINCIPLES

In quoting unedited manuscripts or early printed material, I have modernized punctuation and capitalization and expanded abbreviations. In cases where the manuscript or incunable versions are contemporary with the author, or nearly so, I have retained the orthography, although it may not conform to classical strictures. Translations are my own, with a few clearly identified exceptions.

·Possible Lives·

PLATE 1. Ludovico Foscarini, opening of the passion of Victor and Corona (*Gesta gloriosorum martirum Victoris et Corone*). Baltimore, Walters Art Museum, MS W 393, fol. 68v.

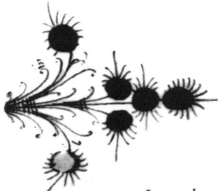

CHAPTER I

Introduction:
Authors, Saints, and Texts

Quidnam igitur humano generi melius, quid utilius dici aut excogitari potest?
quid etiam memoratis dignius mandari litteris? quid, quod magis posteritati con-
sulat, habemus, quam sanctorum doctrinam, institutionem, persecutiones et
miraculas?

What, then, can be thought or declared better or more useful for humankind?
what, indeed, more worthy to record in writing? what do we have more relevant
to posterity, than the teaching, instruction, sufferings, and miracles of the saints?

—Sebastiano Serico, prologue to the life of the Blessed Amato Ronconi (1518)[1]

In the midwinter of 1439, the aspiring historian Tobia
del Borgo wrote a letter to Guarino Guarini, his former teacher. Guarino (1374–1460) encouraged students to keep in touch after they left his school, especially urging them to hone their rhetorical skills by
composing descriptions. The event that Tobia had just
witnessed in Milan certainly deserved a lengthy and—
since a good Renaissance historian was expected to

1. *AASS,* May II (Paris, 1866), 345–351, at 347, col. b, para. 4.

deploy the classics—a densely allusive description.[2] Tobia opened with apologies for not writing more often, but then he got right to work. As he explained to Guarino, it all started with a hunt for manuscripts.[3]

Cardinal Branda da Castiglione spent the days just before Christmas 1438 thoughtfully sifting the contents of the library of St. Thecla in Milan.[4] He was looking for material pertinent to the reunification of the eastern and western churches, for some authoritative text that might help to refute "Greek superstition" ("quibus rationibus pertinacem Graecorum superstitionem elidat ac perterreat"). In the cathedral library, Branda found an ancient manuscript that looked promising, one said to have been compiled and even written out by the fourth-century bishop of Milan, St. Ambrose himself. The cardinal got permission from a priest to use the manuscript for a while (per temporis spatium) and carried it back to his residence to study more closely.

Not two weeks later, the priest (Tobia calls him a *flamen*) learned that Branda da Castiglione was preparing to leave Milan with the manuscript. Regretting his liberality and fearful that a moderate request for the book's return would be ignored, the priest decided on desperate measures, "obscene and execrable force," according to Tobia ("obscena ac execranda vi aggredi ausus est"). He called the citizens by ringing the cathedral bell, an unusual summons that announced a crisis. To capture the emerging drama, Tobia borrowed the classical historians' technique of

2. Sabbadini, *Epistolario*, letter 759, dated by Sabbadini to 1439. Line references below are to this letter. Sabbadini's marginal notes chiefly record Tobia's allusions to Virgil and other poets; allusions to Cicero's speeches and the Roman historians are not indicated. On Tobia Borghi (d. ca. 1451), see Scipione Maffei, *Verona illustrata* (Verona, 1731), 201; he is dismissed in Cochrane, *Historians*, 98. To Borghi, Guarino wrote an important letter, "De historiae conscribendae forma" (Sabbadini, *Epistolario*, letter 796, dated there to 1446), with which Mariangela Regoliosi, "Riflessioni umanistiche sullo scrivere storia," *Rinascimento* 31 (1991): 3–27, at 8–16, demonstrates Guarino's use of Lucian's *De historia conscribenda*.

3. On the educator Guarino, see Remigio Sabbadini, *La scuola e le studi di Guarino Guarini Veronese* (Catania, 1896); Anthony Grafton and Lisa Jardine, *From Humanism to the Humanities* (London: Cambridge University Press, 1986), chap. 1; Paul Grendler, *Schooling in Renaissance Italy* (Baltimore: Johns Hopkins University Press, 1989), 126–129; and G. Pistilli, "Guarini, Guarino," *DBI* 60 (2003): 357a–369b, with a copious bibliography.

4. Tobia begins by noting that his subject, Cardinal Branda da Castiglione (d. 1443), was interested in "sniffing out ecclesiastical libraries" (*ecclesiasticas quotidie bibliothecas olfaceret*, l. 42). The cathedral of St. Thecla was demolished in the Quattrocento to enlarge the square in front of the new Duomo, which was being built as Tobia wrote. On Branda da Castiglione, see Tino Foffano, "Breve nota sull'epistolario del Card. Branda Castiglioni," *Aevum* 2, 62 (1988): 302–309; and idem, "Un carteggio del Cardinal Branda Castiglioni con Cosimo de'Medici," in Rino Avesani, ed., *Vestigia: Studi in onore di Giuseppe Billanovich* (Rome: Edizioni di storia e letteratura, 1984), 1:297–314, with further bibliography. On Branda's adventure at St. Thecla, see Giuseppe Billanovich and Mirella Ferrari, "La tradizione milanese delle opere di sant'Ambrogio," in *Ambrosius Episcopus: Atti del convegno internazionale, Milano, 27 dicembre 1974* (Milan: Vita e pensiero, 1974), 26–34.

representing speech directly, inserting into his letter a version of the priest's address to those who gathered. "Don't be surprised, worthy citizens, if I have called you here in such a sudden and unaccustomed way," the priest began. "The reason is the holy book of blessed Ambrose."[5] Then, in tones alternately injured and inflammatory, the priest recalled for his audience the value of the book, the centuries they had possessed it, the virtue they had received from it. Now, he charged, "that shameless man" (*ille, ille*) had borne away all learning, had absconded with their salvation, had stolen the honor, glory, and ornament of Milan. A mere priest, he himself was unable to oppose a cardinal. That must be the work—indeed, it was the duty—of the citizens ("vestrum hoc opus et officium sit").[6]

Responding to the priest's alarm, the citizens ran to the cardinal's residence and surrounded it. They hurled stones and filth and shouted threats of fire and death.[7] As the crowd grew more violent, bringing up torches, and, Tobia implies, with the capture of the residence impending, the cardinal appeared at a window to ask the reason for the uproar. The gathered people demanded the return of the manuscript. Tobia, saving his rhetoric for the cardinal's paternal remonstration with the citizens, says only that Branda da Castiglione ordered the book given to them ("librum eis dari iussit").[8] Since it is unlikely that a violent and incendiary crowd would have been calmly handed such a book, there may be more truth in a later account: the Milanese historian Bernardo Corio (d. 1513) wrote that the frightened cardinal "threw the book to them from a window" ("per paura gli gettò il libro per una fenestra").[9]

According to Tobia, neither the return of the manuscript nor the cardinal's paternal speech pacified the citizens. They now suspected that Branda had removed folios from the codex and, worse, that he intended to steal their relics of Ambrose as well.[10] As this rumor spread, people of all stations joined the crowd at the cardinal's residence. It looked as though the cardinal would be violently attacked and killed ("nulla fere iam de tanti viri salute spes haberetur").[11] The manuscript had precipitated a riot.

5. ll. 67–69.

6. ll. 83–84.

7. ll. 172–176.

8. ll. 176–180. Tobia does not say that the cardinal was frightened but that he was *admiratus*, full of wonder or amazement. For his paternal remonstration, in direct address to complement the priest's speech, see ll. 180–188.

9. I follow R. Sabbadini, "Il cardinale Branda da Castiglione e il rito romano," *ASL*, ser. 3, 19 (1903): 397–408, quoting Bernardino Corio, *Storia di Milano* (1503), sign. GIv; also given in Sabbadini, *Epistolario*, notes to letter 759 (at 368–370). On Corio (1459–1513), see Cochrane, *Historians*, 117–118. Eugenio Cazzani, *Il cardinale Branda Castiglione* (Saronno, 1988), facing 283, reproduces without comment a somewhat later painting that depicts the moment of the throwing down of the book.

10. ll. 189–198.

11. ll. 67–69.

At this point, thanks to the "great-souled and truly divine" ("magnanimus ac vere divinus") foresight of the prince, city officials intervened.[12] They drove off the crowd and captured the instigator of the plan to force the cardinal out with fire. As a warning to the others, this culprit was hanged from a window of the residence. The priest was imprisoned and tortured. Throughout the reprisals, the cardinal remained a model of mercy; Tobia even attributes to him Christ's injunction, "Forgive them, for they know not what they do" ("parce illis . . . quia nesciunt quid faciant").[13] And in the end the cardinal was not only unharmed but satisfied. Shortly after the incident, the manuscript was found for him safe and sound, "as if in a most pleasant lodging" ("in amoenissmimo diversorio") by Tobia's friend, a member of the cardinal's entourage at Pavia.[14]

One of the many intriguing aspects of Tobia's account is the function of the *libellus*, or little book, at its center. Tobia reports a general belief that the manuscript had been compiled and even transcribed by Ambrose ("ut aiunt, a beato Ambrosio . . . et compilatus et propria manu scriptus est").[15] But Tobia is careful not to credit the saint with its actual authorship, suggesting that the cardinal found the manuscript attractive not just for its theological statements but also for its physical connection to a patristic saint. In fact, both men seem to have approached the object with the reverence normally reserved for relics.[16]

Certainly the citizens of Milan perceived the manuscript as a relic. Tobia makes that clear in several ways, beginning with the emphases of the speech attributed to the priest. The *libellus* was taken from me, says the priest, or rather from your church, or better yet, from all of you, the triplet encouraging in his audience a sense of collective ownership, responsibility, and outrage.[17] The priest reminds his listeners how the object links them to past and future. "For so many centuries," he intones, "you have so piously, so

12. ll. 209–215, describing the prince, naming the officials, and admiring "the authority of great and imposing men" (*Dii boni, quantum magnorum ac gravium virorum valet auctoritas!*).

13. ll. 200–204, comparing the cardinal to the unjustly accused Aristides and Jesus.

14. ll. 283–284, naming Ferufino.

15. ll. 45–47.

16. As a relic, the *libellus* falls into the category of *brandea,* or contact relics; see Henri Leclerq in *DACL* 14, fasc. 2 (1948): 2294–2359, sec. 13; J. M. McCulloh, "The Cult of Relics in the Letters and *Dialogues* of Gregory the Great," *Traditio* 32 (1976): 145–184 at 165–169. For some examples of books used as healing relics, see Thomas Heffernan, *Sacred Biography: Saints and Their Biographers in the Middle Ages* (New York: Oxford University Press, 1988), 16; Alain Boureau, "Franciscan Piety and Veracity: Uses and Strategems in the Hagiographic Pamphlet," in R. Chartier, ed., *The Culture of Print: Power and the Uses of Print in Early Modern Europe,* trans. L. Cochrane (Princeton, N.J.: Princeton University Press, 1989), 15–16; Kathleen Ashley and Pamela Sheingorn, *Writing Faith: Text, Sign, and History in the Miracles of Sainte Foy* (Chicago: University of Chicago Press, 1999), 141.

17. ll. 69–70.

reverently, so faithfully" wished the manuscript "to be guarded, honored, and enclosed [*recludi*]." "Under [its] discipline you have lived for so long and will live."[18] As an object that binds the citizens as guardians and beneficiaries, both past and present, the book is assimilated to a relic.

Speaking in his own voice, Tobia adduces the reliquary nature of the manuscript in order to explain the riot. The locals, he says, understood the cardinal's possession of the manuscript to be criminal violence because they drew an analogy to the theft centuries earlier of their relics of the Three Kings.[19] The day before the riot, ceremonies for Epiphany had taken place at St. Eustorgius, where the relics of the Magi had once been kept; as part of those ceremonies, the empty space they no longer occupied had been formally viewed and lamented.[20] The first time that Tobia mentions the theft of the relics of the Three Kings, he is frankly speculating about why the priest was so easily able to incite the citizens.[21] The second time, however, he depicts the crowd explicitly making the connection; he claims to use their own words ("ut eorum utar verbis") to report that they would not allow a second such insult to Milan.[22]

Tobia also fits the presumed theft of the manuscript into a series of escalating threats to the integral body of Milanese religious practice. In the inflammatory speech attributed to the priest, Tobia represents him playing on apprehension that the cardinal was scheming to end celebration of the Ambrosian rite. "How many times," asks the priest, "has he tried this same tactic, so that the Roman rather than the Ambrosian office would be celebrated at Milan! Now, under the guise of confuting the Greeks, he wants to get past us with these underhanded tricks. How long, how long, mighty citizens, must we bear this?"[23] To the fear of Roman subversion of Milanese liturgical traditions, Tobia adds suspicions that the cardinal had mutilated the manuscript and that he harbored designs on the bodily relics of Ambrose as well.[24] Tied thus to their concern for the integrity of their distinctive liturgy and for the safety of

18. ll. 70–72.

19. Patrick J. Geary, *Living with the Dead in the Middle Ages* (Ithaca, N.Y.: Cornell University Press, 1994), 243–256, notes the possibility that Milan never had these relics and gives earlier bibliography.

20. On the St. Eustorgius ceremony, see Geary, *Living with the Dead*, 243–244 and 255.

21. ll. 86–90.

22. ll. 160–165.

23. ll. 77–80, echoing Cicero's Catilinarian. In fact, as Sabbadini, "Il cardinale," points out, far from being an enemy of the Ambrosian rite, Branda da Castiglione was so interested in it that he had funded a special school to train the singers. Perhaps Tobia does not know of Branda's interests; perhaps he puts untruths into the mouth of a speaker in order to criticize him.

24. ll. 192–193.

their bodily relics of Ambrose, the citizens' suspicion that the cardinal had mutilated the book corresponds to a concern for the wholeness and authenticity of a relic.[25]

Finally, Tobia indicates the reliquary nature of the *libellus* by his own attention to the local nature of religious devotion, that is, to the aspect of pre-Reformation piety that found its most typical expression in the cult of saints and relics.[26] For all the careful compliments that Tobia pays to the cardinal's zeal for the universal Church, the humanist admires the jealous piety of the citizens. Unmoved by the authority of the cardinal's name, unimpressed by his position, unmindful that he was Milanese, these citizens were prepared to die, observes Tobia, for Ambrose's book.[27] Tobia offers his account to his correspondent as an example of the strength of local religion: "You see, Father Guarino, with what strong audacity, what sharp zeal, what determined mind they guarded their honors and, if I may so speak, their household gods [*penates*]."[28] Tobia, the cardinal, the priest, and the Milanese crowd all understood that this audacity and violent zeal was elicited by Ambrose's special position as Milan's patron. Loss of objects associated with him diminished both the honor and the security of the city.

In most instances, this study looks at writings *about* saints rather than writings *by* saints, but the riot over Ambrose's book raises all the fundamental issues that underlie the presentation. The focus of the Milanese incident was an ancient text. The fact that it was not a classical text, and probably not even an authentic patristic text, was of little importance to the participants in the drama. Of course, there is no reason to think that the citizens, intent on their saintly patron, would care about the fine points of what we today call textual reception and criticism. But it is significant that, for a humanist like Tobia, even the tangential connection (both metaphorically and literally) of this book to a church father made it valuable. Humanists interested in the history of their local churches and of the Church at Rome might search for old *vitae sanctorum* (saints' lives) with much the same energy that other humanists displayed in their searches for Cicero's orations and Livy's histories.

The incident at Milan also introduces the complexities of the world into which the classicizing rhetoricians known as humanists cast their

25. On the correspondence beween body symbolism and social forms, see Mary Douglas, *Natural Symbols: Explorations in Cosmology* (London: Cresset, 1970); and John Gager, "Body Symbols and Social Reality," *Religion* 12 (1982): 346–364.

26. The *loci classici* are William Christian, *Local Religion in Sixteenth-Century Spain* (Princeton, N.J.: Princeton University Press, 1981); and Eamon Duffy, *The Stripping of the Altars* (New Haven: Yale University Press, 1992), on Iberia and England respectively; on northern Italy, see Webb, *Patrons*.

27. ll. 79–114. As if to balance his admiration for this unruly display of devotion, Tobia gives a lengthy *laudatio* of Branda's family; see ll. 124–156.

28. ll. 95–97.

narrative propositions about sanctity. The actors in the Milanese drama
were a reforming cardinal, a local priest, and a jealous community; the
recorder was a classicizing historian; his audience was the schoolteacher
Guarino and, by extension, Guarino's network of rhetorically alert cor-
respondents; in the not-too-distant background stood the high politics of
Milan under the Visconti. The interests of all parties converged on a
dubious manuscript that all equated with a saint. Naturally, their reverence for the object was cast in different terms. Tobia's was that of a
humanist with historiographical inclinations; Branda's that of a scholas-
tically trained proponent of Church union; the priest's that of a responsible guardian; the citizens' that of beneficiaries of holy patronage; the
prince's that of a determined manipulator of power both symbolic and
actual. Despite these differences, Tobia's account shows that all participants understood that manuscripts and the texts they housed might
share a functional equivalence with saints. Indeed, more than a functional equivalence, one could fairly speak of a general synecdochic
assimilation of historical saint, saintly narrative, physical book, and
saintly relic in the minds of most people in this period, including some of
the most educated.

In addition, the Milanese incident draws attention to the sensibility that
humanist authors might bring to the cult of the saints. The disturbance
caused by the borrowed manuscript was written up by a humanist rhetorician for a highly educated audience; but despite Tobia's deference toward
the cardinal, he did not compose a piece of proto-Enlightenment mockery
of plebeian superstition. Rather, Tobia's letter records an empathetic interest in the piety of people who may, at least from his point of view, have
been only marginally literate. He acknowledges the profundity of their
devotion, giving a fairly sympathetic description of the passionate and
socially disruptive forms that it might take.

Tobia's interest, attention, and sympathy alert modern readers that
fifteenth-century authors involved in writing or rewriting the lives of
saints were aware of what was at stake in any rhetorical or factual innovations they proposed in the heavily formulaic *vitae sanctorum*. In this
area of classicizing endeavor, as in few others, philology might have
explosive results. There was a Quattrocento audience for a revised
"hagiography," but it was still an audience fervently and pragmatically
devoted to its saintly patrons. Conscious of such possessiveness, humanists took up the writing and rewriting of *vitae sanctorum* with considerable sensitivity to the implications of any changes in style, structure, and
content. They often wrote defensively, expecting criticism from several
sources, including fellow humanists lay and clerical, ecclesiastics with
scholastic training, and the many stations of laypeople who had their
own reasons to be protective of the stories. Pagan gods and pagan mores
could be controversial subjects, but the difficulties they raised were

relatively straightforward when compared with the implications of rewriting the lives of the saints.[29]

Nevertheless, it was work that had to be done, and there was a lot of it. The Quattrocento had inherited an enormous quantity of this literature. It is easy to forget, today, that a sizable proportion of all the written texts in premodern Europe were about saints. Daily, in local churches, priests drew on a wide variety of books to honor "the special friends of God."[30] They used office books such as the sanctorale, the lectionary, and the breviary, for example, to read the abbreviated liturgical lessons (*lectiones*) for a saint's feastday; they announced the day's martyrs using the short notices gathered in passionaries and martyrologies. Preachers turned to Latin and vernacular *legendae* (literally, things to be read, narratives about saints) and collections of instructive anecdotes (*exempla*) to find stories about saints for their sermons (*sermones, orationes*), whether they were speaking in the ornate chapels of popes and kings or outdoors before large, mixed crowds. In the urban confraternities, laypeople recounted the lives and passions of both local and universal saints to one another; they funded, wrote, and

29. For encyclopedic treatments of specific saints and periods, see *BS, GLS,* and, above all, G. Philippart, dir., *Hagiographies: Histoire internationale de la littérature hagiographique latine et vernaculaire en Occident des origines à 1500* (Turnhout: Brepols, 1994–), treating both Latin and vernacular traditions. Richard Kieckhefer gives a helpful English-language introduction to the cult of the saints in "Imitators of Christ: Sainthood in the Christian Tradition," in *Sainthood: Its Manifestations in the World Religions* (Berkeley: University of California Press, 1988), 1–42; see also Tom Head's "Hagiography" section at the ORB Website (http://orb.rhodes.edu/bibliographies/) and international links from the Bollandists' Website (www.kbr.be/~socboll). On the nature of the medieval Latin texts, see D. Townsend, "Hagiography," in F. A. C. Mantello and A. G. Rigg, eds., *Medieval Latin: An Introduction and Bibliographical Guide* (Washington, D.C.: Catholic University of America Press, 1996), 618–628. Also helpful are G. Rocca, A. Vauchez, P. Delooz, and M. Foralosso, "Santità," in *DIP* 8 (1988); G. Philippart, "Martirologi e leggendari," in *Lo spazio letterario del medioevo,* I. *Il medioevo latino,* i, *La circolazione del testo* (Rome: Salerno, 1994), 605–648; S. Boesch Gajano, "Agiografia," in *Morfologie sociali e culturali in Europa fra tarda antichità e alto medioevo* (Spoleto: Centro italiano di studi sull'alto Medioevo, 1998), 2:797–850. The older study by Hippolyte Delehaye, *La culte des saints,* 3d rev. ed. (Brussels: Bollandist Society, 1927; in English translation, by D. Attwater, *The Cult of the Saints* [Dublin: Four Courts, 1998]), is still helpful; Michel de Certeau, "L'hagiographie," in *Encyclopedia universalis* 8 (1968): 207–209, still thought-provoking. The recently updated surveys by René Aigrain, *L'hagiographie: Ses sources, ses méthodes, son histoire,* 2d ed. (Brussels: Bollandist Society, 2000); and Reginald Grégoire, *Manuale di agiologia. Introduzione alla letteratura agiografica,* 2d ed. (Fabriano: Bollandist Society, 1996) offer instructively different views. *SMHM* and the journals *AB* and *Hagiographica* provide guides to research. For a sample of case studies in English, see Stephen Wilson, *Saints and Their Cults: Studies in Religious Sociology, Folklore, and History* (New York: Cambridge University Press, 1983), with a still-useful annotated bibliography.

30. The phrase, popularized by Peter R. L. Brown's *Cult of the Saints: Its Rise and Function in Latin Christianity* (Chicago: University of Chicago Press, 1981), is a reminder that the intercessory function of the saints so evident in Renaissance devotion has roots in the medieval permutations of the classical patronage systems.

enjoyed plays (*sacra rappresentazione*) that retold these stories. They, their rulers, and the local houses of the increasingly centralized religious orders took an interest in narratives promoting the local findings (*inventiones*) and movings (*translationes*) of saintly relics. Both secular powers and religious orders took care to record the evidence of the saints' continuing presence in the form of miracle collections (*miracula*). Saints' lives were retold in prose and verse (*gesta, historia*) to be read in small groups or privately by both laypeople and those in orders. Housed thus in a supple variety of forms, the narration of sanctity moved in all the intermediate spaces hidden by the heuristic oppositions of oral and literate, popular and elite, official and domestic, peripheral and central, Latin and vernacular, local and universal.

It is hard to recover the outlook that found authority and value in this literature. The social functions of holy *vitae* and *passiones* (lives and passions) may continue in our attachment to the idea of role models and mentors, in the manifold ways we have found to exhort ourselves to self-improvement, even in our amusement at the impossibilities announced as fact by the newspapers at the grocery checkout. But—despite the renewed spirituality and the politicized canonizations of the last decade[31]—lives of the saints no longer constitute a living genre. "Hagiography" remains a pejorative in common usage. The combinations of ritual, play, politics, necessity, fact, and invention that made the literary narratives about saints so vigorous in premodern Europe may seem quite foreign.

Possible Lives attempts to recapture the force and vigor of this literature by exploring the accounts of saints written by a particular group of authors during the fifteenth century in Italy. That time and place are central to what is commonly called the Renaissance; the authors are those whose "intention to imitate ancient Latin style" identifies them as humanists.[32] As the

---

31. According to L. Cunningham, "Saints and Martyrs: Some Contemporary Considerations," *Theological Studies* 60, no. 3 (1999), John Paul II has over seven hundred beatifications and more than two hundred canonizations to his credit and has "asked for the compilation of a modern martyrology" to record twentieth-century witness, "not only Catholic but Orthodox and Protestant" (529). For an example of a twentieth-century process, see Catherine M. Mooney, *Philippine Duchesne: A Woman with the Poor* (New York: Paulist Press, 1990).

32. Ronald G. Witt, *In the Footsteps of the Ancients: The Origins of Humanism from Lovato to Bruni* (Leiden: Brill, 2000), at 22, proposes this intention. For earlier attention to "humanist hagiography," see Charles W. Trinkaus, *In Our Image and Likeness: Humanity and Divinity in Italian Humanist Thought*, 2 vols. (Chicago: University of Chicago Press, 1970); Charles L. Stinger, *Humanism and the Church Fathers: Ambrogio Traversari (1396–1439) and Christian Antiquity in the Italian Renaissance* (Albany: SUNY Press, 1977); Cochrane, *Historians*, 416–420; and especially Riccardo Fubini, "Papato e storiografia nel Quattrocento. Storia, biografia e propaganda in un recente studio," *Studi medievali*, ser. 3, 18, no. 1 (1977): 321–351; O'Malley, *Praise*; Remo L. Guidi, "Questioni di storiografia agiografica nel quattrocento," *Benedictina* 34 (1987): 167–252; Diana Webb, "Eloquence and Education: A Humanist Approach to Hagiography," *Journal of Ecclesiastical History* 31 (1980): 319–339; and idem, "The Truth About Constantine: History, Hagiography, and Confusion," *Studies in Church History* 17 (1988): 85–102. Vauchez, *La sainteté*, stops with the early Quattrocento.

arbiters of a Renaissance of pre-Christian letters, the humanists are not generally acknowledged to have been interested in the lives of the saints. Lorenzo Valla (d. 1457), for example, was better known among his contemporaries, as he is today, for his rhetorical *Elegancies* and his attack on the Donation of Constantine than for his sermon about St. Thomas Aquinas or his Latin translation of two Greek passions of the Forty Martyrs of Sebaste. Likewise, Pier Candido Decembrio (d. 1477) was and remains better known as a translator of Aristotle's *Politics* than as the author of a (lost) life of St. Ambrose. Leon Battista Alberti (d. 1472) is the famous author of *Della pittura*, *De architectura*, and *I libri della famiglia*. His martyrdom of St. Potitus did not circulate in his own day; in ours, although a modern edition of the *vita Potiti* has been available for fifty years, it remains largely unexamined. Leonardo Giustinian (d. 1466) enjoyed and still enjoys a much greater reputation as a vernacular poet and translator of Plutarch than as the compiler of a life of St. Nicholas. Lives of saints in general, and these humanists' lives in particular, long ago fell out of the literary canon or were subsumed into the canon in ways we barely perceive.[33] The aim of *Possible Lives* is to recover the extent, the variety, and the significance of the humanists' engagement with the saints.

Despite the longstanding undervaluation, hundreds of fifteenth-century narratives about saints are extant—in Latin and the vernaculars, in prose, verse, and dramatic renderings of all kinds, treating hundreds of saints, written by dozens of authors. These sources can be, as the sociologist Pierre Delooz noted of canonization processes, "exceptionally rich documents, probably among the richest [scholarship] will ever have at its disposal for the comprehension of the past."[34] Scholars have found it easy to agree with Delooz when newly composed or vernacular sources are at issue. For that reason, studies of saints such as the Sienese Catherine (d. 1380) and Bernardino (d. 1444)—both of whom were canonized in the Quattrocento—have proliferated, as has work on the *vitae* (lives) written by contemporaries of those late medieval and early modern women who died "in the odor of sanctity." The study of Renaissance sanctity has become, almost by definition, the study of living women saints (*sante vive*) and canonization. In the past two decades, that focus has profoundly changed the historiography of late medieval and early modern Europe and the Americas, transforming our evaluation of religion in the Renaissance. In a sense, the old *problema religioso*—the nineteenth- and early-twentieth-century debate about Renaissance

---

33. Julia Lupton, *Afterlives of the Saints: Hagiography, Typology, and Renaissance Literature* (Stanford: Stanford University Press, 1996), persuasively argues for this subsumption.

34. Pierre Delooz, "Towards a Sociological Study of Canonized Sainthood in the Catholic Church," reprinted in Wilson, *Saints*, 189–216, at 193.

atheism—has been resurrected but thoroughly recast as an inquiry into the period's pervasive religiosity.[35]

When we turn to the humanists, however, it is evident that the majority of their *vitae* and *passiones* were not fashioned *ex novo*, were not devised to promote canonizations, and were not composed in the vernacular or in epic meters. Their accounts are most often derivative ones in Latin prose. That fact links them solidly to medieval practice: throughout the Middle Ages, authors mostly revised earlier accounts in Latin prose. Medieval revisions have increasingly become an object of scholarship, perhaps because the academic notion of intertextuality and the popular one of sampling have helped us to see the self-conscious skill even of derivative works.[36] In this study, I propose that the Renaissance humanists' secondary, tertiary, and still further derived texts, written in a language and form that—it seems to us—must necessarily have excluded the majority of the authors' contemporaries, also deserve our full attention, and for more than source studies. If we think of the cultural production of a period only in terms of its new literature, we form an unjust estimate.[37] Recent studies of historical memory emphasize that what societies choose to preserve from the past is fully as eloquent as any novelties they contribute to the record. This preservation represents, as historians know, the dialogue of the present with those aspects of the past that can be accommodated, and the terms of that accommodation are themselves historical evidence. The dialogue of the humanists with their inheritance of saints' lives is, however, the opposite of invented tradition, the phenomenon by which societies figure the new as old. People also return to the old for new reasons.

Saints' lives are a commemorative literature, so it is not surprising that few of the Latin prose narratives treated here are original compositions. Many are translations, revisions, epitomes, compilations, or mild retouchings of already existing pieces. Some are simply transcriptions. All these forms—including the transcriptions—are of value for, as the following

35. On the *problema religioso,* see the survey in Carlo Angeleri, *Il problema religioso del rinascimento* (Florence: Le Monnier, 1952); on recent trends in the study of Renaissance religion, see David Peterson, "Out of the Margins: Religion and the Church in Renaissance Italy," *RQ* 53, no. 3 (2000): 821–834, to which I would add the shift in our understanding of humanism, so that it is seen now primarily as a phenomenon of rhetoric rather than philosophy. Kristeller, "Contribution," and O'Malley, *Praise,* early demonstrated the far-reaching implications of this shift. See below.

36. See, e.g., Marc van Uytfanghe, "Le remploi dans l'hagiographie: Une 'loi du genre' qui étouffe l'originalité?" in *Ideologie e pratiche del reimpiego nell'alto medioevo* (Spoleto, 1999), 1:359–411.

37. A point emphasized in Patrick Geary's introduction to S. Sticca, *Saints: Studies in Hagiography* (Binghamton, N.Y.: MRTS, 1996), at 14. For authoritative attention to the significance of rewritten accounts, see H. Delehaye, *Les passions des martyrs et les genres littéraires* (Brussels: Bollandist Society, 1921), chap. 5, esp. 370–372.

chapters make clear, they represent both the fundamental continuity of medieval literature on the saints into the fifteenth and early sixteenth centuries and some of the most striking discontinuities. This study, then, is, predicated on the intrinsic value of this cache of derivative documents. Simply by virtue of quantity, the "sacred biographies" written in Latin prose by Quattrocento humanists deserve our attention.[38]

No one would argue, however, that they constitute great literature. Even by the stylistic standards of their own day, they were rarely aesthetic successes. Nor did they, through any combination of intrinsic virtue, market appeal, or ecclesiastic imposition, become part of the literary canon of the West. Most have lain untouched in manuscript collections for five centuries—and not without reason. Readers today often find humanist literary productions of all kinds distinctly off-putting; this distaste may double before types of narratives like saints' lives, whose social logic is so far removed from our lives. Humanist authors often strike us as self-important pedants, "superfatted bores," as an accomplished scholar once remarked to me. The perception of pedantry is to some extent justifiable. Even individuals who were not professional teachers often had a strongly pedagogical outlook, for the idealistic program of classicizing rhetorical education (the *studia humanitatis*) that had formed them aimed at a thoroughgoing social renewal through changed values in the classroom.[39] But any distaste we may feel for the humanists' self-promotion and ideological jockeying should be balanced against a curiously underestimated fact. Precisely as humanists these authors had been trained to be attentive to their audience's needs and desires. If—as is often the case—the authors were *also* clerics, mendicants, or ecclesiastics engaged in preaching, then they had been still more carefully groomed to nurture their audiences.[40] This attentiveness to

38. Heffernan, *Sacred Biography,* proposes the term "sacred biography" in place of "hagiography." Terminology is a problem: see Guy Phillippart, "Hagiographies et hagiographie, hagiologes et hagiologie: Des mots et des concepts," *Agiografia* 1 (1994): 1–16; Felice Lifshitz, "Beyond Positivism and Genre: 'Hagiographical' Texts as Historical Narrative," *Viator* 25 (1994): 95–113; Marc van Uytfanghe, "Die *vita* im Spannungsfeld von Legende, Biographik und Geschichte," in A. Scharer and G. Scheibelreiter, eds., *Historiographie im frühen Mittelalter* (Munich: Oldenbourg, 1994), 194–221; and idem, "L'hagiographie: Un 'genre' chrétien ou antique tardif?" *AB* 111 (1993): 135–188. Like Cynthia Hahn, *Portrayed on the Heart: Narrative Effect in Pictorial Lives of Saints from the Tenth Through the Thirteenth Century* (Berkeley: University of California Press, 2001), I think that the work of H.-R. Jauss on genre and reception can help us around this terminological impasse.

39. See Craig Kallendorf, ed. and trans., *Humanist Educational Treatises* (Cambridge, Mass.: Harvard University Press, 2002), for the educators' program statements. Classroom realities are another matter. See chap. 4.

40. The fact that a medieval preacher or teacher was taught to fit his material to his audience is fundamental to any appreciation of the extant corpus of sermons and *vitae*. Even when the material was exceptionally difficult and the speaker exceptionally learned, the needs of different audiences had to be accommodated, as A. Minnis shows in discussing the

audience is part of the reason that the humanists' writings about saints
can be useful to the historian. The narratives tell us more than we have
supposed about the conditions of reception, about what the audience or
readership was willing to bear and even to enjoy. As the narratives are not
the artistic productions of genius, they do not raise the interpretive problems associated with the analysis of a literature that transcends the conditions of its making. The humanists' *vitae sanctorum* may not compel
rereading, but they do embody the tensions of changing devotion, religious outlook, and even classroom practice that characterized Europe at
the end of the Middle Ages and the beginning of the Early Modern period.
In some ways, these narratives may elucidate the social and intellectual
contexts of their composition with more immediacy than major literary
works are able to do.

❊ ❊ ❊

The focus of this study is on the authors. Whether the saintly subjects of
the humanists' narratives really possessed the virtues attributed to them—
indeed, whether they even existed—will matter here only when it matters
to the authors.[41] These authors, the humanists, are identified as products,
admirers, or adherents of the *studia humanitatis*.[42] My approach to this
group might be described as sociological: in designating any author as a
humanist, I have drawn on evidence about education, cultivation of
friendships and patronage relations with like-minded people, and intention in a given narrative. I have not relied on current scholarly evaluations
of how successfully an author met the ideal of a classical Latinity. According to my broad definition, a humanist was a person attracted by classical subjects, genres, and stylistic turns and a person who, by the end of
the period considered here, would normally have been competent in

---

scholastic Henry of Ghent, in "Medium and Message," in R. G. Newhauser and J. A. Alford,
eds., *Literature and Religion in the Later Middle Ages: Philological Studies in Honor of
Siegfried Wenzel* (Binghamton, N.Y.: MRTS, 1995), 209–235. For recent emphasis on audience, see the articles gathered in C. Muessig, ed., *Preacher, Sermon, and Audience in the Middle Ages* (Leiden: Brill, 2002), giving earlier bibliography.

41. My model in pursuing the historical aspects of even ahistorical texts is Brigitte
Cazelles, *Le Corps de sainteté d'après Jehan Bouche d'Or, Jehan Paulus et quelques vies des
XIIe et XIIIe siècles* (Geneva: Droz, 1982). This approach is intimated already in Delehaye,
Les passions.

42. I use a mild version of P. O. Kristeller's well-known definition of the humanist as a
person with training in—not necessarily a professional practitioner of—the *studia humanitatis*; see, e.g., Kristeller, "The Humanist Movement," in M. Mooney, ed., *Renaissance
Thought and Its Sources* (New York: Columbia University Press, 1979), 21–32. Webb's "Eloquence," the seminal study in English of humanists' writings on saints, offers a similar but
tighter definition. See the following notes.

Greek.[43] He—for it has turned out that all the authors treated are male—received or gave himself an education that encouraged such interests.[44] He was not necessarily a professional grammarian or rhetorician. One author, the noble ambassador (*orator*) and jurisconsult Ludovico Foscarini (d. 1480), newly arrived to govern Feltre for Venice, apologized in the preface to his account of the martyrs Victor and Corona that it had been a long time since he had studied rhetoric.[45] It had not actually been that long; his apology is, however, a clue that he was aware of the skills expected.

Thus *Possible Lives* differs from many studies of sanctity in beginning not with a place or a saint but with the premise that a sociologically identifiable group of authors produced a body of literature that is distinguished significantly (though of course not solely) by the authors' intellectual formation. A place and its patron saints might well constitute one of an author's commitments, but these authors shared several traits that worked against their full identification with a locality.[46] As humanists, they had a pedagogical

43. The word *umanista* is first attested in the late fifteenth and early sixteenth centuries, with a more restricted meaning than employed here; *umanesimo* only entered Italian in the eighteenth century. See A. Campana, "The Origin of the Word 'Humanist,' " *Journal of the Warburg and Courtauld Institute* 9 (1946): 60–73; Giuseppe Billanovich, "*Auctorista, humanista, orator*: Per l'origine della parola *umanista*," *Rivista di cultura classica e medievale* 7 (1965): 143–163; Rino Avesani, "La professione dell'umanista nel cinquecento," *IMU* 13 (1970): 205–234; M. L. McLaughlin, "Humanist Concepts of Renaissance and Middle Ages in the Trecento and Quattrocento," *Renaissance Studies* 2 (1988): 131–142; Vincenzo Fera, "La filologia umanistica in Italia nel secolo XX," in *La filologia medievale e umanistica* (Rome, 1993), 1:239–273, as well as Kristeller, "The Humanist Movement."

44. I did not set out to study solely male authors, but the criteria by which authors turned up—as I worked toward the authors from *vitae* in manuscript and print—led to this result. It is not surprising: for the association of boys and Latin prose, see Walter Ong, "Latin Language Study as a Renaissance Puberty Rite," *Rhetoric, Romance, and Technology: Studies in the Interaction of Expression and Culture* (Ithaca, N.Y.: Cornell University Press, 1971), 113–141; and Amy Richlin, "Gender and Rhetoric: Producing Manhood in the Schools," in W. J. Dominik, ed., *Roman Eloquence: Rhetoric in Society and Literature* (New York: Routledge, 1997), 90–110. For two famous examples of women's writing on saints in this period, see *In Beati Hieronymi laudem oratio* by Isotta Nogarola, ed. E. Abel, *Isotae Nogarolae opera quae supersunt omnia* (Vienna: Gerold and Associates, 1886), 2:276–289; it is now available in English translation in *Isotta Nogarola: Complete Writings*, ed. and trans. M .L. King and D. Robin (Chicago: University of Chicago Press, 2004), 167–174. See also Camilla-Battista Varano's vernacular treatise on the death of St. Giacomo della Marca, "Del felice transito del B. Pietro da Mogliano," in G. Boccanera, ed., *Camilla Battista da Varano, Le opere spirituale* (Jesi: Scuola tipografica francescana, 1958), 72–111.

45. "Iam diu haec studia non solum intermissa sed penitus abdicata nunquam revocaverim" (Ludovico Foscarini, prefatory letter to Jacopo Foscaro in Baltimore, Walters Art Gallery, MS W393, fols. 65–66, at 65v). The account (*BHL* —) was composed about 1439, when the author was thirty. Foscarini's protestation is a humility trope; such tropes occur profusely in both medieval and Renaissance hagiographic prologues.

46. For the reflection of this same supralocal tendency in humanist historiography, see Mariangela Regoliosi, "*Res gestae patriae* e *res gestae ex universa Italia*: La lettera di Lapo da Castiglionchio a Biondo Flavio," in C. Bastia and M. Bolognani, eds., *La memoria e la città: Scritture storiche tra Medio Evo ed Età moderna* (Bologna: Il Nove, 1995), 273–305.

formation that insisted on its own universal value. The *studia humanitatis*, as a refinement of the medieval *trivium*, promoted not just grammar and rhetoric (deemphasizing although hardly eliminating dialectic) but also poetry, history, and moral philosophy. In theory, these subjects were taught with reference to the Greek and Roman classics. That the authors shared this formation does not mean that their experience of it was the same or that they agreed on all points about it. They are, in fact, notorious for the bitterness of their public disputes about aspects of their common program. But they agreed that basic training in classical texts and proper appreciation of the ethical instruction contained in them ought to be widely shared and would be of self-evident use to Christians able to assimilate it. From this common ground arose the perception that saints' lives needed revising precisely in ways most suited to themselves, possessors of specialized training not just in Latin grammar and rhetoric but also in history and moral philosophy.

Closely related to their self-understanding based on the claims of the *studia humanitatis* is the authors' decision to write in Latin. In the fifteenth century, the vernacular production of saints' lives far overweighed the Latin.[47] But this fact, which we tend to conceive as part of "popular religion," might in practice restrict the audience or the audience's sympathy for a text. Language remained a vital part of local identity in late medieval and early modern Italy, when dialects still overpowered "Italian." Preaching, for example, was done in the vernacular, but texts for preachers continued to circulate in Latin.[48] The case of Pietro Ransano's (d. 1492) abbreviated life of Vincent Ferrer, composed to answer a fellow Dominican's request for reliable preaching material, suggests that the Church's official language was an important part of the authority of the base narrative, no matter how the preacher might subsequently manipulate the text.[49] Latin composition, by increasing the chances that a work would travel successfully, was an appeal to the widest community of Christendom. Thus the decision to focus this investigation on Latin saints' lives stems logically from the broader decision not to focus on a single locality. The humanists sold classicizing Latin as their mark of superiority, which is to say that writing in Latin was a way they consciously escaped the claims of locality, although their subjects and presentations might be unmistakably local.

These authors also tended to be a highly mobile group. As young men,

47. See J. Dalarun and C. Leonardi, eds., *Biblioteca Agiografica Italiana* (Todi: Galluzzo, 2003), now the fundamental guide.

48. On the predominance of preaching in the vernacular from Latin sources see Augustine Thompson, "From Texts to Preaching: Retrieving the Medieval Sermon as an Event," in Muessig, *Preacher*, 17–18, and esp. V. Coletti, *Parole del Pulpito* (Casale Monferrato: Marietti, 1983).

49. For another case involving preaching material and the vernacular, see chap. 5 below.

they trailed after teachers, patrons, and arguments. Those who grew up to become teachers of grammar or rhetoric, or who entered a professional discipline such as medicine or law, frequently moved among cities, courts, and universities and were in any event aware of their peers and colleagues in other sites.[50] Those in orders often passed through houses in various localities, thanks to the common practice of sharing the talents of gifted administrators within an order. Laymen with training in the *studia human-itatis* might hold political office or serve as diplomats or bureaucrats in other localities than their native ones; they arrived in those places expecting to take part in or even to improve the local intellectual culture. As in the case of the Venetian Ludovico Foscarini at Feltre, noted above, that participation might include rewriting the lives of local saints.

Naturally, those humanists who lived off their rhetorical capabilities were professionally required to have exchangeable loyalties. As publicists and propagandists, humanists sold their tongues and pens to the wealthiest and most prestigious powers that would have them. Commerciality of this sort does not necessarily mean that humanist expressions of local pride, so often found in *vitae sanctorum,* were insincere or futile. Contemporaries, at any rate, do not seem to have worried that transferable loyalties made authors cynical about saintly perfections. And even if contemporaries did entertain suspicions, it is a rhetorician's job to be challenged rather than silenced by such doubts.

To underline these universalizing points—the educational and linguistic commitments of the authors, as well as their mobility and professional self-conception—is not to make extreme assertions. It would be nonsensical, speaking of the Quattrocento, to claim that local contexts were irrelevant, that order loyalties uniformly bowed to intellectual ideals, that vernacular hagiography was secondary, or that professional mobility allowed humanists to transcend place. *Possible Lives* suggests, however, that a study of what humanists shared as a group might offer insights otherwise obscured by focus on a single locality, on the vernacular, or on contemporary sanctity. Those insights will touch both the history of sanctity and the history of humanism.

❧ ❧ ❧

What happened when an author with training in the *studia humanitatis* undertook to revise the life of a medieval saint? As the following chapters demonstrate, no single characterization serves to answer the question: it is,

---

50. For an impressive list emphasizing the mobility of teachers in this period, see Robert Black, *Humanism and Education in Medieval and Renaissance Italy: Tradition and Innovation in Latin Schools from the Twelfth to the Fifteenth Century* (New York: Cambridge University Press, 2001), 4.

in fact, hard to define humanist hagiography. A patron's desires, local traditions, available sources, an author's devotion to the saint, financial considerations, even the rawest claims of urban or order politics: all these things frustrate simple definitions. The form itself might intervene, for it was a commonplace that the traditional and didactic literature about saints should observe a certain simplicity (that *sermo humilis* associated with the Evangels) rather than the elegance we expect of humanist prose.[51] For just that reason, singling out only those works that possess an elevated style or philosophical sophistication can obscure the range of humanist engagement with this literature.

Nevertheless, like the centuries of authors who preceded them, the humanists who undertook to revise saints' lives faced some familiar problems and responded in ways that can be discussed as trends or preferences. Taking up their sources, as they created dossiers of evidence about the subject saint, potential rewriters had always considered style, content, and structure.[52] The humanists were no different. In practice, these three aspects of the *vita* are tightly entangled, but a schematic unknotting of style, content, and structure will clarify how the humanists approached their work.

Humanist authors are most characteristic in complaining about the *style* of their sources, which they evaluated by referring to the Latin prosody of Cicero's Rome and to the patristic models of Cyprian, Lactantius, Jerome, and Augustine. Sources that failed this style test (according to their notions of propriety, of course, not ours) were fair candidates for revision, because what was understood to be incompetent Latin was equally understood to damage the credibility of the content.[53] If, as Cicero said, there was no notion so unlikely that it could not be made acceptable by being well expressed, the opposite was also true: there was no element of faith so certain that it could not be made dubious by being poorly stated. Thus the humanists were engaged not simply to persuade but to alter perceived reality. As a cardinal remarked, approving one author's revisions, "What reads elegantly is taken for fact."[54] Inelegance reflected so badly on the saint that

---

51. Eric Auerbach's "*Sermo humilis*," in *Literary Language and Its Public in Late Latin Antiquity and in the Middle Ages*, trans. R. Manheim (New York: Pantheon, 1965), 25–82, is the *locus classicus*. So, for example, Sebastiano Serico, quoted in the epigraph to this chapter, reminds the dedicatee of an earlier translation of Xenophon and of Thucydides's style but declares that the saints require simplicity. See also chap. 4 below.

52. Guidi, "Questioni di storiografia agiografica," gives an excellent overview of the humanists' difficulties on this count.

53. E.g., the humanists shunned rhymed prose for liturgical offices. For the ubiquity of that format in the Middle Ages, see R. Jonsson, *Historia: Étude sur la genèse des offices versifieés* (Stockholm, 1968).

54. "Quod elegans legitur, hoc et factum creditur, pro deliris inconcinna habentur," wrote Cardinal Jacopo Ammannati to Francesco da Castiglione, in Paolo Cherubini, ed., *Iacopo Ammannati Piccolomini Lettere (1444–1479)* (Rome: Ministero per i beni culturali e ambientali, 1997), 2:1227 (letter 376).

another author reminded his patrons not to mistake the shortcomings of the old accounts for the failings of the saints.[55] Such complaints about style had been a justification for rewriting throughout the medieval centuries; if the humanists continued a well-rehearsed excuse, they did so because changing fashions had kept the excuse ever current.[56] The learned ninth-century monk Wandelbert, introducing his life of St. Goar, expressed sentiments very like the fifteenth-century opinion in the epigraph to this chapter.[57] But Wandelbert, no more than the humanist Serico, proposed that the stories of the saints be saved and passed to posterity through devout transcription.[58] Both men had in mind proper *revision*. The humanists merely claimed to be more classically correct, and so more persuasive, in their revisions than their predecessors had been.

The potential author's evaluation of the *content* of his source texts was a complex matter, being at once critical (i.e., concerned with the historical reality of the saint) and rhetorical (i.e., concerned with the choice of topics and presentation to shape the audience's response). Again, concerns about factual and rhetorical truths were not new.[59] Thirteenth-century Dominicans, for example, specialized in the "critical" approach. The annotations that Master General Humbert of Romans made in 1254, as he proposed revisions to the entries about saints in the Dominican lectionary, evince a historiographical astuteness that few humanists equaled.[60] But the same type of critical evaluation so expertly used by Humbert—identifying sources, ascertaining authorship, assessing the literary and cultic presentation on the basis of external evidence[61]—continued in the Renaissance. The

---

55. Raffaele Maffei, treated in chap. 6 below.

56. The tropes of complaint and improvement fill prefaces and dedications; I am completing a study of the humanists' contributions. The survey of prefatory tropes in historiographical genres before the thirteenth century in Gertrud Simon, "Untersuchungen zur Topik des Widmungsbriefe mittelalterlicher Geschichtsschreiber bis zum Ende des 12 Jahrhunderts," *Archiv für Diplomatik* 4 (1958): 52–119 and 5–6 (1959–60): 73–153, includes hagiographic prefaces. On patristic prefaces to *vitae*, see Gerhard Strunk, *Kunst und Glaube in der lateinischen Heiligenlegende. Selbstverständnis in den Prologen* (Munich, 1970).

57. *BHL* 3566; see Bruno Krusch, ed., *MGH, Scriptores rerum merovingicarum* 4, at 410.

58. On transcription, see chap. 3 below.

59. François Dolbeau, "Les hagiographes au travail: Collecte et traitement des documents écrits (IXe–XIIe siècles)," in M. Heinzelmann, ed., *Manuscrits hagiographiques et travail des hagiographes* (Sigmaringen: Thorbecke, 1992), 49–76, efficiently corrects assumptions about medieval gullibility.

60. On Humbert's work, which began in 1246, see M. B. Parkes, "The Compilation of the Dominican Legendary" in K. Elm, ed., *Florilegien, Kompilationen, Kollektionen* (Wiesbaden: Harrassowitz, 2000), 91–106, on Oxford, Keble College, MS 49. Of course, few humanists possessed Humbert's authority to suggest revisions; for one who probably was granted such authority, but failed to rise to the occasion, see remarks on Antonio degli Agli in chap. 2 below.

61. On the scope of critical evaluation, see Parkes, "The Compilation," 96. Looking at literary context *(circumstantia litterae)* was an accepted way to evaluate the authenticity of a text; Humbert's innovation was to apply these scholastic criteria to hagiographical texts (ibid., 93).

novelty was that now this critical proficiency extended deeply into lay circles, feeding into and on the philological expertise that scholars such as Ermolao Barbaro the Younger and Angelo Poliziano were developing at the end of the fifteenth century.[62] That tools so powerful should be in the hands of lay readers necessarily threatened the traditional keepers of *vitae et passiones*. As the Dominican Giovanni Dominici (d. 1419) worried in his *Lucula noctis*, eagle-eyed readers who knew how to identify inconsistencies in the ancient historians would transfer those practices to the lives of the saints. Surely, he warned, the devil wanted nothing else.[63]

Both Humbert and Dominici were Dominicans. The former, addressing an internal audience in the thirteenth century, urged sweeping revisions to the content of received *vitae et passiones* on the basis of critical analysis. The latter, addressing a fifteenth-century lay public, aimed to head off the effects of the new pedagogy and confirm the reverence owed to the traditional accounts and (by synecdochic extension) to the subjects of those accounts. The contrasts in the situations of these two men and in their proposals constitute fine evidence of just how changed the context for *vitae et passiones* was by the early Renaissance. Thanks in part to the success of the *studia humanitatis*, an urban priest could now regularly worry that some part of the congregation was more highly educated than he was. And those people were likely to be vocal about their knowledge. Humanism, like the scholasticism that had formed Humbert, encouraged an agonistic outlook far different from the monastic obedience expected of cloistered authors or the classroom obedience expected of grammar students.

Since the audience's response was fundamental to the success of a *vita* and so to the success of a saint, humanist authors minutely evaluated the *content* of their sources not just for factual errors but also for rhetorical ones. They were critical of overly ambitious use of the *colores rhetorici* (embellishment), figures of speech, tropes, and commonplaces.[64] They also

62. See the overview in Anthony Grafton, *Joseph Scaliger: A Study in the History of Classical Scholarship*, vol. 1 (New York: Oxford University Press, 1983), chap. 1, with further references. Fundamental are Silvia Rizzo, "Per una tipologia delle tradizioni manoscritte di classici latini in età umanistica," in O. Pecere and M. D. Reeve, *Formative Stages of Classical Traditions: Latin Texts from Late Antiquity to the Renaissance* (Spoleto: Centro italiano di studi sull'alto Medievo, 1995), 317–408; idem, "Il latino nell'umanisimo," in A. Asor, ed., *Letteratura italiana*, vol. 5, *Le questioni* (Turin, 1986), 379–408; and eadem, *Il lessico filologico degli umanisti* (Rome, 1973/1985). For a dissenting opinion about the extent to which the humanists may be considered philologists, see E. J. Kenney, *The Classical Text: Aspects of Editing in the Age of the Printed Book* (Berkeley: University of California Press, 1974).

63. Giovanni Dominici, *Lucula noctis*, ed. E. Hunt (Notre Dame, 1940), chap. 46, 178. On the manuscripts, see Karl Loefstedt, "Zur *Lucula noctis* des Giovanni Dominici," *Mittellateinisches Jahrbuch* 34, no. 2 (1999): 119–124.

64. Leonid Arbusow provides a guide to such embellishment in *Colores rhetorici: Eine Auswahl rhetorischen Figuren und Gemeinplätze als Hilfsmittel für akademische Übungen an mittelalterlichen Texten* (Göttingen: Vandenhoeck and Ruprecht, 1948).

What will they be looking for?

checked for quotation or evocation of classical authors such as Virgil, Seneca, and Cicero. Such quotations can be found throughout medieval *vitae*, but the humanists apparently thought that their medieval sources were insufficiently explicit, wide-ranging, and inventive in this regard. To judge from their additions, humanist rewriters also found their sources lacking other elements they understood to be classicizing, such as authors' asides and speeches in direct address. Artificial though these additions may seem to us, they represent the humanists' sense of what would move an audience, and consequently we cannot afford to overlook them. A saint's life aimed, after all, at changing lives; an author's success could be tabulated in conversions. An analogy to advertising today points up the brutal simplicity of the test: if the public does not buy, the ad company has failed at its defining task. The product is, at least momentarily, discredited and must be removed from circulation or handed to a better advertiser. If the product is an article of faith and its success depends on the ability of clerics less educated than their audiences, then discreditation will affect the standing of the Church, not to mention later generations' evaluations of Church "corruption." "Mere" rhetoric, always a question-begging appellation, may be especially so in the case of *vitae sanctorum*.

A humanist author's evaluation of *structure*, as he looked over his source texts, was guided by a handful of prose models. Each was specific to a certain setting, although the boundaries of setting and form were permeable and constantly tested. There are five chief forms to be considered:

1. Classical *vitae* or biographies. Today we understand the classical models for life writing to be complex and contradictory.[65] But there is no explicit evidence that this problem of contradiction occurred to Quattrocento authors. Rather, to judge from the straightforward, even shallow, borrowings they made, these authors rarely appreciated (or dared utilize?) the range of opportunities offered by the classical prose models before them. To take a simple example, Francesco Catellini da Castiglione (d. 1484), canon at San Lorenzo in Florence, evidently meant to echo Plutarch's *parallelae* by composing matched *vitae* of his employer Arch-

---

65. On the complexity of the classical evidence, see articles gathered in W. W. Ehlers, ed., *La biographie antique* (Geneva: Fondation Hardt, 1998); Arnaldo Momigliano's Sather Lectures, *The Development of Greek Biography* (Cambridge, Mass.: Harvard University Press, 1971); and T. A. Dorey, ed., *Latin Biography* (New York: Basic Books, 1967). The strongest competition the saints received in this period was from Plutarch; I do not investigate it here, but compare Plutarch's place at Vittorino's school, discussed by Mariarosa Cortesi, "Lettura di Plutarco alla scuola di Vittorino da Feltre," in V. Fera and G. Ferrau, eds., *Filologia umanistica per Gianvito Resta* (Padua: Antenore, 1997) 1:429–455, with the classroom use of hagiography proposed in chap. 4 below. Cf. F. Leo, *Die griechisch-römische Biographie nach ihrer literarischen Form* (1901; repr. Wollheim, 1965) and, on the tension between classical biographical models and *vitae sanctorum*, Walter Berschin's ongoing *Biographie und Epochenstil im lateinischen Mittelalter* and n. 68 below.

bishop Antonino Pierozzi (c.d. 1523) and his former teacher Vittorino da
Feltre.[66] If that was indeed his aim, then the decision is original and fascinating. But the parallels are not thoroughgoing. A modern reader determined to find much more of Plutarch than the simple claim of parallel subjects will have hard work. It is true that Francesco utilizes the personaliz-
ing anecdote in a way similar to Plutarch, but anecdote is also a feature of
Suetonius and Sallust, not to mention the synoptic Gospels and the majority of late medieval *vitae*. More often than humanist authors borrowed the
structure of classical biography, they simply evoked *sententiae*, or statements of moral guidance, from these sources. But in these instances they
drew chiefly on Sallust and Suetonius, who had also been medieval
favorites.[67] In short, the part played by classical biographical models for
vitae sanctorum appears to be surprisingly limited.[68]

2. Patristic *vitae* and early Christian *passiones*. Here the evidence is
extensive and convincing: the humanists demonstrate respect for these models through transcription, imitation, and, most important, translation.[69]

Transcription constitutes basic but difficult evidence of the continuing
effect of a small group of patristic and early Christian accounts. Dozens of
transcriptions of Jerome's *vitae* of Paul, Hilarion, and Malchus, not to

66. On Francesco da Castiglione, see chap. 2 below.

67. Other borrowings are noted in the following chapters. It is my impression that *sententiae*, when not taken from biographical sources, come most often from Cicero, Virgil, Statius, Seneca, Sallust, Terence, and Valerius Maximus, whether in medieval or in Renaissance
lives of saints. A comparative statistical study of a few key texts from representative centuries
would be revealing.

68. On the relation between classical models and *vitae sanctorum* in Late Antiquity and
the Middle Ages, see Jacques Fontaine, "Alle fonti dell'agiografia europea," *Rivista di storia
e letteratura religiosa* 2 (1966): 187–206; idem, "Comment doit-on appliquer la notion de
genre littéraire à la littérature latine chrétienne du IVe siècle?" *Philologus* 132 (1988): 53–73;
B. R. Voss, "Bemerkungen zu Evagrius von Antiochen: Vergil und Sallust in der *Vita Antonii*,"
Vigiliae christianae 21 (1967): 93–102; idem, "Beruhungen von Hagiographie und Historiographie in der Spätantike," *Frühmittelalterliche Studien* 4 (1970): 53–69; Claudio
Leonardi, "I modelli dell'agiografia latina dall'epoca antica al medioevo," in *Passaggio dal
mondo antico al medioevo: Da Teodosio a San Gregorio Magno*, Atti dei Convegni Lincei
(Rome, 1980), 435–476; Jean-Michel David, "Rhétorique et histoire: L'exemplum et le mod-
èle de comportement dans le discours antique et medieval," *MEFR* 92, no. 1 (1980): 9–179;
and Marc van Uytfanghe, "Modèles bibliques dans l'hagiographie," in P. Riché and G. Lobri-
chon, eds., *Le Moyen Age et la Bible* (Paris: Beauchesne, 1984), 449–488.

69. For introductory material on humanists and patristics, see G. Voigt, *Il risorgimento
dell'antichità classica ovvero il primo secolo dell'umanesimo*, trans. D. Valbusa (Florence:
Sansoni, 1988); August Buck, "Der Ruckgriff des Renaissance-Humanismus auf die Patris-
tik," in K. Baldinger ed., *Festschrift Walther von Wartburg* (Tübingen: Niemeyer, 1968),
1:153–175; and Eugene F. Rice, Jr., "The Renaissance Idea of Classical Antiquity: Humanist
Patristic Scholarship," in A. Rabil. ed., *Renaissance Humanism: Foundations, Forms, and
Legacy* (Philadelphia: University of Pennsylvania Press, 1988) 1:17–29; some specialized
studies are noted below.

mention the pseudepigraphal *transitus Hieronymi* texts, are extant in humanist hands. As the scribes responsible for these transcriptions are rarely identifiable, it is hard to do more than note the warm and continuing use of the variety of Jerome texts.[70] But the example of the jurisconsult Mazo dei'Mazi (Madius; d. 1445)—student of Guarino and friend of Flavio Biondo, Lorenzo Giustinian, and Francesco Barbaro—may be telling. Mazo wrote out in his own hand the lives of two saintly bishops, Zeno and Martin.[71] As we know that he engaged scribes to produce classical manuscripts, it may seem proof of the relative unimportance of saints' lives that he did not employ them in this instance. But we should bear in mind that the life of Martin, at least, is not a brief narrative: Mazo may well have been engaged in transcription as an act of devotion.

Demonstrating imitation is only slightly less divinatory than sorting out the motivations for transcription. Still, it does appear that imitative echoes of the earliest martyrs' *passiones* are intentional in some humanists' compositions. For example, the curialist Leon Battista Alberti, writing about the martyr Potitus, reproduced a salutation found in letters exchanged among the early Christian churches about their martyrs; the Dominican Pietro Ransano, writing about the contemporary martyr Anthony of Rivalto, whom he himself had counseled, may have chosen to cast his *passio* in the form of a letter on the basis of the same early Christian models. The patristic rhetorical model is claimed, however, more often than actually employed. Giovanni Garzoni is typical in this respect: he relentlessly adduces Lactantius and Jerome as his guides, although their greatest effect on his prose seems to be a certain testiness.[72]

About translation we can be quite certain. By translating patristic and early Christian lives of saints, the humanists contributed to the spiritual life and literature of the West in a way that paralleled the effect of their translations of the Greek classics.[73] Here the Camaldolese monk Ambro-

70. See chap. 4 for some examples of these texts and a suggestion of their use. In his library of 388 codices, the humanist and reforming Cardinal Domenico Capranica (d. 1458) had at least five manuscripts that included *transitus Hieronymi* narratives. See the 1480 catalog in BAV, MS Lat. 8184, at f. 7r, items 228–229 and 232–234.

71. Sabbadini, *Epistolario* 3, 60.

72. On Garzoni, see chap. 4 below.

73. On Traversari, see Kristeller, "Contribution," 155–156, and G. C. Garfagnini, ed., *Ambrogio Traversari nel VI centenario della nascita* (Florence, 1988), as guides to earlier literature. On humanist techniques of translation, see Lucia Gualdo Rosa, "Le traduzioni dal greco nella prima metà del Quattrocento," in R. Renard and P. Laurens, eds., *Hommages à Henry Bardon* (Brussels, 1985), 177–193; Livia Martinoli Santini, "Le traduzioni dal Greco," in M. Miglio, ed., *Un pontificato ed una città: Sisto IV (1471–1474)* (Vatican City: Scuola Vaticana di paleografia, diplomatica e archivistica, 1986), 81–114; Mariarosa Cortesi, "La tecnica del tradurre presso gli umanisti," in C. Leonardi and B. Munk Olsen, *The Classical Tradition in the Middle Ages and the Renaissance* (Spoleto: Centro italiano di studi sull'alto Medioevo, 1995), 143–168; cf. Rita Copeland, "The Fortunes of *non verbum*

gio Traversari (d. 1439) had a seminal role: among his dozens of translations of Greek works, five are of *vitae sanctorum*.[74] His first efforts, from 1424–1431, were to translate John Moschus's *Spiritual Meadow* (which Traversari combined with the *Paradisus animae* under the title *Vitae patrum*, lives of the Fathers). Then there followed versions of Simeon Metaphrast's life of Daniel the Stylite; Gregory Presbyter's life of Gregory Nazianzen; an abridged translation of Palladius's dialogic life of John Chrysostom; and Daniel the Monk's life of John the Scholar. Both lay and clerical authors continued the project of translation across the Quattrocento. Among them were Guarino, who translated a Greek life of Ambrose around 1434; George of Trebizond, who translated the meditative life that Gregory of Nyssa had written of Moses; Nicolaus Secundinus, who translated, like Traversari before him, Gregory Presbyter's life of Gregory Nazianzen; Pietro Balbi, who translated Gregory of Nyssa's life of his sister Macrina (Balbi's translation is lost); and Pietro Barozzi, who—probably before his accession to the bishopric of Padua in 1487—translated an unidentified life of Basil. Aldus Manutius's three-volume textbook *Poetae christiani* of 1501–1503, which often presents the Greek with facing-page Latin translation, signals the full arrival of this literature.[75]

3. An authoritative model for any author of *vitae sanctorum* also existed in the canonization *vita*.[76] But this model—which, by the fifteenth century, required a rigid ordering of the events of the life, followed by a survey of the virtues, then an account of the pious death and canonization,

---

pro verbo; or, Why Jerome Is Not a Ciceronian," in R. Ellis, ed., *The Medieval Translator* (Woodbridge, Suffolk: Brewer, 1989), 15–36; Paolo Chiesa, "*Ad verbum o ad sensum?* Modelli e coscienza metodologica della traduzione tra tarda antichità e alto medioevo," *Medioevo e rinascimento* 1 (1987): 1–51; and, on hagiographic texts, François Dolbeau, "Le role des interprètes dans les traductions hagiographiques d'Italie du sud," in G. Contamine, ed., *Traduction et traducteurs au Moyen Age: Colloque international du CNRS, 26–28 mai 1986* (Paris: CNRS, 1989), 143–168. Specialized studies are noted below.

74. Six, if we count the lost life of Athanasius; see the hand list. Elpidio Mioni, "Le *vitae patrum* nella traduzione di Ambrogio Traversari," *Aevum* 24 (1950): 319–331, remains the best study. Traversari's letters reveal as well his interest in the Latin lives of Benedict and Peter Damian, the dialogues of Desiderius, the *Collationes* of Cassian, and Philo's *Vita Moysis*. Cf. the translations of the *vitae patrum* by Angelo Clareno, O.F.M., cataloged by Ronald Musto: "Angelo Clareno, O.F.M.: Fourteenth-Century Translator of the Greek Fathers—An Introduction and a Checklist of MSS and Printings of His *Scala paradisi*," *AFH* 76 (1983): 215–238, 589–645; A. Sottili, "Humanistische Neuverwendung mittelalterlicher Ubersetzungen: Zum mittelalterlichen und humanistischen Fortleben des Johannes Climacus," in A. Buck, ed., *Die Rezeption der Antike* (Hamburg, 1981), 165–185.

75. On all the translations mentioned in this paragraph, see the hand list.

76. On the medieval development of canonization procedure, there is a large literature. For an introduction, see *Enciclopedia cattolica* 3:569–607; *New Catholic Encyclopedia* 3:55–61; *DS* 1:77–85; E. W. Kemp, *Canonization and Authority in the Western Church* (London, 1948); and above all, Vauchez, *La sainteté*.

and finally a coda of miracles—was not embraced by the humanists. They seem, as rhetoricians professionally concerned with persuasion, to have preferred more integrated narratives. For example, these authors rarely echo, in any of their accounts, the massive collection of miracles entailed in the canonization *vita*. Their hesitancy on this point had, I suspect, less to do with an aversion to the miraculous per se, than with the fact that such catalogs were legal documents, constructed by notaries on the basis of witnesses' testimony, and so largely outside the purview of the rhetorician. The case of the layman Niccolò Borghesi (d. 1500) is instructive: of his six saints' lives, only one has an extensive catalog of miracles, and that account is also the only one he wrote about a contemporary saint, Jacopo Filippo Bertoni (d. 1483), a Servite in the convent at Faenza. Niccolò wrote at the request of the prior at Faenza, Taddeo da Anghiari, and shortly after the subject's death. So his concluding catalog may indicate that Prior Taddeo was considering a submission of material to initiate proceedings for canonization. In this instance, Niccolò was probably as useful to the Servites for his political position as for his language skills. In short, if a humanist author engaged in anything like a canonization format, he did so decisively and probably with canonization in his patron's mind, if not his own.

And there is another point to be borne in mind. In the final analysis, no matter what the authors thought of the canonization *vita* format, they were rarely invited to produce such *vitae*. The example of Niccolò Borghesi notwithstanding, lay humanists were rarely engaged by an order to write about that order's saints (although they themselves might choose to write about order saints, as I will show). A fortiori, lay humanists were not invited to compose official *vitae* for the in-house figures who dominated fifteenth-century canonization proceedings. Of those humanists in orders, only one was invited to compose an official canonization *vita*, and his response seems strikingly ambivalent.[77] After Vincent Ferrer's process had been successfully completed, the Dominican Pietro Ransano was recruited to write the official life. The *vita Vincentii* was to consist of four or five books, the first two treating the life and virtues, the third miracles *in vita*, and the fourth miracles *post mortem*. Now, by the fifteenth century, what we call the canonization life was typically written before the process and so contributed to the documentation for the process itself. This reversal of the normal order of composition suggests that the order sought precisely Ransano's rhetorical skills. So perhaps it is not surprising that Ransano barely got further than the third book, abandoning the project just as he arrived at the legalistic catalog. Ransano turned out sev-

---

77. I address other cases of humanist involvement in promoting canonizations in chaps. 5 and 6 below. The cathedral canon Francesco Catellini da Castiglione used the canonization proceedings to write his account of Vincent Ferrer; see the hand list.

eral different kinds of useful narratives about Vincent but left his prestigious commission incomplete.[78]

4. The mendicant encyclopedic model. The relatively short and simply written derivative life known as a *legendum* (legend, without the derogatory overtones of the English word), made familiar by Jacobus de Voragine's *Legenda aurea*, remained powerful in the Quattrocento.[79] The continuity of the mendicant model can be seen most basically in the expanded version of the *Legenda aurea* that was prepared by the Observant Benedictine Ilarione Lantieri at the request of the Chapter General and printed in Milan in 1496 or in the expanded 1506 Venetian edition of Petrus de Natalibus's fourteenth-century legendary.[80] The mendicant model was obviously fundamental to any revision of martyrologies and legendaries, which were by definition collections of abbreviated narratives. But the desire for authoritative and entertaining brevity extended beyond the confines of those compilations. A little mealtime reading, an engaging story before bed, an elementary grammar-school text, a kernel from which to elaborate a sermon, a clutch of virtues for meditation and prayer, a souvenir from the civic event of a *translatio*: epitomes in the form of *libelli* (handbooks) served all these purposes, especially in the second half of the century as printing enlarged the market. Most of the humanists' accounts are, in fact, such abbreviated legends.

5. The fifth structural model used by humanist authors was liturgical.[81]

78. Even so, the account was quite widely distributed (see the hand list). Laura Smoller is completing a study of Vincent Ferrer's canonization, *The Saint and the Chopped-Up Baby: The Canonization and Early Cult of Vincent Ferrer*. In the meantime, see eadem, "Miracle, Memory, and Meaning in the Canonization of Vincent Ferrer," *Speculum* 73 (1998): 429–454; and "Defining the Boundaries of the Natural in the Fifteenth Century: The Inquest into the Miracles of St. Vincent Ferrer (d. 1419)," *Viator* 48 (1997): 333–359. I am grateful to Professor Smoller and to John Coakley for sharing thoughts.

79. On mendicant historiography and abbreviated forms, see H. Pätze, ed., *Geschichtschreibung und Geschichtsbewusstsein im späten Mittelalter* (Sigmaringen: Thorbecke, 1987); and Elm, *Florilegien*. In the enormous bibliography on the *Legenda aurea*, see especially C. Frova and B. Fleith, in S. Boesch Gajano, ed., *Raccolte di Vite di Santi dal XIII al XVIII secolo* (Fasano de Brindisi: Schena, 1990); Barbara Fleith, *Studien zur Überlieferungsgeschichte der lateinischen Legenda aurea* (Brussels: Bollandist Society, 1991); and eadem, "The Patristic Sources of the *Legenda Aurea*: A Research Report," in Irene Backus, ed., *The Reception of the Church Fathers in the West: From the Carolingians to the Maurists* (Leiden: Brill, 1997) 2:231–288, its scope broader than the title suggests; Barbara Fleith and Franco Morenzoni, eds., *De la sainteté à l'hagiographie: Genèse et usage de la Légende dorée* (Geneva: Droz, 2001). An instance of the influence of the *Legenda Aurea* on humanist rewriting is treated in chap. 4.

80. On Lantieri and Petrus de Natalibus (Pietro Nadal), O.P., who compiled the legendary between 1369 and 1372, see the hand list. On Pietro da Chioggia, another important Dominican compiler of the fourteenth century, Albert Poncelet, "Le légendier de Pierre Calo," *AB* 29 (1910): 5–116, remains the only substantial study.

81. For medieval background on liturgical *vitae*, see *SMHM* 59–102; and John Harper, *Forms and Orders of Western Liturgy from the Tenth to the Eighteenth Century* (New York: Oxford University Press, 1991) esp. 51–54, 81 and 240–241. Further bibliography in chaps. 2 and 6.

Saints' names occurred in calendars, which were lists arranged according to the liturgical year; in invocatory litanies; and in parts of the Mass (the Church's eucharistic celebration) according to instructions set out in technical books known as sacramentaries. The humanist rewriters of saints' lives focused, however, on the special office celebrated on the saint's feast-day (such as are found in late medieval and Renaissance breviaries). These offices included a set of readings, *lectiones*, for the service at matins. During the second nocturne of that early morning ceremony, as few as three or as many as twelve *lectiones*, depending on the solemnity of the feast, were read.[82] The *lectiones* might consist of passages from the Bible, of highlights from a *vita* alternating with scripture or patristic homilies, or of a short *vita* broken into sections. Humanists specialized in this last model, which they seem to have approached by composing brief *vitae* and then dividing them into readings.[83] As public texts, *lectiones* especially required evidence of thoughtful intelligence and rhetorical skill applied to the capacities of the audience (and to the capacities of the priests who would present the readings). Learned listeners, including officiants and potential authors, might be scandalized by unfashionable, which is to say, risible and unbelievable, presentations.[84] And the mockery of the learned, it was feared, would infect simpler souls.

To sum up, humanist hagiography continued the medieval use of classical tags and *sententiae* and expanded the medieval use of authorial asides and speeches in direct address. On rare occasions, humanists innovated by borrowing classical forms such as parallel lives; many authors may have felt instead that Plutarch's models had to be countered. Humanists continued medieval attention to *vitae* by and about the Latin fathers and pursued Greek patristic sources with a new enthusiasm. They were concerned, as their medieval predecessors had been, with historical and rhetorical

---

82. On the Renaissance office, see Pierre Batiffol, *History of the Roman Breviary*, trans. A. M. Y. Baylay (London: Longmans, 1989), 220–223, with background in E. Palazzo, *Le Moyen Age* (Paris, 1993).

83. For an example of a traditional scriptural office for a saint, see the office for Crescentius by Giovanni Pietro Arrivabene bound at the end of a printed Roman missal (London, British Library, IB 18578), discussed by D. S. Chambers, "Giovanni Pietro Arrivabene (1439–1504): Humanist Secretary and Bishop," *Aevum* 58 (1984): 397–438, at 432–433.

84. For an example of a risible text, although one that was neither a set of *lectiones* nor about a saint, see O'Malley, *Praise*, 20: during Advent of 1512, a Franciscan gave a sermon in the papal chapel that was "three or four or five times" the normal half-hour length and would not be stopped even by the laughter and loud comments of his audience. O'Malley's study has been a model for this one, although the texts analyzed there were produced under "laboratory" conditions, unlike those treated here. For a mid-Quattrocento report on other such incidents, see P. de Corso, ed., *Timoteo Maffei: In sanctam rusticitatem litteras impugnantem. Introduzione, edizione critica e commento* (Verona: Archivio storico, Curia diocesana, 2000), 177–178; Maffei is discussed in chap. 5 below.

FIGURE 1.1. To judge from the hand list, authors preferred to write about saints from which century?

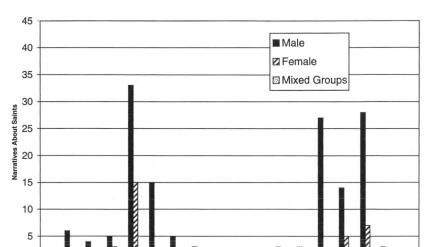

notions of truth, although the changing historiographical and rhetorical context gave Quattrocento attention to *veritas* a different tone.[85] Thus it appears that the effect of the *studia humanitatis* on the field of hagiogra-phy is best described as an intensification and redirection of medieval con-cerns, not as a complete break with, or a series of challenges to, those con cerns. This description makes a certain sense. After all, the early Christian *vitae* that were known throughout the Middle Ages to reading Christians (and to many who did not read)—Athanasius's life of Anthony, Jerome's lives of Paul, Hilarion, and Malchus, and Sulpicius Severus's life of Mar-tin—themselves drew on classical language and forms.

※ ※ ※

To which saints was this concern for the tight knot of style, content, and structure applied? Thanks to the material gathered in the hand list, some rough quantitative responses can be given to that question. Figure 1.1 records the frequency with which humanist authors chose saints from par-ticular centuries as their subjects. Century is assigned by the saint's date of

85. On humanist historiography, see Cochrane's introduction in *Historians*, with earlier bibliography. Specialized studies are noted in the chapters below; in particular, chap. 6 below considers the implications of the changing historiographical context for *vitae sanctorum*.

death; that dating respects the authors' historical understanding rather than current scholarship.[86]

A degree of skepticism about this quantification is strongly encouraged: counting up the narratives, means ignoring differences in their length, format, intended audience, and aesthetic pretensions. Moreover, no figure or discussion can fairly represent everything that might be noticed about this complex evidence. It has proven impracticable, for example, to convert into chart format the hundreds of lives and passions that were gathered into compilations or anthologies by Antonio degli Agli, Giannozzo Manetti, Giovanni Caroli, Bonino Mombrizio, Ilarione Lantieri, Bonifacio Simonetta, Leandro Alberti, and Giovanni Antonio Flamini.[87] For the same reason, my findings about the humanists' preferred subjects are best set out discursively. And even the relatively simple question answered by the single figure given above conceals important findings.

One of the findings that does not appear, for example, is the severe underrepresentation of the Holy Kinship in humanists' compositions:[88] there are no Latin prose narratives about Ann or Elizabeth and very few

86. The y-axis does not represent saints but narratives about saints. A single narrative might treat a single saint, male or female. But a single narrative might also treat groups of saints, and some of those groups consist of both men and women (indicated as "mixed groups" in figure 1.1). In the case of groups treated in a single narrative, such as Pietro Donato Avogaro's 1494 account of Veronese bishops from the first through fourth centuries, the latest date of death determines the century. Data stops at 1520.

87. On the collections, see the hand list; all are addressed to some extent in this study. It is unlikely that consensus could be reached on the sanctity of each figure in such collections. Some pose acute problems of definition: Giovanni Caroli, for example, wrote a collection of lives of Dominicans from his convent in Florence. Only two of his seven narratives have been given *BHL* numbers (official recognition that the accounts are about saints). What Caroli thought of each figure's sanctity would have to be argued case by case. The same problem dogs analysis of Leandro Alberti's *De viris illustribus ordinis praedicatorum* (1517). The crowning difficulty is that fifteenth-century manuscript and printed copies of the *Legenda aurea* and its avatars, as well as of Usuard and the *transitus Hieronymi* texts, should also be borne in mind, to the extent that humanists were engaged as editors or even produced those texts as entrepreneurs. It is not possible to give a scientifically objective count of humanist hagiography.

88. Humanists wrote many biographical treatments of Christ in prose and verse. See, e.g., "De vita et moribus ac miraculis Christ," which forms book 2 of Manetti's *Adversus Judaeos et Gentes* (BAV, MS Urb. lat. 154); the eleven-book epic *Messiade* by Domenico di Antonio (Mazzatinti 30 [1926/67], 179 = Bologna, Bibl. Com. Arch., MS A.445, dated 1472); the extremely popular *Vita e passione di Cristo* by Antonio Cornazzano (Schutte, *PIVRB*, 149; Roberto Bruni and Diego Zancani, *Antonio Cornazzano: La tradizione testuale* [Florence: Olschki, 1992]); and Bonino Mombrizio's *De Dominica passione* (Ganda, *I primordi*, 135, item 35; and chap. 3 below). In addition, the sacred oratory of the Roman Curia between 1450 and 1521 was overwhelmingly delivered for liturgical occasions associated with the birth and passion of Christ and the life and death of the Virgin. See O'Malley, *Praise*, appendix, 245–255, where sermons for saints' days make up only about 15 percent of the total, of which the majority (eleven) are for All Saints' Day (i.e., are not life narratives).

of the Magdalene or Joseph.[89] John the Baptist, as patron saint of Florence, is a special case. But even he, well represented in vernacular sermons and verse—Francesco Filelfo's 1445 *Vita del sanctissimo Johanni Battista*, written at Milan for Filippo Maria Visconti, is a prime example[90]—is treated with relative infrequency in Latin prose. I suspect that the humanists did not write about the Holy Kinship in Latin prose precisely because these figures belonged so intimately to mother-tongue devotions. But humanist composition of saints' lives and passions in the vernacular is probably undercounted, as a result of the classicizing interests of most scholars in the field of Renaissance studies and the nonhumanist interests of most scholars of late medieval sanctity. The case of the humanist Pietro Edo (d. after 1501) may be exemplary. Edo, a priest at Pordenone, in the Friuli, translated local law into the vernacular for the good of his community; he also made his parishioners a vernacular translation of an office for the Virgin.[91] But Ann's popularity with the elite Roman fraternity known as the Coryciade—who annually produced Latin verse in her honor—also suggests that the mother-tongue hypothesis will not fully account for the relative paucity of Latin prose *vitae* about the Holy Kinship.

At any rate, figure 1.1 must not be considered an absolute or final statement. Inevitably, other humanist accounts will be discovered. Readers may disagree now with my attribution of this account to that author, now with my description of that author as a humanist. Most important, I have not included sermons in the catalog, although a *vita* or *passio* might well be

---

89 Ann is a special case: patron saint of the Coryciade, her cult produced a fair amount of humanist poetry in Rome. See John Sparrow, "Renaissance Latin Poetry: Some Sixteenth-Century Italian Anthologies," in C. H. Clough, ed., *Cultural Aspects of the Italian Renaissance: Essays in Honour of Paul Oskar Kristeller* (New York: Zambelli, 1976), 386–405, at 387–388; J. Gaisser, "The Rise and Fall of Goritz's Feasts," *RQ* 48 (1995): 41–57; J. IJsewijn, "Poetry in a Roman Garden: The *Coryciana*," in P. Godwin and O. Murray, eds., *Latin Poetry and the Classical Tradition: Essays in Medieval and Renaissance Literature* (Oxford: Oxford University Press, Clarendon, 1990), 211–231. Catherine Lawless, "'A Widow of God'? St. Anne and Representations of Widowhood in Fifteenth-Century Florence," in C. Meek, ed., *Women in Renaissance and Early Modern Europe* (Dublin: Four Courts, 2000), 15–42, offers an explanation specific to Florence for Ann's underrepresentation. On Mary Magdalene and Joseph, see the hand list. Note that the epideictic orations studied by O'Malley, *Praise*, also do not include these figures.

90. See P. Viti, "Filelfo, Francesco," *DBI* 47 (1997), 622b; Kristeller, *Iter* 1:282b on MBA, MS D 73, with a letter to Giovanni Trivulzio; see also Aristide Calderini, "I codici milanesi delle opere di Francesco Filelfo," *ASL* 5, 2, 42 (1915), 335–411, at items 21 and 45. Schutte, *PIVRB*, 177, records the 1494 incunable.

91. Lilia Sereni, *I tesori della Civica biblioteca* [*Udine. Catalog*] *Mostra di manoscritti e libri rari* (Udine, 1983), 66, no. 13.3. On Edo, see Massimo Miglio, "L'umanista Pietro Edo e la polemica sulla donazione di Costantino," *Bollettino dell'Istituto storico italiano per il Medio Evo e Archivo Muratoriano* 80 (1968): 167–232. Virginia Reinburg, "Liturgy and the Laity in Late Medieval and Reformation France," *Sixteenth Century Journal* 23, no. 3 (1992): 527–547, at 530, mentions French humanists' promoting the use of vernaculars in the Mass. See chap. 7 below.

read in such a way as to function as a sermon, and vice versa.[92] So the figure represents only a rough indication of the preferences that humanist
authors expressed in their writings about saints. It offers not simple facts
but a myriad of trends. *Possible Lives* is designed to explore both the
trends and the anomalies revealed by quantification.

Figure 1.1 shows dramatically that humanist authors favored saints
from the fourth and fifth century and from the thirteenth through the fifteenth century. This emphasis appears to confirm the most traditional
depiction of Renaissance prejudices in favor of (Late) Antiquity and their
own times and against the Middle Ages. But does it in fact? The chapters
that follow will suggest, in various ways, that the humanists' neglect of the
central Middle Ages resulted not from malign intent, not from judgments
about the barbarism of those centuries, but from preoccupations with
other concerns. By avoiding saints from certain centuries, humanists reveal
to us not so much their own as their patrons' and audiences' approbation
of the existing accounts or even lack of interest in those saints.

It is possible to press forward, building on figure 1.1, to ask about the
frequency with which humanist authors writing in Latin prose chose certain types of saints as subjects.[93] There is, of course, no simple typology.
Apostles were martyrs, too; the category of bishops includes archbishops,
popes, and patriarchs (among them, more martyrs); the category of
laypeople includes a range of saints from the emperor Charlemagne to the
humble hermit Amato Ronconi, whose virtues are offered by Sebastiano
Serico in the epigraph to this chapter. Religious orders are diverse, their
early histories notoriously contested, and the adherence of a saintly individual to one or the other of them might well be insecure (and here, too,
are martyrs). I have counted Augustine, for example, among the bishops,
but authors associated with the Lateran Canons and the Augustinian Hermits considered him first of all a founder. Nevertheless, it can be affirmed
that, when writing in Latin prose, the humanists overwhelmingly selected
three subject types: those in orders, martyrs, and bishops.

The first favored group, the regulars, makes up almost the entirety of
the thirteenth- to fifteenth-century *vitae* that show so prominently in figure 1.1. Among these regulars, the preaching orders feature largely; the

92. See the introductory remarks of George Ferzoco, "The Context of Medieval Sermon
Collections on Saints," in Muessig, *Preacher*, 279–280.

93. The categories of type, or *status vitae,* that I have used are ones familiar to the authors
themselves: figures from the Old Testament, apostles, early martyrs, bishops, those in religious orders, and laypeople. These categories are similar to those in Vauchez, *La sainteté,*
although his study is restricted to canonized sainthood, unlike this one. For an introduction
to the standard saintly types, illustrated from medieval and Renaissance manuscripts and
early printed books, see the exhibition catalog edited by Claudio Leonardi and Maria
degli'Innocenti, *I santi patroni: Modelli di santità, culti e patronati in Occidente* (Carugate:
Everprint, 1999).

Benedictines are barely represented. The second most favored group, the martyrs, accounts for the very strong category of fourth-century saints in figure 1.1. Bishops, the third most favored group, occur across the field of humanist composition delineated in the figure, for reasons that will become clear shortly.

The humanists' attention to mendicants and to bishops suggests that these authors (and their patrons) sought to represent a robust, this-worldly spirituality, focused on the male *vita activa*, on reforming manifestations of religious life *outside* the cloister and *in* the city.[94] This emphasis—perfectly in tune with current perceptions of the ethos of the *studia humanitatis*—can be detected even in humanist composition of martyrs' *passiones*. But it is most unambiguously revealed in narratives about bishops.[95]

Roughly 20 percent of the Latin prose accounts by humanist authors treat bishops, and the importance of this group rises when the relative length, complexity, and circulation of some of these narratives are considered. The narratives bear up recent scholarship on humanist reformers' promotion of exemplary ecclesiastics through *specula episcoporum*.[96] The

94. Cf. Samuel K. Cohn, "Piety and Religious Practice in the Rural Dependencies of Renaissance Florence," *English Historical Review* 114, no. 159 (1999): 1121–1142, on rural devotion. Emblematic of the humanists' urban outlook is Ambrogio Traversari's effort to enlist the authority of Eugene IV for removing the recently discovered relics of Maurus and Vitalis from a rural monastery described as *desolatus*. The abbot was evidently a friend of Traversari's and willing to help, but the locals who farmed the monastery's fields were likely to object: "veretur Abbas ipse rusticorum offensam, qui terras ipsius monasterii colunt" (L. Mehus and P. Cannetus, eds., *Ambrosii Traversarii . . . Epistolae . . . [et] Vita . . .* [Florence, 1759; reprint, Bologna: Forni, 1968], letter 3, at col. 12).

95. For statistical evidence of the medieval attention to bishop-saints, see Vauchez, *La sainteté*, 258, and the discussion, 285–310; for an introduction to the genre of episcopal history, see Michel Sot, *Gesta episcoporum, gesta abbatum* (Turnhout: Brepols, 1981); and Reinhold Kaiser, "Die *gesta episcoporum* als Genus der Geschichtsschreibung," in A. Scharer and G. Scheibelreiter, eds., *Historiographie im frühen Mittelalter* (Munich: Oldenbourg, 1994), 459–480.

96. E.g., Raffaele Maffei's posthumous edition of Paolo Cortesi's *De cardinalatu*, on which see G. Ferrau, "Politica e cardinalato in un età di transizione: Il *De cardinalatu* di Paolo Cortesi," in S. Gensini, ed., *Roma capitale (1447–1527)* (Pisa: Pacini, 1994), 519–540; and Gasparo Contarini's *De officio viri boni ac probi episcopi*, written for the new bishop of Bergamo, on which see G. Fragnito, "Cultura umanistica e riforma religiosa: Il *De officio viri boni ac probi episcopi* di Gasparo Contarini," *Studi veneziani* 11 (1969): 75–189 and the English edition by J. P. Donnelly, *Gaspare Contarini, The Office of a Bishop* (Milwaukee: Marquette University Press, 2002). (It is important to keep in mind that Contarini wrote for a thirteen-year-old; his treatise may be fruitfully compared to Erasmus's handbook for the young prince's education.) In a few instances, a family's patronage also plays a role in the composition of bishops' *vitae*: e.g., the life of Zenobius by the layman Naldo Naldi (d.c. 1513), dedicated in 1499 to Raffael Girolami, who claimed descent from the saint's line. See Sally J. Cornelison, "A French King and a Magic Ring: The Girolami and a Relic of St. Zenobius in Renaissance Florence," *RQ* 55, no. 2 (2002): 434–469, with further bibliography.

bishops' *vitae* also signify a strong continuity with the Middle Ages: from the late ninth century, authors throughout the Italian peninsula can be found linking the well-being of the community to the activity of the bishop as urban patron.[97] Episcopal participation in urban politics, which had initiated this shift in the literary phenomena, only increased in later centuries, cementing the trend.

The humanists' *vitae* play up the idealized sociopolitical role of the model bishop in one particularly striking way: by re-creating the scene of the deathbed speech as a testamentary act. Models for this bit of invention could be found in a handful of early *vitae* but are a regular feature in the early *vitae* of the mendicant founders, which often included last words in *oratio recta* (direct address).[98] No matter whether the bishop was a contemporary, as the Dominican archbishop of Florence, Antonino Pierozzi, was for his biographer Francesco Catellini da Castiglione, or a distant and sparsely documented figure, as the fifth-century bishop Zenobius of Flo-

---

97. Jean-Charles Picard, *Le souvenir des évêques: Sépultures, listes épiscopales et culte des évêques en Italie du Nord des origines au Xe siècle* (Rome: BEFAR, 1988), traces the emergence in northern Italy from the eighth to tenth century of the cult of bishops as city patrons (rather than, as they had been, patrons of the local church narrowly conceived). As Picard notes, developments in northern Italy were well behind those in Gaul: there is no equivalent to the Merovingian output of *vitae episcoporum* in the north or central part of the Italian peninsula. Paolo Golinelli, *Città e culto dei santi nel medioevo italiano* (Bologna: CLUEB, 1988), and Webb, *Patrons,* take up the place of bishops as saints in northern Italian cities from the High Middle Ages.

98. S. Dagemark, for example, emphasizes the scene of death in "Possidius's Idealized Description of St. Augustine's Death," in *Vescovi e pastori in epoca teodosiana. XXC incontro di studiosi dell'antichità cristiana Roma, 8–11 maggio 1996* (Rome: Institutum Patristicum Augustinianum, 1997), 2:719–741, but there is no direct discourse. For the virtue of silence, see P. Henriet, "*Silentium usque ad mortem servaret.* La scène de la mort dans les ermites italiens du XIe siècle, *MEFRM* 105 (1993): 265–298. See also Jacques Dalarun, "La mort des saint fondateurs, de Martin à François," in *Fonctions,* 193–215; Pierre Boglioni, "La scène de la mort dans les premieres hagiographies latines," in C. Sutto, ed., *Le sentiment de la mort au Moyen Age: Études présentées au cinquième colloque de l'Institut d'études médiévales de l'Université de Montréal* (Montreal: L'Aurore, 1979), 185–210; and H. Fichtenau, *Living in the Tenth Century* (Chicago: University of Chicago Press, 1991), 213–216. That the development was a real innovation is suggested by the series of fifteenth-century humanist accounts of Zenobius, conveniently listed in C. Nardi, "Un volgarizzamento quattrocentesco della Vita di san Zanobi di Lorenzo di Amalfi (sec. X)," in *La Cattedrale e la città: Saggi sul Duomo di Firenze. Atti del convegno internazionale di studi. Firenze 16–21 giugno 1997* (Florence: Edifil, 2001), 145–174. Such attention to the deathbed speech is not found, for example, in the canonical episcopal *vitae* known to the humanists, such as pseudo-Amphilochius's life of Basil; Possidius's life of Augustine (although, preceding the death of Augustine, Possidius quotes a lengthy letter that might be said to serve as spiritual testament); or Severus's life of Martin (although, of course, Severus also wrote a dialogue on Martin's death). I thank Caroline Bynum for her observation that the *vitae* of charismatic women saints often include a deathbed address; indeed, the humanist G. M. A. Cararra's life of Clare of Montefalco includes an exceptionally long deathbed address. This approved site of women's speech deserves investigation.

rence was for Giovanni Tortelli (d. 1466), Antonio degli Agli, and Naldo Naldi, the deathbed speech became, for many humanist authors, the bishop's literary testament, a moment of public instruction mixing spiritual and temporal concerns. Such concerns were, notably, those of the medieval and Renaissance reformers: residency, conscientious attention to *cura animarum* (care of souls), and the provision for the peace and well-being of the city through charity and justice. The reforming aim is important, as it shows both clerical and lay teachers of the *studia humanitatis* engaged in training up an exemplary episcopacy. In other words, the bishops' *vitae* explicitly use *imitatio*, imitation, as their justification (even if, to preserve the perfection of the saint, they also warn that complete imitation is impossible). As the *Commentaries* of Pius II (d. 1464) suggest by juxtaposing Cosimo de'Medici *mercimoniis intentus* (intent on gain) and the beneficent Archbishop Antonino Pierozzi, the bishop might be presented as the true *pater patriae* (father of his country).[99]

The humanists continued medieval practice in another way when, as ecclesiastics named to episcopal positions, they rewrote the *vitae* of their predecessors. So, for example, after receiving an appointment to Acqui from Alexander VI in 1499, Ludovico Bruni (d. 1508) revised an account of the town's eleventh-century bishop Wido. Alessandro Geraldini (d. 1525), named bishop of Montecorvino, made a collection of all his predecessors' *vitae*, taking care to revise a twelfth-century narrative by one of those predecessors, Bishop Richard of Montecorvino, about *his* predecessor, Albertus. Employing a trope used by centuries of rewriters, Ludovico and Alessandro justified their innovations with a complaint about the style of the older accounts. But engagement with saintly episcopal predecessors did not necessarily entail profound attention to diocesan concerns: neither Ludovico nor Alessandro was a resident bishop.

The exemplary resident bishop Pietro Barozzi (d. 1507) did not write about his predecessors at Belluno or Padua.[100] Rather, during the years between 1471 and 1487, when he held the episcopacy of Belluno, Barozzi held up the model of a "universally" recognized bishop by composing a 375-line Virgilian *carmen de vita Martini*.[101] Later, Barozzi translated a

99. *Pii II Commentarii rerum memorabilium que temporibus suis contigerunt*, ed. Adrian van Heck, (Vatican City: BAV, 1984), 2:151–152, at sec. 29, pointing out the liturgical echo.

100. On Barozzi, see M. L. King, *Venetian Humanism in an Age of Patrician Dominance* (Princeton, N.J.: Princeton University Press, 1986), 333–335. G. De Sandre Gasparini, "Uno studio sull'episcopato padovano di Pietro Barozzi (1487–1507) e altri contributi sui vescovi veneti nel Quattrocento: Problemi e linee di ricerca," *RSCI* 34 (1980): 81–122, is the fundamental study of Barozzi's episcopate. Gaspare Contarini (n. 96 above) is said to have modeled *De officio . . . episcopi* on Barozzi.

101. See Mario Bolzonella, *Pietro Barocio, vescovo di Padova, 1487–1507* (Padua, 1941), at 27–28, on the *carmen Martini*; it was published in 1801, according to F. Gaeta, "Barozzi, Pietro," *DBI* 6 (1964): 512a. I am grateful to the keeper of manuscripts at the Seminario

Greek account of Basil the Great. The piece closes by acknowledging the impossibility of imitating Basil *ad unguem* (perfectly) but rests on the assumptions that a good bishop was like a good teacher and that a good account of that bishop's life made the lesson compelling. Francesco Catellini da Castiglione's biography of Archbishop Antonino Pierozzi, because it is paired in some manuscripts with an account of Francesco's teacher Vittorino da Feltre, makes the principle of *imitatio* still stronger, hinting that the more the bishop was like a humanist pedagogue, the better.[102] In short, bishops appear to have provided the humanist authors with their most straightforward subjects.

Making sense of the large category of *vitae* about those in orders requires some further subdivision so that the predominant orders can be identified. The emphases that result are, in descending order, Dominican, Franciscan, Augustinian, and Servite. The Dominican strength is related to the canonization of Vincent Ferrer (d. 1419; c.d. 1455), the liturgical promotion of Thomas Aquinas (d. 1274; c.d. 1323), and the martyrdom of Anthony of Rivalto (d. 1460; cult approved 1767). The Franciscans show well because of the *vitae* treating contemporaries and canonizations: Bonaventure (d. 1274; c.d. 1482); Bernardino of Siena (d. 1444; c.d. 1450); Bernardino da Feltre (d. 1494; cult approved 1654); and Giovanni Capistrano (d. 1456; c.d. 1724). The numbers of both Dominican and Franciscan *vitae* are increased by accounts from authors outside those orders: for the Dominicans, these authors include Cristoforo Barzizza, Francesco Catellini da Castiglione, Giovanni Antonio Flamini, Giovanni Garzoni (all, except the canon Francesco, laymen); for the Franciscans, Pietro Barozzi, Agostino Dati, Sicco Polenton, Maffeo Vegio, and Raffaele Maffei (all, except the bishop Barozzi and the curialist Vegio, laymen at the time of writing). Lay composition is, in fact, a strong characteristic of Renaissance *vitae sanctorum*; it will virtually disappear in the changed circumstances of the Reformation and Counterreformation.

Another anomaly is worth noting as well. The subjects of the order

---

Gregoriano in Belluno for permission to examine MS 23 (Kristeller, *Iter* 2:496a); Barozzi's poem is the concluding piece in this unified fifteenth-century codex that consists mostly of writings by Gregorio Correr (1409–1464). One contemporary who read the poem was Pietro Dolfin, who wrote to compliment the author in 1475, approving the metric form, which, with its "venustate ac elegantia," delighted the soul more than prose (E. Martène and U. Durand, eds., *Veterum scriptorum et monumentorum amplissima collectio*, vol. 3 [Paris, 1724], letter 21, at col. 976).

102. Antonino had not yet been canonized when Francesco wrote this *vita*. See Stefano Orlandi, "La canonizzazione di s. Antonino," *MD* 81 (1964): 85–115 and 131–162, esp. 88–91 on cult immediately after death. Lorenzo Polizzotto, "The Making of a Saint: The Canonisation of St. Antoninus, 1516–1523," *JMRS* 22, no. 3 (1992): 353–381, treats the difficult process. On the pairing, see p. 21 above.

vitae in Latin prose are overwhelmingly male: barely 5 percent of the Dominican accounts take women as subjects; around 75 percent of the Franciscan accounts treat men.[103] But, in the case of the Augustinian Hermits, the emphasis is reversed: two-thirds of these accounts are about women. It will become evident that the attention paid to women's lives in the Order of Hermits may well have been a deliberate policy.

As I stated earlier, predominance of both the episcopal and order *vitae* makes sense according to our current model of the this-worldly ethic of the *studia humanitatis*. The high proportion of martyrs' *passiones*, however, does not. The martyrs, and especially the early ones, who predominate, would not make good civic humanists. They were often people of low status, of near-anonymity; they were humiliated, criminalized, violated. Moreover, the inherited stories emphasize their aggressively otherworldly outlook: no calculating merchants, prudent patriarchs, or republican citizens here. Accounting for the humanists' emphasis on these figures is the task of chapter 2, "A Renaissance of Martyrs." And the problem is quite acute, for—by eliding the contents of the anthologies and compilations— figure 1.1 badly underrepresents humanist interest in retelling martyrs' *passiones* from the first Christian centuries. The bar for fourth-century saints—almost entirely martyrs—should rise several times higher than it stands.

Once the extent of humanist attention to the martyrs is properly acknowledged, a further problem emerges. Across the medieval centuries, the proportion of martyrs in paraliturgical collections such as the *legendarium* (legendary) steadily decreased throughout Europe, from a highpoint of 95 percent in the ninth century to a low point of 65 percent in the fifteenth.[104] But the two most accomplished Quattrocento collections flout this finding by emphasizing martyrs to an unfashionable degree. The first, a manuscript collection entitled *De vitis et gestis sanctorum* that was composed by the Florentine priest Antonio degli Agli, has over two hundred brief entries, of which more than 80 percent are about martyrs.[105] It is discussed in chapter 2 as part of the investigation of martyrdom.

The later *Sanctuarium*, by the Milanese layman Bonino Mombrizio (d.c. 1480), gathers over three hundred narratives about saints, more than 70 percent of them about martyrs. Mombrizio's work, which is extant not in manuscript but in dozens of incunable copies, differs from Agli's in providing lengthier narratives. It is anomalous in two further ways. First, the

103. The four hundred canonizations from 1185 to 1431 analyzed in Vauchez, *La sainteté*, are similarly dominated by men.

104. See Guy Philippart, *Les Légendiers latins* (Turnhout: Brepols, 1977/1985), 40, on the decline, and 45–50, demonstrating that it was less marked in the legendaries produced on the Italian peninsula.

105. See chap. 2, n. 98 below..

TABLE I.I.   Frequency with which identifiable authors composed, revised, translated, or transcribed a saint's life

Once	Two–Three Times	Four–Ten Times	More
48	21	9	1(9*)

*Authors whose multiple compositions take the form of collections or anthologies of texts: Antonio degli Agli, Leandro Alberti (with Giovanni Antono Flamini), Giovanni Caroli, Cristoforo Garatone, Ilarione Lantieri (Hilarion Mediolanensis), Giannozzo Manetti, Bonino Mombrizio, Bonifacio Simonetta, and Ambrogio Traversari.

Sanctuarium is the largest printed work about saints produced in the time period studied here. Second, it is not a collection of revised texts: current scholarship holds that Mombrizio transferred his medieval sources into print with painstaking exactitude, producing near-diplomatic transcriptions. Chapter 3, "The Last Medieval Legendary," reexamines this interpretation of the *Sanctuarium*, proposing that the Counterreformation success of Mombrizio's collection stands in sharp contrast to its demonstrable bibliographic oddities and the circumstances of its production.

Drawing again on the material assembled in the hand list, one can ask whether authors who chose to write about saints were particularly devoted to turning out this kind of literature. Table I.I records the frequency with which authors composed, revised, translated, or transcribed saints' lives. All the compilations that were excluded from figure I.I are registered in the fourth column in parentheses.

Table I.I shows that few authors wrote more than three Latin prose accounts. In some cases, this tendency to write only one, or at most two or three, accounts reflects an author's genuine misgivings about the form, the saint, or the undertaking. In other instances, however, it appears that composing only one or two accounts fit certain social uses of the saint's life. Writing about a saint was, for example, a rite of passage for young men in orders. Although he represents eastern practice, the émigré cardinal Bessarion (1408–1472) can stand in for the type. He wrote only one saint's life, a Greek account of the hermit Bessarion. It was composed as he finished his novitiate (before 1423) and took his own religious name. Thus it marked his passage to a new identity. The little *vita Bessarionis* was not abandoned as *juvenilia* but traveled with Bessarion to the West, and in 1471 it was translated into Latin by Niccolò Perotti, then systematically collecting the cardinal's works.[106]

106. E. J. Stormon, "Bessarion Before the Council of Florence: A Survey of His Early Writings (1423–37)," *Byzantina Australiensia* 1 (1980): 128–156; and Antonio Rigo, "Le opere d'argomento teologico del giovane Bessarione," in G. Fiaccadori, ed., *Bessarione e l'umanesimo: Catalogo della mostra: Venezia, Biblioteca nazionale Marciana* (Naples: Vivarium,

The fact that a humanist might compose only one or two *vitae* is also related to the need for a saint's intercessory power. The majority of these authors seem to have been just as confident of the availability of that power as were the majority of the people among whom they lived. Thus, humanists—or at least those of them likely to write about the saints—took an active interest in relics. In a letter better known for its reference to the discovery of classical manuscripts, the layman Giovanni Aurispa (d. 1459) wrote from Basel on August 6, 1433, to Iacopino Tebalducci, sending a precious ring that had been touched to relics in Aachen. Aurispa described the manuscripts, but he enumerated the relics just as precisely: "the blouse of Our Lady; the platter that held the head of Saint John, still all stained with that holy blood; the cloth Our Lord was wrapped in at his birth; the column and the rope with which he was bound by the Jews when he was beaten; the Shroud into which He was placed for burial, and many other relics; also [statues of] the Three Kings and many cloaks of the Virgin."[107] Aurispa closed by urging Iacopino to treat the numinous ring with pious care.

In a still more intimate letter, the learned Augustinian Hermit Egidio da Viterbo (d. 1532) wrote to his friend Serafino on July 11, 1505, about his visits to reliquary sites: "I wept at Loreto, I wept at the memorial to Nicolò [Tolentino]. But when I saw the prodigies of the virgin Clara [of Montefalco], I nearly died. Great God! How much she accomplished in God while living, and how much dead! When I see you, you'll understand. [Her] crucifix, three hairs [tresses?], and [her] still (and ever) living blood not only shook tears from me, but tore at my soul and very heart. "[108] Similarly, the learned canon Paolo Maffei (1380–1453) collected a stone and a thorn when he visited Montecassino and sent these relics with a letter on the good example of Benedict to a group of nuns in Venice.[109]

1994), 33–46. On the date of Perotti's translation, see John Monfasani, "Bessarion Latinus," *Rinascimento* 2, no. 21 (1981): 165–209, reprinted in idem, *Byzantine Scholars in Renaissance Italy: Cardinal Bessarion and Other Emigrés* (Ashgate: Variorum, 1995), at 174 and 191. Some Western examples of young men composing saints' lives are discussed in chap. 4 below.

107. This famous letter is reedited by Lidia Caciolli, in "Codici di Giovanni Aurispa e di Ambrogio Traversari negli anni del Concilio di Firenze," in P. Viti, ed., *Firenze e il concilio del 1439: Convegno di studi. Firenze 29 novembre–2 dicembre 1989* (Florence: Olschki, 1994), 639, from Sabbadini, *Carteggio*, Letter LXVI. Note the Marian and Christological emphasis of Aurispa's reliquary tourism. The humanist cleric Venturino de Prioribus similarly touched a cloak to a series of relics in Rome; see Federico Patetta, *Venturino de Prioribus: Umanista ligure del secolo XV* (Studi e testi 149) (Vatican City: BAV, 1950), 66–67. Aurispa also promoted the Most Precious Blood at S. Maria in Vado, a church he held in commenda; see Adriano Franceschini, *Giovanni Aurispa e la sua biblioteca: Notizie e documenti* (Padua: Antenore, 1976), appendix 2, 176, item 13.

108. Martène and Durand, *Amplissima collectio* 3:1234.

109. Martène and Durand, *Amplissima collectio* 3:986–987. On the learned reformer Maffei, see C. D. Fonseca, "I canonici e la riforma di s. Giustina," *Riforma della chiesa, cultura e spiritualità nel Quattrocento Veneto: Atti del convegno per il VI centenario della nascita di Ludovico Barbo (1382–1443)* (Cesena, 1984), 293–308, at 303–307.

As relics mattered, so did names: humanists, like their contemporaries, often bore saints' names and took the link to heavenly patronage seriously.[110] In his magnificent library of Greek philosophical works, for example, the rhetorician, translator, and physician Giorgio Valla (1447–1500) had a single saint's life, of George.[111] The Sienese rhetorician Agostino Dati (1420–1478) wrote several sermons about saints but composed only one saint's office.[112] This single office united a group of saints, who were the name saints of each member of his immediate family: bishops Augustine and Nicholas for himself and his son, virgin martyrs Margaret and Theodora for his wife and his daughter.[113]

When the heavenly patrons responded with favors, offerings were due. Humanists, however, might give narratives as ex-votos rather than wax limbs or pounds of candles.[114] Niccolò Borghesi, the lay politician whom I introduced earlier, wrote several lives of Servite saints but only one about a Dominican: his *vita* of Catherine of Siena was composed out of gratitude for the healing touch of a relic. The Bolognese rhetorician and professor of medicine Giovanni Garzoni (1419–1506), who wrote on many saints, chose a pope for a subject only once, making good on his sickbed vow to Gregory the Great by writing Gregory's *vita*.[115] The protonotary and priest Francesco Negro (1452–ca. 1523) repaid Theodosia's response to his tearful prayers by writing "the history of her passion" (*historia passionis*) and dedicating an office about the martyr to Vittoria Colonna, marquess of Mantua. The lay physician Giovanni Michele Alberto Carrara of Bergamo (1438–1490) set aside his taste for secular verse composition to write a single Latin prose saint's life, thanking Clara of Montefalco for past favors and securing future ones by revising the life written by Berengar. His friend, the *orator* Francesco Diedo (ca. 1432–1484), also wrote one life, a *vita Rochi* meant to enlist St.

---

110. See David Herlihy, "Tuscan Names, 1200–1530," *RQ* 41 (1988): 561–582, on the Florentine fashion of name saints during the High and late Middle Ages. For more on the phenomenon among humanists, see chaps. 4 and 5 below.

111. See item 35 in "Appendice. 1. Indici dei codici greci Pio," in G. Mercati, *Codici Latini Pico Grimani Pio* (Studi e testi 75) (Vatican City: BAV, 1928), 208. The account was by George of Cyprus. Mercati's survey turns up other saints' lives in Alberto Pio's collection, but none appears to have come from Giorgio Valla's library. On Giorgio Valla, a relation of the more famous Lorenzo, see the overview in L. Chines, *La parola degli antichi* (Rome: Carocci, 1998), 175–181, with further bibliography. For the account, see *BHG* 683.

112. See also Webb, *Patrons*, 298–306 passim, on Dati's presentation of his native city's "exemplary piety" in the *Historia senensis*.

113. See Dati's *Opera* (1503), fol. 58, an antiphon and a prayer.

114. One of the best-known ex-votos of this period is the painting commissioned by the canon Tommaso Inghirami (1470–1516), when he survived a fall from his mule. He invoked not a saint, however, but the miracle-working image of Christ, the *Archeropita*, at St. John Lateran. See Deoclecio Redig de Campos, "L'Ex voto dell'Inghirami al Laterano," *Rendiconti della pontificia accademia romana di archeologia* 29 (1956–57): 171–179, reviewed by I. Rowland, *The Culture of the High Renaissance* (New York: Cambridge University Press, 1998), 151–152.

115. Discussed in chap. 4 below.

Roch's protection for plague-stricken Brescia, where the Venetian Diedo was serving as *podestà*. This pragmatic function probably accounts for the success of the printed *vita Rochi*; Diedo's was among the most widely distributed of humanist saints' lives, and manuscript copies were made from the incunable. The life of St. Roch attributed to Marcantonio Sabellico appears to be a similar exercise and—if it did, in fact, once exist—would also constitute Sabellico's sole saint's life.[116] Francesco Catellini da Castiglione, the Florentine canon and prolific author of *vitae sanctorum* mentioned above, wrote only one account in which he expressed a personal interest in the saint's response. Noting that his forebears had honored Vincent Ferrer with their wealth, Francesco hoped that his *vita Vincentii* would induce the saint to return the favor and right his family's financial decline.[117] A humanist's request might be comparatively recherché: the Aristotelian George of Trebizond (1395–1472) closed his single original composition about a saint, a passion of the contemporary martyr Andrew of Chios, by asking the saint to see to the defeat of the Platonists.[118] But even in such a case, the petitioner's need was no less real, the seeking no less sincere than any rural peasant's.[119] The saints were not less present to the educated.

Single accounts, or ones that stand out uniquely in an author's *oeuvre*, can, then, reveal a great deal about the nature of humanist engagement with the cult of the saints. But quantity is important, too, for it tells us about an author as such. Attention is therefore compelled by the sole author to write more than ten accounts that were not part of a collection: the Bolognese humanist Giovanni Garzoni. His thirty-six narratives are especially striking because they failed to secure his reputation as an author of saints' lives.[120] To a degree, the neglect is understandable. His compositions are derivative in content, self-righteous in tone, and riddled with stylistic clichés, both Ciceronian and hagiographic.[121] They give the uneasy impression of being nothing so much as symptoms.[122] It is tempting to imagine that Garzoni's

---

116. Cf. F. Tateo, "Coccio, Marcantonio," *DBI* 26 (1982), 510b–515a, which does not mention a life of Rocco. Cf. Goff A 352, by H. Albiflorus.

117. It was written for Jacopo Ammannati. On the family's decline, see Francesco Bausi, "Francesco da Castiglione fra umanesimo e teologia," *Interpres* 11 (1991): 112–181.

118. See chap. 2 below on George's interest in martyrs.

119. See Leonard Boyle, "Popular Piety in the Middle Ages: What Is Popular?" *Florilegium* 4 (1982): 184–193.

120. Three scholars who have paid attention to Garzoni's *vitae sanctorum* are Luisa Avellini, Florio Banfi, and Charles Trinkaus; see chap. 4 below.

121. Luisa Avellini, "Eloquenza e committenza: Prosa encomiastica e agiografia di Giovanni Garzoni," in *Bentivolorum magnificentia* (Rome, 1984), 136, observes "una personalità certamente non di spicco primario (e una produzione non valutabile qualitativamente alla pari della stupefacente quantità)."

122. Luisa Avellini, "Per uno studio del problema dell'eloquenza nell'opera di Giovanni Garzoni," *Studi e memoria* (Biblioteca de l'Archiginnasio), n.s., 3 (1983): 90 mentions "i manifesti limiti della sua personalità," although she is not here speaking specifically di Garzoni's writings on saints.

defensiveness derived in part from his stutter, that his churchy tone reflected his own struggles with sexuality, and that his sentimentalizing piety was confirmed by, if not due to, the childhood deaths of three of his four sons, all in a single plague year. Renaissance melancholy might well account for this obsessive composing. Chapter 4, "The Teacher's Saints," explores the context in which he wrote to propose an alternative explanation for the unique size of Garzoni's output: his classroom practice.

The material gathered in the hand list reveals another peculiarity of the humanists' *vitae et passiones sanctorum*. The model of humanist attachment to the dignity of man and the considerable evidence that these authors were interested in contemporary secular biography both indicate that there should be a preponderance of accounts about contemporaries striving for sanctity.[123] In fact, it appears that the humanists somewhat neglected these contemporaries—especially given the numbers of them that are elsewhere documented. We arrive here at a real conceptual crux, because figure 1.1 is bound to be unsatisfactory. What exactly was sanctity, according to the Quattrocento humanists?[124] And what, for them, was the use of it?

Drawing on the catalog, I have suggested that sanctity was, for these authors, largely a matter of early martyrs, of exemplary bishops, and of mendicants proposed for canonization. But there are numerous instances of biography that were surely intended as commemorations of remarkable virtue in people who would never be formally recognized as saints. Leonardo Bruni's life of Aristotle is, for example, a partisan paraphrase of Diogenes Laertius, designed to present an admirable secular philosopher who might be set not just against the criticisms of Diogenes Laertius but also against the monastic and eremitical values embodied in such texts as the early Christian *Vitae patrum*.[125] When one turns to contemporary biography, the question becomes still more difficult. The *vita* that young Matteo Bandello wrote about his dear friend Giambattista Cattaneo shows that the problem was not just one of secular versus regular virtues.[126]

123. The humanists' anthropology has been studied by Trinkaus, *In Our Image and Likeness*. On their attention to biography, see Massimo Miglio, "Biografie e raccolte biografiche nel Quattrocento italiano," *Atti della Accademia delle scienze dell'Istituto di Bologna, Classe di scienze morali. Rendiconti* 63 (1974–1975): 166–193; and idem, "Biografia e raccolte biografiche nel '400 italiano," *Acta conventus neo-latini Amstelodamensis* (Monaco, 1979), 775–785, pointing out that it has less to do with any abstract commitment to contemporary excellence or love of humanity than with the search for patronage.

124. Thus Guidi, "Questioni di storiografia agiografica," 205.

125. Gary Ianziti, "Leonardo Bruni and Biography: The *Vita Aristotelis*," *RQ* 55 (2002): 805–832, compares Bruni's Aristotle to that presented in Diogenes Laertius, then (1429) being translated by a reluctant Ambrogio Traversari.

126. On Bandello, see N. Sapegno, "Bandello, Matteo," *DBI* 5 (1963), 667–673, noting the *vita* at 669b; and C. Godi, "Per la biografia di Matteo Bandello," *IMU* 11 (1968): 257–292. The *vita* is edited by Godi, *Matthaei Bandelli opera latini inedita vel rara* (Padua:

Matteo represented his fellow Dominican novice as perfect in Christian virtue. Young Giambattista lacked miracles, of course. But saints without miracles are possible (difficult though they are to promote and preserve in public memory); if humanists wanted to promote saints without miracles, there were precedents to hand.[127] Accounts of secular virtue such as Bruni's Aristotle or perfect monastic virtue such as Bandello's indicate that an audience for alternative kinds of sanctity existed. We could call Bandello's narrative a spiritual biography and consider the problem solved. But since the Quattrocento lacked an explicit category of that sort, we might do better to think of the twenty-year-old Bandello exploring—thanks either to his inexperience as an author or to his blossoming genius—the juncture of medieval saint's life, monastic necrology, humanist funeral oration, and classical philosopher's *vita*. If Bruni's Aristotle shows that monastic virtues were not the only ones recognized, Bandello's suggests that traditional recipes for sanctity were insufficient to meet contemporaries' desires to acknowledge the virtuous humans who lived among them.

All hagiography, like all historiography, is contemporary, of course. But my point is that the category of *contemporary saints' lives* is always uncertain, shifting, and beset with definitional problems: the criteria applied to the hagiography of any period must be reconsidered when contemporary *vitae* are at issue. Perhaps, during the Renaissance, this perennial problem grew more acute. The constituents of virtue were as debated as ever—male or female? in orders or out? *vita activa* or *contemplativa*? miracles or not? learned or *idiotus*? mystic irregularities or quotidian obedience? But, by the fifteenth century, the ground of the debate was complicated: first, by the extensive participation of lay authors; second, by the ever-increasing likelihood that an author in orders had training in the classicizing *studia humanitatis*; and, third, by the inevitable political repercussions of any sort of contemporary promotion. Chapter 5, "The Spectacle of a Woman's

---

Antenore, 1963), 123–181, with a commentary at 1–30. Cf. Gregorio Correr's life of his uncle Antonio, bishop of Ostia (Kristeller, *Iter* 2:259b), addressed by G. Musolino, A. Niero, and S. Tramontin, eds., *Santi e beati veneziani: Quaranta profili* (Venice: Edizione studium cattolico veneziano, 1963), 329–341.

127. Some examples occur in Giulia Barone, "Une hagiographie sans miracles: Observations en marge de quelques vies du Xe siècle," in *Fonctions*, 435–446; Sofia Boesch Gajano, "Uso e abuso del miracolo nella cultura altomedioevale," in *Fonctions*, 109–122; Fernanda Sorelli, "Imitable Sanctity: The Legend of Maria of Venice," in Bornstein and Rusconi, eds., *Women and Religion*, 165–181; K. G. Cushing, "Events that Led to Sainthood: Sanctity and the Reformers in the Eleventh Century," in R. Gameson and K. Leyser, eds., *Belief and Culture in the Middle Ages: Studies Presented to Henry Mayr-Harting* (New York: Oxford University Press, 2001), 187–196.

Devotion," takes up an exemplary case, in which the author chose a type of contemporary saintly subject that his peers largely neglected. By writing about the elderly charismatic Elena Valentini, Giacomo da Udine, the canon of Aquileia, stirred a half-dozen hornet's nests at once, the chief being the strained relations between Venice and Rome and the notorious suspicions that his dedicatee, Paul II, held toward both literary humanists and contemporary saints. Chapter 5 explores the unique way the author responded to such a difficult situation.

If representing sanctity was so difficult and yet so necessary, it was nonetheless in the hands of professional rhetoricians. Why did someone not approach the problem as a pedagogical assignment and simply describe "how to do it" (to borrow a phrase from Rudolph Bell)? In fact, two humanists did just that. Chapter 6, "The Saint as Author," contrasts the instructions for saintly panegyric composed by Aurelio Brandolini with those for the composition of saintly histories by Raffaele Maffei. Brandolini's saints' lives appear to be lost, but Maffei's strangely neglected *vitae* and *passiones* can be tested against his prescriptive ideals. The result is not encouraging: Maffei, it appears, could not unite his twin desires for historiographical and exemplary approaches to the commemoration of sanctity. The failure is especially telling, since it is clear that Maffei's search for effective saintly models was motivated in large part by his own efforts to match his life to just those models.

In conclusion, chapter 7 draws out what these case studies suggest about the state of humanist hagiography on the eve of the Reformation. As I have underlined above, in discussing the formal qualities of their accounts, the authors had inherited some of the obvious problems of composition from the Middle Ages. Others, however, they created for themselves, as they experimented with solutions to the old problems. Their attempted solutions were so remarkably various that the fifteenth century emerges, unexpectedly, as a period of wide-ranging hagiographic experiment and of corresponding encouragement for that experiment. Indeed, the nearest precedent for such manipulation of traditional forms may be the fourth-century shift from a pagan to a Christian literature.[128] But innovation had a cost. Precisely as experiments, the humanists' solutions were without consequence. In the sixteenth century, as authorities on all sides bore down heavily to manage the demands of rhetorical and factual truth claims in the new atmosphere of confessionalized polemic, the humanists' *vitae* and *passiones* often

---

128. In general, see Alastair Fowler, "The Life and Death of Literary Forms," *New Literary History* 2 (1971): 199–216. Robert Browning, "Later Principate," in *The Cambridge History of Classical Literature*, vol. 2, *Latin Literature* (New York: Cambridge University Press, 1982), 693–786; and J. Fontaine, "Comment doit-on appliquer la notion de genre littéraire," *Philologus* 132 (1988): 53–73, are acute on the problem of generic change in Late Antiquity.

looked ridiculous. As experiments, they answered needs that had evap-
orated. As compelling stories, they did not respond to suffering that was
immediate and pressing. Today, as a similarly politicized religious
polemic undoes our own complacency, both the flourishing and the failure of the Renaissance literature on the saints may even help us com-
prehend the ideological shifts around us.

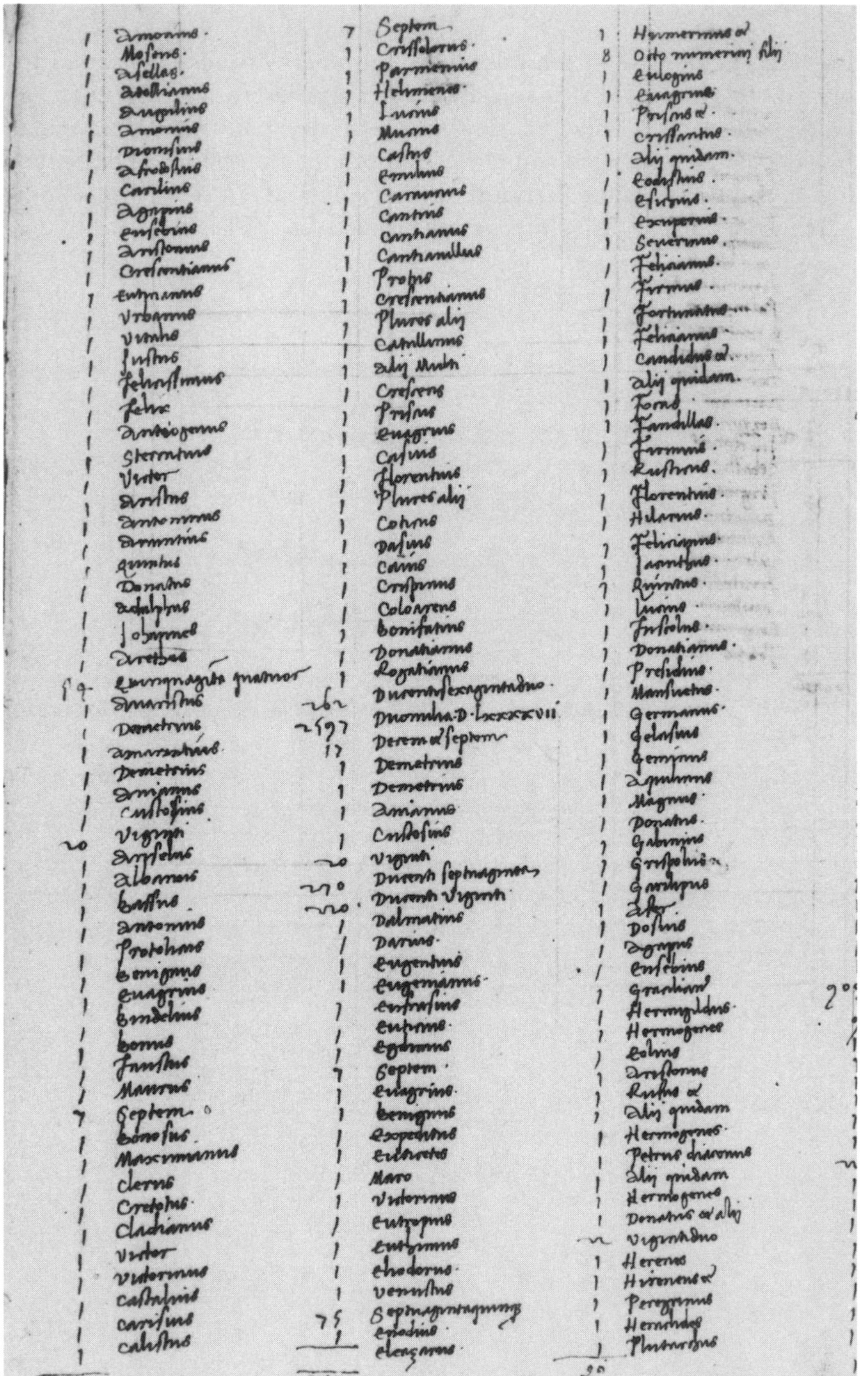

PLATE 2. Giannozzo Manetti's 1426 copy of Usuard's martyrology, one of several folios on which Manetti lists and adds up the martyrs. Biblioteca Apostolica Vaticana, MS Pal. lat. 835, fol. 7r.

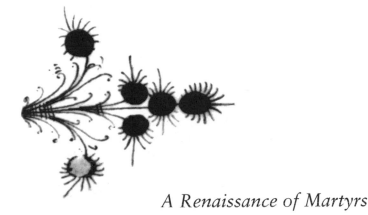

CHAPTER 2

A Renaissance of Martyrs

Quid de martirum nece existimabimus? Cum illi in carcerem coniecti quidvis cruciatus ac mortis subire sint coacti, an eorum interitum censebis miserum?

What shall we think of the death of the martyrs? Since they were thrown into prison and forced to undergo all kinds of torture and death, will you think their death wretched?

—Marcellus to his father, Johannes, in Giovanni Garzoni (d. 1505), *Libellus de christianorum felicitate*[1]

The Quattrocento humanists' focus on martyrdom, and especially on the martyrs of the early Church, represents a strong continuity with the preceding centuries. Alongside its proliferation of Christological and Marian feasts, the calendar of the pre-Tridentine Church favored early martyrs above all other types of saints. This emphasis reflected the foundational role of martyrdom in the Church's past; as Tertullian had said, the blood of the martyrs was the seed of the

---

1. Quoted from the autograph copy of the dialogue in BBU, MS 2648, fols. 75–86 at 85v. The author Garzoni is the subject of chap. 4 below.

Church.[2] Medieval Christians understood that the harvest had been large; a letter purported to be by Jerome and regularly prefaced to Usuard's martyrology, a ninth-century collection widely used in medieval and Renaissance Europe, claimed five thousand for every day of the year.[3] The number was taken seriously: Giannozzo Manetti (1396–1458/9) struggled in the flyleaves and margins of his own copy of Usuard to make the arithmetic work (plate 2).

Martyrs were also prominent because they had geopolitical roles. Many cities on the peninsula traced their Christian origins to an apostle or early bishop who was martyred. By the fifteenth century, such saints had long been fundamental to regional and urban self-definitions. Bologna, for example, honored her fifth-century bishop, Petronius; in the late fourteenth and early fifteenth centuries, when Bologna's aggressive neighbor Milan threatened, Petronius's cult was directed against Milan's ruling family, the Visconti.[4] Milan, in turn, defended its apostle, Barnabas, against challenges from its rival, Florence, that he had not, in fact, ever preached Christianity in Milan.[5] In a late papal variant of this much-studied civic phenomenon, the Renaissance popes, returned from Avignon under Martin V (1417–1431), asserted their legitimacy by promoting the early martyrs of Rome.[6]

Analogies to martyrdom were powerful, too, as crusading—both in rhetoric and in fact—kept quasi-martyrological models of heroic death current and the nostalgic song and literature of chivalry kept them com-

---

2. Tertullian, *Apologia* 50, 13; cf. Clement of Alexandria, *Stromateis*, book 4.

3. *Martyrologium Hieronymianum, epistola praefatoria*, quoted in section 23 of "De festivitate omnium sanctorum," in *LA*, 1101, noting "excepto kalendarum Ianuariarium." One of the stars of humanist panegyric for the saints, the canon Tommaso Inghirami, makes a rhetorical point of the number in his oration for All Saints; see chap. 6 below. Usuard's martyrology is discussed later in this chapter.

4. On Petronius's cult in Bologna, see A. I. Pini, "Un agiografia 'militante'" *Atti e memorie della Deputazione di storia patria per le provincie di Romagna*, n.s., 49 (1999): 245–280; Webb, *Patrons*, 73–80; and, on the early stages, F. Lanzoni, *San Petronio Vescovo di Bologna nella storia e nella leggenda* (Rome, 1907).

5. On the Milanese cult of Barnabas, see P. Tomea, *Tradizione apostolica e coscienza cittadina a Milano nel medioevo: La leggenda di san Barnaba* (Milan: Università Cattolica del Sacro Cuore, 1993). On Barnabas in Florentine and Milanese polemic, see, e.g., A. Sottili, "Ambrosio Traversari, Francesco Pizolpasso, Giovanni Aurispa: Traduzioni e lettere," *Romanische Forschungen* 78 (1966): 56 and n. 78, with further bibliography in Tomea, *Tradizione*, 137–138, n. 169; and Webb, *Patrons*, 105, 110, 152–153. On civic uses of the cult of saints, including martyrs, in the late Middle Ages, see André Vauchez, "Patronage des saints et religion civique dans l'Italie communale à la fin du Moyen Age," in Vincent Moleta, ed., *Patronage and Public in the Trecento: Proceedings of the St. Lambrecht Symposium* (Florence: Olschki, 1986), 59–80; and idem, ed., *La religion civique á l'époque médiévale et moderne (chrétienté et islam)* (Rome: BEFR, 1995).

6. Charles Stinger, *The Renaissance in Rome* (Bloomington: Indiana University Press, 1985), 174–177.

pelling.[7] Beginning in the mid-fourteenth century, waves of plague contributed to the already strong discourse of martyrdom.[8] Reinforced by phenomena such as the *ars moriendi* literature and the Bianchi flagellants, the "new religion of death" that characterized late medieval Europe fed a subjectivity whose long roots reached back to the disciplining of the early penitentials, to late-eleventh-century religious movements, to twelfth-century vernacular literature and Corpus Christi devotions, to the confessional requirements of Fourth Lateran in the thirteenth century.[9] By the Quattrocento, a wealth of literature and art taught the internal and external re-creation, the deliberate imitation, of Christ's suffering.[10] An impartial observer, weighing the evidence for religion as constitutive or reflective of values, might wonder if Christianity had not created in Western Europe a society capable not just of inflicting but also of profoundly appreciating the confessional martyrdoms of the sixteenth century. The least that can be said is that, in the one hundred years before the Reformation, the humanists' choice to write about martyrs appears to be a direct and obvious response to several long-term trends and immediate stimuli.

Nevertheless, the humanists' attention to martyrdom is at odds with three familiar historiographical models. First, scholars of early modern Italy traditionally describe the Quattrocento ethos as active and this-

---

7. See, e.g., C. Erdmann, *The Origin of the Idea of Crusade* (Princeton, N.J.: Princeton University Press, 1977), 20–21, 273–280; H. E. J. Cowdrey, "Martyrdom and the First Crusade," in P. W. Edbury, *Crusade and Settlement* (Cardiff: University College Cardiff Press, 1985), 46–56; and Colin Morris, "Martyrs on the Field of Battle Before and During the First Crusade," in D. Wood, ed., *Martyrs and Martyrologies* (Oxford: Blackwell, 1993), 93–104. For an art-historical view, see Doris Carl, "Franziskanischer Martyrerkult als Kreuzzugspropaganda an der Kanzel von Benedetto da Maiano in Santa Croce in Florenz," *Mitteilungen des kunsthistorischen Institutes in Florenz* 39, no. 1 (1995): 69–91. Adriano Prosperi, "*Miles christianus* nella cultura italiana tra '400–'500," *Critica storica* 26 (1989): 685–704, links chivalric and Christian ethics. Cf. Geoffrey Schnapp, *The Transfiguration of History at the Center of Dante's Paradise* (Princeton, N.J.: Princeton University Press, 1986), on the domestication of the martyr in Dante.

8. On the effect and reality of the plague, see Samuel K. Cohn Jr., "The Black Death: End of a Paradigm," *American Historical Review* 107, no. 3 (2002): 703–738, with further references.

9. I quote from Peter Dinzelbacher, "Die Präsenz des Todes in der spätmittelalterlichen Mentalität," in L. Kolmer, ed., *Der Tod des Mächtigen: Kult und Kultur des Todes spätmittelalterlicher Herrscher* (Paderborn: Schoeningh, 1997), at 27. The phrase is originally Alberto Tenenti's.

10. Brad Gregory reviews this literature and art in *Salvation at Stake: Christian Martyrdom in Early Modern Europe* (Cambridge, Mass.: Harvard University Press, 1999), 50–62. For several centuries' worth of striking examples of such deliberate imitation, including Elena da Udine (who is treated in chap. 5 below), see Peter Dinzelbacher, "Diesseits der Metapher: Selbstkreuzigung und –Stigmatisation als konkrete Kreuzesnachfolge," *Revue mabillon*, n.s., 7 (1996): 157–182.

worldly; a darker vision, one that might support a passive and otherworldly commitment to martyrdom, rarely surfaces.[11] Second, the widespread devotional practices most attuned to the martyrological *imaginaire*, the ones that re-created both in imagination and in ritual the suffering of Christ, that encouraged the *imitatio Christi*, are part of an affective and somatic piety that is not often associated with men, much less with the Quattrocento humanists.[12] Third, scholars of Reformation Europe, struck by the awe-ful quantity of sixteenth-century martyrs and by the competitive quality of the confessional martyrologies, propose that the late medieval idea of martyrdom was weak, as martyrdom itself was rare, reduced to "a frontier phenomenon."[13] In light of these three explanatory models, the task of this chapter is to clarify the circumstances in which humanists wrote about martyrs and the ways in which they chose to present those figures. Since there was a strong martyrological *imaginaire* in late medieval and renaissance Europe and since the humanists seem, by virtue of their emphasis on *passiones*, to have participated in it, what were the terms of their participation?

11. See, for an instance of its surfacing in Italy, Charles Trinkaus, *In Our Image and Likeness: Humanity and Divinity in Italian Humanist Thought* (Chicago: University of Chicago Press, 1970), 173–321, on the dialectic of human dignity and misery. R. S. Kinsman, *The Darker Vision of the Renaissance: Beyond the Fields of Reason* (Berkeley: University of California Press, 1974), emphasizes the later, English audience.

12. Cf. Richard Kieckhefer, "Holiness and the Culture of Devotion: Remarks on Some Late Medieval Male Saints," in R. Blumenfeld-Kosinski and T. Szell, eds., *Images of Sainthood in Medieval Europe* (Ithaca, N.Y.: Cornell University Press, 1991), 288–305. Appreciation of the affective and somatic aspect of late medieval religion has been strongly shaped by the work of Caroline W. Bynum, from *Jesus as Mother: Studies in the Spirituality of the High Middle Ages* (Berkeley: University of California, 1982), through *Holy Feast and Holy Fast* (Berkeley: University of California Press, 1987), *Fragmentation and Redemption* (Cambridge, Mass.: Zone Books, 1991), *The Resurrection of the Body in Western Christianity* (New York: Columbia University Press, 1995), and *Metamorphosis and Identity* (Cambridge, Mass.: Zone Books, 2001); see also Peter Dinzelbacher, ed., *Mittelalterliche Frauenmystik* (Paderborn: Schöningh, 1993). For its aspect on the peninsula, see, e.g., Anna Benvenuti Papi, "La santità al femminile: Funzioni e rappresentazioni tra medioevo ed età moderna," in *Fonctions*, 467–488; and *Temi e problemi nella mistica femminile trecentesca: Convegno del Centro di studi sulla spiritualità medievale, 20* (Todi: Presso l'Accademia Tridentata, 1983); and chap. 5 below. For the contrasting intellectualized piety of the humanists, see Trinkaus, *In Our Image and Likeness*; and W. J. Bouwsma, "The Spirituality of Renaissance Humanism," in Jill Raitt, ed., *Christian Spirituality: High Middle Ages and Reformation* (New York: Crossroad, 1987), 236–251.

13. Quoting Vauchez, *La sainteté*, Gregory, *Salvation*, 62, notes that "actual martyrdom remained remote on the eve of the Reformation." By looking at canonized sainthood, Vauchez's study tends to hide the continuing phenomena of martyrdom; in his conclusion, Vauchez notes the late medieval "obscurity [of] the popular 'martyrs'" (*Sainthood*, 538). Donald Weinstein and Rudolph M. Bell, *Saints and Society: The Two Worlds of Western Christendom, 1000–1700* (Chicago: University of Chicago Press, 1982), 160–163, agree, pointing out that until the sixteenth and seventeenth centuries' renewal of martyrdom, veneration of martyrs declined in the face of the popular cult of "miracle-working healers and intercessors" despite the continuation of martyrdom on external and internal frontiers.

This chapter opens by sketching the extent and the structuring concerns of the humanists' *passiones*. Here, the focus is on accounts that were written singly; my aim is to show the range of approaches employed. I then address *passiones* gathered into collections, to argue that humanists made an important contribution to the history of the martyrology. Whether they wrote *passiones* to stand alone or to be gathered into different sorts of anthologies, these authors paid special attention to classical models, both republican and imperial. In the third and concluding part of this chapter, turning to contemporary experience of martyrdom, I argue that the martyr's heroic exercise of the will—the act of choosing violent death—had a new appeal in the fifteenth-century context of failed Crusades and of rapid Ottoman expansion.

Table 2.1 below draws on the hand list to specify sixty-one Latin prose accounts of martyrs by humanists, including seven that are reliably attested but lost and five that take the form of readings for the saints' festal offices.[14] To this group can be added four large and dissimilar compilations in which martyrs have a commanding or significant place. Three are of interest in this chapter: Antonio degli Agli, *De vitis et gestis sanctorum* (completed 1450?), covers the first through the seventh centuries, and was dedicated to Nicholas V; Giannozzo Manetti, *Adversus Judaeos et Gentes* (1455–1458), covers the first through the fifteenth centuries (bks. 7–9), and was dedicated to Alfonso of Aragon; Bonifacio Simonetta, *De persecutionibus Christianorum* (1492), covers the first through the seventh centuries, and was dedicated to Charles VIII. The fourth, Bonino Mombrizio's *Sanctuarium,* which treats saints up to the fourteenth-century Catherine of Siena, is a special case and will be discussed in chapter 3. Humanist contributions to the printing of Jacobus de Voragine's *Legenda aurea* (*editio princeps* 1470), Petrus de Natalibus's *Catalogus sanctorum* (*ed. pr.* 1493), and Usuard's *Martyrologium* (*ed. pr.* 1486)—all of which contain a majority of entries about martyrs—should also be borne in mind. Bartolomeo Platina's *Liber de vita Christi ac omnium pontificum* and Jacopo Zeno's incomplete *De vitis summorum pontificum* include accounts of martyred popes; they are omitted here because papal *passiones* are a minority of the entries.[15] But

14. See the hand list. At least three, and possibly five, of the *passiones* are translations from the Greek. In the minds of some contemporaries, John Capistran, O.F.M. (d. 1456) and the nonhistorical Rocco (Roch) and Alexius would have belonged in this list of *passiones*; they would increase the number of accounts to nearly seventy.

15. Nor have I considered histories, such as Pietro Ransano's considerable attention to martyrs in *Annales omnium temporum*; for example, he treats early martyrs in Palermo, Bibl. comm., MS 3 Q q C 57, at fols. 225–297, drawing especially on the early medieval compilators Ado, Florus, and Usuard. See also Jacopo Foresti's *Supplementum chronicarum* (ed. pr. Brescia 1484) and Raffaele Maffei's *Commentarium libri 38* (ed. pr. Rome 1506).

these caveats and inclusions, taken together with table 2.1, suggest the conceptual richness of martyrdom in the humanists' hands. The martyr does not have just one meaning.

The dominance of the author Giovanni Garzoni, responsible for almost half of the *passiones*, is explored in chapter 4 below, the civic and liturgical emphases of Raffaele Maffei in chapter 6. For the moment, I am interested less in such specifics than in two general observations.

First, the great majority of the *passiones* in table 2.1 respond implicitly or explicitly to the presence of relics. This fact is a useful reminder that humanists, too, served the theology of immanence that characterized late medieval Christianity. It also suggests that the initial impulse for their compositions, the first audience envisioned, was primarily local or particular.[16] More than half of the accounts listed in table 2.1 name dedicatees, and these dedicatees mostly have hometown or personal reasons for interest in the saint. Of course, the local audience was not the only one envisioned; authors did not set out to limit the honor paid either to the saints or to their own compositions. Bernardo Giustinian's tripartite account of Mark was appended to his history of Venice, and together that history, along with the *vita*, the *translatio*, and the description of the relics, confirmed Venice's own sense of its prestige and represented its greatness abroad. Other less familiar instances are just as impressive in their attention to both local and larger aims. The *Historia sancti Pantaleonis* by the Observant Augustinian Hermit Agostino Cazzuli (d. 1495) recounts the saint's story as well as the *translatio* to Crema, an event which Cazzuli, himself from Crema, had arranged. The *Historia* was published simultaneously in Latin and vernacular versions dedicated to the city of Crema, shortly after the 1492 translation. At the same time he honored his city, Cazzuli promoted his order, claiming to know "per non pochi et certi evidenti segni" that God had chosen Lombardy, "questa nostra terra," as the place to introduce the new Observant Congregation of the Augustinian Hermits. By highlighting Lombardy, Cazzuli also had an eye on the reputation of the Sforza (for whom he sometimes worked as diplomat and spy), who favored his order.[17]

16. Medievalists will recognize this local focus as the "civic Christianity" described by David Herlihy, *Medieval and Renaissance Pistoia: The Social History of an Italian Town, 1200–1430* (New Haven: Yale University Press, 1967), 241–258. The notion of "civic humanism" formulated by Hans Baron to describe the humanists' part in Florentine and Milanese rivalries in the early Quattrocento, adapted by Herlihy, ibid., 258–268, and reviewed in James Hankins, ed., *Renaissance Civic Humanism: Reappraisals and Reflections* (Cambridge: Cambridge University Press, 2000), is not usually thought to be so open to the lives of the saints. It should be noted, however, that the medieval genre of *laus civitatis* included notices of local saints. See J. K. Hyde, "Medieval Descriptions of Cities," in his *Literacy and Its Uses: Studies on Late Medieval Italy* (Manchester: Manchester University Press, 1993), 1–32.

17. See W. Terni de Gregory, *Fra Agostino da Crema, agente sforzesco* (Crema: Vinci, 1950).

TABLE 2.1. Latin prose narratives about martyrs*

Published	Author	BHL	Saint (Century)	Dedicatee
1420–30	Traversari, Ambrogio	2666m	Eugenia (4)	–
1432–34	Alberti, Leon Battista	6912d	Potitus (2)	Biagio Molin
c. 1437	Lapo da Castiglionchio	5111a	Machabees (Bib.)	Card. Johannes
1438	Aurispa, Giovanni	–	Mamas (3)	Janus of Cyprus
1439	Foscarini, Lodovico	–	Victor & Corona (2)	Jacopo Foscaro
1442	Volpe, Niccolò	6642c	Petronius (5)	Bolognese canons
1442	Volpe, Niccolò	6643d	Petronius (5)	Bolognese canons
1446	Valla, Lorenzo	–	Sebastenses (2)	Matteu Pujades
1446	Valla, Lorenzo	LOST	Sebastenses (2)	Matteu Pujades?
c. 1451	Agli, Antonio degli	–	Cosmas & Damian	Cosimo de'Medici
1455	Guarini, Guarino	–	Timotheus (1)	Timoteo Maffei
1460–86	Lolli, Antonio	–	Eugenia (4)	Fr. Tod. Piccolomini
1461	Ransano, Pietro	608b	Antonius de Ripolis (15)	Pius II
1464–85	Hilarion Veronensis	1380d	Blasius (3)	–
1464–85	Hilarion Veronensis	3396	George (4)	–
1464–85	Hilarion Veronensis	6049b	Nazarius & Celsus (1)	–
1464–85	Hilarion Veronensis	3402–3404	George (4)	Teofilo Beaqua
1468	George of Trebizond	444	Andrea da Chio (15)	–
1468	Ransano, Pietro	– (office)	Barbara (4)	Filippo Perdicario
1468–69	Francesco da Castiglione	607	Antonio da Rivalto (15)	Jacopo Ammannati
1469	Ransano, Pietro	917r	Barbara (4)	Filippo Perdicario
by 1471	Francesco da Castiglione	6726	Peter Martyr (13)	Bartolomeo Roverella
1471	Enrichetti, Zaccaria	6642	Petronius (5)	Galeazzo Marescotti
c. 1470–c. 1500	Garzoni, Giovanni	138f	Agatha (3)	–

Table continued on next page

TABLE 2.1. Latin prose narratives about martyrs* (continued)

Date	Author	Code	Saint	Note
c. 1470–c. 1500	Garzoni, Giovanni	LOST	Blasius (2)	—
c. 1470–c. 1500	Garzoni, Giovanni	1678d	Catherina Alex. (4)	—
c. 1470–c. 1500	Garzoni, Giovanni	1496d	Cecilia (3)	—
c. 1470–c. 1500	Garzoni, Giovanni	1759f	Christina (3)	—
c. 1470–c. 1500	Garzoni, Giovanni	1976d	Cosmas & Damian	—
c. 1470–c. 1500	Garzoni, Giovanni	2763d	Eustachius (2)	Johannes
c. 1470–c. 1500	Garzoni, Giovanni	2884m	Felix & Felix (4)	—
c. 1470–c. 1500	Garzoni, Giovanni	3406g	George (4)	—
c. 1470–c. 1500	Garzoni, Giovanni	3519f	Gervasius & Protasius (3)	—
c. 1470–c. 1500	Garzoni, Giovanni	3967d	Hippolytus (4)	Giovanni Trofanino, O.P.
c. 1470–c. 1500	Garzoni, Giovanni	4323cb	Johannes apost. (1)	—
c. 1470–c. 1500	Garzoni, Giovanni	4772d	Laurentius (3)	—
c. 1470–c. 1500	Garzoni, Giovanni	4996d	Lucia (4)	Bonifacio
c. 1470–c. 1500	Garzoni, Giovanni	5309d	Margarita (4)	—
c. 1470–c. 1500	Garzoni, Giovanni	LOST	Mauritanian martyrs (4)	Leandro Alberti?
c. 1470–c. 1500	Garzoni, Giovanni	6067d	Nereus & Achilleus (1)	—
c. 1470–c. 1500	Garzoni, Giovanni	2850d, 6920e	Primus & Felicianus (4)	Giovanni Trofanino, O.P.
c. 1470–c. 1500	Garzoni, Giovanni	6957d	Proculus (6)	Ludovicus
c. 1470–c. 1500	Garzoni, Giovanni	—	Sebastian (4)	—
c. 1470–c. 1500	Garzoni, Giovanni	8715b	Vitus & Hippolytus (4)	Dominican friend
1475	Tiberino, G.M.	7762–67	Simon of Trent (15)	Brescia; Raf. Zovenzoni
after 1475	Garzoni, Giovanni	7767d	Simon of Trent (15)	—
after 1478	Garzoni, Giovanni	6725	Peter Martyr (13)	Vincenzo (Malmignati?)
1493	Cazzuli, Agostino	6446–47	Pantaleon (4)	Crema
by 1494	Garzoni, Giovanni	LOST	Petronius (5)	—
c. 1485–1489	Giustinian, Bernardo	5292	Marcus evangelista (1)	—
c. 1494	Negri, Francesco	—	Theodosia (4)	Vittoria Colonna?

c. 1494	Negri, Francesco	LOST	Theodosia (4)	—
by 1498	Garzoni, Giovanni	8086d	Theodorus (3–4)	Giovanni da S. Gemignano
by 1500	Garzoni, Giovanni	LOST	Symphorianus (4)	—
by 1500	Garzoni, Giovanni	1779b	Christopher (3)	Johannes Blanchfeldus
by 1519	Maffei, Raffaele	—(office)	Linus papa (1)	Volterra chapter
by 1519	Maffei, Raffaele	—(office)	Actinea & Greciniara (4)	Volterra chapter
by 1519	Maffei, Raffaele	—(office)	Victor Maurus (4)	Volterra chapter
before 1524	Marulus, Marcus	2270	Domnius (3)	—
before 1524	Marulus, Marcus	415	Anastasius (4)	—
before 1526?	Flamini, Giovanni Antonio	LOST	Theodorus (4)	—

* See hand list for details.

In still other cases, the local and reliquary status of the *passio* is unstated but may be cautiously inferred: the passions of the Salonitan bishops Domnius and Anastasius (the latter originally from Aquileia), whose relics were kept at Split, were revised or transcribed by the humanist schoolteacher Marko Marulic of Split (d. 1524). Marulic, who had been educated by Italian humanists and maintained close ties to Venetian humanism, may have offered these texts to friends in Venice in order to promote his hometown in the eyes of the governing power. In all these instances, local relics, audiences, and traditions seem to have been paramount. Such *campanilismo* represents a significant continuity with the medieval composition of *passiones*, which also served local interests, and suggests a further continuity with the dialectic of the "particular" and "universal" in Counterreformation hagiology.[18]

The large collections by Agli, Manetti, and Simonetta do not relate so clearly to relics or local practices, and neither are they the traditional sorts of liturgical texts required by the Church Universal. Rather, they are innovative representations of the past that use the martyrs to assert a meaningful connection between the early and the contemporary Church. This claim is explored below.

The second point to notice about table 2.1 is that none of the authors listed there witnessed the passions they describe. As a Dominican and as Anthony of Rivalto's superior, Pietro Ransano felt compelled to write about the neomartyr, but Ransano had not been present at Anthony's death by stoning in North Africa.[19] Ransano composed his epistolary account about a year after the event, which he described as an unheard-of occurrence ("rem novam et a multis iam saeculis inauditam").[20] Nor was George of Trebizond present at the martyrdom of Andrew of Chios at Constantinople. He learned of the event months later, when he arrived in that city. And he wrote the *passio* later still, in 1468, two years after Andrew had kept him safe during the difficult sea voyage home from the East.[21] (George does not discuss his sources, but apparently he composed his *passio Andreae* on the basis of oral reports that he had noted or could

---

18. The dialectic of "universal" and "particular" is a central theme of Simon Ditchfield, *Liturgy, Sanctity, and History in Tridentine Italy: Pietro Maria Campi and the Preservation of the Particular* (London: Cambridge University Press, 1995).

19. E. Hocedez, "Lettre de Pierre Ranzano au Pape Pie II sur le martyre du B. Antoine de Rivoli," *AB* 24 (1906): 364.

20. Hocedez, "Lettre," 364. Ransano adds that Anthony's death made it easy for both Christians and "Saracens" to understand what early Christian martyrdom was like.

21. George arrived in Constantinople in November 1465; Andrew had been martyred there in May. See *AASS* May VII (Brussels, 1868): 181; N. di Grigoli, "Andrea di Chio," *BS* 1 (1961): 1126–1127; John Monfasani, *Collectanea Trapezuntiana* (Binghamton, N.Y.: MRTS, 1984), 597–599.

recall.) Similarly, the authors who wrote about the supposed child-martyr Simon of Trent may have witnessed the aftermath of his death in the persecution of the Jewish community and the miracles attributed to the new saint. But they did not witness the event. Indeed, by definition, Simon's martyrdom had to be a furtive act.[22] We can be sure, however, that in every other case, including the three major collections, the authors rewrote, translated, or transcribed older narratives.

Thus, for all the Quattrocento humanists, the *passio* was not a response to the experience of witnessing a martyrdom. It was an act of the literary and historical—which is to say, the rhetorical—imagination. This fact sets the Quattrocento humanists' *passiones* off sharply from those of the Reformation. In the hierarchy of moral claims on our attention, of course, actual experience trumps imaginings about the past and symbolic enactment. That is one reason the Reformation martyrdoms are so compelling. Nevertheless, the evidence of past experience that remains is not more factual or true than the evidence of past imagination, ceremony, or symbolic enactment.[23]

Both the strength of the martyrological *imaginaire* in which the humanists worked and the problems it poses for analysis are demonstrated by the heroic death portrayed in the passion of the Persian saint James the Dismembered, *Jacobus intercisus*. This account is found in the *Legenda aurea* by the thirteenth-century Dominican Jacobus de Voragine, which was enjoying wider circulation in the fifteenth century than before.[24] James's story opens, as passions usually do, in medias res, with the saint already imprisoned.[25] A densely poetic narrative follows; French scholar Alain Boureau has described it as the pinnacle of Jacobus's *virtuosite*

---

22. See Ugo Rozzo, "Il presunto omicidio rituale di Simonino da Trento e il primo santo 'tipografico,'" *Atti dell'Accademia di Scienze Lettere e Arti di Udine* 90 (1997): 185–223. Note that the first saint of print was a martyr.

23. I agree at least on this point with Philippe Buc's analysis of early Christian martyrdom in *The Dangers of Ritual: Between Early Medieval Texts and Social Scientific Theory* (Princeton, N.J.: Princeton University Press, 2001), especially when he notes at 156 that "cultural characteristics (such as the purpose of martyrdom) are as much facts as events are."

24. On the *Legenda aurea*, see chap. 1, n. 79, and on its circulation, R. F. Seybolt, "Fifteenth-Century Editions of the *Legenda Aurea*," *Speculum* 21 (1946): 327–338; Valerio Manucci, "Manoscritti e stampe antiche della *Legenda aurea* di Jacopo da Varagine volgarizzata," *Filologia e critica* 5 (1980): 30–50; and Barbara Fleith, *Studien zur Überlieferungsgeschichte der Lateinischen Legenda aurea* (Brussels: Bollandist Society, 1991). Of the 153 chapters devoted to saints in the *Legenda aurea*, 91 relate martyrdoms; see Alain Boureau, *La légende dorée: Le système narratif de Jacques de Voragine (1298)* (Paris: Cerf, 1984), 112, and, for a discussion of the difficulties of classification by type, 32–38.

25. *LA*, ch. 170, 1219–1223 [*BHL* 4101]; brief analyses by Boureau, *La légende dorée*, 34, 60; and Bynum, *Fragmentation*, 290–294. Not discussed in Julia Reinhard Lupton, *Afterlives of the Saints: Hagiography, Typology, and Renaissance Literature* (Stanford: Stanford University Press, 1996); her emphasis on mourning is gainsaid by this martyr's celebratory language.

didactique.[26] It is entirely devoted to James's torture, as he is cut apart, piece by piece. The tale is brief, but the process long: one team of torturers is exhausted and replaced by another (a commonplace in *passiones*). Exultantly, James says good-byes to thumbs, fingers, and toes; to feet and hands; to arms and knees. One by one, each severed piece—twenty-eight in all—is directed to the praise of God until, at last, he is decapitated. Readers today may find this account off-putting or amusing, but what was its effect on premodern audiences? No one, of course, has left a report. Nevertheless, what we know both of the learned author and of the use of similar narratives indicates that the text had a reliable and specific function. An experienced preacher such as Jacobus de Voragine would not have included the story in his *Legenda aurea* without an informed estimate of its effect. A literary scholar might note, in this regard, that the narrative represents a public death only insofar as the listening or reading audience accepts the role of witness; for all Jacobus de Voragine tells us, there were no eyewitnesses to James's death except his persecutors. In other words, the absence of an audience inside the story can only be compensated for by the audience outside the story: the narrative invites "onlookers" who imagine themselves as participants of one sort or another.[27]

The effect that Jacobus de Voragine sought can be gauged, if not precisely known, by comparison with similar late medieval devotional texts. For example, the ubiquitous instructions to meditate on the dolorous Passion story, on images of the "Man of Sorrows," and on the *arma Christi* (the instruments of the Passion) suggest that James's story worked simultaneously in contradictory ways.[28] On one hand, a methodical narrative of this sort encouraged a systematic meditation on pain, the humiliation of helplessness, and the horror of consciousness during bodily partition.[29] Just as the devout re-created internally and in physical reenactment a sensual knowledge of Christ's passion thorn by thorn, tool by tool, in each moment of its bloodiness, abjection, and defeat, so they would have known how to re-create in imagination the fullness of James's suffering.

---

26. Boureau, *La légende dorée*, 60.

27. Theater historian Marla Carlson explores such imagined participation in "Spectator Responses to an Image of Violence: Seeing Appolonia," *Fifteenth-Century Studies* 27 (2002): 7–19, giving further references in her notes.

28. See, e.g., Ann Derbes, *Picturing the Passion in Late Medieval Italy: Narrative Painting, Franciscan Ideologies, and the Levant* (New York: Columbia University Press, 1996), on thirteenth-century Franciscan depictions of the Passion; J. Hamburger, *The Visual and the Visionary* (New York: Zone 1998), for the imaginative devotions of nuns; and Louis Gougaud, *Dévotions et pratiques ascétiques du moyen age* (Paris: Desclée de Brouwer, 1925), 200–219, on the desire for martyrdom.

29. The martyr's range of experience of pain and bodily disintegration is variously reported. Some undergo a miraculous anesthetization; others (such as James) endure with miraculous fortitude. See A. Glücklich, "Self and Sacrifice: A Phenomenological Psychology of Sacred Pain," *Harvard Theological Review* 92, no. 4 (1999): 479–506.

(The ways in which they figured such suffering for themselves have, of course, their own histories.)[30] On the other hand, the suffering that readers or auditors imagined was not purposeless. They undertook it for Christ and so imitated Christ's triumph not just over the humiliations of the world but over death itself.[31] We can only speculate that, in the passion of James the Dismembered, the thirteenth-century Dominican preacher sought such an imaginative fusion of the imitator and the model. But other devotional texts indicate that when this fusion occurred, what the world perceived as abject loss was transformed into triumphant *caritas*. The power of the martyr's passion as a literary form seems to have lain (still to lie?) in its ability to reproduce in the hearer this uncanny oscillation between abjection and triumph. The result might be described as an experience of the sublime. For the historian, compelled to honor the contingency of each author or reader and wary of speculating about the internal mechanisms of belief, the constant impinging of one aspect or the other of this oscillation makes the *passio* difficult evidence.

Estimating the Renaissance response to such stories poses special problems. If it is the case that these humanists held to a this-worldly ethic, practiced an intellectualized devotional life, and had no experience of actual martyrdom (although they would certainly have seen criminal executions and difficult deaths at home), then the story of James the Dismembered probably struck them as distasteful or comic. There is indeed evidence that some of them scorned the *Legenda aurea*,[32] and a few withheld full

---

30. For examples of the different ways historians have approached changing late medieval perceptions of Christ's violent death, see Caroline W. Bynum, "Violent Imagery in Late Medieval Piety," *Bulletin of the German Historical Institute* 30 (spring 2002): 3–36; Christopher Ocker, "Ritual Murder and the Subjectivity of Christ: A Choice in Medieval Christianity," *Harvard Theological Review* 2 (1998): 153–192, on Christian identification with Jewish persecutors of Christ; Esther Cohen, "To Die a Criminal for the Public Good: The Execution Ritual in Late Medieval Paris," in B. S. Bachrach and D. Nicholas, eds., *Law, Custom, and the Social Fabric in Medieval Europe: Essays in Honor of Bryce Lyon* (Kalamazoo, Mich.: Medieval Institute Publications, 1990), 285–304, on criminals as martyrs for their cities; and, for theatrical expression, Kathleen Falvey, "Early Italian Dramatic Traditions and Comforting Rituals: Some Initial Considerations," in K. Eisenbichler, ed., *Crossing the Boundaries: Christian Piety and the Arts in Italian Medieval and Renaissance Confraternities* (Kalamazoo, Mich.: Medieval Institute Publications, 1991), 52. The life of Bernardino of Siena (*BHL* 1199), added to the 1506 edition of Petrus de Natalibus, depicts the saint explicitly inviting a youthful audience to martyrdom by ministering to plague victims. For the ubiquity and the didactic quality of criminal punishment in this period, see Mitchell B. Merbeck, *The Thief, the Cross, and the Wheel: Pain and the Spectacle of Punishment in Medieval and Renaissance Europe* (Chicago: University of Chicago Press, 1999).

31. A point nicely captured by E. B. Vitz, "Gender and Martyrdom," *Medievalia et Humanistica*, n.s., 26 (1999): 79–99.

32. Sherry L. Reames, The "Legenda Aurea": A Reexamination of Its Paradoxical History (Madison: University of Wisconsin Press, 1985), esp. 11–42. In chap. 4 below, I will complicate Reames's position considerably.

approval of the ethic of suffering that underwrites martyrdom, even as
they wrote *passiones*. They had to be cautious: the plots of the popular
passiones were well known, so that an author could not easily modify a
story. But in the space traditionally allowed for the presentation of the
text—dedicatory letters, prefaces, introductory remarks—an author who
had reservations could dilute the passive suffering of a violent "red" martyrdom even beyond the ascetic self-mortification that had, since the
fourth century, been designated "white" martyrdom.[33] These brief presentation pieces must be used carefully, for commonplaces and readers' expectations governed what could be said to an exceptional degree, just as they
do in similar material today. So, for example, the Latin into which Giovanni Aurispa cast his translation of a Greek *passio Mamantis* did not
challenge the value of Mamas's suffering, and there is no reason to suspect
that Aurispa did not admire Mamas's martyrdom in its historical reality.
But in his preface, concerned for contemporary readers, Aurispa advised
his audience neither to imitate the martyrs' deaths (advice that he evidently
felt was necessary) nor to practice extremes of self-denial. Instead, they
should transpose the models of extreme suffering into daily forbearance,
patientia in its broadest sense.[34] Let readers learn from Mamas's "special
grace," to be more "constant" in daily life.[35] Aurispa responded similarly
later in life when he translated a Pythagorean text. He thought it quite
compatible with Christianity, even sans miracles, but used his preface to
bracket ascetic aspects of the pagan cult and to promote instead the socia-
ble, secular, and Aristotelian virtues of justice, prudence, dutifulness, kind-
ness, and piety.[36]

Such reservations about literal imitation of the martyr characterize a
surprisingly small number of the passions listed above. Most authors simply avoided the issue. In its place, they expressed some familiar civic and
domestic uses of the cult of the saints. Introducing his passion of Victor

33. Some humanists questioned even the traditional monastic virtues that were often
assimilated to martyrdom, most famously Lorenzo Valla in *De professione religiosorum*, ed.
Mariarosa Cortesi (Padua: Antenore, 1986), although this treatise had almost no circulation.

34. This move is already evident in Maximus of Turin (d.c. 457), whose sermon 82 (*PL*
57, 429–430) defines martyrdom as "witness" in order to argue that death is not a requirement of martyrdom. See M. Pellegrino, "Martiri e martirio in S. Massimo di Torino," *Rivista di Storia e Letteratura Religiosa* 17 (1981): 169–192. The place of Augustine in the definition of white martyrdom is also important; see Carole Straw, "Martyrdom and Christian
Identity: Gregory the Great, Augustine, and Tradition," in W. E. Klingshirn and M. Vessey,
eds., *The Limits of Ancient Christianity: Essays on Late Antique Thought and Culture in
Honor of R. A. Markus* (Ann Arbor: University of Michigan Press, 1999), 250–266.

35. VBM, MS Lat. XIV 244 [4681], fol. 150.

36. Hierocles, *In aureos versus Pythagorae*, where Aurispa's preface is more enthusiastic
about the virtues on display. I used the edition of Venice 1523; the preface occurs at fols.
IV–2v.

and Corona (see plate 1), Ludovico Foscarini explained that he was motivated to write not only by the fact that Victor was the protector of his family ("Victor, a quo me familiamque omnem meam divinitus protectam
sensi") but also because the arrival of the saints' relics in Feltre had led to
the improved health and safety of the citizens ("posteaquam ad hos
montes veneranda illorum corpora aplicuere, multa egregia, cum ad
salutem plurimorum, tum ad patriae deffensionem, secuta sunt exempla").[37] Neither in his dedication to Jacopo Foscaro, who had encouraged
Ludovico to write the passion, nor in his preface, which laments the effects
of studying classical literature and asks for the martyr's intercession, did
Foscarini mention the fact of martyrdom.

Yet a third group of authors rejected the presentations of Aurispa on
one hand and of Foscarini on the other. They did not suspect the martyrs
of being antisocial sufferers, whose passive deaths had to be reformulated
as ordinary virtue in order to have a postpersecution utility. Neither did
they seize on contemporary anxieties about the effects of classical studies
or on contemporary hopes for the martyr's intercession to justify their
attention to these deaths. Instead, these authors explicitly cast the martyrs
as military heroes, as people who suffered violent death in a role easily
recognizable in Quattrocento Italy. They assimilated Christian martyrdom
to the noble deaths of the Romans.

The operative model seems to have been the Roman practice of *devotio*.[38] In this ceremony of self-sacrifice, an individual military man—typically a general—attoned for civic failings and promised victory in times of
crisis by dying in some spectacular way. Marcus Curtius, for example, had
ridden fully armed into a chasm that had opened in the Forum.[39] For the
humanist authors of *passiones*, the *devotio* offered an exemplary death that
was at once powerfully and actively chosen rather than passively suffered,

37. Baltimore, Walters Art Gallery, MS W 393, fols. 67v–68.

38. On the *devotio*, see comparative remarks in Anton J. L. van Hooff, *From Autothana-
sia to Suicide: Self-Killing in Classical Antiquity* (London: Routledge, 1990), 54–57,
126–129, and 185–197; and Jan Willem van Henten and Friedrich Avemarie, *Martyrdom
and Noble Death* (London: Routledge, 2002), 19–21, with further bibliography. Buc, *The
Dangers of Ritual*, 131–141, analyzes texts of early Christian martyrdom as evidence of the
experience of an "imaginary hijacking of the dominant [Roman] political culture" (134), noting the Christian "recycling" of the Roman *devotio* in the passion of Polycarp (137). In many
of the texts studied here, identifying just which culture was being hijacked will require as
much attention to audience as to language.

39. Valerius Maximus, *Dictorum et factorum memorabilium*, 5, 6, 2; cf. Varro, *De lingua
latina* 5, 148–150. Maria Berbera, "Civic Self-Offering: Some Renaissance Representations
of Marcus Curtius," in Karl Enenkel, Jan L. De Jong, Jeannine De Landtsheer, and Alicia
Montoya, eds., *Recreating Ancient History: Episodes from the Greek and Roman Past in the
Arts and Literature of the Early Modern Period* (Leiden: Brill, 2001), 147–165, traces artists'
depictions of an instance of *devotio* in the later Quattrocento and Cinquecento.

Public
vs
Private

publicly enacted rather than privately inflicted, and immediately and tri-
umphantly useful rather than contributing to another life beyond this world.
The fact that of all the authors listed in table 2.1 only Ludovico Foscarini
alludes to the *philosophical* death of Socrates indicates that authors, patrons,
and audiences were mostly attentive to the military aspect of martyrdom.[40]
Quattrocento authors drew from Valerius Maximus and Livy examples of
patrician generals such as the Decii, who had ceremonially sacrificed themselves in order to save Rome. Martyrs compared to such figures could be
shown dying for Christ, with Christ, as Christ in triumph for the *res publica
Christiana*.[41] These figures were far from antisocial. They were the founders
and refounders, in the Machiavellian sense, of Christian communities.[42]

The author who most often compares his martyrs to such pagan heroes
is Giovanni Garzoni, who wrote in the later part of the fifteenth century.
He relies frequently on a form of synkrisis or comparison, the *quanto
magis* (how much the more) trope, that allows him to win twice, as it were.
First, he draws a learned analogy between pagan heroes and Christian
martyrs. Then, he righteously rejects the analogy, since obviously (how
much the more), the Christian martyrs are superior to any pagan. Thus the
martyrs Lucy and Christina are more constant than Marcus Attilius Regulus;[43] George and Theodore more virtuous than Marcus Curtius;[44]

40. Foscarini mentions Socrates "mortiferum potius poculu ellegit quam simulacras illas,
quae ipse mala domina appellabat, deos esse palam profiteri" (Baltimore, Walters Art Gallery, MS
393, fol. 67r–v). Cf. Garzoni's account of Christina, at p. 197 below. Van Henten and Avemarie,
Martyrdom, 12–14, give further bibliography on the model of the philosopher's death. Buc, *The
Dangers of Ritual*, 156, identifies the key point of difference between the military and the philosophical death as the distasteful theatricality of the former. On theatricality, see chaps. 4 and 5
below.

41. A clear humanist statement of the martyr as Christ occurs in Francesco Catellini da
Castiglione's long letter written to Simon *monachus* in answer to theological questions. The
canon Francesco notes of the martyrs' suffering: "in tanta suppliciorum acerbitate non iam
ipsi martyres qui ex se tanta virtute inferiores erant, sed ipse Christus qui in illis vincebat divinis potius quam humanis armis militabat" (BAV, MS Chis. Lat. B IV 57, fols. 2–32; Kristeller,
Iter 2:479a); see the discussion by Francesco Bausi, "Francesco da Castiglione fra umanesimo e teologia," *Interpres* 11 (1991): 112–181, at 157–159. The notion can be traced to the
accounts of early Christian martyrdoms.

42. Again, Maximus of Turin provides a useful contrast. His sermon 81 (*PL* 57, 427–430)
proposes that martyrs do not die just to win the prize (*praemium*) for themselves but also to
provide examples and salvation for the community (*civibus ad exemplum . . . ad salutem*).
The exemplary aspect of the martyrs is attractive to the humanists, but they rarely mention
the martyrs as offering spiritual *salus*, wary, perhaps, of an insult to Christ.

43. Garzoni, preface to the *passio Luciae* in BBU, MS 741, fol. 132; preface to the *passio
Christinae* in BBU, MS 2648, fol. 101r–v, at 101 (also MS 739, fol. 60v and MS 1622, ii, fol.
207). This trope is an old one: Marcus Regulus is praised above Cato as a Job figure by
Augustine, *De civitate Dei*, book I, chap. 24.

44. Garzoni, preface to the *vita et passio Georgii*, in BBU MS 739, fols. 52v–53 (see also MS
1622, iii, fols. 205v–206); idem, preface to the *vita Theodori*, in BBU, MS 2648, fols. 24v–25
(see also MS 740, fol. 55 and MS 1622, iii, fol. 253), listing Mucius Scaevola, as well as the Decii.

Agatha beats out "Scipiones, Decios, Catones, Lentulos, Marcellos," not to mention Lucretia and Hortensia.[45] In the end, it is hard to discern whether pagan or Christian virtue is more fundamental.

In sharp contrast, Lorenzo Valla, writing in the first half of the fifteenth century, proposes imitable martyrdom in language that is at once shorn of explicit classical references and resonant with echoes of the *devotio*.[46] A skilled rhetorician, Valla suited his procedure to both his subject and his audience. His subject is a group of military men known as the Forty Martyrs of Sebaste; his audience, the soldiers employed by Alfonso of Aragon. For this audience, Valla made Latin translations of two Greek texts, Basil's *laudatio* and an unidentified *vita*, that honor the members of the Roman Twelfth Legion.[47] The Forty suffered in what is now Turkey, perhaps during the fourth-century persecutions of Licinius. Because they refused to pay cult to the emperor, they were exposed to be frozen to death in what was understood to be an extraordinarily painful way.[48] Whether Valla had access to the *Testamentum*, long considered authentic, that recorded the names of the Forty, we do not know.[49] Like other Quattrocento readers, he would have estimated the martyrs' authenticity in light of the homilies that Basil, Gregory of Nyssa, and Ephraim (or pseudo-Ephraim) had composed; works by these patristic authors were being translated and circulated by humanists such as Ambrogio Traversari.[50] We can, at any rate, surmise that Valla considered the Forty to be authentically

---

45. Garzoni, preface to the *passio Agathae*, in BBU, MS 1676, fols. 29r–v. In a slightly different move, Garzoni opens his account of Sebastian by relating the history of the ceremonial triumph and proposing that Sebastian, unlike the Roman heroes, really deserves one.

46. See John Monfasani, "The Theology of Lorenzo Valla," in J. Kraye and M. W. F. Stone, eds., *Humanism and Early Modern Philosophy* (New York: Routledge, 2000), 1–23; and Salvatore I. Camporeale, "Lorenzo Valla: *Adnotationes in Novum Testamentum* ed *Encomion s. Thomae.* Alle origini della 'teologia umanistica' nel primo '400," *MD*, n.s., 31 (2000): 71–84. Camporeale, "Lorenzo Valla tra Medioevo e Rinascimento: *Encomion s. Thomae*—1457," *MD* 7 (1976): 21, remarking on Valla's opening meditation in the *Encomion*, suggests that the humanist felt that classical antecedents cast a pall over Christian usage. A similar concern may have kept Valla from explicitly mentioning classical heroes in his *passio* of the Forty, something that his student Garzoni would not hesitate to do in the later part of the Quattrocento.

47. I am grateful to Martin Davies for sharing his transcription. See Mariarosa Cortesi, "*Sanctissimum militum exemplum*: I martiri di Sebastia e Lorenzo Valla," *Bollettino della Badia greca di Grottaferrata*, n.s., 54 (2000): 319–336. Valla's letter to Tortelli mentioning the translation, in O. Besomi and M. Regoliosi, eds., *Laurentii Vallae Epistolae* (Padua: Antenore, 1984), letter 32, at 286, with nn. at 272–273, is assigned to 1446; it bears the date "x kal. martias. Neapoli." If Valla's account was finished by February 20, then it was just in time for the traditional feast day of the Forty, March 9.

48. Thus Basil, in his *laudatio*, PG 31, 513–516, at sect. 5 (see chap. 6 below).

49. Cortesi, "*Sanctissimum militum exemplum*," 320 n. 5.

50. Cortesi, "*Sanctissimum militum exemplum*," 319 n. 2.

historical figures. As he stated in the *Declamatio* on the Donation of Constantine, written about the same time for Alfonso of Aragon, "I neither detract from the wonder of the saints nor deny their divine works. . . . Rather I maintain and defend these things. But I do not allow them to be confused with make-believe."[51]

All that remains of Valla's translations is a fragment of the anonymous prose *passio*[52] along with a brief letter of dedication.[53] The letter is addressed to Matteu Pujades, a Valencian serving as treasurer general in Alfonso's Naples, whose duties, as the dedication makes plain, included serving as paymaster to the troops.[54] The dedication is in some respects traditional. For example, Valla praises his friend's "probity, virtue, and wisdom" ("singulari tua tum probitate tum virtute tum sapiencia"). But other aspects are original and even unique, when considered in light of the humanist *passiones* in table 2.1. Although Valla did not describe martyrdom as a virtue, he clearly thought that the martyr narrative had an immediate social utility, for he proposed that it be turned to the defense of Alfonso's kingdom. To achieve this goal, however, the exemplary lesson must be well taught. So, with a homely pragmatism suited to his audience, Valla suggests that Matteu tell the martyrs' story as part of his customary exhortation when he distributes the troops' pay ("sicuti stipendium militibus numeras").[55] Behind this instruction lay a simple but powerful theory of imitable virtue that Valla enunciates more plainly than any of the authors considered in this study. Matteu could use the example of the martyrs to stir the soldiers to military virtue and constancy ("ita possis, quod facis, magis eos ad virtutem fidemque animare, proposito illis sanctissimorum militum exemplo"). And he would achieve the desired effect, Valla explains, because our nature is such that we are most excited (*incendare*) by models (*exempla*) whose condition in life is like

---

51. "Neque ego admirationi sanctorum derogo nec ipsorum divina opera abnuo. . . . Immo defendo illa et tueor, sed misceri cum fabulis non sino" (Lorenzo Valla, *De falso credita et ementita Constantini donatione*, ed. Wolfram Setz, MGH, vol. X [Weimar, 1976], 151).

52. Salamanca Univ., MS 1530, fasc. 3, fols. 1–4. Davies identifies the fragment as a translation of *BHG* 1201; cf. Cortesi, "*Sanctissimum militum exemplum*," 321 n. 8, and 322–328, demonstrating what I read as a typically loose hagiographic translation.

53. Cortesi, "*Sanctissimum militum exemplum*," at 329, edits the text of the letter.

54. Cortesi, "*Sanctissimum militum exemplum*," 320 and nn. 6–7; and Alan Ryder, *The Kingdom of Naples Under Alfonso the Magnanimous: The Making of a Modern State* (Oxford: Oxford University Press, 1976), 99–100 and 170–171.

55. Valla gives as his second reason for dedicating the work to Matteu: "ut cum quidam quodammodo sis militie princeps, sicuti stipendium militibus numeras, ita possis (quod facis) magis eos ad virtutem fidemque animare, proposito illis sanctissimorum militum exemplo" (Cortesi, "*Sanctissimum militum exemplum*," 329, ll. 10–13).

our own.[56] Thus Alfonso's troops would learn from the Forty Martyrs of Sebaste not passive and solipsistic suffering (that un-Aristotelian virtue that worried Aurispa and, as I will suggest, Leon Battista Alberti) but the group-oriented fidelity and active fortitude that constitute military virtue, precisely the underpinnings of the classical *devotio*.[57] Valla did not, however, explicitly invoke classical figures in presenting the Forty Martyrs, and his proposal also differed from the *devotio* in proposing not individual but group sacrifice. And there is a not-unfamiliar irony in the fact that Valla meant these saintly martyrs to encourage a Christian army to attack Christians, including the pope.

Nevertheless, Valla's achievement in this preface deserves notice. For even if an author decided to draw an analogy between martyr and military hero (or, much more rarely among these authors, between a martyr and a philosopher), the form and content of the *passio* made it hard to fashion a seamless whole of the pagan and Christian ethical systems. Perhaps, as Archbishop Antoninus of Florence remarked, "from the opinions both of the gentiles and of the saints, everyone should know how one ought to live in the world"—but they would not learn this from the *passiones*.[58] After all, the early, authentic martyr stories refute the claims of the classical *vita* by exhibiting utter lack of interest in the subject's life and by representing the subject as similarly rejecting that life. They parade the temporal inadequacy of this world by beginning in medias res (if not much later). *Passiones* attend in detail to the most shameful (by Roman standards) mutilations and loss of public persona, often presenting as heroes people of no social standing or people who do not accept classical strictures concerning behavior. The early Christian martyrs described in Eusebius do not die mounted, in full battle gear. They have, instead, placed all value in the otherworldly, so that their deaths do not redeem the political structures or moral ideals of the republic or empire. Martyrs reject parents, mock social superiors, and flagrantly disobey rulers. The unhistorical martyr Proculus even murders one of his persecutors. Such deaths would seem to have only the most tenuous of connections to the noble deaths of the Decii. Valla's

---

56. "Nam ita natura comparatum est ut vehementius nos incendant exempla eorum qui eiusdem cuius nos sumus conditionis extiterunt" (*ibid.*, ll. 13–15). Camporeale, "Lorenzo Valla tra Medioevo e Rinascimento," 22, points out the persistence in Valla's output of the themes of the *miles Christianus* and the *beatitudo* of Paradise, suggesting that he may be echoing the liturgy, specifically the Common of Martyrs and Confessors.

57. "Hoc si facies, milites ex fidelibus erga Regem fidelissimos, ex fortibus fortissimos reddes magnaque pars ob id victorie debebitur" (Cortesi, "*Sanctissimum militum*," ll. 15–17). The proposal that soldiers might be martyrs lies behind crusading ideology; Erdmann, *The Origin*, 122–123, locates this novel development in the papacy of Leo IX (1049–1054) and the formation of a "papal army."

58. James Bernard Walker, *The Chronicles of St. Antoninus* (Washington, D.C.: Catholic University of America, 1933), 108, without reference.

prefatory letter to Matteu Pujades, by rising above these contradictions while presenting the exemplary military martyr, is a triumph of ideological manipulation, unique among the humanist *passiones*. But Valla's notion that these ancient, precious deaths might be recast to save an earthly institution is not unique at all.

❖ ❖ ❖

Protonotarii primum apostolici, qui gesta martyrum per omnes mundi regiones conscribere debent. In his doctrina requiritur, fides, sanctimonia, ut eorum scriptis publica fides habeatur, non genus, non opes, non divitiae. . . . Protonotarii autem non ambitiose in urbe resideant ad maiores dignitates semper anhelantes, sed per universum mundum vagentur sanctorum vitas subtili scrutinio explorantes easque scriptis fidelissimis commendantes.

Above all, apostolic protonotaries are those who ought to write the deeds of the martyrs throughout all the regions of the world. Of them is required not noble birth, not possessions, not wealth, but learning, faith, and an upright life, so that public trust may be placed in their writings. . . . Protonotaries . . . ought to wander the earth, seeking the lives of the saints with painstaking investigation and commending them in the most trustworthy writings.

—Francesco Negri (d. 1523)[59]

In the late Middle Ages, the ubiquitous liturgical book known as the breviary was dominated by martyrs, both in its introductory section, the *calendar*, or list of saints to be celebrated, and in its closing section of readings for the office at matins, the *sanctorale*.[60] In the allied paraliturgical collection known as the martyrology (*martyrologium*), on which the Church depended for brief historical notices that might also be used as readings, martyrs dominated by definition.[61] The Quattrocento humanists

59. G. Mercati, *Ultimi contributi all storia degli umanisti*, fasc. 2, "Note sopra A. Bonfini, M. A. Sabellico, A. Sabino, Pescennio Francesco Negro, Pietro Summonte e altri" (Studi e testi 91) (Vatican City: BAV, 1939), 70, n. 3.

60. On liturgical readings about saints, see chap. 1. See *SMHM*, 59–102 and 135–180 for a liturgical bibliography. On the development of liturgical books, see A. G. Martimort, *Les lectures liturgiques et leurs heures (Typologie des sources du Moyen Age occidental, 64)* (Turnhout: Brepols, 1992); on the development of the breviary, especially following the twelfth- and thirteenth-century imposition by the curia of the Franciscan reform of the breviary, see S. J. P. Van Dijk and J. H. Walker, *The Origins of the Modern Roman Liturgy: The Liturgy of the Papal Court and the Franciscan Order in the Thirteenth Century* (London: Darton, Longman, and Todd, 1960); and for an important instance of resistance to Roman rite, Archdale A. King, *Liturgies of the Past* (Milwaukee: Brice Publishing, 1959), esp. 1–51 on Aquileia, at 22–27.

61. The origins and ubiquity of the custom of liturgical reading from the martyrology are both uncertain; see Martimort, *Les lectures*, 98–99; Baudouin de Gaiffier, "De l'usage et de la lecture du martyrologe: Témoignage antérieures au XIe siècle," *AB* 74 (1961): 40–59. By the Renaissance, the martyrs' place in the liturgy had long been secured.

served that earthly institution, the Church at Rome, by helping to revise the martyrology. Negri's observation helps to explain why the liturgical importance of the martyrs, evident in these sorts of books, might affect the curial humanists in particular. Increasingly, they made up the ranks of the protonotaries, the corps of papal secretaries, and thus inherited an honorable papal instruction, dating back to the times of the persecutions, to nourish the Church's stock of saints. The humanists' own retellings of popes' lives show that they were aware of this injunction.[62] Indeed, their part in liturgical revision for the universal or Roman Church is well known. It is customarily located, however, at the end of the period covered by this study.[63] During the papacy of Leo X (1513–1521), in connection with the convening of the Fifth Lateran Council (1512–1517), prelates and religious such as Paolo Giustiniani and Pietro Querini—both products of the *studia humanitatis*—urged attention to the liturgy of the Church for a comprehensive healing of head and members.[64] Around the same time, the bishop of Imola, Domenico Cerboni (1511–1533), undertook to revise the whole office.[65] The Benedictine and then Carthusian *manqué* Zaccaria Ferreri (1479–1524) produced a classicizing revision of hymns in the early

62. For Negri's curial ambience, Peter Partner, *The Pope's Men: The Papal Civil Service in the Renaissance* (Oxford: Clarendon Press, 1990), is indispensable. For the part of the early popes in formulating the protonotaries' duty, see L. Duchesne, ed., *Liber pontificalis* 1:xcv–xcvi, 4; Platina's *Liber de vita Christi ac omnium pontificum*, ed. F. Gaida, in *RRIISS* (Città di Castello, 1913), entries 20 (Antherus) and 21 (Fabianus); Jacopo Zeno's lives of the popes, in BAV, MS Lat. 5942, at fols. 15r–v (Antherus) and fols. 15v–16v (Fabianus). Antonio Agli, not a curialist but writing for a papal patron, attributed a similar interest to the still earlier Clement I; see BAV, MS Lat. 3742, fols. 16–17 and FBNC, MS Nuovi acq. 399, fols. 98v–101v (lower left foliation). See also Kelly, *ODP*, 161–167; Eric W. Kemp, *Canonisation and Authority in the Western Church* (London: Oxford University Press, 1948), 10–11; and Thomas F. X. Noble, "Literacy and the Papal Government in Late Antiquity and the Early Middle Ages," in R. McKitterick, ed., *The Uses of Literacy in Early Medieval Europe* (New York: Cambridge University Press, 1990), 84 (on Fabianus). Paul Nelles, "The Renaissance Ancient Library Tradition and Christian Antiquity," in R. de Smet, ed., *Les humanistes et leur bibliothèques: Humanists and Their Libraries* (Louvain: Peeters, 2002), at 167–168, ties the protonotaries' martyrological collecting into Onofrio Panvinio's ideas about the function of libraries. For Jean Bolland's 1643 preface to the *Acta sanctorum*, which similarly identifies Clemens, Fabianus, and Antherus as instigators of the notarial collection of martyrs' acts, see chap. 3 below.

63. Renaissance reform of papal ceremonial, as opposed to the liturgy proper, is dated to the papacies of Nicholas V (1447–1455), Pius II (1458–1464), and Sixtus IV (1471–1484); see, e.g., Joaquin Nabuco, *Le Cérémonial apostolique avant Innocent VIII* (Rome: Edizione liturgiche, 1966), with attention to saints at 91–94 and 126 (Stephen); 113–117 (the calendar); 127 (the Innocents); and 190–191 (canonization).

64. The crucial document is their *Libellus ad Leonem X* (1513). E. Gleason, s.v. "Querini," and N. Minnich, s.v. "Giustiniani," give introductions and further bibliography in H. Hillerbrand, ed., *Oxford Encyclopedia of the Reformation* (New York: Oxford University Press, 1996).

65. Rome, BN, MS Autogr. A 96, 7/2 (see chap. 6 below).

sixteenth century and was said by his publisher to have prepared a thoroughly rewritten breviary.[66] Ferreri's breviary never appeared.[67] Instead, following an abortive effort by the bishop of Chieti, Giovanni Pietro Carafa (later Paul IV, 1555–1559), the first major revision of the breviary was prepared by the Franciscan, Cardinal Francesco Quiñones (1475–1540).[68] His *Breviarium Romanum* was published in 1535 with a pared-down roster of 124 readings (*lectiones*) about saints.[69] Three-quarters of Quiñones's entries were for martyrs.

The humanists' involvement in liturgical reform, with its concomitant emphasis on early martyrs, began much before the sixteenth century. Among the sources that Quiñones consulted for his breviary was a manuscript collection of 228 saints' lives, compiled by the Florentine priest Antonio degli Agli (ca. 1400–1477).[70] The collection is dedicated to Nicholas V

66. Batiffol, *History*, 231 and 235; J. Wickham Legg, ed., *The Second Recension of the Quignon Breviary* (London: Henry Bradshaw Society, 1908), 11; E. Stöve, "Ferreri, Zaccaria," *DBI* 46 (1996), 810a and 811a. On Ferreri's hymns in the context of early printed hymn collections, see Ann Moss, "Latin Liturgical Hymns and Their Early Printing History, 1470–1520," *Humanistica Lovaniensia* 36 (1987): 112–137.

67. Bernardo Morsolin, *Zaccaria Ferreri:. Episodio biografico del secolo decimosesto* (Vicenza: Tip. Reale Gir. Burato, 1877), at 98, only speculates that the project—which had certainly begun under Leo X—continued under Adrian VI.

68. The 1535 edition was edited by J. Wickham Legg, *Breviarium Romanum a Francisco Cardinali Quignonio editum et recognitum iuxta editionem Venetiis A.D. 1535 impressam* (Cambridge: Clay and Sons, 1888); the 1537 edition by idem, *The Second Recension*, with discussion of the 1507 Spires breviary (4), and Carafa's efforts (12–14).

69. Legg, *Breviarium Romanum*, 102–191. The number of readings is based on my own count; I do not include Marian or Christological feasts, and I count multiple saints on the same day only when they are clearly given separate entries.

70. Legg, *Breviarium Romanum*, 203–205, names the sources of Quiñones's texts. The Vatican Library inventory entry of 1533 proves that Quiñones borrowed BAV, MS Lat. 3742; see Giovanni Mercati, "Per la storia del Breviario Quignoniano," reprinted in idem, *Opere minori* III (Studi e testi 78) (Vatican City: BAV, 1937), 30–31. I doubt that the cardinal excerpted from Agli's work and suspect that he was dismayed by what he found there. On Agli's *De vitis*, see the fundamental study of Diana Webb, "Sanctity and History," in P. Denley and C. Elam, eds., *Florence and Italy: Renaissance Studies in Honour of Nicolai Rubinstein* (London: Westfield College, University of London, 1988), 297–308. Scholars disagree on whether Agli should be called a humanist: Webb, "Sanctity and History," assumes that he should; Arthur Field thinks not (personal communication). Agli did not study formally with any recognized teacher of the *studia humanitatis*, and he did get a theology degree, which suggests a scholastic formation. Nevertheless, he clearly recognized and attempted to join in the cultural innovations around him: he corresponded with people central to them; he wrote in genres typically used by the humanists; and he participated in the *certame coronario* organized by Leon Battista Alberti and others to demonstrate the literary excellence of the vernacular. He was chosen to teach Pietro Barbo, the future Paul II, probably because he was not an aggressive classicizer (on Paul II's relation to the humanists, see chap. 5 below). For Agli's possible brief study with the bibliophile Antonio Corbinelli, see Nelson Minnich, "The Autobiography of Antonio degli Agli (ca. 1400–1477)," in Craig Morogh and Craig Hugh Smith, eds., *Renaissance Studies in Honour of Craig Hugh Smith* (Florence: Giunti Barbèra, 1985), 179–180.

(1447–1455), but, in his preface, Agli recalls that the idea for it predated Nicholas's pontificate by at least a decade. The project had been formulated by the Camaldolese abbot Ambrogio Traversari shortly before his death in 1439. Thus the collection may have originated as early as 1430 and almost certainly overlapped with Eugene IV's first extended residence in Florence (June 23, 1434, to April 1436).[71] Its ambitions can be estimated from the fact that Agli's collection treats saints of the first seven centuries, the same period covered by the great Carolingian martyrologies that, in dozens of local recensions, were still authoritative and widely used.[72]

Circumstantial evidence suggests that Agli was not, however, the first person to be handed such a project. He seems to have been preceded by Leon Battista Alberti (1404–1472).[73] At the time Alberti accepted the task,

71. It would also have coincided with the literary quarrel over Christian and secular virtue between Traversari and Bruni: see Gary Ianziti, "Leonardo Bruni and Biography: The *Vita Aristotelis,*" *RQ* 55, no. 3 (2002): 805–832. The *terminus post quem* of 1430 for Traversari's hagiographic project comes from the dating assigned by F. P. Luiso, "Riordinamento dell'Epistolario di Ambrogio Traversari," *Rivista delle biblioteche e degli archivi* 8–9 (1899): 77–79, to a letter in which Traversari refers to Agli slightingly; see also Ludwig Bertalot, "Zwölf Briefe des Ambrogio Traversari," in P. O. Kristeller, ed., *Studien zum italienischen und deutschen Humanismus* (Rome: Edizione di storia e letteratura, 1975), 1:260–261; and Giovanni Mercati, "Un passo non chiarito del Traversari sopra due giovani umanisti toscani," *Ultimi contributi alla storia degli umanisti,* vol. I, *Traversariana* (Studi e testi 90) (Vatican City, 1939), 68–70. Eugene lived in Florence again from January 27, 1439, to March 7, 1443. For Traversari's part in formulating the project, see Webb, "Sanctity and History," 298.

72. An introductory bibliography on these martyrologies appears in *SMHM,* 103–134; see especially Jacques Dubois, *Les martyrologes du moyen age latin* (Turnhout: Brepols, 1978), 37–60; the "Appendix: Martyrologia," in Klaus Gamber, *Codices liturgici latini antiquiores* (Freiburg, 1965); and the indispensable Henri Quentin, *Les martyrologes historiques du Moyen Age : Etude sur la formation du martyrologe romain* (Spoleto: Centro italiano di studi sull'alto medioevo, 2002 [1908]). Traversari may have had a broader conception of the project, something along the lines of the *Acta sanctorum.* As early as the Council of Constance (1414–1418), when other humanists were busily rifling monastic, convent, and cathedral libraries for classical manuscripts, Traversari examined the saints' lives in codices at Lindau. About the same time, he was seeking Aurispa's help to acquire the full set of Simeon Metaphrast's menology (*menologium,* a Greek hagiographic collection). See Sabbadini, *Epistolario* 1:46–47; Remigio Sabbadini, ed., *Carteggio di Giovanni Aurispa* (Rome: Tipografia del Senato, 1931), 11; idem, *Biografia documentata di Giovanni Aurispa* (Noto: Zamit, 1891), 49–52; Charles Stinger, *Humanism and the Church Fathers: Ambrogio Traversari (1386–1439) and Christian Antiquity in the Italian Renaissance* (Albany: SUNY Press, 1977), 269 n. 161. It is odd that Traversari did not seek his menology closer to home. As Walter Berschin makes clear in *Greek Letters and the Latin Middle Ages: From Jerome to Nicholas of Cusa,* trans. J. C. Frakes (Washington, D.C.: Catholic University of America, 1988), several monasteries in southern Italy and nearby Rome continued Greek liturgical and hagiographical traditions.

73. See Anthony Grafton, *Leon Battista Alberti, Master Builder of the Renaissance* (New York: Hill and Wang, 2000), 64; Cochrane, *Historians,* 50 n. 75; Eugenio Garin, "Il pensiero di Leon Battista Alberti: Caratteri e contraste," *Rinascimento,* ser. 2, 11–12 (1971–1972): 13; A. Guarino, "Leon Battista Alberti's *Vita s. Potiti,*" *Renaissance News* 8, no. 2 (1955): 86–89; and, above all, the introduction to Cecil Grayson, ed., *Opusculi inediti di Leon Battista Alberti* (Florence: Olschki, 1954), 27–41.

probably in 1433 but perhaps as late as 1434, he may have been in Rome
or in Florence. He was in minor orders, possessed of a degree in canon law,
and had just begun to work as secretary to Eugene IV's dear friend, fellow
Venetian, and chancellor Biagio Molin.[74] The chancellor evidently asked
Alberti to improve the "accuracy" and "dignity" of the "life of the holy
martyrs" ("sanctorum martirum vita").[75] This phrase, which occurs twice
in Alberti's only known letter to his patron, suggests a sizable assignment.
At the close of the letter, Alberti confidently invited Molin to choose an initial martyr ("iube cuius vitam primam esse velis").[76] That phrasing, too,
indicates that more saints were expected to follow.

Molin gave his secretary the martyr Potitus as a first subject.[77] We do
not know if he also provided the legend that Alberti chose to elaborate,
but it is clear that sources posed a problem. At some unidentified point in
the process of research and composition, Alberti wrote to his friend the
priest and poet Leonardo Dati (ca.1408–1472), complaining that he did
not have books to use ("hac nostra librorum inopia"). If Alberti was writing from Rome, the phrase can only mean that he did not have any that
were helpful.[78] He did consult Eusebius's *Historia Ecclesiastica* and a local
variant of the ninth-century martyrology by Usuard. From these sources,

74. On dating, see Grayson, *Opusculi*, 31–32. Alberti served as Molin's secretary from
late 1432 until Molin advanced from Grado to Jerusalem in 1434. Because of uncertainty
about the dates of Molin's successive episcopal appointments, dating Alberti's composition
is difficult.

75. The phrase "sanctorum martirum vita tuo integerrimo iudicio parum accurate scripta
videtur" occurs in the dedicatory letter (Grayson, *Opusculi*, 63). Note that Alberti does not
say "sanctorum *et* martirum vita." The use of the singular form *vita* when the plural *vitae*
would seem preferable is utterly normal; for a pious explanation, see Gregory of Tours, discussed in Thomas J. Heffernan, *Sacred Biography: Saints and Their Biographies in the Middle Ages* (New York: Oxford University Press, 1988), 6–7.

76. Grayson, *Opuscula*, 64, ll. 12–13.

77. The name Potitus does not occur in this "prefatory" letter. Moreover, all the verbs of
choosing the subject and writing the composition are in the future tense. Thus Alberti's letter to Molin is not a preface (except in the formal sense of being placed in prefatory position).
It is an acceptance letter, a kind of contract, that was not revised or even recopied when the
account was completed (in the manuscript, the preface is written on larger paper than the *vita*
and bear the marks of having been folded into quarters). I am aware of no comparable epistolary prefaces. Potitus is an odd choice: the fact that he occurs in some manuscripts of
Usuard but not others may have led to Alberti's assignment (n. 80 below).

78. Grayson, *Opusculi*, 87, ll. 28–29. Even if we redate the composition to place it in Florence, Alberti's complaint is hard to understand in a literal sense. On Leonardo di Piero Dati
(then serving as secretary to Cardinal Giordano Orsini [d. 1438]), see R. Ristori, "Dati,
Leonardo," *DBI* 33 (1987), 44–52; and Renato Lefevre, "Fiorentini a Roma nel '400: I
Dati," *Studi romani* 20 (1972): 189–191. It is important for an estimate of the nature of this
hagiographic assignment to note that Leonardo Dati, who was a close friend of Antonio Agli,
would have excellent relations with Paul II (Lefevre, "Fiorentini," 190 n. 10); see chap. 5
below.

he gathered a handful of incompatible facts about three different Potituses. One was an early heretic, obviously unsuitable. Another was a fifteen-year-old boy who died among the Martyrs of Lyon in 177, under Marcus Aurelius.[79] The child's name was not right—Ponticus instead of Potitus—but Alberti supposed that the mistake was due to careless transcription, *librariorum negligentia*. In the martyrology, Alberti found yet a third Potitus, a martyr of unknown date who had suffered in an unknown location with the unknown pair Julianus and Celsus.[80] None of these three was Alberti's eventual subject, the Apulian-Sardinian child-martyr who had been the object of an increasingly warm civic cult in Pisa since his translation there in the late twelfth century.[81] And none of them was the figure who may have been of interest to the Venetian Molin, former bishop of Pola and Zara and recently named patriarch of Grado: the ancient Potitus (Polieucte or Hippolytus) associated with the patriarchate of Ravenna.[82]

Unsure what to do, Alberti drafted a narrative that was doubly unsuitable. It failed as a *laus* by being morally ambiguous, intimating far too little sympathy for traditional saintly virtues. And it failed as a *vita*, since

79. Jean Bolland's preface to the *AASS* adduces the acts of the Martyrs of Lyons, inter alia, as proof of the epistolary, i.e., notarial, collection of evidence about the deaths of martyrs (*AASS* Jan. I [Brussels, 1843], xva) that Francesco Negri lauds in the epigraph to this section. The epistolary form was clearly important to Alberti, too. Alberti was right to pay attention to the precise names of the martyrs of Lyons; see Henri Quentin, "La liste des martyrs de Lyon de l'an 177," *AB* 39 (1921): 113–138, for a brilliant effort to reconstitute Eusebius's lost list of their names. The way Alberti mangles the first name in the list—for Blandina he gives Baldina—may be a clue to his source.

80. Potitus is absent from most manuscripts of Usuard and Ado, but cf. *PL* 123, 648, s.v. "*Auctaria*," for three manuscripts that do include him. Or Alberti may have looked in a martyrology similar to the pseudo-Florus adduced by the editors of the *BHL* for January 3; for the text, see *AASS* March II (Paris, 1865), viii; and *PL* 94:801–802. Cf. Poncelet 1909, 169, entry 61 (*BHL* 6910). Celsus and Julianus may be misreadings of place names, although the Latin is ambiguous; see G. Lucchesi, "S. Potito ed una celebre discussion agiografica," *Studi romagnoli* 8 (1957): 457, quoting a ninth-century text in BAV, MS Reg. lat. 482 (not seen). The final *auctaria* entry for January 13 in *PL* 123:650, suggests that abbreviated forms of "Jutta reclusa" might have been misconstrued as "Julianus et Celsus" long before Alberti. Some evidence that Alberti's martyrology was, as he complained, *corruptissimus*, is provided by the fact that the martyrs' names he quotes are in the nominative rather than the genitive.

81. See Grayson, *Opusculi*, 33, on how closely Alberti adheres to his apparent sources (not identified). For Potitus in late medieval Pisa, see Webb, *Patrons*, 109–110; and sermon 78 in Nicole Bériou, dir., *Les sermons et la visite pastorale de Federico Visconti, archevêque de Pise (1253–1277)* (Rome: BEFAR, 2001), 925–926. Pace Grafton, *Leon Battista Alberti*, 64, and idem, "*Historia* and *istoria*: Alberti's terminology in context," *I Tatti Studies* 8 (1999):51, there is no Potitus associated with the city of Rome or martyred under Julian.

82. See Lucchesi, "S. Potito," 459–461. Perhaps the same figure at Padua; see BBU, MS 1622, fols. 292ra–292vb, an entry in a fifteenth-century legendary that closes with the authenticating remarks of the supposed author, "presbiter Marcus," quoted in Florio Banfi, "Vita di san Gerardo da Venezia nel codice 1622 della Biblioteca Universitaria di Padova," *Benedictina* 2 (1948): 327.

Alberti could not improve the historical precision of the account.[83] The latter failure was serious, but the former was fatal. We cannot well understand Alberti's project unless we recognize that, while Alberti describes his narrative, still in progress, as *istoria* and *historia* in his letter to Leonardo Dati, he chooses quite another word to describe it, now finished, in his letter to Marino Guadagni. In the letter to Guadagni (undated but evidently written to accompany a copy of the completed narrative sent as a gift), Alberti refers to his narrative only as a *laus*. He never once uses the words *istoria, historia,* or even *vita*. His narrow choice of a term is odd, since the structure of his account is traditional enough to be taken for a *vita,* and it was customary to designate such accounts as *historiae*. By insisting that he had written a *laus,* however, Alberti declared the unhistorical (even antihistorical) aspect of his *vita Potiti*. His choice of the word *laus* allows us to identify the weakness of the narrative from the point of view of the ecclesiastical patron, Biagio Molin. For if a *laus* was excused from historical precision, it was not excused from its moral task, which was to praise the subject—here the saint—in such a way as to confirm in an already favorable audience the duty to honor and imitate. This task Alberti did not fulfill. The problem that the assignment caused him can, perhaps, be better grasped if it is put in context: Alberti wrote his *vita Potiti* about the same time that he was composing *I Libri della famiglia*.[84] The urban virtues broached in that dialogue are the middling, Aristotelian ones; in fact, they are precisely the Aristotelian virtues that Leonardo Bruni meant to defend in 1429 by writing his *vita Aristotelis,* a partisan work aimed not just at Traversari's translation of Diogenes Laertius (which Traversari had hesitated to undertake on account of its pagan subjects) but also at Traversari's translation of the *Vitae patrum*.[85] It is possible that undercurrents of Bruni's secular Aristotelian ethics troubled Alberti's patron; certainly those ethics had no room for the passive humiliations of Christian martyrdom. Alberti was not engaged to write any more saints' lives.[86]

83. See Webb, "Sanctity and History," 298–299; cf. Grafton, "*Historia,*" 50–53, on Alberti's letter to Dati. On the variable relationships of *historia, vita,* and *laus,* see chap. 6 below.

84. Paolo Marolda, *Crisi e conflitto in Leon Battista Alberti* (Rome: Bonacci, 1988), discussing the *vita sancti Potiti* at 73–77, underlines the coincidence of the two works at 74–76.

85. Ianziti, "Leonardo Bruni," demonstrates the partisan aspect of Bruni's life of Aristotle. Diogenes Laertius's life of Aristotle was being translated by Ambrogio Traversari during the late 1420s and early 1430s; Ianziti notes, but underplays, Traversari's concurrent translation of the *Vitae patrum*. For insight into factional currents and how one might negotiate them, see Arthur Field, "Leonardo Bruni, Florentine Traitor?" *RQ* 51, no. 4 (1998): 1109–1150, and the long note at 1115–1116 n. 24.

86. Note that Molin commissioned a copy of Ambrogio Traversari's *Vitae patrum* in 1435, *after* Alberti had ceased to participate in the martyrological project; see Elpidio Mioni,

Agli got the project next, and he went much further with it than Alberti did. Being recommended by Bruni's critic, Ambrogio Traversari, doubtless helped. But if Agli did not share Alberti's reluctance to celebrate the virtues of martyrdom (Agli's prefaces to books 2 and 3 of his collection read like rebuttals of misgivings about the utility of the martyr as a model of social virtue), he did share Alberti's bedevilment with unreliable sources.[87] The factual vagueness of the early martyrs was compounded by their numerousness. The Carolingian martyrologies contain crushing lists of entries. For January 20, for example, the ninth-century martyrologist Usuard provides:

> At Rome: the birthday [i.e., death] of the blessed Pope Fabianus, who having headed the Church for thirteen years, suffered martyrdom at the time of Decius and was buried in the cemetery of Callixtus. On that same day in the catacombs: [the birthday] of Saint Sebastian the martyr, who although he had the leadership of the First Cohort, was ordered on account of his Christianity by the emperor Diocletian to be bound in the middle of a field and to be shot at with arrows by soldiers and in the end to be beaten until he died. On the Via Cornelia: [the birthday] of the holy martyrs Marius and Martha with their children Audifax and Abacuc, Persian nobles, who came to Rome to pray in the time of the *princeps* Claudius. And after they bore beatings, scorchings, fires, rakings, and the cutting off of their hands, Martha was killed in the nympheum, and the others were beheaded, and their bodies burned.[88]

"Le *vitae patrum* nella traduzione di Ambrogio Traversari," *Aevum* 24 (1950): 325–326, on BAV, MS Lat. 1214. Grafton, *Leon Battista Alberti*, 68–69, observes that "Alberti apparently gained the reputation of an able biographer of saints." He refers to the recommendation by the Benedictine Girolamo Aliotti (1412–1480) that Alberti be engaged by the Camaldulensians to write a *vita* of Ambrogio Traversari; see G. Aliotti, *Epistolae et opuscula* (Arezzo, 1769), 1:33. *Vitae* about contemporaries, however, are a special case (see chap. 1 above); I think it highly unlikely that Alberti's *vita* of Potitus contributed to Aliotti's recommendation (although Alberti may have come to Aliotti's mind because of time Alberti spent with Traversari on Molin's project).

87. For the prefaces, see FBNC, MS Nuovi acq., MS 399, fols. 16r–v and 17v–18r. In the preface to book 2, Agli sets out the standard theological reasons for the necessity of all the terrible deaths, although he admits that he barely manages to convince himself. This preface may draw on Agli's youthful dialogue on the deaths on the martyrs, his first literary undertaking (lost or so far unidentified); see Agli's autobiographical dialogue in Camerino, Bibl. Valentiniana, MS 78, fol. 115v, for this notice. I thank Nelson Minnich for sharing his microfilm of this work with me. In the preface to book 3 of his collection of *vitae et passiones*, Agli refutes those who say that the passions of the martyrs are unsophisticated narratives of no use to anyone except women, children, and the uneducated. See Webb, "Sanctity and History" and Guidi, "Questioni."

88. My translation from *PL* 123:673–674. The text of Usuard is easily available in *PL* vols. 123–124, a reprint of de Sollier's edition from the *AASS*. See Martimort, *Les lectures liturgiques*. For a general introduction, see René Aigrain, *L'Hagiographie* (Paris: Bloud and

Most of Usuard's entries mention at least three and, depending on local variants, sometimes more than a dozen saints, often with much less detail than here. For further information about such entries, humanists turned to what they believed were early Christian sources. So, for example, Agli's entry on Sebastian is not based on Usuard but is a close paraphrase of the legend attributed to Ambrose.[89] His entry for Fabianus drew on the *Liber pontificalis*.[90] Working at Florence, Agli seems not to have known the encyclopedic work of the accomplished Dominican Petrus Calo (da Chioggia, d. 1348) to gather and authenticate *vitae*; during the fifteenth century, a five-codex set was at Santa Maria Minerva in Rome.[91] Neither did he know the twelve-volume Greek menology transcribed at Basel in 1435, at the request of Eugene IV, by the humanist Cristoforo Garatone (d. 1448 at the battle of Kosovo), then serving as papal secretary and legate, as well as bishop of Coron.[92] What Agli did appreciate was the size of the task, for a thoroughgoing revision of the Carolingian martyrologies was a labor that no Quattrocento scholar could misjudge. He may also have estimated the payoff in prestige: by taking up the revision, Agli became heir not just to Usuard but to a line of authorities stretching back through Ado and Florus to Bede, "Jerome," and so to the first collector, Eusebius.

To judge from the results, Agli was directed to collect narratives, to evaluate them critically, and then to compose his own revised versions. The results are not immediately impressive. Often the priest made only minor revisions in the old entries or introduced scholarly and informal comments that would not have been permitted in an official service

---

Gay, 1958), 62–65; and, for an illuminating case study, Janet Nelson, "The Franks, the Martyrology of Usuard, and the Martyrs of Cordoba," in D. Wood, ed., *Martyrs and Martyrologies* (Oxford: Blackwell, 1993), 67–80. For local revisions of Usuard that were printed in the fifteenth century under the supervision of men with training in the *studia humanitatis*, see the hand list s.vv. "Bartolomeo da Palazuolo" and "Vespucci, Giorgio Antonio." These editions suggest humanist participation in the reform of the liturgy through its regularization, a project that can be traced back to Charlemagne's reforms under Alcuin.

89. BAV, MS Lat., 3742, fols. 73–76v; cf. *PL* vol. 17, cols. 1021–1058. Francesco Quiñones, in his sixteenth-century *Breviarium Romanum*, also draws on Ambrose.

90. BAV, MS lat. 3742, fol. 58.

91. Today the Vatican Library holds two of the five volumes that were once at the Minerva; see items 134–137 in Gilles Meersseman, "La bibliothèque des frères prêcheurs de la Minerve au XVe siècle," in *Mélanges Auguste Pelzer* (Louvain: Bibliothèque de l'Université, 1947), 618.

92. Giovanni Mercati, *Scritti d'Isidoro il cardinal Ruteno* (Studi e testi 46) (Vatican City: BAV, 1926), 106–116; Sottili, "Ambrosio Traversari," 56–63, esp. 58 and n. 90. The letter recording Garatone's transcription is dated May 16, 1435. Whether the transcription was brought to Rome and translated, as was intended, I do not know. It is worth pointing out that the menology attributed to Simeon Metaphrast traditionally occurs in ten volumes, not twelve.

book.[93] In his entry for the evangelist Mark, for example, Agli reported hearing Ambrogio Traversari describe an ancient manuscript that related the translation of the relics to Constance, thus implying that Venice's patron and founder was honored in the lagoons with inauthentic relics.[94] He noted that he himself had been present at the 1439 translation of Zenobius, before explaining that there wasn't space to list all the saint's miracles.[95] Such comments can be found in saints' *vitae* and *passiones* throughout the medieval and early modern periods, but they are not typically part of the martyrology entry or the office readings.

Agli's chattiness should not, however, obscure the significance of his project. He worked at the pleasure of a humanist who was notably attentive to sanctity. Nicholas's papacy had begun with the invention and authentification of the relics of Stephen and Laurence at Rome; the pope also forwarded the canonizations of Bernardino of Siena, Francesca Romana, and Vincent Ferrer. He intended to make not just architectural splendor (the space of ritual) but also liturgical reform (ritual itself) his chief legacy.[96] Agli's great novelty as a compiler thus takes on added significance. For Agli did innovate: he removed the saints from their traditional positions as markers of the *circulus anni*, the calendrical time of the fixed feasts.[97] Instead of using the liturgical sequence of the calendar, Agli arranged the entries according to the year of the saint's death, that is, according to a *secular* principle that made no liturgical sense.[98]

93. See Webb, "Sanctity and History," 301 (Matthew, George, Minias, Sylvester, Simon, and Dionysius the Ariopagite) and 302 (Clement I, Fabian and Anterus, and Gregory Nazianzen, noting the odd absence of Jerome and Chrysostom). Agli's entry for Pamphilus, for example, reproduces Florus verbatim.

94. "Quod pluribus elapsis iam seculis quidam Venetias, quae civitas est Italiae in Adriatico sita, alii Constantiam Germanie urbem translatum asserunt. Ego vero ab Ambrosio generali abbate ordinis sancti Romualdi viro probate fidei audivi, cum diceret se argenteas tecas vidisse in monasterio sito in insula quae est in medio lacu iuxta Constantiam legisseque antiquissimis libellum apicibus scriptum quo eius translatio Constantiam ordine ennaratur. Hos vero in medio id relinquimus" (BAV, MS Lat. 3742, fols. 12v–13).

95. "Mille et eo amplius annis post, ex eo loco ubi prius collocatum fuerat, in digniorem honoratioremque locum in eadem ecclesia nobis presentibus est absportatum. Tum quoque miracula quedam facta, sed longiorem esset omnia recensere" (FBNC, MS Nuovi Acq. 399, fol. 71).

96. On Nicholas's desire for a liturgical legacy, see Stinger, *The Renaissance in Rome*, 46–47 and 346 n. 115, expanding Giannozzo Manetti's remarks in his life of the pope.

97. On calendrical order in liturgical books, see John Hennig, "Kalendar und Martyrologium als Literaturformen," *Archiv für Liturgiewissenschaft* 7, no. 1 (1961): 1–44; and idem, "Martyrologium und Kalendarium," *Studia patristica* V. *Texte und Untersuchungen* 80 (1962): 69–82.

98. For some sense of the conceptual changes that such a reordering involved, see Roy Rappaport, *Ritual and Religion in the Making of Humanity* (Cambridge: Cambridge University Press, 1999), 169–235; Buc, *The Dangers of Ritual*, 147–152. For details on how Agli redistributed his saints, see A. K. Frazier, "Katherine's Place in a Renaissance Collection: Evidence from Antonio degli Agli (c. 1400–1477), *De vitis et gestis sanctorum*," in J. Jenkins and K. Alexander, eds., *St. Katherine of Alexandria: Texts and Contexts in Western Medieval Europe* (Turnhout: Brepols, 2003), 228 at n. 28.

He then grouped these rearranged entries into ten books. The first eight books are periodized by the sequence of imperial reigns. A ninth book consists of ten entries about saints who suffered during the Vandal persecutions. In the tenth and final book, Agli placed entries for saints whose year of death could not be ascertained, figures such as Reparata, Euphrosina, Genevieve, Sigismund, and Simeon the Stylite. Although this final book partially returns to organization by feast date and Agli's estimates of chronology elsewhere in the collection are sometimes inaccurate, his overall accomplishment is remarkable. He presented the martyrology as a lay historical document. This feat evidently required someone with a modicum of sympathy for the virtues presented. Thus it was not Leon Battista Alberti but Antonio Agli, the lesser intellect and the priest, who articulated a new model of Christian history.

Whether Agli succeeded is another matter. It is difficult to tell what sort of document he thought he was creating. The length of the entries varies a great deal, from barely fifty words for Pionius, martyred under Antoninus Verus, to several hundred on Florence's fifth-century bishop Zenobius. That range bespeaks a model such as Jerome's *De viris illustribus* rather than, say, the *Legenda aurea* of Jacobus de Voragine. The presentation of saints according to a secular chronology may also represent the influence of world history. Both Vincent of Beauvais's thirteenth-century *Speculum historiale* and Antonino Pierozzi's fifteenth-century *Chronicon*, for example, wove a year-by-year presentation of saints into their histories.[99] The recurrence of liturgical elements throughout *De vitis* suggests at the same time that Agli did not abandon the expectation of a traditional liturgical function: canonical feast dates are usually provided, as are ritual closings ("Ad laudem et gloriam etc."), and feast date remains a sporadic principle of order within the books.[100] Because it incorporates elements of such disparate formats, Agli's collection should be described as a deliberate experiment in genre. Because it fails to articulate a coherent alternative to the liturgical martyrology, it should also be described as a failure.

Agli deposited a manuscript of his saints' lives and passions in the Vatican Library before or shortly after the death of Nicholas V (1455). It was a mere sketch for a revised martyrology, as he himself acknowledged by describing it so casually when he later cataloged his own writings.[101] The project then lay fallow for some years, until it was taken up again under Paul II

99. J. B. Walker, *The Chronicles of St. Antoninus: A Study in Historiography* (Washington, D.C., 1933), at 55–56, notes Archbishop Antonino Pierozzi's reliance on Vincent of Beauvais, which is then amply documented throughout Walker's study. Walker also observes fundamental ways in which Antonino's structure differs from Vincent's, including the fact that "hagiography is, as a rule, kept apart from the general narrative" in the *Chronicon* (93–94).

100. Cf. Vespasiano da'Bisticci's report on the collection discussed in Webb, "Sanctity and History," 299; and Frazier, "Katherine's Place," 233 n. 52.

101. Frazier, "Katherine's Place," 226–227.

(1464–1471).[102] Early in 1469, Cardinal Jacopo Ammannati (who would later preside over the canonization inquiry for Bonaventure) tried to enlist the canon of San Lorenzo in Florence, Francesco Catellini da Castiglione, to revise the martyrology.[103] "You know how many martyrdoms of saints [*sanctorum martyria*] are read in the church, how big is the volume that holds them," he wrote. Would Francesco "take up this work" of rewriting and "vindicate the precious deaths" (*pretiosas mortes*)?[104] The cardinal congratulated Francesco on his stirring account of the contemporary martyrdom of Anthony of Rivalto, especially in their own spiritually lukewarm times (*his tepentibus saeculis*). He noted that Francesco was appropriately interested in Christian rather than pagan literature and that his accomplished style would lend credibility. Ammannati flattered Francesco: "You're the right age for the task, you're a hard-working intelligent man, and you're skilled in letters." He also offered the inducement of a preliminary work "prepared by someone else" in which the lives of the saints had been collected and ordered.[105] Francesco would clear up obscurities, tighten the exposition, improve the diction, and revise to suit the listener's "soul and ears."

Ammannati had settled his hopes on an unlikely figure. Francesco had already told the cardinal of his intentions to imitate his learned teacher Vittorino da Feltre, who humbly chose not to increase the world's burden of reading.[106] Now Francesco, acknowledging the force brought to bear,

102. Agli's disengagement must be inferred; there is no precise evidence of when or why he abandoned the project. Unlike Alberti, Agli continued to write about saints, composing a lengthy panegyric on Francis for Sixtus IV (BAV, MS Lat. 3698, the dedication copy).

103. In describing Quattrocento work on the martyrology, I have linked episodes to papacies. But Eugene IV, Nicholas V, and Paul II do not seem *themselves* to have asked humanists to do this rewriting; intermediaries such as Molin, Traversari, and Ammannati show up instead. On this author, Francesco Bausi, "Francesco da Castiglione," *DBI* 49 (1997), 713a–715b, and idem, "Francesco da Castiglione fra umanesimo e teologia," are essential. The chapels of San Lorenzo were the site of innovative attention to saints; see Robert Gaston, "Liturgy and Patronage in San Lorenzo Florence," in F. W. Kent and P. Simons, with J. C. Eade, eds., *Patronage, Art and Society in Renaissance Italy* (New York: Oxford University Press, 1987), 111–134, especially 115–119.

104. Letter 376, January 25, 1469, in Paolo Cherubini, ed., *Iacopo Ammannati Piccolomini Lettere (144–1479)* (Rome: Ministero per i beni culturali e ambientali, uffizio centrale per i beni archivistici, 1997) 2:1227–1229. Quotations in this paragraph are drawn from the letter.

105. Webb, "Sanctity and History," 304, considers the possibility that this preliminary work was Agli's. A less likely but intriguing candidate is Manetti's Usuard (plate 2) with its lists and marginal annotations.

106. "Studebam enim imitari Victorinum praeceptorem, qui quamquam esset in omni doctrina et scientiae facultate doctissimus, numquam tamen ad scribendum aliquid se contulit quod posteritati prodesse posset. Satis enim superque in omni doctrinae genere conscriptum esse asseverabat ut aetas hominis ad illa etiam perlegenda non sufficiat" (Florence, Bibl. Laurenziana, MS S. Marco 408, fol. 51r–v; FBNC, MS Magliab. XXXVIII, 142, fol. 65; FBNC, MS Conv. soppr. J VII 30, fols. 106–108). Francesco reiterated the point at the end of a second letter: "Satius esset profecto mutire quam prava *kai akromola* secundum

refused his powerful patron: "You wish that I would illustrate the Church's lives and passions of the saints, which are are not so elegantly written, in some more accessible, not to say more learned, style. I do not possess such a style."[107] Neither did he have the means or the time. But Francesco also justified his refusal in terms that the cardinal must have found discouraging. None of the Fathers, Francesco argued at length, had undertaken to write such massive collections of brief narratives. Men such as Athanasius, Gregory Nazianzen, Paulinus of Milan, Ambrose, and Jerome had written about one or at most two saints at a time; they produced *libelli*, booklets or handbooks, not martyrologies or legendaries. Of course, they were learned enough to write about the martyrs. But as learned people should, they chose to write about things they knew well and about figures who could be studied in reliable sources. These two requirements were missing in the case of the early martyrs, who were often so poorly documented that their accounts could not be chronologically ordered and had even, in some cases, been declared by the Church itself to be apocryphal. To seal his point, Francesco appealed to the principle of *congruitas*. Each genre, he said, has its rule: poetic and encomiastic composition is regulated by the author's inventive gifts (*amplitudo*); legal speech (*civiles causae*) by verisimilitude and the probable; history by truth (*veritas*) and narrative order (*ordinem rei gestae*). The cardinal was asking for a commitment "of months and years" for a project that was implausible by the standards of rhetorical historiography and inauthentic by the standards of patristic hagiography. Francesco, despite his poverty, would not accept the call.

To judge from the experiences of Leon Battista Alberti, Antonio Agli, and Francesco da Castiglione, at least some influential Quattrocento ecclesiastics thought that refashioning the canon of literature associated with the cult of the saints was a necessary and significant aspect of reform. No opposing voices have left a record. So we cannot say that anyone questioned assigning the revision to men trained in the *studia humanitatis*, men

---

Victorini praeceptoris sententiam scribere" (Flor., Bibl. Laurenziana, MS S. Marco 408, fol. 59v; see also FBNC, MS Conv. soppr. J VII 30, fols. 113v–116; FBNC, MS Magliab. XXXVIII, 142, fols. 70–75), I. A. Orsi, ed., *Francisci castilionensis martyrium Antonianum* (Florence, 1728). See also the remarks of Cherubini, *Iacopo Ammannati*, 2:1229.

107. "Laudasti officium meum verbis amplissimis, egisti pro parvulo munusculo gratias ingentes, fecisti ut res minima magna esse videretur. Collegisti omnes locos quibus persuasio fieri possit, ut id ad quod me hortaris magno animo et cum fiducia aggrediar. Velles enim ut martyria vitasque sanctorum qui habentur in ecclesia quae minus eleganta scripta sint denuo aliquo faciliori, ne dixerim disertiori stilo—quod in me non est—illustrarem" (FBNC, MS Conv. soppr. J VII 30, fol. 113v; see also FBNC, MS Magliab. XXXVIII, 142, fols. 70–87; and Flor., Bibl. Laurenziana, MS S. Marco 408, fols. 46v–49v). The discussion below draws on this letter. See Webb, "Sanctity and History," 304–305.

who possessed acknowledged rhetorical and critical skills. The candidates themselves did not reject the place of the saints in the liturgy, much less the prevailing system of belief. What troubled them were documentary difficulties, the proposal of imitable martyrdom, and the inauthenticity of the martyrology as a patristic genre.

It must have been difficult to work in such an atmosphere, at once eager for improvement and hypercritical on both moral and historiographical grounds. In that sense, at least, it is not surprising that the curial project for a new martyrology failed in the Quattrocento. Success would not come until the second half of the sixteenth century, in the vastly changed context of Reformation martyrdom, when Cesare Baronio developed a revised *Martyrologium Romanum* in conjunction with the reforms of the Council of Trent. Baronio did not retain the humanists' single great innovation, the secular chronology. Nevertheless, that chronology demands attention, hard as it can be now to appreciate what a profound change it represented. The new chronology was not a precious antiquarian revival. Neither, of course, does it prove that the Church was infested with people who were pagans at heart. Rather, the curia's persistent efforts to get help with the martyrology suggest that reordering and authenticating had somehow become of fundamental importance to the institution's sense of its mission.

Two quite different works, both composed outside the realm of liturgical reform, may help to clarify and support this hypothesis. The first is *Adversus Judaeos et Gentes* by the Florentine layman Giannozzo Manetti (1396–1458/1459). This treatise, planned as a twelve-book defense of Christianity, may have been intended for Nicholas V. After the pope's death, Manetti dedicated it instead to Alfonso of Naples, at whose court he spent the last years of his life.[108] Manetti organized *Adversus Iudaeos et Gentes* by topic, but the topics were set out in rough chronological order.[109] The first book would address pre-Christian thought, both classical and Jewish; then would follow three books on Christ's life, teachings, Passion, and Resurrection; two on authors of the Christian era, both

---

108. Manetti, in voluntary exile from Florence since 1453, spent time first with Nicholas V and then, at the pope's death in 1455, in Naples. Although Nicholas V was clearly the ideal dedicatee for *Adversus Judaeos et Gentes*, I am unaware of any scholarly argument that he was originally intended or that Manetti's attention to saints—described below—was connected with the curial hopes for a revised martyrology or with Manetti's own painstaking notes in his Usuard in BAV, MS Pal. lat. 835.

109. For the full plan, see BAV, MS Urb. lat. 154, fol. 84v, quoted in Gianfranco Fioravanti, "L'apologetica anti-giudaica di Giannozzo Manetti," *Rinascimento* ser. 2, 23 (1983): 8–9. Fioravanti's fundamental study argues the originality of Manetti's apology, which "in niente corrisponde al tipo 'normale' dell'opera di controversia" (8) against the Jews. On Manetti's anti-Jewish arguments, see also Ricardo Fubini, "L'ebraismo nei riflessi della cultura umanistica: Leonardo Bruni, Giannozzo Manetti, Annio da Viterbo," *Medioevo e Rinascimento* 2 (1988): 288–296.

sacred and profane; four books of saints, predominantly martyrs; and two final books on popes and emperors. The saints, in "vertiginously" extended lists, are found in books 7 through 10.[110] Here, the dilemma of identifying and dating comes again to the fore.

Manetti's roughly chronological topics collapse when he arrives at books 7–10, because chronology is, for the humanists, the defining problem of the early saints. These books are arranged instead by saintly type. The traditional arrangement places apostles first, followed by martyrs, then confessors, and finally virgins. Manetti begins by modifying this order somewhat, lumping together apostles and confessors under the title "confessors": his first entry is for the apostle Iacobus *maior*, Judas Thaddeus (book 7). This book goes on to discuss confessors such as Anthony (d.ca. 356) and Hilarion (d. ca. 371). Then Manetti backs up, chronologically speaking, to martyrs whose death dates are known, "secundum ordinem temporum," and opens book 8 with the protomartyr of the first century, Stephen. Martyrs without order, *sine ordine*, follow in book 9; the first are the presbyter Severus and the deacon Johannes, whom he can at least place under the empress "Eudocia" (d. 460) and the prefect Saturninus. Finally come virgins and virgin martyrs, and Manetti recommences yet again, now with Mary (book 10). Once the type-based groupings are achieved, Manetti imposes a secular chronology; that is, within each of the books in this central group, he organizes by year of death rather than day of feast. The arrangement of the martyrs "without order" in book 9 caused the most difficulty. Since secure imperial dating was not possible, Manetti set out these figures first by prefect, "a prefectis," then by barbarian persecution, "barbarum gentium persecutiones," and then simply by any available data, "quantum fieri poterit . . . ponemus."[111] Although the secular chronology and some aspects of his solutions to chronological difficulties are reminiscent of Agli's procedure, I do not see evidence that Manetti used Agli's work. In fact, Manetti's entries are, on the whole, even briefer and more derivative than Agli's, as he struggled to account for the "multitudes of martyrs, troops of the dead, masses of murdered Christians, such that it can

---

110. The characterization is from Fioravanti, "L'apologetica," 8. My emphasis on these books is not intended to supplant Fioravanti's identification of book 1 as the interpretive key to the anti-Judaic argument of *Adversus Judaeos et Gentes* (ibid., 24) or to contradict the interpretation in Fubini, "L'ebraismo," 291–293, that, overall, Manetti is less interested in hewing to Eusebius than in countering Josephus. I consider here a restricted part of Manetti's *apologia*, the final four books. Some Franciscan entries from books 5, 7, and 10 have been edited; see the hand list. Both editors point out how unoriginal and often faulty Manetti's entries are.

111. From the introduction to book 9 in BAV, MS Urb. lat. 154, fol. 182v and 184.

hardly be told."[112] Late in book 10, Manetti declared himself "panting with an inexpressibly great desire for the end of this long and prolix work" ("[nos] huius longi ac prolixi operis finem supra quam dici potest miro quodam desiderio anhelantes").[113] Finally, the martyrs wore him out: he left the *apologia* incomplete, without the projected eleventh and twelfth books on popes and emperors.

The second extracurial collection addressing martyrdom is the *Persecutionum christianorum historia* by the Milanese Cistercian Bonifacio Simonetta (fl. 1460). Simonetta declares his subject as "the persecution of the Christians and the popes."[114] "But because this same material has been treated by others," notes the presbyter and canon Stefano Dolcino (1462–1508) in a prefatory letter, "he has interspersed letters to friends" on topics of "history and the natural world."[115] In this eccentric format, following lives of Moses and Mohammed (no entry addresses Christ or Mary), Simonetta presents two books of learned references to the early martyrs, set out rigorously emperor by emperor to make seventeen periods of persecution. He breaks up these efficiently factual accounts by interspersing letters on topics such as drunkenness, the vestal virgins, climate, philosopher-kings, giants, and the plague.[116] The remainder of the collec-

---

112. BAV, MS Urb. lat. 154, fol. 196v: "quante martirum multitudines, quante defunctorum copies, quante denique trucidatorum christianorum summe per singulas provintias efficerentur, haud quamquam recenseri poterat," continuing, "Si igitur certus omnium martirum numerus vere fideliterque recenseretur, qui sub decem illis famosis celebratisque, ut alias omittamus (qua plurimas fuisse non dubitamus), Neronis, Domitiani, Traiani, Antonini, Severi, Maximini, Decii, Valeriani, Aureliani, Dioclitiani, et Maximiani persecutionibus varia tormentorum genera pertulerunt, celorum stellis et arene maris quemadmodum de israhelitarum cetibus per hyperbolem sacri litteris scriptum legimus nimirum coequaretur." This lengthy digression late in book 9 is set off by an even longer rumination on Peter Martyr, O.P., as a renovator of martyrdom (BAV, MS Urb. lat. 154, fol. 196)

113. In the life of Scholastica, BAV, MS Urb. lat. 154, fol. 214.

114. Sign. a2. The work was published in Milan by Antonio Zarotto in January 1492 (H 14750; IGI 9011; Goff S530). There is no title page; I use the title given by Ganda, *I primordi* #174; cf. Rogledi Manni, *La Tipografia*, # 919; and *BMC* 6:722. The work is described by Girolamo Tiraboschi in vol. 6, part 1 of *Storia della letteratura italiana* (Rome: Salvioni, 1783), 283, as "scritta in un modo singolare, e di cui forse non troverassi altro esempio."

115. "Sed quoniam ab aliis haec eadem tractata fuit materia, interpositis ad amicos epistolis, rem iam pene vulgarem novo invento illustravit. Epistolae enim ipsae tanta tum historicarum tum physicarum rerum copia redundant" (sign. a[r]). I cannot identify the vernacular work that apparently served as the model for Simonetta's gimmick. The Cremonese Dolcino, canon at S. Maria alla Scala, also edited an edition of Ambrose's works, printed by Zarotto in 1491 (HC *899; GW 1601; IGI 425; Goff A553; Ganda, *I primordi*, #173). See Enrico Cattaneo, "Lo studio delle opere di s. Ambrogio a Milano nei secoli XV–XVI," in *Studi storici in memoria di Mons. Angelo Mercati, Prefetto dell'Archivio Vaticano* (Milan: Giuffrè, 1956), 156.

116. Drunkenness and vestal virgins in book 1, epistles 5 and 6; climate, philosopher-kings, giants, and plague in book 2, epistles 5, 7, 9, 11.

tion, books 3 through 6, is a papal chronology from Peter to Innocent VIII cribbed from the *Liber Pontificalis,* with its own complement of miscellaneous letters.[117]

Manetti and Simonetta chose a broader historical stage than Agli's assignment allowed. They echo Agli, however, in imposing a secular chronological structure. Moreover, both use the period of martyrdom as a structuring principle of that new secular chronology, making it the fulcrum of the world-historical shift from keeping time by emperors to keeping time by popes. (Manetti intended to conclude his apology with two books on popes and emperors; Simonetta actually does so.) It is true that both seem somewhat embarrassed by the example of the martyrs: Simonetta distracts his reader with marvels and jokes, while Manetti is more engaged by the history of authorship and Christian doctrine than by the chronological mess and unseemly quantity of the martyrs. Nevertheless, by putting the martyrs into a secular chronology and therefore on the same world-historical stage as the pagan heroes and secular rulers, the three humanist authors of martyrological collections—whether they conceive their work as liturgical, polemical, or entertaining—revive the conceptual world of the fourth century in the fifteenth.[118] They return to the chronological format of the first Church historian, Eusebius. Thus, what at first appears a secular format is, on reflection, just the opposite.

By reinstating Eusebian imperial chronology, these authors similarly reinstate his emphasis on the struggles of the *ecclesia* in the *saeculum.* The fifteenth-century roster of these struggles is well known. Although the Great Schism was over, the activities of councils continually threatened to renew it. The return of the papacy to Rome in 1420 had raised expectations of reform that the institution, politically insecure and short of cash, was in a poor position to meet. Increasing levels of literacy and a growing urban middle class made unprecedented demands on a priesthood whose spiritual commitment and level of education were an endless source of concern. The Observant movement, potentially a strong ally for reforming

---

117. In book 3, epistolae 20 and 22, Simonetta criticizes his rival as a papal historian, Bartolomeo Platina. Simonetta's praise of the Sforza in the concluding letters suggests that the work should be analyzed in light of Gary Ianziti, *Humanistic Historiography Under the Sforzas* (Oxford: Clarendon Press, 1988); Bonifacio was a nephew of Cicco Simonetta, discussed in chap. 3 below.

118. On the importance of the fourth century for the historical conceptualizations of the fifteenth, see Diana Webb, "The Truth About Constantine: History, Hagiography, and Confusion," *Studies in Church History* 17 (1981): 85–102, and Robert Black, "The Donation of Constantine: A New Source for the Concept of the Renaissance," in A. Brown, ed., *Languages and Images of Renaissance Italy* (New York: Oxford University Press, 1995), 51–86. Buc, *The Dangers of Ritual,* structures the first part of his study in reverse chronological order so as to work back into the redefinition of public ceremonial that accompanied the conversion of Constantine in the fourth century.

popes, also generated competition and ill feeling among the orders. Powerful families and territorial states continued, understandably, to put their own political needs before those of the papacy. And above all these institutional crises loomed renewed evidence that God apparently intended Islam to thoroughly humiliate Christianity, if not to triumph over the West *tout court*. This psychological bind—how to make sense of "the successes of a flourishing rival civilization"—was an old one.[119] In the Quattrocento, the dilemma was sharpened by an escalating series of Ottoman successes, most famously under Mehmed II (1432–1481), who brought the Roman Empire in the East to an end when he captured Constantinople in 1453; Mehmed's father, Murad II (d. 1451), and grandfather, Mehmed I (d. 1421), had also pursued expansionist policies.[120] The ecumenical union achieved at Florence in 1439 can be seen, at base, as the most coherent institutional response that the West could manage to Murad's successes.[121] But other sorts of responses were imagined as well, ones that may help to explain the intensifying emphasis on martydom in the second half of the Quattrocento, after the fall of Constantinople, documented in table 2.1 above.

❊ ❊ ❊

Dum feror eloquii Graii succensus amore
Dum linquo Italica, Graiaque tecta colo,
Occubui Thomas viridi Arretinus in aevo,
Spes quondam patriae nunc dolor ipse meae.
Externa in patria quid me cecidisse doletis
Omnibus externa vivitur in patria.
Vos tanquam peregrine mortales vivitis istic.
Hic patria, hic longae meta suprema viae est.

---

119. John V. Tolan, *Saracens: Islam in the Medieval European Imagination* (New York: Columbia University Press, 2002), traces European responses to Islam through the thirteenth century, noting the psychological bind at xiv–xv. For the Renaissance, recent historiographical trends emphasize rather the shared culture of Italy and the East; see Daniel S. Goffman, *The Ottoman Empire and Early Modern Europe: New Approaches to European History* (New York: Cambridge University Press, 2002). Awareness of this shared culture might, paradoxically, feed the "psychological bind."

120. Turan Osman, "The Ideal of World Domination Among the Medieval Turks" *Studia islamica* 4 (1965): 77–90. I am grateful to Islamicists Geoffrey Schad and Denise Spellberg for sharing their expertise.

121. Franz Babinger, *Mehmed the Conqueror and His Time*, trans. R. Manheim, ed. W. C. Hickman (Princeton, N.J.: Princeton University Press, 1978), 3–63, discusses the Balkan and Greek campaigns of Murad's sultanate, from the time of his accession in 1421 until his death in 1450; see also Halil Inalcik, *The Ottoman Empire: The Classical Age, 1300–1600* (London: Phoenix, 1973/2000), esp. 23–34. For an analysis of how Ottoman conquests drove the project for Church union, see H. Jedin and J. Dolan, eds., *Handbook of Church History* (New York, 1970), 4:491–497.

As I am borne afire with love of Greek eloquence,
As I leave my Italian homes, and dwell in Greek ones,
I, Tommaso d'Arezzo, died in the bloom of youth:
Once the hope of my country, now its very grief.
Why do you lament that I fell in a foreign country?
Everyone lives in a foreign country.
You mortals live as strangers in your place.
Here is my country, here the final goal of the long road.

—Maffeo Vegio (1407–1458), epitaph for Tommaso d'Arezzo,
martyred in 1437[122]

A couple of decades before the fall of Constantinople, in the spring of
1435, around the same time that Alberti was relinquishing and Agli taking up the reform of the martyrology, the humanist cleric Tommaso made
the scholars' familiar journey to Constantinople, hoping to improve his
Greek and collect manuscripts.[123] With him was a compatriot from
Arezzo, Giovanni Tortelli, then in his midthirties, accompanied by his little brother.[124] Tortelli, who had already studied Greek with the well-
known humanists Vittorino da Feltre and Francesco Filelfo, now continued under the prelate Johannes Eugenicus. We do not know if Tommaso
d'Arezzo joined Tortelli with other foreigners in the classroom, but both
men had some success with manuscripts. Tortelli received a Thucydides
from his teacher. Tommaso's daily prowls through "various places and
monasteries" turned up the works of Justin, Marcus Aurelius's orations,
and even a fragment of Athenagoras, bought cheap from a merchant who,
according to Tommaso, was using disjecta to wrap his salted fish.[125]

122. Vegio's poem was first edited in *Carmina illustrium poetarum italorum* X (Florence,
1724), 311; and subsequently by Luigi Raffaele, *Maffeo Vegio* (Bologna: Zanichelli, 1909),
185; and then G. Mercati, "Da incunaboli a codici," in L. Donati, ed., *Miscellanea bibli-
ografica in memoria di Don Tommaso Accurti* (Rome, 1947), reprinted in Mercati's *Opere
minore* (Vatican City: BAV, 1984), 6:211. On Vegio, a devoted Vergilian and a prolific author
of liturgical saints' lives, see the hand list.

123. Much of the story told here derives from Tommaso's *Tractatus*, discussed further
below. More than three decades ago, O. Capriotti, in a *tesi di laurea* that I have not seen, confirmed Mercati's identification of Tommaso as the author of the *Tractatus* and announced a
plan to edit it; see O. Besomi, "Un nuovo autografo di Giovanni Tortelli: Uno schedario di
umanista," *IMU* 13 (1970): 95, 98. The *Tractatus* is discussed as an anonymous work by E.
Randolph Daniel, *The Franciscan Concept of Mission in the High Middle Ages* (New York:
Franciscan Institute, 1992), at 118–127.

124. G. Mancini, "Giovanni Tortelli: Cooperatore di Niccolò V nel fondare la Biblioteca
Vaticana," *ASI* 78, no. 2 (1920): 173–174; and also Mariangela Regoliosi, "Nuove ricerche
intorno a Giovanni Tortelli," *IMU* 12 (1969): 137 and 139; Besomi, "Un nuovo autografo,"
96–98.

125. For the quoted phrase and the story about the fish, see [Tommaso d'Arezzo], *Tractatus de martyrio sanctorum* (Basel: Jacobus Wolff, about 1492) (HC 10864*; IGI 6256;

Then, in the late summer of 1437, Tommaso's friend John of Ragusa, a Dominican who had also been in Constantinople for two years, collecting manuscripts and working as a legate for the Council of Basel, approached the young man with a secret.[126] A movement was afoot to reform the Church in a literally revolutionary way, by initiating a new era of martyrdom. The person who had devised this most holy project, its "innovator" ("huius sanctissime rei innovatorem"), was the humanist Alberto da Sarteano (ca.1385–1450).[127] Tommaso may have recognized the name and may even have met the Observant Franciscan, who is now considered a *beatus*.[128] Alberto da Sarteano was not just a sought-after preacher, Bernardino of Siena's most beloved disciple; he was also

---

BMC III, 776; Goff M331), sign. g4v. The passage is edited by Mercati, "Da incunaboli," 6–7, repr. in Mercati, *Opere minori*, 6:205. On Tommaso's finds, see André Vernet, "Les manuscrits grecs de Jean de Raguse (d. 1443)," *Basler Zeitschrift für Geschichte und Altertumswissenschaft* 61 (1961): 79–80 and esp. 97–98, item 47. For the Thucydides, see Mercati, "Da incunaboli," in Donati, *Miscellanea*, 14 and n. 1, reprinted in Mercati, *Opere minori*, 6:210 and n. 1; Vernet, "Les manuscrits," 95–96, item 44. Mercati, "Da incunaboli," 5–8, also points out that, except for the Athenagoras, all Tommaso's references to early Church writers can be traced to Jerome's *De viris illustribus*. Athenagoras is, therefore, a measure of Tommaso's seriousness as a manuscript hunter and may also reflect his closeness to John of Ragusa (see below), who described his own mission as searching for "original Greek books to verify the authorities [presumably on the *Filioque*] we have from them," quoted in E. Cecconi, ed., *Studi storici sul concilio di Firenze* (Florence, 1869), 1:ccx–ccxi, letter 78, dated February 9, 1436, from John of Ragusa to Cardinal Giuliano Cesarini, the legate leading the Council of Basel.

126. On the conciliarist John of Ragusa (Giovanni Stojkevic, d. 1443), see Kristeller, "Contribution," 143; Aloysius Krchnák, *De vita et operibus Joannis de Ragusio* (Rome: Facultas Theologica Pontificiae Universitatis Lateranensis, 1960); Bonaventura Duda, *Joannis Stojkovic de Ragusio, O.P. (d. 1443): Doctrina de cognoscibilitate ecclesiae* (Rome: Pontificium Atheneaeum Antonianum, 1958), who gives earlier bibliography. For his part in the Council at Basel, see also Joseph Gill, *The Council of Florence* (Cambridge: Cambridge University Press, 1959), *ad indicem*. For his manuscripts, bequeathed to the Dominican convent at Basel, see Vernet, "Les manuscrits"; and R.W. Hunt, "Greek Manuscripts in the Bodleian Library from the Collection of John Stojkovic of Ragusa," *Texte und Untersuchungen zur Geschichte der altchristlichen Literatur* 92, no. 7 (1966): 75–82. For Tommaso's filial relationship to John, see the preceding note and n. 131 below, also quoted in Besomi, ""Un nuovo autografo," 96 and n. 5.

127. On Alberto da Sarteano, see E. Cerulli, "Berdini, Alberto," *DBI* 8 (1966): 800–804. From Cerulli's bibliography, see especially articles by Floro Biccellari and Ricardo Pratesi. Add to that bibliography Pierre Santoni, "Albert de Sarteano, observant et humaniste envoyé pontifical à Jerusalem et au Caire," *MEFR, Moyen Age, Temps Modernes* 86 (1974): 165–211; Jean Richard, *La papauté et les missions d'orient au moyen age (XIIIe–XVe siècles)* (Rome: BEFAR, 1977), 267ff.; and Remo Guidi, "Sottinesi e allusioni tra Poggio e il Sarteano a proposito di una polemica mancata," *AFH* 83, 1–2 (1990): 118–161.

128. Mercati, "Da incunaboli," 10 n. 2 and 15, speculates that Tommaso had already met Alberto da Sarteano, because Tommaso alludes to Alberto's letter in defense of martyrdom and plan for a major treatise (*Tractatus*, chap. 18, sign. h4).

a papal diplomat, friend to Eugene IV, and an accomplished Latinist, student of Guarino Guarini. John of Ragusa knew that only the year before, in 1436, Alberto himself had sought martyrdom in the Holy Land.[129] Now John wanted to introduce young Tommaso to the three Franciscans from whom he had first learned of Alberto's plan.[130] They were in Constantinople on their way to martyrdom. John thought that Tommaso should write up their project or, rather, Alberto da Sarteano's. For secrecy's sake, the three Franciscans thought this treatise should be in Greek.[131]

The Franciscans were anxious to be off, so Tommaso composed the *Tractatus de martyrio sanctorum* in haste.[132] He knew that Eusebius's discussion of the early Christian martyrs in the *Historia ecclesiastica* was vital to "our" treatise but could not find a copy, even in Greek.[133] He had, however, read Eusebius before and knew some passages by heart.[134] Similarly, for Cyprian and Lactantius, he depended on notes made at an earlier read-

---

129. For Alberti's first effort at martyrdom, as well as a second attempt two years later in Egypt and the hope of a third, in the 1440s, in Spain, see B. Neri, *La vita e i tempi del Beato Alberto da Sarteano* (Quaracchi: Tipografia del Collegio di S. Bonaventura, 1902), 89–90, 93–94. Neri is factually unreliable. Nevertheless, what he has to say about Alberto as would-be martyr is not discussed by Floro Biccellari, "L'Opera del B. Alberto da Sarteano per la pace e per la Regolare disciplina," *Studi francescani* 36–37 (1939–40): 212–229; or in Cerulli's *DBI* entry; cf. Santoni, "Albert de Sarteano," 184 and especially 194, asserting that Alberto da Sarteano's thirst for martyrdom in Cairo was Franciscan mythology, promulgated in the *Chronica* of Mariano da Firenze. Santoni does not, however, address Alberto's first attempt, in 1436 in Jerusalem. For my assessment of Tommaso d'Arezzo's *Tractatus*, what matters is the evidence of contemporary belief that Alberto had sought martyrdom as part of a larger project. For another Tommaso associated with Alberto, a Tommaso who got himself martyred in 1447, see R. Lioi, "Tommaso da Firenze," in *BS* 12 (1969): 580–582.

130. *Tractatus*, chap. 18, at sign. h5: "Vidi prefatos patres in Constantinopolitana hac urbe, qui et in ecclesia sancti Petri, que latinis concessa est, pro tempore degebant. Vidit et illos clarissimus vir frater Johannes de Ragusio sacre theologie professor. . . . Admirabatur his illorum mores, humilitatem, religionis amore, zelum fidei, et alia quibus illi mirabiliter decorantur; admirabar et ego. Cogitabat hic prudentissimus vir quod non sine grandi negotio tales viri huc applicuissent . . . et ut breviter concludam, . . . secreta omnia propalarunt . . . que audita re nova quasi perterritus plusculum stupidus siluit cogitavitque intra se rem et tandem opus sanctissimum confirmavit et plurimum laudavit."

131. "Et ut deo placuit aliqua secretissima grece scribi illi fratres optabant, que cum prefato magistro Johanni narraverint, curavit ille ut talia ego scriberem. Fidebat enim de me ut de filio suo et quia rem ex huiusmodi scriptura cognoscere oportebat, illi consentientibus, omnia secreto mihi propalavit" (*Tractatus*, chap. 18, sign. h5).

132. *Tractatus,* chap. 18, sign. h4v, "festinat hora recessus a Constantinopoli."

133. "Quesivique potissimum Ecclesiasticam Eusebii Historiam quam tractatui nostro necessariam noveram, et nec grece saltem illam ut prius compilata fuerat commode reperire valui" (*Tractatus*, chap. 18, sign. h4v). In contrast, Tommaso had no trouble finding a Latin Qur'an (ibid., sign. e2v; see n. 153 below).

134. "[*Sci.* notitiae,] que ex Eusebii historia et aliis, que prius legeram, memorie fideliter mandaveram et recordari potui" (*Tractatus*, chap. 18, sign. h4v).

ing.[135] He excerpted from other texts, including pseudo-Eusebius's letter on the death of Jerome, and decorated his argument with references to Cicero, Virgil, Quintilian, Homer, Herodotus, Xenophon, and Hesiod.[136] The Franciscans contributed stories about exemplary martyrs.[137] Tommaso's many quotations from *passiones* found in Jacobus de Voragine's *Legenda aurea* and Vincent of Beauvais's *Speculum historiale* may represent their help.[138] But it must have been Tommaso's decision to choose one of these stories to retell at by far the greatest length and to place most prominently in the penultimate chapter, just before he closes with his own autobiographical justifications: the story of the methodical cutting to bits of the Persian martyr James the Dismembered.[139]

The Franciscans also provided Tommaso with his thesis: as the early Church had been founded and augmented by the blood of Christ and the martyrs, so would the contemporary Church be saved. God's servants, Tommaso complains, seduced by peace (*pacis ocio*), have been wasting their time in sterile scholarship and the quarrels of secular princes. They have neglected to address the devil's chief triumph, the spread of Islam, which "holds the greatest part of the world and . . . grows daily," conquering "not with disputations but with the sword" ("non disputationibus sed gladio").[140] In the thirteenth century, St. Francis of Assisi had proposed to confound this enemy with martyrdom and the cross of Jesus Christ ("nulla re magis quam martyrio et cruce Jesu Christi illorum perfidia confundi poterit").[141] Now—

135. "Nec aliud, temporis angustia, quam excerpta quedam extra martyrii causam ex Cypriana et Lactantiana, que ipse dum olim horum libros legerem annotaveram, habere permisit" (*Tractatus*, chap. 18, sign. h4v).

136. Pseudo-Eusebius (*BHL* 3866) is among the popular *Transitus Hieronymi* texts; Tommaso quotes it in concluding *Tractatus*, chap. 18, sign. h4.

137. "Et interim hi venerabiles fratres exce[r]pta alia ex sanctorum vitis tradiderunt" (*Tractatus*, chap. 18, sign. h4v). Cf. Vernet, "Les manuscrits," 100, items 54 and 55, two Greek martyrologies from John of Ragusa's legacy to the Dominicans of Basel (not seen).

138. The identification of these thirteenth-century Dominican sources is my own. Cf. Vernet, "Les manuscrits," 104, item [5], with remarks on Basel, UB, MS XI. 3 [AO 13].

139. Lightly revised from the *LA*, with attention to direct address as given by Jacobus de Voragine and followed by a passage from the *Transitus Hieronymi*; see *Tractatus* chap. 17, sign. h2v–h4v.

140. *Tractatus*, preface, sign. a2v.

141. Ibid. See also sign. a2v–a3: "Attendite igitur, Christiani fideles, quia non armis, non curribus, non diversorum generum propugnaculis illorum inifidelitatem faciliter vincemus, qui quotidie ob nostra peccata nos superant ac conculcant, vendunt, et sine martyrio occidunt, sed sanguine potissimum nostro, et cruce Jesu Christi." On Francis's own search for martyrdom in Cairo, see L. Lemmens, "De sancto Francisco Christum praedicante coram sultano Aegypti," *AFH* 19, no. 2 (1926): 559–578; and Miri Rubin, "Choosing Death? Experiences of Martyrdom in Late Medieval Europe," in Wood, *Martyrs and Martyrologies*, 157–161. For the extension of the model in the Franciscan and other orders, see Tolan, *Saracens*, 214–232; among the Dominicans, Vauchez, *La sainteté*, 341–342; and for the model

to the alarm of his teacher Guarino Guarini and his friend Francesco Barbaro—Alberto da Sarteano was renewing that model of individual sacrifice.[142]

The eighteen chapters of the *Tractatus* open with Tommaso drawing on Cyprian, Lactantius, Maximus of Turin, Jerome, Augustine, and Ambrose to explain the meaning, origin, and kinds of martyrdom, as well as its special virtues.[143] It quickly emerges that the *apologia* is also a practical handbook, a guide to being a martyr, as Tommaso lapses into the second person singular as well as the first person plural. Excerpting his authorities and frequently adducing the Evangels, the Old Testament prophets, and the Maccabees, Tommaso identifies the virtues that "you" should exhibit as a martyr, urges constant readiness for martyrdom, and warns against arrogance.[144] He sets out the types of martyrdom, comparing its rewards to the Muslim paradise.[145] He explores impediments, including how to deal with pain or doubt in extremis.[146] Tommaso devotes special care to

among the humanists, the fine study by Franco Gaeta, "La figura di s. Francesco nell'umanesimo," in *L'immagine di Francesco nella storiografia dall'Umanesimo all'Ottocento* (Assisi: Università di Perugia/Centro di studi francescani, 1983), 41–75.

142. For Francesco Barbaro's dismayed response to the personal plans of his good friend Alberto da Sarteano to seek martyrdom by preaching in Syria, see Barbaro's letter to Guarino Guarini (who had taught both men) dated August 22, 1435, letter 20 in Remigio Sabbadini, ed., *Centotrenta lettere inedite di Francesco Barbaro* (Salerno: Tipografia nazionale, 1884), 76–77.

143. *Tractatus*, chap. 1, "Quid est martyrium"; chap. 2, "Qua ex causa, et a quo ortum habuerit martyrium, et unde dicatur"; chap. 3, "Quot sunt genera martyrii"; chap. 4, "Quot modis perficitur martyrium." Tommaso quotes several times from "Maximus in sermone martyrum" (*Tractatus*, chap. 1, sign. a4), including the evocative "fides nostra mater martyrum est" (chap. 2, sign. a6v). A study of Maximus of Turin in humanist hands is needed. Chap. 5, "Que decorant seu magnificant martyrium." Martyrdoms are distinguished by the importance of the place (Rome is greater than Alexandria, for example) and by the age and status of the victim. Henceforward, all references in this discussion are to chapters in *Tractatus*.

144. Chap. 6, "Quibus virtuosis dispositionibus martyrium est suscipiendum." Required are *magnanimitas, alacritas, liberalitas, charitas,* and a magnificent soul, *magnificus . . . animus.* Chap. 7, "Quibus respectibus debemus semper promptos esse ad martyrium." Here, aside from the Old Testament figures of Moses and Phineas, Tommaso adduces several early Christian martyrs briefly, but treats at length Sanctulus from Gregory's *Dialogues* and the Virgin of Antioch (Pelagia) from Ambrose's *De virginitate*. Chap. 8, "Quod nemo impudenter et sua virtute confidens nisi tractus a deo presummat accedere ad martyrium."

145. Chap. 9, "De gradibus martyrii," which are (1) infants; (2) those who might flee guiltily but do not; (3) those who might flee guiltlessly but do not; and (4) the perfect, i.e., those who offer, *tradere,* themselves freely out of charity. This chapter is especially reliant on the *Legenda aurea,* but Tommaso also refers, for the only time, to Anselm's *Cur Deus Homo* and Aquinas's *Summa.* He closes by recalling the sixty Franciscans who had been martyred recently ("pauci admodum sunt anni elapsi") in the vicinity of Jerusalem ("in hierosolyme partibus"), as well as Francis's followers who died in Morocco (these would be canonized in 1481, following the Otranto massacre; see below). Chap. 10, "De premiis martyrii et paradiso Moameth."

146. Chap. 12, "De impedimentis retrahentibus nos a martyrio"; chap. 13, "De his qui Christum negarunt, quomodo debent redire ad penetentiam"; chap. 14, "De crebra invocatione nominis Jesu tempore martyrii."

the language problem, because merchants, although they know foreign languages, aren't likely to want to help. But the prospective martyr might spend a couple of years among the infidels learning their language or write out an explanatory *cedula*—Tommaso includes a sample text—for locals to translate and discuss.[147] He knows of several recent martyrs who have used *cedulae* to explain their cause.

In the longest chapter, "Refutations of typical arguments made against contemporary martyrdom," Tommaso helps the candidate answer skeptics.[148] These are just the sorts of arguments that we, today, are most likely to imagine humanists such as Leonardo Bruni and Leon Battista Alberti making against the contemporary value of martyrdom. They are the arguments that Giovanni Aurispa could not state explicitly in his preface to the passion of Mamas. According to Tommaso, opponents will say that the martyrdom of the early Church cannot be reproduced today, because there is currently no persecution of Christians. Rather, many Christian merchants live peacefully with their families among the Muslims.[149] Opponents will also argue that there is no clear benefit (*fructum uberrimum*, presumably mass conversions) to be gained from voluntary death. Christian virtue now means staying home, either raising your family devoutly or keeping your religious vows with love.[150] The latter argument Tommaso meets with a burst of idealism about what preaching and exemplary death might accomplish. The former argument is his chief concern. At length, he counters that there is contemporary persecution of Christians. Look at the closing of churches *in Europe partibus* (in European parts): "Daily the faith dies, that is, the number of believers, nor is there anyone who wishes to save it" ("Pereat quotidie fides, hoc est credentium numerus, nec est qui velit succurrere").[151] Look, above all, at the blasphemy in the Qur'an.[152] How, asks Tommaso, giving extensive quotations from a Qur'an "clearly

147. Chap. 17, "Quis modus habendus his qui ignorant linguam eorum infidelium ad quos caritatis et martyrii ardore accedere cupiunt." The *cedula* occurs at sign. g6v–h.

148. Actually several chapters address potential objections; chap. 2, for example, refutes the proposition that martyrdom is "contra naturam" (sign. a6v). But objections are formulated explicitly in chap. 11.

149. "Nulla est contra christiano persecutio" (chap. 11, sign. c4). For merchant families among the Muslims, see chap. 11, sign. c4v.

150. Rather than convert, "Heathens will allow no preaching or instruction but will kill you with less thought than they give to killing a dog, because their spiritual precepts tell them that paradise is given to those who kill at least a hundred Christians" (chap. 11, sign. c4). On the same page, Tommaso presents his critics' view of Christian virtue, modeled by the married layperson, the secular cleric, and the regular. These are the people whom he wants to draw into the new scheme for martyrdom.

151. Chap. 11, sign. d5: e.g., Greece and Dacia, in contrast with Armenia where, he admits, the infidel permits the practice of Christianity as long as tribute is paid.

152. Chap. 11, sign. d5v–d6 and e1v–e3.

and faithfully translated," can he read these things daily and not respond?[153] Tommaso recalls with approval the Franciscan at Jerusalem who waited until the mosque filled for prayer and then entered carrying a crucifix, so amazing the Muslim faithful ("insolito miraculo stupentes") that they did not react.[154] "Belt on your sword," he urges. "Together let us go to war" and win "eternal crowns for our victory."[155]

Tommaso compounds the novelty of his argument that "martyrdom is especially necessary *now*" ("Martyrium hoc tempore maxime necessarium esse") with another so unorthodox that it may not have originated with him or even the Franciscans.[156] Tommaso probably thought that the idea came from Alberto da Sarteano. The way of the martyr, he claims, is open to all Christians. It is not confined to mendicants or learned bishops, that is, to those who, according to canon law, were competent to preach. Secular clerics like himself can be martyrs, and so can laypeople, learned and even unlearned.[157] Martyrdom is a special calling, as Tommaso acknowledges, but his treatise envisions an effective wave of martyrs.[158]

Tommaso closes with apologies for the state of his Latin, which he had been meaning to brush up with Quintilian, and his Greek, for he had not been long in Constantinople.[159] The Franciscans have advised him, however, that the plain truth will suffice. So he is content to set out these things simply and artlessly, almost as though speaking in the vernacular, "simpliciter haec et inepte et, ut ita dicam, pene vulgaria explicuisse contentor."[160] Anyway, Tommaso adds, John of Ragusa will give the *Tractatus* to the person who inspired it, Alberto da Sarteano. Alberto will emend

153. Chap. 11, sign. c1v; on the translation of the Qur'an, see also sign. e2v: "Sed video, nec ut tu facere videris, fingo me non audire. Quesivi et reperi alchoran de arabico in latinum egregie et fideliter traductum. Nec difficile fuit, cum plures habeant illum. Et lego et perlego, non ut Christi blasphemias audiam, sed ut eorum ineptias et perfidiam . . . cognoscam." No Latin Qur'an is listed among Giovanni da Ragusa's books, but see Vernet, "Les manuscrits," 86–86, item 19; 101–102 items AN 63 and AN 14.

154. Chap. 11, sign. c1v.

155. The concluding words of chap. 11, at sign. e3.

156. Chap. 11, sign. c4.

157. Chap. 15, "Qui sunt abiles ad martyrium"; cf. chap. 16, "An fratres minores pre ceteris obligentur ad martyrium." For the transgression involved in such an extension of the call to martyrdom through preaching, see Michel Lauwers, "Praedicatio—Exhortatio: L'Eglise, la réforme, et les laics (Xie–XIIIe siècles)," in R. M. Dessi and M. Lauwers, eds., *La parole du prédicateur, Ve–XVe siècle* (Nice and Paris: Centre d'études médiévales, 1997), 187–232, on the restricted office of the preacher and on the difference between preaching and exhorting, with further bibliography.

158. On martyrdom not being for everyone, see chap. 8, sign. c2v.

159. Chap. 18, sign. h4v.

160. Ibid., sign. h5.

or rewrite it as he sees fit, or even tear up and hide the little work if that seems the better course.[161]

It was time for the Franciscans to be off. The Dominican John of Ragusa was prevented from joining them by his vow of obedience; his superiors had commanded him to return to Basel.[162] But Tommaso's life, as he explains in his concluding chapter, was his own to give. He asked the Franciscans to accept him as a fourth member. When they did, Tommaso divested himself of his worldly ties. The Franciscans helped him sell his belongings.[163] With conscious intent, he set aside his attachment to his widowed mother, his siblings, and his friends.[164] Finally, he handed over his precious manuscripts, including the *Tractatus*, to John of Ragusa.[165]

Exactly when, or how, or in what direction the four companions set out to meet death is not known. The epitaph by the curialist Maffeo Vegio, given at the head of this section, is the only record of Tommaso's success. In late 1437, John of Ragusa carried the *Tractatus* with a collection of Greek manuscripts to Basel, where it was eventually deposited, according to the terms of John's will, in the library of the Dominican convent.[166] One of the prelates in attendance at the council, the archbishop of Milan, Francesco Pizzolpasso (d. 1443), made a Latin copy—the only extant manuscript.[167] Despite

161. "Ad illum [Albertum] ex consilio dictorum patruum [Franciscanorum] post discessum ex hac vita portandum curavimus, ut si corrigi potest, illum corrigat et emendet, et ut placuerit, reformet. Si incorrigibili videatur, laceret et abscondat. Nec te labor iste gravabit, dulcissime patre, quin saltem aliquid ad aliorum edificationem de hoc sancto martyrio tuo gravi stilo et auctoritate solitaque charitate conscribas." Ibid., sign. h5.

162. John pled with the council at Basel to be released from his duties to fulfill his "ingens desiderium . . . visitare sepulchrum domini nostri Iesu Christi" (Mercati, "Da incunaboli," 12 n. 4, repr. in Mercati, *Opere minori*, 6, 209, n. 4); I assume that he could hardly afford to reveal his plan to join the new martyrs. Cf. the frank report that the papal diplomat Cristoforo Garatone made to Eugene IV: "quidquid secrete in materia temptaverit, non explicare possem." The most obvious secret had to do with topics of dissension between the pope and the council. But Garatone may have guessed at the other secret, for he closes, "Deus prebeat, ut dignum peccatorum suorum penitentiam illic [in Jerusalem] valeat adimplere" (ibid.). See also John of Ragusa's description of Islamic doctrine and of Christian suffering at Muslim hands in Cecconi, *Studi storici*, letters 78, 80, and 93 at ccliv, as well as his extraordinarily lengthy letter of self-justification, read aloud to the council in Basel on January 29, 1438, after his return there: ibid., letter 178.

163. Chap. 18, sign. h5v.

164. "Sicque amorem dilectissime matris vidue charumque germanorum et dulcissimorum amicorum dedi"(chap. 18, sign. h5v).

165. B. Altaner, "Zur Geschichte der Handschriftensammlung des Kardinals Johannes von Ragusa," *Historisches Jahrbuch* 47, no. 4 (1927): 730–732; Vernet, "Les manuscrits"; Besomi, "Un nuovo autografo," 96, with nn. 3 and 6, and 98 n. 4.

166. Konrad Escher, "Das Testament des Kardinals Johannes de Ragusio," *Basler Zeitschrift für Geschichte und Altertumswissenschaft* 16 (1917): 208–212; Vernet, "Les manuscrits," 82–104, with additions and corrections in Hunt, "Greek Manuscripts."

167. Tommaso's autograph (in Greek?) is lost; Pizzolpasso's copy (his own translation?) is MBA, MS C 17 sup., fols. 1–85, fully described in Louis Jordan and Susan Wool, *Inventory*

Tommaso's explicit instruction (which remains in both the manuscript and the incunable edition of the treatise), there is no evidence that Alberto da Sarteano received the *Tractatus*. Alberto neither published the major *apologia* for martyrdom that he himself had been promising nor, so far as we know, promoted Tommaso's.[168] Neither did Giovanni Tortelli, who as the oldest of the group of language students from Arezzo had some responsibility for Tommaso's well-being, respond to the sacrifice of his "most faithful companion."[169] Tortelli, known today for his work as Vatican librarian, his close friendship with Lorenzo Valla, and his widely circulated textbook *De orthographia*, did go on to get a degree in theology. He also wrote two saints' lives, but not about martyrs. Instead, Tortelli told the stories of two early Christian bishops who died piously in their beds, full of prudent advice for their urban flocks.[170] There is no record of his response to his friend Valla's portrayal of the Forty Martyrs, but perhaps the model bishops constituted a reply to Tommaso's enthusiasm.

❊ ❊ ❊

Aside from the fall of Constantinople in 1453 and of Negroponte in 1470, the greatest opportunity the fifteenth century offered humanists for reflection on contemporary martyrdom occurred in August 1480, when the

---

of Western Manuscripts in the Biblioteca Ambrosiana, Part Two C–D superior (Notre Dame: University of Notre Dame Press, 1986), 18–22. See also Besomi, "Un nuovo autografo," 98 and n. 4; Mirella Ferrari, "Un bibliothecario milanese del quattrocento: Francesco della Croce," *Archivio ambrosiano* 42 (1982): 207.

168. For Alberto's intention to write a four-part treatise urging the imitation of the martyrs, see Francis Harold, ed. *Beati Alberti a Sarthiano O.M. reg. obs. vita et opera* (Rome, 1688), 250–258, letter 37, to Eugene IV, dated by Harold to 1435. Harold's note II emphasizes Alberto's active search for martyrdom. See also Martène and Durand, *Amplissima collectio* 3:795–800, letter to Bishop Nicholas of Rimini, meant to accompany a longer "adversus vituperatores martyrum epistola"; and Santoni, "Albert de Sarteano," 181.

169. Tortelli refers to Tommaso as "fidelissimo socio" in the ownership note of his Thucydides; see Mercati, "Da incunaboli," 15–16, on the secrecy all round.

170. See the hand list. For the importance of bishops' *vitae* in the humanists' hagiographic output, see chap. 1 above. For early history of the genre, see Reinhold Kaiser, "Die *gesta episcoporum* als Genus der Geschichtsschreibung," in A. Scharere and G. Scheibelreiter, eds., *Historiographie im frühen Mittelalter* (Munich: Oldenbourg, 1994), 459–480. Cf. the gift of a translation of the life of Ambrose, another bishop who died in his bed, from Guarino to Alberto da Sarteano in 1437, just after the incident with Tommaso (for the dating, see Sabbadini, *Epistolario*, 3:313), and Buc, *The Dangers of Ritual*, 152, on martyrological elements in Paulinus's *vita Ambrosii*.

Turks captured Otranto, in the south of Italy.[171] The event was potent for three reasons. First, it was not hidden on the periphery. It occurred at home, in the Kingdom of Naples, implicating the Venetians and the Florentines and eliciting immediate responses from the papacy and the Aragonese, as well as plans for an emergency council in England. Second, it could be cast on a grand scale, reminiscent of martyrdoms under the Roman Empire. Scholars now agree with what contemporaries on the peninsula recognized at the time: that the invasion of Puglia was part of a plan of Turkish expansion westward. After his triumphant capture of Constantinople in 1453 and successes against Venetian holdings in the Greek islands, after he had taken Negroponte, Albania, and Serbia, Mehmed II aimed to extend his empire to Rome, fully appreciating what such an advance would mean to the Christian West.[172] Thus, when Otranto was captured, the curialist Jacopo Gherardi reported fears in Rome that all Italy would go up in flames ("incendium toti Italie formidandum"), that Christendom would be lost.[173] Sixtus IV (1471–1484) made emergency plans to evacuate to Avignon.[174] Such was God's punishment for Italy's sins, lamented Vespasiano da'Bisticci in vernacular prose and verse.[175]

171. Otranto is mentioned in passing by Jacob Burckhardt in *The Civilization of the Renaissance in Italy,* tr. S. G. C. Middlemore (London: Penguin, 1990), 76, but not in Gregory, *Salvation.* On the taking of Otranto, see Pastor IV, 333–342; Jedin and Dolan, *Handbook,* 546–547; Babinger, *Mehmed,* 390–392; Inalcik, *Ottoman Empire,* 30; and the introduction by L. Gualdo Rosa to her edition of Ilarione da Verona, "Copia Idruntine expugnationis," in L. Gualdo Rosa, ed., *Gli umanisti e la guerra otrantina* (Bari: Dedalo, 1982), 39. On the extent of the Ottoman Empire in the fifteenth century and on its generally friendly relations with the Italian territorial states, see the overview by Nejat Diyarberkirli, "Les Turcs et l'occident au XVème siècle," in C. D. Fonseca, ed., *Otranto 1480* (Galatina: Congedo, 1986), 1:17–27, and the following notes.

172. Diyarberkirli, "Les Turcs," 23; and Cemal Kafadar, "The Ottomans and Europe," in Thomas A. Brady, Heiko A. Oberman, and James D. Tracy, eds., *Handbook of European History, 1400–1600* (Grand Rapids, Mich.: Eerdmans, 1994), 1:595–596.

173. For the threat to Italy, see Osman, "The Ideal," and Jacopo Gherardi, *Diario Romano,* ed. E. Carusi, *RRIISS* 26, part 3, 23. Jacopo also gives a contemporary's estimate of the dates of landing and capture. Estimates of the size of the Turkish force vary from sixteen to eighteen thousand; see Gualdo Rosa, ed., Ilarione, "Copia Idruntine expugnationis," 39 n. 1. Cf. Donato Moro, "La vicenda otrantina del 1480–81 nella società italiana del tempo: Aspetti letterari e civili," in Alessandro Laporta, ed., *Otranto 1480* (Lecce: Capone, 1980), 73–136; and F. Tateo's measured estimate of the event in his introduction to Gualdo Rosa, *Gli umanisti,* 5–16.

174. Pastor IV, 334.

175. Edited in Laporta, *Otranto,* 15–31, from Frati's edition of Vespasiano da Bisticci's *Vite* (Bologna, 1892–1893), 3:306–325. As Laporta points out (11–12), Vespasiano's lament is "uno dei pochi, se non l'unico in prosa nel suo genere." See also Aulo Greco, "Il *Lamento d'Italia per la presa d'Otranto* di Vespasiano da Bisticci," in Fonseca, *Otranto,* 2:343–360.

Third, the capture of Otranto, by a force under Gedik Ahmed Pasha (d. 1482), a Slav who had converted from Christianity, was violent.[176] This point is delicate, for we cannot know for sure, today, just how violent it was. It is worth considering that the city fell after two weeks of siege, that three days of pillage were allowed by religious law, that the Turks had arrived in Puglia on the heels of a defeat by the Venetians at Rhodes, and that any landing on the peninsula would require a forceful presence. Whatever actually happened at Otranto, some of the deaths were immediately adapted to the language of crusading polemic and Christian martyrdom by humanist chroniclers, poets, and letter writers and then were further magnified both out of fear and in service to peninsular politics.[177] Almost everyone was killed, "cese fere cives omnes et indigene," wrote Jacopo Gherardi in his *Diario Romano*. Others were taken into slavery.[178] Virgins and young boys were violated.[179] All the priests were slaughtered, some on the very altars, like oblations, holding the host.[180] The archbishop was murdered, *extinctus est*, wrote the Benedictine humanist Ilarione da Verona (ca. 1440–after September 30, 1485); rumor had it that he was quartered.[181] Others reported that he was struck down by sword as he celebrated Mass; by the time this news reached Rome, Jacopo Gherardi knew that he stood for some time without his head, terrifying his attackers.[182]

176. Theoharis Stavrides gives a brief entry on Gedik Ahmed Pasha in *The Sultan of Vezirs: The Life and Times of the Ottoman Grand Vezir Mahmud Pasha Angelovic (1453–1474)* (Leiden: Brill, 2001), 65–66; see also Ettore Rossi, "Notizie degli storici turchi sull'occupazione di Otranto," *Japigia* 2 (1931): 184–186, 188–190, and accompanying notes; Maria Corti, "La guerra d'Otranto: 'Variazione' in chiave turca," *L'Albero*, n.s., 16, no. 47 (1971): 113–123; and Moro, "La vicenda otrantina del 1480–81," 76–77 n. 7.

177. See Aldo Vallone, "L'eccidio otrantino tra canoni retorici e invenzione narrativa," in Fonseca, *Otranto*, 1:283–319.

178. Cf. Charles Verlinden, "La présence turque à Otrante (1480–81) et l'esclavage," in Fonseca, *Otranto*, 1:148–149, suggesting fifteen hundred slaves taken from a town of not more than six thousand inhabitants. He relies on two ambassadorial reports from Naples. A recent textbook can report erroneously (by all contemporary accounts) that "all the male inhabitants . . . were put to death" (see also n. 183 below).

179. Ilarione da Verona, "Copia," 272.

180. Antonio de Ferrariis, Il Galateo, *De situ Iapygiae* (1511), excerpted in Francesco Tateo, "L'ideologia umanistica e il simbolo 'immane' di Otranto," in Fonseca, *Otranto*, 1:248–251. See also the more extensive description, with names of victims, in Giovanni Michele Marziano's *Successi dell'armata turchesca nella città d'Otranto nell'anno MCCC-CLXXX*, excerpted in Gualdo Rosa, *Gli umanisti*, 201.

181. Lucia Gualdo Rosa, "Una lettera di Ilarione da Verona sulla presa di Otranto," in Fonseca, *Otranto*, 1:272: "genus mortis dubium. Id tamen vulgatissimum est, esse eum exquartatum."

182. Galateo, *De situ Iapygiae*, 258; cf. Gherardi, *Diario Romano*. Pietro Colonna's eyewitness reminiscence in 1524 of the archbishop's exchange with the Muslims who burst into the cathedral during Mass is edited by Antonio Antonaci, *I processi nella causa di beatificazione dei martiri di Otranto (1539–1771)* (Galatina: Editrice Salentina, 1960), 197, from BAV, MS Lat. 5567, fols. 147–148v.

Then, on the morning of August 12, eight hundred citizens who would not convert to Islam were put to death on a hilltop outside the city.[183] All were men over the age of fifteen, recalled an eyewitness, the learned Franciscan Cardinal Pietro Colonna (1460–1540), more than four decades later.[184] His recollection was part of an anti-Muslim commentary on Revelations, written in 1524 at the request of Cardinal Francesco Quiñones and dedicated to Charles V. There, the learned Colonna described a brave group, comforting and strengthening one another, as they "[chose] rather to die any sort of death for Christ, than to deny [their] faith."[185]

The Eight Hundred Martyrs lay unburied for more than a year, as long as the Turkish force held Otranto. Then, in May 1481, Mehmed II died. While Rome celebrated the fortuitous death with special masses and reliquary processions, the Aragonese quickly retook Otranto. The bodies of the Eight Hundred could now be gathered and honored. In his late, apocalyptic recollection, Pietro Colonna described how the victims were found: unwounded and whole, as he himself had seen ("illesa et integra, sicut ipse vidi"). All were face up, looking toward heaven ("inventi sunt omnes coelum versus vultus respicientes habere"). Far from appearing sad or terrified, their faces were happy, as if they were laughing ("nemoque eorum tristiciam aliquam praeseferre videbatur, immo adeo letam hylaremque faciem praetendebant, ut ridere crederentur").[186] Other eyewitnesses, speaking even later, at the 1539 inquiry for canonization, remembered that at night, as the bodies lay unattended, torches had shone mysteriously around them.[187] Alfonso of Calabria translated one hundred fifty (or two

183. But see the lengthy note in Moro, "La vicenda otrantino," 89–91, on several problems that dog our understanding of the martyrdom of the Eight Hundred and the translation of their relics. On the Eight Hundred, see N. Del Re, "Otranto, martiri di," *BS* 9 (1967): 1303–1306; *AASS* Aug. III (Anvers, 1737), 179–198. For an insider's account of their cult, see Gabrielle Monaco, *I Beati martiri di Otranto nel 5 Centenario del loro glorioso trionfo* (Naples, 1980). The date of the martyrdom is disputed.

184. Antonaci, *I processi*, 198. All those who survived the initial sack, says Antonio de Ferrariis (Tateo, "L'ideologia," 248). On Colonna, see C. Colombero, s.v. "Colonna, Pietro," in *DBI* 27 (1982), 402b: Colonna was in his early twenties and already in orders at the time of the massacre. Did he know the six Franciscan conventuals who were among the martyrs (*Commentarium O.F.M. Conv.* 61 [1964]: 172–173). One must ask the awkward question: how did Colonna manage to escape alive? And one might wonder what part trauma and guilt play in his deep but eccentric learning later in life.

185. Pietro Colonna quoted in Antonaci, *I processi*, 198. Antonio de Ferrariis describes a similar scene, if less fully, and mentions the celebration of a feast over "reliquias sive fragmenta" gathered at the site and kept in a chapel at Otranto; see Tateo, "L'ideologia," 250; cf. Moro, "Le vicende," 89–91 n. 31. The martyrs are still honored there today (Monaco, *I Beati martiri*).

186. Colonna, quoted in Antonaci, *I processi*, 198.

187. Antonaci, *I processi*, 161, quotes the 1539 deposition of Francesco della Cerra, who said he was twelve years old when he saw the massacre. The original records of this sixteenth-century inquiry are lost; Antonaci's edition is based on late-eighteenth-century copies.

hundred forty) of the Otranto Martyrs to the Neapolitan church of the Magdalene, which was then renamed in their honor. There, they bore witness to the continuity of Christian martyrdom but especially to Alfonso's victory.

The Eight Hundred Martyrs of Otranto are not among the saints listed in table 2.1, for no *passiones* were written to honor them. They were commemorated in phrases worked into letters, histories, epic poems, and, as in the case of Pietro Colonna, into exegetical treatises; in sum, they were treated in passing. As Francesco Tateo has observed, the problem was precisely the Aragonese connection: the martyrdoms were discussed to the extent that they could be used to magnify the Regno. As a result, those who counted themselves among Alfonso's enemies had difficulty acknowledging the deaths. And even Alfonso's friends slighted them: the most notable Pugliese humanist, Antonio de Ferrariis, il Galateo (1448–1517), barely recalled the Martyrs in the *Paternoster* written for Alfonso's daugher, Isabelle of Aragon, although he did mention the glorious retaking of Otranto.[188] Neither did Galateo write a passion of his relative, the archbishop Stefano Pentinelli, a man whom Sigismondo de'Conti (1432–1512) described as "to be numbered among the holy martyrs and honored on feast days" ("vir profecto sacris martyribus annumerandus, et aniversariis sacris colendus").[189] In his *Copia Idruntine expugnationis,* a letter from Naples describing the taking of Otranto, Ilarione da Verona (Niccolò Fontanelli) passed up the opportunity to echo the early Christian letters on local martyrdoms. In fact, he did not mention the Eight Hundred at all. The events were uncertain, the politics complex, and the Turk as much an object of fascinated admiration as of horror. Sixtus IV's response is telling. The taking of Otranto interrupted the Franciscan pope's carefully nursed project to canonize a fellow Franciscan, Bonaventure (d. 1274).[190] In the brief interim before Bonaventure's process was resumed

188. Tateo, "L'ideologia," 247. See P. Ghinzoni, "Alcune rappresentazioni in Italia nel secolo XV," *ASL* ser. 2, 4, 20 (1893), 966, for a play performed in Naples on February 19, 1482, "probabilmente per celebrare la liberazione."

189. Tateo, "L'ideologia," 238.

190. On Bonaventure's canonization, see Lorenzo Di Fonzo, "Il processo di canonizzazione di s. Bonaventura da Bagnoregio, O.Min. (1474–1482)," and Stanislao Da Campagnola, "Fonti e cronache francescane nei processi di canonizzazione di s. Bonaventura," in A. Pompei, ed., *S. Bonaventura maestro di vita francescana e di sapienza cristiana* (Rome, 1976), 1:227–289 and 291–304. The interruption is reported by Di Fonzo at 256–257 and n. 77. Bonaventure, rewriting the first *vita* of St. Francis, toned down those aspects of Francis's image—such as his radical poverty and fundamentally anti-institutional outlook—that had fostered extremism among the Franciscan Spirituals. One aspect of Francis's life that did not trouble Bonaventure, however, was the founder's fascination with martyrdom; see E. Randolph Daniel, "The Desire for Martyrdom: A Leitmotiv of St. Bonaventure," *Franciscan Studies* 32 (1972): 74–87.

and concluded (1482), Sixtus recognized not the Eight Hundred but the five comrades of St. Francis who were martyred in Morocco in 1216.[191] Long-dead Franciscans could be used to support an anti-Turkish crusade, but Sixtus was no friend of the Aragonese. The Otranto martyrs, politically difficult, were not beatified until 1771.

***

It is now possible to return to the question posed at the beginning of this chapter about the nature of the humanists' presentation of martyrdom. There, observing that the focus on martyrs was not a novelty but an area of continuity with the late Middle Ages, I noted two fundamental aspects of humanist *passiones*. First, they were largely motivated by relics, that is, by the physical presence of the saint in a particular place for particular people. Second, the *passiones* were based not on eyewitness experience of martyrdoms but on the revision or translation of older narratives and thus on the imaginative re-creation of the past. The focus of this chapter has been on the latter, textual aspect.

Behind the relatively simple notion of imaginative re-creation lie the complexities of individual presentations. Authors returned again and again to two issues, imitation (the problem of the martyr as model) and documentation (the problem of the martyr as historical figure). The martyr as imitable model was the subject of disagreement. Valla, for example, approved it; Aurispa did not. In order to dissent, of course, any author had first to agree that the point mattered, to take seriously the possibility of fully imitable martyrdom. There were certainly authors, such as Ludovico Foscarini, who were concerned only to enlist the martyr as intercessor and who therefore did not address imitability. Indeed, intercession remained, thanks to the omnipresence of relics, a sine qua non for the employment of humanist hagiographers.

Authors who disapproved of the martyr as model preferred virtues that were more Aristotelian, more useful to the formation of citizens. This position, cautiously adopted by Aurispa and subversively intimated by Alberti, is the one that we readily accept as "humanist." It appears to be a novelty in comparison with medieval retellings of *passiones*. If more humanists did not write about saints, the controlling place of the martyr in the hagiographic pantheon might help to explain their silence. Again, such an explanation entails that potential authors—even those who disapproved of the model of passive and otherworldly suffering—took the lesson of fully

191. See G. Odoardi, "Berardo, Pietro, Ottone, Accursio, e Adiuto," *BS* 2 (1962), col. 1272.

imitable martyrdom seriously: what one proposed to an audience might be enacted. Just why fully imitable martyrdom might have become, in the Quattrocento, a troublesome topic for men professionally trained to persuade audiences is a tricky question. The answer may be found in the new reality of martyrdom posed by the success of Islam.

And yet even an author who disapproved of the martyrological model might still write *passiones*. For such authors, the dilemma was not *whether* to indicate disapproval but *how*—especially given audience expectations and the traditional nature of the stories. An author could, like Giovanni Aurispa on Mamas or Antonio degli Agli on Cosmas and Damian, use the preface to propose to the patron (in these cases, Janus of Cyprus and Cosimo de'Medici of Florence) something other than violent death. Aurispa substituted daily forbearance; Agli, writing in old age to the elderly Cosimo, urged that both men use *passiones* to begin their own turn away from the world, their move from *vitae commentatio* to *meditatio mortis*.[192] Toning down "red" martyrdom in this way, hedging the violence with a moderating preface or conclusion, had been traditional throughout the Middle Ages from the time of the confessors. In the Quattrocento, one resourceful author, Leon Battista Alberti, expressed his reservations about martyrdom and his preference for the civic Aristotelian virtues in a new way, undercutting and even mocking his subject by conspicuously failing to rise to the expected heights of *laus* in the body of the *passio* itself.

But it was also possible for humanists to approve the martyr as a fully imitable model. Indeed, the second striking contribution of the humanists to the history of the *passio* lay in their reclamation of the heroic self-sacrifice of pre-Constantinian Christians as a fully imitable act of contemporary value. The early Christian centuries, in other words, were perceived to have immediate relevance to the present. Valla is the outstanding example. He proposed the Forty Martyrs to Alfonso's troops *in order* to elicit imitation. Decades later, Valla's student, Giovanni Garzoni, did so in a more literary form, for a more educated audience, explicitly naming the classical models—the Curtii, the Decii, and Lucretia. Valla knew these models well: he discusses them in another, better known work that was also written for Alfonso, the attack on the Donation of Constantine. Evidently, in a passion, these references were unsuitable. For Valla particularly, author not just of the *Declamatio* but also of the attack on monastic virtue in *De professione religiosorum*, the secular status of many pre-Constantinian martyrs may have been part of their attraction. And there

---

192. FBNC, MS Nuovi acq. 399, fols. 280v–281. In fact, assuming that this draft manuscript was written during the pontificate of Nicholas V at the latest, Agli would live for another twenty years and Cosimo for another ten.

is some evidence that a similar secular expansion of the model was more widely attractive. Tommaso d'Arezzo (and, behind him, possibly Alberto da Sarteano) suggested in his treatise and in his own death an analogous secularization of the Franciscan model of martyrdom, proposing the value of voluntary death even to contemporaries who were not in orders. On the symbolic level, Antonio degli Agli explored a similar shift when he revised the martyrology for Eugene IV and especially Nicholas V: by substituting a secular chronology for the liturgical one, he reinstated the historiographical reality of the pre-Constantinian Church, the conceptual world still evident in Eusebius.[193] These three examples—Valla, Tommaso d'Arezzo, and Agli—do not represent secularization as a turning-away from Christianity but as the "broadening of a religious vision" to include parts of society excluded by a strictly monastic or mendicant ethics.[194]

With regard to the second problem, that of documentation—that is, the authenticity of the martyrs themselves—humanists agreed that the difficulties were so great and grave as to be nearly insoluble. The requirements of documentation defeated even Antonio degli Agli and Giannozzo Manetti, who, of all the authors treated here, made the most serious efforts to impose order on the early history of martyrdom. One could prop up a dubious figure, or an authentic figure of whom dubious claims were made, by writing well; hence the concern for style that so often occurs in prefaces to *passiones*.[195] When Leon Battista Alberti described his *vita Potiti* not as *historia* but as *laus,* he intimated that authenticity, conceived both as a matter of documentation and of style, impinged as well on the issue of imitation: inauthentic saints made unconvincing models.[196] This double dilemma of authenticity and conviction made reform of the martyrology urgent. Once, the blood of the martyrs had been the seed of the Church; now, the stories of the martyrs would strengthen the Church in its

193. Black, "The Donation," concludes that Petrarch's synthetic genius included the creation of such a pre-Constantan program. Ronald Witt, *"In the Footsteps of the Ancients": The Origins of Humanism from Lovato to Bruni* (Leiden: Brill, 2000), esp. 229–291, comes from a different angle to a similar conclusion about Petrarch's place in the origins of the Renaissance.

194. Black, "The Donation," 85. I return to the problem of secularization in chap. 7 below.

195. Among several clear complaints about the damage that poor style has wrought on the cult of the saints, see especially Antonio Lolli's preface to his translation of the Greek passion of Eugenia, dedicated to Francesco Piccolomini: "Saepenumero me plures interrogarunt . . . quid in causa sit cur sacre littere et historie martyrum apud doctos et elegantes viros nullius pretii habeantur, et cur potius quam ad sanctorum vitam ad poeticas fabulas mira quadam celeritate cucurrant. Respondi id ex crassa (ut aiunt) minerva et dicendi inconcinnitate [procedi]. Nam ut plurimum sacre littere et historie virgirem crassiori stilo composite nauseam legentibus afferunt, non quod eos materia, sed sermo inornatus offendat" (BAV, MS Chis., F IV 83, fo. 1r–v).

196. See chap. 6 below.

Quattrocento trials. But that could only happen if the stories were reliable. Thus it was a powerful rejection when Francesco Catellini da Castiglione refused to help reform the martyrology by alleging the inauthenticity of the genre itself. He was evidently not convinced that even the new secular chronology employed by Antonio degli Agli and Giannozzo Manetti had managed to secure the historical reality of the early martyrs. Yet Francesco had written with conviction about an authentic contemporary martyr, the Dominican Anthony of Rivalto.

Contemporary martyrdoms were occurring, and humanists were engaged in promoting them. While it may be true that these pre-Reformation martyrdoms occurred mostly on the peripheries, it is also true that, decade by decade, those peripheries were moving toward the center. The success of Islam, and specifically the Turkish advance over the course of the late fourteenth and fifteenth centuries, coupled with contemporaries' perceptions of Turkish designs first on Constantinople and then on Rome, contributed significantly to how the humanists thought about the composition of *passiones*. The martyr's story became real in a new way: hence the fascinating conjunction, in Tommaso d'Arezzo's treatise, of James the Dismembered and Tommaso's own brief life story. Moreover, by creating opportunities for martyrs' deaths, the Turkish advance made the rhetorician's skilled narration of martyrdom dangerously liable to be effective. One could not offhandedly praise voluntary death without the likelihood of inciting imitation among such impressionable students as Tommaso d'Arezzo. Thus, by making the possibility of martyrdom more immediate, the Turkish advance also shaped humanists' reservations about the utility of the martyrological model. That model, after all, argued the absolute value of individual self-sacrifice, and those who were convinced either embraced it, as Tommaso d'Arezzo did in his treatise and his body, or refashioned it, as Lorenzo Valla did by offering the model of a corps of military martyrs. Thus, although Leon Battista Alberti's subversive *vita Potiti* may suit our notions of Quattrocento humanism, I will close this chapter by suggesting that Tommaso d'Arezzo's *Tractatus de martyrio sanctorum* and Lorenzo Valla's translations of the passions of the Forty Martyrs of Sebastea should be factored in as well. For both explored a more intimate kind of knowledge about early Christianity. The martyrs, and above all the possibility of a fully imitable martyrdom, allowed a more than imaginative re-creation of the early fourth century. To revive that world was to revive as well the moral and institutional dilemmas of the first Christian centuries.

We are accustomed to describe Renaissance Europe as a region poised on the brink of takeoff, and it is true that within a century European empires would be established around the world, empires that even in their absence influence politics today. But the story I have told here suggests that such a description is possible only retroactively. Rather than perceiving the imminence of global glory, the Quattrocento perceived the possibility of destruction and subjection.[197] I suspect that this point is relevant to each of the chapters that follow. That things did not turn out as expected is a useful truism to contemplate as well.

---

197. James Hankins, "Renaissance Crusaders: Humanist Crusade Literature in the Age of Mehmed II," *Dumbarton Oaks Papers* 49 (1995): 111–209, is indispensable for grasping the humanists' perceptions. Hankins has identified "more than 400 texts written by more than 50 humanists, and this material is by no means complete" (112 n. 3).

PLATE 3. Bonino Mombrizio, passion of Katherine of Alexandria (*Peri tes Aekaterines*), opening image of the saint and Bianca Maria Visconti-Sforza. Brussels, Royal Library of Belgium, MS 10975, fol. 5.

CHAPTER 3

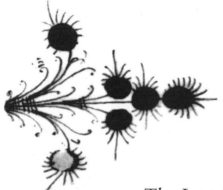

The Last Medieval Legendary

Boninus Mombritius Mediolanensis duo ingentia volumina edidit, quibus Acta Sanctorum complexus est, ut ea in manuscriptis codicibus reperit, ita fideliter, ut ne menda quidem scriptionis correxerit, quae minus iucundam lectionem reddere solent. Dicavit illud opus, quod Sanctuarium inscripsit, honestissimo Equiti Cicho Simonetae Ducum mediolanensium Secretario.

Bonino Mombrizio of Milan put forth two huge volumes in which he gathered the acts of the saints, just as he found them in manuscript codices, and so scrupulously that he did not even correct the scribal errors, which usually make the reading less pleasant. He dedicated this work, which he entitled *Sanctuarium*, to the worthy knight Cicco Simonetta, secretary of the duke of Milan.

—Jean Bolland, *Praefatio generalis in vitas sanctorum* (1643)[1]

Of all the Quattrocento humanists who worked with medieval *vitae et passiones*, the Milanese rhetorician Bonino Mombrizio (1424–ca. 1480) was by far the most successful. The reasons are not hard to understand. Mombrizio's is the largest collection of extensive narratives made by any of the authors discussed in

1. *AASS* Jan II (Brussels, 1883), xxib.

this study, encompassing 326 lives and passions whose subjects range from the apostles of the first century to Catherine of Siena (d. 1380; c.d. 1461).[2] More important, unlike Antonio degli Agli's *De vitis et gestis sanctorum*, which has languished in manuscript despite its place in liturgical history, Mombrizio's collection was printed during his lifetime.[3] The *Sanctuarium* was issued in two folio volumes from "the Printer for Boninus Mombritius" in Milan, probably in 1477.[4] At least eighty copies of the incunable, some intact, some fragmentary, some constructed from dismembered volumes, survive today.[5]

Mombrizio's success—including the survival of so many copies—was sealed in the seventeenth century by the words of the Catholic scholar Jean Bolland (1596–1665), quoted at the head of this chapter. The context of those words was crucial to the reception of the *Sanctuarium*: Bolland enunciated his judgment in the introduction to the first volume of the *Acta sanctorum*, that immense project, continuing today, to evaluate all the historical evidence of sanctity.[6] In the second and third parts of the introduction, Bolland treats the critical principles guiding the *Acta sanctorum*, but, in the first part, the learned Jesuit traces the antecedents of the project. These antecedents, Bolland argued, reached as far back as the second-century popes who had assigned the protonotaries to collect

2. There are 143 entries in volume 1 and 187 in volume 2, for a total of 330 entries. I subtract from this total the entries "Cathedra sancti Petri," "S. Crucis Inventio," "S. Crucis Exaltatio," and the "Dedicatio Basilicae s. Michaelis" (not saints' lives, narrowly speaking). In the first study to urge critical attention to Mombrizio's collection, Serena Spanò Martinelli, "Le raccolte di vite di santi fra XVI e XVII secolo," *RSLR* 27 (1991): 446, gives the number of 334 persons treated (*figure trattate*) by Mombrizio. Here, as throughout this study, I count entries rather than persons; an entry might treat several persons. Moreover, a single figure might receive two entries: see p. 143 below on Inventius. I thank S. Boesch Gajano for notice that Spanò Martinelli is preparing a major study of Mombrizio.

3. Agli's collection is discussed in chap. 2.

4. H*11544; Pellechet Polain 8106; *BMC* 6:736; *IGI* 6690; Rogledi Manni 689; Goff M810. The date of the edition and the conditions of publication are discussed below.

5. The number and nature of the extant copies are the subject of a census still in progress; the size of the print run cannot be estimated from the survival rate. In 1910 the Benedictines of Solesmes reissued the *Sanctuarium* in an important edition that includes prefatory material about Mombrizio and extensive appendixes tracing sources for many of the texts; this edition will be cited here as Mombritius 1910. The Solesmes edition was itself reissued in 1978.

6. On the Bollandists' project, see David Knowles, *Great Historical Enterprises: Problems in Monastic History* (London: Nelson, 1963), 1–32; Baudouin de Gaiffier, "Hagiographie et critique: Quelques aspects de l'oeuvre des Bollandistes au XVIIe siècle," in *Études critiques d'hagiographie et d'iconologie* (Brussels: Bollandist Society, 1967), 209–310; and introductory bibliography in D. Sullivan, "Jean Bolland (1596–1665) and the Early Bollandists," in H. Damico and J. B. Zavadil, eds., *Medieval Scholarship: Biographical Studies on the Formation of a Discipline* (New York: Garland, 1995), 3–14. On the preface discussed here, see the finely articulated study of Sofia Boesch Gajano, "Dai leggendari medioevali agli 'acta sanctorum': Forme di trasmissione e nuovi funzioni dell'agiografia," *Rivista di storia e letteratura religiosa* 21 (1985): 219–244, with remarks on Mombrizio at 220–221 and 227.

acta,[7] and as far forward as the Belgian Jesuit Héribert Rosweyde (1569–1629), who had first drawn up a proposal for a critical *De vitis sanctorum* in sixteen volumes and secured papal approval.[8] To a few intermediary figures Bolland devoted special attention: the fourth-century "princeps in hoc genere," Eusebius of Caesarea; the tenth-century Greek rhetorician known as Simeon Metaphrast, "celeberrimus eo in genere"; the thirteenth-century Dominican theologian Jacobus de Voragine, *eruditus*; and the sixteenth-century editor Laurentius Surius, unequaled in *studium* and *industria*.[9] Among those predecessors was the unexpected figure of a Quattrocento humanist, Bonino Mombrizio.[10]

In Bolland's unambiguous estimate, the value of the *Sanctuarium* lay in its reliable reproduction of medieval manuscripts. Mombrizio did not revise or ornament his sources. (He was a good humanist, we might say, to the extent that he did not, in this instance, behave as a humanist.) Mombrizio did not even intervene to correct obvious errors. This part of Bolland's evaluation is double-edged.[11] On the one hand, Bolland implies that the presence of obvious errors in the imprint proves the reliability of Mombrizio's transcriptions. On the other hand, it is clear from Bolland's appreciation of both Simeon Metaphrast and Jacobus de Voragine that the learned Jesuit was prepared not just to tolerate but even to defend considerable editorial intervention. He approved, for example, of Simeon Metaphrast's addition of speeches (historians were allowed to do that) as well as miracles[12]; he also

---

7. *AASS* Jan. I (Brussels, 1883), xiva–xvb. For the humanists' appreciation of these early protonotaries, similarly based on the *Liber pontificalis*, see chap. 2 above.

8. *AASS,* Jan. I (Brussels, 1883), xxiiia–xxiiia; see especially xxiiia–b for Bolland's quotation of Rosweyde's *modus tractandi*; and Gian Domenico Gordini, "L'opera dei Bollandisti e la loro metodologia," in G. D. Gordini, ed., *Santità e agiografia: Atti del VII Congresso di Terni* (Genoa: Marietti, 1991), 49–74.

9. *AASS,* Jan. I (Brussels, 1883), xvb–xvia (Eusebius); xxiia–xxiiib; xvia–xixa (Simeon). On Ludwig Sauer's collection, see Serena Spanò Martinelli, "Cultura umanistica, polemica antiprotestante, erudizione sacra nel 'De probatis sanctorum historiis' di Lorenzo Surio," in S. Boesch Gajano, ed., *Raccolte di vite di santi dal XIII al XVIII secolo: Strutture, messaggi, fruizioni* (Fasano di Brindisi: Schena, 1990), 131–142.

10. Bolland's remarks on Mombrizio are followed by notice of Jacques Lefèvre d'Étaples's *Martyrum agones*, which Bolland had not seen; Georg Witzel's *Hagiologium*, which Bolland found insufficiently documented; and Aloysius Lippomanus's multivolume collection, which Bolland admired, although not as much as Surius (*AASS,* Jan. I [Brussels, 1883], xxib–xxiia).

11. To the extent that Mombrizio was faithful to his sources, Bolland says, he produced a collection tedious to read. Raw evidence suggesting such tedium can be seen in the copy of the *Sanctuarium* held at the Biblioteca Angelo Mai in Bergamo (Inc. 1.184): in crude drypoint, a sixteenth-century reader has carved the dates of his slow progress through the text into the thick paper of the edition.

12. *AASS,* Jan. I (Brussels, 1883), xviiib, arguing that the Metaphrast omitted things he found untrustworthy but did not add anything; then, at xixa, allowing that he had embellished the *colloquia* of the martyrs with their persecutors "ad legentium utilitatem ac voluptatem." Such additions were allowed to historians: "an est quisquam qui id non permittat historico?"

sanctioned Jacobus's epitomizing (although he withheld his full approval of the *Legenda aurea*).[13] So when Bolland noted that Mombrizio did *not* intervene in his manuscript sources, we can surmise that Mombrizio was at once being praised for accurate transcription and criticized for withholding the benefit of his scholarly intelligence.

Bolland's praise for Mombrizio's accurate transcription carried the day. Its force has been upheld by the fact that most of the narratives in the *Sanctuarium* had their *editio princeps* there; several have not been edited elsewhere to this day. In consequence, Mombrizio's name occurs frequently in both the *Acta sanctorum* and its companion catalog of medieval Latin hagiography, the *Bibliotheca hagiographica latina*. Such repetition, occurring in such authoritative sources, has thoroughly secured Mombrizio's reputation as a forefather of the Bollandists' project.[14]

Scholars have also gone beyond Bolland's brief estimate to describe Mombrizio's achievement as a philological and critical success.[15] It is true that accurate transcription is the first step in a philologically informed critical edi-

13. Bolland's discussion of the *Legenda aurea* is largely defensive. For example, Bolland claims that Jacobus's famous etymologies were added by someone else: "Sed addidit alius (ut puto) quispiam vitis nonnullis ineptam et ridiculam nominum interpretationem, indignam sane Jacobi eruditione" (*AASS*, Jan. I [Brussels, 1883], xxa). And so were other things: "Omitto cetera non minus absurda; quae cum indocti homines pro pulpitis identidem declamarent, nauseam et risum movebant eruditis, seque ipsos et Sanctorum historias in summam adducebant contemptionem." But he also adds: "Ego certe non omnia probo quae ille [Jacobus] scribit; quin tamen vetera secutus sit monumenta, non dubito" (xxb). For an important examination of Bolland's position, see Sherry L. Reames, *The Legenda aurea: A Re-Examination of Its Paradoxical History* (Madison: University of Wisconsin Press, 1985).

14. Thus E. Sannazzaro, "Mombrizio, Bonino," in *Enciclopedia cattolica* 8 (1952), 1233–1234; and J. Cambell, "Mombritius, Boninus," in *LTK* 7 (1962): 532. In Giovanni Treccani degli Alfieri, dir., *Storia di Milano* (Milan: Fondazione Treccani per la storia di Milano, 1953–1966), vol. 7, *L'Età Sforzesca dal 1450 al 1500* (hereafter *L'Età Sforzesca*) part 4, 571 n. 2, the *Sanctuarium* is "una raccolta . . . ove le fonti sono trascritte con cura rigorosa"; Adriano Bernareggi, *Enciclopedia ecclesiastico* (Milan: Vallardi, 1942), 1:64a, more cautiously calls the collection "abbastanza genuina." Maria Teresa Graziosi, editing Paolo Cortesi's *De hominibus doctis dialogus* (Rome: Bonacci, 1973), 128–129, slightly elaborates on Bolland to note that "egli [Mombrizio] infatti raccolse le vite dei santi, ricercando gli Atti dei Martiri con tale scrupolo da riportare gli errori dei copisti." About Mombrizio's *ricerca* we know nothing.

15. The paleographer Mirella Ferrari, "Tra i *latini scriptores* di Pier Candido Decembrio," in R. Avesani and Giuseppe Billanovich, eds., *Vestigia: Studi in onore di Giuseppe Billanovich* (Rome: Edizione di storia e letteratura, 1984), 1:247–296, refers to the *Sanctuarium* as "un monumento filologico per l'agiografia" (259). Remo Guidi, an expert on Renaissance religious literature, adduces Mombrizio's "sincerità" and "scrupolo filologica" in "Questioni di storiografia agiografica nel quattrocento," *Benedictina* 34 (1987): 179–180. The learned medievalist and scholar of Manichaeanism Samuel Lieu describes Mombrizio's *Vita Sylvestri* as an instance of "critical stud[y]" in "From History to Legend and Legend to History: The Medieval and Byzantine Transformation of Constantine's Vita," in S. N. C. Lieu and D. Montserrat, eds., *Constantine: History, Historiography, and Legend* (London: Routledge, 1998), 138.

tion of a text. But did Mombrizio *intend* such a first step? Bolland does not say so. Nothing that Mombrizio himself says in the *Sanctuarium* supports such a deduction. The humanist's own words are limited to three brief poems, two at the opening of the first volume and one in penultimate position in the second volume (they are addressed below). Some of the *vitae* and *passiones* open with prefaces, but these are just the traditional prefaces associated with the narratives, not interventions by the editor.[16] There are no printed glosses and no footnotes. Marginal comment in Mombrizio's hand has not yet been identified.[17] Marginalia left by contemporary readers do not indicate that they perceived a critical rigor in the presentation of the narratives, either by approving the accuracy of the "editions" or by criticizing them.[18] The immediate context of Bolland's remark in the *Acta sanctorum* preface suggests that Cardinal Bellarmine was the source of his judgment and that the cardinal considered the *printed* aspect of Mombrizio's work most significant. Nevertheless, Bellarmine's own writings do not, so far as I have determined, mention Mombrizio.[19]

A manuscript text of the *Sanctuarium* contemporary with the imprint might aid scholars in estimating the meaning of Mombrizio's precise transcriptions. It might, by its layout and markings, demonstrate that Mombrizio was transcribing in order to collate and emend, in other words, that he was indeed working with philological intent. Or it might indicate that he was being so careful with the texts out of reverence for the narratives and their subjects, much as a monastic transcriber in the Middle Ages.[20]

16. François Dolbeau, "Les prologues de légendiers latins," in J. Hamesse, ed., *Les prologues médiévaux: Actes du colloque international organisé par l'Academia Belgica et l'Ecole française de Rome avec le concours de la FIDEM (Rome, 26–28 mars 1998)* (Turnhout: Brepols, 2000), 345–393, develops a typology of legendaries in order to analyze their prologues and discusses Mombrizio's organization, but not his prefatory poems, at 385–386.

17. In the course of preparing this study, I have been able to examine, sometimes only cursorily, about half of the extant copies of the *Sanctuarium*.

18. As Paul Needham points out to me, the correct term for the *Sanctuarium* is "edition." Most readers of this study will not be bibliographers, however, so, to avoid the misapprehension that Mombrizio edited his texts (Bolland describes *transcription*), I will refer to the *Sanctuarium* throughout as an imprint. By noting the absence of marginal response, I will not argue from silence about Mombrizio's intentions. But, in the context of this study, it is of interest that other authors working on *vitae et passiones*—for example, Celso (Maffei) of Verona, whose ownership note can be found in the copy of the *Sanctuarium* held at Verona, Biblioteca capitolare, shelf mark 143—did not respond.

19. I have not found references to Mombrizio's collection in Bellarmine's *Chronologia de scriptoribus ecclesiae* (Lutetiae Parisiorum: S. Cramoisy, 1631) or his *De felicitate sanctorum libri quinque* (Antwerp: Plantin, 1616). For an example of the deployment of Mombrizio as an authority in local arguments about Church history during the Counterreformation, see J. A. Castileonaeus, *Mediolanenses Antiquitates* (Milan, 1625), 81.

20. Early medieval transcription of saints' lives is discussed in Michael Lapidge, "Editing Hagiography," in C. Leonardi, ed., *La critica del testo mediolatino* (Spoleto, 1994), 239–258; on the conditions of textual fluidity, see J. E. G. Zetzel, *Latin Textual Criticism in Antiquity* (New York: Arno, 1983), 249–250.

Or it might lead us to consider that he was copying because he was busy and could not be bothered to revise. Unfortunately, no contemporary manuscript is extant.[21] The eighteenth-century secretary and *érudit* Filippo Argelati (1685–1755) states that he saw such a manuscript, a "codex [that] appears to be [Mombrizio's] autograph, or at least written during the fifteenth century," in the library of the Augustinian Hermits at S. Marco in Milan. Although there is no reason to distrust his witness, this description (discussed below) is too vague to allow a critical assessment of Mombrizio as an editor. We cannot even deduce from it that the manuscript preceded rather than followed the printing of the *Sanctuarium*.[22] And Bolland does not seem to have known Argelati's codex.

Nevertheless, those who maintain that Mombrizio's transcription had a philological aspect do so with good reason, for we have impressive evidence of this humanist's textual practice. Mombrizio identified the value of an "old and hard-to-read" tenth-century manuscript of Avienus and transcribed it with near-photographic accuracy.[23] The ability, first, to recognize a significant manuscript and, second, to take such care in transcribing it, places Mombrizio among the handful of exceptionally aware textual critics in the second half of the fifteenth century. Of such men—among them, Giorgio Merula, Angelo Poliziano, and Ermolao Barbaro the Younger—it could fairly be said that an accurate transcription might constitute a first step toward critical emendation. The case of Mombrizio's

21. Attempts began early to identify a source manuscript. In his preface to Mombritius 1910, A. Brunet noted that Domenico Magri (1604–1672) had recorded in his *Hierolexicon* (Rome, 1677), under the entry *birrus*, that Mombrizio based his legendary (and not just the *vita Cypriani* that was the subject of discussion) on an "antiquo passionario in pergameno manuscripto, in archivio Lateranensi conservato" (x, quoting Magri's 1677 entry, 83b). Magri does not demonstrate but only asserts Mombrizio's use of the eleventh-century manuscript. In the vernacular edition of Magri's dictionary, *Notizie di vocaboli ecclesiastici* (Bologna: Longhi, 1682), 70–71, s.v. *birra*, there is no mention of Mombrizio. Brunet rejects Magri's identification.

22. Argelati, in Mombritius 1910, xxvi. Dolbeau, "Les prologues," 386 n. 154, plausibly elaborates on Argelati's description when he characterizes this manuscript as "une première ébauche," but the manuscript might have been compiled after the imprint in order "correct" it. Like Dolbeau, I wonder what happened to this manuscript and hope that by alerting scholars it might be found. Consequently, I record here the fact that Argelati saw the manuscript in the older Augustinian convent of S. Marco rather than in S. Maria Incoronata, the newer Observant convent that had become, during Mombrizio's lifetime, the object of Sforza patronage.

23. Avienus (not to be confused with the fabulist Avianus) is not a saint but a fourth-century Latin poet who translated the *Phaenomena* of Aratus and the *Descriptio orbis terrarum* of Dionysius Periegetes. Mombrizio's transcription of Avienus (MBA, MS D 52 inf.) was made from Vienna, Österreichische NB, MS Palat. 107. See Jean Soubiran, "Sur les deux manuscrits d'Avienus," *Revue de philologie* 49 (1975): 217–226; Giuseppe Billanovich, "Terenzio, Ildemaro, Petrarca," *IMH* 17 (1974): 58; and Ferrari, "Tra i *latini scriptores*," 260 and nn. 28–29, from which I translate the quoted phrase.

Sanctuarium is different, however, because the accurate transcription was made *in print*.[24] Is it plausible to conclude from Mombrizio's care to produce a diplomatic manuscript copy of the tenth-century Avienus manuscript that he intended the same sort of reproduction in print of his manuscript sources of medieval saints' lives (many of which, as I will discuss, were far from rare or ancient)?[25] A comparison with classical texts may be germane: is there an *incunable* of a classical text that intentionally and faultlessly reproduces a rare manuscript?[26]

The situation was bound to be still less scholarly in the case of hagiography. As this study of humanist *vitae et passiones sanctorum* shows again and again, Quattrocento authors were not often interested in making the sorts of corrections that would require collation and emendation; their revisions were more often, as Bolland implied, rhetorical. When humanists did collect manuscripts as part of the thoroughly traditional process of compiling a saint's dossier and claimed in prefaces to offer factual corrections, audience expectations kept them from taking those corrections too far.[27] Moreover, humanists' "improvements" in rhetoric or fact, whatever their objective value, do not constitute critical emendation. The two-volume, folio-sized, unillustrated, Latin *Sanctuarium*, which sold for roughly the price of bread for one person for a year, was obviously not a

24. Cf. Anna Modigliani, *Tipografi a Roma prima della stampa: Due società per fare libri con le forme (1466–1470)* (Rome, 1989), 122–123, on Vito Puecher as an exceptionally careful Quattrocento editor of legal texts, seeking to supply correct editions (not transcriptions of faulty manuscripts) to his readers.

25. There is not space here to assess the evidence of corrections made to the text during printing. But note one example: the title for the entry on Nicholas Tolentinas (*BHL* 6230) appears in at least two distinct forms. Nicholas, canonized in 1446, was the titular of Bianca Maria Sforza's church at Santa Maria Incoronata; see Maria Luisa Gatti Perer, *Umanesimo a Milano: L'Osservanza agostiniana all'Incoronata* (Milan: Arte Lombarda, 1980), 93–94.

26. For the humanists' textual practice with regard to the classics, see Silvia Rizzo, *Il lessico filologico degli umanisti* (Rome: Edizioni di storia e letteratura, 1973/1985); and Vincenzo Fera, "Problemi e percorsi della ricezione umanistica," in G. Cavallo, P. Fedeli, and A. Gardini, eds., *Lo spazio letterario di Roma antica* (Rome, 1990), 3:513–543. In contrast, E. J. Kenney, *The Classical Text: Aspects of Editing in the Age of the Printed Book* (Berkeley: University of California Press, 1974), 1–20, and Anthony Grafton, *Joseph Scaliger: A Study in the History of Classical Scholarship* (New York: Oxford University Press, 1983), chap. 1, emphasize its weaknesses: Kenney follows Willamowitz; Grafton singles out Poliziano as an exceptional case.

27. On the compilation of dossiers as standard medieval practice, see François Dolbeau, "Les hagiographes au travail: Collecte et traitement des documents écrits (IX–XIIe siècles)," in M. Heinzelmann, ed., *Manuscrits hagiographiques et travail des hagiographes* (Sigmaringen: Thorbecke, 1992), 49–76. Well known today is Erasmus's more successful (in our terms) approach to factual correction in myth and saints' lives; see P. G. Bietenholz, *Historia and Fabula: Myths and Legends in Historical Thought from Antiquity to the Modern Age* (Leiden: Brill, 1994), esp. 153–157.

popular devotional work.[28] But we should not therefore assume that it represents the application to *vitae sanctorum* of standards of classical scholarship that the humanists still rarely achieved in the 1470s.

The *Sanctuarium* is a mystery, both in its origins and in its renewed success during the seventeenth century. This chapter undertakes to establish the grounds for a reevaluation of the incunable. It surveys what is known about the editor and the nature of publishing in Milan around 1477, examining the *Sanctuarium* qua intentionally produced object, offering a preliminary analysis of dedication, structure, and contents. In what is bound to be a more controversial move, it replaces the legendary in its narrowly political context. The point of the reevaluation is neither to detract from Bolland's achievement in the *Acta sanctorum* nor to question the significance of the *Sanctuarium* for the critical study of saints' lives. Whatever Mombrizio intended, the *Sanctuarium* as it was printed and Bolland's judgment together had the effect of creating the collection as a critical monument for Counterreformation scholars. In other words, what is at stake in this chapter is not the integrity of post-Tridentine hagiology but our grasp of fifteenth-century humanists' approaches to medieval texts about saints. On that point, one thing is clear: the *Sanctuarium* is, by virtue of being at once large and printed, an impressive example of humanist engagement with the cult of the saints. This chapter attempts a more precise evaluation. Setting out what is known about the author and reexamining the *Sanctuarium*'s structure, content, and context may improve our understanding of the balance of tradition and innovation in Mombrizio's engagement with the saints and clarify the place of humanist philology in the transmission of saints' lives.[29]

❋ ❋ ❋

28. Tino Foffano, "Per la data dell'edizione del *Sanctuarium* di Bonino Mombrizo," *IMH* 22 (1979): 509–511, records the price of "libris XVIII, solidis X" for a bound copy of the *Sanctuarium*. Gregory Lubkin, *A Renaissance Court: Milan Under Galeazzo Maria Sforza* (Berkeley: University of California Press, 1994), xix, records that in 1463 eight soldi—there were twenty in a pound—would buy bread for one person for two weeks, so in 1478 the cost of two bound volumes of the *Sanctuarium* on paper (I know of no parchment copies) might be estimated at a year's supply of bread for one person. Cf. Arnaldo Ganda, "La prima edizione del messale ambrosiano (1475): Motivi pastorali e aspetti commerciali," *La Bibliofilia* 83 (1981) 101 n. 15, for the 1474 price of a manuscript copy of the Ambrosian Missal on parchment, twenty-five ducats. For the sharply contrasting format and contents of less expensive vernacular devotional works at this time, Schutte, *PIVRB*, is fundamental.

29. Arnaldo Ganda has begun this reevaluation by filling out the biography of Mombrizio himself. Contrast *L'Età Sforzesca* 571—"il gentile e pio Bonino Mombrizio, l'infaticabile editore, l'accurato e candido raccoglitore di vite e leggende di santi, il mite poeta cristiano"— with the picture of Mombrizio that emerges in Arnaldo Ganda, "Il tipografo del Servius H14708 ha un nome," *La Bibliofilia* 87 (1985): 227–265.

Dominus Boninus de Montebreto filius quondam domini Bertole porte Ticinensis parochie sancti Maurilii Mediolani . . .

Lord Bonino de Mombrizio, son of the late Lord Bertola of the Ticino Gate, in the parish of Saint Maurilio in Milan . . .

—Opening of notary Tommaso Giussani's printing contract between Mombrizio and Vespolate, July 12, 1475[30]

Bonino Mombrizio was born to a father named Bertola, probably in 1424.[31] His name appears to be his own vernacular devising, based on his latinization of the family name Montebretti or Mombretto.[32] Several Montebretti were notaries in Milan and Pavia, so Bonino may have been born in either city and destined early for law.[33] To judge from the recurrence of the Montebretti name in records of property transactions, some branches of the family were well-off, even recently ennobled, as Bonino and his father, Bertola, apparently were.[34] Bonino himself dealt in a few

30. Ganda, "Il tipografo," 250: a contract to produce the elementary school text, Priscian's *De octo partibus orationis.*

31. For his father's name, see n. 30 above. The birthdate occurs in Donato Bossi's *Chronica mediolanensis,* at sign. q5v: "Hoc item anno Boninus Mombretus eximius poeta Mediolani nascitur." Bossi's chronicle was published in Milan by Zarotto in 1492 (H* 3667; Polain 844; *GW* 4952; *BMC* 6:722; *IGI* 2017; Goff B1040; Ganda, *I primordi,* #175). His dating is confirmed (or borrowed?) by a genealogy known to Filippo Argelati; see the passage reproduced in Mombritius 1910, xxv–xxix, that traces the family from 1365 to 1484.

32. Archival documents bear up Joannes Fabricius, *Bibliotheca Latina mediae et infimae aetatis,* vol. 5 (Florence: Baracchi, 1858), reprinted in Mombritius 1910, xviii.

33. E.g., ASM, notarial *busta* 386, for Lanzellotto q. Antonino Montebretto; 1378 for Ottorino q. Ippolito Montebretto; and 3523 for Ippolito q. Ottorino Montebretto. According to the *Statistica degli atti custoditi nella sezione notarile* (Venice: Naratovich, 1886), 365, Lancilloto was active around 1435 as an imperial notary in Milan. The imperial connections may be important, if they indicate that family connections were known to be Ghibelline (see below). See R. Maiocchi and N. Casacca, *Codex diplomaticus Ord. E. S. Augustini Papiae* 1 (1905), ix, for a Monfredo Mombreto, O.E.S.A., teaching in the theology faculty at Pavia in 1437 and named deacon in 1454; Maiocchi and Casacca, *Codex* 2 (1906), *ad indicem,* for the same Manfredino Mombreto, prior at the O.E.S.A. convent of S. Pietro in Ciel d'Oro at Pavia; Galvagno Mombreto, his brother, son of a Iohannolus "civis et notarius papiensis"; and a notary, Pietro Mombreto. Michele Ansani, "La provvista dei benefici (1450–1466): Strumenti e limiti dell'intervento ducale," in Giorgio Chittolini, ed., *Gli Sforza, la chiesa lombarda, la corte di Roma: Strutture e pratiche beneficiarie nel ducato di Milano (1450–1535)* (Naples: Liguori, 1989), 38, 64, and 97 (chart), records an *economo* of Piacenza before June 14, 1453, named Giampiero da Montebreto.

34. C. Godi, "Notai e famiglie milanesi nel MS Braidense AG.X.26 di Giovanni Sitoni di Scozia," *Aevum* 63, no. 3 (1989): 531–545, a survey of the families listed in Sitoni's study of Milanese nobility, does not include any Montebretti. Cf. F. Calvi, *Il patriziato milanese secondo nuovi documenti deposti negli archivi pubblici e privati,* 2d ed. rev. (Milan: Mosconi, n.d.), at 371–386, a list of "cives Mediolani qui sunt, et etiam intelliguntur Consilium 900 Comunis Mediolani" made July 22, 1388. In this list, the family name

properties.[35] He also made his living as a rhetorician and author, producing literature and providing books for the Milanese court. It is, for example, from a dunning letter of 1472, written to remind Duke Galeazzo Maria Sforza of an overdue payment for books, that we learn of Mombrizio's four daughters and can conclude that he was or had been married.[36] He made his home in a southern neighborhood of Milan, the Ticino Gate, in the parish of S. Maurilius.[37] If the genealogy mentioned by Filippo Argelati is correct, then Mombrizio had no sons or at least none who outlived him, and the patriarchal line of his branch ended with his death.[38]

As a young man, Mombrizio studied with Guarino Guarini at Ferrara.[39] Pier Candido Decembrio, in an affectionate letter of March 2, 1468 (when Mombrizio was spending time in an unidentified rural setting), applauds this early education in the *studia humanitatis,* observing that it had superbly formed his friend's character.[40] Decembrio's recourse to Mombrizio's

---

Montebretto appears under the parishes of S. Pietro in Curte and S. Alessandro in Palazzo. Caterina Santoro, *Gli offici del comune di Milano e del dominio visconteo-sforzesco (1216–1515)* (Milan: Giuffrè, 1948), 124, lists a "Nob. Petrus de Montebreto, civis Mediolani" appointed to the "Officium bulli et potestaria fornacum" on January 1, 1465, by letter of October 8, 1464 (Reg. duc. 167, fo. 11v). Thus the family's definitive move upward dates from Visconti rule.

35. Ganda, "Il tipografo," 230 n. 21, recording rental property in Rosate and land purchases in 1473.

36. Evidence of daughters in ASM, Autografi, 144, *filza* 28, item 1, a letter dated September 13, 1472, from Mombrizio to the *illustrissime princeps* Galeazzo Maria Sforza asking for help—"o in denari, o drapi o zioe saltem sin a la summa de ducati 38"—with the expense of marrying one of his daughters. Bonino justifies the amount by reminding the prince that "quali sono le spese de questi mei ultimi libri donati a vestra excellentia di sua voglia, computata quella accomodatissima opereta io scrisse per il natale dil Illustrissimo conte vestro primogenito" (GianGaleazzo Maria had been born June 20, 1469). Mombrizio's daughter Lucretia was apparently married in early 1475 (ASM Notarile, T. Giussani, rubrica 2489, entries for January 25 [1475]). Another, Appolonia, may be mentioned just below in the entry for [October 6] 1475. The appendix "Atti della visita pastorale di Amicus de Fossulanis alla città e diocesi nel 1460" in Xenio Toscani, *Aspetti di vita religiosa a Pavia nel secolo XV* (Milan: Giuffrè, 1969), 125, transcribing the record of a visitation to the Augustinian Hermits' convent of St. Martin in Pavia, records a professed nun, Margarita de Mombreto. Altogether the family seems to have been closely tied to Pavia and loyal to the Augustinian Hermits.

37. Given in the epigraph to this section. Giuseppe Sassi reports that in 1470 the humanist swore an oath of fidelity to Galeazzo Maria "cum aliis incolis nobilibus Portae Ticinensis"; see the passage edited in Mombritius 1910, xxvi and xx.

38. Mombritius 1910, xxvi.

39. Antonia Tissoni Benvenuti, "Schede per una storia delle poesia pastorale nel secolo XV: La scuola Guariniana a Ferrara," in F. Alessio and A. Stella, eds., *In ricordo di Cesare Angelini: Studi di letteratura e filologia* (Milan: Il Saggiatore, 1979), 126 n. 1.

40. "Sic enim eruditus es, sic a puero institutus, ut nihil nisi pium, nisi sanctum, nisi memoria et laude dignum possis cogitare" (MBA, MS I 235 inf., fol. 126v). The letter, known to Sassi and Argelati (e.g., Mombritius 1910, xvii), is numbered A253 by V. Zaccaria, "L'Epistolario di Pier Candido Decembrio" *Rinascimento* 3 (1952): 85–118 at 113. I have not seen the poems from Mombrizio to Decembrio, noted by Argelati in Mombritius 1910, xxviii. On Mombrizio as a poet, see previous note.

expertise proves that flattery was not the only point of the communication. In the same letter, Decembrio announces that he will shortly be sending Mombrizio a new composition.[41] From another, undated letter, we learn that an unnamed work submitted to Mombrizio was returned with exhaustive corrections: you allow nothing to pass without emendation ("nihil inemendatum transire sinas"), Decembrio observes testily.[42] But the best measure of Mombrizio's intellectual accomplishment is his devotion to Virgilian verse and expertise in Greek, both evident in several of the compositions, translations, and editions that are discussed below.

According to Ferrante Borsetti (1682–1764), Mombrizio attended the university in Ferrara, receiving degrees *in utroque*.[43] An ownership note in the humanist's transcription of Avienus's *Descriptio orbis terrae* confirms this professional identity.[44] Giuseppe Sassi (1675–1751) records that a contemporary funeral oration for the legal expert Petrus Crassus (Pietro Grassi) includes Mombrizio among Petrus's "aequales et condiscipulos" — Francesco Filelfo, Cola da Montano, Gabriele Pavero Fontana, and Francesco Puteolano—as a *dissertissimus professor*.[45] As a lawyer, a man

41. V. Zaccaria, "Sulle opere di Pier Candido Decembrio," *Rinascimento* 7 (1956): 57, on a life of Ambrose (see also n. 198 below).

42. MBA, MS I 235 inf., fol. 60 (Zaccaria, "L'Epistolario," 110 = A115 in Zaccaria's enumeration). Decembrio objects that the witness of the ancients on several points of orthography is not so univocal as Mombrizio thinks (thus we have evidence of Mombrizio's great care for correct orthography, which might help to evaluate his work on the *Sanctuarium*, a point to be touched on briefly below). From a third letter (ibid., fols. 63r–v), dated September 29, 14⟨6⟩0 (Zaccaria, "L'Epistolario," 110 = A122), we learn that the two men also argued about the degree of orderliness that exists in human affairs. Mombrizio seems to have held, with reference to the opinions of certain *docti viri*, that the world is without a stable order. Decembrio opposed this viewpoint passionately, from an explicitly Christian position. Any reductive understanding of Mombrizio's spirituality must be called into question by this exchange.

43. Ferrante Borsetti, *Historia almo Ferrariae Gymnasii* . . . (Ferrara: Pomatelli, 1735), 2:298, without documentation. Mombrizio is not mentioned in Maria Gigliola di Renzo Villata's survey "Scienze giuridici e legislazione nell'età sforzesco," in *Gli Sforza a Milano e in Lombardia e i loro rapporti con gli stati italiani ed europei (1450–1535): Convegno internazionale Milano, 18–21 maggio 1981* (Milan: Cisalpino-Goliardica, 1982), 65–146. According to Borsetti's *Historia*, Bonino returned to Milan in 1460; cf. n. 48 below. That he was a medical doctor has been deduced from a puffery poem at the head of a *Testamento preservativo e curativo per defensione . . . dal morbo pestilentiale*, printed in Milan by Antonio Zarotto before August 29, 1477 (R 1407; *IGI* 9487; Ganda, *I primordi*, #62); see also Mombrizio's *Trenodia*, published in Milan in 1504 by Alessandro Minuziano, sign. e4r, l. 2, "Sim mihi laudatae medicus non utilis artis," and the interjection into the prayer of Katherine of Alexandria quoted below, n. 264.

44. See n. 23 above; Giuseppe Billanovich, "Terentius," 58, on MBA, MS D 52 inf.; see also Ferrari, "Tra i *latini scriptores*," 260 and nn. 28–29.

45. Sassi, in Mombritius 1910, xvi; cf. M.G. Di Renzo Villata, "Grassi, Pietro" in *DBI* 58 (2002): 685a, 685b. I have not seen this oration by Ludovico Sangallo, which is not known to George McClure (personal communication); not listed in John McManamon, *Funeral Oratory and the Cultural Ideals of Humanism* (Chapel Hill: University of North Carolina Press, 1989); and not indicated in Di Renzo Villata's bibliography.

expert in Latin and Greek, and classed in such company, Mombrizio may have participated in the branch of the university at Pavia that was located at the Milanese court. No record of him as an independent teacher of grammar or rhetoric has turned up. Evidence does exist that he worked as an *arbitrator* for notarial prorogations,[46] turned out courtly compositions in manuscript,[47] took positions with the flourishing Milanese bureaucracy,[48] and—as the *Sanctuarium* shows—participated in the new technology of print. In fact, he seems to have planned with characteristic prudence for this last undertaking by contracting on January 8, 1471, just as printing was introduced to Milan, to learn goldsmithing from Giovanni Crivelli.[49] Thus at the end of his life he paired an appointment as professor of rhetoric at the Milanese university (in 1481, if the notice is reliable) with a position as a functionary in the "Treasury for Extraordinary Accounts."[50] More will be said below about Mombrizio's participation in the morally dubious activities of the *Entrate Straordinarie* under Galeazzo Maria Sforza; its functionaries had extensive administrative and jurisdictional powers.[51] For the

46. Mombrizio is named as *arbitrator* in several *prorogationes compromissorum* (amendments to or cancellations of previously drawn-up contracts) in ASM Notarile, rubr. 2489, Tommaso Giussani, e.g., for September 30, October 15, and October 30, 1476. See also Ganda, "Il tipografo," 230 n. 21.

47. His compositions are surveyed below. Mombrizio's name does not appear among courtiers recorded by Lubkin, *A Renaissance Court*.

48. His name occurs among those in the office of *Contrascriptor ad trafigum salis* with appointments on January 1, 1458, and December 9, 1462, each time for a one-year term, the first letter of appointment specifying a salary of five florins a month; see Caterina Santoro, *Gli uffici del dominio Sforzesco* (Milan, 1948), 130 and 131, citing ASM, Reg. duc. 153, fols. 125 and 106, fol. 38. Mombrizio is the only one of these officials whose salary is specified. This 1458 appointment contradicts Borsetti's claim, repeated by Foffano, "Per la data," 509, that Mombrizio only returned to Milan from Ferrara in 1460. Then around 1470 he served as *Cancellarius intratarum extraordinarium* with a monthly salary of eight florins; see Santoro, *Gli uffici*, 81, citing Reg. Beltrami, fol. 36, and further below.

49. Ganda, "Il tipografo," 230 n. 21. Giovanni Crivelli had his degree from the University of Parma in 1470; according to Emilio Motta, "Un tipografo a Milano nel 1469," *ASL,* ser. 3, 22, no. 5 (1895): 150–155, he may have been the brother of Galeazzo Crivelli, a Piedmontese physician whose name occurs in one of the earliest printing contracts drawn up in Milan, dated March 14, 1469. The timing of Mombrizio's metalworking lessons suggests that he was privy to the council discussions about the introduction of print into Milan (n. 52 below) and therefore close to the upper circle of power in Milan. Cf. early printing associations in Rome that included *orefici* anxious to protect technical secrets (Modigliani, *Tipografi,* 66–77).

50. On the bureaucratic structure of treasury and mint, see Caterina Santoro, *Gli Sforza* (Milan, 1968), 219–221, 224, and bibliography in the following notes.

51. Franca Leverotti, "'Governare a modo e stillo de' Signori . . .': Osservazioni in margine all'amministrazione della giustizia al tempo di Galeazzo Maria Sforza duca di Milano (1466–1476)," *Archivio Storico Italiano* 157 (1999): 43–74, is a fundamental analysis of Galeazzo Maria's co-optation of the *Entrate Straordinarie* to collect money from condemnations and overdue payments. See ibid., 55 n. 147, for her notice that Mombrizio served as the first chancellor to Michele da Cremona already in 1469 but apparently left that appointment because he fell ill. Leverotti does not note Mombrizio's reappointment (or continued participation?) in

moment, it is sufficient to note that, although this dual professional track may be unique, those familiar with early printing will find it eloquent: in addition to his literary accomplishments, Mombrizio had technical knowledge about metals, as well as access to cash and connections. All were valuable to the first generation of scholars involved with printing.[52]

A large part of what we know about Mombrizio comes from his presence in Milanese incunables. He worked as editor, *revisor*, or *corrector* with most of the printers operating in Milan during the 1470s, including Christoph Valdarfer, Filippo Lavagna, Domenico Vespolate, Antonio Zarotto, Johannes Bonus, and perhaps Pachel and Scinzenzeller. Despite his law degrees, Mombrizio seems not to have pursued the lucrative publishing of law books, probably because the noble Pietro Antonio Castiglione had already cornered this sector of the Milanese market.[53] Mombrizio was engaged in a minor way with the publication of elementary schoolbooks.[54] His work with the printers is taken up below in connection with the evidence of his dedications.

The date of Mombrizio's death has been variously set at 1482, 1484, 1496,

---

the office: in ASM, Autografi, gener. 144, *filza* 28, item 3, a letter dated December 12, 1478, Giovanni Pietro Panigarola describes Bonino as "cancellero ad la camera ex[tra]or[dinar]ia et sopra le monete." Preceding Mombrizio, the holder of the position in 1463 was Prospero Lampugnani, a family name that will recur below.

52. Arguments about control of the technology—the political and economic implications of which escaped no one—began in council meetings from at least March 1469. The tenor of discussions in council reflected Milan's rivalrous enmity toward Venice, which was the most important center of fifteenth-century printing; see Paul Needham, "Venetian Printers and Publishers in the Fifteenth Century," *La Bibliofilia* 100 (1998): 157–200. The two cities were engaged at the time in economic warfare by means of counterfeiting: see Reinhold C. Mueller, "Guerra monetaria tra Venezia e Milano nel Quattrocento," in G. Gorini, ed., *La Zecca di Milano: Atti del convegno internazionale di studio. Milano 9–14 maggio 1983* (Milan: Società numismatica italiana, 1984), 341–355; Franca Leverotti, "Scritture finanziarie dell'età sforzesca," *Squarci d'archivio sforzesco* (Como, 1981), 121–137; Ernesto Bernareggi, "Notizie sulla produzione della zecca di Milano nel periodo sforzesco in documenti di archivio," *Annali dell'istituto italiano di numismatica* 18–19 (1971–1972): 265–279; and idem, "La politica monetaria e l'attività della zecca a Milano nel periodo sforzesco," *Annali dell'istituto italiano di numismatica* 16–17 (1969–1970): 171–197. On the Venetian public's suspicions of associations between minters and printers, see Martin Lowry, *Nicholas Jenson and the Rise of Venetian Publishing in Renaissance Europe* (Oxford: Blackwell, 1991), 107–111. The earliest history of printing in Galeazzo Maria's Milan is shadowy and much discussed; for bibliographical guidance, see Rogledi Manni, *La tipografia*, and above all the many studies by Ganda. Recent studies suggest that the first book was printed in Milan in 1468 by Filippo da Lavagna; see Ugo Rozzo, "Il libro a stampa nelle biblioteche friulane," in G. Lombardi and D. Nebbiai Dalla Guarda, eds., *Libri lettori e biblioteche dell'Italia medievale (secoli IX–XV): Fonti, testi, utilizzazione del libro. Atti della tavola rotonda italo-francese (Roma 7–8 marzo 1997)* (Rome, 2000), 192 n. 4.

53. Arnaldo Ganda, "Marco Roma, sconosciuto editore dei prototipografi milanesi (1473–1477) e un nuovo incunabulo: Il catalogo di vendita dei suoi libri," *La Bibliofilia* 82 (1980): 104–106 and n. 33.

54. Ganda, "Marco Roma"; and idem, "Il tipografo." On Tommaso Grassi's charity school and its connections to textbook printing, see n. 129 below.

and 1500.[55] The Bossi chronicle, which records a birth date, does not have an entry for Mombrizio's death.[56] Certainly, the date must be after December 24, 1478, when Mombrizio made his testament with the notary Tommaso Giussani.[57] Sassi argued that, since Mombrizio followed Francesco Filelfo (d. July 31, 1481) into the chair of rhetoric at the Milanese *studium* in 1481, and Giorgio Merula (1424–1494) was given that chair in 1482, it must be that Mombrizio died in the intervening period.[58] But as I have noted, Sassi assumed Mombrizio's appointment on the basis of the phrases in a funeral oration. Telling against the appointment is the fact that the humanist's name is not recorded among the professors in the lists of Milanese appointments kept at Pavia.[59] And it is odd that the death of even a small-time professor holding an appointment between the greater lights of Filelfo and Merula is not recorded in a contemporary document. So a conservative death date respecting the *terminus post quem* provided by the testament may be preferable.

❈ ❈ ❈

Qui cupit annosi prius abdita tempora mundi
Noscere, transcriptos hos emat aere libros.
Non calamo speret volucri non condere penna.
Plurima, qui temptet, menda patere solet,
Seu sibi praescriptam servet non linea sedem
Sive sua reges a statione cadent

Whoever wants to know the once-obscure ages
of the world, so full of years,
Let him buy these books transcribed in metal.
Let him not hope to preserve [past ages] with a reed or a quill.
He who tries often suffers many errors,
either the line does not use the place drawn in for it,
or the kings fall from their order.

—Bonino Mombrizio in *Chronica Eusebii*[60]

55. The 1484 date seems to rely on the dedication of "Suetonius," *De viris illustribus* (see below), and perhaps on a genealogy known to Argelati (that may itself rely on the *De viris illustribus* dedication). The date of 1496 is simply wrong; see Sassi in Mombritius 1910, xx. Cosenza, s.v., dates the death to 1500, without reference, as do Sannazzaro, "Mombrizio, Bonino," and Cambell, "Mombritius, Boninus."

56. See n. 31 above: cf. Bossi's entries for Decembrio and Filelfo, which give death dates but not birth dates (sign. fol, 6v; sign. t1r).

57. ASM, Notarile, Tommaso Giussani, rubr. 2489, final entry for that year. A letter from Giovanni Pietro Panigarola to Cicco Simonetta, referring to Bonino's illness "in tanto che de sua vita si dubita assai" is dated two days before (ASM, Autografi, gener. 144, *filza* 28, item 3).

58. Sassi in Mombritius 1910, xvi and xx. Tiraboschi follows Sassi and Argelati in accepting 1482.

59. Paul Grendler, personal communication.

60. First lines of Bonino Mombrizio's second poem to the reader, introducing his edition of the *Chronica Eusebii, Hieronymii, Prosperi et Matthei Palmieri*, published in Milan with Filippo da Lavagna (H 6716; GW 9432; BMC 6:703; IGI 3752; Goff E116; Rogledi Manni

In the premodern period, contemporary titles are clues to function, and this is especially the case with Latin religious works.[61] Not surprisingly, Mombrizio's incunable has no title page.[62] It also lacks the heading where, in imitation of manuscript practice, authors of early printed works customarily named their compositions, themselves, and their dedicatees. The initial dedicatory poem does have such a heading, but it names only Mombrizio and his dedicatee, not the work itself. Nor does the word *sanctuarium* occur in the body of the dedicatory poems, for it would offend the metric scheme. Instead, in those poems, Mombrizio describes the work in traditional terms as "sanctorum vitas maxima gesta virum" and "sanctorum historias"—lives, deeds, and histories of saints.

The now-familiar title *Sanctuarium* derives from the heading of the *tabula*, or index, that is placed at the front of each volume: "Tabula in sequens Sanctuarium." If this heading is owed to Mombrizio, then he might have chosen it from Papias's *Vocabularium*, an eleventh-century dictionary he had edited in early December 1476. Papias defines a *sanctuarium* as "a place or little room in which holy things are done."[63] Another meaning, "relic," derived from the Latin of Gregory the Great, is also attested for the late Middle Ages.[64] But the most likely derivation of the name *sanctuarium* is on the model of *legendarium* (legendary) and *passionarium* (passionary). Similar to both of these, a *sanctuarium* offered a handy, compendious, and authoritative collection of saints' lives and passions for liturgical or paraliturgical use.

Contemporary usage supports this generic meaning. In the Jenson *Breviarium romanum* published in 1478, the editor, Georgius Spatharius,

415, dating to 1474–1476). The verse, which is also given in Mombritius 1910, xxiii, indicates that Mombrizio appreciated printing for the opportunity it gave to avoid the usual sorts of scribal errors in transcription—not to repeat them. The word *linea* might refer to a horizontal line or vertical column. Since the *Chronicon* is largely set out in columns, the latter meaning may be preferable here. See also R. W. Burgess, "Jerome Explained: An Introduction to His *Chronicle* and a Guide to Its Use," *Ancient History Bulletin* 16 (2002): 1–32, mentioning Mombrizio's *editio princeps* at 9 but not using that edition because it is too faulty.

61. See *SMHM* 61–62, a list of the types (names) of thirteenth-century liturgical books; the word *sanctuarium* does not occur there, which suggests the devolved late medieval quality of Mombrizio's title. For Jean Gielemans's choice of the equally new *Sanctilogium* in 1487, see the remarks of Dolbeau, "Les prologues," 383.

62. On the late-fifteenth-century emergence of the title page, see M. M. Smith, *The Title Page: Its Early Development, 1460–1510* (London: British Library; New Castle, Del.: Oak Knoll, 2000).

63. "Sanctuarium: locus vel cubiculum ubi sanctae res geruntur," in *Papiae Glossarium* or *Vocabularium*, printed December 12, 1476, in Milan by Domenico Vespolate (H 12378; *BMC* 6:732; *IGI* 7204; Rogledi Manni 748).

64. Cited incidentally from Jean Gobi in Carlo Delcorno, "Nuovi studi sull'*exemplum*: Rassegna," *Lettere italiane* 46, no. 3 (1994): 469 n. 32; cf. John M. McCulloh, "The Cult of Relics in the Letters and *Dialogues* of Gregory the Great: A Lexicographical Study," *Traditio* 32 (1976): 158–165.

titled the *sanctorale*, or section of the breviary devoted to readings for saints' days, "Sanctuarium where the deeds of the saints [are narrated]."[65] Spatharius repeated this defining phrase in a note above the colophon, defending his adjustments to the *lectiones* (readings) by explaining that he had used an authoritative source: "We carefully reviewed the *sanctuarium* where the deeds of the saints are narrated and did so all the more carefully because we had the exemplars of the holy man Lorenzo Giustinian, of happy memory," that is, manuscript breviaries owned or compiled by the Blessed Lorenzo Giustiniani (1380–1456), patriarch of Venice.[66] A contract drawn up in Perugia in 1478, in which a patron hired a scribe to "write a *santuaro* from the breviary, or rather, to be clearer, the whole section of the saints' feasts,"[67] also indicates a liturgical book and further suggests that the word was a neologism. Its meaning continued to evolve, as in the 1502 *Sanctuarium, sive sermones de sanctis per totum annum*, an anonymous collection of sermons published in Brescia by J. Britannicus,[68] and the 1505 *Papie Sanctuarium* (*Pavia Sanctuarium*) by the Milanese *doctor de utroque* Jacopo Gualla, a historical defense of Pavia's relics, published there by Jacopo de Burgofranco.[69] So it seems fair to conclude that, in the last quarter of the fifteenth century, a work entitled *Sanctuarium* was a set of readings for preaching and liturgical use, an expansion of the *sanctorale*, and that its narratives were understood to authenticate local religious practices and relics.[70] One might reasonably expect a sim-

65. I consulted the parchment copy of the *Breviarium romanum* printed in Venice in 1478 by Nicholas Jenson that is held by the Morgan Library, inc. 16292 (H 3896, Pellechet Polain 2922, *BMC* 5:179; *GW* 5101; Goff B1112). At sign. 2a1, Spatharius has entitled the section of readings on the saints "Sanctuarium ubi gesta sanctorum secundum ritum romane curie per anni circulum." My attention was drawn to this instance by Lowry, *Nicholas Jenson*.

66. "Sanctuarium vero ubi sanctorum gesta narratur accurate revolvimus et eo accuratius quo felicis memorie sancti viri Laurentii Justiniani . . . exemplario habuimus" (ibid.). For an anonymous contemporary *vita*, arranged as an overview of the *opera*, see A. Derolez, ed., "Un bio-bibliographie de saint Laurent Justinien edité d'après le manuscrit New York Public Library 82," *Latomus* 55, no. 4 (1996): 786–805.

67. Olga Marinelli Marcacci, "Codici e copisti a Perugia nel secolo XV," in R. Creytens and P. Kuenzle, eds., *Xenia medii aevi historiam illustrantia oblata Thomae Kaeppeli O.P.* (Rome, 1978), 2:565–566: "scribere uno santuaro de breviario, overo per meglio intendere tucto il festivo."

68. Not seen but listed in the MBA copy of Pietro Nurchi's manuscript "Catalogo parziale delle cinquecentine custodite nella biblioteca Ambrosiana . . . ," 98, no. 827. See F. E. Cranz, *A Microfilm Corpus of . . . Catalogues of Latin Manuscripts before 1600 A.D.* (New London, Conn., 1982), reel 157, item 4.

69. For the possibility that Gualla's work may hold a clue to Mombrizio's, see n. 150 below.

70. See also Davide Gutierrez, "De antiquis ordinis eremitarum sancti Augustini bibliothecis," *AA* 23 (1953–1954): 273: the 1480 inventory of the O.E.S.A. convent library at S. Maria del Popolo in Rome lists Leonardo da Udine's *sanctuarium*. As the Dominican preacher Leonardo da Udine wrote no known work with that title, the reference is likely to his widely circulated collection of sermons.

ilar local and liturgical focus to Mombrizio's collection. Mombrizio himself nowhere refers to the collection as a *legendarium* or *passionarium*; he may have approved, or even coined, the generic *sanctuarium*. Modern acceptance of that title was secured by Jean Bolland, by the usage of the *BHL* catalog of 1898–1899, and by the Solesmes edition of Mombrizio's *Sanctuarium* in 1910.

The publisher and publication date of the *Sanctuarium* are also unknown. Like many incunables, the volumes lack the colophons where such information was typically placed. But scholars have long assigned the imprint to Milan and dated it to around 1478, when its dedicatee (as we will see) fell from power.[71] No archival documents have yet surfaced to provide a date for any *pacta* between Mombrizio and his printer, to identify members of a publishing syndicate that might have produced the incunable, or even to clarify the nature and extent of Mombrizio's participation in the printing venture. Some sort of association was almost surely established by contract. Not only were these fluid groupings typical of early printing in Milan as elsewhere, but the size of the *Sanctuarium* suggests that the initial outlay for paper must have required wealthy backers or the connections to secure a considerable loan.[72] Arnaldo Ganda's research into early Milanese printing shows that Mombrizio had the money to enter several such *pacta* and that he was a prudent minder of his

---

71. Cf. the earliest attribution "Milan, Filippo Lavagna, 1476," from *Diario eruditorum Italiae*, 10:446, as recorded by a late annotating hand on the third flyleaf of *Sanctuarium*, vol. 1, copy held at Chatsworth House, shelf mark 14.C.

72. For an overview of early associations and production matters, see A. Colla, "Tipografi, editori, e libri a Padova, Treviso, Vicenza, Verona, Trento," in N. Pozza, ed., *La stampa degli incunaboli nel Veneto* (Vicenza, 1984), 37–80, noting that the outlay for paper might be one-half to three-quarters the cost of an edition (34–40); cf. the more restrained estimate in Melissa Conway, *The Diario of the Printing Press of San Jacopo di Ripoli, 1476–1484: Commentary and Transcription* (Florence: Olschki, 1999), covering startup costs for a press at 20–26, including paper for one edition at 26. The *Sanctuarium* was printed before *cartolai* in Milan organized into a guild—see C. Santoro, "Appunti e documenti per una storia dei cartai milanesi," in B. Maracchi Biagiarelli and D. E. Rhodes, eds., *Studi offerti a Roberto Ridolfi direttore de La Bibliofilia* (Florence: Olschki, 1973), 421–426—so organizing paper supplies may have been facilitated by the fact that Mombrizio had an official position and had worked with the ducal paper supplier, Melchior Squassi, and his son Giovanni in producing the Priscian, *De octo partibus orationis*, of 1475 (H*13354; BMC 6:730; IGI 8047; Goff P963; Rogledi Manni 826; Ganda, "Il tipografo," 230). See the Priscian contract, which declared Mombrizio's duty to fund ink (5 lire) and paper (4.5 lire per ream *forme maioris*), and the workmen's pay, all given in Ganda, "Il tipografo," 231, 232 and doc. 4 at 250. On the term "forma maioris," see appendix 3 of Paul Needham's "*Res papirea*: Sizes and Formats of the Late Medieval Book," in *Rationalisierung der Buchherstellung im Mittelalter und in der frühen Neuzeit: Ergebnisse eines buchgeschichtlichen Seminars Wolfenbüttel 12.–14. November 1990* (Marburg an der Lahn: Institut für Historische Hilfswissenschaften, 1994), 141–145.

investments.[73] He would therefore recognize that, while a run of 425 copies of the school text Priscian or 240 copies of the *Fioretti* of St. Francis would sell easily, hundreds of copies of a two-volume Latin text might prove a liability.[74] And such liabilities were to be avoided: he himself had briefly secured the imprisonment of Vespolate when that printer fell into his debt.[75]

A model for entrepreneurial thinking about liturgical books in Milan exists in the process leading to the publication of Antonio Zarotto's 1475 Ambrosian missal.[76] The preceding year, in 1474, Zarotto had produced Italy's first liturgical imprint, a Roman missal. Zarotto and his editor therefore had a basis on which to calculate the market for these sorts of books before proceeding with the Ambrosian missal. Indeed, the market was identifiable enough to encourage speculation, and in this instance we know something about the speculator: the Ambrosian missal was backed by the medical doctor and agricultural entrepreneur Marco Roma.[77] Roma's investment was fairly safe, because the Ambrosian missal was, at least in part, produced to meet a subscription list that had been compiled to meet diocesan need estimated during pastoral visits (although the list of secured subscribers amounted only to about forty names and the print run is unlikely to have been that restricted).[78] This model of financial backing secured by a subscription list may be relevant to two other liturgical publications: Arcangelus Ungardus's *Litanie secundum ordinem Ambrosianum*, tentatively dated to 1476, and Johannes Bonus's *Breviarium romanum* of

73. For Mombrizio's prudence, see Ganda's explicit estimate, "Il tipografo," 230 n. 21, discussed further below.

74. Ganda, "Il tipografo," 231 and 232, gives print runs of smaller books that preceded the *Sanctuarium*: 425 copies of Priscian's *De octo partibus orationis*, 300 copies of Cicero's *Familiares*.

75. Ganda, "Il tipografo," 237–238 and doc. 12 (drawn up in Mombrizio's home) at 259, showing Mombrizio turning this debt to his advantage in the printing and sale of the *Filocolo* of July 14, 1476, and the earlier Priscian. Vespolate and Mombrizio continued to work together, producing the Papias by December 12, 1476 (239).

76. This discussion draws primarily on Ganda, "La prima edizione"; see also Ganda, *I primordi*, 59–65. The Roman missal was edited by the priest Gabriele Orsini and the humanist pedagogue Cola da Montano, whose name will appear below.

77. Ganda, "Marco Roma," 100–101, shows that the noble Marco da Roma, a member of the college of physicians in Milan, speculated in the management of monastic properties and in printing and that his wife helped with these investments.

78. Ganda, "La prima edizione," 99–100, but without information on the size of the run; 110–111 for the subscription list; 109 for Roma's ultimate gain on his investment. The diocesan visits and the list were made by Bishop Daniele in his capacity as aide to the absent archbishop of Milan, Stefano Nardini (98–99). Several diocesan churches subsequently refused to make the promised purchase, and their representatives were called before the vicar and Marco Roma's procurator to explain (111–112).

March 1478.[79] It may also apply to the *Sanctuarium*. But even if the *Sanctuarium* had neither a backer nor a subscription list, the success of liturgical printings in Milan probably influenced Mombrizio's decision to print. As Ganda has shown, Mombrizio was a profit-oriented man.

The Latin typeface of the *Sanctuarium* is a well-proportioned roman font substantially the same as that used by Arcangelus Ungardus,[80] who produced five editions at Milan in 1476–1477.[81] Ungardus's type, identified by Haebler as 107R, seems to have been "recast on or leaded to a body of 112 mm," that is, the lines of print in Mombrizio's compilation occur at a slightly larger distance from each other than in the Ungardus imprints.[82] The technical point is not minor: in the *Sanctuarium,* the Mombritius printer offered an open and graceful presentation of the page, just the sort of look that market pressures were actively eliminating in the 1470s.[83] The generous left, right, and center margins of the *Sanctuarium,* the lack of concern to fill the final columns of each gathering completely, and the moderate use of abbreviations likewise suggest that the *Sanctuarium* was solidly enough backed to be relatively free from market pressures.[84] The lay-

79. The *Litanie* (H 10121; *BMC* 6:734; *IGI* 5767; Goff L230; Rogledi Manni 570; *BMC* 6:xxv "not later than November 1476"), which is dedicated to Stefano Nardini, cardinal of S. Adriano, opens with a letter from Ungardus to Romano de' Barni in which the printer refers to himself as *presbiter* and *sacerdos* and explains "me huic imprimendorum librorum arti addixi, qua nihil Christus Iesus dominus noster studiis liberalium artium conducibilius monstravit in terris" (sign. a1v). The *Breviarium romanum,* published in Milan by the Augustinian Hermit of German origin, Johannes Bonus, in octavo (Rogledi Manni 208; *IGI* 2114A), is described in A. Veneziani, "Notizie sul tipografo Johannes Bonus ed un suo Breviario Romano sconosciuto ai bibliografi, " *La Bibliofilia* 72 (1970): 247–252. Ganda, "La prima edizione," 106, speculates that a subscription list was applied, perhaps retroactively, to the Zarotto *Missale romanum* of 1474. For Johannes Bonus as printer at the Incoronata in the 1470s, see chap. 5 below.

80. Mombrizio did not use Greek in this imprint as often as he apparently intended to or might have done. A single word occurs in Greek lettering in the *Sanctuarium* (passion of Chrysanthos and Daria, in vol. 1, at sign. c7v, a39). On occasion, Mombrizio left blank spaces rather than supply the Greek type, as in the passion of Dionysius, Rusticus, and Eleuterius, in vol. 1, at sign. d4, a30 and a33. He passed up opportunities to insert Greek type, e.g., at sign. 3a2r, a47, transliterating "apodixen" in the passion of Agnes. The copy held at Parma, Bibl. Regia, shelf mark 1184, has a contemporary note of Latin explanation added in the margin at this point.

81. *BMC* 6:xxiv and 374–375.

82. *BMC* 6:736–737; K. Haebler, *Veröffentlichungen der Gesellschaft für Typenkunde des XV Jahrhunderts* (1907–1936; repr. Osnabruck, 1966), table 2178. Haebler makes a genealogical connection between these typefaces being used in Milan and one used in Pavia (table 1956).

83. On the winnowing of publishers during this period, see Lowry, *Nicholas Jenson,* chap. 7, and Rozzo, "Il libro a stampa," 196 and n. 18. Scholars of printing history disagree about how much influence ought to be attributed to early market forces.

84. Ganda, "Il tipografo," 239, notes a similarly generous layout for the Papias. The folios that remain blank recto and verso in some copies today represent protective papers that were not cut away during binding.

out cannot be attributed to inexperience. Rather, the printer's failure to fill his folios is related in every instance to the sequence of signatures for each gathering as these are aligned to the organization of the contents (see below).

The close relationship of the typeface in Mombrizio's legendary to that used by Ungardus allows some speculation about dating, for the two men had documented business connections.[85] Although most of Ungardus's editions are undated, the latest one bearing a date is Dictys's *Historia Trojana* of May 19, 1477.[86] If Ungardus did pass on his matrices to the "Printer for Boninus Mombritius," then the *Historia Trojana* may provide a *terminus post quem* of May 1477 for that sharing.[87] As for a *terminus ante quem*, that is securely grounded. More than twenty years ago, Tino Foffano discovered a copy of the *Sanctuarium* with a purchase note dated September 14, 1478.[88] The date allows a rough comparative calculation to be made.[89] Notarial documents show that it took three months for the 188-leaf bifolio *Missale romanum* of 1474, edited by the humanist schoolteacher Cola da Montano and the priest Gabriele Orsoni for Antonio Zarotto, to go from contract to sales. This *Missale* was roughly one-quarter the size of the *Sanctuarium*, which implies a year's production time for Mombrizio's compilation. But adding presses or farming out composition units to other workshops (even as far afield as Pavia, since the court and the humanists moved back and forth constantly) might considerably reduce this time. In 1473 Gerardus Cremonensis's translation of Avicenna, *Canon de medicina*, was printed by the Lavagna workshop to meet a contract that stipulated three and a half months production time, on three presses.[90]

85. Ganda "Il tipografo," documents a business connection between Ungardus and Mombrizio in 1476.

86. H 6156; *GW* 8326; *BMC* 6:735; *IGI* 3422; Goff D 185; Rogledi Manni 376. The edition includes a dedicatory letter from the editor, Masellus Venia, to Bartolomeo Calco.

87. Such a scenario is implied by the chronological presentation of the *BMC* entries for the two presses, which places Ungardus just before the "Printer for Mombritius."

88. Foffano, "Per la data," on Inc. 18 of the library of the Università Cattolica di Milano, a remarkably clean copy of *Sanctuarium* vol. 2. The imprint was bought by the famous preacher Blessed Bernardino Caimi after his return from the Holy Land, for the Observant Franciscan convent of s. Bernardino near Caravaggio, east of Milan.

89. The census (n. 5 above) includes bibliographical description; see G. Thomas Tanselle, "Printing History and Other History," *Studies in Bibliography* 48 (1995): 269–289. Colla, "Tipografi," 43, observes, on the example of Maufer at Padua, that a well-organized workshop in the 1470s would have four to six presses going. For their "vasto e ambizioso programma editoriale" of May 1477, to produce school, law, and liturgical books in Milan, Marco da Roma and Antonio Zarotto had six presses (Ganda, "Marco Roma," 118 and doc. 31 at 238–239).

90. *BMC* 6:700b–701a. This imprint (H *2200; *GW* 3115; *BMC* 6:700; *IGI* 1115; Rogledi Manni 119) had a two-column format, similar to the *Sanctuarium*, but a gothic rather than a roman font. The contract stipulating the number of presses and the production time was drawn up on September 26, 1472; see Emilio Motta, "Di Filippo di Lavagna e di alcuni altri tipografi-editori milanesi del Quattrocento (nuovi documenti)," *ASL*, ser. 3, 25, no. 18 (1898): 28–72.

Lavagna's *Canon* was a work in three volumes, with a total of 573 leaves; Mombrizio's *Sanctuarium*, in two volumes, had 714 leaves of text. Postulating, for the sake of the calculation, a similar three presses to produce the *Sanctuarium*, we can estimate a production time of about four months for Mombrizio's compilation. Any increase in the number of presses or workshops involved—or in the amount of type available, so that each forme did not have to be broken down to compose the next one—could dramatically reduce even this calculation. But working backward from the purchase date discovered by Foffano, we can speculate that printing commenced, at the latest, in the spring or summer of 1478. So, even if the *terminus post quem* of the typeface is dismissed, the *ante quem* of the purchase note of mid-September 1478 suffices to demonstrate that the *Sanctuarium* was compiled, printed, and sold during a period of political unrest that was exceptionally severe, even for Milan. To that situation I now turn.

❧ ❧ ❧

Nunc tandem ut discas saeuis ex ordine coeptis
Quam multum scelus a paucis sit ciuibus actum:
Accipe flagitii quam longa incendia narrem.

Now, at last, that you may know, without pause, about the bloody happenings,
How great a crime was committed by a few citizens,
Hear how I tell of the lengthy conflagrations of the crime.

—Bonino Mombrizio, *Trenodia*[91]

In June of 1476, while Galeazzo Maria Sforza was meeting with his *consiglieri* in Pavia, an unsuccessful attempt was made on his life.[92] The second attempt that year succeeded: on December 26, St. Stephen's Day, the duke of Milan was murdered as he attended Mass.[93] The assassins were

91. Bonino Mombrizio, *Trenodia*, published in Milan by Alessandro Minuziano, March 2, 1504, sign. A2v, 5–7. This poem is discussed below.

92. Riccardo Fubini, "Osservazioni e documenti sulla crisi del ducato di Milano nel 1477 e sulla riforma del consiglio segreto ducale di Bona Sforza," in S. Bertelli and G. Ramakus, eds., *Essays Presented to Myron P. Gilmore*, vol. 1 (Florence: La Nuova Italia, 1978), 69 n. 3, with further references; Maria Nadia Covini, *L'esercito del duca: Organizzazione militare e istituzioni al tempo degli Sforza (1450–1580)* (Rome: Istituto storico per il medioevo, 1998), 346 and n. 311.

93. This account of politics at Milan in 1476–1480 depends chiefly on Marcello Simonetta, ed., *Carteggio degli oratori mantovani alla corte Sforezca (1450–1500)*, vol. 11, 1478–1479, dir. F. Leverotti (Rome: Archivi di stato, 2001); Leverotti, "Governare"; Covini, *L'esercito*; Lubkin, *A Renaissance Court*; Gary Ianziti, *Humanistic Historiography Under the Sforzas* (New York: Oxford University Press, 1988); Fubini, "Osservazioni" and "L'Assassinio di Galeazzo Maria Sforza nelle sue circostanze politiche," in *Lorenzo de'Medici Lettere*, vol. 2, 1474–1478 (Florence: Giunti-Barbèra, 1977), 532–535; Camillo Marazza, "Molinet e l'uccisione di Galeazzo Maria Sforza," *Bibliotheca dell' Archivum Romanum* 123, 1975:

three young Milanese, Giovanni Andrea Lampugnani, Gerolamo Olgiati, and Carlo Visconti.[94] Two of these men had close ties to the notorious "republican" humanist and early printing enthusiast Cola da Montano.[95] Lampugnani, the ringleader, was a friend of Cola's; Olgiati had been a student.[96] In addition, the assassins were perceived to have support among factions of the Milanese nobility: Galeazzo Maria was disliked among nobles not so much for curtailing their access to governing institutions as for deforming those institutions to serve his own will.[97] Factional suspi-

---

61–85; Vincent Ilardi, "The Assassination of Galeazzo Maria Sforza," in L. Martines, ed., *Violence and Civil Disorder in Italian Cities* (Berkeley, 1972); *L'Età Sforezca*; Bortolo Belotti, *Il dramma di Gerolamo Olgiati* (Milan, s.a. [1929]). I follow Fubini's analysis of factional politics under Galeazzo Maria; Lubkin (204–205), expresses reservations. Leverotti, "Governare," gives ample evidence of reasons for resentment against the duke.

94. The official description of the St. Stephen's Day event is contained in a letter from Orfeo da Ricavo to Sforza Bettini, reprinted in Eugenio Casanova, "L'uccisione," *ASL* 26, 24 (1899): 302–308; see also Marazza, "Molinet e l'uccisione"; cf. Belotti, *Il dramma*; Fubini, *Lorenzo de' Medici Lettere*, 523–535; idem, "Osservazioni"; Lucia Fontanella, "La relazione di Roberto Sanseverino sull'assassinio di Galeazzo Maria Sforza," *Pluteus* 6–7 (1988–89): 67–77; and Lubkin, *A Renaissance Court*, 239–241. The letter from Bona and Cicco to Sixtus IV describes the assassination occurring "inter spectandum dum res divina perageretur"; see Ludovico Frati, "Una lettera della duchessa Bona di Savoia a Papa Sisto IV," *ASL*, ser. 2, 4, no. 17 (1890): 943. This description could be calculated for the papal audience; other sources describe the moment differently. For an overview of external and internal political strains during 1475–1476, see Covini, *L'esercito*, 337–348.

95. On Cola, see Belotti, *Il dramma*, 34–50, with documentation in Girolamo Lorenzi, *Cola Montano: Studio Storico* (Milan, 1875); the letter from Orfeo da Ricavo to Sforza Bettini does not name him but describes Giovanni Andrea Lampugnani as studying the Catalinarians for four months before the assassination and mentions "the sect [*cierto*] that wants to imitate those ancient Romans and be liberators of the country [*patria*]" (Casanova, "L'uccisione" 307). It was reported among contemporaries that Olgiati's confession had included a recollection of Cola's critique of servility under tyrants; see Belotti, *Il dramma*, 38; Corio, *Storia*, 3:304 for the passage from the confession; Lorenzi, *Cola Montano*, 46–88, gives the entire text. Cola had been a student of George of Trebizond: the first Milanese edition of George's *Compendium de partibus orationis ex Prisciano* (attributed to the press of Filippo da Lavagna, after October 29, 1471 [Rogledi Manni 467]), was dedicated to Cola; see John Monfasani, *George of Trebizond* (Leiden: Brill, 1976), 231. The letter of dedication was reprinted at the end of the 1472 edition attributed to the press of Antonio Zarotto (Rogledi Manni 468; Ganda 1985, # 9) and in the 1474 and 1478 editions attributed again to Lavagna (Rogledi Manni 469–470).

96. Belotti, *Il dramma*, 51–52; cf. Fubini, *Lorenzo de' Medici Lettere*, 2:525. Visconti is described by primary and secondary sources as a lower-class ruffian and "simple," but he had, in fact, been favored by the duke. On the vicissitudes of the nobles Francesco and his son Carlo under Galeazzo Maria, see Fubini, "Osservazioni," 60; and, most important, Leverotti, "Governare," 106–107.

97. On the "unjust justice" expertly practiced by Galeazzo Maria (its success can be measured in the wealth of his treasury, despite the deep debt of the Milanese state), see Leverotti, "Governare." She argues that Galeazzo Maria probably increased the size of some administrative bodies with honorific appointments. He also made appointments that guaranteed insecurity and distrust among the appointees, so that the traditional alliances of the ruling families were destroyed.

cions were aggravated by the fact that the Ambrosian Republic was only twenty-five years distant, still in living memory, still structuring allegiances.[98] Girolamo Olgiati, the assassin who had been educated by Cola da Montano, confessed that he had prayed before a statue of St. Ambrose before the assassination.[99]

In the months following the assassination, Galeazzo Maria's widow, Bona of Savoy, was in an extremely difficult position. Not only was Milan itself uncertain, but her husband's siblings were overtly hostile, her children were minors, the subject cities—Genoa especially—threatened to swing out of orbit, and major powers such as Naples were maneuvering to benefit from Milan's difficulties. To maintain control, both of perception and in fact, Bona relied of necessity on the long-time head of the *Consiglio ducale*, Cicco Simonetta (1410–1480).[100] So it happened that in the days following Galeazzo Maria's death—just as in the days following the death of his father, Francesco—the continuity of Sforza rule rested in the person of Simonetta.[101] With his team of two secretaries and about a dozen chancellors, first secretary Simonetta oversaw the whole range of state matters, from diplomatic and military arrangements abroad to law and order in the

98. Cf. Leverotti, "Governare," which sets Galeazzo Maria's "decennio di autoritarismo imperante" (132) in contrast to Francesco's reforms, rather than to the events of 1447–1450, as Fubini does in "Osservazioni."

99. It was important to contemporaries to note this connection to Ambrose, as it was almost fifty years later to Niccolò Machiavelli (d. 1527), who included a version of the prayer in his *Istorie fiorentine*, which had been commissioned by the Medici in 1520 (the prayer is quoted in the epigraph to the concluding section of this chapter).

100. Bona's independence and competence are defended by Lubkin, *A Renaissance Court*, 226–227, which gives further references. But Cicco's power was intrinsic to the ducal chancery: in 1450 Francesco Sforza and Cicco had cofounded the *Consiglio ducale*, and Cicco had written the handbook of chancery duties. On the history of the Milanese notariate, see Alberto Liva, *Notariato e documento notarile a Milano dall'alto medioevo alla fine del settecento* (Rome: Consiglio nazionale del notariato, 1979); for an overview of Simonetta's contribution, see Ianziti, *Humanistic Historiography*, 152, with further references, as well as, e.g., Belotti, *Il dramma*, 24; Lubkin, *A Renaissance Court*, 242 et seq., and, in depth, Francesco Senatore, *"Un mundo de carta": Forme e strutture della diplomazia Sforzesca* (Naples: Liguori, 1998). A. R. Natale, ed., *I diari di Cicco Simonetta* (Milan: Giuffrè, 1962), xiii–xv, gives biographical data on Cicco.

101. For two years after Francesco Sforza's death, poor relations between Galeazzo Maria and his mother persisted, finally settling in Galeazzo Maria's favor by December 1467/January 1468: see Leverotti, "Governare," 10–27. The question of legitimacy was also crucial: Galeazzo Maria had not been invested by the Holy Roman Emperor, and this had internal as well as external repercussions. See H. Angermeier, "Die Sforza und das Reich," in *Gli Sforza a Milano*, 165–192, esp. 176; and J. E. Law, "Un confronto fra due stati 'rinascimentali': Venezia e il dominio sforzesco," in ibid., 397–414, esp. 403, with bibliography in n. 25. Bona represented a connection to France that was not universally desired, and her eldest son was only eight years old at the time of the assassination. Thus, following Galeazzo Maria's death, whatever legitimacy Francesco had acquired for the Sforza dynasty stood most clearly in the first secretary appointed by Francesco and kept on by Galeazzo Maria.

territories and at home. The historian of Milan's administrative institu-tions, Caterina Santoro, described him during the Regency as the "vero padrone dello Stato."[102]

In Milan, retribution for the assassination was a deliberate spectacle of violence, at least to judge from contemporary writings. Lampugnani had been killed on the spot. Contemporary sources report that his body was then mutilated by the mob and left to be eaten by pigs and that his severed right hand was burned and nailed to a post.[103] Over the course of a week in which official pressures were applied to their families and friends, his two accomplices and an implicated servant were hunted, captured, and tortured.[104] Bona's secretary, Bartolomeo Calco, wrote the letter arranging their executions by drawing and quartering.[105] Contemporary histories record that, as the executioner began to cut into his chest, the young humanist Olgiati first fainted but then found strength by projecting himself into history in terms suitable for both martyrs and patriotic Romans: *Stabit vetus memoria facti. Mors acerba, fama perpetua.*[106] His corpse, along with those of the others, was dis-played for what was perceived to be an abnormally long time through-out an unusually wide area of the city: members posted above the city gates, heads affixed to the *campanile* of the Broletto, the administrative building.[107]

Despite the lingering spectacle of retribution and a series of further exe-cutions, banishments, and confiscations, Milan continued unstable through 1477. Bona oversaw, guided by Cicco Simonetta if not by her sec-retary, Bartolomeo Calco (who delivered the letter informing the mem-bers), an expansion of the *Consiglio segreto* that was intended to neutral-

102. Santoro, *Gli uffici*, "Domini de consilio secreto," 8 n. 2; Filippo Argelati, *Biblio-theca scriptorum mediolanensium* (Milan, 1745), vol. 2, col. 2164, at D: "ejus arbitrio fier-ent universa."

103. Fontanella, "La relazione," 75 n. 22, citing Molinet, the source of "particolari più crudi di quella morte." See also Casanova, "L'uccisione," 306, with Leverotti, "Governare." Retributory spectacles were common practice throughout Europe at the time.

104. On the pressures applied, see, e.g., Belotti, *La dramma*, 122–124.

105. Belotti, *La dramma*, 126–128.

106. The equivalency of martyrs and Roman generals is discussed in chap. 2. For the quo-tation, see Belotti, *La dramma*, 127, drawing on the 1492 *Cronaca* of Donato Bossi. Cf. the 1503 description by Bernardo Corio, in *Storia di Milano* (Milan, 1857), 3:313: "Il detto Girolamo quando il maestro di giustizia col ferro che mal tagliava cominciò a percuoterlo sul petto, smarrendosi quasi del tutto stette come morto. Tuttavia riprendendo alquando lo spir-ito pronunciò queste parole: 'Collige te Hieronime: stabit vetus memoria facti. Mors acerba, fama perpetua.'" See also Olgiati's Latin confession (ibid., 304–313).

107. Belotti, *La dramma*, 127–128, drawing again on Bossi's chronicle. In *Storia*, 313, Corio notes only "le membra degli altri [that is, excepting Lampugnano] furono inchiodate sulle porte della città, e le teste sul campanile del Broletto nuovo."

ize the opposing factions.[108] But this yearlong restructuring, during which the *Consiglio* met with striking infrequency, failed to put an end to factional politicking in favor of Bona's brothers-in-law.[109] In May, the brothers-in-law attempted a coup against her government. They did not succeed. The Florentine ambassador wrote home in June 1477 that Simonetta had confirmed and concentrated his power.[110] Then evidence surfaced of further plots, including more than one to murder Cicco.[111] Resident ambassadors reported rumors of impromptu militia groups, of house sackings, of the threat of anarchy, but also a degree of normalcy in bureaucratic functions.[112] Power, however, was shifting: over the course of 1478, as Cicco came under attack from a noble faction favorable to the dynastic claims of Lodovico Maria Sforza, the duchess's secretary, Bartolomeo Calco, moved prominently to the fore.[113]

The remainder of the story falls beyond the *terminus ante quem* of the *Sanctuarium* but is relevant to the work's reception. In September 1479, pressed by the noble faction that had welcomed Francesco Sforza but chafed under his son Galeazzo Maria, Bona risked reconciliation with her brother-in-law Lodovico Maria Sforza.[114] Lodovico, Il Moro, arrived in Milan on September 10.[115] He removed Simonetta from the chancery three days later; after more than a year in prison, Simonetta was beheaded in late October 1480.[116] Bartolomeo Calco became the new first secretary of the *Consiglio ducale*. Calco now served, as Simonetta had, to mediate

---

108. These factions are described in Fubini, "L'Assassinio," as Guelf (Sforza) and Ghibelline (Visconti/Ambrosian Republic). Cicco, as first secretary of the *Consiglio ducale*, was a member of the *Consiglio segreto*. Insofar as Bona's reorganization allowed any power to the Ghibellines (i.e., to those Visconti aristocrats such as Pietro da Pusterla who had favored Francesco Sforza, despised Galeazzo Maria, and were now willing to welcome his brother Lodovico Maria Sforza), it posed a threat to Cicco. For the vicissitudes of the *consigli* under Galeazzo Maria, see Leverotti, "Governare," 84–103 (*Consiglio segreto*) and 103–122 (*Consiglio di giustizia*).

109. The official establishment of the new *Consiglio* occurred in an *ordinatio* of December 31, 1478 (subscribed January 28, 1478), but the revised council had actually been instituted fully on October 7, 1477; see Fubini, "Osservazioni."

110. Fubini, "Osservazioni," 51 and n. 11.

111. C. Magenta, *I Visconti e gli Sforza nel castello di Pavia e loro attinenze con la Certosa e la storia cittadina* (Milan, 1883), 2:389–392; Ianziti, *Humanist Historiography*, 223–224; and especially Fubini, "Osservazioni," 59–60 and 98, with notes and further references.

112. Fubini, "Osservazioni," doc. 5. Normalcy was emphasized in the official report, the letter from Orfeo da Ricavo; see Casanova, "L'uccisione," passim.

113. On this secretary, see A. Petrucci, "Calco, Bartolomeo," in *DBI* 16 (1973), 526b–527a.

114. For the "Ghibelline" pressures on Bona to reconcile with Lodovico Maria, see Corio, in *Storia*, 3:347–348 and the note at 383–384.

115. Simonetta, *Carteggio*, vol. 11, 32, and letters 219–220.

116. Santoro, *Gli Sforza*, 179–187; Ianziti, *Humanistic Historiography*, 211, 222.

between the duke and the administration and became what Simonetta had been, "the most important official" in Lombardy.[117] In the meantime, Lodovico Maria moved against Bona. He transferred his nephew Gian-Galeazzo Maria from the duchess's guardianship into his own, and Bona retreated from Milan to her family's home in Savoy. The young man served as figurehead until his death in 1494, when Lodovico Maria took full power.

Was the *Sanctuarium* published before or after the assassination of Galeazzo Maria? That question cannot be securely answered. Three aspects of the *Sanctuarium*, however, offer tentative support to a post-assassination dating: the dedication, the physical presentation of the texts, and the nature of the contents. Each will be examined in turn below. The implications of this examination are far-reaching. Mombrizio's work may well have had a political aspect, by which I mean that it was, *in part*, a response to the administrative and factional exercise of power at Milan in 1476–1478. This proposal is not prima facie improbable: throughout the Middle Ages, saints' lives, like their relics, were deployed in the exercise of authority in the secular as in the ecclesiastical realm.[118] Nevertheless, the proposal entails a great adjustment in our understanding of the *Sanctuarium*. Milanese political history is so notoriously the object of overheated speculation (most engagingly and instructively in Jacob Burckhardt's learned presentation of Milan as the perfect type of tyranny) that some readers may dismiss this proposal out of hand as so much conspiracy theory.[119] So I have tried to frame the discussion below in such a way that, even if readers disagree with the interpretation, they will find the clarification of the context, structure, and contents of the *Sanctuarium* helpful. That, in turn, will contribute to a fuller understanding of the compilation as a significant example of humanist hagiography.

❈ ❈ ❈

Dum satis ista meo tandem sint credita Cicho.
It is enough, in the end, that all be credited to my Cicco.

—Bonino Mombrizio, *Sanctuarium* [120]

---

117. Petrucci, in *DBI* 16 (1973), 527b.

118. See, e.g., R. Folz, *Les saints rois du Moyen Age en occident (Vie–XIIIe siècles)* (Brussels: Bollandist Society, 1984); P. Corbet, *Les saints ottoniens: Sainteté dynastique, sainteté royale, et sainteté feminine autour de l'an mil* (Sigmaringen: Thorbecke, 1986); J. Petersohn, *Politik und Heiligenverehrung im Hochmittelalter* (Sigmaringen: Thorbecke, 1994); Webb, *Patrons*; D. R. Bauer and K. Herbers, eds., *Hagiographie im Kontext: Wirkungsweisen und Möglichkeiten historische Auswertung* (Stuttgart: Steiner, 2000).

119. Burckhardt, *Civilization of the Renaissance in Italy*, 44, briskly summarizes the story of Galeazzo Maria's reign; the whole of his part 1 famously explores tyranny as art.

120. Thus Bonino Mombrizio concludes his second poem to Cicco Simonetta in the *Sanctuarium*, in the penultimate position in volume 2.

All of Mombrizio's own compositions and translations, and many of his editions, bear dedications.[121] Like any other Renaissance author or editor, he aimed these dedications high, seeking effect, careful not to risk offense, too professional to waste time or effort. His aim was not exclusively Milanese. The Latin translation of Hesiod, for example, was dedicated to Borso d'Este, ruler of Ferrara.[122] Mombrizio also nurtured ties to Rome.[123] One Latin epic, on Jerome, was dedicated first to Paul II (1464–1471) and then, when Paul died, to his successor Sixtus IV (1471–1484).[124] A second Latin epic, the Virgilian *De dominica passione*, also went to Sixtus IV.[125]

For the most part, however, the humanist sought the attention of the Sforza rulers of Milan. In 1451 and 1455—after the Sforza succession had become clear but while he himself was still living in Ferrara—Mombrizio wrote epithalamia for the marriages of Francesco Sforza's illegitimate sons Sforza Secondo and Tristano.[126] In the early 1460s, after he had moved (back?) to Milan, Mombrizio dedicated a vernacular epic about Katherine of Alexandria to Francesco's wife, Bianca Maria, and made a metric Latin translation of Janus Lascaris's Greek textbook, the *Erotemata*, for Francesco's daughter Ippolita Sforza.[127] In the late 1460s he dedicated a series of poems, the *Bucolica*, and a lengthy metric, *De varietate fortuna*,

---

121. Sassi and Argelati give a partial list in Mombritius 1910, xxi–xxix.

122. Sassi, in Mombritius 1910, xix and xxiv; Argelati, in ibid., xxvii. The text of the dedication is edited in *Bibliotheca Smithiana*, cxxix–cxxx. This translation of the *Theogeny* was first published in Ferrara by Andreas Belfort in 1474 (*IGI* 4725), with Mombrizio's preface to Borso d'Este (d. 1471). Cf. London, BL, MS Harl. 3397, a fifteenth century manuscript of the translation (Kristeller, *Iter* 4:170a).

123. From 1461 to 1484 the archbishop of Milan, Stefano Nardini, was absent from the city, serving in Rome, but I have not found evidence that Mombrizio's papal dedications were connected to Nardini's proximity to the curia.

124. Argelati, in Mombritius 1910, xxvii. *De vita Hieronymi carmen* is extant in four manuscripts, two bearing dedications to Paul II and two to Sixtus IV. I consulted MBA, MS Trotti 390, to Paul II (Kristeller, *Iter* 1:350b); and BAV, MS Lat. 3722, to Sixtus IV (Kristeller, *Iter* 2:323a); cf. Kristeller, *Iter* 1:50b and 2:583a. The *terminus ante quem* must be July 26, 1471, the death of Paul II.

125. Sassi, in Mombritius 1910, xxiii–xxiv; Argelati, in ibid., xxvii. The epic was printed in Milan by Antonio Zarotto c. 1474 (H 11542; *BMC* 6:712; *IGI* 6689; Rogledi Manni 688; Ganda, *I primordi*, #35). Many copies are extant, as are at least four manuscript copies, three transcribed from the incunable. The dedication copy to Sixtus IV is BAV, MS Ottob. lat. 826 (Kristeller, *Iter* 2:415a).

126. Sassi, in Mombritius 1910, xviii; Argelati, in ibid., xxvii. I have not seen the poems; they are in MBA, MS C 42 sup., fo. 47–67. See Louis Jordan and Susan Wool, *Inventory of Western Manuscripts in the Biblioteca Ambrosiana from the Medieval Institute of the University of Notre Dame, the Frank M. Folsom Microfilm Collection*, vol. XXII/2 (Notre Dame: University of Notre Dame Press, 1986), 71–72.

127. On the *Erotemata*, see Sassi, in Mombritius, 1910, xix and n. 1, giving a poem in Lascaris's praise by Mombrizio; Argelati, in ibid., xxvii. There is a sole manuscript, MBA, MS N 264 sup. (Kristeller, *Iter* 1:303b). Two editions of Lascaris's *Erotemata* were published in Milan on January 30, 1476, and September 29, 1480 (*IGI* 5690 and 5691); Mombrizio seems to have had a hand in neither.

to the new duke, Galeazzo Maria, as well as a twelve-part poem on the virtues and vices of women, the *Momidos*, to the duke's wife, Bona.[128]

In a few instances, Mombrizio stepped outside the charmed circle of ruler-patrons. He contributed brief Latin poems "to the reader" in six incunables:[129] Paul of Venice's *Summularium*,[130] Eusebius's *Chronica*,[131] the *Vocabularium* of Papias,[132] a vernacular treatise on the plague,[133] Boccaccio's *Il Filocolo*,[134] and Luctatius's commentary on Statius.[135] The poems are evidence that he edited or reviewed the texts or had an entrepreneurial or organizational part in their production. As in the case of the *Sanctuarium*, Mombrizio's precise role is unclear; he may have combined editorial and entrepreneurial tasks.[136] The range of subject areas is striking and suggests a calculated attempt to gauge the market, whether on Mombrizio's part or on the part of his business partners.

Except for these six instances, Mombrizio chose dedicatees who were not members of ruling families only four times. In 1469 he dedicated to Giovanni Borromeo—a new feudal lord of considerable wealth and a known opponent of Cicco Simonetta—an epic on the aristocrat's name

---

128. On the *Bucolica*, see Argelati in Mombritius 1910, xxvii. *Momidos* is extant in a single incomplete manuscript (MBA, MS G 113 inf.); there may have been others that were complete, since the poem was known to contemporaries such as Jacopo Filippo Foresti and Alessandro Minuziano. Sassi in Mombritius 1910, xviii, finds in it evidence that Mombrizio was celibate; see also Argelati, in ibid., xxvii. The poem is discussed further below.

129. Incunables to which Mombrizio did not contribute poems or dedications but with which he is associated through the "Printer for Boninus Mombritius" include the *editio princeps* of the school text, Prosper of Aquitaine, *Epigrammata de virtutibus et vitiis* (*IGI* 8094; Goff P 1020; Rogledi Manni 831), published c. 1477 and backed financially by Marco da Roma. See Ganda, "Marco Roma," 122 and n. 94, on the basis of the entry "Prosperi" in Roma's "Lista de Libri Stanpiti," reproduced at 111. Ganda argues from the "Lista" and the notarial evidence that Marco da Roma set out deliberately to corner a clearly identifiable market, students of the new Scuole Grassi. Tommaso Grassi established this school by legacy in 1473, providing a house in which to educate 250 poor boys and lands to support the bequest. The only study known to me, Alessandro Giulini, "Tommaso Grassi, le sue scuole e le relazioni sue cogli Sforza," *ASL* ser. 4, fasc. 35, anno 39 (1912): 271–283, includes no information about teachers or curricula; see Ganda, "Marco Roma," 108 n. 41, and F. Bacchelli, "Grassi, Tommaso de'" in *DBI* 58 (2002): 693b.

130. Printed at Milan by Christoph Valdarfer, December 14, 1474 (H 12500; R 6:110; *IGI* 7349; Goff P220; Rogledi Manni 764). Ganda, "Marco Roma," 113–114, suggests that this imprint may have been one of the motivating factors in making Roma a speculator in print. In fact, the subject of Mombrizio's appended dedicatory poem is precisely the utility of printed schoolbooks.

131. See n. 60 above.

132. See Sassi, in Mombritius 1910, xxi–xxii; Argelati, in ibid., xxvii; Ganda, "Il tipografo."

133. See n. 43 above. Not recorded in Mombritius 1910.

134. Milan, Vespolate, June 14, 1476 (H 3927; *GW* 4464; *BMC* 6:732; *IGI* 1786; Rogledi Manni 172). See also Ganda, "Il tipografo." Not recorded in Mombritius 1910.

135. Luctatius Placidus, *Interpretatio in Statii Thebaida*, published in Milan c. 1480 (*BMC* 6:736; *IGI* 5634; Goff L19; Ganda, *I primordi*, 230; Rogledi Manni 589). I follow Ganda's dating.

136. Modigliani, *Tipografi*, 36–39, discusses the mixed role of entrepreneur and editor in Roman incunables.

saint, John the Evangelist.[137] This poem has never been edited. Around 1475 Mombrizio dedicated the edition of Solinus's *Polyhistor* to the canon lawyer and commendatory patron of San Antonio, the noble Antonio Trivulzio.[138] At an uncertain date, perhaps more than a year after the assassination, as the growing influence of Bona's secretary became evident, he dedicated—with exceptional warmth—the edition of Statius's *Thebaid* to Bartolomeo Calco.[139] And at some unspecified time before mid-September 1478, Mombrizio dedicated the most voluminous undertaking of his scholarly and publishing life, the *Sanctuarium*, to the man who acted so powerfully in the wake of the assassination: the first secretary of the *Consiglio ducale* and *padrone* of the Regency, Cicco Simonetta.

Only one other editor working in Milan dedicated printed books to Cicco Simonetta.[140] Unlike Mombrizio, the humanist Buono Accorsi of Pisa made his dedications to the first secretary repeatedly—five in 1475, one (a reissue) in 1476, and one in 1477.[141] All but one of Accorsi's dedications to Cicco predate the assassination. Liturgical interests are nowhere evident, for the dedicated works are Lorenzo Valla's *Elegantiae* (in compendium),[142] Agostino Dati's *Elegantiolae*,[143] Ovid's *Metamor-*

137. The *Vita divi Iohannis evangelistae* is extant only in MBA, MS F 207 inf. (Kristeller, *Iter* 1:291b). The dedication names Borromeo as "Aronae comitem ducaleque consiliarium," indicating a *terminus post quem* of January 5–10, 1469. For this date, the family's extensive if new holdings and Giovanni's consequent ability to snub Galeazzo Maria Sforza, see G. Chittolini, "Borromeo, Giovanni," in *DBI* 13 (1971): 54a; Lubkin, *A Renaissance Court*, 7. New nobles such as Borromeo were deliberately created as part of the political changes instituted in the late fourteenth century by Gian Galeazzo Visconti; see Luigi Prosdocimi, *Il diritto ecclesiastico dello stato di Milano, dall'inizio della signoria Viscontea al periodo Tridentino (sec. XIII–XVI)* (Milan, 1941; anastatic reprint, Milan: Cisalpino-Goliardica, 1973), 152–153. Giovanni Borromeo was both wealthy and wise enough to renounce his salary when he joined Galeazzo Maria's highly manipulated *Consiglio segreto*; see Leverotti, "Governare," 85–86 n. 266.

138. Printed in Milan c. 1475, according to Rogledi Manni 936 (H *14873; *BMC* 6:728; *IGI* 9086; Goff S618); see Sassi, in Mombritius 1910, xvi and xxiv. At this date Trivulzio opposed Sforza and Simonetta, although other members of the family were extremely close to Galeazzo Maria; see, e.g., Lubkin, *A Renaissance Court*, 193.

139. Milan, Printer for Mombritius, traditionally assigned to 1476–1477 (H 14990; *BMC* 6:736; *IGI* 9156; Goff S700; Rogledi Manni 940).

140. Cf. the Pavian imprint Johannes Campegius Bononiensis, *Tractatus de iure dotum ad Ciccum Simonetam ducalem secretarium* of 1477, recorded in Siro Comi, *Memorie bibliografiche per la storia della tipografia Pavese del secolo XV* (Pavia: Bolzani, 1807), 11; H 4294; *GW* 9455; *BMC* 7:1000; *IGI* 2389.

141. Argelati, *Bibliotheca*, 2167. Accorsi is best known for his Greek editions, none of which were dedicated to Cicco Simonetta.

142. Published by Lavagna in 1475 (H *63; *GW* 168; *BMC* 6:701; *IGI* 36; Goff A26; Rogledi Manni 9); cf. Rogledi Manni 10.

143. Published by Lavagna in 1475 (H *5989; *GW* 8047; *BMC* 6:701; *IGI* 3343; Rogledi Manni 365). The dedication to Simonetta persists in the Lavagna edition of March 5, 1476 (H5991 = 5992; *GW* 8052; *IGI* 3346; Goff D63; Rogledi Manni 366), but falls out in the succeeding editions of 1478–1492 by other Milanese printers (Rogledi Manni 367–373).

phoses,[144] Valerius Maximus's *Facta et dicta,*[145] the *Scriptores Historiae Augustae,*[146] and (after the assassination) Ovid's *Opera.*[147] As Simonetta took great interest in his sons' education, these titles—for the most part, advanced fare of the *studia humanitatis*—probably reflect the first secretary's fatherly concerns.[148] But whatever the motivations for Accorsi's repeated dedications, they throw into sharp relief Mombrizio's singular dedication of a paraliturgical work to the first secretary.

Galeazzo Maria would have been a much more logical dedicatee for the *Sanctuarium,* and not just by virtue of status. Given his attention to art and music in the ducal chapels at his castles in Milan and Pavia, the duke may have been nursing for some years a plan for new liturgical books.[149] Galeazzo Maria had a well-documented gift for all the varieties of ideological imposition and may even have envisioned replacing the traditional legendaries of the regional churches, monasteries, and convents around Milan. Still more intriguing is the possibility that Mombrizio's *Sanctuarium* began as a textual collection paralleling and supporting Galeazzo Maria's reliquary collection. At least two hundred of these relics, distributed into *capsette,* or ampoules, were to be inserted into an enormous *ancona,* or roodscreen, planned for the castle chapel at Pavia.[150] There is,

144. Published by Lavagna in 1475 (H 12157; *BMC* 6:701; *IGI* 7114; Goff O178; Rogledi Manni 736).

145. Published by Zarotto in 1475 (H *15777; *BMC* 6:713; *IGI* 10059; Goff V27; Rogledi Manni 1059; Ganda, *I primordi,* # 41); cf. Rogledi Manni 1060–1063, without the dedication to Simonetta.

146. Published by Lavagna in 1475 (H *14561; *BMC* 6:702; *IGI* 8847; Goff S340; Rogledi Manni 904).

147. Published by Zarotto on September 11, 1477 (Rogledi Manni 716); cf. Ganda, *I primordi,* # 64.

148. See nn. 152–153 below on the library lists.

149. Evelyn S. Welch, "Sight, Sound and Ceremony in the Chapel of Galeazzo Maria Sforza," *Early Music History* 12 (1993): 151–190, makes a point of "the sums which Galeazzo Maria was willing to invest in his chapel" (153) and gives several examples of his attention to liturgical accoutrements, including books, for both chapels. She overemphasizes his dislike of humanists; the new duke simply cleared out his father's men in as many venues as he could (Leverotti, "Governare," is good on this clearing). Galeazzo Maria liked docile humanists. See also G. D'Adda, *Indagine storiche, artistiche e bibliografiche sulla libreria visconteo-sforzesca del Castello di Pavia* (Milan: Brigola, 1875–1879), 1:127–128 and 2:80–82, recording that twenty-five ducats were spent to make liturgical books for the ducal chapel in 1478. A more specific date would be helpful, but this is, at any rate, *after* the assassination.

150. Evelyn S. Welch, "The Image of a Fifteenth-Century Court: Secular Frescoes for the Castello di Porta Giova, Milan," *Journal of the Warburg and Courtauld Institute* 53 (1990): 163–184, records that after the assassination, "in 1477, Bona of Savoy . . . refused to complete the vast polyptych in the Pavian chapel" (without reference). On the *ancona* and its vicissitudes, the best study remains C. J. Ffoulkes and R. Maiocchi, *Vincenzo Foppa of Brescia, Founder of the Lombard School: His Life and Work* (London, 1909), 93–107. These authors misdate Jacopo Gualla's *Papiae Sanctuarium* (Brescia: J. Britannicus, 1505) to the seventeenth century. But Gualla's work exists, in part, as an inventory of the relics that had

however, no evidence that Mombrizio intended the *Sanctuarium* for the duke. Sense must be made of the dedication to Cicco Simonetta.

Two aspects of Cicco Simonetta as a person with an interest in books are relevant to any estimate of Mombrizio's intentions and Cicco's participation in them.[151] First, three inventories of his library, drawn up at Pavia and Abiategrasso in the 1470s, suggest a pragmatic reader but one with a lively conscience.[152] All the lists include legal and geographical or historical reference books and, for the children, textbooks of grammar and rhetoric.[153] The third inventory, of 1476, is most intimately Cicco's: it lists books kept in a chest in his dressing room. The location is suggestive, although we do not know if he actually read a single one of these books. In his private room at the Pavia retreat, Cicco kept such books as one large

---

been assembled for insertion into the *ancona*. A notary's inventory was one of the formalities involved in their removal from one storage location in the castle at Pavia to another in the Pavia Cathedral. I have not seen a notary's list of the relics intended for the *ancona*.

151. Also relevant is Cicco's part in the introduction of printing in Milan; for example, his signature occurs on letters arranging for Pamfilo de Castaldi to meet Galeazzo Maria, and he himself met with Pamfilo during the early negotiations. See Emilio Motta, "Pamfilo Castaldi—Antonio Planclla: Pietro Ugleimei ed il vescovo d'Aleria. Nuovi documenti per la storia della tipografia in Italia tratti dagli archivi milanesi," *Rivista storica italiana* 1, no. 2 (1884): 266 and 267.

152. Carlo Magenta, *I Visconti e gli Sforza nel Castello di Pavia e loro attinenza con la Certosa e la storia cittadina* (Milan: Hoepli, 1883), 2:343–348, doc. 355, three inventories. The first was drawn up on June 26, 1472, at Pavia (in three parts); the second on March 15, 1472, at "Abia" (i.e., Abiategrasso; also in three parts); and the third on August 24, 1476, at Pavia. Unlike the inventories of 1472 and 1473, which include the children's books, the 1476 inventory lists books kept in Cicco's dressing room at Pavia ("repositi in la camera de le asse verso la strata dove el se veste el prefato domino Cicho" and now moved "nel capsono grande novo" whose key is kept by "Iohanne de Dexo factore").

153. For example, the inventories dated June 26, 1472, and March 15, 1473, parts of which were drawn up by the children's tutor, include Bartolus, Hostiensis, the *Digest*, and the *Decretals*, as well as Cicero on oratory, Martial, Livy, Valla's *Elegancies*, the letter by "Lentulus" describing Christ, Pompeius Sextus, Plautus, Priscian, Virgil, Servius, Ovid, Tortelli's *Orthography*, Donatus on Terence, Terence himself, a *Doctrinale*, Juvenal, Persius, *De Ludo* [*scacchorum*], Gasparino Barzizza's *Regule*, Guarino's *Regule*, Aesop, and so on. Note that one section of this list indicates a set of printed books in ornate matched bindings: "Tucti li soprascripti libri sono in papero facti in stampa et ligati ad uno modo tucti, coperti de coyro rosso, stampati et con broche piatte" (Magenta, *I Visconti*, 344). These books are Tortelli's *Orthographia*, Virgil's *Opera*, Ovid's *Opera*, Servius on Virgil's *Opera*, Cicero's *Familiares*, Valla's *Elegancies*, a complete Priscian in one volume—with the teacher's note that he did not previously have a complete Priscian, or at least not one in this format—Donatus on Terence, and Terence (ibid., 344). As the list was made in early 1473, the information about what was then available in print at Pavia and Milan and the fact that Simonetta intentionally acquired or was given it (to judge from the decision to match bindings) are important. Note as well that only one book in any of these inventories is described as being in Greek, It is the textbook:"IIII quinterneti in grego di Crotimani [*sci.* Erotemata] secondo Chrisorla [Manuele Chrysoloras]." See ibid., 345, in a list of "Libri portati a Pavia per li figlioli de domino Cicho per maistro Augustino de Lonate" (i.e., Honate?).

and one portable Bible; a *De Conceptione Virginis*; a Lactantius (unspecified); a *De Trinitate*, not specified but presumably by Augustine, Ambrose,
or Hilarius;[154] two *Antonine* (one Latin and one vernacular), that is, selec-
tions from Archbishop Antonino Pierozzi's popular *Confessionale*;[155] two
copies of Celso Maffei's *Scrutatorium* "circa la confessione dei peccati"
(one Latin and one vernacular);[156] yet a third book "containing things pertinent to the conscience, that is, to confession" ("continens quedam ad
conscientiam pertinentia, idest de confessione"); and a ceremonial for
blessing rulers, territorial lords, and churches.[157] These titles allow a
glimpse of a first secretary who might have cared to receive the dedication
of a massive collection of saints' lives that was historical in scope, ethical
in content, and useful for liturgical reference.[158]

Second, Cicco Simonetta was deeply involved in the production of official Sforza historiography.[159] In the years preceding the assassination, he
secured the services of Francesco Filelfo, Piercandido Decembrio, Lodrisio
Crivelli, and Giovanni Simonetta, although the authors met with varying
degrees of success. He helped some of them with sources and then evaluated the results with a piercing eye for the Sforza reputation.[160] So we
have, on the one hand, a learned author who took demonstrable care to

154. No editions of the Bible, of *De conceptione virginis*, of Lactantius, or of *De Trinitate*—whether by Ambrose, Augustine, or Hilarius—had been published in Milan by 1476.

155. Possibly Rogledi Manni 78.

156. No edition published in Milan.

157. Magenta, *I Visconti*, 347. On the publication of confessional manuals in Milan, see
Roberto Rusconi, "Manuali milanesi di confessione editi tra il 1474 ed il 1523," *AFH* 65
(1972): 107–156.

158. For further evidence of Simonetta's traditional piety, see Pier Giacomo Pisoni, ed.,
*Un Libro-Cassa per Cicco Simonetta (1478–1479) e altre note del tesoriere Leonardo da
Giussano* (Germignaga: Verbano, 1981). The first entry is for April 22, 1478, the last for September 6, 1479; therefore the account book begins well after the assassination and covers
roughly the year and a half preceding Simonetta's fall. Most striking are monthly payments
for candles supplied to priests saying masses for Cicco (fourteen masses a month seems to be
the norm, although the number occasionally rises to twenty-eight or more) and repeated payments to proxies going to Santa Maria de Loreto. Cicco was having masses said for himself
at several churches in the city, including San Marco (his favorite) and Santa Maria degli Car-
meni. On October 6, 1478, Cicco made a gift of a bound breviary printed on paper to Fra
Tadeo da Vezana "del'ordine de Santa Maria dela Pace" (21). I thank Marcello Simonetta for
notice that, during his year of imprisonment, Cicco read the book of Job.

159. Ianziti, *Humanist Historiography*, is fundamental. He argues that the historiography
was pursued to legitimize the uninvested Galeazzo Maria by demonstrating the legitimacy of
his father, Francesco, also uninvested.

160. Cicco's support, essential to an author's success, was selectively applied: compare his
treatment of Decembrio, on the one hand, and of Giovanni Simoneta, his own brother, on
the other (Ianziti, *Humanist Historiography*, 74–76 and 146). Evidence of Cicco's dedication
to and painstaking care in recording the diplomatic events of his own times is given by P.-M.
Perret, "Le manuscrit de Cicco Simonetta (Manuscrit latin 10133 de la Bibliothèque
nationale)," *Notices et extraits des manuscrits de la Bibliothèque du roi* 34 (1891): 323–368.

place his dedications with those in power and, on the other, a patron who was aware of the pedagogy of the *studia humanitatis* and who took an active, not to say invasive, interest in public writing.

It has been asserted that Mombrizio and Cicco Simonetta were friends.[161] The internal evidence of the two dedicatory poems addressed to Simonetta hardly implies familiarity, but perhaps the men did discuss the *Sanctuarium*. Dedications require delicate handling, of course. Nevertheless, these poems deserve attention as the sole words in the compilation declaredly from Mombrizio's pen. Thus, on the question of friendship, it must be noted that the poems to Simonetta have an abject quality absent from Mombrizio's other dedications. The first poem addresses Simonetta as the wielder of power on an imperial scale by invoking not Milan or even Lombardy but Latium, that is, Rome ("regum Latiae moderator habenae").[162] The chancellor controls ingress and egress, Mombrizio says, and is in a position to return peace to the world.[163] The final line, in which Mombrizio begs permission to "cherish [his] Maecenas," suggests that the chancellor made or was expected to make a financial contribution to the collection.[164] The allusive promise that Simonetta would find something pleasing in the collection ("Inuenies aliquid quod et inuenisse iuuabit") is too vague to support an argument about the nature of the contents.[165]

The final dedicatory poem to Simonetta poses similar problems of interpretation. It opens with an apology:

Forgive the metals gathered to write these things,
   Forgive them. You see, a great enough work is extant.
Nor think to ask me, nor to imagine yourself,
   Taking up these books, whence all these things came.
It is enough that, in the end, all be credited to my Cicco. [166]

---

161. In A. G. Spinelli, "Carmen in morte di Cico Simonetta," *ASL* 2, 12, 3 (1885): 515, mildly defending his attribution of the "Carmen" to Mombrizio.

162. Cf. "Latiae diffisus habenae," in Silius Italicus, 13, 34, and Aulus Gellius 14, 1, 4; and Lucretius 2, 1096. A similar phrase in Ovid, *Metamorphoses*, 15, 481, "populi Latialis habenas," refers to Numa, perhaps significant in this liturgical context.

163. "Ciche potens rerum, rerum quo cardine postes / Claudere nunc aditum, nunc aperire solent / Tu potest optatae mundo commercia pacis / Reddere. Tu valida cogere bella manu. / Mars tamen Italia vacat Erigoneaque caelo / Saturno rursus cum sene lapsa reddit." Mombrizio 1910, 1:10.

164. The subjunctive rather than indicative mood governs the second line of the poem, as Mombrizio invites Cicco "mei tutor sis, sine labe ducis." Ibid.

165. The poem concludes: "Est aliquid quod te legisse per otia malim / Sanctorum vitas maxima gesta virum. / Invenies aliquid quod et invenisse iuvabit. / Nil Cicho fateor dignius esse meo." Ibid.

166. "Parcite compositis haec ad scribenda metallis, / Parcite. Sat magnum, cernitis, extat opus / Nec mihi iam queri, nec uobis omnia fingi / Undelibet sumptis posse putate libris. / Dum satis ista meo tandem sint credita Cicho." Mombrizio 1910, 2:653.

Mombrizio's concern that the multiply reproduced object not offend his dedicatee suggests that Simonetta had nothing to do with the decision to print the *Sanctuarium* and expected, or would have preferred, to receive the compilation in manuscript.[167] If Cicco did patronize the edition, then his contribution probably did not take the form of a speculative sharing in a publishing syndicate, such as would be documented in notarial sources. In addition, the third and fourth lines of this difficult poem suggest that Mombrizio collected the sources for his compilation without help from the chancellor. The existence of a dedication does not, of course, entail the patron's participation in the making of the gift. But no client would risk neglect or reprisal by inappropriately dedicating a work to a patron who was uninterested or hostile. On the basis of what we know about Mombrizio as an alert entrepreneur in the printing world and as a careful director of dedications both in manuscript and print, we can surmise that the *Sanctuarium* was not a complete surprise to the first secretary. But if such an enormous legendary had been compiled with Simonetta's engaged participation and guidance, then the two dedicatory poems to the first secretary would likely be less abject, distant, and apologetic, and the editor would have been careful to thank the first secretary for his help with manuscript sources.

The second dedicatory poem, the one "to any reader," *Ad quemlibet lectorem*, reveals quite another aspect of the production. Here, Mombrizio joins the centuries' long discussion of the place of the classics in Christian education.

> Reader, you seek in this volume the fodder
> That may feed and nourish the snowy flock of Christ.
> Let others recite fables and with elegant trifles
> Waste the days bestowed for better things,
> Or narrate to themselves the Decii dead for their fatherland,
> And the one who freely burnt his hand in the hungry flame.
> We believe that Christ and his generals, most clear lights
> For the world, are more worthy to be read.[168]

---

167. Cf. Borso d'Este's preference for manuscript books, described by Martin Lowry, "Cristoforo Valdarfer tra politici veneziani e cortigiani estensi," in Amadeo Quondam, ed., *Il libro a corte* (Rome: Bulzoni, 1994), 273–284. Cicco, too, might have been an antiprinting snob to whom some tactical dedications of printed works were made. In light of the Buono Accorsi dedications and the children's bound set of printed textbooks (see n. 153 above), it may be that Cicco thought print fine for schoolbooks.

168. "Queris in hoc quae sit farrago volumine, lector / Quae niueum Christi pascat alatque gregem. / Fabellas alii recitent nugisque decoris / Largitos perdant ad meliora dies, / Aut sibi pro patria Decios occumbere narrant / Quique libens auido coxit in igne manum. / Nos Christum Christique duces, clarissima mundi / Lumina, credidimus dignius esse legi." Mombrizio 1910, 1:10–11.

I have noted in the preceding chapter the use of Roman military models in humanist *passiones*; such references were not uncommon in the final quarter of the fifteenth century. And I will show in the next chapter how the place of saints' lives as worthy reading matter exercised Aldo Manuzio at the end of the Quattrocento, just as it had Coluccio Salutati and Giovanni Dominici at the beginning. The arguments may seem weary to us now— all those manuscript and incunable copies of Basil's *De legendis* in Bruni's translation![169]—but for the disputants each sally was invigorating precisely to the degree that it implicated particular schools, teachers, and students: in short, local urban livelihoods.

Or even lives. In the wake of the assassination, the republican associations of the murderers were much discussed. "Republicanism" helped contemporaries make sense of the event, just as "tyranny" provided a historical context by which to evaluate Galeazzo Maria (his contemporaries all knew the neologism *tiranizzare*). Historians today do not argue that the humanist Cola da Montano caused the assassination by teaching classical texts.[170] But Cola's student, the assassin Olgiati, introduced this charge, and his contemporaries seized on its explanatory power. Mombrizio himself, in the poem entitled *Trenodia* (quoted in the epigraph to this section and discussed below), set out the widely held perception that Olgiati had learned his republican sentiments as a defenseless child at school. Studying, as Mombrizio's readers would have known, under Cola da Montano, young Olgiati was taught to appreciate classical history ("repetens de more vestutas historias") and especially the figure of Brutus, the assassin

169. James Hankins, *Renaissance Civic Humanism: Reappraisals and Reflections* (New York: Cambridge University Press, 2001), 147, notes that more than 440 manuscripts and 91 printed editions of Basil's treatise are known. Filippo da Lavagna's ca. 1474 Milan edition of *Ad adolescentes* (H 2693; GW 3703; IGI 1414; Rogledi Manni 151) seems to have been published without Vergerio's treatise, *De ingenuis moribus,* but it appears that all subsequent versions in Milan and elsewhere in Italy (in contrast to the north) were bound with Vergerio. I have not confirmed this hypothesis by examining all the extant editions. Cf. the practice of the humanist schoolteacher Giorgio Antonio Vespucci, of regularly inscribing his pre-Christian texts with an excerpted phrase from *De legendis* as if to sanitize the material. Further exploration of this ritual usage by other humanists would be interesting.

170. Cola does not make an appearance in the structural analysis of Leverotti, "Governare." Cf. Corio, *Storia*, 3:304: Girolamo Olgiati's confession opens with remarks on how Cola influenced his opinion of the duke by encouraging the young man not to be servile but to bear in mind "quamplurimorum atheniensium carthaginensium et romanorum vestigia, imitando quos pro patria fortissime facientes fuisse laudem eternam consequtos aiebat." Olgiati alleged that Cola took advantage of his student's youth in this instance: "Itaque per longum spacium eo die ipse talia recitante forte prospiciens me ut tenellus eram faciliter ad voluntatem suam inclinatum me dimisit, pollicitusque est multa alia pulcherrima alias narrare, tantummodo tacite ad virtutem et animi fortitudinem, Hieronyme mi, dixit, persevera, eo tum talem de ipso preceptore fidem habebam habuique magis ut ita dicam verbis ejus quam evangelio fidem."

of Caesar whom Dante had placed in the lowest circle of hell.[171] Outsiders appreciated the republican references, too: the Mantuan ambassador, for example, reported that Lampugnani's *differentia* with those in power had driven him to organize a conspiracy "in the manner of Catiline" ("de modi di Catilina").[172] Like the ambassador, contemporaries in the princely cities of the peninsula understood that classicizing teachers—laymen most culpably—formed impressionable young people according to republican ideals and that children who received such educations might well grow up to put the peace of those cities at risk. There was an obvious corollary: an education based on Christian grammatical and rhetorical texts would not have this effect. As Machiavelli would darkly observe, Christians were politically passive.[173]

Mombrizio, in the dedicatory poem to the reader, names two classical exemplars, the Decii and Mucius Scaevola,[174] whom he denigrates as trivialities, fashionable fables, outdone both in numbers and in accomplishments by the Christian saints collected in the *Sanctuarium*. The point is clichéd in the extreme. The pagan exemplars—and these ones in particular—had a busy afterlife in the *quanto magis* comparative tropes that littered the prefaces to medieval and Renaissance *vitae et passiones sanctorum*.[175] In post-assassination Milan, these classical exemplars were powerful because they were still more suspect, not because of their pagan but because of their republican significance.[176] Such identifications may account for the elementary and overstated terms of the second dedicatory

171. Bonino Mombrizio, *Trenodia*, sign. cIv, 7–14: "cur est adeo crudelibus inquis / moribus : impubis quem vis adoleverit aetas? / Digna rogas. studium certe tam nobile miror / Infami sordere luto : deceptus ab ipsis sensibus est : ut qui repetens de more vetustas / Historias : teneris & adhuc sit iunior annis / Aemula Romanis audax cognomina Brutis / Vindicat : & tantum patria differre fatetur." At sign. c2, Mombrizio adduces the economic motives of another conspirator, Giovanni Andrea Lampugani; cf. Belotti, *Il dramma*, 92, for Lampagnani's wish merely to frighten the duke.

172. A. Bertolotti, "Spedizioni militari in Piemonte sconosciute o poco note di Galeazzo Maria Sforza duca di Milano," *ASL* 10, no. 3 (1883): at 637–638, transcribes the document.

173. *Discorsi*, book 2, chap. 2. Twenty to forty years after the assassination, Machiavelli's friendships with Guicciardini and Soderini must have given him plenty of opportunity for informed discussions of the Milanese crisis, because members of those families had held honorary appointments (which is not to say any power) in the Milanese government under Galeazzo Maria Sforza.

174. Muzio Attendolo, the *condottiere* who was Francesco Sforza's father, had been cast as "Mucius," and a fanciful genealogy had been developed to make him a descendent of the Scaevola; it is unlikely that Mombrizio intended any reference to this fantasy.

175. On this comparison and the tension between pagan and Christian exemplars, see chap. 2 above.

176. For example, the Ambrosian Republic (1447–1450) had as one of its founding fathers Oldrado Lampugnani, who died a "martyr," executed when rule passed to the *popolo* (Bellotti, *Il dramma*, 77, quoting Enea Silvio Piccolomini).

poem.[177] Mombrizio, as the author of *De dominica passione,* the editor of the Gospel of Nicodemus, the author of the *Bucolica,* the translator of Hesiod, and the editor of Statius, hardly needed to mention classical exemplars at all in his capacity as "the last medieval collector of saints' legends," that is, the maker of a compilation that was not a set of aggressively classicizing revisions but an anthology constructed from traditional texts.[178]

Mombrizio's poem to the reader also reveals the distance between his intended audience and the audience envisioned by Jacobus de Voragine in the thirteenth century for the *Legenda aurea.* That is not to say that Jacobus wrote for a religious and Mombrizio for a secular audience—far from it. The surviving copies of the *Sanctuarium* that have near-contemporary purchase notes indicate an audience of regulars, whether in monasteries, convents, or cathedral chapters. But by the 1470s, more and more of those clerics, priests, canons, monks, and friars would have had at least some inkling of the *studia humanitatis.* By both recognizing and rejecting the classical precedents, Mombrizio made his poem effective and his collection valuable, whether a reader approved or disapproved of education in the classics for members of orders. The collection itself, insofar as it presented texts that had been spared humanist intervention, would have been recognized as traditional and conservative.

To understand the tone of the poem to the reader, it will also help to bear in mind the delicate positions held by humanist educators in cities such as Florence, Venice, Rome, and Milan. Like his friend Pier Candido Decembrio, who came under the prince's suspicion in 1473, Mombrizio was a layman.[179]

---

177. Cf. the verses by the Benedictine Ilarione Lantieri, following the index in *Legendarium nonnullorum sanctorum abbreviatum supplementum illius de Voragine secundum kalendarium Monasticum* (H 8661; IGI 4776; Rogledi Manni 501), which was printed in Milan in 1494, about seventeen years after the *Sanctuarium,* explicitly to provide the Benedictines with a more comprehensive legendary:

Multorum Vitas, mores, & nomina, Lector,
Sanctorum, nostri cerne laboris ope.
Non musas, non falsa Deum cunabula canto,
Nec uanas latebras his Heliconis habes;
Nil fictis inseritur, tantum obseruatio facti
Panditur, ut ueterum pagina certa docet.

178. Gerhard Eis, *Die Quellen für das "Sanctuarium" des mailander Humanisten Boninus Mombritius: Eine Untersuchung zur Geschichte der grossen Legendensammlungen des Mittelalters* (Berlin: Ebering, 1933), 15: Mombrizio is "der letzte grosse Legendensammler des Mittelalters." Cf. Boesch Gajano, "Dai leggendari medioevali," 227: it is probably neither the last of the medieval legendaries nor the first of the modern ones.

179. For Galeazzo Maria's suspicions about Decembrio, see Belotti, *Il dramma,* 46. On the friendship between Decembrio and Mombrizio, see M. Borsa, "Pier Candido Decembrio e l'umanesimo in Lombardia," *ASL* 2, no. 20 (1893): 413–414. Cf. the Venetian suspicion of Paul of Venice as the organizer of a cult of professorial personality, discussed by Bruno Nardi, "Letteratura e cultura veneziana del Quattrocento," in *La civiltà veneziana del quattrocento*

His bureaucratic appointments suggest that he was relatively powerful (the dunning letter to Galeazzo Maria, noted above, is not shy). Employed in the Office of Extraordinary Accounts, he was implicated in the regime's injustices in a way that would make it difficult for him to find safe ground as factional politics grew heated over 1477–78. His work with many Milanese printers, his self-identification as a humanist, and his close connections to the court are strong evidence that he would have known the republican Cola da Montano and members of the assassin's family, the Lampugnani. In the wake of the assassination, such a man might find it wise to assert publicly and under the auspices of Cicco Simonetta that civic virtues derived not from the ethics of republican Rome—the Rome in which tyrants were assassinated and orators such as Cicero were martyred for their learned ideals—but from the authentically Christian figures of the saints.[180]

It rarely possible to make definitive arguments on the basis of dedicatory verse, and I do not claim to do so in this instance. Nevertheless, it would be negligent to avoid addressing these three poems. In the present state of research, they are the only evidence we have for Mombrizio's thoughts about the *Sanctuarium*.

❖ ❖ ❖

Gratam materiam rerumque vocabula late
Exibit, exhibitis non minus ordo placet.

(Papias) offers engaging matter and a range of words for things,

and the order pleases no less than what is offered.

—Bonino Mombrizio, editor of Papias, *Vocabularium* [181]

(Florence: Sansoni, 1957): 99–146. On Francesco Filelfo's cult of personality during his teaching at Florence and its associated republican ideology, see Arthur Field, "Leonardo Bruni, Florentine Traitor? Bruni, the Medici, and an Aretine Conspiracy of 1437," *RQ* 51, no. 4 (1998): 1120 and n. 46.

180. Cf. the case of Gabriele Paveri Fontana, one of the group of humanists associated both with the branch of the University of Pavia operating at the Milanese court and with the "republican" pedagogue Cola da Montano through early printing ventures. On February 20, 1477, not two months after the assassination, Paveri Fontana was dismissed from his position as *corrector* for the joint publications of Marco da Roma and Antonio Zarotto. It was probably early in the very next month that he printed his own commemorative volume on Galeazzo Maria's death (n. 215 below). Ganda observes of the dismissal, "se ne ignora il motivo" ("Marco Roma," 110). But it is not beyond possibility that the reason was political and that Paveri Fontana intended his commemorative volume as a self-rehabilitation. If so, his case of implicit guilt would parallel that of Mombrizio, discussed below.

181. So concludes Mombrizio's poem to the reader at the head of his 1476 edition of Papias, *Vocabularium*, published in Milan by Vespolate (n. 75 above; nn. 187–188 below).

TABLE 3.1.   Mombrizio's *Sanctuarium* by Month*

Month (saints)	Number of Entries	from LA	from SH
November (Martinus to Andreas)	15 (12)	1	2
December (Bibiana to Sylvester)	25 (14)	0	8
January (Concordius to Iulius sacerdos)	37 (20)	3	14
February (Brigida to Matthias)	13 (16)	1	2
March (Herculanus to Regulus)	11 (9)	1	3
April (Abundius to Donatus episcopus)	20 (11)	3	3
May (Philippus to Sisinnius et socii)	24 (18)	0	5
June (Erasmus to Sirus)	30 (16)	2	6
July (Processus et socius to Germanus)	32 (22)	2	3
August (Eusebius Ver. to Felix & Adauctus)	48 (27)	2	10
September (Lupus episcopus to Jerome)	31 (18)	3	6
October (Remigius to Quintinus)	29 (13)	4	8
November (Benignus to Theodorus martyr)	8 (6)	0	3
TOTAL	323 (202)	22	73

* Months assigned according to feastdates of the Roman Martyrology (with ref. to Frei's edition of the *Sanctorale* and to the *Liber notitiae sanctorum mediolanensium, LNSM*). Parentheses in the second column indicate the number of entries for that month in the calendar pages of the Roman use missal copied by Fra Ignatius of Milan for the Augustinian Hermits of S. Maria Incoronata in 1476. On San Marino, Huntington Library, MS HM 1068, see C. S. Dutschke, *Guide to Medieval and Renaissance Manuscripts in the Huntington Library* (San Marino, Calif.: Huntington Library, 1989), 2:313–316. The calendar is at fols. 1–6v; I count all primary entries in contemporary hands.

The actual printing of the *Sanctuarium* should not be confused with the planning that, to some degree, must have preceded it. The size of the collection demonstrates that Mombrizio aimed at a certain comprehensiveness. Table 3.1 groups the *Sanctuarium* texts loosely into the traditional liturgical presentation by month (columns 3 and 4 record how many texts reproduce entries in the thirteenth-century compilations *Legenda aurea* [LA] and *Speculum historiale* [SH]).[182] The list begins with the feast of St. Martin of Tours on 11 November because that is the traditional start of the Ambrosian Calendar.

182. Mombritius 1910 notes seventy-three accounts drawn more or less precisely from *SH* and twenty-two from *LA*. Germani duo and Therenus are not in *LNSM* and not counted here. The standard Milanese and Roman feast dates that have governed my distribution of saints throughout the months may not have been the dates on which these saints were celebrated in any given Milanese parish, such as Mombrizio's own St. Maurilius. The breakdown in the table is unlikely to match local practice perfectly. Comparison to the Roman use missal is a similarly imprecise tool, but it underlines the variable nature of the calendar.

Any church's calendar will show an imbalanced distribution of saints, month by month, although Mombrizio's collection reveals a striking range from fifty entries for August to nine entries for March. We cannot know if the unbalanced distribution was intentional or if it represents work left incomplete, but, in either case, the *Sanctuarium* as we have it must have been tremendously time-consuming to prepare. Working alone (especially if we assume that he was searching through manuscripts for texts similar in value to his tenth-century Avienus), Mombrizio could not have assembled such a variety of saintly narratives in a month's or, for that matter, a year's trawl through the Duomo library.[183] If he searched outside the Duomo—at the recently inventoried Bobbio library, for instance—then still more preparation time would have been required.[184] And if some of these texts were revised throughout, however lightly (say, just with regard to orthography), then we probably need to posit several months, if not years, as an absolute minimum before the printing.

But in the wake of the assassination, even work painstakingly begun might have been hastily concluded and earlier plans reconsidered under the pressure of events. Perhaps the order of the collection reflects such a scenario. Argelati's brief report on the fifteenth-century manuscript of the *Sanctuarium* reveals that the texts were originally set out "in a different order, and with several words changed, too. [The codex] begins with St. Martin the bishop [f.d. November 11], then follows as given: 'Passion of saint Romanus, priest and martyr [f.d. November 18], of Clement martyr and bishop [f.d. November 23], of Andrew the Apostle [f.d. November 30], of Nicholas bishop and confessor [f.d. December 6], the life of saint Ambrose bishop and confessor [f.d. December 7].'"[185] I have added feast dates to the precious excerpt, to show that in the lost manuscript the saints were arranged according to the liturgical calendar (as given in the list of saints per month above). But the printed *Sanctuarium* does not follow that layout. For all its attention to tradi-

---

183. Did Francesco della Croce, librarian at the Duomo, take an interest in the *Sanctuarium*? In a letter of March 28, 1473, della Croce, who had been vicar to Francesco Pizzolpasso, told Galeazzo Maria Sforza of his desire for a better-educated clergy that had passed through good schools; see Mirella Ferrari, "Un bibliothecario milanese del quattrocento: Francesco della Croce," *Archivio ambrosiano* 42 (1982): 179–181.

184. Mirella Ferrari, "Segnalibri del secolo XV in codici Bobbiesi," *IMU* 12 (1969): 325. BAV, MS Vat. lat. 5771 is a ninth-century Bobbio Passionary said to be the source of Mombrizio's account of Sirus. If Mombrizio did use this manuscript for Syrus, he or his workshop made spelling corrections and slight rearrangements of phrasing (cf. Katherine of Alexandria, below). See N. Everett, "The Earliest Recension of the Life of S. Sirus," *Studi medievali* 3, 43, 2 (2002): 857–957.

185. Argelati, in Mombritius 1910, xxvi.

tional texts, the imprint presents the saints in an untraditional alphabetical order.[186]

This principle of organization might seem, at first glance, to be good evidence about Mombrizio's intentions for his transcriptions. After all, alphabetical order is often perceived as objective and impartial, the sign of developing rationalization in the ordering of knowledge. Moreover, Mombrizio seems to have appreciated this rationalization himself. As I have mentioned, before the *Sanctuarium*, Mombrizio had produced in contract with Domenico Vespolate the *Vocabulista*, or *Elementarium doctrinae rudimentum*, of Papias.[187] Not only did this edition give Mombrizio the opportunity to consider the techniques and the utility of alphabetization, but also the couplet from his poem to the reader (given in the epigraph to this section) indicates that he saw alphabetization as a potential selling point, for that work at least.[188]

Perhaps Mombrizio meant to create a comparable reference work by alphabetizing the narratives in the *Sanctuarium*. This possibility is supported by the evidence of the signature system, which is itself alphabetized (proceeding "a, aa, aaa, aaaa . . . ," "b, bb, bbb, bbbb . . . ," etc.), similar to Adolf Rusch's signature system in the glossed Bible printed at Strasbourg in 1480/1481.[189] Unlike Rusch, however, Mombrizio linked his sig-

186. Dolbeau, "Les prologues," 386 n. 154, notes that fifteenth-century manuscripts of the liturgically ordered *Sanctilogium Angliae* of John of Tynemouth (ca. 1350), have been rearranged into alphabetical order. He proposes alphabetical order, along with "a return, insofar as possible, to complete texts" (rather than abbreviated ones) as part of the "solution" Mombrizio offered to the problem of swelling legendaries that featured reworked texts, such as that by Petrus Calo.

187. See V. de Angelis, ed., *Papiae Elementarium: Littera A* (Milan: Cisalpina-Goliardica, 1977).

188. On Papias as a milestone in the history of alphabetization, see M. A. Rouse and R. H. Rouse, "*Statim invenire*: Schools, Preachers, and New Attitudes to the Page," in *Authentic Witnesses: Approaches to Medieval Texts and Manuscripts* (Notre Dame: University of Notre Dame Press, 1991), 193–194; idem, "*Ordinatio* and *compilatio* Revisited," in M. D. Jordan and K. Emery Jr., eds., *Ad litteram: Authoritative Texts and Their Medieval Readers* (Notre Dame: University of Notre Dame Press, 1992), at 122 and 126–127; and further bibliography in n. 193 below. De Angelis, *Papiae Elementarium*, xviii–xx, records—significantly for any estimate of Mombrizio as a reliable editor—that a gathering has been inadvertently dropped from the *princeps* and that there are many cases "di manifesta interpolazione mombriciana," "abbastanza pesante" but exhibited "in modo discontinuo" so that sometimes obvious errors are left uncorrected. I have not confirmed de Angelis's description.

189. I thank Paul Needham for calling my attention to the signature system of Adolf Rusch's glossed Bible; see Karlfried Froelich and Margaret T. Gibson, ed., *Biblia Latina cum Glossa ordinaria: Facsimile Reprint of the Editio Princeps, Adolph Rusch of Strassburg, 1480/81*, 4 vols. (Turnhout: Brepols, 1992); and the overview by Karlfried Froelich, "An Extraordinary Achievement: The *Glossa ordinaria* in Print," in K. Van Kampen and P. Saenger, eds., *The Bible as Book: The First Printed Editions* (London: British Library, 1999), 15–22.

natures to the content of the imprint, matching "A" saints to "a" signatures, "B" saints to "b" signatures, and so forth. Thus, again unlike the case of Rusch's glossed Bible, Mombrizio's signatures would support the use of the *Sanctuarium* as a reference work; running titles, of course, would have been the traditional way to support that usage.[190] Or perhaps, by putting the saints in alphabetical order rather than in the order of the Roman or Ambrosian liturgies, Mombrizio meant to increase the universal appeal of his text. This tactic would be good for sales in a competitive market, which is an aspect of book production that we know this editor appreciated.[191] There is a third possibility. By putting the saints in alphabetical order, Mombrizio avoided having to choose between presenting them according to the Roman or Ambrosian liturgical calendar. In Milan, the Ambrosian order would have republican implications; a Roman order, in consequence, would not be neutral.[192] These three possibilities are not mutually exclusive.

The *Sanctuarium* is the first alphabetized legendary in print. But alphabetized legendaries in manuscript were not unknown. Already in the thir-

190. This signature system had a cost. In order to fit their alphabetized gatherings, the narratives' rate of abbreviation sometimes rises sharply toward the end of a gathering. At the other extreme, final columns are sometimes left unfilled. One text, Nicasius (*BHL* 6079), is left incomplete: some readers wrote out the conclusion of the entry; in the eighteenth century, two different tipped-in sheets were designed to correct the lack.

191. I thank Robert Babcock for pointing out to me that alphabetization might encourage sales; I am also indebted to him for help with the Beinecke copy of the *Sanctuarium*.

192. The hypothesis that liturgical order had political meaning may be borne out by Milan's publication history during this period. It is possible that no service books for the Ambrosian rite were published between 1477 and 1479, when the postassassination regime directed by Cicco collapsed. The two possible exceptions are undated. One, the *Litaniae secundum ordinem Ambrosianum*, printed by Arcangelus Ungardus in Milan (H 10121; *IGI* 5767; Rogledi Manni 570), is assigned the *terminus ante quem* of November 1476 by *BMC* 6:734–735. Cf. Carlo Marcora, "Stefano Nardini, arcivescovo di Milano, 1461–84," *Memorie storiche della diocesi di Milano* 3 (1956): 318, proposing 1475, a date taken up by Ganda, "La prima edizione," 102 n. 20. The second, the *Rituale Ambrosianum* attributed to Pachel and Scinzenzeler (*IGI* 8382), is dated to around 1478 by Rogledi Manni 863 on the basis of M. Magistretti, "Di due edizione sconosciute del rituale dei sacramenti secondo il rito ambrosiano," in *Miscellanea Ceriani: Raccolta di scritti originali per onerare la memoria di M.r. Antonio Maria Ceriani* (Milan: Hoepli, 1910), 88–120. It may, therefore, contradict the hypothesis.

193. E.g., London, BL, MS Add. 41070, a legendary compiled by a thirteenth-century Franciscan for Dominican use. Alphabetical format, long familiar in medical compilations, was extended in the thirteenth century to collections of *exempla* and of heresies, and thence to legendaries; see H. G. Pfander, "The Medieval Friars and Some Alphabetical Reference-Books for Sermons," *Medium Aevum* 3 (1934): 19–29; L. C. MacKinney, "Medieval Medical Dictionaries and Glossaries," in J. L. Cate and E. N. Anderson, eds., *Medieval and Historiographical Essays in Honor of James Westfall Thompson* (Chicago: University of Chicago Press, 1938), 240–268; M. B. Parkes, "The Influence of the Concepts of *ordinatio* and *compilatio* on the Development of the Book," in J. J. G. Alexander and M. T. Gibson, eds., *Medieval Learning and Literature: Essays Presented to Richard William Hunt* (Oxford: Clarendon Press, 1976), 132; Guy Philippart, *Les Légendiers latins et autres manuscrits*

teenth century such collections of notices about saints were being made.[193] One of these, the *Liber notitiae sanctorum mediolani*, a topographical encyclopedia of Milanese saints, their churches, altars, and relics, had entered the library of the Duomo around 1450, and so was available as a model.[194] So perhaps more noteworthy than recourse to alphabetical order per se in the *Sanctuarium* is Mombrizio's evident lack of concern for the perfection of that order. Papias, which Mombrizio had edited immediately before the *Sanctuarium*, had alphabetized to the third letter; in the *Sanctuarium*, however, there are series that barely apply the rigor of the alphabet beyond the first letter of each saint's name.[195] The twenty-three entries under the letter "I" are a good example. The first three saints are named Iacobus and are reasonably organized, but another Iacobus occurs in twenty-second place. The bishop Innocentius, in sixth place, is preceded by one Iohannes and followed by four. Then come two Iustinas, before Inventius and Ionius at fourteenth and fifteenth place. In fact, there are two entries for the confessor Inventius (Viventius, of Burgundy; surely Iuventius of Pavia is expected). He is the only saint who is repeated in the *Sanctuarium* with nearly identical entries; but they are separated by seven intervening ones.[196]

Perhaps some Quattrocento editors were incapable of grasping in a thoroughgoing way the combination of saints, on the one hand, and alphabetization, on the other. It is difficult, however, to argue that Mom-

hagiographiques (Turnhout: Brepols, 1977), 44 and 81; R. H. Rouse, "La diffusion en occident au XIIIe siècle des outils de travail facilitant l'accès aux textes autoritifs," in *L'Enseignement en Islam et en Occident au Moyen Age* (Paris, 1978), 113–147; J.-C. Schmitt, H. Bremond, and J. Le Goff, *L'Exemplum* (Brepols: Turnhout, 1982), 60–61; Carlo Delcorno, *Exemplum e letteratura tra Medioevo e Rinascimento* (Bologna: Il Mulino, 1989), 15 and n. 39; Ana Maria Mussons, "Estudio del *Recull de exemples y miracles per alfabeto*," in *Literatura medieval: Actos do IV congresso da associaçao hispanica de literatura medieval* (Lisbon, 1993), 2:105–110.

194. The *Liber*, attributed to Goffredo da Bussero, is extant in Milan, Biblioteca del capitolo metropolitano, MS II. E.2.8 (not seen) and edited by Marco Magistretti and Ugo Monneret de Villard, *Liber notitiae sanctorum mediolani: Manoscritto della Biblioteca* (Milan: Allegretti, 1917). See also the brief entry by Mirella Ferrari in Marco Navoni, ed., *Dizionario di liturgia ambrosiana* (Milan: NED, 1996), 267–270; Dolbeau, "Les prologues," 377–378; and E. Cattaneo in the Treccani *Storia di Milano* III, 751–754. The alphabetical order may be a precocious fourteenth-century "improvement" to the thirteenth-century compilation.

195. Cf. not only the edition of Papias (which includes entries for Andrew, Bartholomew, John the Baptist, and Stephen properly alphabetized to the third letter) but also—in connection with Mombrizio's legal training—the *Supplementum* by Nicholas of Osimo, published in Milan in 1479 (*BMC* VI, 746; *IGI* 6876; Goff N69; Rogledi Manni 701), a well-alphabetized list of legal terms, with a well-alphabetized guide to legal abbreviations in the back.

196. Mombrizio 1910, 2:80–81 and 90; cf. Everett, "Earliest Recension," on Iuventius of Pavia.

brizio shared that incapacity. First, he was the appreciative editor of Papias; the epigraph given at the head of this section emphasizes the virtues of Papias's alphabetical order. Second, he was a man with two law degrees, and therefore accustomed to thoroughly alphabetized legal indices. He could have encouraged a better presentation.

This problem cannot be solved in the current state of our knowledge. Perhaps the loose alphabetization of the *Sanctuarium* indicates that Mombrizio did not think that priests needed the sort of strict alphabetical order useful to lawyers or dictionary users.[197] Or perhaps it indicates that Mombrizio had nothing to do with the decisions about signatures (which are primarily instructions for workmen assembling the book) or alphabetized texts: composition units may have been alphabetized at different workshops with different capacities for the book at hand. Or perhaps, as the doubled entry for the unlikely saint Inventius suggests, it indicates haste and carelessness all round.

The imperfect alphabetization does have some strange effects, most notably at the opening of the collection. According to strict alphabetical principles, the martyrs Abdon and Senen should be in first place; instead, they come fourth. If alphabetization were intentionally loose, St. Martin, representing the start of the Ambrosian liturgical year, or St. Peter, representing the commanding place of Rome, might appear as the first entry. But Martin and Peter are tucked into their respective alphabetical slots. A semialphabetized collection put together in Milan might well open with the city's patron, Ambrose, representative of the city's ancient Christianity. Ambrose was difficult, however. Even before the assassination, a collection that led off with Ambrose would have evoked the republic. As it happens, Ambrose is rather

---

197. Cf. Novara, Bibl. capitolare del Duomo, MS XCII, an alphabetized *Dizionario dei santi padri* compiled by an anonymous cleric for the bishop of Novara, Giovanni Arcimboldo (1468–1473; then cardinal; d. 1488). I am grateful to the keeper of manuscripts at the Duomo for permission to examine the manuscript. According to the preface, it was Arcimboldo who requested alphabetical order and suggested the model of Festus's collection of Virgilian vocabulary.

198. The entry for Ambrose raises a further problem: Argelati's report on the manuscript describes the account of Ambrose there as much longer than the one included in the printed *Sanctuarium*. Still, Mombrizio's printed account of Ambrose (*BHL* 377) is not negligible: at around 6,200 words, it is longer than those of the comparable figures Augustine (ca. 4,100 words; *BHL* 792) and Jerome (ca. 2,700 words; *BHL* 3871b), although shorter than the account of Martin, taken from Sulpicius Severus (ca. 20,500 words). The *vita Ambrosii* in manuscript must have quite expansive. Pier Candido Decembrio composed a life of Ambrose in 1463–1468, as a counterblast to a minor *vita* translated from the Greek by Guarino (*BHL* 379). In November 1466 Decembrio wrote to the canon of the Duomo in Milan, Francesco de la Croce, harshly criticizing Guarino's *vita Ambrosii* (Argelati in Sassi, *Historia*, col. cxlix). To this same letter, Decembrio attached a preface that he had published at Genoa in a "Missa B. Ambrosii" (unidentified). Then, in 1468, Decembrio wrote from Ferrara to Francesco Marescalchi, mentioning that he had worked on the *vita* for three years; see Carlo de' Rosmini,

well alphabetized, in fifteenth place among the "A" saints.[198] Some humanist authors, making compilations, opened with the Virgin.[199] She is not represented at all in the *Sanctuarium* (legendaries typically included Marian feasts; martyrologies typically did not). Instead, the honor of leading off the collection, of appearing next to the dedicatory poems to Cicco Simonetta and to the reader, goes to Abundius (d. 468), the best-known of the early bishops of Como.[200]

Abundius's placement may well, along with the less than rigorous alphabetization, be an unconsidered matter, an accident. After all, simply doubling the "b" of Abundius, as in the Italian "Abbondio," would secure the bishop of Como an initial position, and that is just the sort of decision a compositor might make. But the early bishop had strong associations for Mombrizio's contemporaries, especially in the year preceding and the year following the assassination. Even as an accidental placement, the initial position of Abundius would have been disconcertingly meaningful to those clerical and regular readers who were likely to have access to the *Sanctuarium* immediately upon its publication. Such readers knew that the contemporary bishop of Como, Abundius's fifteenth-century equivalent, was Branda da Castiglione (bishop from 1466 to 1478).[201] And they would have had an inkling of the bishop's favor with the regime.

Branda, a relatively long term member of the *Consiglio ducale* and the *Consiglio segreto*, had accompanied Galeazzo Maria into St. Stephen's on the morning of the assassination: he was one of the people nearest the duke

---

Vita e disciplina di Guarino Veronese (Brescia, 1806), 2:186–188 n. 304, esp. 187 col. b. Such a long composition period suggests but does not prove lengthiness. Decembrio intended to send the *vita Ambrosii*, which was dedicated to Francesco della Croce, to his friend Mombrizio. But the life is no longer extant. It is listed as a lost work by Paolo Viti, "Decembrio, Pier Candido," *DBI* 33 (1987): 496a; and by Zaccaria, "Sulle opere" 57, no. 31.

199. For example, Jacopo Filippo Foresti's *De claris scelestisque mulieribus*, printed in Ferrara by Laurentius de Rubeis, April 29, 1497 (H 2813*; *IGI* 5071) places the Virgin first, although his chronological order starts formally with Eve; this work is discussed further in chap. 5 below.

200. *BHL* 15; Mombrizio 1910, 1:1–4. On his feastdate, see C. Pasini in *GLS* 1:2. In contrast to series A, the first entries for the series B, D, F, I, L, M, N, O, Q, R, T, V, X, and Z are adequately alphabetized, even though alphabetization becomes less rigorous later in each series. The series C, E, G, H, P, and S are, like A, faulty at the beginning, some more so than others.

201. Branda had been made bishop of Como by Paul II (1464–1471), who admired him greatly (Ughelli 5:313–314, entry 76); cf. Niccolò Machiavelli, *Istorie fiorentine*, ed. F. Gaeta (Milan: Feltrinelli, 1962), Book 7, chap. 33, 503, recording that Paul II gave the abbey to "uno suo propinquo." See also F. Petrucci, "Castiglioni, Branda" *DBI* 22 (1979): 126–129 and Marina Cavallera, *Morimondo: Un'abbazia lombarda tra '400 e '500* (Milan: Cisalpino, 1990), 64–65 and 71–75.

202. Branda's position near the duke is mentioned in Casanova, "L'uccisione," 304. Alfio Rosario Natale, *Acta in consilio secreto in castello Porta Jovis Mediolani*, vol. I, *7 ott. 1477–10 apr. 1478* (Milan: Giuffré, 1963): xxviii et seq., records Branda's regular appearance on the lists of those attending *Consiglio segreto* meetings from 1469; cf. Leverotti,

at his death.[202] Afterward, Branda had celebrated the funeral mass for the prince. Branda had also, in his capacity as commendatory abbot of the Cistercian abbey of Morimondo,[203] benefited in the legal case that had provoked Galeazzo Maria's assassination.[204] This abbey, which lay to the southwest of Milan, between the castles of Abbiategrasso and Binasco, had been founded in 1134 and then refounded following Bernard of Clairvaux's 1135 visit to Milan.[205] In its first century, Morimondo was a prosperous site with an active scriptorium, but then came earthquakes, political violence, and a series of attacks by neighbors.[206] By the fifteenth century Morimondo had sunken to become a hunting grounds and country house for the ruling family and their guests, and a source of personal enrichment for its

"Governare," 87. The significance of this regularity in the months following the assassination is argued in Fubini, "Osservazioni," e.g. 58 and 72 n. 42. As Cicco's power was coming under attack throughout 1478, Branda aligned himself with the aristocrats, that is, with Giovanni Borromeo and Pietro Pusterla, who led the attack. He even joined them to urge Cicco's arrest and execution. See Corio, Storia, for 1479–1480. With a dedication to Cicco and a first entry about a bishop of Como, the Sanctuarium is unlikely to have been printed after spring 1478.

203. P. F. Kehr, Italia pontificia, 6, 1 (Berlin: Weidmann, 1913/1961), 129, says 1476; Cavallera, Morimondo, 73, says 1475. Morimondo began to be held in commenda from about 1450: see Laura Airaghi, "Gli ordini religiosi nel secolo XV," in A. Caprioli, A. Rimoldi, and L. Vaccaro, ed., Storia religiosa della Lombardia: Diocesi di Milano (Brescia: "La Scuola," 1991), part 1, 357; Paolo Calliari, L'Abbazia cistercense di Morimondo (Casorate Primo: Multigrafia GBR, 1991), 238; Cavallera, Morimondo, 30. Cf. Antonio Cavagna Sangiuliano, dating the commenda to the 1460s, "L'Abbazia di Morimondo," part 1, "La storia," Rivista storica benedettina 3 (1908): 603, perhaps referring to the first nonresident commendatory abbot, Matteo Castiglioni (1463).

204. Machiavelli, Istorie, book 7, chap. 33 at 502–504, discussed in Belotti, Il dramma, 64–65; cf. Calliari, L'Abbazia, 239–240; Cavallera, Morimondo, 71. By May, Galeazzo Maria had decided to forgo involvement in the dispute between Branda and the Lampugnani syndicate using the goods of Morimondo (Belotti, Il dramma, 66, referring to ASM, Serie famiglie, Lampugnani, appendice, doc. 6). By October, Giovanni Andrea Lampugnani informed Galeazzo Maria that he and Branda could not come to any accomodation (ibid., 93, citing ASM, Prov. Sov., GM Sforza, Busta 805, app. 7).

205. Kehr, Italia pontificia, 6, 1, 128–132; on the location, see Diego Sant'Ambrogio, "La badia di Morimondo," ASL ser. 2, fasc. 8, anno 18 (1891): 129.

206. See Mirella Ferrari, "Lo scriptorium di Morimondo" and Sandrina Bandera, "Gli inizi dello scriptorium di Morimondo" in Un abbazia lombarda: Morimondo la sua storia e il suo messaggio. Convegno celebrativo nel VII centenario del termine dei lavori della chiesa abbaziale 1296–1996 (Fondazione Abbatia Sancte Marie de Morimundo, 1996), 103–111 and 113–130 respectively, and Mirella Ferrari, "Biblioteche e scrittoi benedettini nella storia culturale e della diocesi Ambrosiana: Appunti ed episodi," Ricerche storiche sulla chiesa ambrosiana (Archivio ambrosiano) 9 (1980): 241–244 and 283–287. On the attacks of 1245, 1266, and 1314, see Sant'Ambrogio, "La badia," 132; on the late-thirteenth- and early-fourteenth-century earthquakes, see Giulio Porro, "Alcune notizie sul monastero di Morimondo," ASL 2, no. 8 (1881): 627.

207. Cavagna Sangiuliano,"L'abbazia," 603; Porro, "Alcune notizie" 628.

abbot and his lay tenants.[207] Branda, appointed commendatory abbot in 1475, was not the first or the last to try to reassert ecclesiastic usufruct.[208] But his attempts ran counter to strong claims to Morimondo by the Lampugnani family, which had established a syndicate to control the totality of the abbey's goods, both moveables and immoveables.[209] In the face of Branda da Castiglione's efforts to dislodge them, one member of the family, Giovanni Andrea Lampugnani, appealed repeatedly over the course of 1476 to Galeazzo Maria for recognition of his family's claim.[210] The prince did not provide justice. Rather, he referred the matter to Branda himself and so, by implication, to Rome, a court in which the Lampugnani had no standing. By late 1476 Giovanni Andrea had given up hope of peaceful settlement, organizing instead his conspiracy to "frighten" the duke into some favorable response. As we have seen, the plot was brave but pointless. Far from damaging any claim the bishop of Como might have had on Morimondo, the assassination spurred rigorous repression, including the threat to exile the entire Lampugnani family. Branda's rights were confirmed.

Branda's ecclesiastical position would have been known to clerical readers of the *Sanctuarium* in Milan and its surrounding cities, and it would not have been odd for them to recognize Abundius as his symbolic equivalent. There is, however, no proof that Abundius was intentionally placed at the opening of the collection. For one thing, the strongest case for intentional placement requires that it have been done *after* Galeazzo Maria's assassination, and we do not know when the edition was printed. Second, the web of signification—identifying Abundius with Branda, Branda with the Morimondo dispute, the Morimondo dispute with Galeazzo Maria's assassination—is dense. If Abundius's initial position was meaningful, it must have been transparent and eloquent to a restricted readership, and only briefly.

❊ ❊ ❊

208. Serious reform was undertaken in 1490 by the commendatory abbot Giovanni de'Medici (later Leo X), who introduced monks from the austere Cistercian monastery of Settimiano in Florence that had been reformed by Domenico Capranica (Cavagna Sangiuliano, "L'abbazia," 603; Cavallera, *Morimondo*, 104–121). Ferrari, "Biblioteche e scrittoi," 247 (without reference) dates the reform at Morimondo earlier, to 1465, and associates with it the compilation of a new library inventory; for ducal efforts at reform in the 1460s, see Cavallera, *Morimondo*, 91seq.. The connection between reforming and inventorying is suggestive in this hagiographic context.

209. Leverotti, "Governare," 105 n. 315, refers to her own unpublished research demonstrating that the Lampugnani commanded the "totalità dei beni dell'abbazia di Morimondo." Movables would include codices.

210. Belotti, *Il dramma*, 66–68; see also n. 204 above.

Vir nam omnino piissimus & excultissimus in omni fere uita perpetuis fortunae plagis oblisus est.

For this utterly pious and learned man (Bonino Mombrizio) was crushed throughout his whole life by unending blows of fate.

—Alessandro Minuziano to Iacopo Balsamo, 1503 [211]

No matter when the *Sanctuarium* was published or what its loose alphabetization means, there is evidence that Mombrizio himself had connections with the Lampugnani family that were close enough to be incriminating. His weak position during Bona's regency is most clearly indicated in the *quadernus,* or notebook, begun by the notary Tommaso Giussani in March 1478.[212] There, under the date April 23, 1477 (*sic*), Tommaso announced that the next entry would be in Bonino's own hand: *Boninus manu propria.* In his small and graceful script, Bonino wrote:

I, Boninus Mombritius, shortly after the death, not less lamentable than horrible and cruel, of the illustrious and warmly remembered lord Galeazzo Maria Sforza, duke of Milan, inflicted by the evil and unspeakable Giovanni Andrea then called Lampugnani, wished to record both the detestable crime as well as the merits of that divine prince. So I thought it worthwhile to declare not the cruelty of his crime but those disreputable conspirators. And to do so in such a way that you who come afterward would have before you with sharp truth the nature of their conversation, their family origins. I fully revealed from whom their manners and family origin came. And among other things that the most damnable even of the conspirators themselves belongs not to the Lampugnani, as he himself, though falsely, proclaimed, but took his origin from the obscure Lissi. This I set out, according to the unsuppressible truth of history, in a certain work entitled *Threnody.*[213]

211. Alessandro Minuziano (?), prefatory letter to Iacopo Balsamo, explaining the decision to print Boninus Mombritius, *Trenodia* (Milan: Minuziano, 1504), facing sign. A2r. Of Mombrizio's works, this letter mentions only the long poems *Momidos, Dominicae passionis libri sex,* and *De fortuna libri decem.*

212. ASM, Notarile, 862, Tommaso Giussani, entry for March 16, 1478.

213. "Cum ego, Boninus Mombritius, paulo post non minus comiserandam quam horendum atrocissimamque cedem recolande memorie Illustrissimi domini Galeazmarie Sforcie ducem Mediolani, per scelestissimum et inominandum Johannemandream tunc appelatum de Lampugnano inflictum, cuperem tam detestabile facinus tamquam de vivo ipso principe benemeritus mandare memorie, opere pretium putavi non eius tantum inaudita sceleris seriem quam infames illos coniuratos declare, ita ut posteros qui fuerint, qualis eorum conversatio, quibus ducti familiis, exquisita veritate vos videbantur conveniendos duxi, a quibus quidquid ad eorum mores familiarumque originem facit abunde opertum habui. Interque cetera nefandissimum et coniuratorum ipsorum pertinens non ex Lampugnanorum, prout ipse falso predicabat, sed ex obscuris Lyssiis originem trahit, quod et ego historie veritatem

The efforts of the Lampugnani family to disassociate themselves from the assassin are well known, and Mombrizio's literary contribution, the *Threnody*, has long been acknowledged.[214] The focus on the Lampugnani, however, has obscured the personal nature of Mombrizio's efforts to help them achieve this dissociation. Many authors—including the humanist Gabriele Paveri Fontana—commemorated the assassination.[215] But Mombrizio seems to be the only one who found it advisable not simply to commemorate but to mark his commemoration out as an accusation of the illegitimacy of Giovanni Andrea Lampugnani.[216] Mombrizio alone found it prudent not only to accuse the assassin but also to record explicitly both his own intentions in writing a commemoration and his immediate execution of them. Mombrizio alone did so in his own hand, in a legal document, that is, a dated notarial register of the sort admissible in court as conclusive evidence, although one in which the date of his entry cannot be

---

sequens in opusculo quodam meo cui *Trenodie* titulus est non silendum expressi." I have regularized punctuation and capitalization but have not interfered with Mombrizio's spelling. I am grateful to Arnaldo Ganda for correcting my hasty transcription.

214. See, e.g., Belotti, *Il dramma*, 56–60, esp. 57 on Mombrizio's part; Emilio Motta, "Un documento per il Lampugnano, uccisore di Galeazzo Maria Sforza," *ASL*, ser. 2, fasc. 4, anno 13 (1886): 417.

215. For some commemorations of the assassination, see G. D'Adda, "Canti storici popolari italiani tratti da manoscritti o da rarissimi testi a stampa dei secoli XV e XVI," part 2, "La morte di Galeazzo Maria Sforza," *ASL* anno 2, fasc. 3 (1875): 284–294. Cornazzano's *Capitolo sulla morte di Galeazzo Maria Sforza* is now recorded in Roberto Bruni and Diego Zancani, *Antonio Cornazzano, La tradizione testuale* (Florence: Olschki, 1992), 131–132. On Paveri Fontana, a student of Filelfo's, see above, n. 180. His *De vita et obitu Galeaz Mariae Sfortiae Mediolani ducis* (H 12473; BMC 6:734; IGI 7370; Rogledi Manni 768), is an octavo of twenty-eight leaves printed by Ungardus, who had printed the Ambrosian *Litanie* shortly before the assassination (nn. 79 and 192 above).

216. The *Trenodia* is not extant in manuscript, and so we are at the mercy of the sixteenth-century editor, Alessandro Minuziano (n. 211 above). As the text stands in the edition, there are barely two lines on Giovanni Andrea's family origins: "Andreas . . . cuius quamvis vilescat origo / Lissia, degeneres et avos in sanguine ducat, / Lampugnana tamen falso cognomina fingens" (*Trenodia*, sign. b1r, ll. 17–20, with the printed marginal *nota* "Andreas lis/sius qui lam/pugnanum / se esse finxe/rat"). Kristeller, *Iter*, 1:349b, identifies a manuscript copied from the printed edition. On Minuziano, who became an important printer only in the following decade, see Carlo Dionisotti, "Notizie di Alessandro Minuziano," in *Miscellanea Giovanni Mercati*, vol. 4, *Letteratura classica e umanistica* (Vatican City: BAV, 1946), 327–372, 218. The Lampugnani first requested that the *Consiglio segreto* recognize Giovanni Andrea's family of origin as the Lissi rather than the Lampugnani on April 21, 1478; the request was discussed at both morning and afternoon meetings (Natale, *Acta*, 2:35). Cf. the date of April 23, 1488 (sic for 1478?) recorded in Giussani's notebook. Mombrizio's name does not occur in the records of this meeting (or of any others I have seen), which suggests that his poem was not a crucial intervention in the Lampugnani case. If it was not, then his notarial entry is still more convincingly interpreted as a private document, related to his compromising personal relations to the family.

reconciled with the opening date of the register. I do not know of a similar entry in another notarial notebook. As a man trained in law, as a man who worked regularly with notaries drawing up legal documents, Mombrizio must have been acting with great deliberation. Who were the Lampugnani to him, to elicit such an intervention?

Mombrizio's decision to turn his authorship of the *Threnody* into an oath of allegiance is hard to understand, given how little we know about this humanist, especially about his implication in Galeazzo Maria's injustices through the *Entrate Straordinarie* appointment and about the precise role he played in his many printing ventures. The interpretation of these years is vexed, even among experts in Milanese history. It would help simply to know when the *Threnody* was written, but, as it was not printed until 1504, dating its composition is tricky. Bayot and Groult date it to the very day of the assassination. Their dating is called into question not only by the starting date of the notary Giussani's *quadernus* and by Mombrizio's own phrase "shortly after" but also by the fact that it took several months for the implications of Giovanni Andrea's crime for the well-being of the Lampugnani family to become clear. Only then could they formulate a way to evade those implications by seeking formal recognition that Giovanni Andrea was not a member of the Lampugnani clan.[217] We can assume that Mombrizio succeeded in demonstrating, first, his own distance from the criminal and, second, his support of the regime, if indeed he won a university appointment in 1481. But until that appointment is documented, all that is certain about his death is a *terminus post quem* of late 1478, when he made his testament with this same Giussani (see above, p. 114). Altogether, Mombrizio's subject, his declaration of intent, and his claim of an immediate composition do less to help the Lampugnani than to clarify his own pacific relationship to the regime. The *Sanctuarium* may do so as well, although obviously it is a different kind of gesture from the legal document.[218] Unfortunately for Mombrizio, the regime he wished to placate did not last much past the printing of the *Sanctuarium*.

217. I have not been able to establish a precise connection between Mombrizio and Lampugnani. He may have initiated a friendship with members of the family in courtly and humanistic circles before 1458–1460, while he was at school in Ferrara: the Lampugnani held property there, as can be deduced from the record of the *Consiglio segreto* meeting of April 9, 1478 (Natale, *Acta*, 1:295). One printed work, a "Suetonius" *De viris illustribus* (see Rogledi Manni nos. 114–116), opens with a prefatory letter that explicitly links a member of the Lampugnani family to Mombrizio in the shared work of printing, but the publication raises more questions than it answers (n. 55 above).

218. I thank Daniel Bornstein for helping me to clarify this point. For his finances, Mombrizio cared that the *Sanctuarium* sold; for his safety, Mombrizio cared that Simonetta accepted the dedication of the paraliturgical work qua paraliturgical work. In contrast, the notarial document lay ready for use if matters took a legal turn.

❀ ❀ ❀

O padrone di questa nostra città, tu sai la intenzione nostra e il fine a che noi
vogliamo metterci a tanti pericoli. Sia favorevole a questa nostra impresa, e
dimostra, favorendo la giustizia, che la ingiustizia ti dispiaccia.

O, (Ambrose,) patron of our city, you know our intention and the end for which
we are willing to put ourselves in so many dangers. Be favorable to our enter-
prise, and show by favoring justice that injustice displeases you.

—Niccolò Machiavelli, *Istorie fiorentine* 7, 34 [219]

If Mombrizio's *Sanctuarium* was issued in ostensible support of a regime
that was in a crisis, by someone who feared being mistaken for a contribu-
tor (even on the symbolic level) to that crisis, then individual saints in the
Sanctuarium may bear political and personal meaning. The concluding section of this chapter pursues that possibility. Two questions about the contents of the *Sanctuarium* require attention: first, the range of texts presented;
and second, the range of saints represented by those texts. As the legendary
contains hundreds of entries, both questions can be answered here only
superficially. Even a tentative reevaluation, however, must offer some rationale for the array of texts and saints that Mombrizio chose to include.

In the case of the range of texts, a rationale is badly needed. This chapter opened by considering at length Bolland's estimate of Mombrizio as a
humanist devoted to the reliable printed transmission of *vitae sanctorum*
from manuscript. Especially if Mombrizio was acting as a philologically
aware humanist in making his transcriptions, it must follow that he sought
ancient and rare texts in singular manuscripts. His decision to transcribe
Avienus demonstrates that he recognized this aspect of text-critical work.
It is surprising, then, to note that in more than ninety instances—roughly a
quarter of the entries—Mombrizio's *Sanctuarium* reproduces derivative
and widely available texts from the thirteenth-century *Legenda aurea* and
Speculum historiale (see table 3.1, above). These narratives have no appre-
ciable value for anyone interested in the oldest traditions of the
early martyrs—precisely the figures who dominate the collection to a
degree atypical of late medieval legendaries.[220] Almost 70 percent of the
entries in the *Sanctuarium* feature pre-sixth-century saints, above all martyrs of the third and fourth centuries. Mombrizio's collection is unfashionable in another way, too: the members of the Holy Kinship—Mary, Joseph,
Ann, and Elizabeth—are absent. Franciscan or Dominican influence does

---

219. The prayer of the conspirators of 1476 before the statue of St Ambrose at the church
of St. Stephen; I quote the English from Machiavelli's *Florentine Histories*, trans. L. F. Ban-
field and H. C. Mansfield Jr. (Princeton, N.J.: Princeton University Press, 1988), 314.

220. See chap. 1, p. 35.

not appear to influence Mombrizio's design, since neither Bernardino of Siena (d. 1444; c.d. 1450) nor Vincent Ferrer (d. 1419; c.d. 1458) have entries. The Hermits are better represented: Niccolò da Tolentino (d. 1305/6; c.d. 1446) is present, as is Monica (but Augustine's mother is clearly an afterthought, badly out of order in the ultimate position).[221]

In a second group of instances, however, Mombrizio did print the text of important original narratives rather than second- or third-hand derivations. Such was the case for example, with the lives of Catherine of Siena, Francis, Malachy, Martin of Tours, and Nicholas of Tolentino.[222] Even so, none of these entries presents a rare text. Mombrizio's *passiones* for Katherine of Alexandria and Therenus represent yet a third sort of entry.[223] They are not taken from mendicant historiographical works, and neither are they texts by recognized authors. They are apocrypha in the medieval sense, that is, texts appearing without an author's name. In sum, the texts edited by Mombrizio and dedicated to Cicco Simonetta are an eclectic mix: original sources with named authors who are mostly members of the religious orders, apocryphal sources (some derivative themselves), and derivative sources by Dominican encyclopedists. It is hard to deduce a critical editorial program from this mix. In some cases, Mombrizio used highly authoritative sources; in other cases, he seems to have used such texts as came to hand.[224] This eclecticism may indicate carelessness, or a greater concern to fill gatherings than to present valuable texts, or a hasty change of plan. Any of those three cases suggests that a start might be made at reconstituting the lost fifteenth-century manuscript of Mombrizio's work by subtracting from the *Sanctuarium* the accounts traceable to the *Legenda aurea* and the *Speculum historiale*. The core that remains may indicate the editor's desires for the collection, although at some remove that still must be estimated.

If the political implications of saints' cults matter, as I have suggested, we

---

221. Nicholas in Mombritius 1910, 2:310–326, with notes at 2:704–705 (*BHL* 6230b). Monica in ibid., 2:53–55, with notes at 2:758 (*BHL* 5999). Lives of Monica published in Milan are part of the polemic between Hermits and Canons discussed in chap. 5 below; the decision to append a *vita Monicae* suggests that the response of the Augustinian Hermits to the *Sanctuarium* was calculated by the editor, entrepreneur, or printer. If the absence of Clare of Montefalco (d. 1308; c.d. 1881) reflects the fact that she was not yet canonized, then the official quality of Mombrizio's *Sanctuarium* is further underlined.

222. Catherine of Siena in Mombritius 1910, 1:297–332, with notes at 1:637–638 (*BHL* 1704); Francis of Assisi in ibid., 1:489–532, with notes at 1:665–669 (*BHL* 3107); Malachy, ibid., 2:143–169, with notes at 2:684–688 (*BHL* 5188); Martin of Tours, ibid., 2:196–231, with notes at 2:692–694 (*BHL* 5610); on Nicholas of Tolentino, see n. 221 above.

223. Katherine of Alexandria in Mombritius 1910, 1:283–287, no note (*BHL* 1657); Therenus, ibid., 2:598–599, no note (*BHL* 8129).

224. The fact that Jerome is represented by *BHL* 3870 is an instance of striking conservatism, given the amount of humanist attention to Jerome (including Mombrizio's own epic poem, n. 124 above). On "Plerosque nimium," see Rice, *Jerome, ad indicem*.

should consider not just the texts but the saints they represent. Obviously, the polyvalence of the saints poses an obstacle at this point.[225] Moreover, in studying such a secretive and faction-ridden place as Quattrocento Milan, it is dangerously easy to overinterpret the already proliferating meanings imputed to the heavenly patrons. The initial placement of Abundius is a good example of how one person's reasonable interpretation may be another's conspiracy theory. A similar instance is the life of Bernard of Clairvaux, which holds the symbolic center of volume 1 and is by far the longest account in either volume, at more than 42,000 words.[226] (Francis is a distant second, at just over 24,500 words.)[227] Bernard, as I have noted, was associated as founder with Morimondo, the Cistercian monastery over which the Lampugnani syndicate and the commendatory abbot Branda da Castiglione were fighting in the year before the assassination. Similarly, the saint most out of alphabetical order in the *Sanctuarium*, Augustine's mother, Monica, was especially important to the Augustinian Hermits; in Milan, the Hermits, in their new monastery of S. Maria Incoronata, were patronized both by the Simonetta and the Sforza families.[228] Such coincidences are grounds for speculation rather than argument.

Oddly enough, an absent saint provides the clearest indication of political intent in Mombrizio's *Sanctuarium*: the military martyr George is missing. In his description of the fifteenth-century manuscript, Argelati records an entry for George and notes its absence from the printed version of the work: "There follows a life of St. George the Martyr [f.d. April 23 in Rome; April 24 in Milan], which is lacking in the

225. A further complication, raised by anthropological approaches: the choice of saints will be hard to interpret because, as Catherine Bell points out in *Ritual Theory, Ritual Practice* (Oxford: Oxford University Press, 1992), the ritualized body (in this case, the Christian worshiper familiar with representations of saints) is equally capable of submission or resistance. That is to say, inclusion of any saint may equally represent approval or criticism.

226. Mombritius 1910, 1:175–210, with notes at 1:631–632 (*BHL* 1220), the so-called second recension of Bernard's life.

227. See n. 222 above. The entry for Francis occupies three gatherings, the signatures F, FF, and FFF. This composition unit is often misbound: the layout of the volume suggests that Francis was intended to open the saints whose names begin with "F," but his story is usually found at the end of that group. The earlier "F" saints fall under "f, ff, fff . . . " signatures. The intended order may be indicated by the presence of a fanciful "Finis" at the conclusion of the last account in the F/f series, that for the martyrs Fides and Caprasius. There is no "Finis" at the end of the life of Francis, so it was probably not intended to close the F series. The initial F gathering has an anomalous watermark—a bunch of grapes—rarely found elsewhere in the copies I have examined. This watermark may indicate that the F, FF, FFF composition unit was produced at another workshop. See U. Monnaret de Villard, "Le filigrane delle carte milanesi dalle più antiche alla fine del XV secolo," *ASL* ser. 8, 5–6 (1954–1956), 24–55, "uva" (518); cf. C.-M. Briquet, *Les filigranes: Dictionnaire historique des marques du papier* (New York: Hacker, 1977; repr. of 2d ed. 1923), no. 13048 (1444).

228. Maria Luisa Gatti Perer, *Umanesimo a Milano: L'Osservanza agostiniana all'Incoronata* (Milan: Arte Lombarda, 1980), passim.

imprint."[229] If Argelati describes a manuscript of the *Sanctuarium* prepared *before* printing, then it is obvious that George was removed before the legendary was printed, and so he will be of great interest as a "censored" saint.[230] If Argelati describes a manuscript of the *Sanctuarium* prepared *after* the printed edition, then George's absence from the imprint troubled at least one contemporary reader enough that an insertion was arranged. Moreover, it does seem that no saint has been inserted into the printed *Sanctuarium* to hold the feast date given to George in the Milanese calendar. But even if Argelati's witness is set aside, George's absence from Mombrizio's compilation is surprising. He could not have been omitted by accident.

George was of ancient cult in Milan. He is not, it is true, recorded in the thirteenth-century *Liber notitiae sanctorum mediolanensis*. But he had a secure place in the traditional Milanese liturgical calendar and is listed in the ninth-century *Sanctorale Ambrosianum*.[231] Anyone supposing that Mombrizio was engaged in a philologically minded examination of hagiographic manuscripts might think that, for just that reason, Mombrizio would be sure to include the military martyr. And George had a church, San Giorgio al Palazzo, in Mombrizio's own neighborhood of the Ticino Gate. This church is incorporated into the series of ritual processions set out in the *Litanie secundum ordinem Ambrosianum* published by Ungardus, even if George himself is not invoked in the course of the litanies.[232] Mombrizio's local attachments, then, might also have encouraged him to include George.

229. "Sequitur Vita sancti Georgii martyris, quae deest in impressis." The quotation continues, "Habentur aliorum Vitae, inter quos sancti Syri episcopi Ticinensis [f.d. December 9] satis longa." The account of Sirus (*BHL* 7976) in the printed *Sanctuarium* is around three thousand words long. See n. 184 above.

230. George's inclusion in the manuscript draft (if it represents a *prior* draft) is evidence that Mombrizio's original project was a paraliturgical collection sufficiently sympathetic to the Sforza that it might, as hypothesized above, have been undertaken at Galeazzo Maria's behest. As recorded by Argelati, however, George seems to occur badly misplaced in the manuscript draft organized by the liturgical year. I do not know what to make of this placement, unless Argelati is just offhandedly rather than rigorously noting George's inclusion in the manuscript.

231. For the antiquity of his cult in Milan, see Otto Heiming, "Die ältesten ungedruckten Kalendar der mailandischen Kirche," in B. Fischer and V. Fiala, eds., *Colligere fragmenta: Festschrift Alban Dold zum 70. Geburtstag am 7.7.1952* (Beuron, 1972), 218 and 228; Judith Frei, *Das ambrosianische Sakramentar D.3.3 aus dem mailandischen Metropolitankapitel* (Münster: Aschendorf, 1974), 91 and 100; E. Cattaneo in Treccani, *Storia*, vol. 3, *Dagli albori del commune all'incoronazione di Federico Barbarosa* (Milan, 1954), charts following 828. See also Gualla, *Papie Sanctuarium*, book 5, chap. 13, fol. 62, "De sancto Georgio," aligning the martyr with Curtius and Codrus, "qui pro salute sue patrie sponte morti se exposuerunt," and fol. 62v, recalling Ambrose's praise of George.

232. See n. 79 above. The *Litanie*, fol. 182v, lists saints to be invoked when the procession reaches San Giorgio al Palazzo (I preserve the spelling): Maria, Stephanus, Georgius, Teodorus, Iovita and Faustinus, Petrus, Marcelinus, Latina, Tegla, Cecilia, Galdinus, Ambrosius. Of these figures, George, Faustinus and Iovita, and Latina are not in the *Sanctuarium*, which further suggests that Mombrizio did not complete his work.

Most important, George was the patron saint of the Sforza dukes. On his feast day, the ducal standards were customarily blessed in the Duomo, and, under Galeazzo Maria, the celebrations had grown especially grand.[233] In the first half of the 1470s the duke regularly oversaw large and elaborate celebrations for George's festival.[234] The high point came in 1475: Galeazzo Maria "planned for over 4,000 soldiers to participate in the display," many in specially made costumes in Sforza colors and with Sforza insignia.[235] To the nobles who participated, securing a favorable place in the ceremony mattered profoundly, for proximity indicated the duke's favor. Art historian Evelyn Welch has clarified this point by analyzing the duke's fresco plan, drawn up in 1474 for the renovated Porta Giovia palace; it called for a representation of the San Giorgio festival featuring many more identifiable portraits than any of the courtly scenes set out in earlier programs.[236] One reason the frescoes were never executed, Welch speculates, is that they would have become outdated immediately, so quickly did Galeazzo Maria's favor ebb and flow.

The San Giorgio festival has thus served historians as a gauge of the political current in Milan. To the extent that the Sforza dukes promoted St. George, Sforza opponents found George a problem.[237] Those nobles who felt keenly the illegitimacy of Galeazzo Maria's rule wanted the duke to pay more attention to Ambrose.[238] Among the citizens of Milan, the festival of San Giorgio was perceived as yet another of Galeazzo Maria's unwelcome and expensive impositions. So it is not surprising that, as tensions grew in Milan over 1476, the celebration was scaled back.[239] Cicco Simonetta's diary entry for April 24, 1476 (shortly before the first, failed assassination attempt at Pavia in June), records that the customary blessing of the stan-

---

233. Covini, *L'esercito del duca*, 318, notes that the blessing of the standards was transformed under Galeazzo Maria into an "occasione di trasmettere un messaggio di potenza, di ricchezza e di sfoggio militarista, rivolto sia ai sudditi sia ai potentati italiani ed esteri."

234. Motta, "Un documento," 417, and Covini, *L'esercito del duca*, 318–322.

235. Lubkin, *A Renaissance Court*, 215–218 at 215.

236. Welch, "The Image of a Fifteenth-Century Court," 180–181, with further references; Covini, *L'esercito del duca*, 322–327.

237. The point is emphasized in Lubkin, *A Renaissance Court*; see the reservations expressed in Covini, *L'esercito del duca*, 321–322, about the sources. In Milan's restive subject city, Genoa, the same St. George had inverse implications: he was an anti-Sforza, pro-liberty saint. See Bertolotti, "Spedizioni militari," 625–626.

238. Lubkin, *A Renaissance Court*, 219, argues that Galeazzo Maria "had little attachment to the capital's patron saint."

239. Belotti, *Il dramma*, 85, citing AS Mantova, Arch. Gonzaga, Aff. Est., Busta 1625; Lubkin, *A Renaissance Court*, 218–219; Leverotti, "Governare," 18, records that Bianca Maria had counseled that the celebrations be cut back in 1467 for political reasons, so there was precedent for thinking about the festival as a potential excuse for unrest.

dards was restricted that year to the "the guard of the family, and not other soldiers," and further specifies that the crossbowmen who accompanied the standards into the Duomo were *desarmata*.[240]

In 1477, following the assassination, the festival of San Giorgio appears not to have been celebrated. Bona and Cicco Simonetta (perhaps Bartolomeo Calco also had an opinion) may have feared that the traditional armed knightly assemblies would be co-opted by the dead duke's brothers, who at that point were perceived as a threat to Milanese stability. But at the end of March 1478, on short notice, less than a month before George's feast day, the celebration was reinstituted.[241] Or, rather, it was emphatically marked out: San Giorgio had been chosen for the "enthroning" of the minor duke.[242] The knightly families of Milan and some of the subject cities were summoned to honor the occasion, and instructed to behave; their expenses would be borne by the treasury. Plans must have been made at this time to feature select members of the nobility in the celebration itself, as the event of April 24 included the induction of more than two dozen nobles as *cavalieri aurati*.[243] The hasty decision to celebrate San Giorgio in April 1478 by enthroning the minor duke and placating the nobles was public notice that power was legitimately in Sforza hands.

If the *Sanctuarium* printing were begun during Galeazzo Maria's lifetime, the omission of George (even in a work dedicated to the prince's chancellor rather than to the prince himself) would have appeared treasonable. If the printing occurred after March 1478, when the forceful reinstitution of San Giorgio with its civic spectacle was in effect, then the omission of George would have been dangerously insensitive. But in the preceding months, and especially in 1477, when the festival appears to have been suppressed, removing George from the *Sanctuarium* might have made sense. It would echo the prudent suppression of the feast; it would

240. Natale, *I diari*, 201.

241. See the *Consiglio segreto* entry for March 31, 1478, given in Natale, *Acta*, 1: 275.

242. The decision was made, or at least formally announced, at the end of March: see the preceding note. Simonetta's diary entry April 24, 1478, does not mention San Giorgio or any ceremony (Natale, *I diari*, 232). Corio, *Storia*, 3:323, notes the enthroning but not the festival. In contrast, Donato Bossi's chronicle, published in 1492, describes the 1478 celebration (fol. 292) but does not mention those of 1475–1477. Milan was still so volatile that it was not politically expedient to give Galeazzo Maria a public burial: see Sabine Eiche and Gregory Lubkin, "The Mausoleum Plan of Galeazzo Maria Sforza," *Mitteilungen des kunsthistorischen Instituts in Florenz* 31, no. 3 (1988): 547–548 and 551.

243. See, e.g., Felice Calvi, *Famiglie notabili Milanese*, vol. 3 (Milan: A. Vallardi, 1875–1885), Famiglia Landriani, table 8, s.n. Gallassio, son of Antonio, brother of Palamede. Gallassio was one of those named *cavalieri aurati* on this occasion; Calvi notes several others.

TABLE 3.2.   Argelati's list of *Sanctuarium* manuscript contents*

Date of Feast	Saint
November 11	Martin of Tours
November 18	Romanus
November 23	Clement
November 30	Andrew
December 6	Nicholas
December 7	Ambrose

* Feast days assigned according to the liturgical calendar of Rome.

likewise have been of a piece with the reorganization of the *Consiglio seg-reto*, insofar as both were aimed at short-circuiting the ambitions of Bona's brothers-in-law.

Suppressing George would also have marked Bona's regency, in a placating way, as mildly Ambrosian in its ostensible ideology.[244] Thus the absence of George may make the printed *Sanctuarium* a more Ambrosian collection than has been acknowledged heretofore. But it is unlikely that George's absence from the imprint declares Mombrizio's sympathies with the "republican" assassins. No matter what his personal, professorial, or printing associations with Cola da Montano or the Lampugnani, Mombrizio was not foolhardy. We must ask, however, if anyone producing a historiographical genre—that is to say, any authoritative representation of Milan's Christian past—for Cicco Simonetta, the vigilant minder of Sforza success and its literary depictions, could dispense with the Sforza patron without permission.

The problem of George's absence has a parallel in the presence of Katherine of Alexandria. Table 3.2 notes the liturgical order of the contents of the lost fifteenth-century manuscript, as Argelati recorded it. The six saints in Argelati's list occur in the incunable *Sanctuarium*, although we cannot know if the texts that represent the six are also the same ones Argelati saw. But setting out dates and saints in this way reveals that Katherine of Alexandria was omitted from the draft. If Mombrizio had included her in it, she would have appeared between Clement and Andrew, since her feastdate is November 25. Present in the imprint but not in the manuscript, the learned virgin martyr thus poses the opposite problem to George, who was present in the manuscript but disappeared from

244. Bona and the *Consiglio segreto* were immediately aware of the need to placate. See Leverotti, "Governare," 115, for the practical measures taken: reduction of the prices of salt and livestock; reduction of taxes; suspension of certain legal cases.

the imprint (or, if the manuscript postdates the imprint, then Katherine was felt, for some reason, to be unsuitable).[245]

Katherine was a popular saint, and that is reason enough for Mombrizio to have included her in the *Sanctuarium*. But she was not originally part of the Ambrosian liturgy.[246] Moreover, because her historical status was insecure, some humanist authors preferred not to treat her.[247] And since the *Sanctuarium* excluded other popular saints (for example, Ann, although one of Galeazzo Maria's daughters was named after Jesus' maternal grandmother), we may suspect that Katherine's presence represents more than a generalized popularity. In the fifteenth century, popular saints (that is, those who were widely revered, whether or not they were also officially recognized) always had local meanings that gained strength by capturing and controlling universal meanings. Such symbolic deployment is evident, for example, in the Sforza use of George.

Mombrizio was not averse to Katherine, for he had written on her twice previously. On both of these occasions, he courted the patronage of the Sforza women. In a minor reference, Mombrizio names Katherine among the virgin martyrs at the conclusion of a moralizing poem *Momidos*, which was addressed to Bona, Galeazzo Maria's wife, in 1468–69.[248] The twelve books of *Momidos* are divided six against and six for women, some bearing descriptive titles such as "De mulierum avaricia" and "De ingenio mulierum." Book 11, which has no descriptive title, ends with praise of the Sforza women, especially Bianca Maria and Bona, while the concluding book 12 briefly treats the virgin martyrs, among them Katherine. And

245. Argelati's list suggests that Mombrizio's draft manuscript of the *Sanctuarium* was missing not only Katherine but also Antoninus of Piacenza (November 13 in the Ambrosian calendar); Vitalis and Agricola (November 14); Elizabeth of Hungary (November 20); Cecilia (November 22); and Chrysogonus (November 24), all of whom, except Antoninus, were locally important figures and most of whom have entries in the incunable *Sanctuarium* (*BHL* 8682, 2506, 1495, 1795). On Mombrizio's neglect of Antoninus of Piacenza, see B. de Gaiffier, "Deux passionaires de Morimondo conservés au seminaire de Côme," *AB* 83 (1965): 142–156 at 154 n. 2.

246. Katherine is missing from the ninth-century *Sanctorale Ambrosianum* but seems to have been incorporated into the Milanese calendar of feasts by the mid-thirteenth century. The *Liber notitiae*, at 199a, records three churches, fifteen altars, and one feast in Milan and, at 202b, three churches, thirty altars, and two feasts in the diocese. In the circa 1476 *Litanie*, fols. 172r–v, Katherine is invoked when the procession reaches San Vitus (the 1494 Italian edition of the *Litanie* also names her at Santa Agata, and once more, at the final station).

247. Alison Frazier, "Katherine's Place in a Renaissance Collection: Evidence from Antonio degli Agli (c. 1460–1497), *De vitis et gestis sanctorum*," in J. Jenkins and K. Lewis, eds., *St. Katherine of Alexandria: Texts and Contexts in Western Medieval Europe* (Turnhout: Brepols, 2003), 221–223. See the survey of Katherine's cult in F. Baudot and L. Chaussin, *Vies des saints et des bienheureux selon l'ordre du calendrier, avec l'historique des fêtes par les rr. pp. Benedictins de Paris* (Paris: Letouzey and Ané, 1935), 11:854–882.

248. See n. 128 above.

before composing *Momidos*, the humanist had written at length on Katherine. At some point between 1450 and 1466, Mombrizio composed a substantial vernacular epic of 1,405 lines, *Peri tes Aikaterines*, for Bona's mother-in-law, Bianca Maria Visconti-Sforza.[249] This work stands out in Mombrizio's oeuvre as the sole extant vernacular composition and also as the only original work by this humanist to have a Greek title. The preface to the epic closes by describing Bianca Maria as "la divota sua [*sci.* of Katherine]."

The single manuscript of Mombrizio's vernacular epic on the virgin martyr is Brussels, Bibliothèque Royale, MS 10975, written on fine parchment, with initials decorated in red, blue, and gold; it is probably the presentation copy.[250] Bianca Maria willed the manuscript to her daughter-in-law Bona, and it must have traveled with Bona back to Savoy in 1479, after Ludovico il Moro entered Milan, as Bona later gave it to her niece.[251] The manuscript opens with a miniature of Bianca Maria kneeling, facing the saint (plate 3), which can be compared to a fresco portrait of Bona by Bernardo Benizi, in which the duchess is depicted kneeling in front of but facing away from an unidentified virgin martyr, whose wedding ring indicates Katherine and whose stance is protective.[252] These manuscript and fresco images suggest that Katherine's place in the *Sanctuarium* represents not only the saint's general popularity but also her importance to the women of the Sforza household. If so, then her inclusion in the *Sanctuarium* may be Mombrizio's gesture of homage to the memory of Bianca Maria Visconti-Sforza and the regency of Bona.[253]

Mombrizio's vernacular epic on Katherine is especially important for our understanding of the *Sanctuarium* entry on Katherine. *Peri tes Aikaterines* shows that he knew the popular traditions about the saint, including the extravagant late narratives that gave her a Constantinian genealogy and

249. Dating from Alphonse Bayot and Pierre Groult, eds., *La légende de Ste Catharine d'Alexandrie, poème italien du XVe siècle* (Gembloux: Duculot, 1943), 8.

250. Kristeller, *Iter*, 3:118b; there is a full description in Bayot and Groult, *La légende*, 5–9; see also Simonetta Cerrini, "Libri dei Visconti-Sforza: Schede per una nuova edizione degli inventari," *Studi petrarcheschi* 8 (1991): 239–281 at 261–263. I am grateful to Sally Whitman for help with this manuscript.

251. Bayot and Groult, *La légende*, 6–8.

252. *L'Età Sforzesca*, plate facing 250, a partial reproduction; reattributed to Zanetto Bugatto by Luke Syson, "Zanetto Bugatto, court portraitist in Sforza Milan" *The Burlington Magazine* 138 (1996): 305 fig. 9 and 308. Syson proposes that the saint depicted is Bona of Rheims.

253. See also Paolo Cherubini, ed., *Iacopo Ammannati Piccolomini, Lettere (1444–1479)* (Rome: Uffizio Centrale per in Beni Archivistici, 1997), 1:340, letter 7 from Ammannati to Bianca Maria Sforza, dated September 6, 1460, from Siena. Evidently, Bianca Maria had made two requests of Ammannati. First, she had pressed him for information about an "offitio de Sancta Catharina." Second, and in immediate sequence, Bianca Maria had asked about a curial post for "Petro de Monbreto da Pavia." On this figure, see ibid., 341 n. 6 and n. 33 above.

a mystical marriage.[254] These later plot developments, present in the vernacular epic, are not included in the Latin *Sanctuarium* account. But neither does the *Sanctuarium* reproduce unchanged any *vita Katherinae virginis et martyris* yet identified in manuscript.[255]

As noted above, the relationship of Mombrizio's printed texts to his manuscript sources is the crucial problem posed by the *Sanctuarium*. Katherine of Alexandria allows us to make a cautious test of one instance. In 1965 the Bollandist Baudouin de Gaiffier speculated, based on the rarity of the *Sanctuarium* narratives about Therenus, Pelagia (*virgo antiochena*), Reparata, and Eusebius of Vercelli, that these and others in the *Sanctuarium* might be traceable to two medieval legendaries now held at the Episcopal Seminary in Como.[256] De Gaiffier did not live to test his hypothesis by collating these *Sanctuarium* entries with Como 5 and 6. Nor did he note that Como 5 and 6 are partial witnesses to one of the most important and widely disseminated medieval legendaries, the *Magnum Legendarium Austriacum* (*MLA*), a late-twelfth-century Cistercian collection organized by the liturgical year, starting with January 1.[257]

The Cistercian scholar Jean Leclercq had earlier suggested that Como 5 and 6, which he dated to the twelfth/thirteenth centuries, were already in the library at Morimondo when the first inventory was made there in the twelfth century.[258] They might have been present, that is to say, at the very monastery that was the bone of contention between Giovanni Andrea Lampugnani and

---

254. A. Linder, "The Myth of Constantine the Great in the West: Sources and Hagiographic Commemoration," *Studi medievali* ser. 3, anno 16, fasc. 1 (1975): 80–84, succinctly describes the elaboration of the narrative.

255. Thanks to Eis, *Die Quellen*, 41–43, and B. de Gaiffier, "Au sujèt des sources du *Sanctuarium* de Mombritius," *Mittellateinisches Jahrbuch* 14 (1979): 278–281, texts have been found that match each of Mombrizio's entries very closely. Yet somehow Katherine of Alexandria eluded these investigations, for the collations done by Eis show that, while the *Magnum Legendarium Austriacum* may be a relatively close match, it is less perfect than others. See below.

256. Como, Biblioteca del Seminario vescovile, MSS 5 and 6. I thank the staff of the Episcopal Library for their generous help. In B. de Gaiffier, "Deux passionnaires," the heading on 147, "MS 5," should read "MS 6"; that on 152, giving "MS 6," should read "MS 5."

257. The *MLA* exists in several versions: see A. Poncelet, "De magno legendario austriaco," "De martyrologio Wolfhardi Haserensis," and "De legendario Winderbergensi," *AB* 17 (1898): 24–96, 5–23, and 97–122, respectively (the latter two articles describing sources from which the *MLA* derives); and J. van der Straeten, "Le 'Grand Légendier Autrichien' dans les manuscrits de Zwettl," *AB* 113 (1995): 321–348. G. B. Bronzini, "La leggenda di s. Caterina d'Alessandria," *Atti della Accademia nazionale dei Lincei: Memorie. Classe di Scienze morali, storiche e filologiche* 8, 9, 2 (1960): 257–416, argues that *BHL* 1657 is close to the Greek; HermannVarnhagen, *Zur Geschichte der Legende der Katharina von Alexandrien* (Erlangen: Junge, 1891), 2–3, points out the closeness of *BHL* 1657 to a tenth- or eleventh-century manuscript at Montecassino (not seen).

258. Jean Leclercq, "Textes et manuscrits cisterciens dans les bibliothèques des Etats-Unis," *Traditio* 17 (1961): 176–180, edits the twelfth-century inventory from Morimondo. It does not include these manuscripts, although Leclercq warns that the inventory is not a foolproof guide to the holdings (176). Leclercq is more certain that the seventeenth-century inventory recorded by Ughelli does include these two legendaries; see 181–182, entry 36, with reference.

Bishop Branda da Castiglione and therefore played a signal part in the assassination of Galeazzo Maria Sforza.[259] De Gaiffier expressed the Morimondo connection of Como 5 and 6 with more certainty; the paleographer Mirella Ferrari, noting that some sixty manuscripts traceable to Morimondo are extant to serve as controls, with more caution.[260] The Morimondo connection is not necessary for the following examination, although, if it can be maintained, it entails the availability of the manuscripts to the Lampugnani family and, through them, to the scholarly and publishing world of Quattrocento Milan. In that case, the elusive connection between Mombrizio and the Lampugnani might be located, at least in part, in the access that the humanist was allowed to Morimondo manuscripts. But that speculation aside, briefly testing an entry in the *Sanctuarium* against these possible manuscript sources allows a cautious and preliminary estimate of what editorial restraint might have meant in Mombrizio's approach to *vitae et passiones sanctorum*.

Katherine of Alexandria is not in the more accomplished Como MS 6. If Mombrizio did use the account of Katherine from Como MS 5 or a similar *Magnum Legendarium Austriacum* manuscript, then he or his compositors made several sorts of changes. First, the *Sanctuarium* mildly adjusts vocabulary, orthography, and word order. Mombrizio's version of the *vita Katherinae* everywhere corrects the aspiration in *nichil* and *michi*, omnipresent in Como MS 5, to *nihil* and *mihi*. On the other hand, *rethores* is retained in the *Sanctuarium* whenever it occurs in the manuscript; whenever the *Sanctuarium* deviates from the manuscript, however, the properly classical spelling *rhetores* occurs.[261] Names of ancient authorities are cor-

259. Jean Leclerq, "Manuscrits cisterciens dans les bibliothèques d'Italie," *Analecta sacri ordinis cisterciensis* 7 (1951): 71–77, dates the manuscripts, noting that they "n'ont plus l'exlibris, ayant perdu leur dernier feuillet; ils viennent très probablement aussi di Morimondo, mais n'y furent pas écrits" (71). He describes the two manuscripts at 72–73.

260. De Gaiffier, "Deux passionnaires," 144; cf. Ferrari, "Biblioteche e scrittoi," 241 and 266 n. 92. The consensus seems to be that the manuscripts were not produced at Morimondo but were probably there by the fifteenth century.

261. For *michi-mihi* and *rethor-rhetor*, see the following comparison. Note that only when the text of the *Sanctuarium* diverges from Como MS 5 does the correct spelling *rhetor* occur, e.g.,

TABLE 3.3

Como, MS 5, fol. 84ra, ll. 32–36	*Mombritius 1910, 1:285, ll. 6–9*
Et dixit ad eos imperator. Si obscurum uerbum in uobis et fuco plenum est, dictionalis mulier apud nos gloriosa,	et dixit ad eos Imperator : Si est in uobis obscurus sermo et fusco plenus : dicite mihi : est enim apud nos mulier quaedam gloriosa spetie fulgida omni scientia et rhetorico sermone decorata
et fuco plena scripture. calammoco rethorico, sursum ymaginaria, et robuste docta. Si est ergo	Si est ergo

rected throughout the *Sanctuarium* entry: *Scolapius* becomes *Aesculapius*;
Galhenus becomes *Galen*; *Sybilla* and *Sibilla* become *Sibylla*.[262] And
phrases are made more mellifluous: the manuscript's "ut cognoscitis
propositum quod positum est" is rewritten, for example, as "ut cognoscis
praeceptum: quod positum est."[263] Nevertheless, Katherine's final prayer
indicates that the *Sanctuarium* might follow the *MLA* family of manuscripts very closely, even with regard to punctuation and spelling.[264] But
other forms of direct discourse, *oratio recta*, represented in the *Sanctuarium*'s account of Katherine deviate more radically from the manuscript. In

---

262. Compare the list of authorities that Katherine refers to in her refutation of the fifty
philosophers:

TABLE 3.4

Como, MS 5, fol. 84va, ll. 32–35	*Mombritius 1910, 1:285, ll. 30–32*
dictionum homerii . et aristotilis . scolapii . et galheni . dionisii . iamnes et mambres . phylistonis . et sibille . platonis . et eusebii . que ego conitiens	dictionum Homeri dicere graeca lingua Aristotilis . Aesculapii . et Hippocratis . Dionysii . Platonis . et Ianni . et Mambris et Phylistonis : et Sibylae .
	omnia ista
sub calcaneo meo posui	sub calcaneo meo posui

Mombrizio's *graeca lingua* echoes an earlier phrase from the manuscript. Compare this list
of authorities to one given earlier in the narrative, a list of Katherine's learning: "Hec
didicerat librum virgilii et homerii . et scolapii . galieni . aristotilis . platonis . eusebii . iamnes
et mambres . dionisi . sibille . nicromantie, rationem etiam rethorum sciebat, et omnis narratio septuaginta duarum linguarum volvebatur in ore eius" (Como MS 5, fol. 83rb, ll.
22–28), which is removed in the *Sanctuarium*: "Haec didicerat omnem scientiam omnium
artium tam poetarum quam philosophorum : et omnis interpretatio lingue etiam uoluebatur
in ore eius" (Mombritius 1910, 284, ll. 15–17).
263. Cf. Como, MS 5, fol. 83a, ll. 26–27, and Mombritius 1910, vol. I, 283, l. 53.
264. Compare the following:

TABLE 3.5

Como MS 5, fol. 86va, ll. 10–27	*Mombritius 1910, 1:287, ll. 27–37*
Sancta autem catherina extendit manus suas ad celos, et dixit . Domine deus exaudi me . et tribue omnibus memorantibus nomen meum catherinam . pro tuo amore, habundantiam panis et uini, sanitatem corporis . seruitium quadrupedum . Repelle ab eis omnem infirmitatem . omnem auram tenebrosam, et da omnibus colentibus nomen meum ut non	Sancta autem Catherina extendit manus suas ad caelos : et dixit : Domine deus exaudi me: et tribue omnibus memorantibus nomen meum Catherinam : pro tuo amore abundantiam panis et uini . sanitatem corporis . seruitium quadrupedum . repelle ab eis omnem morbum et omnem auram tempestatum : et da omnibus colentibus nomen meum : ut non possint a subitanea morte : nec careant aliquo membrorum : nec mulier patitur abortum : nec in partu pereat:

Table 3.5 continued on next page

Como MS 5, the longest exchanges are between the young virgin and the fifty philosophers, called together by the emperor to refute her Christian arguments against the pagan gods.[265] These speeches appear to represent a mystical excess of meaning, if not an intermediary's simple incomprehension of a Greek original. The *Sanctuarium* often completely rewrites them, reducing ecstatic nonsense to rational discourse.[266] Aside from these apparent interventions to make grammatical and rhetorical "improvements," Mombrizio or his compositors made a few minor factual changes, removing or adjusting dates and numbers.[267] In short, if Mombrizio had recourse to Como MS 5 for his account of Katherine, he does seem to have inter-

sit sterilitas fructuum in civitate aut in regione illa, sed celestis ros sit super eam die ac nocte, et da eis remissionem omnium peccatorum. Quod si recordatus fuerit nominis ancille tue catherine . in hora obitus sui, angeli tui deducant eum in sanctam requiem paradisi. Et cum finisset	et non sterilitas fructuum in ciuitate aut in regione sed caelestis ros sit super eam die ac nocte : et da eis remissionem omnium peccatorum : quod si recordatus fuerit aliquis nominis ancillae tuae Catherinae in hora exitus sui : angeli tui deducant eum in paradisi sanctam requiem. Et cum finisset

265. Como, MS 5, fol. 84vb, l. 6–fol. 85b, l. 9.
266. Compare the following:

TABLE 3.8

Como, MS 5, fol. 84rb, ll. 27–33	*Mombritius 1910, 1:285, ll. 22–26*
Et aperiens os suum dixit . Ex aquoso elemento consistunt maria . fucate robuste et multum latenter re[peri]unt[ur] . et congregantur in uiuo pelago . Hoc est enim maximum capitulum . et obscurissiumum homerii . Ait enim in aristotelis splendidissimus rhethor . Ita euidenter affero duplam maximamque uisionem sonantem acerrime . Solatam in canalibus uoraginum subterraneum . . .	Et aperiens os suum dixit : Stulte non legisti quia scriptura dicit : Compraehendam in astutia eorum : et apostolus Paulus dicite uidite : ne quis uos decipiat per philosophiam et inanam falaciam : et iterum : Sapientia huius mundi stultitia est apud deum.

The incomprehensible remainder of Katherine's first speech as presented in Como 5 is simply excised in Mombrizio's account (Como, MS 5, fol. 84rb, l. 28–fol. 84va, l. 25).

267. First, dates: The queen's martyrdom is dated "mense novembris die vicesima tertia fera quinta" (Como, MS 5, fol. 86va, ll. 18–19); cf. Mombritius 1910, 287, l. 14. The martyrdom of Porphyrius and his two hundred troops is dated "mense novembris die vicesima quarta sexta feria" (Como MS 5, fol. 86va, ll. 34–35); cf. Mombritius 1910, 287, ll. 21–22 (retaining the number of two hundred soldiers earlier, at l. 15). Katherine's martyrdom is dated "mense novembris vicesimo quinto die feria septima hora diei tertia" (Como MS 5, fol. 87ra, ll. 5–7); cf. Mombritius 1910, 287, ll. 49: "septimo calendas decembris." Next, numbers:

vened in the narrative. His interventions are typically humanist; that is, they touch on classicizing orthography, direct address, and minor points of fact. That would not be a philologist's procedure. Moreover, these interventions are such minor and expected ones that many editors of the period—and some compositors—might have made them.

❊ ❊ ❊

The *Sanctuarium* that was printed in Milan around 1477 by a consortium that included Bonino Mombrizio is, unmistakably, an extensive collection of holy lives. This chapter has suggested that it is also, in some fundamental ways, an unfinished or hastily finished edition. On the basis of the inclusion of fifty saints for the month of August, for example, we might speculate that Mombrizio planned for more than five hundred entries. Alternatively, on the basis of the unfinished *ancona* for Galeazzo Maria's chapel at Pavia, we might speculate that he only intended to treat about two hundred saints. If the lost manuscript known to Argelati was indeed produced before the imprint, then we can further say that the anthology was meant to be in liturgical order; since Argelati noted that the manuscript opened with St. Martin, we can surmise that the order was Ambrosian. Whether the imprint appeared before or after Argelati's manuscript, certain saints seem to have posed a problem; they needed to be cut out or included. The fact that these troublesome saints are George and Katherine, figures of particular importance to the Sforza dynasty, seems to confirm the hypothesis that some political meaning attached to the production of the paraliturgical collection.

It is difficult to say in just what kind of spirit Mombrizio intended to offer his texts. Bolland's description of the *Sanctuarium* as a transcription of sources so exact as to include manuscript errors is, in some instances, fully borne out.[268] Moreover, the evidence of the Avienus transcription encourages the conclusion that Mombritius recognized the rarity of some of his hagiographic sources and therefore reproduced them carefully on

---

Where Como MS 5, fol. 86rb, ll. 31–32, says that the broken parts of Katherine's wheel "interfecerunt multitudinem militum quasi quattuor milia," the *Sanctuarium* says only "interfecerunt multos ex gentilium militibus." For a corrected number, compare Como MS 5, fol. 83ra, ll. 20–22— "Temporibus maxentii impiissimi imperatoris . anno tricesimo quinto imperii eius"—and Mombritius 1910, 283, l. 50: "Temporibus Maxentii impiissimi imperatoris anno quinto imperii eius."

268. My collations of the *Sanctuarium* entries for the rare narratives treating Therenus, Reparata, and Pelagia with Como MSS 5 and 6 are too technically complex to be reproduced here. The results are varied. Cf. W. Weismann, "Die *Passio Genesii mimi* (BHL 332)," *Mittellteinisches Jahrbuch* 12 (1977): 36, n. 62.

that account. Such recognition—which would constitute philological attentiveness to medieval saints' lives—would also suggest a great deal of time spent in research and reading. In other instances, notably that of Katherine of Alexandria, the *Sanctuarium* suggests more typically "improving" humanist interventions. These improvements, minor as they are, would also have been time-consuming to prepare. If my collation of the Katherine text stands, then it is best to hesitate before deciding that the collection was intended to reproduce all its ancient sources in a photographic manner or as a preparatory stage for later *castigationes* of *vitae et passiones sanctorum*.

A more fundamental problem exists, however. Bolland made an assumption about Mombrizio's role in the production of the *Sanctuarium*. In fact, we do not know what part Mombrizio played in the printing venture. On the basis of his earlier printing work, we can deduce that Mombrizio helped to fund the publication: he was a speculator and entrepreneur. On the same basis, we can deduce that he may also have served as *revisor* for the proofs; that is, he had some editorial capacity.[269] That combination of tasks was not unusual in the Quattrocento. But we do not know if he was assigned or took upon himself the task of collecting the manuscripts; we do not know if Morimondo's library played a part, or Bobbio's library or even Montecassino or the Morimond mother-house in Burgundy. We do not know how many presses or workshops were involved, or how closely Mombrizio supervised the production of composition units. And we do not know how seriously he took his editorial work in this instance.

It does seem likely that the political events of 1476–78 intervened in the printing of the *Sanctuarium*. I have hypothesized that Mombrizio's own standing with the interim regime needed to be secured; that hypothesis will account for his haste in publishing and his dedication to Simonetta. There may have been time only to remove the politically sensitive saint George and to add accounts from the *Legenda aurea* and *Speculum historiale* in order to fill out gatherings or to represent saints on whom he had not yet worked. Inclusion of a *vita Katherinae* as well as its mild touching-up are both consonant with this hypothesis.

But we should also ask a yet more fundamental question: was the sort of editorial accomplishment credited to Mombrizio by Jean Bolland even *possible* in the Quattrocento? Was perfect transcription of a text about a saint (as opposed to a classical text) *thinkable* as such, that is, as consciously undertaken labor at once preservative and critical in intent? That the labor

---

269. The problem of Inventius / Iuventius (p. 148 above) suggests a misunderstood instruction, for example.

should be both preservative and critical is important: simple preservation may be an act of reverence, and of that sort of labor we have abundant evidence for the whole of the Middle Ages and Renaissance. Canonical narratives about saints had been copied with great care for centuries. But as Michael Lapidge has argued, the body of medieval *vitae et passiones sanctorum* also included some of the more labile texts that a scribe might face.[270] Scribal intervention in noncanonical accounts is to be expected, for only a handful of canonical texts were copied with the kind of precision that we associate with critical transcription but that medieval monks associated with their vows of obedience and humility. In the Quattrocento, a literate copyist, especially a layman, might be hard put to restrain his urge to revise an egregiously ungrammatical, infelicitous, or unbelievable saint's life.

We know, however, that such laymen existed. In 1456 the humanist schoolteacher Guarino Guarini was invited by a friend to revise a twelfth-century account of Guarino's own name saint, the thirteenth-century Guarinus or Warinus.[271] The old narrative of the saintly canon and cardinal Warinus had been discovered by a former student, the Lateran Canon Timoteo Maffei, and Timoteo had sent it as a gift to his elderly teacher. Guarino was deeply touched. Writing in thanks to Timoteo, Guarino recalled his childhood experience of his father's death and how his mother had consoled him with a reminder that the boy possessed his father's name: Guarino. Now he had the saint, to confirm the virtue of the name. We have, in short, unusual evidence of Guarino's profound identification with this saint and of the circumstances in which a humanist might publicly acknowledge such identification. Another of Guarino's friends, the Lateran Canon Cyprian of Bologna, naturally thought that the humanist would be interested in encouraging the Bolognese saint's cult by rewriting the narrative. But here is the crux: Guarino told Cyprian that, on the contrary, the life of Warinus ought *not* to be rewritten in "another style and rhetorical form" ("alio stilo et orationis genere").[272] In a lengthy and impassioned letter, Guarino made his point by describing analogous improprieties: what if Cyprian's fellow monks dressed in white sandals and purple robes? The *vita* would be suspicious with its hair curled and its cheeks rouged.[273] The truth of this account lay precisely in its humble character, its *tenuitas*. In a case of such virtuous authenticity, Guarino claimed, to rewrite would be to falsify: both *historia* and saint required

---

270. See n. 20 above.

271. Sabbadini, *Epistolario*, letter 904, 2:646–648, with notes at 3:496–497. Sabbadini dates Guarino's letter to 1456.

272. Sabbadini, *Epistolario*, 2:648, ll. 71–72. Cyprian must have asked for a panegyric.

273. Sabbadini, *Epistolario*, 2:648, ll. 74–77. For analogies between clothing and hair, on the one hand, and rhetorical style, on the other, I have learned a great deal from talking to Christine Krause about her work on Caesar.

attention to deeds, not words.[274]

How would Mombrizio have responded to this argument? Did he think of his collected texts with such warm devotional care? For Guarino's argument to preserve is not made on the basis of any text-critical notions. Rather than being explicitly philological, it takes a great part of its effect from the fact that Guarino was elderly—in his mid-eighties—and was recalling the death of his homonymous father. Perhaps, in this instance, Mombrizio would have agreed with his teacher. Perhaps he even thought that devotion and philology made good bedfellows; humanists certainly exhibited, on occasion, such devotion to their classical sources that a reliquary sense might be inferred. But in the Quattrocento context of these *vitae*, it is unlikely that, even if Mombrizio did agree with Guarino's restraint in some cases, he would have agreed in all. As his prefatory poem in the *Chronica* shows, Mombrizio thought of the printing press as a reliably correcting form of scribe, not as an unthinking one. His position was, in fact, close to Bolland's. Like the seventeenth-century Jesuit scholar, the fifteenth-century bureaucrat, poet, and printing entrepreneur also expected responsibly improved versions that attended to audience as well as to history. Philology alone will not account for the *Sanctuarium* as we have received it.

274. Sabbadini, *Epistolario*, 2:648, ll. 78–86.

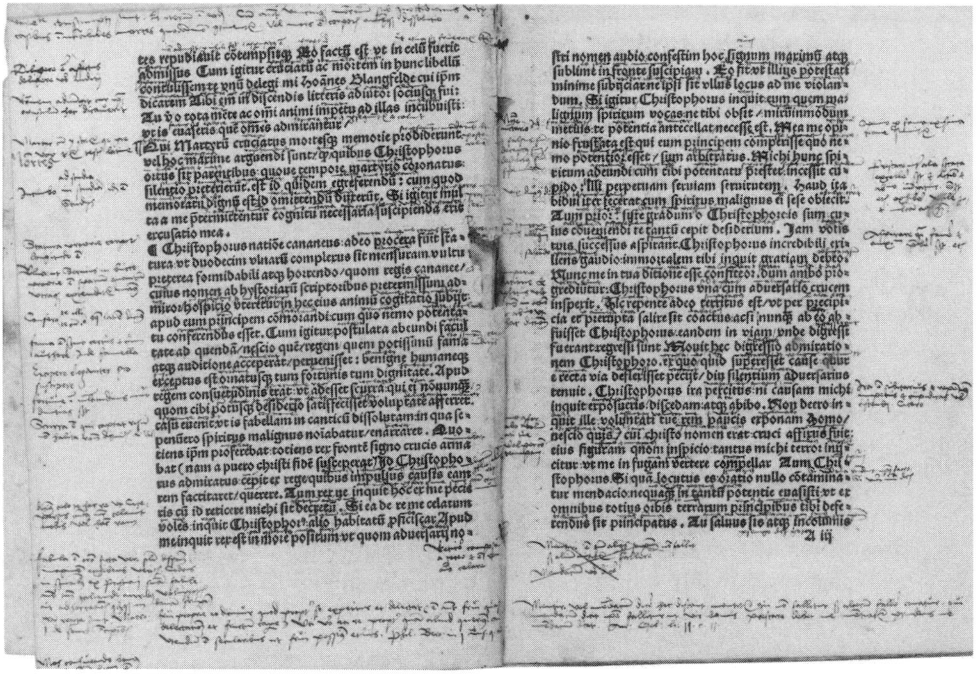

PLATE 4. Giovanni Garzoni, *Gloriosissimi martyris Christophori Cananei vita ab J.G. elegantissime conscripta* (Leipzig: Martinus Herbipolensis, 1510). London, British Library, T.943 (1), sign. 2v–3.

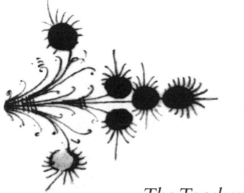

CHAPTER 4

The Teacher's Saints

To narrative forms is given the useful task of upholding or destroying things, which is called confirmation and refutation. And this can be done not only to things handed down in myth and poetry but also even in histories.

—Quintilian, *Inst. orat.* II, iv, 18

It can even be asked about religious subjects, such as Susanna, Tobia, and Judith. And likewise about more recent histories, such as Saint George, and many others, where there are many arguments to be disproved.

—Lorenzo Valla, *postilla ad locum*[1]

The preceding chapters have shown authors engaged with dozens, even hundreds, of saints' lives and passions at a time. The encyclopedic projects undertaken by Antonio Agli, Giannozzo Manetti, Bonino Mombrizio, and others, although dissimilar in concept and intent,

1. "Narrationibus non inutiliter subiungitur opus destruendi confirmandique eas, quod *anaskeue kai kataskeue* uocatur. Id porro non tantum in fabulosis et carmine traditis fieri potest, uerum etiam in ipsis annalium monumentis" and Valla's annotation, "Hoc queri potest etiam in rebus ecclesiasticis, ut de Susanna, de Tobia, de Iudit. Item de historiis recentioribus, ut Sancti Georgii, et aliorum multorum, ubi plura sunt argumenta ad improbandum," quoted from L. Cesarini Martinelli and A. Perosa, eds., *Lorenzo Valla: Le postille*

are equally impressive in scope. But if we consider accounts that were meant to stand alone, uncollected, unabsorbed into larger codicological schemes, then it must be said that the most impressively prolific humanist author of prose *vitae et passiones sanctorum* was a married layman, physician, professor of medicine, and teacher of rhetoric. Giovanni Garzoni of Bologna composed more saints' lives and martyrs' passions than any other Quattrocento humanist.[2]

In the prefaces to his *vitae* and *passiones*, Garzoni often declares his purpose. These justifications are not profound. In the introduction to his life of John the Evangelist, for example, he says straightforwardly:

> For if pagan writers, who had no idea of the truth, wrote the deeds of Greek and Roman princes, I do not see why I should pass over in silence the outstanding deeds of such great men, deeds accomplished for the purpose of increasing and maintaining the Christian republic. It has not escaped me that many men, utterly ignorant of liberal studies, have taken upon themselves this weighty duty. I find in their writings

---

all'*Instituto Oratoria di Quintiliano* (Padua: Antenore, 1996), 52. See G. L. Spalding, ed., *De institutio oratoria* (Paris, 1821–1825), 1:278. Cf. Priscian, *Praeexercitamina*, "De refutatione," in C. Halm, ed., *Rhetores Latini minores* (Leipzig: Teubner, 1863), 554. De *institutio oratoria*, book 2, chap. 4, Quintilian's overview of twelve *progymnasmata*, or grammatical and rhetorical exercises, is a valuable section for anyone considering Valla as a teacher. *Anaskeue* and *kataskeue* are relatively advanced exercises; see George Kennedy, *A New History of Classical Rhetoric* (Princeton, N.J.: Princeton University Press, 1994), 202–208, esp. 204–205, discussing Apthonius's use of the exercises.

2. On Garzoni, see are Dionysius Sandellius (pseud. for Vincenzo Domenico Fassini), *De vita et scriptis Joannis Garzonis Bononiensis . . .* (Brescia: Vescovo, 1781); Giovanni Fantuzzi, *Notizie degli scrittori Bolognesi* 4 (Bologna: S. Tommaso d'Aquino, 1784), 78–100; Florio Banfi, "Un umanista bolognese e i domenicani," *MD* 52 (1935): 365–378 and 53 (1936): 69–80; Guglielmo Manfré, "La biblioteca dell'umanista bolognese Giovanni Garzoni," *Accademie e biblioteche d'Italia* 27, no. 4 (1959): 249–278 and 28, nos. 1–3 (1960): 17–69; Pearl Kibre, "Giovanni Garzoni of Bologna (1419–1505), Professor of Medicine and Defender of Astrology," *Isis* 58 (1967): 504–514; H. S. Matson, "Giovanni Garzoni (1419–1505) to Alessandro Achillini (1463–1512): An Unpublished Letter and Defense," in E. P. Mahoney, ed., *Philosophy and Humanism* (Leiden: Brill, 1976), 518–530; Luisa Avellini, "Per uno studio del problema dell'eloquenza nell'opera di Giovanni Garzoni," *Studi e memorie: Istituto per la storia dell'Università di Bologna. Biblioteca de "L'Archiginnasio*," n.s., 3 (1983): 83–104; eadem, "Eloquenza e commettenza: Prosa encomiastica e agiografia di Giovanni Garzoni," *Bentivolorum magnificentia* (Rome, 1984), 135–154; Alfonso D'Amato, *I Domenicani a Bologna* (Bologna: Studio Domenicano, 1988), 1:465–471 passim; A. J. Hunt, "A Token of Friendship from Giovanni Garzoni to Politian: His Dialogue on Alexander the Great and the Romans," *Pluteus* 6–7 (1988–89): 133–199; and Lind, *Letters*. Hunt, "A Token," 144, corrects the traditional birthdate of 1419 to ca. 1428, convincingly, in my opinion; Lind, *Letters,* evidently did not know Hunt's study (although both men were in touch with P. O. Kristeller). Hunt's revised birthdate entails some refiguring of the biography given by Lind at iv–xv. Lind's edition of the letters—without which this study could not have been written—must be used carefully. The recent entry in *DBI* 52 (1999), 438b–440a, is a summary of older scholarship, without reference to Hunt or Lind.

none of the dignity required by elegant composition. I will overlook weightiness of precept, of which I see nothing, so that it is embarrassing that they took up such a great office. Therefore, although I have little learning in eloquence, I thought I might assume that burden, for the sake of exercising my small wit.[3]

In his typically self-righteous way, Garzoni claims to write because no one else is honoring the holy subjects appropriately. Unfortunately, the gist of this explanation—as well as the comparative trope with which it opens and the gesture of humility with which it closes—might have been uttered by any of the authors who undertook similar revisions in the preceding dozen centuries. Garzoni's preface does not, in other words, help us to account for the abundance of his *vitae et passiones* in comparison to those by earlier authors or in comparison to those by his contemporaries. It does not clarify his choice of a Latin prose format: the verse epics by Baptista Mantuanus or the hymns by Zaccaria Ferreri strike us as more typically "humanist."[4] The preface does not shed any explanatory light on the fact that this prolific rewriter of saints' lives was a layman, a phenomenon perhaps perhaps less surprising in fifteenth-century Italy but rare in the centuries before and after. And the preface contains no hints to help us understand why the simple fact of quantity did nothing to ensure Garzoni's reputation as an author of saints' lives.[5] There are, then, many questions. This chapter will suggest that humanist pedagogy, the *studia humanitatis* in its classroom manifestation, may help us make sense of such a prolific author.

In the present state of scholarship, most of what we know about Garzoni comes from his many writings and especially his *epistolae familiares*.[6] The ten books of letters reflect the activities and concerns of his middle and old age; the earliest letter that can be dated is a brief *responsio* of 1466,

---

3. From the preface to the life of St. John the Evangelist in BBU, MS 1676, fols. 1–2. Garzoni's hagiographic prefaces are edited in A. Frazier, "Italian Humanists as Authors of *vitae sanctorum*, 1417–1521" (PhD diss., Columbia University, 1997), 615–664.

4. Until more work is done on Latin metric *vitae sanctorum* across the Middle Ages, it will be hard to evaluate humanist contributions to saintly epic. See François Dolbeau, "Un domain négligé de la littérature médiolatine: Les textes hagiographiques en vers," *Cahiers de civilisation médiévale* 45 (2002): 129–139.

5. Aside from the catalogs of Manfré and the Bollandists, only Avellini, "Eloquenza," has addressed the body of *vitae sanctorum*, although she, like Banfi, "Un umanista," concentrates on "le tre vite più importante, in quanto più estese e testimoniate da un maggior numero di copie": the lives of Dominic, Thomas Aquinas, and Peter Martyr.

6. A critical biography of Garzoni based on archival sources has yet to be written; in consequence, the information presented here remains tentative. For a survey of the *opera*, see Sandellius, *De vita et scriptis*, 20–36; and Fantuzzi, *Notizie* 4:78–101. Lind's edition of the *epistolae familiares* gathers almost five hundred letters, a fraction of the total composed by Garzoni during his mature working life.

when Garzoni, then in his late thirties and following his father's professional path, received his medical degree from the University of Bologna.[7]
With few exceptions, he stayed in Bologna from that time, teaching practical medicine at the university until his death.[8] On a faculty where there
were real stars, Garzoni was hardly among the most active, innovative, or
well-paid teachers of medicine. His professional skills were respected,
however. He consulted for the Bentivoglio and, from 1477, served as
physician to the Hermits of San Giacomo.[9] Private patients of both sexes
sought him out, and he advised clients in the allied field of astrology.[10] But
if the letters confirm the professional success of his mature years, they also
demonstrate that medicine—*studia haec stercoralia*—was neither Garzoni's first calling nor the one he preferred.[11]

Garzoni's earliest and deepest enthusiasm was for rhetoric, the *studia oratoria*.[12] Perhaps he "received his early education at home," tutored by his
learned father, Bernardo, or his father's friend Giovanni Lamola (d. 1449).[13]
Garzoni does recall that, as a boy ("nundum tertium decimum annum age-
bam"), he heard Leonardo Bruni (d. March 9, 1444) advise a virtuous young
Florentine that to achieve eloquence, he ought to read and reread Cicero.[14]

7. Banfi, "Un umanista," 377 n. 2; Lind, *Letters*, letter 285. On his father's medical career
and acquaintance with Lorenzo Valla's friend Giovanni Tortelli, see Celestino Piana, *Nuove
ricerche su le Università di Bologna e di Parma* (Florence: Quaracchi, 1966), 146–147, item
45 and n. 1; and David A. Lines, "The Importance of Being Good: Moral Philosophy in the
Italian Universities, 1300–1600" *Rinascimento*, ser. 2, 36 (1996): 175.

8. Garzoni's name "is listed from 1466 to the year of his death, 1505, as a professor of
medicine in the rolls of the University," according to Lind, *Letters*, x.

9. On service to the Bentivoglio, see Lind, *Letters*, x; for his relatively few appearances on
doctoral committees, see ibid., xii–xiii; for difficulties with his service to the Augustinians,
see ibid., letter 128. See also L. R. Lind, *Studies in Pre-Vesalian Anatomy: Biography, Translations, Documents* (Philadelphia: APS, 1975), 26–27; Matson, "Giovanni Garzoni," on
Garzoni's part in the career of Alessandro Achillini; and Lind, *Letters*, letter 120, in which
Garzoni complains of salary inequity about 1490.

10. See, e.g., Lind, *Letters*, letter 155, for an example of medical advice; Kibre, "Giovanni
Garzoni," on astrology; and, for astrology in his library, see Manfré, "La biblioteca," 18–19
(BBU, MS 132); 26–27 (MS 467); and 30–31 (MS 731, 2).

11. Garzoni complains to Francesco Tranchedino that his rhetorical skills are suffering
because of his profession: "Quod enim solatium mihi esse putas quum saepenumero a me illa
quaerantur an aegrotus totam noctem dormierit, an urinam fecerit, an cibi reliquias degusta-
verit, et mille huiusmodi, que praetereo nequid iniocunditatis habeat oratio?" (Lind, *Letters*,
letter 51, dated by Lind to 1490–99). For similar sentiments, see ibid., letter 123. For medical notes and manuscripts in his library, see Manfré, "La biblioteca."

12. The phrase *studia oratoria* occurs in Lind, *Letters*, letter 424, and passim. References
to his early education are thin: e.g., ibid., letters 44, 99, 123, and 192.

13. Lind, *Letters*, ix, speculates on Lamola's tuition; the letters do not mention it. On the
close relationship between Lamola and the elder Garzoni, see Ezio Raimondi, *Codro e l'u-
manesimo a Bologna* (Bologna: Zuffi, 1950), 54. On Bernardo's library, see BBU MS 921.

14. Lind, *Letters*, letter 3. On the basis of the 1419 birthdate for Garzoni, Lind, *Letters*,
ix, dates his visit to Florence to 1431, but Pope Eugene IV was not in Florence that year, as
required by the letter. See the following note.

The recollection, which occurs in a letter that must have been written when Garzoni was at least sixty-five, describes an event of around 1439.[15] Then, as Garzoni notes, Florence was home to such major figures as Carlo Marsuppini, Ambrogio Traversari, Flavio Biondo, and George of Trebizond. But Garzoni merely lists these names, without recording meetings or further impressions.

Similarly, Giovanni Garzoni reminisces hardly at all about his adolescent years in the Rome of Nicholas V (March 6, 1447–March 24, 1455). His father had been called to serve as one of the pope's physicians, and the boy was lucky enough to be taken along.[16] Some sense of young Garzoni's intellectual attainments at the time can be gathered from a codex that he compiled in late 1450.[17] The bulk of this manuscript, nearly three hundred folios, is occupied by a widely used textbook that Garzoni "transcribed, corrected, and emended," the *Tractatus*, or *Summulae logicales*, by Petrus Hispanus, later John XXI (1276–1277).[18] Because the *Tractatus* was a university-level introduction to Aristotelian logic, it is possible that Giovanni spent some time at the *studium urbis* in Rome, at university in Bologna, or even (as I will note) in Ferrara. But his codex suggests that he was also acquainted with other sorts of teachers in other sorts of ways. The handful of folios following the *Tractatus* sport an array of humanist ephemera: short poems, mostly in honor of Giovanni Lamola (who had died in Bologna in 1449), by Francesco Filelfo, Guarino Guarini, Niccolò Perotti, and even Giovanni Garzoni himself;[19] the odd letter by Giovanni

15. The letter is to Frater Leandro Alberti; the word *frater* shows that it postdates 1493, when Alberti joined the Dominicans as a novice. If Garzoni was born around 1428, he was at least sixty-five by 1493. Hunt, "A Token," 144, proposes that Garzoni's visit to Florence occurred in 1439 (when Garzoni would have been about eleven) on the basis of Garzoni's mention that Ambrogio Traversari (d. October 21, 1439) was still living.

16. Bernardo joined the *familia* of his old university friend, the humanist bishop of Bologna, Tommaso Parentucelli, now Nicholas V. Lind, *Letters*, viii, implies the date of 1443 for the beginning of Bernardo's appointment to Nicholas V, impossible because Nicholas only became pope in 1447.

17. See Manfré, "La biblioteca," 60–62, a description of BBU, MS 1619.

18. The Paris-trained logician and professor of medicine Petrus Hispanus is best known today for his intervention, as pope, in the Paris faculty disputes and for his commentary on Aristotle's *De Anima*. There is a critical edition of the *Tractatus* by L. M. de Rijk, ed., *Petrus Hispanus Portugalensis, Tractatus, Called Afterward Summulae Logicales* (Assen: Van Gorcum 1972); and a brief discussion in idem, *La philosophie au moyen age* (Leiden: Brill, 1985), 185–192. Peter Mack, *Renaissance Argument: Valla and Agricola in the Tradition of Rhetoric and Dialectic* (Leiden: Brill, 1993) *ad indicem* identifies aspects of the *Tractatus* that were adopted or rejected by humanist logicians. See also Paul Grendler, *The Universities of the Italian Renaissance* (Baltimore: Johns Hopkins University Press, 2002), 257–260.

19. BBU, MS 1619, fols. 287v, 289, 290. Of these authors, Perotti, too, had a connection to Bernardo Garzoni; see Loredana Chines, *La parola degli antichi: Umanesimo emiliano tra scuola e poesia* (Rome: Carocci, 1998), 88–89 and n. 74.

Aurispa, by Guarino, by Filelfo (several on Lamola's death); miscellaneous *sententiae*; and an excerpt from Antonio Beccadelli's controversial work of 1425, the *Hermaphroditus*.[20] These names are suggestive, although they do not, of course, constitute proof that the authors even met, much less befriended or taught Garzoni. Nevertheless, his father's appointment as physician to Nicholas V probably facilitated Giovanni's meetings with major humanists resident in Rome. Late in life, for example, Giovanni recalled that Theodore Gaza had been exceptionally kind and close to him ("summa erat benivolentia summaque familiaritas"), even showing the young man his personal library.[21]

Into that same manuscript, Giovanni Garzoni also wrote a list of books, the contents of his own library around 1450.[22] It is very much a bachelor's collection. Predominant are the early staples of scholastic logic, including a commentary on the *Summulae*, by Henry of Ghent (d. 1293); Herveus Natalis (d. 1323) on first and second intentions; the *Commentaria in totam artem veterem Aristotelis* by Giovanni Graziadio d'Ascoli, O.P. (fl 1450); a "complete" Walter Burley (d. 1345); and two miscellanies featuring logical works by Paul of Pergola (d. 1455) and Paul of Venice (d. 1429).[23] The classical authors are represented by Cicero, although not the rhetorical but the "philosophical writings" (possibly his father's copy of the *Tusculan Disputations*), and by Ovid's *Epistolae ex Ponto*.[24] These were supplemented by two later works: a *De viris illustribus* attributed to Pliny (but probably Aurelius Victor) and Eutropius's *Roman Histories*. Giovanni owned a single textbook associated with the *studia humanitatis*: the *Orthographia* by Gasparino Barzizza (ca. 1360–1431).[25] It is striking that Valla's *Elegantiae* (completed ca. 1441) and George of Trebizond's *Compendium* of Priscian (composed in the early 1430s)—works that Garzoni is known to have possessed—are not present in this list. However, these and other texts may have been tucked into the manuscripts. The mis-

20. BBU, MS 1619, fol. 288v, 290v, 291r (letters); fols. 290v and 292 (*sententiae*); f. 291v (Beccadelli).

21. In Garzoni's *Vita divi Antonii*, printed in Bologna by Hector in 1503, at sign. B4 (bound at the end of BBU, MS 732; see also BBU MS 741, fols. 17v–18).

22. Manfré, "La biblioteca," 60.

23. Logic preceded moral and natural philosophy and other studies in the university curriculum; see Paul Grendler, *Schooling in Renaissance Italy: Literacy and Learning, 1300–1600* (Baltimore: Johns Hopkins University Press, 1989), 268–269, and Lines, "The Importance," 150 and nn. 50–53. See Manfré, "La biblioteca," 53, for Bernardo's Paul of Venice, BBU, MS 920, also used by Giovanni's son.

24. Manfré, "La biblioteca," 29, a description of Bernardo's *Tusculans*.

25. On Barzizza, see G. Martelotti, "Barzizza, Gasparino," *DBI* 7 (1965): 34b–39a, and on the textbook, W. Keith Percival, "The *Orthographia* of Gasparino Barzizza," *AION* 14 (1992): 263–282. Garzoni's copy seems to have disappeared from his library by the time of his death. For the grammatical works he held late in life, see Manfré, "La biblioteca," 254.

cellaneous additions to Garzoni's *Summulae logicales* of 1450 are a reminder that a codex need not contain only the work by which it is named and that the title may not even be a reliable guide to the additional material. Moreover, Garzoni's acquaintance with books was not limited to these listed works: other sources, for example, reveal that about this same time he was reading Jerome's *De viris illustribus* and that it was guiding his intellectual explorations.[26]

The books named in Garzoni's library list suggest that Bernardo intended his son for one of the professions—medicine, law, or theology—providing the young man with the foundation of a philosophical (i.e., dialectic-based) education that would normally have followed preliminary training in grammar and rhetoric. But the codex itself shows that Giovanni grew up in an environment where the fascination of humanist rhetoric was overwhelming. The admirable men he encountered seem to have been teachers associated with the *studia humanitatis.* The result must have been painful, for Giovanni would have had to demonstrate exceptional textual brilliance to compensate for his impediment in oratorical delivery. Perhaps someone consoled him by pointing out that even Demosthenes had a stutter.[27]

Garzoni studied with two teachers who embodied the best of the *studia humanitatis.* The first was Guarino Guarini (1374–1460), with whom, perhaps using a manuscript that had been transcribed decades earlier by his father, Garzoni studied Juvenal ("audivi hunc librum").[28] As Guarino was in Ferrara during 1449, the year specified for the study, Garzoni must have been absent from Rome for some length of time while his father was still serving in the curia. He may have studied—for weeks or months but probably not years—in Ferrara in the late 1440s and may even have transcribed his *Summulae logicales* at the university there. By the mid-1450s he had returned to Rome. There, during the pontificate of Callixtus III (April 8, 1455–August 6, 1458), when Giovanni himself would have been in his late twenties, he spent four years with a second teacher, Lorenzo

26. See n. 47 below.

27. On Garzoni's stutter, see Lind, *Letters,* letters 29, 50, and 89 and p. 422.

28. For the quotation, see Manfré, "La biblioteca," 52, from BBU, MS 876, note on flyleaf. There Garzoni refers to Guarino as "praeceptore meo" without specifying Guarino senior. See also Sabbadini, *Epistolario* 3:438, and Lind, *Letters,* ix and 568–569, a note to letter 488 from Battista Guarino to Garzoni. In fact, Garzoni says that he studied with Battista. But that makes the date 1449 difficult: Battista would have been fifteen years old, and Garzoni about twenty (or, if the traditional birth date of 1419 is accepted, thirty). Luigi Piacente, "Battista Guarini: l'uomo e il letterato," in P. Castelli, ed., *"In supreme dignitatis . . . " per la storia dell'università di Ferrara 1391–1991* (Florence: Olschki, 1995), 196, dates Battista's first steps as a teacher later, to 1452. Manfré, "La biblioteca," 25, 26, and 42 describes BBU, MSS 466, 467, and 748, collections of Cicero's orations and letters that formed part of Garzoni's library at his death. All bear annotations that may be traceable to Guarino's teaching.

Valla (d. 1457).[29] The connection to Valla was a point of pride, reiterated in several letters.[30] The master would naturally have taught his student to appreciate Quintilian. But neither Garzoni's library notes of around 1450 nor the catalog of his mature library include so much as excerpts from Quintilian. The library notes mention Cicero; in the mature library, Cicero predominates even over the doctor's medical books.[31] By the late Quattrocento, decades after the controversy between Poggio and Valla, Garzoni found it easier to harmonize than to contrast the two great figures of Latin rhetoric. He alleges in *De proprio Ciceronis imitandi studio*, for example, that many are amazed to find him cultivating Ciceronian Latin; they expect him to be a Quintilianist (evidently, then, contemporaries did acknowledge his study with Valla). But in uncharacteristically mild self-defense, he simply points out that Quintilian admired Ciceronian Latin.[32]

Another staged controversy that lived on anticlimactically in Garzoni's recollection was Valla's polemic with George of Trebizond about the relative military skills of the Romans and Alexander the Great.[33] When Garzoni composed a dialogue on that venerable dispute—could Alexander the Great have defeated the Roman army at the height of its powers?—he sided patriotically with his former teacher on the greater merit of the Latins over the Greeks.[34] But, again, the student was not overawed by his

29. Lind, *Letters*, ix. Subtracting four years of study from Valla's death in 1457 requires that Garzoni had returned to Rome by 1453, if accurate chronologies are to be expected. See Avellini, "L'Eloquenza," 91–92.

30. Cf. Banfi, "Un umanista, " 376 n. 3 : V. Del Nero, "Note sulla vita di Giovan Battista Pio (con alcune lettere inedite), " *Rinascimento* 21 (1981) : 247–263, letter 1; Lind, *Letters*, letters 65, 127, 135, 172, 215, 257, 407, and 417 (a letter that provides rare evidence for the link of Valla and Quintilian in Garzoni's mind; for this reason, it is of interest that the letter closes with Garzoni determining to write a *vita Pauli*). None of these letters is dated.

31. Manfré, "La biblioteca," 252, notes that Cicero is represented in eleven of the codices. Garzoni's *De elocutione ad nobilem virum Leonardum* (BBU, MS 1622, i, fols. 245–248) opposes Valla's position on Quintilian's clausulae (Manfré, "La biblioteca," 253). Avellini, "L'Eloquenza," 99–103 at 102.

32. Garzoni's brief *apologia* is edited in Hunt, "A Token," 195; and again in Lind, *Letters*, 570–571. Quintilian's admiration of Cicero (*Inst. orat.* 10.1.112) is repeated in *ibid.*, letter 31. For the context, see John Monfasani, "Episodes of Anti-Quintilianism in the Italian Renaissance," *Rhetorica* 10, no. 2 (1992): 119–138, reprinted in his *Language and Learning in Renaissance Italy* (Aldershot: Ashgate, 1994).

33. Lind, *Letters*, letter 424, to Angelo Poliziano; see John Monfasani, *George of Trebizond* (Leiden: Brill, 1976), 80. Drawing on Plutarch, Garzoni also wrote a treatise comparing Alexander and Julius Caesar (BBU MS 752, iii, fols. 203–220v). See the following note.

34. Garzoni's dialogue with his son Marcello was sent to Poliziano; no response is extant. Hunt, "A Token," edits the dialogue. He draws on Monfasani, *George of Trebizond*, to suggest that the original dispute between Valla and George took place in 1448–1451 (ibid., 161 and 162 n. 52); this dating suits the situations of Trebizond and Valla but cannot be reconciled with Garzoni's recollection of study with Valla during the pontificate of Callixtus III.

master. He owned two copies of George of Trebizond's popular *Compendium* of Priscian, alongside Valla's *Elegantiae*.[35]

In fact, no copy of the *Elegantiae* is extant among the inventory of codices in Garzoni's mature library, and it is not named in the ca. 1450 list. But from an undated letter to a Hungarian, Panonius, it becomes evident that Garzoni had long and thorough acquaintance of the work. This Hungarian, perhaps a student, is reprimanded for failing to return a precious book, Garzoni's own copy of the *Elegantiae*, transcribed before he was sixteen ("nondum enim quintum decimum egrediebar annum").[36] If Garzoni's memory serves him well, then he made his copy about 1443, probably in Bologna. Valla was still in Naples: 1443 would have been more than a decade before the period of Garzoni's study with him in Rome. Young Garzoni may have had access to an exemplar of the *Elegantiae* that had come into Lamola's hands, perhaps via Giovanni Tortelli or Niccolò Volpe.[37]

Another aspect of Garzoni's intellectual formation can be glimpsed in the subscription that closes a vernacular manuscript of Florus.[38] In this note, dated 1455 (that is, during a year in which Garzoni claims to have been studying with Valla in Rome), a "Iovane de garzoni" records his employment by Cardinal Domenico Capranica (1400–1458).[39] The connection to Capranica may explain Garzoni's otherwise mysterious trip to

35. For Priscian, see Manfré, "La biblioteca," 52, on BBU, MS 796, an *Institutio de arte grammatica* from Garzoni's library, and ibid., 51, describing two manuscript copies of George of Trebizond's *Compendium de partibus orationis ex Prisciano* from Garzoni's library, now BBU, MSS 794 and 795 (not seen). On George's popular *Compendium*, see Monfasani, *George of Trebizond*, 27–28; and idem, ed. *Collectanea Trapezuntiana* (Binghamton, N.Y.: MRTS, 1984), 478–480, listing Garzoni's manuscripts as nos. 4 and 5.

36. Lind, *Letters,* letter 294: "Quas in opus redegeram Laurentii Vallensi Elegantias (nondum enim quintum decimum egrediebar annum) tibi mutuo dedi," going on to threaten the remiss student. Florio Banfi, "Giovanni Garzoni ed il Cardinale Tomaso Bakócz Primate d'Ungheria," *L'Archiginnasio: Bulletino della Biblioteca comunale di Bologna* 31, nos. 1–3 (1936): 120–139, speculates that this student was one of the nephews of Bakócz, the archbishop of Esztergom, who nearly beat out Leo X for the papacy. Garzoni was reluctant to share his copy of the *Elegantiae* even with his good friend Giovanni Torfanino; see Lind, *Letters,* letter 210, in which the humanist describes his daily reliance on "Elegantiae meae." The Hungarian's request must therefore have been weighty.

37. On the successive drafts of the *Elegantiae,* originally composed in 1441, see Mariangela Regoliosi, *Nel cantiere del Valla: Elaborazione e montaggio delle Elegantiae* (Rome: Bulzoni, 1993), with the review by Silvia Rizzo in *Roma nel Rinascimento* 1993, 5–16.

38. VBM, MS Lat. XIV 172 (4627), fols. 19–46v, an Italian version of Florus (Kristeller, *Iter,* 2:266a). A print from microfilm, provided by John Monfasani, confirms that this manuscript is in Garzoni's hand.

39. See Hunt, "A Token," 145 n. 24A. A. Strnad, "Capranica, Domenico," *DBI* 19 (1976), 147b–153b, which depends on M. Morpurgo-Castelnuovo, "Il cardinal Domenico Capranica," *Archivio della R. Società Romana di Storia Patria* 52 (1929, printed 1931): 1–146. Capranica received a degree in canon law from the University of Bologna, probably in 1422, and so may have known Bernardo Garzoni.

Naples—with an exotic stop to visit a woman teacher of the *studia humanitatis* at Frosinone—during this same period, for the cardinal went to Naples twice as Callixtus's legate (July 18, 1453; November 6, 1454).[40] Garzoni would have worked alongside Jacopo Ammannati on these legations, but the collected letters reveal nothing about the ambience of the cardinal's *familia* (Ammannati's correspondence is thin for these years, too).[41] The connection to Capranica might also explain Garzoni's relative openness to George of Trebizond, despite his years of study with Trebizond's old enemy Lorenzo Valla.[42]

Growing up in Nicholas V's Rome, studying with Valla and Guarino, working in the *familia* of Capranica, Garzoni could not have missed the importance of Greek. He does not seem to have arrived in Rome with any competence in that language, however, and so is unlikely to have studied Greek as a boy in Bologna under Giovanni Lamola.[43] Garzoni himself confessed to Theodore Gaza, sometime between early 1450 and spring 1455, that he did not know Greek.[44] No Greek works are inventoried in his mature library. Neither do Garzoni's familiar letters suggest that he ever acquired much proficiency. References to Greek philosophy, for example, are usually secondhand through Cicero's *Tusculans* or through works commonly used in translation, such as Aristotle's *Ethics*. All substantive

40. Strnad, "Capranica,"; for the woman schoolteacher, see Lind, *Letters,* letter 451 (although Lind's speculation about dating may be too late).

41. On Ammannati's time with Capranica from 1448–1455, see Paolo Cherubini, ed., *Iacopo Ammannati Piccolomini, Lettere (1444–1479)* (Rome: Ufficio centrale per i Beni Archivistici, 1997), 135–136, 1289 n. 5, and *ad indicem*, with full bibliography. Garzoni does not appear in Ammannati's letters or in Cherubini's notes.

42. These quarrels should not be exaggerated, however. George had dedicated a translation of *De anima* to the cardinal and had found in Capranica a reliable ally for his own anti-Turkish projects. See A. V. Antonivics, "The Library of Cardinal Domenico Capranica," in C. H. Clough, ed., *Cultural Aspects of the Italian Renaissance: Essays in Honour of Paul Oskar Kristeller* (New York: Zambelli, 1976), 144 and n. 67; see also Monfasani, *George of Trebizond,* 56 and n. 125; idem, *Collectanea,* 436.

43. Lind, *Letters,* ix, speculates that Lamola might have tutored Giovanni in Greek. Chronologically, the tuition is possible: Lamola, who died in Bologna in 1449, was teaching there during the decade before Bernardo took his son to Rome; see Chines, *La parola,* 87 n. 71, for the dates of Lamola's *studium* appointments.

44. See Banfi, "Un umanista," 376 n. 1. Garzoni learned from Jerome about a letter from St. Anthony to the inhabitants of Arsinoe and asked Theodore Gaza if he had read it. Gaza, he recalls, took him by the hand to his library ("me ad bibliothecam suam deduxit manu prehendens") and showed him an ancient codex ("vetustissimo codice") of letters by Origen, Paul, Basil, Anthony, and Athanasius, which he himself had transcribed while a boy ("quas a puero excripsi"). When Giovanni admitted "ego graece . . . nescio," Gaza—we are led to believe—made him a translation. Garzoni recalls this event and appends Gaza's translation of the letter to his life of St. Anthony published in Bologna by Hector in 1503, at sign. B4. For Ambrogio Traversari's interest in these letters in 1433, see Charles L. Stinger, *Humanism and the Church Fathers: Ambrogio Traversari (1396–1439) and Christian Antiquity in the Renaissance* (Albany: SUNY Press, 1977), 129 and n. 163.

mentions of Basil are to a single work, *De legendis libris gentilium*, widely available in Leonardo Bruni's 1403 translation.[45] A passage from Herodotus in the letters appears to derive from Valla's translation of the *Histories*,[46] while the famous description of Christ from Josephus's *Antiquities*, translated by Garzoni in a letter complaining about Jewish obstinacy, may draw on Jerome's *De viris illustribus*.[47] We might suspect that if Garzoni read the *Iliad* in Greek, he also knew the translation begun by Valla and completed by Griffolini.[48] Epistolary references to Hesiod's *Works and Days*, as well as to the *Iliad*, may also bear on Garzoni's friendship with Antonio "Codro" Urceo (1446–1500), who lectured on those authors at the Bolognese *studium* in the last two decades of the fifteenth century.[49] In sum, if Garzoni acquired some Greek, he did so late in life, and he never taught it.[50] Neither did he consult Greek sources for his *vitae et passiones sanctorum*.

Even without Greek, Garzoni's formation was sufficient to make his public practice of rhetoric a success when, following the deaths of Lorenzo Valla, Callixtus III, and Domenico Capranica, he returned home to Bologna.[51] He entered the political life of his city shortly after returning and composed orations for the events connected to the handful of public

45. Lind, *Letters*, letters 116, 137, 159, 179, and 191.

46. Lind, *Letters*, letter 39, identifying a reference to Herodotus 7.46; cf. a vague allusion to the same passage in letter 107.

47. Lind, *Letters*, letter 255, undated, to Giovanni Torfanino, O.P., includes the *Testimonium Flavianum* from Josephus, *Antiquities*; cf. Jerome, *Gli huomini illustri*, ed. and trans. A. Ceresa-Gastaldo (Florence: Nardini, 1988), chap. 13, at 101–102. The passage is virtually transcribed into Garzoni's *Passio Luciae* (BBU, MS 741, at fol. 126), which otherwise relies on the *Legenda aurea*. Cf. Valla's judgment of the *Antiquities* in his *postille* to Quintilian, *Inst. orat.* III, vii, 21, in Cesarini Martinelli and Perosa, *Lorenzo Valla*, at 84.

48. Garzoni refers in passing to Homer in Lind, *Letters*, letters 2, 143, 159, 187, 311, 312, 412, 430, 431, 438, and 439. None of these references requires knowledge of Greek.

49. On Hesiod, see Lind, *Letters*, letter 85, and the oblique reference in Garzoni's passion of Vitus (BBU, MS 732, fol. 151). On the *Iliad*, see the preceding note. For Codro's teaching at Bologna, see Raimondi, *Codro*, and Chines, *La parola*, chap. 3. For an inquiry from Garzoni asking Codro's advice about *persona*—probably with reference to Valla's *Elegancies*, book 6, chap. 34—see Lind, *Letters*, letter 448, undated.

50. Leandro Alberti, for example, mentions that his logic teacher, Vincenzo dei'Barattieri, O.P. (also a student of Garzoni's), was skilled in Greek but does not comment on Garzoni's proficiency; see Lind, *Letters*, 426.

51. Hunt, "A Token," 145, dates the return to 1458. The earliest archival proof of Garzoni's return is his appearance on the governing board of the Anziani in 1461 (Lind, *Letters*, x). His father had died at some point after 1456, the last year that Bernardo is recorded teaching at the University of Bologna (Manfré, "La biblioteca," 251). Capranica was expected to succeed Callixtus III as pope, a position that would have secured members of his *familia*, such as Garzoni, jobs in Rome; he himself died, however, shortly after Callixtus; see Morpurgo-Castelnuovo, "Il cardinale," 69 and n. 2.

offices that came to him throughout his adult life there.[52] During the years of his medical professorship, he provided the brief formal speeches expected for university occasions such as the granting of degrees in medicine and even in theology.[53] He celebrated his friends' and patrons' weddings, and he offered consolation at more than two dozen funerals.[54] Such a record of public speaking suggests that Garzoni learned to manage his stutter, although he did not always deliver his own compositions.

On his return to Bologna, Garzoni also began to teach Latin rhetoric. The nature of his classroom remains obscure, but he seems to have boarded some students in his home and to have employed them as scribes.[55] The exhortatory style of his letters to present and former students shows that he was a fond and conscientious teacher, and in his old age he continued to delight in his students.[56] Young men came to him from the Germanies, Hungary, and the cities of the peninsula. From Hungary may have come two nephews of Cardinal Tamás Bakócz; from Croatia an "Udalricus meus"; from Bohemia, Rodericus Dubravus.[57] His students of local origin included, notably, Leandro Alberti (1479–1552), the historian and geographer. If Alberti's case is typical, then Garzoni's *pueri* arrived about the age of ten and so were presumably equipped with the first elements of Latin. Perhaps, similar to Alberti, they stayed about four years. Then they might have entered orders, as Alberti did in 1494, leaving Bologna for his novitiate at Forlì. Or they might have passed on to higher instruction, as did Johannes Blanchfeldus of Berlin, taking a degree in civil

52. Banfi, "Un umanista," 377, gives his appointments; Sandellius, *De vita et scriptis*, 34, items 46.5, 7, 14, 15, 16, 20, 21, and 24, the civic speeches.

53. Sandellius, *De vita et scriptis*, 34, item 46.18, 22–23, and 25–26, all as unoriginal as the occasion demanded. The layman Garzoni composed speeches for theology students to present. In several, e.g., "Cum dantur insignia in theologia" (BBU, MS 2648, fols. 65v–66), Garzoni describes the ceremony.

54. Sandellius, *De vita et scriptis*, 4, item 46.6 (wedding oratory). See Lind, *Letters*, x, for the public offices, and xiii, for the university committees. John McManamon, *Funeral Oratory and the Cultural Ideals of Italian Humanism* (Chapel Hill: University of North Carolina, 1989), 271–273, lists twenty-nine funeral orations; see also Lind, *Letters*, letter 121.

55. Banfi, "Giovanni Garzoni," 127, gives a reasonable description of the school—"una scuola particolare," where Garzoni taught "filosofia, oratoria, poesia, belle lettere" and took "una larghissima affluenza di goliardi universitari, italiani e stranieri"—but provides no source. For a student certainly in Garzoni's home, see the subscription in BBU, MS 2648, "Bononie in domo preceptoris mei Iohanni Garzonis xii Octobris anno sancto videlicet 1500" (fol. 73v).

56. Lind, *Letters*, letter 99, to Leandro Alberti: "Senectus mea stipata est studiis iuventutis ex quibus summam voluptatem percipio."

57. On the Bakócz nephews, see n. 36 above. For Udalricus Croatus, see Lind, *Letters*, letter 187 (a recommendation); cf. ibid., letter 141. For Rodericus Dubravus, see ibid., letters 483 and 484 (cf. letter 19).

law at the University of Bologna, or as "Marcus Attilius" did, moving on to study with Giovan Battista Pio at Mantua.[58] From our vantage point, Garzoni's most renowned student was Girolamo Savonarola, who achieved his subdiaconate and diaconate, stages in the novitiate, at San Domenico in Bologna in 1476–1477.[59] He appears in Garzoni's letters as Frater Hieronymus Ferrariensis. If Savonarola's case is typical, then Garzoni also took students who were already novices. These young men—perhaps his students Vincenzo dei'Barattieri and Francesco da Ferrara should be counted among them—were tutored under the auspices of the Dominicans.[60] Another Bolognese humanist, Niccolò Volpe— like Garzoni, a layman—performed similar services for the Servites.[61] The prior of St. Dominic monitored student-teacher relations closely, in one instance advising Garzoni to reprimand a student who read his teacher's histories rather than Livy, Sallust, and Curtius Rufus.[62] Some part of Garzoni's characteristic defensiveness is probably related to his vulnerable position as lay teacher for the Dominicans.[63] But he maintained good rela-

58. On Blanchfeldus, see Lind, *Letters*, letter 62; on Marcus, see *ibid.*, 251 (cf. Del Nero, "Note sulla vita," letter 3), 262 and 275.

59. On this period of Savonarola's life, see Celestino Piana, "Il diaconato di fra Girolamo Savonarola (Bologna, 1 marzo, 1477)," *AFP* 34 (1964): 343–348; and idem, "Il suddiaconato di fra Girolamo Savonarola (Bologna 21 sett. 1476)," *Rinascimento*, ser. 2, 6 (1966): 287–294; it is not discussed in Giulio Cattin, *Il primo Savonarola: Poesie e prediche autografe dal Codice Borromeo* (Florence: Olschki, 1973). In light of the classroom argument that I make here, Bonaventura Kruitwagen, "Le *Speculum exemplorum* (Deventer 1481) entre les mains de Savonarole à Brescia," in *Miscellanea Giovanni Mercati*, vol. 4 *Letteratura classica e umanistica* (Vatican City, 1946), 209–244, provides intriguing evidence of how Savonarola read a printed legendary as sermon material. See also Armando F. Verde, ed., *Il breviario di Frate Girolamo Savonarola: Postille autografe* (Florence: SISMEL, 1999).

60. See Lind, *Letters*, letters 182 and 299.

61. Volpe ran a school for *adolescentes* starting around 1438 and also taught at the Bolognese *studium* from 1439; see Loredana Chines, ed., *I lettori di retorica e "humanae litterae" allo Studio di Bologna nei secoli XV–XVI* (S. Giovanni in Persiceto: Il Nove, 1992), entry 267. Ludovico Frati, "Di Nicolò Volpe," *Studi e memorie per la storia dell'università di Bologna* 9 (1926): 204–205, says that he may have been teaching Servite novices, including his brother Lorenzo, both letters and chant in Bologna around 1449. Francesco Filippini, "Il P.M. Fr. Taddeo Garganelli Bolognese, 1430–1469," *MOSSM* 1, no. 4 (1933): 178, proposes that Giovanni Tortelli was also teaching in the Servite convent in Bologna about 1445.

62. See Lind, *Letters*, letters 31 and 32, which must be dated before 1501 if Barattieri (the subject of 31 and recipient of 32) left Bologna in that year.

63. See, e.g., Lind, *Letters*, letter 102, to the Dominican Johannes Torfaninus, praising Dominicans: "Quid loquar de Vincentio Ferrariensi ac de Bonifacio Casaliensi, qui *quamquam praeceptionibus meis instruerentur numquam tamen a religioni defecerunt?*" (my emphasis; a joke, perhaps, but a tellingly defensive one). He acknowledges that his correspondent studies only sacred literature: "Non te oratorum studia, non poetarum ingenia, non diversarum philosophorum sententiae sed sanctarum litterarum cognitio delectat." Approving this choice, Garzoni goes on to praise other students of his who, as early as the age of thirteen, showed talent and went on to join the order.

tions with the convent throughout his life and, shortly before his death, was admitted as an *eques Christi* (knight of Christ), perhaps a member of the Compagnia della Croce, the Dominican confraternity that had been revived in 1450 as part of the Observant reform in Bologna.[64]

Garzoni may have made a practice of encouraging younger students such as Alberti to enter orders. His declared aim in tutoring the Dominican novices was to produce accomplished preachers, what he called *oratores* and *concionatores*.[65] Such an interest is not surprising; like other lay humanists, he was a keen observer of contemporary preaching style. He wrote to Johannes Paxius, his longtime friend among the Hermits, of a *Jacobus tuus* (presumably a novice) who had, in a preaching exercise, wittily impersonated the popular oratorical style exemplified by Mariano da Gennazzano, Roberto da Carracioli, and a "Paulus"—probably another contemporary, the Lateran Canon Paolo Maffei.[66] Listening to this Jacobus, Garzoni had bitten his tongue for a long time but then had to laugh until he wept and wet his pants; he predicted great things for the young man.

Garzoni's attitude toward the advantages of the *studia humanitatis* in forming preachers is typical of his status group. The verisimilar comments that Poggio Bracciolini (1380–1459) attributes to papal secretaries Antonio Loschi, Cincius Romanus, and Bartolomeo da Montepulciano at the opening of the dialogue *De avaritia* show humanists critically thoughtful about preaching style.[67] Their points found an echo in Garzoni's appreciation of his students' progress. As Loschi admired Bernardino's ability to excite the full range of an audience's emotional response and Cincius approved the moral content but worried that such preachers sought the gratification of their own egos rather than the "curing of sick souls" ("egris

64. The confraternity is not specified in Lind, *Letters*, letter 96, to Johannes Torfaninus, O.P. (dated to September 1503 by Lind). The Compagnia della Croce received both men and women and had a special devotion to a fragment of the Crown of Thorns, given to the convent in 1245 by Louis IX. D'Amato, *I Domenicani*, 1:394–99, notes the requirement of thrice-yearly confession and the recitation, five times a day, of both the Pater and the Ave Maria in honor of the Five Wounds. Not mentioned in M. Fanti, *Confraternite e città a Bologna nel medioevo e nell'età moderna* (Rome: Herder, 2001) and not known to Nicholas Terpstra, whom I thank for notice that Garzoni's name does not turn up in the archival records of Bolognese confraternities that he reviewed.

65. Although Garzoni wrote a great many orations, he seems to have left only two that might be called sermons (besides those on saints mentioned below): an *Oratio de laudibus beatae virginis Mariae* (BBU, MS 732, fols. 116v–125) and an *Oratio in nativitate domini* (BBU, MS 741, fols. 40–42v). The latter was sent to a Girolamo Palmieri at Genoa, whose comment Garzoni hoped to receive (see Lind, *Letters*, letter 438, which precedes the *oratio* in BBU MS 741).

66. Lind, *Letters*, letter 411.

67. *De avaritia* is a polemical work that represents a lay ethics; Riccardo Fubini, "Poggio Bracciolini e San Bernardino" in *Umanesimo e secolarizzazione da Petrarca of Valla*, (Rome: Bulzoni, 1990), 183–219. The verisimilar opening serves Poggio's purpose.

animis"), so Garzoni encouraged students to hone a sophisticated range of delivery and content but to put those skills in the service of pastoral duty.

Thus, in blessed ignorance of the future, Garzoni promised Frater Hieronymus (Savonarola) that if he persisted and did not make war on Priscian, he would become a great *orator*.[68] Similar encouragements were offered to Alberti: "The [Dominicans] have famous and outstanding philosophers and theologians," he told the new novice. "But they have no *orator*. You alone will be the one showered by all with immortal praises for this brilliant achievement."[69] We learn from other letters that Garzoni followed his students' progress as officiants at the Mass and as preachers, ready with praise but also, when needed, with helpful and specific criticism. "I went happily to see you celebrate the Mass [*Christi solemnia*]," he tells Filippo Musotti, O.P., a former student, "judging that you would perform such an important ritual [*tanto sacrificio*] with no less solemnity than distinction. But I was wrong. You rushed through the ceremony with such haste that I and many others were amazed and upset."[70] *Gravitas* and *dignitas*, above all, he advises the young friar. Searching for a way to impress on him Cicero's counsel that the audience will be drawn to you if you speak just a little slowly, Garzoni offers the image, as memorable as it is unlikely, of a beautiful woman delighting onlookers with her self-consciously slow steps.[71] Filippo should deliver his liturgical lines with just that alluring tension: delivery, delivery, delivery, admonishes Garzoni.[72]

---

68. Lind, *Letters*, letters 182 and 299. Unlike Roberto Ridolfi, *The Life of Girolamo Savonarola*, trans. C. Grayson (London: Routledge and Paul, 1959), 35, I take Garzoni's reprimand to be playful; cf. Lind's note to letter 182. Garzoni seems to have taught his own students both Priscian (perhaps from George of Trebizond's popular *Compendium*) and Valla's *Elegantiae*.

69. Lind, *Letters*, letter 5, which must be dated after November 1493, when Alberti left Garzoni's tutelage.

70. Lind, *Letters*, letter 29.

71. Garzoni quotes the pseudo-Ciceronian *Rhetorica ad C. Herennium.*, ed. G. Calboli (Bologna: Patron, 1993), 3.11.19, adding, "Nam ut mulier formosa si, dum iter suscipit, nulla festinatione utitur, prospectantes mira voluptate afficit, sic sacerdotes dum Christi solemnia faciunt, si tardiusculi fuerint eos qui astant vehementer oblectant."

72. Garzoni borrows from Cicero, *De oratore*, 3.213 and *Orator*, 56, in Lind, *Letters*, letter 29, ll. 15–19. For the problem of liturgical pronunciation taken up by a student of Guarino's several decades earlier, see the undated *epistola* from the lay humanist Bartolomeo Casciotti (fl. 1427–1447), *Admonitio ad clericum qui nuperime sacerdotium inceperit* (VBM, MS Lat. XIV 218 [4677], fol. 70).

Cum ad ea quae ad missarum solemnia pertinent legenda advenerint, tanquam excordes et penitus insani omnia ita corrupte et inepte pronunciant, ut non de deo gravissime et prudentissime verba facere putentur, sed potius turpissime et malevolentissime religionem Christi veram vituperare credantur. . . . Pauci admodum sunt in ecclesia sacerdotes, ut alia reticeam, qui omni *kyrie eleison* pronunciare velint, non absurde illud exprimant et aliud quam debeat significare faciant. Adde quod syllaba longior pro brevi tractabitur, et quae brevis fuit longi temporis spatio metietur. Itaque fit,

The repeated word "delivery" (*pronunciatio*) leads him to reflect on his own shortcoming: "How many times I have cursed Nature, who brought me into this world bereft of suitable pronunciation. If only she had thought to give me such an endowment! Then my situation would be better."[73]

I quote at length from this letter not just because it reveals Garzoni's concern to form competent priests but also because it suggests his virtues as a teacher. He cared about the boys' success, following their work even after they left his tutelage; he was thoughtfully, humorously, and optimistically inventive about helping them improve; and he freely offered himself as an example, even as a counterexample. This evidence of his pedagogical ethic is important for any estimate of his saints' lives.

As a working physician, Garzoni wrote medical *practica*. But what survives in quantity are his compositions in the favorite forms of the humanists: not just several hundred letters and dozens of orations but also dialogues, short treatises, and histories.[74] In addition to the dialogue with his son Marcello on Alexander's military capacity, Garzoni wrote another, also with Marcello, treating Christian happiness, as well as a third, with his adopted son Giovanni and his long-time friend, Johannes Paxius Ripanus, O.E.S.A., addressing the Aristotelian and Ciceronian topic *De amicitia*.[75] When he wrote short treatises, Garzoni clung to the expected classroom subjects, including the imitation of Cicero, the office of the prince, human misery, and fate.[76] A prolific

---

ut tanta sit in eis ipsis discordia, ut quae sit longa vel brevis ipsis pessime et sine ullo ordine legentibus agnosci nequiat. Ex quo plurima etiam his qui mediocriter litteras noscunt confusio nascitur. Nam cum vir non parum eruditus eos ipsos presbyteros illa ignorare perviderit, quae quisque provectior puer teneat, magnopere admiratur et multa cogitatione invenire satagit. . . . Cum hanc eorum tarditatem amplissime cognoverint, religionem nostram rem commentitiam esse diiudicant.

73. Lind, *Letters*, letter 29, which I paraphrase slightly. See also Maria Luisa Gatti Perer, *Umanesimo a Milano: L'Osservanza agostiniana all'Incoronata* (Milan: Arte Lombarda, 1980), 42, noting that the Milanese chapter of the Hermits, meeting in 1471, had ordered that *frati* who did not known how to read well should not officiate before a large congregation, especially "se fra essi vi sono persone istruite," so as not to cause a scandal.

74. Sandellius, *De vita et scriptis*, 20–35, surveys Garzoni's oeuvre by genre.

75. BBU, MS 2648, fols. 75–86, on Christian happiness, is dedicated to the apostolic protonotary Antonio Galeazzo Bentivoglio (b. 1472; apostolic protonotary from July 16, 1483; d. 1525). BBU, MS 2648, fols. 47–62v is on friendship.

76. On princes, see BBU, MS 735, discussed by Lynn Thorndyke, "Giovanni Garzoni on Ruling a City and On the Office of Prince," *Political Science Quarterly* 46 (1931): 277–280, 589–592. On human misery, see the 1505 Strassburg imprint of *De miseria humana* of Ioannes Grueninger, which includes the dedication to Giovanni Battista Fabelli, apostolic protonotary and governor of Bologna; cf. Thomas Brady, *Protestant Politics: Jacob Sturm and the German Reformation* (Atlantic Highlands, N.J.: Humanities Press International, 1994), 27 and n. 82. On fate, see *Quod fatum nihil est*, in BBU, MS 732, fols. 161–164, dedicated to his Dominican friend Giovanni Torfanino. Cf. *De varietate fortunae*, in BBU, MS 740, fols. 1–30v, and *Quod fortuna nihil est*, in BBU, MS 742, fols. 124–125v (not seen).

historian, he was influenced in his choices of political and military content and treatment by Caesar, Sallust, and Livy, as well as by Curtius Rufus, Cornelius Nepos, and Florus. Although he wrote histories for friends, as well as for distant patrons,[77] he concentrated on local history for the Bentivoglio and, especially, on Bologna's wars.[78]

Even more than moral philosophy and warfare, Garzoni was fascinated with life writing.[79] The numerous funeral orations—which gave the speaker an opportunity to review the achievements of the deceased—are an aspect of this fascination, as are, obviously, the biographies, for example, of lay princes such as Giovanni Bentivoglio, of ecclesiastical princes such as Bishop Egidio Albornoz, and of rebellious citizens such as Petrus Cossolinus.[80] Contemporaries acknowledged Garzoni's skill at life writing: he was urged to write a *vita* of Louis, king of France (but declined),[81] and he may have been invited to undertake a *vita* of his former student, Girolamo Savonarola.[82] He also worked in forms that incorporated elements of life narratives, vituperating the life of Mohammed in a treatise that features an elderly friend describing a visit to hell;[83] making Latin

77. For his friend Johannes Paxius, Garzoni wrote a history of Rivalto; for Ferdinand of Aragon, an account of the conquest of Granada, *Expugnatio urbis Granatae, sive de bello Mauritano* (BBU, MS 732, fols. 3–54). Cf. Fantuzzi, *Notizie*, 4:85, an "Urbis Granatae expugnatio sive de Bello Mauritano" dedicated to Bartolomeo Ghislardi. For Frederick of Saxony, he wrote *De bello ab Alberto principe cum Federico et Theodorico liberis gesto libri duo* (BBU, 743, fols. 2–24v); for Mattias Corvinus, *De bello ab [Mattia Corvino] cum Johanne Sagona . . . libellus* (BBU, MS 753, fols. 188–195).

78. In print are *De bello in mutinensis*, edited in appendix to L. Frati's *La prigionia del re Enzo a Bologna* (Bologna: Zanichelli, 1902); *De rebus Ripanis* (revised by T. Quatrini, and published in 1576 in Ancona); *De rebus Saxoniae* (Basil: Froben, 1513); *De dignitate urbis Bononiae commentarius* (ed. F. Argelati, *RRIISS* 21, 1143–1168). For other editions of these works, see Lind, *Letters*, 576–579. For other historical works, see BBU, MS 752 and 753.

79. Manfré, "La biblioteca," 255, discusses historiographical holdings in Garzoni's library, several of which also fall into the category of life writing: Cornelius Nepos, excerpts from Hegesippus, excerpts from Aurelius Victor's *Epitome de caesaribus*. Garzoni also owned a copy of Cassian's *Collationes*, which includes holy lives (Manfré, "La biblioteca," 268, 269).

80. BBU, MS 753, fols. 4–45v; 46–57; for the lives of Bentivoglio and Cossolinus, see also BAV, MS Vat. lat. 7185.

81. Lind, *Letters*, letters 397–399, all dated by Lind to 1498–1499 on the basis of Garzoni's reference to Benedetto Collucci, then teaching at Bologna. In these, Garzoni explained his refusal to write a life of Louis, perhaps St. Louis IX (c.d. 1297), who had given the Bolognese Dominicans an important relic, rather than Garzoni's contemporary Louis XII (who was not, of course, a saint).

82. See Lind, *Letters*, letter 307, in which "FH" would be, I speculate, "Frater Hieronymus." Garzoni's misgivings suit the case. See also letter 309bis.

83. *Adversus eos qui nullos esse inferos arbitrantur . . . libellus*, in BBU, MS 741. See also Lind, *Letters*, letters 109 and 137.

translations of stories from Boccaccio's *Decameron*;[84] and writing up *vitae* or critical assessments (*invectiva*) of classical or mythological figures and of contemporaries. These included a life of Hercules; an attack on Seneca; a pornographic story about a Bolognese pimp, "Heliogalbalus"; and a six-part attack on another contemporary, "Poliphemus."[85] Such protonovelistic narratives allowed him to clarify virtues and vices, to sort out tensions between Christian and classical values, and to expound on motive and choice—what we would call psychology. Through life writing, he could address the absolutes that haunted moral philosophy and the contingencies that operated in warfare, but in an organically satisfying form, one that exercised his evident love of, or need for, drama.[86]

The *vitae et passiones sanctorum*, to be discussed shortly, offered the same opportunity. So, to a lesser extent, did a variety of ancillary pieces that touched on saintly lives. Garzoni's letters incorporate *exempla* about saints for whom he did not write orations or *vitae*.[87] In one, he took the *passio* of Agnes as an extended model for his own unworldliness.[88] With a reference to *vetustis historiis*, ancient histories, he recalls in another the well-known example of Martin of Tours, who shared his cloak with a poor man.[89] In a third letter, the humanist physician matter-of-factly records St. Matilda's aid to women in childbirth.[90] A fourth describes the

84. BBU, MS 752 (II.B.35), fols. 93–114v, of *Decameron* IV, i; VI, vii; VIII, ii. Cf., from Garzoni's library, BBU, MS 313, fols. 68–77, which is Leonardo Bruni's translation of *Decameron* IV, i, all listed by G. Tournoy, "Le versioni latine del *Decameron*," in G. Tarugi, ed., *Teoria e prassi della poetica dell'umanesimo: Onoranze a Giovanni Boccaccio* (Florence: Olschki, 1981), 125–126.

85. Hercules: BBU, 752 (II.B.35), fols. 185–201, dedicated to Ercole Malvizzi, who had consoled Garzoni after some great loss. Seneca: BBU, MS 732, fols. 91–93 (fragment). Heliogabalus: BBU, MS 746, fos. 48v–56v, in a student's hand to which Garzoni has made corrections. The sexual tortures described here (Garzoni relates them in the person of a hidden observer) resemble the tortures inflicted on his virgin martyrs. Poliphemus: BBU, MS 734, fols. 1–111 (Manfré, "La biblioteca," 32; not seen).

86. Avellini, "Eloquenza," 150, notes, "La teatralità, il gusto per la 'pittura' della scena o del personaggio sono del resto una costante della scrittura sia encomiastica sia storica del Garzoni" (discussing the life of Thomas Aquinas).

87. Garzoni mentions that a "sanctissimi libellum Bernardi," probably a devotional work, was read and discussed at a dinner given by the Venetian ambassador Antonio Vinciguerra (Lind, *Letters*, letter 303, dated February 23, 1498, when Garzoni would have been about seventy years old). The vernacular life of St. Jerome recorded as part of Garzoni's library by Manfré, "La biblioteca," 269, item 16, is a published work of 1511, six years after Garzoni's death; it must have been added to his library by his son.

88. Lind, *Letters*, letter 223, to Leandro Alberti.

89. Lind, *Letters*, letter 336 (undated), also mentioning Paul.

90. Lind, *Letters*, letter 489. It is striking that Garzoni does not adduce Margarita (Marina) in this capacity; he wrote her passion, and she is the expected reference for parturition. Garzoni also wrote an account of the doctor-martyrs Cosmas and Damian. The preface to their *passio* situates it as a unique hagiographic contribution to the *disputatio* over the relative value of the arts, a quarrel in which, as Garzoni would have learned from Valla, the place of medicine was not high.

virtues of Catherine of Siena (about whom Garzoni did not write) to a Dominican correspondent.[91]

Beyond these brief epistolary treatments, Garzoni addressed the saints in epideictic forms that he called *laudationes*, to distinguish them from the *vitae et passiones*. These orations praise Paul, Jerome, and Dominic (there are two *laudationes* on Dominic).[92] Other ancillary pieces are also extant. For a Dominican friend, he wrote a brief treatise on the search that Constantine's mother, Helena, made for the True Cross,[93] and, for a friend who was an Augustinian Hermit, he composed an equally brief treatise on a fourth-century anti-Semitic miracle involving the Host.[94] He offered an *oratio* (in the sense of "prayer") to Thomas Aquinas, perhaps intended to precede the public reading of his life of Aquinas.[95] Another work is harder to categorize: Garzoni's account of Diocletian's persecutions in North Africa, *De Diocletiani crudelitate, qua in Mauritania usus est*, is no longer extant, but the title indicates a treatise mixing invective with stories about martyrs.[96]

❊ ❊ ❊

91. Lind, *Letters*, letter 420. Catherine's canonization in 1461 provides a *terminus post quem* for the letter to Marcus Peregrinus, O.P. In his note, Lind misattributes a life of Catherine of Siena to Garzoni, who wrote instead about Katherine of Alexandria; the *libellus* mentioned by Garzoni in letter 420 is probably *De christiana felicitate*.

92. The *laudationes* of Paul and Jerome have been assigned BHL numbers, although Garzoni entitled neither a *vita* (see below for Garzoni's intention to write a *vita Pauli*). The oration on Jerome was provoked by an attack on that father; see Lind, *Letters*, letter 70, to Johannes Paxius Ripanus, O.E.S.A., which Lind dates to the 1470s; and letter 71, similarly dated, to Vincenzo Malmignati, O.P. One *laudatio* of Dominic has been edited by Lind, *Letters*, as letter 81; the other is in BBU, MS 732, fols. 107v–115v. See Poncelet, 1924, item 4; Manfré, "La biblioteca," 31. See also Lind, *Letters*, letter 214 (undated), sending a copy of the lengthy *De beati Dominici laudibus oratio* to Giovanni Torfanino, O.P.

93. *De sanctissimae crucis inventione*, in BBU, MS 732, fols. 81–90v (mutilated at the beginning). See Lind, *Letters*, letter 217, on the problem of the dedication, promised to Johannes Torfaninus but possibly retracted.

94. *De signo a Christo optimo maximo perpetrato*, in BBU, MS 740, fols. 37–48v (pencil foliation), dedicated to Lodovico Orlandini, whom Garzoni had known for forty years (fol. 38) and who urged him to write on this subject (fol. 37v).

95. Lind, *Letters*, letter 284, describes it as a "proem," but here I would translate *oratio* (an ambiguous word in any event) as "prayer." The more common word is *prex* or *deprecatio*. In BBU, MS 741, from which Lind edits the *oratio*, the lengthy work that follows is not an oration (*oratio* and *laudatio* are Garzoni's own terms for orations) but a transcription of Garzoni's life (*vita*) of Thomas Aquinas, which was read at the Dominican convent.

96. Sandellius, *De vita*, 25, item 28. Garzoni dedicated the work to former student Leandro Alberti, "quod in his Gentilium studiis tantum profecisti." See Lind, *Letters*, letter 153: "Instituenti igitur mihi quicquam litteris mandare libuit Dioclitiani crudelitatem qua in Mauritanis usus fuerat memoriae prodere."

Thirty-two of Giovanni Garzoni's *vitae* and *passiones* are extant.[97] These narratives might be classified in several ways. For example, twenty-five have male subjects, while only seven are about women; twenty-three are martyrs' *passiones*, but only nine are *vitae*;[98] fifteen have dedications, and seventeen do not.[99] A type-based schema can be imposed: one pope, two child-martyrs, three Dominicans, and so on.[100] The narratives can be ranked by length, ranging from an efficient passion of Primus and Felicianus (ca. 250 words), to a life of Anthony (ca. 3,500 words).[101] Or the narratives might be addressed chronologically, from first to fifteenth century, according to the date Garzoni assigned to the saint.[102] Such an ordering would reveal Garzoni's typically humanist focus on traditional figures from the early Church. Only two of Garzoni's accounts are about contemporaries and even those two are not Bolognese: Garzoni overlooked the controversial bishop of Bologna Corradino Bornada, O.P. (d. 1429),

97. See Poncelet, "Catalogus"; Manfré, "La biblioteca"; and Frati, "Indice." Lind, *Letters*, xv, mentions "forty-five saints' lives" but does not explain his method of counting. I count narratives rather than the number of saints included in them: for example, although the *passio* of Eustachius (BHL 2763d) also relates the martyrdom of his wife and two children, I count it once; cf. Primus and Felicianus (BHL 2850d and 6922e), which I count twice, not because there are two martyrs in the narrative but because Garzoni wrote two *passiones* about these paired figures. See the hand list. Three early martyrs' passions, attested in the letters or in manuscript catalogs, are lost: Blasius (Lind, *Letters*, letter 173); Petronius (Poncelet, "Catalogus," 329); and Symphorianus (Lind, *Letters*, letters 188, 154, and 156). Another, on Mauritius (Lind, *Letters*, letter 4) may also have been written. For these and other lost lives and for Garzoni's intentions to write about still other figures, see the hand list.

98. For a list of the martyrs' passions, see chap. 2 above. The *vitae* treat Alexius, an ambiguous subject because often depicted in a confessor role so extreme as to be martyrdom; Anthony Hermit; Augustine; Dominic; Gregory I; Helena utinensis; Johannes apostolus et evangelista; Nicholas; Thomas Aquinas. Women feature in *passiones* rather than in *vitae* in a proportion of 6:1; men in a proportion of 18:7.

99. The dedicatees are not always named: the life of Gregory I, discussed below, is to a *praestantissimus pater*. Note as well that the dedicatees were changed in some instances: the life of Augustine was dedicated to Johannes Paxius Ripanus, O.E.S.A., and then rededicated to Cardinal Tamás Bakócz. The lost life of Symphorianus was also rededicated; see the hand list.

100. I have not included Garzoni's life of the Virgin (BHL 5347r) in my count of the *vitae*, choosing to preserve the Marian devotion of the humanists as a category for separate study. Although Garzoni refers to it as a *vita*, Frati, "Indice," 255, item 424, calls it an "oratio de laudibus BVM." The exemplar in BBU, MS 746, fols. 29–37v, has no title inscribed at fol. 29, but in Lind, *Letters*, letter 368 (undated), Garzoni tells his correspondent "I have written her life [*vitam*]. . . . Receive this book [*libellus*] as your guest" and "give it every honor." In conjunction with what will follow below, note that Garzoni's source appears to be the *LA*, especially chaps. 1, 6, 15, 37, 50, 115, 127, and 152.

101. In counting words, I do not include the prologues. Because I have not counted the words in all the accounts, the extremes noted here are merely suggestive.

102. Garzoni offers specific dates for Cecilia (225), Christine (287), and Proculus (520); other passions are located by emperor (Decian, Trajan, Domitian, Diocletian, Arcadius and Honorius).

and the Franciscan tertiary and later Poor Clare Caterina de' Vigri (d. 1463; c.d. 1712),[103] preferring to write about "foreigners"—the alleged child-martyr Simon of Trent (d. 1475) and the Augustinian tertiary Elena of Udine (d. 1458)—neither of whom he knew.[104]

The *vitae et passiones* might be analyzed according to the patrons or groups for whom they seem to have been written. As Garzoni was a layman, those accounts written for religious orders are most striking. The two accounts drawn up for Augustinians are addressed in the following chapter. For Dominicans, he composed an important group of three lives: Dominic, Thomas Aquinas, and Peter Martyr of Verona.[105] All were read in the refectory at the Dominican convent, but the reading of the *Vita Dominici* is best documented. An unnamed *lector* performed it at a mealtime *convivium*; the audience was diverse: "theologians, ambassadors, philosophers, lawyers, knights, doctors, and many of the most outstanding citizens ("theologi, oratores, philosophi, iure consulti, equites, medici

103. On Corradino, see S. M. Bertucci, "Bornada, Corradino," *BS* (1963), 3:362–363. The lay rhetorician Cristoforo Barzizza (fl. 1475) had written his life at the request of a family member, and his cause was being promoted by the Dominicans from the 1470s; see *AASS*, Nov. I (Paris, 1887), 402, para. 2. On Caterina, see S. Spanò, "Caterina da Vigri," *DBI* 21 (1979), 381–383. Garzoni also did not write about the Dominican Matteo Carreri (d. 1470), whose commemoration was allowed by Sixtus IV in 1481 at the urging of Garzoni's friend Salvo Casetta; see A. Foa, "Casetta, Salvo," *DBI* 21 (1978), 461b, and Angelo Walz, "Carreri, Matteo," *BS* (1963), 712. Another interesting omission from Garzoni's hagiography—although not, in this instance, of a contemporary—is the fourth-century matron Juliana, known to Ambrose and Augustine. She was associated with a convent of Franciscan nuns in Bologna, and her relics in Bologna were reconfirmed (following a bull of Celestine III in 1195) by Sixtus IV in 1477; see G. D. Gordini, "Giuliana di Bologna," *BS* 6 (1964): 1170–1171. Garzoni also neglected popular saints tied to important local relics, such as Ann, whose head relic had been given to his father's friend Niccolò Albergati at the Council of Arras in 1435, as a gift to the city of Bologna; see Webb, *Patrons*, 231, with n. 131.

104. On Simon of Trent, see also Lind, *Letters*, letter 19. For a variety of readings of Simon's case, compare Ugo Rozzo, "Il presunto omicidio rituale di Simonino da Trento e il primo santo 'tipografico,' " *Atti dell'Accademia di scienze lettere e arti di Udine* 90 (1997, but 1998): 185–223; R. Po-Chi Hsia, *Trent 1475* (New Haven: Yale University Press, 1992); Miri Rubin, *Gentile Tales. The Narrative Assault on Late Medieval Jews* (New Haven: Yale University Press, 1999); and I. Rogger and M. Bellabarba, eds., *Il principe vescovo Johannes Hinderbach (1465–1486) fra tardo Medioevo e Umanesimo: Atti del convegno promosso dalla Biblioteca Comunale di Trento, 2–6 ottobre 1989* (Bologna: Dehoniane, 1992). Garzoni's life of Elena of Udine is discussed in chap. 5 below.

105. Banfi, "Un umanista," is fundamental on Garzoni's Dominican ties, with Luisa Avellini, "Note sui Domenicani, i libri e l'umanesimo a Bologna," in V. Fera and G. Ferraú, eds., *Filologia umanistica per Gianvito Resta* (Padua: Antenore, 1997), 1:107–128. She singles out Gaspare Sighicelli as the crucial link between lay humanism and the Bolognese Dominicans (122–125). Sighicelli actually joined the order; Garzoni, admittedly a lesser intellect, remained *in saeculo*.

permultique praestantissimi cives").[106] Thus, with this account, Garzoni
achieved a degree of civic and scholarly recognition that seems otherwise
to have eluded his saints' lives.[107] Part of the local impact had to do with
his authoritative restatement of the Dominicans' position (then under
challenge from the Franciscans) that their founder's body was indeed in
Bologna. But the reading as performance should also be compared to those
rhetorical occasions at the start of the Bolognese school year, when
humanist luminaries such as Codro or Beroaldo gave their *praelectiones*,
or introductory lectures, to great acclaim. That context helps to suggest
the kind of appreciation that Garzoni sought and received when he added
to the saint's life classicizing vocabulary and references (for example,
Dominic quotes Ovid before effecting a miracle and Cicero before
dying),[108] digressions on the office of the historian, asides on theology and
philosophy, simultaneously vehement and cautious, and lengthy instances
of *oratio recta*.[109]

106. Lind, *Letters*, letter 387. Apparently, this reading was the second inside the convent:
see Lind, *Letters*, letter 196, in which Garzoni reprimands Frater Leandro Alberti for not
inviting him to a mealtime reading of the *Vita Dominici* there. See also Lind, *Letters*, letter
69 (undated), to Vincenzo Bandello. Lind believes that the harshly criticized *libellus* referred
to in letter 197 is the life of Dominic, but Garzoni does not so specify, and he does not call
this *vita* a *libellus* elsewhere.

107. Compare Garzoni's Dominican *vitae* with the *vita* and *narratio de translatione* of
Petronius composed in 1442 by the lay humanist Niccolò Volpe (n. 61 above), teacher of Nic-
colò Perotti. Volpe's account of Petronius was read before a large and varied audience in the
Lateran Canons' church of San Giovanni in Monte. It was then transcribed into their office
book and so can also be said to have entered their canon; see the hand list. Like Dominic,
Petronius was a universal saint with great local significance; see Webb, *Patrons*, 173–180;
and Pierre Kerbrat, "Corps des saints et controle civique à Bologne du XIIIe au début du
XVIe siècle," in A. Vauchez, ed., *La religion civique à l'époque médiévale et moderne (chrétienté et islam): Actes du colloque organisé par le Centre de recherche "Histoire sociale e culturelle de l'Occident, Xie–XVIIIe siècle" de l'Université de France (Nanterre, 21–23 juin
1993)* (Rome: BEFR, 1995), 165–185.

108. See L. Alberti and G. A. Flamini, *De viris illustribus* (Bologna, 1517), fol. 19v: "Otia
si tollas periere cupidinis artus [*sic*] / Contempteque iacent et sine luce faces" (Ovid, *Reme-
dia amoris*, ll. 139–140). This couplet has a history of productive misinterpretation by
monastic writers that deserves investigation. On his deathbed, Dominic quotes Cicero, see
ibid., fol. 20v: "In eam sententiam [*sci.* Pauli apostoli] M. Tullius consentit, qui ipsa [*sci.* car-
itas] sublata, nihil iocundum arbitratur." Although it is true that pairing Cicero and Paul is
a medieval trope, I do not know of any other saints' lives—much less lives of Dominic—that
represent saints quoting Cicero by name on their deathbeds.

109. Again, Niccolò Volpe (nn. 61 and 107 above) can help us appreciate Garzoni's
efforts: Volpe described the style of his *Libellus de Vita Petronii* "non penitus oratorio, non
ecclesiastico, sed medio quodam stilo conscripsimus ut hominibus vitae secularis et pariter
religiose non displiceret," according to G. Teste-Rasponi, "Note marginali al *Liber pontificalis*," part 2, "Codice della R. Biblioteca Universitaria di Bologna, non catalogato," in *Atti
e memorie della R. deputazione di storia patria per le Romagne* 4, no. 2 (1912): 232. Note,
however, that Volpe opens his account with an etymology of Petronius that takes the *Legenda aurea* as its model. Volpe was undoubtedly a "better" humanist than Garzoni. But it is

Garzoni's letters reveal that the life of Dominic was well received by contemporaries both inside and outside Bologna. From Rome, the learned humanist Pomponio Laeto (d. 1496) wrote to offer Garzoni his friendship on the basis of the *vita*, observing that several Spaniards had taken copies home with them and recommending a strategic rededication to Ferdinand II of Aragon.[110] Inside the convent, the chronicler and prior Girolamo Albertucci de'Borselli, O.P. (1432–1497), named the layman Garzoni in his list of Dominican authors who had written canonical accounts of the order's founder.[111] Such formal recognition of a lay *vita* about the founder of any order had no precedent; nor, so far as I know, has it ever been repeated. The final evidence of Garzoni's success lies in the fact that his rhetorical project for the Dominicans continued after his death. His former pupil Leandro Alberti, O.P., sought out another lay humanist pedagogue and author of saints' lives, Giovanni Antonio Flaminio, and eventually brought him to Bologna to teach and to write on Dominican sanctity.[112]

Garzoni, writing probably fifty years later, who produces an account that dispenses with the fixture of etymology and includes explicitly classicizing detail. Cf. Valla on etymology in his *postille* to Quintilian, *De institutio oratoria* I.25 (Cesarini Martinelli and Perosa, *Lorenzo Valla*, 20–23) and I.33–35 (ibid., 36–37). The hagiographical envelope was being pushed to its extreme.

110. Lind, *Letters*, letter 68, undated.

111. On Borselli, see G. Rabotti, "Borselli, Girolamo," *DBI* 1 (1960), 763; *DHGE*, 1:1594–1595; Albano Sorbelli, "Una raccolta poco nota d'antiche vite di santi e religiosi domenicani," *Rendiconti della R. Accademia dell'Istituto di Bologna, Classe di scienze morali* 2, no. 6 (1922): 79–108; and G. Pasquali, "Gerolamo Albertucci de'Borselli, OP (1432–1497): Ricerche bio-bibliografiche," *RSCI* 25 (1971): 59–82. One of the virtues of D'Amato, *I Domenicani,* is the use of Borselli's *Cronica magistrorum generalium ordinis fratrum praedicatorum* (BBU, MS 1999) as a source. The *Cronica* remains unedited, but Borselli's list of authors of *vitae Dominici* is given in the preface of A. Sorbelli, ed., *Cronica gestorum ac factorum memorabilium civitatis Bononiae*, in *RRIISS* 23, no. 2 (1912): xxxvii. Borselli's list is in effect the canon of *vitae Dominici* accepted by late-fifteenth-century Dominicans and suggests the ideal list of sources available to Garzoni. Of all these sources, Garzoni drew almost exclusively on Theodoric of Apoldia in composing his *Vita Dominici*. Because Albertucci de'Borselli omits Theodoric from his list but includes Garzoni, Garzoni may have set out to replace Theodoric's account with Albertucci de'Borselli's knowledge. My study of Garzoni's account suggests that he also used Petrus Calo (a copy, now at the Marciana, was then held at the Bolognese convent of San Eustorgio) as a source for three miracles traceable in their original to Sister Angela. For the 1494 inventory of San Eustorgio, see Thomas Kaeppeli, "La bibliothèque de saint-Eustorge à Milan à la fin du XVe siècle," *AFP* 25 (1955): 5–74, giving the Calo legendary at 23–24, items 23–26. See n. 118 below.

112. On Flamini, see V. de Matheis, "Flamini, Giovanni Antonio," *DBI* 48 (1997), 278b–281a; and Chines, *I lettori*, entry 85. Flamini was Alberti's coeditor for the 1517 *De viris illustribus ordinis praedicatorum* and went on (after the closing date of this study) to write more extensive accounts; see the hand list. Pieter F. J. Obbema, "A Flaminius Manuscript in Leiden: Autograph and Printer's Copy," in *Quaestiones Leidenses: Twelve Studies on Leiden University and Its Holdings. Published on the Occasion of the Quattrocentenary of the University* (Leiden, 1975), 209, n. 4, also notes Alberti's part in bringing Flamini to Bologna.

Garzoni's Dominican *vitae* are important evidence that religious orders patronized lay humanists; this sort of patronage would evaporate with the confessionalization of the sixteenth century, as the context of composition changed radically. But grouping Garzoni's *vitae et passiones* by dedicatee does not serve the oeuvre well, because more than half the accounts lack dedicatees. And these undedicated accounts include some of the most problematic ones, narratives so simple-minded as to defy explanation as works by a philologically or historiographically sensitive humanist.

Nor is it fruitful to discuss the narratives in order of composition, because Garzoni's *vitae et passiones* are nearly impossible to date. Most are so derivative that the internal evidence is slight. Of those that name a dedicatee, none can be assigned a precise date of composition. Often, when Garzoni mentions the *vitae* in his collected letters, those letters are themselves undated.[113] For the majority, only *post* or *ante quem* dating is possible. But the *vitae* do appear to have been composed after his return to Bologna and especially in his late middle and old age. Although imprecise, this observation is significant, for it means that Garzoni was composing all the *vitae et passiones*—not just the better-known Dominican ones—at the same time that he was teaching rhetoric in Bologna.

As a result of this coincidence, a structural fact about the *vitae et passiones* also takes on significance, for the compositions reveal Garzoni to be far more dedicated to paraphrase than to epitome. Both these forms of rhetorical manipulation were typically practiced by the humanists in their appropriations of earlier texts of all sorts. But in the field of *vitae et passiones*, epitome is a characteristic of mendicant encyclopedists, whose ambitions to encompass all knowledge required compression of texts. Humanists who made hagiographic epitomes—Agli in his revision of the martyrology, for example—may be said to exercise mendicant formats. Paraphrase, it will be recalled, was one of those *progymnasmata* dear to Quintilian.[114] It was an exercise that slipped indiscriminately between the written and the oral, eluding any simple categorization as primary or secondary rhetoric. And it was a highly adaptable exercise, appropriate for all levels, as suited to to the elementary grammar student struggling with vocabulary and syntax as to the accomplished rhetorician extending his facility in invention, *copia*, and delivery.[115] The following discussion, then, considers the nature of Garzoni's paraphrase, proposing that three levels

113. E.g., Lind, *Letters*, letters 67, 77, 173, 193, etc.

114. Above, n. 1. See J. F. Cottier, "La paraphrase de Quintilien à Érasme," *Revue des Etudes Latines* 80 (2002): 237–252.

115. Michael Roberts, *Biblical Epic and Rhetorical Paraphrase in Late Antiquity* (Liverpool: Cairns, 1985), chaps. 2–3, surveys classical theory about *progymnasmata*, of which the paraphrase formed a part. The division of classical opinion about paraphrase, at least as the

of paraphrastic practice are evident in his *vitae et passiones* and that the evidence suggests classroom use of *vitae et passiones*.

❊ ❊ ❊

The major source—and for at least half the *vitae et passiones*, the sole source—for Garzoni's paraphrasing work was the thirteenth-century *Legenda aurea* by Jacobus de Voragine, O.P.[116] Garzoni never reveals his reliance on the *Legenda aurea* and mentions it explicitly only once. In the second preface to the twinned accounts of Vitus (a child martyred with his nurse, Crescentia, and an incidental Modestus) and Hippolytus (an adult, martyred with his elderly nurse Concordia), sent in a *libellus* to a Dominican friend for the convent library, Garzoni complains: "I am, moreover, completely amazed that some unknown *frater* Jacobus de Voragine, ignorant both of letters and of all doctrine, thought that he ought to take upon himself such an outstanding, such a noble, such an important task. But leave him to his ignorance."[117] The Dominicans who received the *passiones* may have been taken aback by this description of their learned master general, whose sermons and *legenda* about saints were available in every Dominican convent and in the convents of many other orders as well. But our surprise is bound to be less. In choosing Jacobus as his defining other, Garzoni shared the opinion of most humanists, both those who wrote about saints and those who—perhaps dismayed by the parade of

---

humanists received it, can be simply stated: Cicero found paraphrase unhelpful, but Quintilian recommended it. On the range of practices that could be called paraphrase, see Antonio V. Nazzaro, "La parafrasi agiografica nella tarda antichità," in G. Luongo, ed., *Scrivere di santi: Atti del II Convegno di studio dell'Associazione italiana per lo studio della santità, dei culti e dell'agiografia. Napoli, 22–25 ottobre 1997* (Rome: Viella, 1998), 72. The similarity of paraphrase to humanist notions of translation is also underwritten by classical theory; see, e.g., Ermolao Barbaro's dedicatory letter to his *Paraphrasin in Themistius* in *Orationes Praelectiones et Praefationes et Quadam Mithicae Historiae Philippi Beroaldi* (Paris: Jehan Petit, 1505), fol. i6r.

116. On the *LA*, see sources cited in chap. 2; and on the diffusion of the manuscript, especially in Bologna, see Barbara Fleith, *Studien zur Überlieferungsgeschichte der lateinischen Legenda aurea* (Brussels: Bollandist Society, 1991), 75–76 (= LA 74 and LA 75), 165–166 (= LA 426), 213–214 (= LA 601, perhaps written in Bologna), and 214–215 (= LA 601a, LA 604). R. F. Seybolt, "Fifteenth-Century Editions of the *Legenda aurea*," *Speculum* 21 (1946): 327–338, gives a list of Latin and vernacular incunables, none published in Bologna.

117. "Sum autem vehementer admiratus cum fratrem nescio quem Iacobum voraginem et litteraturae et omnis doctrinae indoctum, tam egregiam, tam nobilem, tam praestantem provinciam sibi suscipiendam duxerit. Sed relinquendus cum ignorantia sua" (BBU, MS 732, fol. 155v). Then, with his closing words, Garzoni made a gift of his own narrative to the convent library (*ibid.*, fol. 158).

problems that would have to be rectified in the *Legenda aurea*—could not be persuaded to do so.

Garzoni's *vitae et passiones* were shaped by his enemy to an extraordinary degree. Why was this? He could have chosen other sources. If a critical approach to the historical saint had been his intent, for example, the learned fourteenth-century compilation by the Dominican Petrus Calo, Pietro da Chioggia, was at his disposal in the library of the Bolognese Dominicans (which had long been open to laymen).[118] If showy elegance were his aim, then he might have taken as his models the early Christian poets, such as Prudentius or Sedulius, or his contemporaries Baptista Mantuanus and Ugolino Verino.[119] But the evidence suggests that he intentionally followed Jacobus de Voragine, and not out of ignorance or laziness.

What, then, did Garzoni do with the *Legenda aurea*? The first level of his paraphrasing technique is represented by his life of St. Christopher, the *Vita Christophori Cananei*, which very nearly reproduces Jacobus de Voragine's account. Aside from the addition of a brief prayer in *oratio recta*, Garzoni troubles only to substitute a classicizing vocabulary and slightly more intricate syntax.[120] His *Vita Christophori* is not, in other words, an epitome (or at least no more so than his source) but a grammatical paraphrase, a model of the sort of exercise that beginning students in Latin could be given.[121]

118. On Petrus Calo's legendary, see A. Poncelet, "Le légendier de Pierre Calo," *AB* 29 (1910): 5–116; and n. 111 above.

119. On Mantuanus, see Mario Chiesa, "Agiografia nel Rinascimento: Esplorazioni tra i poemi sacri dei secoli XV e XVI," in Luongo, *Scrivere di santi*, 206–212, with bibliography. On Verino, see Francesco Bausi, "Umanesimo e agiografia: Il carme di Ugolino Verino in lode di Antonino Pierozzi," *MD* 29 (1998): 99–158, esp. 107: Verino undertook his *Poema sacrum*, a verse paraphrase of the Old and New Testaments, at the urging of Garzoni's old pupil Savonarola. On the early Christian precedent, see Roberts, *Biblical Epic*. A critical edition of Teofilo Folengo's *Hagiomachia* is being prepared by Claudio Marangoni and Alberto Cavarzere. See also A. Fritsen, "Ludovico Lazzarelli's *Fasti christianae religionis*," *Myricae: Essays on Neo-Latin Literature in Memory of Jozef IJsewijn* (Leuven, 2000), 115–132.

120. Garzoni often adds prayers in direct address to his accounts, as though to teach a vocabulary for prayer in classical Latin. The text here (as Christopher asks not to be tempted by the two prostitutes sent to corrupt him) is typical: "Ne, inquit, sinas me, o Christe, a duabus vilissimis scortis tanta labe inquinari. Tibi hanc animulam, hoc corpusculum dedidi, vovi, dicavi" (I add punctuation and capitalization). The pleonasm is typical of Garzoni's paraphrasing and typically pedagogical.

121. On the problem of the *LA* as a school text, see Carla Frova, "Problemi e momenti della presenza della letteratura agiografica nella scuola medievale," in S. Boesch Gajano, ed., *Raccolte di vite di santi dal XIII al XVIII secolo* (Fasano da Brindisi: Schena, 1990), 101–109; and Evelyn B. Vitz, "From Oral to Written in Medieval and Renaissance Saints' Lives," in T. Szell and R. Blumenfeld-Kosinski, eds., *Images of Sainthood in Medieval Europe* (Ithaca: Cornell University Press, 1991), 97–114. Fleith, *Studien zur Überlieferungsgeschichte*, 413–417, records evidence that a *pecia* system was in place, probably in Bologna, in the thirteenth and fourteenth centuries, to reproduce the *LA* on a large scale. I would suggest that, by the last quarter of the fifteenth century, after the publication of Malermi's vernacular version, *any* evidence that the *LA* was read in Latin rather than the vernacular practically guarantees that it was being approached less as a devotional or preaching text than as a classroom grammar or rhetoric text.

The exemplar of Garzoni's life of Christopher held by the British Library demonstrates how such an account might be used in the classroom (plate 4). A confident cursiva hand, near-contemporary with the 1510 publication, has written interlinear and marginal glosses throughout Garzoni's text (not just at the opening, as so often in school texts). These annotations are largely devoted to providing simple synonyms for Garzoni's mildly elevated vocabulary. Jacobus, for example, opens his account: "Christophorus genere Cananeus procerissime stature uultuque terribilis erat et XII cubitos in longitudine possidebat."[122] Garzoni remodels the sentence thus: "Christophorus, natione cananeus, adeo procera fuit statura ut duodecim ulnarum complexus sit mensura, in uultu preterea formidabili atque horrendo,"[123] slightly expanding the description but also logically regrouping, so that all information about height occurs in one clause (with an explanatory *adeo*), and further balancing the clauses with *praeterea*. There is, in fact, quite a bit of teaching that might be done on the basis of this single elaborated sentence, which is a typical example of Garzoni's procedure. The annotator has responded simply, noting above *procera*, "tanta longitudine corporis fuit"; above *mensura*, "longitudinem." In the margin, the annotator has continued, "Statura proprie corporis longitudo est."[124] He is not always so reductive. Other marginal notes refer to Aulus Gellius, Cicero's *De natura deorum*, Virgil's Georgics, Macrobius's *De somno Scipionis*, and Boethius's *De consolatione philosophiae*, as well as to Josephus's *Antiquities*, Valla's *Elegantiae*, and Garzoni's Bolognese contemporaries Beroaldo and Codro.[125] The annotator, in other words, may have studied in Bologna; at any rate, he knows the Bolognese intellectual context and finds the tiny *vita* a worthy reflection of it.

This text might not have been so carefully read, however, if the annotator had not mistaken the Bolognese medical doctor Garzoni for the incomparably better known theologian Jean Gerson (d. 1429), chancellor of the University of Paris (a misperception revealed by the brief biography of Gerson that a contemporary hand has written on the title page).[126] The error is disconcerting, especially in light of the marginal references to university professors in Bologna. But the error does not vitiate the evidence that contemporaries recognized the pedagogical significance of

122. *LA*, 664, v. 2.

123. *Vita*, sign. A2v; I have modernized punctuation.

124. Other examples of vocabulary notes: "Excipere: eleganter pro suscipere"; at *scurra*, an interlinear *ioculator* (sign. A2v); at *dactilos*, an interlinear *fructus palme* (sign. 4r).

125. E.g., "fabula est oratio ficta, veri plurimum differans, imaginem exhibens veritatis. Codro in sermonibus ex Prisciani" (sign. A2v), incipit of the *Praeexercitamina*.

126. Garzoni's name is given as "Joanne Garzone" on the title page; that he was indeed author of the *Gloriosissimi Martyris Christophori Cananei vita* is demonstrated by the letter of dedication to former student Johannes Blanchfeldus (sign. A2r–v).

hagiographic paraphrase. Nor does it impugn a more speculative corollary: that Latin prose *vitae sanctorum* might, in certain circumstances, be part of the humanist classroom. Indeed, given the defensive posture of humanist educators before more traditionalist educators in the orders, we might wonder if such texts did not play a larger part in the humanist classroom when novices were present than they did in the medieval classroom.[127]

Garzoni did not usually compose such close paraphrases but deviated more boldly from the *Legenda aurea*. In these cases—at a second level of his paraphrastic technique—he may have had slightly more advanced rhetorical training in mind, whether narrowly, in the classroom, or more diffusely, as public reading aloud would accomplish. The chief characteristic, at this further level of remove from his thirteenth-century source, is the addition of *oratio recta*. Thus, for example, the accounts of Christina, Lucia, and Katherine of Alexandria, which also rely on Jacobus de Voragine, feature extended episodes of direct address, as the virgin martyrs denounce their persecutors.

Of course, direct address in saints' lives was nothing new. Jacobus de Voragine's passion of Christina itself bristles with short exchanges: "Her father said to her, 'My daughter, if you sacrifice to just one god, the others will be angry with you.' She answered, 'Although you don't know the truth, you speak truly; I sacrifice to the Father, the Son, and the Holy Spirit.' Her father said, 'If you worship three gods, then why not others?'"[128] "Her mother tore her clothes and coming to the prison fell at her daughter's feet, saying, 'My daughter Christina, light of my eyes, have mercy on me!' She replied, 'Why do you call me your daughter? Do you not know that I have the name of my God?'"[129] Scholars have proposed that the quick pace of Jacobus's dialogue maintains interest and that the content offers the occasion for teaching doctrine. Jacobus's narrative can also be described as efficient in the manner of the encylopedists and "historical," even in the whimsy of the father's imperfect grasp of the Trinity. In contrast, Garzoni's paraphrase is courtly in its learned but not overweighted content, concerned to include classicizing trivia (for the purpose of education? for verisimilitude?), and, above all, luxuriously emotional.

Far from epitomizing, Garzoni's major contribution to the chain of rewriting is to slow the pace and, as Leon Battista Alberti had done decades earlier with his account of Potitus, to enter imaginatively into the cares of pagan parents and rulers in ways that might engage and

---

127. I am grateful to my colleague Marjorie Curry Woods for this suggestion.
128. *LA*, 646, vv. 11–14.
129. *LA*, 647, vv. 22–25.

instruct readers. After tattling servants reveal Christina's apostasy to her father, Urbanus, he spends a sleepless night ("totam noctem insomnens egit"). The next day, the agonized father is careful to conduct his early questioning of her secretly ("in secretum"). And when she refuses to honor his gods, he thoughtfully considers his options ("diu silencium tenuit"). None of these refinements is found in Jacobus. Garzoni further draws out the pain of the father's position, as he pleads with his daughter in direct address:

> If you think that honor must be paid to one god, I fear that you will incur the enmity of the others. Put before your eyes that man who was judged wisest of all by the Apollonian oracle, Socrates of Athens. For so long as he embraced our gods with great and divine honors, he was respected by the Athenians. But when he spoke less liberally about them . . . he was stained with considerable infamy and, thrown into prison, was forced to drink the poison that killed him. Such was the death of such a great philosopher who, if he had not sunk to such insanity, would have joined the gods. So recall yourself soon from these errors, lest Diocletian decide to inflict upon you the bitterness of all punishments.[130]

Christina rejects her father first briefly and then, following her first tortures, at length:

> You, she said, have a shameless character. God hates you greatly. The tortures you have inflicted have exhausted the men [her torturers]. Let your gods, if they can, restore them. This unstained body you ordered to be stripped and beaten by these nameless barbarians who consider nothing splendid, nothing elegant, nothing fine. There is no shame in you. Christ himself, the Best and Greatest, to whom your thoughts are known and manifest, will seek the most bitter punishments for you. You will not escape his hands, if you consider in your mind the destruction of the Roman princes whom you imitate. You

---

130. BBU, MS 2648, fol. 102v:

Si ad unum deum honorem deferendum censes uereor ne ceterum minnas sis susceptura. Pone igitur ante oculos illum qui Apollinis oraculo omnium sapientissimus indicatus est, Socratem Atheniensem. Etenim quamdiu deos nostros immortales eximiis et diuinis honoribus complexus est, tam diu apud Athenienses in gloria fuit. Ubi uero minus liberales de ipsis sermones protulit [. . .] non mediocrem infamie maculam subiit atque in carcerem coniectus uenenem, quo decessit, coacta est bibere. Hic fuit exitus tanti philosophi, qui si ad tantam insaniam non declinasset, deum celestium numerum auxisset. Quare te aliquando ab hiis erratis revoca, ne te Dioclecianus omnium suppliciorum acerbitate afficiendum curet.

should never have taken up such iniquity. You must not cast aside memory of Nero, who, when he had killed the Christians so ignominiously, found his own death between the via Sallaria and Numentana. Domitian, similarly cruel to the Christians, was killed in his palace and borne out ignobly by the corpse bearers, so that the Roman people toppled his images to the ground and spoke publically of his shame. The Caesar Trajan . . . died in agony of a stomach flux. It is not my intention to relate the deaths of the other emperors; that they were foul and shameful can be discovered by anyone.[131]

Christina's mother is given a speech of equal length and greater pathos, beseeching Christina not to render her maternal old age wretched.[132] In response, Christina is dismissively curt. As a result of these familial exchanges, the weight of Garzoni's presentation falls on the tragedy of the family's situation rather than on the martyr's suffering per se.[133] When the tortures come, he does not stint in describing them, but their effect has been arranged for by means of these speeches. Garzoni's paraphrase has minimal doctrinal content. The elision of doctrine is prudent, perhaps, for

---

131. BBU, MS 2648, fol. 103r–v:

Inverecundum, inquit, possides ingenium. Maximo apud deum es in odio. Qui me cruciatu affecerunt fractis sunt viribus. Dii tui, si possunt, eos reddant incolumes. Hoc tu corpusculum nulla labe inquinatum a barbaris nescio quibus (nichil enim est apud eos lautium, nichil elegans, ni[chi]l exquisitum) et nudari et affligi iussisiti. Nullo es pudore. Ipse Christus Optimus Maximus cui cogitacionis tue note sunt ac manifeste acerbissimas a te penas est expetiturus. Haud ex eius manibus effugies, si romanorum principum quos imitaris calamitates cum animo tuo consideresses. Nunquam tantam iniquitatem induisses. Debuisti profecto nullam Neronis memoriam abijcere, cum Christianos indigna nece occidisset, inter Sallariam et Numentanam viam sibi mortem conscivit. Domicianus cum in Christianos eadem fuisset crudelitate in palacio occisus est, et per vespiliones ignobiliter asportatus, quin populus Romanus eius imagines in terram deiecit, et per ignominam publice contulerant. Traianum cesarem dum respondent Domiciano acerbissimis doloribus vexatum ventris profluvium oppressit. Non est mei consilii ceterorum imperatorum exitus referre, quod eos turpes et ignominiosos fuisse quivis exploratum habet.

Cf. a similar speech in Lucy, with similar references to Nero and Domitian, in BBU, MS 741, fol. 127r–v; and in Katherine, BBU, MS 738 fols. 6r–7v. It is striking, in describing the persecutors, that Garzoni relies on Suetonius rather than Lactantius's *De mortibus persecutorum*.

132. BBU, MS 2648, fols. 103v–104, with poetic echoes. Marjorie Curry Woods suggests a parallel with the pseudo-Quintilian major declamations (personal communication).

133. Similarly attentive care for the hard, repeated choice to abandon family for Christ (only now the dilemma is whether or not to join an order or remain in cloister rather than whether or not to persevere unto martyrdom) can be found in the extremely popular pseudo-Augustinian *Sermones ad Heremitas* (I read the edition published in Venice by Vincentius Benalius, January 26, 1492/93 = HC 2004*; IGI 1037; *BMC* 5:525; GW 3006; Goff A1317). See especially sermon 6, "De misericordia," at fol. 12vb–13ra: brothers are driven by their capacity for mercy to leave the monastery in order to help their struggling families but must refrain. The author is sensitive to their dilemma.

a lay author at a time when the orders were aggressively centralizing and reforming. But it is also worth considering that the emotional development of the narrative, achieved by these stately speeches, would be stunted by the presence of doctrinal discussion. Without overevaluating a minor bit of humanist invention, we can notice that, in the absence of doctrine, the reader has been drawn into the family through direct discourse that is almost operatic in its grandiose exploration of intimate grief.

For there can be no doubt that emotional impact was one of Garzoni's chief aims (and even that this aim may help to account for the predominance of martyrs in his work). Garzoni sent another passion to Johannes Paxius Ripanus, O.E.S.A., with the warning-cum-invitation that it would make his friend weep: "If you read this book [about the martyr Theodore], you will not be able to contain your tears. How often it has shaken tears from me!"[134] He used the same phrase in a letter to his former student Leandro Alberti, describing the effect of his own *Passio Symphoriani*: reading and rereading the words of the adolescent martyr before his persecutor (precisely the speeches he himself had written), Garzoni confessed, "wrings tears from me."[135] The humanist author, lingering over his compositions to weep, was hardly immune from his surroundings, from the theatricality of the grammar-school classroom, from the warmth of late medieval devotion. In a similar way, the model bishop of Belluno and Padua, Pietro Barozzi (1441–1507), confessed in his preface to the life of Basil that he had hardly been able to keep the ink from blotting, so frequent were his tears.[136]

The delights of emotional surrender to an imaginative text are ancient. The humble school exercise that directed boys to cast themselves as historical or fictional characters at moments of crisis and to declaim appropriately is known to us from Augustine's reminiscence of his tearful identifications; recent studies suggest that similar declamations may have been standard classroom practice throughout the Middle Ages.[137] They are

134. Lind, *Letters*, letter 338, undated.
135. Lind, *Letters*, letter 156. See also Garzoni's preface to the passion of Hippolytus (discussed below), describing the pleasure (*voluptas*) with which he first came upon the narrative (*historia*) of Hippolytus: "Setting aside all my domestic duties, I read and reread it" (BBU, MS 732, fol. 155r–v).
136. On Barozzi, see chap. 1 above, n. 100. Cf. the brief dedicatory preface from Padova, BU, MS provv. 206, facing fol. 1, in which the author confesses, "tanto animi fremitu commotus pro lacrymarum incontinentia illud evasis obliterationibus haud facile reddere potuerim."
137. Augustine, *Confessiones*, I, ix and xiii. See Marjorie Curry Woods, "Boys Will be Women: Musings on Classroom Nostalgia and the Chaucerian Audience(s)," in R. F. Yeager and C. C. Morse, eds., *Speaking Images: Essays in Honor of V. A. Kolve* (Asheville, N.C.: Pegasus, 2001), 143–166; and eadem, "Weeping for Dido: Epilogue on a Premodern Rhetorical Exercise in the Postmodern Classroom," in C. D. Lanham, ed., *Latin Grammar and Rhetoric: From Classical Theory to Medieval Practice* (New York: Continuum, 2002), 284–294.

more likely to have been emphasized than curtailed in the Renaissance, when classical orators were recovered and reevaluated; when classical drama was revived and classicizing imitations on Christian dramatic themes were composed for school performances; and when the full text of Quintilian—which encouraged such oratorical exercise—was found, disseminated, and discussed.[138] Garzoni seems to have made the characters of the saints similarly available. For the casual reader, there was the opportunity for a more intimate level of emotional engagement with a familiar story. For the student, there was a demonstration of how a poor speech, properly paraphrased, might become moving. Garzoni would have the boy Augustine weep for Christina.

At yet another remove from his source text, the third level of his paraphrastic technique, Garzoni intervenes in the first person.[139] A good example is the revison he made of the *Legenda aurea* accounts of Vitus and Hippolytus for his long-time Dominican friend Giovanni Torfanino.[140] Because Vitus is a child, the prefect Valerianus calls in his father before proceeding judicially. "And the prefect said to the father, 'Correct your son, lest he die badly," narrates Jacobus.[141] As though provoked by such a laconic utterance, Garzoni responds by spinning out an oration of more than one hundred twenty words, including rhetorical questions and advice on the duties of fathers.[142] Such speechifying, just a step beyond the grammatical paraphrase, is now what we expect from this author. But, in addition, the humanist intervenes in his own voice at some length. These asides are flags: they tell us either that Garzoni himself is reacting strongly or—what I suspect is the case—that he knows his audience will and so wants

---

138. For an example of Latin school theater about a saint in the Quattrocento, see Karl Schlebusch, ed., *Petrus Domitius: Augustinus* (Frankfurt am Main: Peter Lang, 1992). I thank Dr. Schlebusch for several helpful conversations. Maria Esposito Frank, *Le insidie dell'allegoria: Ermolao Barbaro il Vecchio e la lezione degli antichi* (Venice: Istituto veneto di scienze, lettere ed arti, 1999), rightly emphasizes the degree to which theater stands behind the *Orationes contra poetas*. For theater and spectacle at Rome, see Ingrid Rowland, *The Culture of the High Renaissance: Ancients and Moderns in Sixteenth-Century Rome* (New York: Cambridge University Press, 1998), 204–206, on Tommaso Inghirami, with further bibliography. On the whole question, see chap. 5 below.

139. I thank Martin Camargo for notice that, at Oxford University in the fourteenth and fifteenth centuries, teachers of rhetoric, and particularly of the *ars dictaminis*, used an exercise that involved the progressively more elaborate rewriting of the same letter. "One feature of the heightened style," according to Camargo, "is . . . first-person interventions" (personal communication).

140. Garzoni notes in the first, general preface that he has already written about many such accounts: "prioribus annis plurium martyrum tormenta mortesque memoriae prodidissem" (BBU, MS 732, fol. 145v), so we might guess that these accounts are relatively late (ca. 1500?) and the fruit of extensive familiarity with the *LA*.

141. *LA*, 87, vv. 18–19, my translation.

142. BBU, MS 732, fols. 147–148.

to help them articulate a correct response. Whatever the meaning of this third level of paraphrase for Garzoni himself, we are bound to note that it would have been valuable practice for preachers, which is to say, it would have been useful for the novices.

In adding first-person interventions to his paraphrase of the *passiones* of Vitus and Hippolytus, Garzoni seems especially inspired by the challenge of miracle, an aspect of the *Legenda aurea* that, along with Jacobus's "iron" or "leaden" prose, has traditionally been understood as most offensive to the humanists.[143] No doubt many humanists, like many scholastics, did worry about gullibility and miracle. But we should not equate willingness to criticize with blanket condemnation. Garzoni is willing, as I have mentioned, to attack Jacobus's prose and to elide Jacobus's doctrinal passages. But he hotly defends Jacobus's miracles, turning his scorn instead on the late Roman belief system. In Vitus's passion, for example, the young saint is fed by an eagle. In a lengthy aside, Garzoni observes that pagans mocked this sort of thing.[144] But, he objects, their mockery was unjustified and illogical, as their own writings show. Those many pagan books, although called "histories" ("plures gentilium libri, quas historias vocant"), are obviously untrustworthy.[145] Look at the unlikely events they credited: the apparitions in battle of Castor and Pollux, described by Livy; Valerius Maximus's story about the vestal Tuccia, who carried water in a sieve to demonstrate her purity; the account, in Suetonius, of the soldier Cynegirus who, bereft of hands, held back a ship with his teeth; and other extravagances in Pliny's *Natural History*.[146]

By pointing out that there are pagan inverisimilitudes as well as Christian ones, Garzoni has hardly created a defense of miracle. Now he must resort to bare authority to save the appearances. So he simply proclaims that miracle pertains to Christianity: if *veritas* is Christian, then *miraculum* stands.[147] His friend Torfanino can trust that Garzoni finds no lies in Christianity and, consequently (the prose waxes triumphant), that the saints' *miracula* can be believed. This progression (it can hardly be called

143. Sherry L. Reames, *The Legenda Aurea: A Re-examination of Its Paradoxical History* (Madison: University of Wisconsin Press, 1985), discusses humanists' evaluations of the collection at 49–52. Her explanation of Nicholas of Cusa's remarks (50) is unconvincing: the narratives that he singles out as especially damaging—those of Blaise, Barbara, Katherine, Dorothea, and Marina/Margaret—are suspicious not because they are full of miracles but because they are unhistorical.

144. Cf. *LA*, 529–531, 29. In BBU, MS 732, fol. 150r–v, Garzoni points out that pagans accepted an eagle in the story of Ganymede.

145. BBU, MS 732, fol. 153v.

146. BBU, MS 732, fols. 153v–154.

147. A tautology: "Res quae miraculo sunt ad religionem christianam spectant" (BBU, MS 732, fol. 154v), "occurrences that are miracles have to do with Christianity."

an argument) does not amount to philosophical fideism, and no student of
Petrus Hispanus's scholastic logic would consider it reliably achieved.
Assuming, as we must, that Garzoni was not a fool, then it seems that he
counts on the emotional force of his prose to carry conviction. He is teaching, after all, rhetorical technique: not just the mechanics of the page but
the dramatics of the pulpit. The task of rhetoric is to persuade. Left to his
own devices, Jacobus is unpersuasive, even damaging to the faith. But he
can be saved by a moving and emphatic delivery, so long as the speaker
demonstrates that he shares—or even bests—the audience's frame of classical reference.

❊ ❊ ❊

Miracle is treated with similarly inconclusive vehemence in several of Garzoni's accounts. But we can better understand the function of these vehement passages by looking briefly at two accounts that appear to belong to
the extracurricular sphere. These two narratives, which include but do not
dwell on miracle, are the only *vitae* that Garzoni composed to record his
own experience of the miraculous. Strikingly, these *vitae* are among the
most restrained in addressing supernatural interventions.[148]

Both narratives—one about Bishop Nicholas of Myra and the other
about Pope Gregory the Great—rely on Jacobus of Voragine's *Legenda
aurea*. In the account of Nicholas, Garzoni places the miracle (a relative,
rescued at sea) prominently at the center of the story but seems otherwise
distracted by his desire to present a model bishop.[149] Gregory, however,
had intervened to save Garzoni himself during a fatal illness, a more intimate matter that resulted in a more complex text. In the course of the *vita*,
the humanist notes Gregory's healing intervention and remarks briefly on
it. Moreover, he retains the famous miracles of Gregory's lifetime, such as
the vision of the angel atop Castel Sant'Angelo. But Garzoni comments on
none of these events and simply excises Jacobus's coda of posthumous miracles. His energy goes not to recording miracles or producing first-person

148. Garzoni also enjoyed favors from the Virgin and Nicholas of Tolentino, O.E.S.A.
(c.d. 1446); see Lind, *Letters*, letter 129. Pace Lind, this Nicholas is not a contemporary
physician. Rather, the saint is "parenti nostro" because Garzoni's correspondent is an Augustinian and because of Garzoni's friendship with Augustinians: "Tuus ille Nicolaus auctor fuit
salutis meae. . . . Ille me a morte ad vitam, a desperatione ad spem, ab exilio ad salutem
vocavit." See also letter 436. But Garzoni did not write a life of Nicholas of Tolentino.

149. Garzoni's *Vita Nicolai* awkwardly breaks the *Legenda aurea* text to explain the
1087 translation of relics to Bari and then to tell the story of his seafaring relative. The model
bishop is delineated by means of three brief interventions promoting education, friendship
(i.e., networking), and conscientious residency (sermons and writings that nourish the flock).
In comparison with humanist accounts of Athanasius or Zenobius, Garzoni's depiction is
impoverished, and not a good example of the "model bishop" genre (see chap. 1 above).

digressions in defense of miracles. Rather, in his life of Gregory, Garzoni saves his first-person interventions for more pressing subjects.

This procedure may reflect the fact that, unlike Nicholas, Gregory was an unusual choice of subject:[150] in striking contrast to the vernacular tradition that evinced widespread and warm devotion to Gregory, few fifteenth-century humanists chose to write, revise, or transcribe Latin prose *vitae Gregorii*.[151] Papal historians such as Bartolomeo Platina and Jacopo Zeno could hardly bypass him, of course;[152] and Antonio Agli and Bonino Mombrizo included Gregory in their paraliturgical collections.[153] Is it possible that the humanists were silent because they shared Garzoni's concern (expressed in the opening humility trope of his preface) that readers might accuse them of arrogance if they competed with the authoritative early accounts?[154] Probably not. Pride is not a sin that frightened

150. The best-known humanist life of Nicholas is by Leonardo Giustinian; it was the sole fifteenth-century piece to be incorporated into Aldus Manutius's *Poetae Christiani* (see below), a singular honor. The account is said to be a translation of Simeon Metaphrast, but I have not collated the two texts and have not yet seen a copy of the *Poetae christiani* that gives facing-page Greek. Moreover, Leonardo himself says he is working from several sources, and Aldus does not say that Simeon Metaphrast is the source, although in the context of the printed collection, such an identification would be a selling point. Agli and Mombrizio both give accounts of Nicholas; Leonardo Dati wrote a *de laudibus*; Michael Canensis and Nicholas Bonavia composed hymns; and there are many Latin orations.

151. Cf. the many editions of the *Dialogues* that include Domenco Cavalca's vernacular translation of John the Deacon's *Vita Gregorii*, listed in Schutte, *PIVRB*, 195–196.

152. Giacinto Gaida, ed., *Platynae historici liber de vita Christi ac omnium pontificum*, *RRIISS* 3, 1–2 (Città di Castello: Lapi, 1932); the entry for Gregory can be found at 96–98. Zeno's history of the papacy, *De vitis summorum pontificum*, dedicated to Paul II (but also with a prefatory letter to Cardinal Battista Zeno), covers Peter through Clement V. In BAV, MS Lat. 5942, Gregory is treated in fols. 63–67v. Throughout this account, as in others, Zeno names his sources, pointing out their inconsistencies and judging among them. Here, his sources include Paul the Deacon, Martinus Polonus, Ptolemy of Lucca, Hostiarius, Petrus de Natalibus, Matteo Palmieri, and Flavio Biondo.

153. Agli's account is in BAV, MS Lat. 3742, fols. 175v–176v, a lightly emended transcription of FBNC, MS Nuovi acq., 399, fols. 58–59v. On this collection, see chap. 2 above. On Mombrizio's *Sanctuarium*, see chap. 3 above; the *Vita Sancti Gregorii Papae* edited in Mombritius 1910, 1:588–596 is an interpolated version of that by Paul the Deacon (*BHL* 3640).

154. Garzoni opens his preface by defending his account: "Vereor equidem ne sint qui me impudentissimum existiment, si Gregorii primi pontificis maximi vitam litteris mandare instituero, cum tot eloquentissimi viri, cum quibus minime sum conferendus, tam officiosam sibi provintiam depoposcerint. Non ea sum ratione impulsus, ut his preferri cupiam. Nunquam id in animum meum induxi. Dementissimam profecto temeritatem subirem, si his quorum scripta et gravissimis sententiis referta sunt et summo deducta ornatu me aequandum, nedum anteponendum, censerem" (BBU, MS 737, fol. 57). Presumably, he has in mind Paul the Deacon [*BHL* 3639] and John the Deacon [*BHL* 3641], not the *LA*. By virtue of its considerable explanatory energy and specificity, this preface suggests that Garzoni had an audience in mind; he wrote in (but later cancelled) a dedication to a "praestantissime doctor."

humanists, and, more to the point, they did not otherwise neglect Gregory. His works were widely read in Latin as well as the vernacular. His relics were honored: in 1464, the humanist pope, Pius II (Enea Silvio Piccolomini), celebrated a *translatio* of Gregory's *corpus* to a rebuilt altar in St. Peter's, one that had been prepared two years earlier to receive the head relic of Andrew.[155] And humanists, just like the humblest of their contemporaries, arranged to have masses of St. Gregory said for their own souls and the souls of their friends.[156] They did so because Gregory's compassion, drawn forth by a miraculous vision of the suffering Christ granted him during Mass, promised his supplicants relief from purgatory.[157] Simply out of personal devotion, humanist *vitae Gregorii* might be expected.

Apparently, Garzoni alone wrote out of personal devotion. Seriously ill and expecting to die, he made a vow. Gregory responded, and therefore the humanist, some time after his cure, wrote an ex-voto *vita* of the pope.[158] Although he was probably moved to choose the pope as thau-

155. Pierre Jounel, "Le culte de saint Grégoire le Grand," in J. Fontaine, R. Gillet, and S.-M. Pellistrandi, eds., *Grégoire le Grand* (Paris: Cerf, 1986), 672; Louise Rice, *The Altars and Altarpieces of the New St. Peter's: Outfitting the Basilica* (New York: Cambridge University Press, 1997), 36 n. 89 and 221b. Such occasions typically called forth humanist oratory, but Gregory's *translatio* was not as fortunate as Andrew's.

156. Cassandra Fedele's vernacular will included a request that "le messe dela Madona e di San Gregorio" be said over her body; Cesira Cavazzana, "Cassandra Fedele erudita veneziana del Rinascimento," *Ateneo veneto* 29 (1906): 396. See also the letter from Jacopo Ammannati, dated by Cherubini to September 5, 1465, announcing to Cardinal Francesco Piccolomini the death of Cardinal Louis d'Albret: Ammannati has arranged for thirty masses of St. Gregory to be said for their friend's soul and urges Piccolomini to do the same (Cherubini, *Iacopo Ammannati*, letter 183, at 805). Early the following year, Ammannati promised Bianca Maria Sforza that he would say masses of St. Gregory for her husband, Francesco Sforza, just deceased (ibid., letter 201, at 856).

157. The story of Gregory's compassion for Trajan (below) is the origin of the purgatory topos; it is greatly developed in the *LA*. See Uwe Westfehling, *Die Messe Gregors des Grossen: Vision, Kunst, Realität: Katalog und Fuhrer zu einer Ausstellung im Schnutgen-Museum der Stadt Köln* (Cologne: Schnütgen-Museum, 1982), 29, for an Umbrian panel depicting the Man of Sorrows, with a painted caption in which Gregory the Great's compassion constitutes the link to the image. Westfehling reproduces several images of the miraculous mass of St. Gregory that include inset scenes of diminutive souls freed from purgatory as a result of the saying of the mass. See also Caroline W. Bynum, "Seeing and Seeing Beyond: The Mass of St. Gregory in the Fifteenth Century," in J. Hamburger and A.-M. Bouché, eds., *The Mind's Eye: Art and Theology in the Middle Ages* (Princeton, N.J.: Princeton University Press, forthcoming).

158. For other humanist ex-voto lives, see chap. 1 above. Garzoni provides a *terminus post quem* of 1478, the year of his illness (BBU, MS 737, fol. 57r–v): "A natali domini salvatoris anni agebantur mille et quadrigenti ac septuaginta octo, cum in febrem incidi et satis molestam." Garzoni acknowledges that his vow resembled the Roman practice of making vows to Fortuna or to Sospita (fol. 57v). He does not linger over this point, but, having acknowledged the similarity, he has calmed his own (or his audience's) frisson of recognition.

maturge by the association of Gregory with testamentary requests for masses of Gregory, no eucharistic or purgatorial associations emerge in the telling.[159] For the first half of the account, Garzoni forthrightly paraphrases Jacobus de Voragine.[160] The early years;[161] the founding of the seven monasteries; the poor sailor exemplum; the Angles sold as slaves in the marketplace;[162] the ascent to the cardinalate; the flood and plague in Rome; the ascent to the papacy and the use of litany to end the plague; the misson to convert the "Britons"; the turn to discussing the virtues of humility and charity, including the miraculous thirteenth guest at the charitable meals; and Gregory's compassion for Trajan with its attendant passages on purgatory,[163] all follow the *Legenda aurea*.

But when Jacobus de Voragine abandons narrative for posthumous miracles, Garzoni abandons Jacobus. The dismissal is curt: "Gregory performed many miracles, not only while he lived but also after his death; these I will forgo, because books are full of them."[164] It is striking that Garzoni bothers neither to contend with nor to defend Jacobus at this

---

159. Ibid.. For important corrections to current appreciation of the eucharistic aspects of the Gregory mass, see Bynum, "Seeing and Seeing Beyond."

160. *LA*, 285 306. With minor divergences, Garzoni follows Jacobus from vv. 8–75 (where he diverges to improvise on *humilitas*), from 94–110 (Garzoni exchanges what Jacobus has to say about *caritas* for a brief encomium of that virtue), from 111–146 (then condensing 147–154, and omitting 156–158), from 159–176 (then condensing 177–187), and from 188–192.

161. *LA*, v. 8, mentions only philosophy. Garzoni adds "grammatica rhetorica dialectica" before "ad philosophiam animum appulit," but the change is unremarkable: he might have found the phrase in Mombrizio's edition (*BHL* 3640).

162. Garzoni seems to misunderstand Gregory's series of puns (*Anglici/Angelici*; *Deiri/de ira eruendi*; *Aelle/alleluia*), so that all the charm of the famous story is lost. But Gregory's puns are close to etymologies, and Garzoni excises these everywhere. In other words, we learn about Garzoni's reading *habitus* and about his knowledge of how his students and his audience read, if we do not leap to the conclusion that he is simply dull-witted here. One egregious etymology, the story of the locust interrupting Gregory's reading in the woods outside Rome, so that the saint decides to make that place his hermitage (*locusta = locus sta*) is not even in Jacobus; see *PL* 75, col. 51, para. 20 (Paul the Deacon); col. 72, para. 24 (John the Deacon), with notes.

163. Jacobus is deeply concerned about purgatory; Garzoni compresses this section but keeps Gregory's decision, when offered the choice by an angel, to suffer physical ailments all his life rather than spend two days in purgatory; cf. *LA*, vv. 188–191 and and BBU, MS 737, fol. 70. Both Jacobus and Garzoni hedge this story with *cavete* verbs: "Fertur" says Jacobus; Garzoni, more compliantly, "Illud constante famam atque omnium sermonem celebratus."

164. Jacobus's account continues with miracles from *LA*, vv. 192 to 295, but Garzoni uses none of this material, breaking abruptly: "Multa sunt ab eo, non solum cum celo terraque fruebatur, verum etiam morte obita signa perpetrata, que dedita opera pretereo, quod eorum pleni sunt libri" (BBU, MS 737, fol. 70v). As a result of abandoning the *LA*, Garzoni does not tell the miracles of the doubting woman (*LA*, vv. 199–206) and of the corporal cut with a knife (vv. 207–210), the two miracles that seem to be confusedly at the origin of the mass of St. Gregory devotion (cf. Westfehling, *Die Messe Gregors*, 16; Bynum, "Seeing and Seeing Through," 5–6 and nn. 14–16).

point, although we have seen him vehement in defense of the miraculous in other, apparently classroom-related, paraphrases of the *Legenda aurea*. Instead, he turns to another source, much more flatly factual: the entry for Gregory in the *Liber de vita Christi ac omnium pontificum* by Bartolomeo Platina.[165] Garzoni follows Platina closely, again without acknowledging his source, borrowing almost verbatim Gregory's institution of new usages for antiphons, for the Kyrie Eleison, the Alleluia,[166] the major litanies (*supplicationes*, says Garzoni, studiously avoiding the Greek in Platina as he had avoided it in Jacobus and thereby teaching a word), most of the stations, the old office,[167] and who celebrated a synod attended by twenty-four bishops.[168] Garzoni strictly segregates Church history from political-military history, omitting passages about the latter that Platina had borrowed from Flavio Biondo's *Decades*.[169]

Other historical aspects of the account, however, he found compelling. First, Platina reminded him of another face of the pope: Gregory as the scourge of antique art.[170] Today, Gregory strikes us as an unlikely enemy of art. Recent scholarship has focused on the two epistles to Serenus that defend the use of images in churches, as well as on the mass of St. Gregory, which linked the pope to two powerful late medieval devotional images, the Veronica and the Man of Sorrows.[171] But, beginning in the thirteenth century, Dominican chroniclers manipulated the *vita* to emphasize a past in which Gregory, by actively combating pagan culture, might seem implic-

165. Platina, *Liber*, entry 66, at 96–98.
166. BBU, MS 737, fol. 70v; cf. Platina, *Liber*, 96, ll. 27–30.
167. Ibid., fol. 70v; cf. Platina, *Liber*, 96, l. 31–97, l. 2.
168. Ibid., fol. 21; cf. Platina, *Liber*, 97, ll. 5–6.
169. Platina, *Liber*, 97, ll. 8–35 et seq.; there is similar material in Jacobus de Voragine. I have not located a source of Garzoni's first-person interpolation about clerical behavior and the proper manners for litanies (BBU, MS 753, fols. 71–72). The latter point particularly troubles him: if people today will laugh and talk and joke during the litanies, then of course, there will be wars and famine and plague (71v).
170. This discussion depends on Tilmann Buddensieg, Gregory the Great, the Destroyer of Pagan Idols," *Journal of the Warburg and Courtauld Institutes* 28 (1965): 44–85.
171. Gregory's letters to the iconoclastic Bishop Serenus of Marseilles, written in 599 and 600, are edited by D. Norberg, *Corpus Christianorum Series Latina* 140A (Turnhout: Brepols, 1982), nos. IX and XI. See also C. M. Chazelle, "Pictures, Books, and the Illiterate: Pope Gregory I's Letters to Serenus of Marseilles," *Word and Image* 6, no. 2 (1990): 138–153; eadem, "Memory, Instruction, Worship: 'Gregory's' Influence on Early Medieval Doctrines of the Artistic Image," in J. C. Cavadini, ed., *Gregory the Great: A Symposium* (Notre Dame, Ind.: University of Notre Dame, 1995), 181–215, analyzing the polemical use made of the letters in the eighth and ninth centuries. On the Veronica and the Man of Sorrows, see Jeffrey Hamburger, *The Visual and the Visionary: Art and Female Spirituality in Late Medieval Germany* (New York: Zone, 1998); and H. W. van Os, *The Art of Devotion in the Late Middle Ages in Europe, 1300–1500*, trans. M. Hoyle (London: Merrell Hilberton, 1994). Westfehling, *Die Messe Gregors*, and especially Bynum, "Seeing and Seeing Beyond," give further bibliography.

itly to authorize their own campaigns against heretics.[172] This manipulation, the fountainhead of all stories about Gregory the scourge of classical art, appears to originate in the *Chronicon pontificium et imperatorum* (Chronicle of popes and emperors), by the Dominican Martinus Polonus (d. 1278). Martinus recorded that Gregory "had caused the heads and members of demonic images to be knocked off throughout Rome, lest the seed of ancient error be increased in another way."[173] Martinus's *Chronicon* was widely diffused, so it is not surprising to find this passage quoted in the *Flores chronicorum* by the Dominican inquisitor Bernard Gui and then traveling outside the order, to appear in Augustinian and lay chroniclers.[174]

By the early fifteenth century, thanks to the success of these works, Gregory was known to be at once a defender of and figure in devotional art and an enemy of classical art. The combination is important: a devotional image of the warmly compassionate pope was joined to another, harsher image developed in the context of mendicant struggle against heresy. And this combination was firmly in place, ready to be deployed against the new and articulate champions of classical culture, the overwhelmingly unheretical intellectuals who had been educated in the *studia humanitatis*. How would these clerics and laymen respond?

Several positions circulated simultaneously in the fifteenth century regarding Gregory's alleged mutilations.[175] The two that are relevant here are associated with Giovanni Dominici, O.P. (d.c. 1420) and the layman Sicco Polenton (d. 1447). In the polemical *Lucula noctis*, Dominici followed the historiographical tradition of his order by identifying Gregory as a destroyer of pagan artifacts; he also agreed with mendicant tradition that the devastation had been beneficial. Dominici developed his argument as part of a well-informed attack on Coluccio Salutati's program of classical studies for schoolboys. Dominici, in other words, set the mendicant's image of Gregory against the human-

172. See Buddensieg, "Gregory the Great," 48 and n. 13.

173. Ibid., 47 and n. 9; my translation.

174. Ibid., 48 and n. 14: the *Chronica* by the fourteenth-century Venetian doge Andrea Dandolo.

175. According to Buddensieg, they were: (1) Gregory had destroyed pagan artifacts, and a good thing, too; (2) Gregory had done so, but the loss was tragic, and the act epitomized the narrow-mindedness of ecclesiastics; (3) Gregory, a learned man, would never have done such a thing (this skeptical position was first explicitly formulated in the fifteenth century); (4) Gregory did destroy pagan artifacts, and, in revenge, his enemies burned his books. These four positions coexisted; there was not a straightforward progression of sentiment, with one argument effectively silencing another. In the early sixteenth century, as Buddensieg points out, the thirteenth-century description of Gregory as a statue smasher was declared reasonable (*verosimile*) by the learned curialist Raffaele Maffei (on whom, see chap. 6 below).

ist classroom.[176] In consequence, he made one major modification in the traditional Dominican argument: the artifacts Gregory had destroyed were not statues but books, and in particular he "burned whatever books by Livy he could find."[177] Dominici's refinement was a crucial one, taking the polemical representation of Gregory to a new plane.[178] By focusing on books, Dominici laid the burden of refutation—or, at any rate, justification—squarely at the feet of those humanist pedagogues who were using classical texts—even the relatively uncontroversial Livy—in their classrooms. Dominici had, by association, all the moral weight of the devotional images of Gregory on his side (and Dominici, who recommended that families pin up pictures of saints for the moral instruction of children, was thoughtful about the power of images).[179] With characteristically sharp insight, Dominici had aimed the thirteenth-century antiheretical representation of Gregory to meet what he perceived to be the major threat to Church authority in his own day: the secular classicizers.[180]

They responded. Dominici's attention to the lost books of Livy likely precipitated the formulation of a novel doubt about the veracity of the chronicle tradition that attributed acts of cultural destruction to Gregory. In his literary history, *Scriptores illustri latinae linguae libri XVIII*, the layman Sicco Polenton, speculating about the pope's character, argued that Gregory was not the sort of person to have committed such outrages. He overlooked the charge of statue smashing to address the alleged destruction of Livy: thus, like Dominici, he neglected images for texts. He pointed

176. Ronald G. Witt, *Hercules at the Crossroads: The Life, Work, and Thought of Coluccio Salutati* (Durham, N.C., 1983), 410–413, at 411 points out the "highly scholastic" nature of Dominici's *Lucula noctis*; cf. Peter Denley, "Giovanni Dominici's Opposition to Humanism," *Studies in Church History* 17 (1981): 103–114. In the sixteenth century, Jacopo Sadoleto referred to Giovanni Dominici as a humanist.

177. Giovanni Dominici, *Lucula noctis*, ed. E. Hunt (Notre Dame: Notre Dame University Press, 1940), chap. 13, 122.

178. This move from images to texts can be found already in John of Salisbury's *Policraticus*, whose concern was with the "mathematicorum via" (Buddensieg, "Gregory the Great," 46 and n. 8). John records the charge that Gregory was responsible for the destruction of the Palatine Library.

179. See David Freedberg, *The Power of Images: Studies in the History and Theory of Response* (Chicago: University of Chicago Press, 1989), 4–5 and 11–12.

180. The effect that Dominici feared from classical studies in the classroom was systematic doubt: students would learn a skeptical approach to texts and that, as Valla recognized in annotating Quintilian, was a transferable skill (see chapter epigraph). In other words, it seems to be the broad and unregulated teaching of this transferable skill, rather than the content of the texts studied, that threatens faith. Witt, *Hercules*, 410, notes that in disputing with Dominici in 1406, "Salutati was far more ambivalent toward the pagans than he had ever been." Dominici had struck a nerve.

out the illogic of the charge of book burning, arguing coolly that there was no challenge to Christian doctrine in Livy.[181]

Did Bartolomeo Platina, the biographer of the popes, know the book-based arguments of either Dominici or Polenton? If he did, he chose not to use them in his entry on Gregory. After drawing on the *Liber pontificalis*, Ptolemy of Lucca's fourteenth-century *Historia ecclesiastica*, and Biondo's *Decades* for information about the pope, Platina turned in closing to the problem of Gregory's destructiveness but ignored books. Rather, good Roman antiquarian that he was, Platina focused entirely on the *vetera aedificia* and *monumenta*, specifically mentioning *arcus triumphales*. Ancient buildings, he protested, collapsed on account of age, or they were torn apart by greedy men, Roman as well as barbarian, who had heard of the custom of placing pots of coins, "ollas cum nummismatibus," in the foundations. But Gregory loved his *patria* more than life itself (although second to God) and so could not have been responsible for architectural losses in Rome.

Giovanni Garzoni could hardly refuse the opportunity that Platina offered him to expatiate on antiquity, but he was not in Rome; he was in Bologna as a lay teacher, chiefly of Dominican religious or of boys who might join them. So, in composing his lengthy aside, he briefly gathered up Platina's archaeological points and denied the destruction of "palatia, templa, turres," arguing instead for the ravages of time and greedy men in search of "ollas cum nummismatibus." Then he turned to the books that mattered to him as a schoolteacher: "poetas et oratores et historiarum scriptores."[182] He argued, as humanists so often did in such instances, from analogy. Cyprian, Lactantius, Ambrose, Jerome, and Augustine were all learned in both "doctrina et gentilium studiis." Like them, Gregory, too, wrote well because he knew pagan authors.[183] And Garzoni argued from verisimilitude: there had been great losses, but the real culprits lay elsewhere.

> If we are deprived of the poets, the orators, the historians, the charge must be laid against the barbarians, who brought Rome such destruction that it makes a person wretched to think of it. [Those who accuse Gregory] know well that Totila not only razed the city's walls to the ground but also burned the Capitoline, the Forum, the

---

181. Buddensieg, "Gregory the Great," 55–56 and n. 25. Although they did not mention Livy, the humanists Guarino and Sabellico shared Polenton's belief that Gregory was too learned to have engaged in cultural destruction (ibid., 56–57 and nn. 34–35); see also Boccaccio's *De genealogiis deorum gentilium*, quoted in ibid., 49 and n. 16. See, too, Pietro Ransano, *Annales omnium temporum* (Palermo, BC, MS 3 Q q C, fasc. 59, fol. 523r–v).

182. BBU, MS 753, fol. 72v.

183. Ibid., fol. 73.

Suburram, and the Via Sacra. No one is so crazy or heedless of himself that he would deny that the great part of the [lost] books were burned in that fire. How many times did barbarian peoples come into Italy? Who doubts that they carried off codices? We were lacking Quintilian, Silius [Italicus], Asconius [Pedianus]. But thanks to that fine man Poggio of Florence, they were borne back to Italy. So Gregory must be freed from the charge.[184]

And then Garzoni gives, briefly, the catalog of Gregory's writings, as though to demonstrate the successful domestication of the gentile woman.

This catalog leads to another first-person intervention, as Garzoni notes that Gregory's writings teach "bene beateque vivendum." The theme is a favorite of Garzoni's: to live well and blessedly, a person must recognize a transcendent reality and not mistake the *brevia, fugatia, caduca*, the short-lived, fleeting, deceptive things of worldly happiness, for truth.[185] To admonish and reform those who have chosen the world, Garzoni will demonstrate heavenly happiness, "divinae domus felicitas." He does so by listing the characteristics of life in heaven: all honors are justly given in a hierarchy of the more and less virtuous; cymbals and song resound, as everyone tirelessly praises God in a tranquil and quiet peace; no one is hurt or envious, no one lustful, insolent, avaricious, or ignorant; there is no free will. . . . It is, in short, a sermon. Elementary in the extreme, as though for an audience that might just follow the Latin if the clauses were short, it operates with the slightly elevated vocabulary and syntax that I noted in the *Vita Christophori*.

His interest in Gregory's life apparently exhausted, Garzoni draws the account to a perfunctory close. He dispenses with Gregory's death in a couple of sentences and simply stops, saying not a word about relics or posthumous miracles. The translation in Rome under Pius II is not mentioned; Garzoni had left Rome himself before then and probably knew nothing of it. The author's debt to the thaumaturge has, however, been paid.

Garzoni's account of Gregory shows him at a relatively sophisticated

---

184. Ibid., fol. 73r–v:

Si poetas, si oratoribus, si historiarum scriptoribus priuati sumus, in barbaros crimen conijicant, qui urbem Romanam ea clade affecerunt, ut ipsam commemorare miserrimum sit. Non sunt nescii Totilam non modo illius menia ad solum euertisse, sed etiam capitolium incendisse, forum, suburram, uiam sacram conflagrasse. Nemo est tam demens nec tam de se parum cogitans, quin fateatur magnam librorum partem ui ignos fuisse consumptam. Quotiens barbare gentes in Italiam iter contulerunt? Quis ambigit ab eis codices non esse deportatos? Carebamus Quintiliano, Silio, Asconio. Sed uirtute elegantissimi uiri Poggii Florentini, in Italiam delati sunt. Est igitur Gregorius culpa liberandus.

185. Ibid., fols. 75–76v, is the digression, keyed to the insertion point on fol. 74.

third level of remove from simple paraphrase: he has combined two sources rather than following the *Legenda aurea*, and he has added two lengthy and educational asides. The first aggressively defends the classical past against monastic detractors and educational traditionalists. To bring Gregory into the humanists' camp was, in fact, a strong move: Garzoni's part in the Quattrocento controversy over that pope deserves recognition. The second lengthy aside that Garzoni adds allows him to reiterate themes from his two compositions on the *vita beata* so as to counter interpretations of Stoic, Epicurean, and Aristotelian philosophy such as might be met in the university atmosphere of Bologna. Both these points are important in themselves, but, for the purpose of this chapter, it is fundamental to notice the fact that, when writing for his own purposes, Garzoni really does not seem to care much about miracles at all. He certainly believes in them. But, in these instances, rather than defending the possibility of miracle, he defends the values of the *studia humanitatis* and Christian orthodoxy, calming at the same time any worries that classicizers like himself necessarily import heretical descriptions of the nature and reality of the Christian afterlife. In other words, when Garzoni does focus on miracles in his asides, we may fairly suspect that he is helping his novices learn a vocabulary and method for defending supernatural occurrences.

❊ ❊ ❊

What light does this brief survey of Garzoni's three levels of paraphrase shed on his intentions for the revision of *vitae et passiones sanctorum*? It is immediately clear that he was not interested in establishing an authoritative text for any of his accounts, although he often protested his trustworthiness. He did not care even to discuss, much less to evaluate, the complex evidence for the reality of his early martyrs, although he occasionally alluded to Roman history. He made no dossiers, collected no documentation. Thus, in his scholarly approach to the saints, the humanist fell far below the achievement of many medieval authors who similarly revised *vitae et passiones*.

But we have impoverished our understanding of the *studia humanitatis* by ignoring this body of work on the grounds that it is philologically uninformed and historiographically frivolous. The evidence of a hierarchy of paraphrastic technique suggests that we might better consider the narratives as literary efforts designed for audiences, including student audiences, of widely differing capacities. At every level, the narratives reflect Garzoni's desire to impart lessons in virtue: no audience was immune from his anxious moralizing. But the audience capacities that most concern Garzoni are chiefly those of language: of grammar and rhetoric. Garzoni's paraphrases reflect the concerns of the humanist classroom. The sense of these *vitae et passiones*—the explanation of their abundance, their format, their

production by a layman, and even of their obsessions—lies in the pedagogy of the *studia humanitatis*.

Is it possible, then, that Garzoni used saints' lives in his teaching? The
proposal may seem, at first glance, surprising, but a moment's reflection
will show that it is not. Evidence for the classroom use of humanist epic
poetry about saints, for example, has been with us for five centuries, even
if it has never been systematically analyzed: of the many incunable editions
of Baptista Mantuanus's *Parthenices* that are extant, a sizable percentage
have interlinear glossing that indicates Christian instruction in Virgilian
and Ovidian vocabulary and metrics.[186] Saints also figured in the plays
that humanist schoolteachers, such as Pietro Domizi of Mantua, wrote for
their students to perform.[187] Schoolboys were set orations on saints for
special occasions: the grammar teacher Orlando da San Gimignano, for
example, composed three speeches on Katherine of Alexandria for his
pupils in Volterra to deliver on the saint's feast day; and in Venice another
youngster, addressing the "patres et cives honorandi" on the subject of St.
Nicholas of Myra, quoted from Basil's *De legendis libris* and Cicero's *De
officiis* in defense of the knowledge to be gained from lives of saints.[188] A
concerted effort to locate student orations would no doubt turn up many
more for saints.

As for Latin prose hagiography in the classroom, manuscript evidence
shows that canonical Latin *vitae*—those by Jerome, for example—were
used. The Milanese schoolteacher Girolamo Calchi shared a collection of
Latin lives of Jerome (including the one by Jacobus de Voragine) with his

186. A survey of this evidence is a *desideratum;* indeed, a full-length study of Mantuanus's
Parthenices remains to be done. The appropriateness of poetry for younger students is a truism of late antique and medieval education; Quintilian assigns poetry to grammarians, for
example, and prose (*historia*) to rhetoricians. For a striking Renaissance example, see
Lorenzo Valla's unsuccessful effort to compose a *Doctrinale* in verse, discussed in Silvia Rizzo
and Mario De Nonno, "In margine a una recente edizione di versi grammaticali del Valla,"
in V. Fera and G. Ferraú, eds., *Filologia umanistica per Gianvito Resta* (Padua: Antenore,
1997), 3:1583–1630. For the larger point, that poetry was easier not just to remember but
also, in this teaching environment, to understand, see Ronald W. Witt, *"In the Footsteps of
the Ancients": The Origins of Humanism from Lovato to Bruni* (Leiden: Brill, 2000),
132–133. For hagiographic poetry as a monastic school exercise, see Jean Leclerq, *The Love
of Learning and the Desire for God*, trans. C. Misrahi (New York: Fordham University Press,
1961/1988), 161–162; and Jean-Yves Tilliette, "Les modèles de sainteté du IXe siècle, d'après
le témoignages des récits hagiographiques en vers métrique," *Settimane* (1988), 406.

187. For Domizi's *Augustinus*, see n. 138 above; *Zenobius* is still in manuscript. Saints in
vernacular *sacre rappresentazioni* are legion.

188. For Orlando, see Hunt, "Two Teachers," at 46, discussing Florence, Bibl. Riccardiana, MS 974; at 48–49, setting out the context for the students' orations on Katherine;
then, at 80–82, 83–85, and 85–88, editing the orations themselves. For the intrepid Venetian
quoter of Basil and Cicero, see VBM, MS Lat. XI 80 (3057), fols. 287v–288. For another student oration on Nicholas, see Rome, Bibl. Angelica, MS 1503 (V 3 10), fols. 240–243.

students.[189] Another fifteenth-century Milanese codex pairs George of Trebizond's edition of Priscian with Jerome's *Vita Pauli*.[190] A fifteenth-century Bergamese manuscript makes the point emphatically by combining two important educational treatises—Guarino's translation of Plutarch's *De liberis educandis* and Pier Paolo Vergerio's *De ingenuis moribus*—with Jerome's lives of Saints Paul, Malchus, and Hilarion.[191] A peninsular manuscript now at the John Rylands Library groups Pius II's *Andreis,* Bessarion's oration on the translation of Andrew's head, Leonardo Giustinian's life of Nicholas, and Jerome's lives of Paul and Malchus with Bruni's *Cicero novus* and Aesop.[192] One of the codices in the library of Garzoni's early employer, Cardinal Domenico Capranica, is especially telling: it opens with the educational treatises by Basil, Plutarch, and Pierpaolo Vergerio and closes with the invectives exchanged between Cicero and Catiline but sandwiched between, along with orations by Aeschines, Demosthenes, and Libanius, are saints' lives about Gregory the Theologian and Jerome.[193] A lost work suggests this classroom use of saintly subjects and paraphrase as well: cataloging his own writings, Antonio degli Agli declares that his first work, completed when he was a *iuvenis*, barely an *adolescens*, was a "certain dialogue in which it is shown that it was not without great cause that God allowed the tyrants to inflict tortures and almost intolerable punishments on the martyrs" ("dialogus quidam quo ostenditur non sine magna causa deus martyrum cruciamenta ac supplic[i]a pene intollerabilia tyrannis inferri permiserit").[194]

Incunables provide further evidence for the classroom use of both metric and prose *vitae et passiones*. The Parma 1491 collection of *Opuscula* by

189. MBA, MS E 21 sup., six items, beginning with Jacobus de Voragine's life of Jerome; on fol. 1v: "Hic liber est Domini Hieronymi Calchi et scholae cius."

190. MBA MS E 48 sup.; John Monfasani, *Collectanea Trapezuntiana* (Binghampton, N.Y.: MRTS, 1984), 478.

191. *Codici e incunaboli miniati della Biblioteca civica di Bergamo* (Bergamo: Credito Bergamesco, 1989), 270–271, no. 115, MS MA 71 (Delta II.15).

192. Kristeller, *Iter,* 4:239–240, MS Lat. 347. The codex is all in one humanist hand.

193. From the 1480 catalog of Capranica's library in BAV, MS Vat. lat. 8184, at fol. 38v, describing the contents of volume 318. On Capranica's library, see A. G. Luciani, "Minoranze significative nella biblioteca del cardinale Domenico Capranica," in C. Bianca and P. Casciano, eds., *Scrittura, biblioteche e stampa a Roma nel Quattrocento: Atti del seminario 1–2 giugno 1979* (Vatican City, 1980), 1:167–182; A. V. Antonovics, "The Library of Cardinal Domenico Capranica," in Clough, ed., *Cultural Aspects,* 141–159.

194. Camerino, Bibl. Valentiniana, MS 78, with Agli's autobiography at 93–138v, containing the list of his works at 115v–119 and giving this dialogue at 115v. I thank Nelson Minnich for sharing his microfilm of this manuscript with me. On Agli, see chap. 2 above; this youthful dialogue on martyrs may have contributed to his being chosen to take up the reform of the martyrology. Agli addresses this same subject in the second preface to *De vitis et gestis sanctorum*; see FBNC, MS Nuovi acq. 399, fol. 16r–v; BAV, MS Lat. 3742, fols. 27v–28.

Augustine includes a life of that fifth-century saint by the Regular Canon
Eusebio Corrado as one of the texts explicitly offered for classroom use at
all levels.[195] Still more ambitious is the three-volume collection of *Poetae
christiani* published by Aldus Manutius in Venice between 1501–1503.[196]
For "studious adolescents" and "all desiring to learn holy manners
together with Greek letters,"[197] the press produced a first volume given
over to the *Peristephanon* by Prudentius and a third volume that concluded
with the *Vita Nicolai* by Leonardo Giustinian. In the second volume, a dedicatory epistle to the Ragusan schoolteacher Daniel Clarius of Parma
declares Aldus's classroom intention: "If instead of the pagan and lascivi-
ous poets, these our Christian poets should take a place in the schools
where the tender souls of boys are taught, everyone would easily become
good."[198] The early Christian texts were to supplant, we must assume,
beginners' study of Persius, Juvenal, Terence, Plautus, and even Virgil. That
a determined publisher of the classics such as Aldus should proceed thus is
certainly unexpected. But the educational concerns of his market—divided
between lay humanists, on the one hand, and monastic educators, on the
other—must be borne in mind. Moreover, the supplantation of classical
school texts by the classicizing paraphrase of Christian texts has a long history. As is well known, the effort to guarantee goodness by substituting a
Christian literature for pagan classroom texts can be traced to the fourth
century, when it blossomed especially in response to Julian's notorious edict
forbidding Christians to teach in schools. The content of *Poetae Christiani*
shows that Aldus had this early Christian precedent in mind. But his concerns were also contemporary. Indeed, they were remarkably similar to
those of the 1455 *Orationes contra poetas* by Ermolao Barbaro (1407–1471),

195. IGI 1018; GW 2867; Goff A1220. This imprint, whose polemical character will
become evident in chap. 5 below, is also of interest because it contains the life of St. Warinus
(Guarinus) mentioned at the end of chap. 3 above.

196. Largely unanalyzed, but see Lee Piepho, *Holofernes' Mantuan: Italian Humanism in
Early Modern England* (New York: Lang, 2001), 18–19; and, for editions of the prefaces
with some helpful notes, *Aldo Manuzio editore: Dediche, Prefazione, Note ai testi*, ed., trans.,
and ann. G. Orlandi, intro. C. Dionisotti (Milan: Il Polifilo [Verona, 1975]), vol. 1, item xxii
(with notes in 2:332–333) and item xxiii (with notes in 2:333).

197. *Poetae christiani*, vol. 3 (1504), fol. 1: "Aldus Romanus omnibus una cum graecis
literis sanctos etiam mores discere cupientibus S.P.D.," naming "studiosi adolescentes" as the
intended audience and instructing them in how to use the collection: "cum graeco diligenter
conferatis, nam & graece simul discetis, & christiane vivere . . . instituunt."

198. Ibid., vol. 2, fol. 1v , a letter dated Venice, June 1502: "Aldus Manutius ro. Danieli
clario Parmensi in urbe Rhacusa bonas literas publice profitenti, S.P.D." and "si in locum
Gentilium lascivorumque poetarum hi nostri Christiani poetae in scholis ubi teneri puerorum
animi instituuntur succederent, facile in bonos plerique omnes evaderent" (*Aldo Manuzio*,
vol. 1, item xxiii). We should not take the noun "poetry" too literally; "art prose" or even
those parts of Livy that discuss religion ("mythology") might qualify as well; see chap. 5
below. Aldus also dedicated his edition of Demosthenes's orations to Clarius.

which was dedicated to Pietro Barbo, the Venetian cardinal of San Marco. (In a delicious mirroring of Julian's edict, this dedicatee would, as Paul II, ban the study of pagan poets by Christian children in Rome.)[199] As Aldus explained: "We publish the most holy books, unknown for almost one thousand years, so that they may be loved and widely used in schools and so that it may happen now not as before, when fables, by which the tender youth of boys is filled, were taken for history (which I think is the chief reason why so many learned men are corrupt and unbelieving). Rather, let falsities be held to be false and the truth to be true. . . . If from their youngest years, boys are taught these Christian poets, they will be imbued with divine things, so that when, well taught, they turn to pagan readings, they will find some good in those books."[200] It is striking that Aldus uses here none of the obvious language of exemplarity, so common in mendicant moral literature; neither does he rely on the allegorizing that had so often "saved" pagan authors. If his prose is more elegant than Garzoni's, nevertheless their arguments are similar, pairing fable and history, false and true, not as historiography or philology but as rhetorically convincing narrative at work in the service of virtue.

That virtue was civic and Christian. As Leonardo Giustinian makes clear in the lengthy preface to his *Vita Nicolai myrensis*, included in the Aldine *Poetae christianae*, beginning Greek students were not to be misled by the most popular of Plutarch's *Parallel Lives*. The adolescent dream of military glory is disparaged: "Shall I, who may never see an army, expend great effort to learn the arts of military strategy, but neglect to learn how to manage pride, extinguish anger, defeat greed and the other diseases of the soul?" In fact, Giustiniani claims that there is Plutarchan glory to be won in writing saints' lives.[201]

But how, precisely, were *vitae et passiones* used in the classroom? This question has been most incisively studied by scholars seeking to reconstruct how the *Legenda aurea* was taught. Their answers tend to locate the pedagogic value of Jacobus's text in *exempla* and, to a lesser extent,

---

199. On Barbaro's *Orationes* and the dedication to Pietro Barbo, see chap. 5 below. Note that Paul's banning of pagan poets in education followed not the firing of the papal abbreviators but the discovery of Platina's "plot" against the pope's life; this chronology is relevant to suspicions about the effects of humanist pedagogy on political loyalties, as discussed in chap. 3 above.

200. "Nam sanctissimos libros, qui circiter mille annos latuere, publicauimus, ut amenter larganturque in scholis, fiatque non ut antehac, cum fabulae quibus tenera puerorum aetas imbuitur pro historia habebantur, quae est potissima, ut puto, causa, quod quamplurimi e doctis & uitiosi sunt, & infideles. Sed contra pro falsis falsa habeantur, & uero pro ueris. . . . Si a teneris annis hosce Christianos poetas pueri doceantur, imbuanturque diuinis. Nam cum ad gentiles iam bene instituti legendos se conferent, bona quaecumque inuenerint legendis illis" (*Poetae christiani* [Venice: Aldus, 1504], lv).

201. *Poetae christiani* (Venice: Manutius, 1501), sign. H2r.

in doctrine.[202] But Garzoni's hierarchy of paraphrase suggests a different emphasis: in the humanist classroom, a text such as the *Legenda aurea* might be brilliant material for learning Latin vocabulary and syntax by rewriting. Garzoni could teach his students to criticize Jacobus's narratives and to pillage them simultaneously. Beginning students could practice vocabulary and syntax with simple transpositions, and the more advanced novices could work out sermon topics in their first-person interventions. At all levels, students could practice creating and delivering speeches as martyrs and persecutors, as budding saints in situations that might reflect some of the tensions of their own experiences on the cusp of entering orders.

There is no direct evidence that *vitae sanctorum* were set for paraphrase in the secular classrooms of the humanist pedagogues. In his recent path-breaking study of Tuscan educational manuscripts, Robert Black does not identify any saints' lives with schoolroom glosses.[203] In any period, classroom paraphrase is not the sort of text that is likely to survive; moreover, given the extreme changes in literary fashion that marked the Counter-reformation, children's classicizing paraphrases of saints' lives were not likely to be counted of any value by those in the business of assembling early modern European libraries. But it is worth noting that the *Patrologia Latina* preserves examples of rewritten *vitae sanctorum* that smack of paraphrastic exercise by medieval novices. Cardinal Bessarion's life of the hermit Bessarion demonstrates the continuity of this rite of passage in the East.[204] Servite novices seem to have made a practice of retelling their order's founding as part of their own passage into religion. In the spring of 1461, when Paolo Attavanti (ca. 1440–1499) was about twenty and so presumably finishing his novitiate, he rewrote the received accounts of the Servite founders. Attavanti not only elaborated the vocabulary and syntax but also shifted the format or genre of the work, from treatise to dialogue. Taddeo Adimari (d. 1517) fashioned a more traditional revision of the

---

202. See n. 121 above. On the theme of education in the fourth-century life of Anthony, see Philip Rousseau, "Antony as Teacher in the Greek *Life*," and Samuel Rubenson, "Philosophy and Simplicity: The Problem of Classical Education in Early Christian Biography," both in T. Haegg and P. Rousseau, eds., *Greek Biography and Paneygric in Late Antiquity* (Berkeley: University of California Press, 2000), 89–109 and 110–139, respectively; and, for the theme of education in early medieval *vitae sanctorum*, see Martin Heinzelmann, "*Studia sanctorum:* Education, milieu d'instruction et valeurs éducatives dans l'hagiographie en Gaule jusqu'à la fin de l'époque mérovingienne," in M. Sot, eds., *Haut Moyen-Age: Culture, Education et Société. Etudes offertes à Pierre Riché* (La Garenne-Colombes: Erasme, 1990), 106–138. None of these informative studies address the use of hagiographic texts for training in grammar or rhetoric.

203. Robert Black, *Humanism and Education in Medieval and Renaissance Italy: Tradition and Innovation in Latin Schools from the Twelfth to the Fifteenth Century* (New York: Cambridge University Press, 2001).

204. See p. 36 above.

founding story into classicizing prose for the same abbot. More than three decades later, Cosimo da Firenze (d. 1526) completed his revision of the same narrative when he was not yet fifteen.[205] Similar exercises can be found in a Dominican context. Garzoni's student Leandro Alberti and his schoolteacher friend Giovanni Antonio Flamini drew young authors into the compilation of *De viris illustribus ordinis praedicatorum*, which they put together over the course of 1516 and published in 1517. Giovanni Flamini's son Marcantonio (1498–1550) wrote an account of the fourteenth-century Dominican Maurizio of Hungary. Niccolò Bagnatorio, who may have been a novice and student of Alberti's or Flamini's, wrote for the same collection on his near-contemporary Conradinus of Brescia (d. 1429). Another teacher, Sebastiano Flamini, contributed a life of the thirteenth-century Dominican Ambrose of Siena to the collection.

Circumstantial evidence suggests that in Guarino's classroom and perhaps that of Vittorino da Feltre, saintly paraphrase may have been such a set exercise. Not only did these two pedagogues turn out a relatively high number of learned and conscientious prelates, but they also produced many men, lay and clerical, who engaged in the paraphrase or revision of saints' lives after leaving the school.[206] So, for example, when Jacopo Foscarini (1409–1480), a former student of Guarino's, made a paraphrastic translation of the martyrdom of Victor and Corona, he said nothing about how the devotional or historically suspect nature of the text might impede him (as a man who was neither a cleric nor a historian but the governor of Feltre for Venice). He apologized only that he had not been a student of rhetoric for a long time, that is, he brought to mind only the classroom connection.[207]

Similarly, when another student of Guarino's, Ermolao Barbaro (ca. 1410–1471), was asked by the nuns of Santa Croce di Giudecca to improve their *Vita Athanasii*, he did not seek out Greek lives of that fourth-century church father, and neither did he compile a dossier of Latin ones. As bishop of Verona, he might easily have commandeered the necessary manuscripts or asked secretaries to assemble a dossier. Instead, he took the assignment as a schoolroom exercise and produced a mild paraphrase.[208] The nuns had

205. Cf. the Servite Taddeo Garganelli of Bologna (ca. 1430–1469), above, n. 61, who wrote a series of six hymns on saints around 1450, with a letter of dedication mentioning another humanist teacher who also wrote saints' lives, Giovanni Tortelli (d. 1466).

206. Remigio Sabbadini, *La scuola e gli studi di Guarino Guarini veronese* (Catania, 1896), chap. 15, remains a useful introduction to sacred studies at Guarino's school. Sabbadini notes the *Vita Ambrosii* and the *Vita Timotei* but does not speculate on the use of *vitae sanctorum* in the classroom.

207. See p. 14 above.

208. Barbaro paraphrases book 10 of Eusebius's *Historia Ecclesiastica*, which was a Latin addition by Rufinus to Eusebius's Greek.

asked, after all, for a text to honor more appropriately the saint whose relics they guarded, and rhetorical paraphrase took propriety as its goal.

We might also consider texts that are otherwise difficult to explain. Guarino's 1434 translation of an unremarkable Greek life of Ambrose into simple Latin for Alberto da Sarteano, O.F.M., for example, provides a base text for preachers to elaborate paraphrastically.[209] Guarino and a former student, the Canon Regular Timoteo Maffei (ca. 1415–1470), exchanged name saint *vitae*: Guarino translated a Greek *vita* of the apostle Timothy for Maffei, and Maffei sent Guarino a twelfth-century life of Cardinal Warinus.[210] Their sense of the appropriateness of the gifts may have depended on classroom familiarity.[211]

Nor is there direct evidence that Giovanni Garzoni assigned hagiographic paraphrase in his classroom, either to his Dominican novices or to his younger secular students. Again, such texts would not likely survive. But here, too, are hints: notice in a letter that Garzoni had received a *Vita Simonis Pueris* from a former student, Frater Rodericus of Bohemia, suggests a continuation of classroom practice.[212] And to the evidence of the life of Christopher, which was dedicated to a former student, can be added Garzoni's *passio* of the knight Proculus, also dedicated to a former student, Ludovicus. Moreover, Garzoni's attention to the *Legenda aurea* is not unique among humanists. Egidio da Viterbo frequently refers to it. All Valla's knowledge of Thomas Aquinas's life, at least as it is expressed in the *Encomion* that caused such a stir at the curia in 1457, is traceable to the *Legenda aurea*.[213] Certainly, Valla's *postilla* to Quintilian's passage on advanced paraphrase suggests that attention to the lives of saints, including difficult cases such as George, interested the Roman humanist. Is it possible that Garzoni learned from Valla to use the *Legenda aurea* for composition practice in his classroom?

That possibility must remain for now mere conjecture. About Garzoni's work with saints' lives, we can be more certain. Whatever we may think of his personality or his prose, Garzoni's education and his work as a

---

209. Evidence of the diffusion of Guarino's *vita Ambrosii* in the Franciscan order has not been systematically gathered. For an example, see Naples, BN, MS VI G 15, 2va–3rb (preface) and 3va–7ra (life) (Kristeller, *Iter*, 1:423a = 5:112b).

210. On this life of St. Guarinus, see chap. 3 above.

211. Cf. the metric account of St. Antoninus of Piacenza, composed by Francesco Bernardino Cipelli (1481–ca. 1540?) for his student Gaspare Anguissola and published at Milan in 1521 (not seen). Loredana Chines, *Le parole degli antichi* (Rome: Carocci, 1998), 189–190.

212. Lind, *Letters*, letter 19; cf. letters 483 and 484, to another Rodericus, not a *frater*. The former Rodericus apparently wrote the *Vita Simonis* after leaving Garzoni's classroom but even so sent a copy to his former teacher.

213. See Remo L. Guidi, "Questioni di storiografia agiografica nel quattrocento," *Benedictina* 34 (1987): 185 n. 34.

teacher argue success. His fellow citizens gave him political offices; his professional colleagues sought his participation in university affairs, not just in the medical faculty but also in the faculty of theology, where, as a layman and a humanist, he would have been an outsider. He served friends as well as patrons in celebration and consolation and was offered the same in return. He was asked to write histories, orations, and biographies. His foreign students went home with warm memories of his help and contributed to a minor circulation of his writings in the north of Europe. Niccolò Burzio (ca. 1450–ca. 1520), in *Bononia illustrata* of 1494, praised the still-living Garzoni, among all the professional men of the city, for his work as a rhetorician.[214] Most important in this context, through his teaching of novices, Garzoni linked lay humanism and the Dominican order, making Ciceronian Latin and classical notions of delivery part of the experience of young men at a leading Observant convent in Italy. One of the most broadly conceived aspects of this educational project, which indeed moved outside the Dominican orbit, was Garzoni's narration of saints' lives. Here, too, he was successful, if we take him on the terms under which he operated. I have suggested that these terms were not so much historiographical or philological, in the sophisticated sense represented by major intellects such as Valla or Poliziano, but pedagogical. Simple classroom practice was not, however, incompatible with more elevated approaches. Garzoni's narratives show that the *anaskeue* and *kataskeue*, or refutation and confirmation, of Quintilian's *Institutes* II, 4, could be achieved in the Quattrocento in ways we no longer credit: through varieties of paraphrase. Through his hierarchy of exercises in paraphrase, Garzoni refuted the moral and rhetorical failings of the *Legenda aurea* as he confirmed the authenticity of Christian virtue and miracle represented by the saints.

214. Bologna: Francisuis de Benedictis, 1494. *IGI* 2274; GW 5794; Goff B 1329.

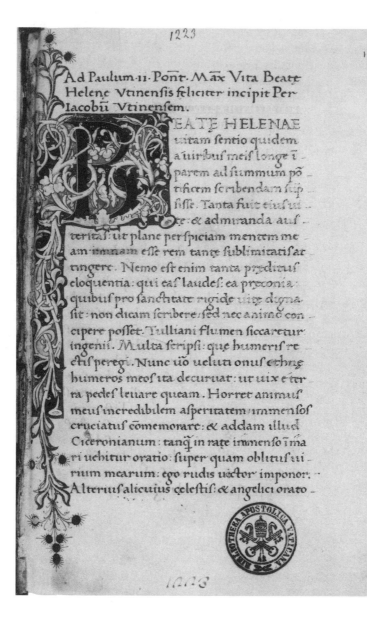

1223

Ad Paulum·II·Pont·Max Vita Beatę
Helenę Vtinensis feliciter incipit Per
Iacobū Vtinensem.

EATĘ HELENAE
uitam sentio quidem
a uiribus meis longe ī
parem ad summum pō
tificem scribendam sus
sisse. Tanta fuit eius ui
tę: & admiranda aus
teritas: ut plane perspiciam mentem me
am· immanam esse rem tantę sublimitatis at
tingere. Nemo est enim tanta prędituf
eloquentia: qui eas laudes: ea pręconia:
quibus pro sanctitate rigide uitę digna
sit: non dicam scribere: sed nec animo con
cipere posset. Tulliani flumen siccaretur
ingenii. Multa scripsi: quę humeris re
ctis peregi. Nunc uō ueluti onus ethnę
humeros meos ita decuruat: ut uix e ter
ra pedes leuare queam. Horret animuf
meus incredibilem asperitatem/immensof
cruciatus comemorare: & addam illud
Ciceronianum: tanq̃ in rate immenso ī ma
ri uehitur oratio: super quam oblitus ui
rium mearum: ego rudis uector imponor:·
Alteriusalicuius cęlestis & angelici orato

PLATE 5. Giacomo da Udine, opening of the *Vita Helenae utinensis*. Biblioteca apostolica
vaticana, MS Vat. lat. 1223, fol. 1.

CHAPTER 5

The Spectacle of
a Woman's Devotion

quasi omnes qui se litteris dederunt inter Epicureos, qui vero litteras aspernantur inter Antonios atque Macarios numerandos

as if all who devoted themselves to letters are to be counted among the Epicureans, but those who spurn letters, among the Anthonies and Macariuses

—Timoteo Maffei, Can. Lat. (d. 1470), *In sanctam rusticitatem*, preface[1]

The most innovative of the Quattrocento humanists' *vitae et passiones sanctorum* was written by Giacomo da Udine (ca. 1415–1482), a canon of the cathedral at Aquileia.[2] The account is unique in its rhetorical display and correspondingly hard to assess. Humanism in the

1. Patrizia Sonia De Corso, ed., *Timoteo Maffei, In sanctam rusticitatem litteras impugnantem* (Verona: Archivio storico, Curia diocesana, 2000), 138, ll. 18–20.

2. On Giacomo da Udine, see G. G. Liruti, *Notizie delle vite ed opere scritte da letterati del Friuli* (Venice, 1760), 1:365–369; but especially Andrea Tilatti, "Il canonico Giacomo da Udine e una sua orazione ad Eugenio IV," *Metodi e ricerche* (Udine), n.s., 7, no. 1 (1988): 61–65, and notes below. I am grateful to Professor Tilatti for his learned advice and generosity. Edward Muir provides a structural introduction to the Friulese context of this chapter in *Mad Blood Stirring: Vendetta and Factions During the Renaissance* (Baltimore: Johns

Friuli is relatively understudied,[3] and the author is little known.[4] The dedicatee, Paul II (1464–1471), is famous for his relative hostility to humanist *literati*.[5] The subject is an elderly contemporary widow of charismatic virtues, a saintly type that did not typically appeal to humanists.[6] And experts have judged the narrative harshly: "less a life of the *beata* than an amateurish stew or rather rhapsody," wrote Daniel Papebroek (1628–1714), "regret[ting] the loss of time and effort" that the Bollandists had taken to transcribe it.[7] Today, more than three centuries after that dismissal, an unsuspecting reader might still take Giacomo's narrative for a stew or rhapsody. This chapter will propose instead that the *vita* is a learned experiment, an unusually rich example of humanist incursions into *vitae et passiones sanctorum*. Indeed, Giacomo's narrative is such a dense knot of fifteenth-century concerns that its implications go well beyond the specialized territory of the hagiologist.

Giacomo was an experienced author in his fifties when he took up his saintly subject, so we cannot easily account for his experiment on the basis

---

Hopkins University Press, 1993), 15–107; see also A. Tagliaferri, dir., *Relazioni dei rettori Veneti in terraferma, 1. La patria del Friuli* (Milan: Giuffré, 1973), "Introduzione storica," for Udine's relations with Venice, and Giuseppe Trebbi, *Il Friuli dal 1420 al 1797: La storia politica e sociale* (Udine: Casamassima, 1998), esp. 3–44. On the fabric of the cathedral at Aquileia in this period, see G. Bergamini, "La basilica patriarcale tra quattro e cinquecento," in A. De Cillia and G. Fornesir, eds., *Il patriarcato di Aquileia tra Riforma e Controriforma: Atti del Convegno di studio, Udine, Palazzo mantica, 9 dicembre 1995* (Udine: Arti Grafiche Friulane, 1996), 131–158. On the history of the cathedral chapter, see P. Cammarosano, F. De Vitt, and D. Degrassi, *Il medioevo* (Udine: Casamassima, 1988), 177–180, with bibliography. For the complex politics of the patriarchate in the Quattrocento, Girolamo de Renaldis, *Memorie storiche dei tre ultimi secoli del patriarcato d'Aquileia (1411–1751)*, ed. G. Gropperio (Udine: Tipografia del patronato, 1888), remains helpful.

3. For example, P. Findlen, M. M. Fontaine, and D. J. Osheim, eds., *Beyond Florence: The Contours of Medieval and Early Modern Italy* (Stanford, Calif.: Stanford University Press, 2003), includes no entry on the Friuli. The best recent study of the Friuli in English, Muir's *Mad Blood*, is a social history of unrest among the impoverished and their feudal warlords. Muir's approach, although a welcome counterweight to the predominance of elites in Renaissance scholarship, may lead to the impression of a land without schools or intellectual traditions. Cf. Claudio Griggio, "L'umanesimo friuliano," *Lettere italiane* 47 (1995): 641–659, and Cesare Scalon, *Libri, scuola e cultura nel Friuli medioevale* (Padua: Antenore, 1987).

4. See Tilatti, "Il canonico"; in "L'elezione del Doge Pasquale Malipiero e l'orazione di Giacomo da Udine in nome della Patria del Friuli," *Metodi e ricerche*, n.s., 8, no. 2 (1989): 40, Andrea Tilatti identifies Giacomo's father as a notary working at Udine.

5. Paul II's antipathy to humanists is discussed below. For a sense of how poorly scholars still estimate Paul in comparison to his papal successors' and predecessors' support of the new cultural currents, see the invidious comparisons made in passing in articles collected in Massimo Miglio, ed., *Un pontificato ed una città. Sisto IV (1471–1484): Atti del Convegno, Roma, 3–7 dicembre 1984* (Vatican City: Scuola vaticana di paleografia, diplomatica e archivistica, 1986).

6. See chap. 1 above.

7. *AASS*, April III (Paris, 1866), 248, para. 4. I do not know if Papebroek's copy is still extant.

of naïveté or adolescent impulsiveness.[8] He had been writing for patronage since his youth, after abandoning a law education when funds ran out.[9] At that point, he left the Friuli to seek his fortune in Rome, where he joined the *familia* of the wealthy and politically astute Cardinal Ludovico Trevisan.[10] The cardinal, bishop of Trau from October 24, 1435, then archbishop of Florence from August 6, 1437, was named patriarch of Aquileia in mid-January 1439. So, by the time he was about twenty-seven, Giacomo had parlayed his curial connections into a position as cathedral canon at Aquileia.[11] It was a potentially weighty appointment, because the nominal church at Aquileia was a pivotal piece in Venetian terraferma expansion and Roman response.[12] Thus, for professional as well as personal reasons, the new canon would maintain his Roman, Venetian, and Udinese connections throughout his life. But he was not a mere opportunist. His fellow canons, who included the humanist book collector, Guarnerio d'Artegna (ca. 1410–1466), acknowledged Giacomo's liturgical competence and respected

8. The date of the composition cannot be precisely determined. Tilatti, "Il canonico," 64–65, narrows the *terminus ante quem* to May 1469, the date of Leonardo da Udine's death. In the *vita*, Giacomo implies that Leonardo is still alive by using the present tense "theologiae monarcha est." See BAV, MS Lat. 1223, fols. 69r v (hereafter, this unitary manuscript is identified by the siglum G); the verb is slender evidence. Presumably the *vita* was written after the dedicatee, Paul II, acceded to the papacy. At any rate, Giacomo was probably in his fifties when he wrote. Certainly he presents himself as an experienced author: "Multa scripsi . . . " (G fol. 1).

9. See degli Agostini, *Notizie* 1:77–78, for Giacomo's letter to the Commune of Udine asking for a subvention to support his studies. According to degli Agostini, this first application was made to the Udinese patrician Urbano Savorgnan through Leonardo Contarini, lieutenant in Udine for Venice. For the problem of identifying this Leonardo, see F. Rossi, "Contarini, Leonardo," *DBI* 28 (1983), 230a. When his petition failed, Giacomo asked Ludovico Foscarini (1409–1480) to exert influence in Udine on his behalf; degli Agostini also edits this letter, with its fulsome praise of Foscarini and mention of Bernardo Bembo (whom Giacomo calls *dominus meus*), as well as of Bembo's mother, Lisabetta Paruta, and father, Nicolò Bembo (*Notizie* 1:47–48, 50). Despite Giacomo's connections, funds were not forthcoming. Two years later, the Commune did offer support on the grounds that Giacomo's father had died bravely fighting the Hungarians (that is, in the series of military actions that preceded the Venetian takeover of the Friuli in 1420). But Giacomo does not seem to have completed his law degree.

10. See Pio Paschini, "Umanisti intorno a un cardinale," *La Rinascita* 1 (1938): 52–73, for the way in which Trevisan's wealth created a web of humanist attachments: "Più che cercare gli umanisti ed i letterati, furono questi che cercarano lui" (53). For Paschini, this effect was exactly the opposite of the one created by Paul II (72). See also Paschini, *Ludovico Cardinal Camerlengo (d. 1465)* (Rome, 1939), 50–63, recapitulated in John Easton Law, *Venice and the Veneto in the Early Renaissance* (Ashgate: Variorum, 2000), 15.

11. Tilatti, "Il canonico," 262, notes that Giacomo first appears in the chapter records at Aquileia on May 2, 1442.

12. Venice's expansion onto the mainland, on which there is an enormous bibliography, receives a succinct and nuanced treatment in Elisabeth Crouzet-Pavan, *Venice Triumphant: The Horizons of a Myth*, trans. L. G. Cochrane (Baltimore: Johns Hopkins University Press, 2002), chap. 3.

his rhetorical skill.[13] Well-known lay figures appreciated his qualities as well. In a letter from Florence, dated February 6, 1439, Poggio Bracciolini wrote to Giovanni Spilimbergo, the Udinese humanist and schoolteacher who was related by marriage to Guarino Guarini, recalling Giacomo as a "most cultured and engaging man" ("vir humanissimus atque amicissimus").[14]

A similar appreciation seems to have led Cardinal Trevisan's old school friend, the learned Venetian patrician Francesco Barbaro (1390–1454), to commission a history of the church in Aquileia from Giacomo.[15] The project might have been important for Giacomo's career: the topic was serious and complex, and the patron was a man who could judge quality work. Barbaro himself had studied under Giovanni Conversino da Ravenna, Gasparino Barzizza, and Guarino Guarini; he had employed George of Trebizond and Flavio Biondo. Moreover, at the time of the commission, in 1448, Francesco Barbaro was serving as lieutenant in Friuli and prefect in Padua.[16] But Giacomo's response to the commission was halfhearted:

13. According to Tilatti, "Il canonico," 62, Giacomo was a responsibly resident canon; cf. de Renaldis, *Memorie storiche,* 92 and 134, noting that the canons were allowed annual absences of six months on account of the bad air. Tilatti, ibid., records that Giacomo passed his examination for liturgical competence. Not everyone did: de Renaldis, *Memorie storiche,* 127, records a fellow canon who could not and would not pass. Guarnerio d'Artegna, who seems to have become a priest by about 1445, was Trevisan's vicar *in spiritualibus* at Aquileia from late 1445 to about 1456; see G. Scalon, "Guarnerio d'Artegna," *DBI* 60 (2003): 417a–b. On his library, see L. Casarsa, M. D'Angelo, and C. Scalon, *La libreria di Guarnerio d'Artegna* (Udine: Casamassima, 1991), and the overview in Scalon, "Guarnerio d'Artegna."

14. H. Harth, ed., *Poggio Bracciolini Lettere* (Florence: Olschki, 1987), 2:345, which places Giacomo da Udine in Florence in late January/early February 1439. He may have arrived there January 27 with Eugene IV's entourage. For Giovanni Spilimbergo as a pedagogue and relation of Guarino's, see Sabbadini, *Epistolario, ad indicem.*

15. On Barbaro, see Margaret L. King, *Venetian Humanism in an Age of Patrician Dominance* (Princeton, N.J.: Princeton University Press, 1986), 323–325 and *ad indicem;* and G. Gualdo, "Barbaro, Francesco," *DBI* 6 (1964), 101–103. In a letter dated "Venetiis VI kalendas maias [April 26,] 1446," edited in Claudio Griggio, *Francesco Barbaro Epistolario* (Florence: Olschki 1999), letter 223 at 2:465, ll. 6–10, Francesco's son Zaccaria Barbaro writes to Lauro Quirini, who had recommended Giacomo da Udine, promising to help Giacomo. Francesco's continuing attention to Giacomo is indicated by his letter 318 of January 31, 1448, in ibid., 644. There Francesco praises Giacomo for his progress "in virtute et bonis artibus," his winning speech, and his diligent letters, especially a recent one about the "cardinal[es] . . . nuper designat[i]" under Nicholas V (1447–1455). These cardinals would have included Latino Orsini, Filippo Calandrino, and Nicholas of Cusa; see Alphonse Chacon, *Vitae et res gestae pontificum romanorum et s.r.e. cardinalium ab initio . . .* (Rome, 1677), 2:974–977. This letter suggests that Giacomo was absent from Aquileia for a period, presumably on official business.

16. King, *Humanism,* does not mention the prefecture at Padua; it is noted but not dated by G. Gualdo, "Barbaro, Francesco," 102a. The records of Barbaro's lieutenancy (1448–1449) are lost; cf. *Relazioni dei rettori veneti in terraferma,* vol. 1, *La patria del Friuli (Luogotenenza di Udine)* (Milan: Giuffré, 1973), which opens with 1525.

De antiquitatibus aquileiensibus libellus is only a letter, an *epistola*.[17] It does include a preface, in which Giacomo addresses Barbaro as *praetor* and adduces Poggio, Pierpaolo Vergerio, and Guarino in order to compliment Barbaro for writing *De re uxoria* in merely twenty-five days.[18] The letter even has a *peroratio*. But in the end the history was no more than a series of notes excerpted from chronicles: Giacomo, who evidently had considerable critical capacities, mistrusted his sources.[19]

Giacomo also delivered orations, a handful of which are extant. At some time between October 1435 and August 1437, a period when Eugene IV (1431–1447) was resident first in Florence and then, briefly, in Bologna, Giacomo petitioned the pope to support his university studies.[20] A reference to Trevisan in this speech of barely four hundred words shows that Giacomo had already established ties to his patron. Then, after the nomination to Aquileia, Giacomo was chosen to represent the Friuli by giving a congratulatory oration for the new doge Pasquale Malipiero (1457–1462);[21] in 1470 his fellow canons selected him to deliver an oration to congratulate the new patriarch of Aquileia, Paul II's nephew Car-

---

17. *De antiquitatibus* is not mentioned in Cochrane, *Historians*, nor in Eduard Fueter, *Storia della storiografia moderna*, 3d ed. rev., ed. M. A. Spinelli (Naples: Ricciardi, 1944). Cf. *De vetustate Aquileiae* by Marcantonio Coccio, Sabellico (d. 1506), composed in 1478; Cochrane, *Historians*, 83; F. Tateo, "Coccio, Marcantonio," *DBI* 26 (1982): 511; cf. Fueter, *Storia*, 39. I have seen only late manuscripts of Giacomo's *De antiquitatibus*: Venice, MS Marc. lat. X 131 (3231) and MS Marc. lat. XIV 49 (4270); and Brescia, Biblioteca Queriniana, MS C.V.11, at fol. 97, a copy made by Cardinal Querini. See also Kristeller, *Iter*, 1:332b, for a fifteenth-century miscellany that includes this work: MBA, MS J 28 sup., fols. 25–35v (not seen). For an edition, see G. M. Lazzaroni, *Miscelanea di varie operette* (Venice, 1740–44), 2:99–134.

18. VBM, MS Lat. XIV 49 (4270), fol. 70v. Cf. Claudio Griggio, "Copisti ed editori del *De re uxoria* di Francesco Barbaro," in V. Fera and F. Ferraú, eds., *Filologia umanistica per Gianvito Resta* (Padua: Antenore, 1997), 2:1033–1055, on the circumstances of the writing "in un paio di mesi" (1034), with further bibliography.

19. "Missas etenim facio nugas paene infinitas in quibusdam cornicis—non cronicis—descriptas, quae cum inpudentissimis mendaciis refertissimae sint, ne referenda quidem illarum fuit opinio" (VBM, MS Marc. lat. XIV 49 [4270], fols. 78r–v; Lazzaroni, *Miscelanea*, 133–134).

20. Edited in Tilatti, "Il canonico," from a San Daniele manuscript (Kristeller, *Iter*, 2:568a–b). Cf. Mazzatinti, *Inventari*, 6:217, on Arezzo, Biblioteca della Fraternità dei Laici, MS 226, a fifteenth-century manuscript (not seen), not corroborated by Kristeller (*Iter*, 1:3a). Also trailing after Eugene IV during his travels at this time was Pietro Barbo (later Paul II); see Giorgio Zippel, ed., *Le vite di Paolo II di Gaspare da Verona e Michele Canensi* (Città di Castello, 1904) at 83 and n. 4. About this time, Eugene was considering a removal of the Basel council to Florence or Udine; see Pastor, *History* 1:312.

21. Tilatti, "Il canonico," 63; in "L'elezione," 41, Tilatti records three copies of the text, identifies an autograph, and edits the oration (44–48), as well as giving precious notice of Giacomo's other ties to Udine.

dinal Marco Barbo (1420–1491).[22] Giacomo was not, it appears, the person who delivered a speech in the persona of Rome before Paul II.[23]

Giacomo wrote on military matters as well. He dedicated to Federico Montefeltro, count of Urbino from 1444, a treatise on warfare entitled *De militari arte apud Graecos, Carthaginenses, Romanosque et armis contra Turcos sumendis*.[24] A collection of biographies about great mercenary generals, *condottieri*, announced as "in progress," is no longer extant and may have been interrupted by Giacomo's death.[25]

Among Giacomo's extant works, the saint's life is by far the most ambitious: in length, in format, and in choice of dedicatee. It is also Giacomo's sole venture into *vitae sanctorum*. In this respect, he is like many of the other authors to be found in the catalog; comparisons might be drawn, for example, with Leon Battista Alberti, who wrote a single, equally hard-to-evaluate saint's life.[26] Giacomo's account also does not appear to have circulated. Extant in one manuscript, his narrative does not seem to have contributed to the reputation or promotion of its subject and, for all its learned novelty, had no effect on the development of hagiographic forms. It is dedicated to Paul II but gives no sign of having been commissioned, although Ludwig Pastor warns that any dedication to Paul II should be taken to indicate his prior approval. Pastor's caution is especially significant since Giacomo da Udine's career had been founded on the patronage of Ludovico Trevisan, and Trevisan was a determined enemy of Pietro Barbo.[27] Finally, Papebroek sealed the fate of the *vita* by so sharply dismissing it in the *Acta sanctorum* entry on Elena.

❋ ❋ ❋

Et sane Paulos et Antonios semper habens prae oculis, quamvis comitata, in solitudine perpetuo degebat.

And rightly having the Pauls and Anthonies always before her eyes, she lived in perpetual solitude (although accompanied).
—Paolo Olmi, O.E.S.A. (d. 1484), *vita Magdalenae*[28]

---

22. Not edited; Barbo's date of appointment is from King, *Venetian Humanism*, 327; Tilatti, "Il canonico," 63; Zippel, *Le vite*, 174 n. 1; Pompeo Litta, *Famiglie celebre italiane* (Milan and Turin, 1819–1885), 11 vols., with *Seconda serie* (Naples: Richter, 1903–23), 3 vols., vol. 9 (Milan, 1868), table 4.

23. Kristeller, *Iter*, 2:93a = Rome, Biblioteca Angelica, MS V V 7.12 (inc. 546), in fasc. 6 (not seen); Zippel, *Le vite*, 193–194, appendix 5.

24. Tilatti, "Il canonico," 64–65. The treatise is extant in BAV, MS Urb. lat. 933 (not seen).

25. Tilatti, "Il canonico," 65.

26. On Alberti's *Vita Potiti*, see pp. 67–70 above.

27. Zippel, ed. *Le vite*, 24–26; Paschini, *Lodovico Cardinal*, at 50 and 206–207.

28. *BHL* 5132, quotation from *AASS* May III (Rome, 1866), at 253, para. 4. Olmi is discussed below.

Giacomo's *vita Helenae utinensis* represents an unusual choice of subject, for authors associated with the *studia humanitatis* paid relatively little attention to their contemporaries who strove after sanctity and still less to the subgroup of aspirants who happened to be married women.[29] Elena of Udine (1395/96–April 23, 1458) may have been a predictable subject insofar as she belonged to the noble family de Valentinis: throughout the Middle Ages, *vitae* were rarely written about laypeople who were politically unimportant.[30] But she was not a virgin, not a martyr, and not a nun. She had been married for three decades to Antonio Cavalcanti, a wealthy cloth merchant of Florentine extraction who made himself more dangerously prominent by his outspoken opposition to the Venetian takeover of his city.[31] After Antonio's death in September 1441, Elena was required by the terms of his will to take financial responsibility for their six children and to live with them in the family home.[32] She gradually divested herself of this worldly duty and at a certain point began living in the house of her widowed sister Profeta, near the church and convent of Santa Lucia, which belonged to the Augustinian Hermits (Ordo Eremitarum Sancti Augustini,

29. On the late medieval model of female sanctity, see Vauchez, *La sainteté*, 215–256, and bibliography below.

30. For the historical reality of Elena, I draw heavily on the publications of Andrea Tilatti. I also follow Tilatti in urging that the conventions of the *vitae* not be mistaken for archival data, although my emphasis in this chapter is on the image of the saint that the humanist wishes to present to Paul II rather than on her historical reality as deducible from the archives. See especially Tilatti, "*Per man di notaro:* La beata Elena da Udine tra documenti notarili e leggende agiografiche," *Cristianesimo nella storia* 8 (1987): 501–520; and idem, "Il canonico," 24–25 and 127 nn. 1–2; see also N. Del Re in *BS* 12 (1969): 886–887 and *AASS* April III (Rome, 1866): 249–260. For Elena's lineage, see Andrea Tilatti, ed., *Simone da Roma, Libro over legenda della beata Helena da Udene* (Tavagnacco: Casamassima, 1988), 28–29. For the rare cases of lay saints from the humbler classes, see Vauchez, *La sainteté*, on Homobonus (d. 1192; c.d. 1199) and Petrus Pettinaius (d. 1289). Webb, *Patrons, ad indicem,* describes their places in the civic pantheon. The most successful lay saints were royal; for analysis of this fact, see Gabor Klaniczay, *Holy Rulers and Blessed Princesses: Dynastic Cults in Medieval Central Europe,* trans. E. Palmai (New York: Cambridge University Press, 2002).

31. According to Tilatti, *Simone da Roma,* 24, Elena was married in 1411. For Cavalcanti's Florentine roots, see Tilatti, "I toscani nelle fonti notarili udinesi del XV secolo: I Cavalcanti ed i Vanni degli Onesti, prospettive per una ricerca," in A. Malcangi, ed., *I Toscani in Friuli: Atti del convegno Udine, 26–27 gennaio 1990* (Florence: Olschki, 1992), 102–104, esp. 102. G. Biasutti, *Profilo spirituale della beata Elena Valentinis da Udine (con cenni storici inediti) nel V centenario della morte* (Udine, 1958), 14; and Tilatti, *Simone da Roma,* 25, note that he was one of ten deputed to serve in ambassadorial positions to Venice and that it was immediately following his first trip to Venice (a visit long sought by the Venetians whom he had so maligned) that he sickened and died.

32. Antonio Cavalcanti died soon after August 27, 1441, according to Biasutti, *Profilo spirituale,* 33–34. On his will, see Tilatti, "*Per man di notaro,*" 506 and 507, and n. 17, pointing out that Antonio provided for Elena to live outside the home if domestic relations deteriorated.

O.E.S.A.).[33] Perhaps the prior of Santa Lucia, Antonio da Milano, was Elena's confessor during these early years, as she adopted the life of a *pinzochera*: without formal affiliation to an order and without taking vows or living in strict claustration, the widow probably practiced chastity, voluntary poverty, frequent prayer, and asceticisms such as restricted eating and sleeping.[34] Such *pinzochere*, the southern European equivalent of the Beguines, were familiar figures in the Quattrocento cities, living withdrawn but not solitary lives. From about 1449, a small group of women, all of elevated social class, and many her kin, joined Elena in her pious withdrawal.[35]

More than a decade after her husband's death, Elena formalized her relationship to the Augustinian Hermits, so that she spent the last six years of her life as a mantellate, a member of the Hermits' Third Order.[36] The impetus for this decision, according to the earliest *vita* (discussed below), was a preaching tour by the otherwise unrecorded Angelo da Sancto Severino, O.E.S.A..[37] Elena was the first woman in Udine to become an Augustinian tertiary, although others from her group seem to have followed her path about the same time.[38] Now, as a mantellate, Elena may have increased her devout exercises, but they would also have been more closely monitored. The Dominican who is known to have been her confessor, Leonardo Mattei of Udine (d. 1469)—famous preacher and promoter of the sanctity of the thirteenth-century ascetic Benvenuta Boiani of

33. On the gradual divestiture, see Tilatti, *"Per man di notaro,"* 506–507, and at 514 dating it to 1444–1446.

34. Her confessor was, at any rate, named Antonio; see Tilatti, *"Per man di notaro,"* 507. On her asceticism, see ibid., 508–510. For studies of similar women, see Daniel Bornstein and Roberto Rusconi, eds., *Women and Religion in Medieval and Renaissance Italy* (Chicago: University of Chicago Press, 1996); and for an overview of the "semi-religious" phenomenon, see Kaspar Elm, *"Vita regularis sine regula:* Bedeutung, Rechtstellung und Selbstverständnis des mittelalterlichen und frühneuzeitlichen Semireligiosentums," in F. Smahel and E. Müller-Lackner, *Häresie und vorzeitige Reformation in Spätmittelalter* (Munich: Oldenbourg, 1998), 239–273, with copious bibliography. Noting that "nothing so clearly divided the ranks of the saints as gender," Donald Weinstein and Rudolph M. Bell, *Saints and Society: The Two Worlds of Western Christendom, 1000–1700* (Chicago: University of Chicago Press, 1982), 220, devote their concluding chapter to mapping that divide according to criteria such as charity and asceticism.

35. See Tilatti, *"Per man di notaro,"* 510 and n. 23, and 511 nn. 25–26, for archival evidence of this circle; and idem, *Simone da Roma,* 155 n. 8, emphasizing their social status.

36. Tilatti, *"Per man di notaro,"* 507, 513 n. 30, and 514; he proposes that she became a tertiary in the fall of 1452. The period of six years as a tertiary is recorded explicitly by Jacopo Filippo Foresti (on whom see further below). So she lived unenclosed as a widow and *pinzochera* a full eleven years after Antonio's death. Andrea Tilatti, "La regola delle terziarie agostiniane di Udine (sec. XV)," *AA* 54 (1991): 65–79, edits her group's *regula.*

37. Tilatti, *Simone da Roma,* 129–130.

38. Tilatti, *"Per man di notaro,"* 514 and n. 32; idem, *Simone da Roma,* 130 and n. 9; further below.

Cividale—may have intervened in these last years to advise that Elena moderate her diet and discipline.[39] Between home and church, she pursued her devotional life with a typically late-medieval mixture of affectivity and rationality. She used number symbolism, for example, in her ascetic *imitatio Christi*: the earliest *vita* reports that she made a pilgrimage to Rome for the 1450 Jubilee with thirty-three pebbles in her shoes (she went by boat).[40] Giacomo da Udine mentions that she kept two clocks, the better to maintain a tight schedule of praying, weeping, and reading.[41] That reading appears to have been solely vernacular.[42] She received the special charisms of tears and long-suffering patience before the onslaughts of the devil. Her small group was aware of those virtues, but Elena told only her sister Profeta of her mystic visions.[43]

Was Elena an aspiring *santa viva*, a living saint?[44] Her own intentions cannot be discerned from the group of near-contemporary *vitae*. In an eighteenth-century process, the Church formalized her status as a *beata*, not a saint.[45] But if sanctity is indeed in the eye of the beholder, then we can surmise from the Hermits who guided Elena in her last years that she was recognized in Quattrocento Udine as a *santa viva*. Her final will states her desire to be buried in the Hermits' church of Santa Lucia so forcefully

39. Giacomo of Udine names Leonardo da Udine "her longtime confessor" ("qui diu extitit confessor eius") and describes him as a moderating influence who advised against strict solitude ("qui eam tendentem ad vastam aliquam solitudinem avocavit") and counseled the temperance in diet recommended by her doctors (G fol. 69r–v). See also Andrea Tilatti, *Benvenuta Boiani: Teoria e storia della vita religiosa femminile nella Cividale del secondo Duecento* (Trieste: Lint, 1994), 120–121 and 124–125, with further bibliography on Leonardo. Leonardo's learning can be traced in his books; see, for example, the catalog of the Cividale Dominican library that he made in 1440, edited in Scalon, *La biblioteca,* 40–49. It is striking, in the context of this study, that Leonardo's *Sermones aurei* open with an oration on his own name saint, and that his preface to the sermon collection mentions Xenophon, Pythagoras, Democritus, Plato, Cicero, and Zeno to explain the gifts the saints have brought the Church.

40. Tilatti, *Simone da Roma*, 36; repeated by Giacomo da Udine (G fol. 53, quoted below).

41. G. fol. 60. Of her early *vitae* (that by Simone da Roma, that by Giacomo, and others discussed below), only the humanist Giacomo da Udine mentions the two clocks: "Duo horalogia, alterum domi, alterum in aecclesiam, semper habebat, totque horas ad orationem, tot ad planctum, tot ad lectionem ipsa constituerat, ne beneficio temporis ingrata sit."

42. Tilatti, *"Per man di notaro,"* 512; see below.

43. Tilatti, *"Per man di notaro,"* 507.

44. On living saints, see the classic studies by Gabriella Zarri, "Le sante vive: Per una tipologia della santità femminile nel primo Cinquecento," *Annali dell'Istituto storico Italo-Germanico di Trento* 6 (1980): 371–445; eadem, "Les prophètes de cour dans l'Italie de la Renaissance," *MEFR* 102 (1990): 649–675; and eadem, *Le sante vive: Cultura e religiosità nella prima età moderna* (Turin: Rosenberg and Sellier, 1990).

45. For the history of the eighteenth-century beatification, see Tilatti, *Simone da Roma*, 92–110.

as to suggest that the order had reason to protect her relics.[46] Further archival evidence that Elena died in the odor of sanctity and that the Hermits seized the opportunity can be found in notarial records of their expenses in 1458 for paper to write her miracles (although notarial evidence of miracles *in vita* is not extant, records of three posthumous miracles have been found among a notary's documents).[47] In the same year, the Hermits also spent money for a painting of Elena, an altar, and a chapel.[48] She was their first, best hope for a *beata*, if not a saint, in Udine.

The Hermits were wise to keep an eye both on Elena's devotions *in vita* and on her posthumous reputation, for an elevation in her status promised an elevation in theirs as well.[49] Although they had held the church of Santa Lucia in Udine since 1381, at the time of Elena's entry into their care the Hermits did not yet have a convent for tertiaries or nuns.[50] In contrast, the Franciscans, whose institutional arrival in Udine postdated that of the Hermits, were more successful there (as throughout Italy) at organizing religious women. The Franciscans did have a convent, Santa Croce, for their nuns.[51] And they had made prominent "acquisitions" in Udinese society, notably among the noble Savorgnan family. The Savorgnan and their allies supported Venice and were known political enemies of the anti-Venetian Cavalcanti, the family into which Elena Valentini had married.[52] By the time Elena entered the third order of the Hermits, there was a decades-long history of rivalry between the Savorgnan and the Cavalcanti.[53] Thus it

---

46. Tilatti, *"Per man di notaro,"* offers this interpretation of her will.

47. Discovered and edited by Tilatti, *"Per man di notaro,"* giving the three posthumous healing miracles at 519–520. The *vitae* discussed below do record miracles *in vita* but are not trustworthy witnesses in the legal terms required for canonization in the Quattrocento.

48. Tilatti, *"Per man di notaro,"* 516 and n. 36.

49. A thumbnail sketch of O.E.S.A. history in Italy from 1244 is given in Tilatti, *Simone da Roma,* 123 n. 1; see the discussion and notes below for Quattrocento developments.

50. Tilatti, *Simone da Roma,* 131 n. 9, observes that archival documents do not suggest the existence of the Augustinian convent of San. Agostino for tertiaries in Udine until 1464. I am grateful to Prof. Tilatti for notice that another convent, San Nicolò, had been founded in the mid-fourteenth century to receive women, such as former prostitutes; its status in the fifteenth century is not clear.

51. Tilatti, *"Per man di notaro,"* 514–515, is cautious on the question of a competition between the orders for influence with the women of important Udinese families. Giuseppe De Piero, *Brevi note storiche sulle antiche parrocchie della città di Udine* (Udine: Graphik, 1982), 118–119, treats the churches and convents of Santa Croce and Santo Spirito.

52. On the Savorgnan, see most conveniently Muir, *Mad Blood,* 77–107, with bibliography. At this period they controlled politics both in Aquileia and in Udine. Elena's brother, serving as *capitano* at Udine, had besieged the stronghold of Tristano di Savorgnan in 1413 (Tilatti, *Simone da Roma,* 127 n. 1). Elena was also related by marriage to the Savorgnan clan, although it is not clear to me to which of the four branches (ibid., 127 n. 2 and 130 n. 6).

53. Intimated by Biasutti, *Profilo spirituale,* 30 and n. 25.

looks as though the Hermits' competition with the Franciscans for holy women in Udine found an opportunistic fit with rivalries between the Valentini/Cavalcanti and the Savorgnan. If family rivalries based on pro- and anti-Venetian stances found echoes in order rivalries, then the case for Elena's sanctity may also have played into the tense diplomatic relations between Rome and Venice, especially with regard to the patriarchate of Aquileia, where Giacomo was a canon.

The strongest evidence for the proprietary nature of the Hermits' hopes for Elena is the fact that, immediately upon her death, they did not ask her confessor, the widely respected Dominican Leonardo da Udine, to write her *vita* but invited a theologian from their own order.[54] Simone da Roma, O.E.S.A., who taught at the University of Padua, had occasionally preached in Udine.[55] Perhaps he had confessed Elena and so had some personal experience on which to draw; he does not say so. In fact, he never once mentions personal knowledge of Elena but writes only that he was "summoned after the *beata*'s death . . . by the prior of Santa Lucia in Udine."[56] It is odd that the Hermits, recognizing potential sanctity, did not have an in-house confessor to hand. Women dying in the odor of sanctity in the late Middle Ages were typically written up by their confessors within the relevant order, men who had supervised the prospective saint's lifetime devotions and thus held the privileged legal status of eyewitnesses.[57] The Udinese prior at the time of Elena's death, a man named Bartolomeo, was somehow not qualified, and Simone, even if he had met Elena on occasion, was not a long-term eyewitness. So, summoned to write the *vita* but unfamiliar with the woman who was its subject, Simone da Roma was surely given documents from which to work. The numbering of visions and temptations in his account, for example, echoes the format of documentary evidence, as does his frequent use of quotations attributed to Elena. But Simone does not mention any documentation,

54. On Leonardo da Udine, see n. 39 above.

55. That Simone was from Padua is not disputed. It is curious, then, to find that in *R* fol. 1, the identifying "Padoa" has been scraped away from his name (Tilatti, *Simone da Roma*, 124). On *R* see n. 56 below.

56. Tilatti, *Simone da Roma*, 124, with n. 4; my translation from the vernacular. Simone also attests in his prologue that the prior of Santa Lucia "mi chiamo per predicare la vita et miracoli per essa [*add. ABCD, sed deest R*: beata] operati." For manuscript *sigla* ABCD and *stemma*, see Tilatti, *Simone da Rosa*, 111–119; *R* = BAV, MS Ross. 48 (VII a 40). On *R* see n. 66 below.

57. On Elena's spiritual fathers, see Tilatti, *Simone da Roma*, 167. On male confessors as authors of female vitae, see John Coakley, "Friars as Confidants of Holy Women in Medieval Dominican Hagiography," in R. Blumenfeld-Kosinski and T. Szell, eds., *Images of Sainthood in Medieval Europe* (Ithaca, N.Y.: Cornell University Press, 1991), 222–256, and studies gathered in Catherine M. Mooney, ed., *Gendered Voices: Medieval Saints and Their Interpreters* (Philadelphia: University of Pennsylvania Press, 1999).

and, if it ever existed, it all appears to be lost. Without a collection of notarial documents or confessor's notes, Elena promised to be an exceptionally difficult case for a Quattrocento canonization.[58]

Simone probably recognized this problem. As a theologian who taught at a major university, as a man sufficiently respected that he would thrice be named prior of the convent of Sant'Agostino in Rome, Simone would have known that undocumented holiness, unapproved and unregulated devotions, could be dangerous to the Hermits' hopes for a saint, especially a woman saint.[59] He may have heard of the unsuccessful application on behalf of a holy matron and charismatic widow with a political background just as awkward as Elena's: three processes had been attempted for Francesca Bussi da Ponziano of Tor de'Specchi in Rome (1440, 1443, and 1451).[60] He surely knew about the successful case of the widowed matron Birgitta of Sweden (d. 1373; c.d. 1391; reaffirmed 1417), because her prophetic writings were widely circulated.[61] Shortly after Simone composed his account, there would be another example of a woman successfully promoted: the virginal Dominican tertiary Catherine of Siena (d.1380; c.d. 1461).[62] Both Birgitta and Catherine succeeded with Latin

58. The procedures for requesting papal attention to a local saint were known and quite precise. Local administrators and local religious would cooperate. Notarial records of Elena's devotions, miracles, and visions would have to be gathered, ordered, approved by interested local bodies, and submitted to the pope. With these documents would go a sort of cover letter in the form of a *vita*. In receipt of the notarial documents and the *vita*, the pope might respond in one of three ways: he could deny the application, allow limited observation of her feast, or set in motion a series of formal inquiries as the first step of canonization proceedings. Elena's supporters naturally hoped for the third outcome, which just might—although years of testimonies, reconsiderations, and expenditures could intervene—result in her inscription in the catalog of saints. As we will see, the Hermits' attention to propriety in commissioning a *vita Helenae* suggests that they were not fumbling for guidance on procedural matters.

59. Cf. Tilatti, *Simone da Roma*, 124. On Simone's Roman appointments, see ibid., 20–21 and n. 10.

60. For a brief introduction to the political significance of Francesca's sanctity, see the argument of Giulia Barone, "Le culte de Françoise Romaine: Un exemple de religion civique?" in A. Vauchez, ed., *La religion civique à l'époque médiévale et moderne (chrétienté et islam): Actes du colloque organisé par le Centre de recherche 'Histoire sociale et culturelle de l'Occident', XIIe–XVIIIe siècle de l'Université de Paris X–Nanterre et l'Institut universitaire de France (Nanterre, 21–23 juin 1993)* (Rome: BEFR, 1995), 367–373, that the cult was not "civic" in the accepted sense, although its "couche sociale" was limited to an economic status group that had "un rôle important dans la crise politique de la fin du XIVe siècle" (372). On Francesca's supporters, Arnold Esch, "Die Zeugenaussagen im Heiligsprechungsverfahren für S. Francesca Romana als Quelle zur Sozialgeschichte Roms im frühen Quattrocento," *QFIAB* 53 (1973): 93–151, remains fundamental.

61. See D. Pezzini, "The Italian Reception of Birgittine Writings," in B. Morris and V. O'Mara, eds., *The Translation of the Works of St. Birgitta of Sweden into the Medieval European Vernaculars* (Turnhout: Brepols, 2000), 186–212, for vernacular circulation in Italy. For guidance on Birgitta's cult, see K. E. Borresen, "Brigida di Svezia," *GLS* 344–348.

62. For an introduction to a flourishing subject, see S. Boesch Gajano, "Caterina da Siena," *GLS* 397–405.

vitae written by their confessors and notarized miracles, but only after some years had elapsed.[63] In short, proprieties had to be observed if Elena's canonization was even distantly envisioned. The Augustinian Hermits in Udine were clearly familiar with those proprieties as well. When Simone da Roma completed his account, they had it notarized so that it became a legal instrument. They also had it formally acknowledged by the Hermit's provincial, the theologian Andrea da Ferrara.[64]

Why then did the theology professor Simone choose, or why did the Hermits direct him, to write his life of Elena in the vernacular rather than Latin? Most likely, the order hoped to use his account to propagate Elena's cult in and around Udine.[65] Vernacular accounts were especially aimed at women, and the Hermits may have hoped to win converts to their Third Order by telling Elena's story. The fact that the vernacular account was notarized also suggests that such versions were felt to be authentic in legal terms. But the cases of Birgitta of Sweden, Catherine of Siena, and Francesca Bussi indicate that a vernacular account would not have been sent to Rome, at least not unaccompanied by a Latin narrative, if and when approval for Elena's cult was sought.[66] Fifteenth-century practice demanded a Latin account.[67]

The fact that there was (and is) no confessor's life in Latin to support Elena's cause must affect any estimate of Giacomo's retelling of her life. But what looks like disorganization may actually reflect a plan. Similar

63. See also the case of Veronica da Binasco: bibliography in Gabriella Zarri, "Veronica da Binasco," *GLS* 1924–1925. See n. 69 below.

64. Tilatti, *"Per man di notaro,"* 515–517. On Andrea da Ferrara, like Simone da Roma a product of the University of Padua, see ibid., 516; idem, *Simone da Roma,* 180 n. 3; and Tomás Herrera, *Alphabetum Augustinianum* (Rome: Pubblicazioni agostiniane, 1989–90; orig. pub. Madrid, 1644), 1:50.

65. Thus Tilatti (personal correspondence). See the comparable vernacular account about Chiara da Rimini, edited by Jacques Dalarun, *Lapsus linguae: La légende de Claire de Rimini* (Spoleto: Centro italiano di studi sull'alto medioevo, 1994), 19–54. But the author in Chiara's case is anonymous, his subject's affiliation apparently of no interest to him, and his intentions for the use of the account as yet undeciphered. Cf. the vernacular lives of Chiara Gambacorta (d. 1419/1420), a *beata* of the Dominicans, and of Eustochia Calafato (d. 1485), a Clarisse of Messina, and Colomba da Rieti (d. 1501), a Dominican *beata,* compositions probably intended for local use.

66. Cf. Dalarun, *Lapsus linguae:* no contemporary copies of Chiara's life exist. Note that there is a contemporary copy, *R,* of Simone's account of Elena. The Candido da Udine who transcribed it is probably the notary who drew up Elena's first testament (Tilatti, *"Per man di notaro,"* 506 n. 13) and Profeta's testament (ibid., 510 n. 22). A very similar hand is found in Giacomo's *vita Helenae* (*G*). *R* has handwritten notes at the end that record the entry of women as Augustinian nuns at Santa Lucia in Udine from 1494.

67. For examples of humanists' Latin accounts that seem to have been prepared for such submissions, see the hand list under Raffaele Maffei (on Umiliana dei Cerchi) and Agostino Cazzuli da Crema (on Johannes Bonus).

cases of what appears to be poorly managed paperwork characterize most of the Hermits' interactions with religious women in the northern Italian cities during the Quattrocento.[68] The Latin *vitae* of Maddalena Alberici (d. 1465) and Cristina the Penitent (Agostina Camozzi, d. 1458), for example, were composed not by confessors but by learned Hermits with more exalted positions in the order: Paolo Olmi (who is discussed below) wrote on Maddalena and Ambrogio da Cora on Cristina.[69] So it is possible that the Hermits managed the difficult sanctity of charismatic women by encouraging the production of local vernacular lives as both propaganda and legal documents and then treated these documents as source material on which to base the official *vitae* required by Church tradition to secure formal recognition of sanctity.

At any rate, under the Hermits' sponsorship, Elena's cult was immediately successful at the local level. Elena died in April 1458. By the end of that year, the Hermits had not only arranged to have her life recorded and authenticated and her miracles written up but had also begun construction of a dedicated chapel. That chapel was still a going concern twenty years later, when Elena's son mentioned it in his will.[70] Beginning in 1465—that is, early in Paul's pontificate—Elena's feast began to be celebrated annually in Udine. The Bollandists record that her feast date was entered in one copy of the 1478 Roman Missal published at Venice.[71]

It is unclear whether any of this cultic activity proceeded with papal approval. No written record of approval has been found, so perhaps it was given orally. Oral approval might have come from Callixtus III before his death in August 1458, from Pius II, who succeeded Callixtus that very month, or even from Paul II.[72] Or perhaps Elena's cult was tacitly approved, simply by virtue of noninterference in local devotion. By the second half of the fifteenth century, however, tacit approval was becoming less common, as reforming bishops monitored local practices and the

---

68. There is, for example, no extant contemporary life of Rita of Cascia (ca. 1380–1457). See the remarks of Claudio Leonardi in *Santa Rita da Cascia: Storia, Devozione, Sociologia: Atti del congresso internazionale in occasione del I. centenario della canonizzazione, celebrato a Roma, 24–26 settembre 1998* (Rome: Institutum historicum Augustinianum, 2000), 18; and L. Scaraffia, "Rita da Cascia," in *GLS*, 1710.

69. All these figures, prospective saints as well as authors, were associated with the Lombard Observancy. For a striking contrast to Elena's case, consider the Observant Dominican Isidoro de Isolanis's excruciatingly elegant Latin life of the Augustinian nun Veronica da Binasco (d. 1497; c.d. 1517). Isidoro was not Veronica's confessor.

70. Tilatti, *Simone da Roma*, 84–85, and n. 6.

71. Tilatti, *"Per man di notaro,"* 518; and idem, *Simone da Roma*, 85 and n. 7.

72. Tilatti, *Simone da Roma*, 84–85 and nn. 3–6. Tilatti, the scholar most familiar with Elena's case, does not believe that Paul II approved her cult, even orally (personal communication).

increasingly highly educated administrators of centralizing orders such as the mendicants oversaw their provinces more aggressively.[73]

* * *

Scripsi hanc uitam, Sanctissime Pater, tuo nomine, in qua siquid minus perite aut inepte positum sit, a te emendari cupio atque oro. . . . Haec profecto scripta est longe inferior divino ingenio tuo, quod longe praestantiori elegantia et aurea aliqua eloquentia dignum esse certum habeo.

I wrote this life, Most Holy Father, in your name. If anything has been put unskillfully or awkwardly, I beg and desire you to emend it. . . . For this writing is far inferior to your far superior divine intelligence, which I know deserves a sophisticated and golden eloquence.

—Giacomo da Udine, *peroratio* to the *vita Helenae utinensis*[74]

If Giacomo da Udine chose an unusual subject in the contemporary matron Elena of Udine, he chose an unlikely dedicatee in Paul II. Many dissonances would have struck those at the curia or in orders. Most obviously, Paul was well disposed *not* to the Augustinian Hermits— Elena's order—but to the Augustinian Canons, in particular, their Observant wing, the Lateran Canons.[75] As cardinal, Paul had been protector of the Lateran Canons; as pope, he restored the Lateran Canons to San Giovanni Laterano, following their eviction by Callixtus III.[76] Both Lateran Canons and Augustinian Hermits thought of St. Augustine as founder and patron. But Hermits and Canons had sharply differing ideas about the fifth-century bishop of Hippo, and these smoldering disagreements sometimes ignited into quarrels over authenticity and precedence. There was no love lost between the Canons and the

73. So, for example, in 1488 Bishop Pietro Barozzi prohibited the unapproved local cult paid to Lorenzino da Marostica at Vicenza, and would not allow a church at Padua to be named after the popular plague saint Rocco, because he had not been canonized. See Giovanni Mantese, *Memorie storiche della chiesa vicentina* III, iii (Vicenza: Neri Pozza, 1964), 481 and n. 88, and G. Penco, *Storia della chiesa in italia: Il Quattrocento* (Milan: Jaca Book, 1978), 522 and n. 159. This aspect of the pre-Tridentine Catholic Reformation needs a systematic interregional study.

74. G fol. 83v.

75. On the Observant Lateran Canons, Nicola Widloecher, *La congregazione dei Canonici Regolari Lateranensi: Periodo di formazione (1402–1483)* (Gubbio, 1929), remains the fundamental study.

76. San Giovanni Laterano was historically the prerogative of the Canons Regular. Eugene IV had attempted to have it reformed by evicting them in favor of the Lateran Canons. But he had only partial success, for the Lateran Canons were in turn expelled by Callixtus III, only to be reinstated by Paul II. Their final expulsion occurred in 1481. See Widloecher, *La congregazione,* and further below.

Hermits.[77] Giacomo's dedication to Paul, patron of the Lateran Canons, of a life about a holy woman associated with the Augustinian Hermits, is therefore quite odd.

Still more seriously, Paul was unmoved by the cult of contemporary saints. He did not welcome the constant pressure put on the curia to create new saints and made it known that there would be no canonizations on his watch. Thus his policy with regard to promotions contrasted sharply with both his predecessors and his successors. Lists can be tedious, but in this case a simple list makes impressively clear that Paul held firm in his decision not to entertain these procedures at any stage.

Of Paul's immediate predecessors, Nicholas V (1447–1455) opened his pontificate with the *inventio* of Stephen and Laurence at Rome, recognized the cult of S. Wendelinus, oversaw the canonization of Bernardino, began a third process for Francesca Romana, and initiated the deposition of witnesses preparatory to a process for Vincent Ferrer.

Callixtus III (1455–1458) moved Vincent Ferrer's process along, began preparations for processes for Rosa of Viterbo and Gabriele Ferretti of Ancona, canonized Osmund of Salisbury, and allowed *cultus* to be paid to Alberto degli Abati of Trapani.

Pius II (1458–1464) published the bull of canonization for Vincent Ferrer; named Albertus Magnus a *sanctissimus doctor*; presided at the canonization of Catherine of Siena, giving an oration himself; translated Andrew's head and the body of Gregory I in Rome; and made a gift of the arm of St. John the Baptist to his hometown of Siena.

Then, following Paul, the Franciscan Sixtus IV (1471–1484) issued a bull approving the cult of San Aquilino in Milan, made the feast of St. Francis a holy day of obligation, translated the relics of Bernardino of Siena, confirmed the cult of Alberto of Trapani and the authenticity of the relics of the widow Juliana at Bologna, received the relics of the Otranto Martyrs (1481) at Santa Maria Maddalena; "canonized" Joseph; canonized the five Franciscans martyred in Morocco in 1216; allowed cult paid to Matteo Carreri (d. 1470), and canonized Bonaventure.

Innocent VIII (1484–1492) received requests to canonize Colette of Corbie and Henry VI of England and canonized Leopold III of Austria.

In sharp contrast to Nicholas, Callixtus, Pius, Sixtus, and Innocent, Pope Paul II appears to have intervened only to give permissions for trans-

---

77. For the Hermits' formulation of their identity, see Eric L. Saak, *Highway to Heaven: The Augustinian Platform Between Reform and Reformation, 1292–1524* (Leiden: Brill, 2002), 160–344; for a late-fifteenth-century incident that reignited bad feelings, see Kaspar Elm, "*Augustinus canonicus—Augustinus eremita*: A Quattrocento *cause célèbre*," in J. Henderson and T. Verdon, eds., *Christianity and the Renaissance: Image and Religious Imagination in the Quattrocento* (Syracuse, N.Y.: Syracuse University Press, 1990), 83–107. The subject is discussed further below.

lations (e.g., for the relics of Raimondo of Fitero to be moved to Monte Sion in Toledo), to declare indulgences (e.g., of seven years to anyone visiting the tomb of Peter the Hermit in Trevi), or to permit local cult of ancient martyrs (e.g., of Sergius and Bacchus at Heiligenstadt). He received no dedications of *vitae* with contemporary subjects other than Giacomo's.[78] Of course, a relative lack of interest in saints does not indicate impiety, emotional coldness, or disbelief in miracles. Paul's cultic attachments might actually be considered thoroughly up-to-date, that is, Marian and Christological. He patronized, for example, the basilica associated with the miraculously transported house at Loreto, site of the Annunciation.[79] And his emotional lability was so marked that Pius II used to call him "Weeping Mary," *Maria pientissima*.[80] But Paul's lack of interest in contemporary sanctity is unmistakable, and, on that count, too, Giacomo's dedication is unusual.

Barbo family interests in the Friuli may have influenced Giacomo's decision to dedicate the *vita* of an Udinese woman to the pope. In 1429 the future pope's father, Niccolò, served as *podestà* at Marano, a fortress town on the lagoons south of Udine and east of Aquileia; Niccolò organized a Friulani army against the Hungarians, as well.[81] In 1436 Pietro Barbo and his older brother, Paul, received from Eugene IV a part of the feudatory of

78. Paul's lack of attention to the cult of Niccolò Albergati (d. 1433; beatified 1744) is striking confirmation of his distaste for contemporary sanctity. As cardinal, Pietro Barbo received the dedication of the *vita* of Niccolò Albergati (*BHL* 6096) written by Jacopo Zeno, Pietro's relative and client. Albergati, a reforming Carthusian dedicated especially to education in the orders, strongly influenced Tommaso Parentucelli. Parentucelli, in turn, shaped the vocation of Zeno; then Parentucelli, as Nicholas V, raised Pietro Barbo to the cardinalate. Despite all these ties, Paul did not press for Albergati's canonization or even make a gesture toward the cult. For Zeno's life of Albergati, see *AASS* May II: 467–474; and the dedication copy, BAV, MS Lat. 3703. S. Spano, "Nicolò Albergati," *GLS* 1475–1476, provides introduction to and bibliography on the saint. Zeno also dedicated his lives of the popes to Paul II; see Massimo Miglio, *Storia pontificia del Quattrocento* (Bologna: Patron, 1975), 181–183, editing the preface, and BAV, MS Lat. 5942, the collection. Bonino Mombrizio intended to dedicate his epic life of Jerome to Paul II, but the pope's death led to a rededication to Sixtus IV; see n. 92 below and chap. 3 above.

79. Floriano Grimaldi, *La chiesa di santa Maria di Loreto nei documenti dei secoli XII–XV* (Ancona, 1984), 124–125, doc. 32, is a sixteenth-century version of Paul's lost concession of indulgences dated November 1, 1464. The funds were to be used to improve the reception of pilgrims. This indulgence was one of Paul's first acts as pope.

80. Cf. "Maria pietosa," given by Litta, *Famiglie*, vol. 9, table 4. Names are important for Paul: see Pastor, *History*, 4:12–13 and notes there; and, on Paul's gentleness, ibid., 33–34. To estimate Paul's virtues, it helps to know that he was named testamentary executor by Nicholas of Cusa, Pietro del Monte, and Giovanni da Mella.

81. Litta, *Famiglie*, vol. 9, table 4; cf. table 3: the Giovanni who married Maria Loredan and then Orsa Bernardo also served as *podestà* at Marano, in 1471. I have not been able to determine if Giacomo da Udine's father served in the force organized by Paul II's father (see n. 9 above).

Règhena in the diocese of Aquileia.[82] Then, in 1441, Eugene named the young cardinal deacon of Santa Maria Nova to be the first commendatory abbot at Santa Maria in Sesto al Règhena (to the southwest of Udine, north of Portogruaro).[83] In 1448 he was appointed commendatory abbot at San Gallo di Moggio (to the north of Udine), also in the diocese of Aquileia.[84] Pietro Barbo held Sesto for more than twenty years. Scholars have assumed that he was never resident at the Benedictine abbey, without evidence to determine either way. Certainly, he contributed to upkeep: his coat of arms is painted in several places, including the chancery wall; and he renovated the tower and the abbatial palace, which may have been frescoed during his tenure.[85] As pope, Paul continued to show concern for the Friulian ecclesiastical fabric, decreeing in 1471 that eight years' worth of income from two vacant canonicates and benefices in Cividale be directed to the construction (or reconstruction) of the church of Santa Maria there.[86] Paul also brought Friulani to Rome: at the curia, he would have no Venetians among his guards, but he gave Friulani positions of special trust.[87] Such ties to the Friuli are intriguing, although they do not explain Paul's dedication.

The most compelling reason for the dedication is that Elena and Paul

82. Zippel, *Le vite*, 365 n. 2.

83. On Sesto, see Gian Carlo Menis and Andrea Tilatti, eds., *L'Abbazia di Santa Maria di Sesto fra archeologia e storia* (Fiume Veneto: GEAPprint, 1999), superseding earlier studies and providing a rich bibliography, especially Andrea Tilatti, "Gli abbati e l'abbazia di Sesto nei secoli XIII–XV," 149–189, and Giovanni Spinelli, "L'età della commenda (1441–1789)," 192–194. Giuseppe Bergamini, *L'Abbazia di Sesto al Reghena: Storia e arte* (Udine: Arti grafiche friulane, 1997), 31, notes that the Venetian conquest of the Friuli in 1418–1420 signaled the definitive decline of Sesto, as its goods were annexed and eventually passed to the papacy.

84. See E. Degani, "L'Abbazia benedettina di Sesto in Silvis," *Nuovo archivio veneto* n.s. 14 (1907): 3–7, 258–323; Spinelli, "L'età della commenda," 193–194.

85. See Tommaso Gerometta, *L'abbazia benedettina di S. Maria in Sylvis in Sesto al Règhena: Guida storico-artistica,* 2d ed. (Portogruaro: Castion di Franceschina e Sartor, 1964), 133. Spinelli, "L'età della commenda," 193b, notes that he also restored the tower and the abbatial palace; see especially Paolo Piva, "Sesto al Reghena: Una chiesa e un'abbazia nella storia dell'architettura medioevale," in Menis and Tilatti, *L'Abbazia di Santa Maria di Sesto,* 246–247, 300 with n. 425, and 306–307. The frescos depict the Last Judgment and have been compared to Dante's *Commedia*—Dante, as I will point out, has a considerable part in Giacomo's *vita Helenae*. See Bergamini, *L'Abbazia,* 59–60, for a description; and Piva, "Sesto," 237. As there are no known documents relating to the frescos, scholarly discussion and dating have proceeded on the basis of the "Giottesque" style.

86. Alberto Starzer, *Regesti per la storia ecclesiastica del Friuli dal 1413 al 1521,* trans. G. Loschi (Udine: Domenico del Bianco, 1894), 25.

87. Pastor, *History,* 4:113, reports the absence of Venetian guards; Zippel, *Le vite*, 193 n. 2, names Doimo da Valvasone, Progne, and Cristoforo, the counts of Polcenigo, and the handsome youth Guglielmo as Friulians brought with Paul II to Rome. On Progne, who served as *scutifer praecideus*, see also ibid., 212 n. 2; on Doimo, see also ibid., 214 n. 7.

were related. Giacomo says so explicitly in his preface, making it a point of papal honor: "Sicut enim artifex in suo artificio praeclaris operibus laetatur, sic tibi, qui sanctitatis lumen et es et haberis, Helenam in seriem tuam uenisse gratulandum superque congratulandum est" ("Just as the artist delights in work made outstanding by his art, so you, who are the light of sanctity and will be so considered, must be congratulated again and again that Elena came into your line").[88]

The "line" (series) to which Giacomo refers is Paul's genealogy.[89] Evidently, a saint in the family might override a distaste for contemporary holiness, even if it was not enough to secure canonization. Perhaps Giacomo's genealogical assertion is factually inaccurate or makes too much of a distant blood relationship; I have not yet established a genealogy that would bring Elena into Paul's family. But an author seeking patronage is unlikely to have adduced such a connection if it was obviously false or insulting. Giacomo's witness should, therefore, be taken seriously.

There is, however, a further problem with Paul as the dedicatee that throws even family relations into question as sufficient to explain this particular saint's life. Giacomo's narrative is the most flagrantly literary of the *vitae Helenae*—perhaps of the whole body of extant *vitae sanctorum* in the West. But it is dedicated to a pope with a poor reputation as a supporter of humanist authors.[90] Paul was an enthusiastic student of classical histories and classical antiquities: sculptures, inscriptions, medals. He brought printing to Rome and received Giovanni Andrea Bussi's lengthy dedications to incunable editions of Apuleius's *Metamorphoses*, Caesar's *Commentaries*,

88. G fol. 2.

89. The word *series* is unusual and difficult to interpret. It might mean "line of popes," although chronologically that claim is awkward (unless Paul II was indeed the pope who approved Elena's cult, an inference supported by Giacomo's analogy with artistic "making"). Or it might be equivalent to *acies*: Elena has joined the pope's serried ranks of battle. I do not think that Giacomo refers to the pope and Elena here as saints together. The simplest solution is the one I have given: that *series* refers to a blood connection of some sort.

90. The character assassination achieved by Bartolomeo Platina in his account of Paul II in the *Liber de vita Christi ac omnium pontificum* no longer controls scholarly understanding of this pope's relations to cultural developments, although the suppression of the Roman Academy and firing of the protonotaries remain difficult topics. Roberto Weiss, *Un umanista veneziano: Papa Paolo II* (Venice, 1957), establishes Paul's antiquarian interests, and A. J. Dunston, "Pope Paul II and the Humanists," *Journal of Religious History* 7 (1983): 287–306, esp. 291, notes Paul's interest in Roman and Greek historians. See also R. J. Palermino, "The Roman Academy, the Catacombs, and the Conspiracy of 1468," *Archivum historiae pontificiae* 18 (1980): 117–155; Paola Medioli Masotti, "Callimaco, l'Accademia Romana e la congiura del 1468," in *Callimaco Esperiente poeta e politico del '400: Convegno internazionale di studi (San Gimignano, 18–20 ottobre 1985)* (Istituto nazionale di studi sul Rinascimento, Atti di Convegni, 16) (Florence, 1987); eadem, "L'accademia romana e la congiura del 1468," *IMH* 25 (1982): 198–204; A. Esposito, "Paul II," in P. Levillain, *The Papacy: An Encyclopedia* (New York: Routledge, 2002), 2:1122; and the following notes.

Livy's *Histories*, Strabo's *Geography*, and Pliny's *Natural History,* whether or not he actually read the prefaces.[91] Latin epigrams, lyrics, inscriptions, and even epics were composed for him.[92] He received several well-known humanists' translations from the Greek of Gregory of Nyssa, Athanasius, and Basil.[93] But in comparison with the popes who preceded and followed him, Paul is still accepted as a learned pontiff who was aggressively uninterested in the humanists' classicizing compositions. What Quattrocento author, painstakingly constructing networks of patronage, would be so foolhardy as to write an artistic *vita* for such a man?

❀ ❀ ❀

Omnes quaerebant eius audire et perdiscere vitam.
Everyone wanted to hear her life and learn it by heart.

—Giacomo da Udine, *vita Helenae utinensis*[94]

In order to appreciate just how artistic Giacomo's account is, it will help to consider the other *vitae Helenae* written by Quattrocento humanists. All the later authors seem to depend on Simone da Roma's vernacular account, although it is impossible to be sure if they had firsthand knowledge of it. The problem is that an important *vita Helenae utinensis*, one mentioned by a reliable contemporary, Jacopo Filippo Foresti (ca.

---

91. For contemporary recognition that Paul introduced printing in Rome, see Zippel, *Le vite,* 57–58, with n. 3. For the seven prefaces from Giovanni Andrea Bussi to Paul II, see Massimo Miglio, ed., *Giovanni Andrea Bussi: Prefazioni alle edizioni di Sweynheym e Pannartz, prototipografi romani* (Milan: Il Polifilo, 1978), 3–28 and 29–41. Bussi remarked that he did not think the pope would read the prefaces: "ab eo tamen lectum iri non putabam" (lviii).

92. So, for example, Bonino Mombrizio's epic on Jerome was dedicated first to Paul; see chap. 3 above. For an example of lyric, see the poems in BAV, MS Lat. 3611, including verses by Antonio Geraldini Amerini, brother of another humanist hagiographer, Alessandro (see hand list). For Paul's edict against the teaching of pagan poetry and for another report on the plot, see the witness of Giovanni Garzoni (the subject of chap. 4 above), in a dialogue *De christianorum felicitate* (BBU, MS 2648, fol. 81r):

> Paulus secundus Pontifex Maximus, cum nonnullorum qui se poetas profitebantur poemata legisset, instituerat ne quis in posterum (si ei vita longior contigisset) gentilium studiis operam impertiretur, quod multa a poetis interdum litteris mandarentur quibus iuuenum ingenia corumperentur, insolencia atque auaricia cum felicitate obsit uehementer tibi [*sic, sine nomine*] exilio mulctanda est. Nulla quippe nacio est apud quam in summo non fuit odio. Ab hiis enim coniuracionis descidio, ciuiles discordie, uenenorum pociones proficiscuntur. Hinc maximo animi cruciatu agitur uita, id quod felici minime congruit.

93. E.g., Marco Vattasso and Pio Franchi de Cavalieri, *Bibliotheca apostolica vaticana, Codices vaticani latini* (Rome: Typis Polyglottis Vaticanis, 1902–88), vol. 1, MSS 256, 261, and 302, all presentation copies.

94. G fol. 71.

1434–1520), is missing. Although it is risky to speculate about the nature of a lost account, the authority and traditional character of this one can be deduced from the status of the author. Paolo Olmi (Ulmeus, Lulmius) of Bergamo (1414–1484) was, like the Paduan theologian Simone di Roma who first wrote about Elena, an Augustinian Hermit.[95] Paolo had studied law at Padua, become a cathedral canon in Bergamo, and then, in 1449, joined the Observant Lombard congregation of the Hermits. His administrative capacities were acknowledged, and his learning can be surmised from his extant writings and appointments. He served as prior at the Observant Incoronata in Milan (1463–1469), an Augustinian convent richly patronized by both male and female members of the Sforza dynasty and known for its attention to books and study: the convent housed a scriptorium and perhaps a *tipografia* where the German Hermit Johannes Bonus produced his early imprints.[96] In 1472, during the pontificate of Sixtus IV, Olmi, along with fellow Hermits Taddeo d'Ivrea (d. 1503) and Agostino da Crema (Cazzuli) of Milan (d. 1495), was sent to conduct an Observant reform of Santa Maria del Popolo in Rome.[97] Olmi was the first prior there (1474) and held the position again in 1478 and 1479. Notably, it was Olmi who initiated the inventory of the convent library in 1480.[98] He went on to hold the position of vicar general of the Hermits seven

95. On Olmi, consult Herrera, *Alphabetum,* 334; Johannes Felix Ossinger, *Bibliotheca augustiniana historica, critica et chronologica* (Ingolstadt, 1768), 522–524; Girolamo Tiraboschi, *Storia della letteratura italiana* (Rome: Salviani, 1738), vol. 6, part 1, 176; Zeno, *Dissertazioni* 2:47; Luigi Torelli, *Secoli agostiniani* (Bologna, 1682), 6:214; D. A. Perini, *Bibliographia Augustiniana: Scriptores Itali* (Florence, 1935) 3:36. See also Giovanni Mercati, *Ultimi contributi* (Studi e testi 90) (Vatican City: BAV, 1939), 73 n. 3. For a printed book with Olmi's note, see Alberto Petrucciani, *Gli incunaboli della Biblioteca Durazzo: Atti della società ligure di storia patria* n.s. 28, no. 2 (Genoa: Società ligure di storia patria, 1988), 215. The Bollandists were unable to find Olmi's *vita* of Elena; see *AASS* April III (Paris, 1866), 239, para. 2. It is mentioned in Foresti's *Supplementum chronicarum* (quoted and discussed below). An outspoken contemporary thought Foresti unreliable: see Mariano da Firenze's *Defensorio della verità,* which disputes Foresti's polemical claim that Francis of Assisi had begun his religious life as an Augustinian Hermit. D. Cresi, "L'opusculo *Defensorio della verità* da Mariano da Firenze," *Studi francescani* 61 (1964): 173–174, 186–187, and 210–211.

96. On Johannes Bonus, see G. Dondi, in *DBI* 12 (1970), 281a–282b. He was a member of the community at Santa Maria del Popolo from 1480 to 1482; see Anna Esposito, "Centri di aggregazione: La biblioteca agostiniana di S. Maria del Popolo," in Miglio, *Un pontificato,* 593; Maria Luisa Gatti Perer, *Umanesimo a Milano: L'Osservanza agostiniana all'Incoronata* (Milan: Arte Lombarda, 1980), 73 and n. 121. On the *tipografia,* see ibid., 36. Gatti Perer mentions letters on the subject of studies exchanged between Alessandro da Sassoferrato, cardinal of Santa Susanna, and Paolo [Olmi] da Bergamo (41–42 and n. 88).

97. See the letters and briefs cited in Enzo Bentivoglio and Simonetta Valtieri, *Santa Maria del Popolo a Roma* (Rome: Bardi, 1976), 196.

98. Esposito, "Centri di aggregazione," 573 and n. 14, and 574 with n. 16; Davide Gutiérrez, ed., "De antiquis ordinis eremitarum sancti Augustini bibliothecis," *AA* 23 (1953–1954): 257–291, lists a rich collection of manuscripts and incunables.

times; his fellow reformers at Santa Maria del Popolo, Taddeo d'Ivrea and Agostino Cazzuli, held it nine times and five times, respectively.[99] Clearly, Paolo belonged to a select group.

Paolo Olmi is also known to scholars as a participant in the polemic between the Hermits and the Lateran Canons, both of whom claimed the epithet "Augustinian." This legal and historiographical quarrel, which I have touched on above, had a long history. It ignited immediately upon the institutional formation of the Hermits in the thirteenth century.[100] The Hermits, like the Franciscans and Dominicans, were a mendicant order, centralizing, urban based, and dedicated to preaching. The Regular Canons, on the other hand, were not formalized as an order and so did not have a centralizing bureaucracy or ideology (although they were more formalized and more centralizing than the secular canons).[101] Regular Canons were usually attached to urban cathedrals and so often had teaching and preaching duties; their income was personal and came from benefices at those cathedrals. Both Hermits and Canons promoted education: humanists can be found in the ranks of each group. And both participated in the ambitious reforming movements of the fifteenth century.

It may at first glance appear obvious that the Canons had the superior claim to authenticity by virtue of seniority: after all, the Hermits were a thirteenth-century phenomenon, whereas Canons could be found already in the early Middle Ages. Such logic appealed to the Canons, but it was irrelevant to the Hermits. Instead, the Hermits relied on the priority of hermitical practice in Augustine's own life to establish their seniority. The Canons

99. Gatti Perer, *Umanesimo*, 73 and 207. Agostino Cazzuli de Crema (ca. 1423–1495) is an important figure as a Hermit and writer about saints, especially in contrast to Paolo Olmi and Simone da Roma; see the hand list.

100. The story tends to get told from the Hermits' point of view, as in Saak, *Highway*, and Kaspar Elm, "Elias, Paulus von Theben und Augustinus als Ordensgründer: Ein Beitrag zur Geschichtsschreibung und Geschichtsdeutung der Eremiten- und Bettelorden des 13. Jahrhunderts," in H. Pätze, ed., *Geschichtsschreibung und Geschichtsbewusstsein im späten Mittelalter* (Sigmaringen: Thorbecke, 1987), 371–397; and idem, "Italienische Eremitengemeinschaften des 12. und 13 Jahrhunderts: Studien zur Vorgeschichte des Augustiner-Eremitenordens," in *L'eremitismo in occidente nei secoli XI e XII: Atti della seconda settimana internazionale di studio. Mendola, 30 agosto–6 settembre 1962* (Milan: Vita e pensiero, 1965), 491–559. The importance of the Augustinian Hermits for Petrarch and thence for the *studia humanitatis* is well known; see, e.g., G. Mazzotta, "Humanism and Monastic Spirituality in Petrarch," *Stanford Literature Review* 5, nos. 1–2 (1988): 57–74; A. M. Voci, *Petrarca e la vita religiosa: Il mito umanista della vita eremitica* (Rome, 1983); P. Courcelle, "Pétrarch entre saint Augustin et les Augustins du XIVe siècle," *Studi petrarcheschi* 7 (1961): 51–71; P. O. Kristeller, "Augustine and the Early Renaissance," reprinted in *Studies in Renaissance Thought and Letters,* 2d ed., (Rome: Edizioni di storia e letteratura, 1969).

101. For the distinction between Regular and Secular Canons, see Agnes Gerhards, *Dictionnaire historique des ordres religieux* (Poitier: Fayard, 1998), 134a–137b, "Chanoines"; Charles Dereine, "Chanoines," *DHGE* 12:353–405.

responded by denying that Augustine had been a hermit in any meaningful sense and argued that he had not provided a rule for the hermitical but for the canonical life. This polemic was reignited in 1474–1476, when the Fabbrica del Duomo in Milan decided to commission a statue depicting Augustine in the distinctive garb of a Hermit.[102] Both Hermits and Canons turned with alacrity to the printing press to justify their claims through polemical analysis of Augustine's works and reconstructions of *vitae Augustini*. Olmi's contribution was an *Apologia* to counter the attacks of the Canons against the authenticity and priority of the Hermits; it was printed at Rome in 1479, while he was serving as prior at Santa Maria del Popolo.[103]

As an author, however, Paolo Olmi had a less recognized specialization of relevance to this study: he wrote women's *vitae*.[104] Olmi composed accounts of Augustine's saintly mother, Monica; of Maddalena Alberici da Como (d. 1465); and of Maria da Genoa (lost).[105] He also promoted the cult of Clara of Montefalco (d. 1308) around Brescia, probably by preaching. The physician and humanist poet Giovanni Michele Carrara (1438–1490) of Bergamo, who rewrote the first *vita* of Clara, recalled that he had been introduced to her virtues by Olmi.[106]

Paolo Olmi's administrative standing, his participation in the Augustinian controversy, and his evident desire to promote women associated with the Hermits all suggest that his lost *vita Helenae utinensis* was an authoritative account. Olmi probably wrote it in Latin, following a traditional structure and terminology for Elena's virtuous progress and drawing on Simone's vernacular narrative. Only the roughest dating can be proposed

---

102. Elm, *"Augustinus Canonicus."*

103. Olmi's *Apologia religionis fratrum heremitarum ordinis s. Augustini contra falso impugnantes,* printed in Rome by Francesco de Cinquinis with the colophon date of July 18, 1479, survives in many copies (H 16086*; *IGI* 10020; Goff P162; IERS 591). An epitome by Ambrogio da Cora, O.E.S.A., was printed as the *Defensorium ordinis sancti Augustini* in Rome by Herolt, probably in 1481 (HC 5684*; *IGI* 437; Goff C877; *IERS* 675).

104. Was this specialization a function of his own penitential practice, said to have been very harsh, so that he had a reputation for sanctity himself? See Esposito, "Centri di aggregazione," 574 and nn. 19–20; and at 594 and n. 108, noting a miracle of conversion attributed to Olmi.

105. Olmi's life of Monica is often found bound with his *Apologia* (n. 103 above), fols. 45–60, and is dedicated to Giovanni da Siena, confessor to Sixtus IV. See also *IERS* 589 and 590. The *vita* is told in the first person by Augustine about his mother, and so should be compared to a similar treatment by the twelfth-century prior Walter of Arrouais (*BHL* 6000). Olmi describes Maddalena as "priscarum Aegypti Eremicolarum imitatrix" in his life of the abbess (*BHL* 5132), said to have been published at Rome in 1484 (not seen; *IERS* p. 252). Cf. Maria of Venice's pursuit of martyrdom in the account by Tommaso Caffarini, which has, in its presentation of "ordinary" virtue, been an interpretive puzzle for scholars: see Fernanda Sorelli, "Imitable Sanctity: The Legend of Maria of Venice," in Bornstein and Rusconi, *Women and Religion,* 165–181.

106. C. Alonso, "La biografia inédita de Santa Clara de Montefalco por el humanista Giovanni Michele Alberto Carrara (s. XV)," *AA* 54 (1991): 7–61, at 58.

for Olmi's lost account. It was surely composed after Simone's of 1458; the safest *terminus ante quem* is Olmi's death at Cremona in June 1484. Since it is unlikely that Simone's vernacular *vita* would have been sent alone to Rome as the first step in seeking recognition of Elena's cult, perhaps Paolo Olmi was responsible for a Latin version that could be respectfully submitted. If so, then he may have written between the composition of Simone da Roma's account in 1458 and 1465, when Elena's cult began to be celebrated annually in Udine. But that is only speculation: Olmi's account is missing, papal approval of Elena's cult cannot be demonstrated, and the nature of Paul's interest in Elena remains unclear, so it cannot be said with certainly whether Olmi wrote before or after the strange narrative that Giacomo of Udine—who as a cathedral canon most certainly was not a Hermit—composed for the pope between August 1464 and May 1469.[107]

At the end of the Quattrocento, three decades after Giacomo da Udine's composition, two other humanists wrote Latin *vitae* of Elena. One was a Hermit, the learned Jacopo Filippo Foresti of Bergamo, author of two frequently reprinted works, a *Supplementum Chronicarum* and *Confessionale*.[108] Foresti entered the Hermits in Bergamo in 1451/52 and so would have known Paolo Olmi. His entry on Olmi in the *Supplementum Chronicarum* is therefore persuasive evidence for the quondam existence of a *vita Helenae* by Olmi: Foresti himself wrote a life of Elena and so is unlikely to have mistaken Olmi's contribution.[109] The entry is also reason to suspect

107. The *terminus post quem* for Giacomo's *Vita Helenae* is most reliably deduced from the dedication to Paul II, who acceded in August 1464.

108. On Foresti, see L. Megli Frattini, "Foresti, Jacopo Filippo," *DBI* 48 (1997), 801b–803a. His much-reprinted chronicle is addressed in Achim Krümmel, *Das Supplementum chronicarum des Augustinermönches Jacobus Philippus Foresti von Bergamo* (Herzberg: Bautz, 1992). His penitential guide, the *Confessionale*, was almost as successful; it was published in Venice by Benali in 1500 and then, in vernacular translation, five further times before 1542 (Schutte, *PIVRB*, 179).

109. Foresti's life of Elena is discussed below. For Foresti's entry on Olmi, see *Supplementum chronicarum* (Venice, 1506), book 15, fol. 200v:

> Paulus Lulmas conterraneus noster, vir dicendi facundissimus et bonarum litterarum, in quibus excellebat, valde insignis, et ipse per hoc tempus tum [patriam] tu[m] religionem nostram in qua (sicut de religioso magis prodesse quam praesse) se plurimum defatigavit. Scripsit et ipse ex ingenii sui magnitudine quosdam libellos salibus conditos, et primo *De floribus eremi liber I*; *De spirituali ascensu ad deum liber I*; *Ad serenissimum Christophorum Maurum Venetiarum ducem liber I*; *De laudibus presentis vitae per dyalogum liber I*; *De appologia religionis contra impugnantes liber I*; *De vita et miraculis beatae Mariae de Genua Liber I*; *De vita beatissimae Monicae liber I*; *De norma et regula poenitentium liber I*; *De spirituali viridario sponsarum Christi in vulgari liber I*; *De vita et miraculis beatae Magdalenae de Como*, ac *Beatae Helenae de Utino nostri ordinis liber I*. Tandem enim 33 quadragesimus continue in populo declamasset. Anno domini 1484 de mense Iunii Cremonae prior existens migravit ad dominum.

(I expand abbreviations, modernize punctuation, and italicize book titles but do not regularize spelling.)

that Foresti drew on Olmi's narrative when he composed his own life of Elena, which occurs in the final section on contemporary women of his *De plurimis claris scele[s]tisque mulieribus*. This encyclopedic collection, dedicated to Beatrice of Hungary, wife of Matthias Corvinus, was published in Ferrara with the colophon date of April 29, 1497.[110] In it, Elena is an unusual entry: to judge from the other contemporary subjects in this concluding section, Foresti preferred to write about the learned women of courtly families. Elena was, of course, a special case, a *beata* of Foresti's own order. In his outline of her pious progress and in his spiritual emphases, Foresti drew on Simone, or perhaps on a version of Simone prepared by Paolo Olmi.

The second late Quattrocento humanist life of Elena appears, in turn, to draw on Foresti. It was written by the lay physician and teacher of rhetoric Giovanni Garzoni of Bologna (ca. 1428–1505), whose classroom use of *vitae sanctorum* is proposed in the preceding chapter. At some point between 1497, when Foresti's account was published, and mid-April 1501, Garzoni acceded to the request of an old friend, the Bolognese Hermit Johannes Paxius, that he write up Elena's *vita*.[111] Paxius provided Garzoni with a source, explaining in a letter that he had used a Latin text to prepare a vernacular life of Elena, adding and subtracting material "according to the opinions of those who were present" ("secutus eorum sententiae qui affuerunt").[112] He wanted Garzoni to translate this vernacular life back into appropriate Latin. Paxius did not divulge the reason for such a roundabout procedure, he did not name his advising committee, and he did not indicate who had written his Latin source. The new Latin *vita Helenae* composed by Garzoni closely echoes Foresti's account. So Paxius may have provided the humanist with a vernacular adaptation of the entry from *De claris mulieribus*. Several parts of Garzoni's account,

---

110. Goff 5204; *IGI* 5071; *BMC* VI, 613. See Hélène Wieruszowski, "*De claris mulieribus*: Lebens- und Bildungsideale der italienischen Frau im Zeitalter der Renaissance," in *1903–1928: Festschrift zür Feier des 25 Jahrigen Bestehens der gymnasialen Studienanstallt in Köln-am-Rhein* (Cologne, 1928), 15–29; and V. Zaccaria, "La fortuna del *De mulieribus claris* del Boccaccio nel secolo XV: Giovanni Sabbadini degli Arienti, Jacopo Filippo Foresti e le loro biografie femminile (1490–1497)," in F. Mazzoni, ed., *Il Boccaccio nelle culture e letterature nazionale* (Florence, 1978), 519–545. A helpful overview of the genre is Marta Ajmar, "Exemplary Women in Renaissance Italy: Ambivalent Models of Behaviour?" in L. Panizza, ed., *Women in Italian Renaissance Culture and Society* (Oxford: European Humanities Research Center, 2000), 244–264.

111. Lind, *Letters*, letter 458. Lind gives the *terminus ante quem* as 1497, but since Garzoni appears to have drawn on Foresti (see below), he must have written after the publication of *De claris mulieribus* (I am assuming that Foresti would not have drawn on Garzoni, whose account was not printed and does not seem to have circulated at all). In his letter, Garzoni promises to write the *vita* soon, when he has some free time.

112. See Lind, *Letters*, letter 457.

however, could only come from the vernacular of Simone or, since Paxius did say he was working with a Latin text, from the lost *vita Helenae* by Paolo Olmi. (Indeed, Paxius may be a second witness to Olmi's lost account.) For example, Garzoni states that Elena was married for twenty-seven years. Jacopo Filippo Foresti does not say how many years she had been married; Giacomo da Udine says twenty-two. Only Simone da Roma (and Olmi?) give the number twenty-seven.[113]

The official commission from Paxius did not ignite Garzoni's enthusiasm. His letter of response has an uncharacteristically flat tone, and the preface to his *vita Helenae* is similarly disengaged.[114] In the life itself, Garzoni's close quotations from Foresti also suggest a lack of interest, for as I noted in the preceding chapter, Garzoni was a tireless reviser of other authors' Latin. Garzoni's account of Elena is extant in two manuscripts, although not much can be made of such a small distribution, since almost none of Garzoni's *vitae et passiones sanctorum* were widely diffused. If a "Ciceronian" *vita* was supposed to help disseminate Elena's cult among the Hermits' novices and among educated Bolognese men (as Simone's vernacular was presumably meant to guide a less-educated Udinese audience, especially those women disposed to join the mantellate), then it failed. But Garzoni's classicizing narrative does draw attention to a problem that Giacomo da Udine's account seems designed to solve: how were highly educated readers to be presented the exemplary life of an elderly widow of charismatic virtue who, though she was evidently literate in her vernacular, could not be called learned in any sense recognizable in humanist or university circles? Indeed, the great problem seems to have been that the

---

113. On the chronological difficulties of ascertaining the length of Elena's marriage, see Tilatti, *Simone da Roma,* 24–25. A more detailed comparison of the accounts of Foresti and Garzoni with that by Simone is given below.

114. Lind, *Letters,* letter 458. Garzoni's *Vita Helenae* is listed in the hand list. I quote from Garzoni's draft, BBU, MS 752, (hereafter E), fols 56r–57r, with reference to the later MS 1622, iii (hereafter D). The preface reads:

Summum illum opificem aedificatoremque mundi deum, cuius ea uis est ut qua quisque [D quis] mente sit non ignoret, non mediocre desyderium subit ut omnes in [D deest] illam aeternam domum discedamus. Atque eorum qui se delitiis [D delictis] inquinant, quo ab illis reuocentur, mentibus praefert lumina. Testantur hoc apostolus Paulus, ac princeps ille et magister omnium theologorum Aurelius Augustinus, caterique sanctissimi uiri, qui cum e recta uia aliquando deflexissent resipuissentque morte obita deorum [E add. in marg.] caelestium numerum auxerunt. Tantam eorum felicitatem cum animo suo consyderans Helena Vtinensis huius mundi illecebras contempsit [D comptensit] seque ad deum tota mente conuertit. Quo factum est ut sempiterna beatitudine fruatur. Eius uitam litteris mandare constitui. Neque enim quae ab ea acta sunt cum memoratu digna existant silentio praetereunda duxi. Cui [D Cum] uero opusculum ipsum dicarem, tu mihi ante alios in mentem uenisti, praestantissime pater, qui cum omni doctrina sanctissimisque moribus polleas, multa de spe decido quin magna ex eo sis uoluptatem percepturus. Vale. [Cui . . . percepturus add. in marg. E]

saintly type embodied by Elena—elderly, female, charismatic, and *illiterata* (ignorant of Latin)—was commonly perceived to represent an extreme form of opposition to the inclusion of the *studia humanitatis* into training for religious.

The *vitae* by Foresti and Garzoni also draw attention to the unique form of Giacomo's narrative. In emphasizing Giacomo's uniqueness, I do not mean to underestimate the innovations of Foresti and Garzoni. It is significant, for example, that Foresti's *vita Helenae* occurs in a humanist's encyclopedia but opens with what appears to be a martyrology entry for Elena and closes with the author's prayer to the *beata*.[115] In the case of Garzoni, it is significant that he appears to be the only Quattrocento layman invited by a religious order to write about its contemporary holy women. His patron, a Hermit *magister* in the Bolognese convent of San Giacomo, deliberately sought out a classicizing *vita* of an elderly charismatic widow. An advisory committee of some sort also wanted this *vita*. Any study of humanist contributions to the writing of saints' lives would want to acknowledge these innovations.

Nevertheless, the accounts by Foresti and Garzoni may be considered traditional in several respects. Both men wrote short accounts, epitomes. Giacomo, in contrast, wrote at great length, warning Paul II in the first preface that he ought not to be surprised to receive such a big book, "tam amplum volumen," since that same God who had multiplied the loaves and fishes had forwarded his composition.[116] Both Foresti and Garzoni wrote chronologically ordered narratives in Latin prose. Giacomo's is also in Latin prose but includes many quotations in the vernacular; and, while Giacomo's is chronologically ordered, it is hardly straightforward. In fact, Giacomo describes his account as written *poetice*, although it is in prose, not meter. So, at this point, it will be useful to summarize, on the basis of Simone's account, the structure and content of Foresti's and Garzoni's narratives. That brief overview will lay the foundation for an evaluation of the more complex retelling by Giacomo da Udine.[117]

Both the Hermit Foresti and the layman Garzoni open with a few words on the city of Udine and its region, "Sapadia," and then relate Elena's

---

115. Foresti's *vita* is preceded by a brief entry in martyrology format, *inc.*: "Helena Utinenesis nostri ordinis heremitarum . . . a scriptura agminibus." His prayer is given at fol. 148v; cf. Tilatti, *Simone da Roma*, 178, "Pregamo te adonche. . . . "

116. G fol. 2.

117. In the following discussion, I use these *sigla* for convenience:

S   Simone da Roma, ed. Tilatti, *Simone da Roma*, 123–180
F   Foresti, *De claris mulieribus*, 146–147v
E   Garzoni, BBU, MS 752, iv, fols. 56–81 (*siglum* from Lind, *Letters*)
G   Giacomo da Udine, BAV, MS Lat. 1223, fols. 1–83v

noble origin, early virtue, and marriage at fifteen to Cavalcanti.[118] They note the peaceful and fruitful character of her marriage, and they tell how, at the death of her husband, Elena's grief was followed by conversion.[119] Both say that her conversion was caused by Augustinian preaching, and both report that she entered the Hermits' third order under the supervision of Angelo de Sancto Severino.[120]

118. Cf. S 123; F fol. 146v; E fol. 57r–v. F and S—the *vitae* by Hermits—barely touched on early virtue, a notable distinction between lay and regular authors.

119. S 128; F fol. 146v, emphasizing the happy marriage; E fols. 57v–59; F emphasizes the widow's grief; E gives Elena a speech in direct address:

> Breve admodum tempus, mi uir, una fuimus. Is quo te semper complexa sum amor, ut a me his donis muneribus efficit, ea in sepulchrum deportate. Unum illud tibi constanti animo polliceor, me in posterum nulli unquam uiro nupturam. Dicabo hanc animam, hoc corpus Christo optimo maximo eique, quantum in me fuerit, et castam et integram et perpetuam seruitutem seruiam. Qui in his fragilibus caducisque bonis (diuturna enim esse non possunt) spem collocant, imprudentia labuntur. Quare omnes hortor, ut illis contemptis ad illud sanctorum concilium cetumque omnia consilia sua referant.

Here Garzoni completely rewrites the direct address that Simone attributes to Elena (S 128). Foresti alludes to Simone's speech later in order to explain how Elena carries out her works of charity by drawing on "sua omnia iocalia in auro et argento uestibus tum sericis tum auratis" (F fol. 147; see S 147).

120. Cf. S 129–130, in great detail about the contents of the sermons. Foresti treats the matter briefly. E fols. 59–60v names Angelo de Sancto Severino:

> Angelus quidam Picenus, quem nullum scientiarum genus latebat (erat is Augustini religioni addictus) Utinum praedicatum iter contulit. Eo in oppido templum est Luciae sacrum, in quo qui Augustino dicantur uitam suam colunt. Cum huic de quo loquor Angelo de christiana ueritate uerba facienda erant, nunquam aberat Helena. . . . Casu accidit ut Angelus in religionis sermonem incideret, cum ex ea quae praemia reportarentur expresisset, ad Aurelii Augustini religionem orationem contulit. Nec Monacham [*sic*], quae Augustino mater fuerat, intactam reliquit. Quanta fuisset religione, quanta charitate, quanta integritate omnibus ante oculos posuit, quae illi pro sanctissimis laboribus suis munera tribuerentur minime praetermisit. Ex quo nulla de spe deciderent, quin religionem profiterentur. Affirmabat homo sanctissimus, qui religiose uitam instituissent, quin eis bene feliciterque euenisset, se nullos uidisse. Tandem beneficiorum, quibus Augustino dicati afficiuntur, mentionem habuit, quae de industria praetermisi, quod nimis orationem meam prouexissem. Igitur Helena, quae ab Angelo proferebantur mente agitans ad Christi crucem aduolare instituit. Ut dei laudibus orationibusque finis impositus est, multis cum lachrymis ad Angeli genua procidit, non postulans sed flagitans ut se miseram in earum quae Christo atque Augustino et Monachae dicatae essent numerum adscriberet, imitata Magdalenam.

F fols. 146v–147, naming "Angel[us] ex Sancti Severino oppido in Piceno" as her "pater spiritualis." S 130 notes the inclusion of her sisters, followed by E fols. 61v–62: "Demum diem qua tunicam sumptura esset, praestituit quae ut illuxit duas Helenae sorores quarum alteri Danieli, alter(i) Perfectae nomen erat . . . Angelus et qui cum eo erat monasterii princeps, compluresque religiosi tunica ad idipsam facta Helenam induerunt." Garzoni also notes that other women followed her: "Non multo post matronae quaedam uirtute, estimatione, nobilitate principes Helenae secutae sunt uestigia."

At just this point, following Simone da Roma's model, both Foresti and Garzoni deflect the simple chronological progress of their narratives to a more topical format, in order to trace Elena's heroic virtues. Thus, like the Hermit Simone, they, too, suggest that these virtues did not precede but followed her entry into the Third Order.[121] They add no virtues that cannot be found in Simone, although they present the virtues in a more fluid order. In all cases, charity is addressed first.[122] Both Foresti and Garzoni note the penitential character of Elena's devotional life but underplay poverty, at least in comparison to Simone.[123] Both record her harsh diet, fasting, and drinking of vinegar and gall.[124] Both note that objection was made to the dangerous strictness of her asceticisms.[125] Following Simone, Foresti says that she practiced the discipline, wore a crown of nails, and had a maid tie her hands and lead her through the house by a rope about her neck, in memory of Christ's sufferings.[126] Garzoni omits these enactments but preserves (unlike Foresti) Simone's oblique recollection of Jerome's penitence in the desert: Elena practiced penitential self-flagellation by beating her chest with a stone.[127] The authors join again, following Simone, to say that she frequently prayed and attended church; they also note that she wept copiously, especially at her frequent communions.[128] Her devotions included reading.[129] Foresti discourses vaguely

---

121. Tilatti, *"Per man di notaro,"* 509, points out that Simone, Foresti, and Giacomo da Udine locate her private devotional practices (*vita contemplativa*) after her entry into the Augustinian Hermits' Third Order; so does Garzoni. See also ibid., 513, on her public activities (*vita activa*), placed before her life as a tertiary only by *G* fol. 26.

122. Following *S* 133; *F* fol. 147; *E* fols. 62v–64.

123. *S* 135–137; *F* fol. 147; *E* fols. 64v–65v.

124. *S* 139; *F* fol. 147; *E* fol. 66r–v, quoting *F* on a six-year fast, and, at 68v, specifying three-day fasts.

125. *S* 139; *E* fols. 66v–67, appearing to quote *F.* None of these authors names Leonardo da Udine at this point.

126. *S* 136–37, giving a speech in direct address; *F* fol. 147. Neither Foresti nor Garzoni record the thirty-three stones in her shoes mentioned above; cf. *S* 136. For another instance of a woman whose penitential practice included binding the hands and being led by a rope around the neck, see Chiara da Rimini, in Dalarun, *Lapsus linguae*, 40–41.

127. *E* fol. 68v: "pectus durisimo lapide verberabat, ut ingens vis sanguinis emanaret"; see *S* 145.

128. *S* 141–143; *F* fol. 147, more briefly; cf. *E* fol. 67r–v, which adds that she had a little house or cell, *aediculum*, built for herself inside Santa Lucia, with a window from which she could observe the Host and watch the Mass and Office. On her weeping, see *E* fol. 67v: "Referam rem inauditam. Intra diem et noctem in lachrymis fletuque horas nouem conterebat," following *S* 141, who explains the symbolism of the number nine.

129. *S* 142; *F* fol. 147, lightly paraphrased by *E* fol. 68: "Quod dabatur ocii, id litterarum studio suppeditabat. Legebat libros duos, quorum alterum crucis speculum vocant, alteri de humilitate est inscriptio" (cf. *F:* "alterum quorum crucis speculum vocant, alter vero de humilitate inscriptus est"). But *F* goes on to note her reading of the Evangel ("tamquam Cecilia"); Garzoni omits this point. And *F,* following Simone, uses her reading to make an explicit reference to Jerome: "[Helena] sciens quoque beatum Hieronymum precepisse orationi lectio lectioni succedat ratio."

on her obedience; Garzoni demonstrates it by repeating the story, given in Simone, of how she received permission for a vow of silence, pursuing it strictly even with her children at a special Christmas visit.[130] Both Foresti and Garzoni take some time over her persecutions by the devil, not a theme that either addresses in other *vitae*.[131] Both note her final three, bedridden years, as well as her vision at that time of Christ and the Virgin accompanied by Augustine and Niccolò da Tolentino.[132] At this point in the narrative, Garzoni records three miracles performed by Elena during her lifetime, not mentioned by Foresti.[133] Then both men tell of her preparations for death in the presence of the prior of Santa Lucia.[134]

Foresti simply announces her death. Garzoni, following Simone, attributes to her a deathbed speech in direct address, records that her passing was witnessed by two religious, Heliseus and Paraclitus, as well as by her fellow tertiaries Antonia and Honesta, and says that she died at the moment the priest read Christ's words, "Into your hands I commend my spirit."[135] Both

130. *S* 149; *E* fols. 68v–69:

Casu accidit, ut qui sese religioni Augustini dediderant Utinum euocarentur prouincialis iussu. Erat hic uir grauis integer summaeque auctoritatis. Ad hunc uisendum cum Helena quam mulieres complures deo dicatae prosecutae erant, iter contulisset. "Si qua sunt," inquit, "filia, quae tibi usui consolationi honori futura putes, ea uerbis sinodi et polliceor et defero. Neque ego dissentiam. Uniuersam religionem nostram castitatis, pudiciciae, sanctitatis, fidei, integritatis, tuae fama peruasit, ut ea sis quam cuncti admirari possunt et debent. Obsequentur omnes studiis tuis." Tum Helena illi amplissimis uerbis gratias egit, unum se solum postulare, ut ei, ne inscio confessore suo cum quopiam uerba facere liceret, praeciperet, quin silentium teneret. Concessit ille in sententiam suam.

131. Five episodes are noted: the devil shouts and shakes from the roof; chases her; tries to push her out a window; tempts her in the appearance of an angel; tries to drown her on her way to Santa Lucia. *F* fols. 147r–v; *E* fols. 70–72v, following *F* closely but including two instances of direct address, the words with which Elena bests the devil. Cf. *S* 153–159, at temptations 1, 2, 3, 4, 5; note that Simone's eighth temptation—the devils break Elena's leg— is what sends her to bed and eventually to her death.

132. *S* 175; *F* fol. 148; *E* fols. 72v–73, closely paraphrasing *F* on years in bed. *S* 163–167 gives ten visions, of which only the second appears in these late Quattrocento accounts. *F* fol. 148; *E* fol. 73v: "Quippe ad orationem incumbenti sese Christus, Virgo illa sanctissima, Augustinus, Nicolaus Tolentinas obtulerunt."

133. *E* fol. 74r–v, the healing of an epileptic, "Helenus Calceretus" of Udine; fols. 74v–75v, the granting of fertility to Benvenuta of Udine (cf. *S* 171–172); fols. 75v–76, the healing of Cristoforo de Fanis of Udine (cf. *S* 172–173). Cf. *S* 169–173, five miracles.

134. Not named specifically by *S* 175–176, who notes that "el sacerdote suo padre spirituale" brought her the viaticum and that "tutti li fratti de l'Ordine che erano in Sancta Lucia andareno processionalmente a casa sua como usanza in lo nostro Ordine."

135. On direct address: *E* fols. 76v–78, relying on *S* 175 (or Olmi?). Garzoni's fidelity to Simone (or Olmi?) can be judged by comparing Simone's list of "tutti li patriarchi e propheti, apostoli, martiri, confesori, verzene sante e spiriti beati della corte celestiale" with Garzoni's "Patriarchae prophetae apostoli martyres confessores uirgines uniuersaeque caelestis turba" (*E* fol. 77v). She is lying on a little straw; *F* fol. 148 says "super nudam humum iacens"; *S* 175 says "iacendo sul suo letto de sassi sopra delle quali non era altro se non un poco de paglia." On witnesses: *S* 176–177; *E* fol. 78v–79, describing Honesta as the princeps of those dedicated to Augustine. On moment of death, cf. *S* 177–178; *E* fol. 79.

men follow Simone's legalism by recording the date of death in full.[136] The women who prepared her body noted the fearsome signs of her discipline and witnessed a miracle, for when they placed a cross on her chest, her head raised up and could not be pressed down.[137] Foresti gives his brief personal prayer and then, writing for a female patron, records two posthumous miracles given to women, before concluding. Garzoni, writing for a male patron, records one posthumous miracle granted to a man and goes on to add a vision associated with her funeral.[138] Plans for a burial at the main altar were made by the abbot at Santa Lucia and the provincial, but the two brothers assigned to guard her body overnight were advised by Elena herself that if they insisted on burying her there, she would leave them.[139] She preferred to be buried in her own oratory inside the church, and her posthumous wishes, Garzoni notes in concluding, were obeyed.[140]

It is clear from this description that the *Vitae Helenae* composed by the humanists Garzoni and Foresti include some ascetic practices that we do not normally associate with the humanists' more intellectualized forms of piety. Even so, the *vitae* are thoroughly predictable in their structure, being similar, in fact, to confessors' accounts of holy women. This quality, this predictable and recognizable structure, is generically important. Predictability can be a form of authentication in narrative as precedent is in law. The confessor's *vita* typically traces childhood signs of virtue; supervised development of the maturing woman; evidence of especially desired virtues such as charity and humility, with lifetime miracles (just a few); and the exemplary death publicly witnessed (posthumous *beneficia* were the province of the notary, not the confessor). Beginning in the late thirteenth century, confessors' *vitae* on this model at first suggested and then later followed a framework for the collection of depositions about the prospective saint. Over time the narrative format of the canonization life grew rigid, so that it provided a recipe for achieving sanctity, both for

---

136. *S* 178; *F* fol. 148; *E* fol. 79v.

137. *S* 179; *F* fol. 148v; *E* fols. 79v–80. I give phrases that appear to be quoted from Foresti in italics: "*Mulieres* consilio inter se *de lauando* corpore habito *summo opere ulceratum inspiciunt* quod *ea de causa accidisse* se existimo quod *tot annos humi iacuerat* . . . cum mulieres *supra pectus* crucem *posuissent subito caput extulit.* Nunquam *demitti potuit.*"

138. Cf. the prayer in *S* 178. Following *S* 179, Garzoni describes the healing of the arm of a certain Giovanni of Udine ("Joannis cuiusdam Utinensis," at *E* fol. 80). Foresti describes (as posthumous?) the healing of an epileptic, Helena Calcereto of Udine, and the *in vita* miracle noted above, conception granted to an infertile woman, Benvenuta of Udine (*F* fol. 148v). Cf. Tilatti, "*Per man di notaro,*" 519–520.

139. Unlike *S* 180, *E* fol. 80v does not use the word *visio* or describe the means by which Elena imparted her posthumous desires. Tilatti, *Simone da Roma,* 180 n. 2, on the two testaments.

140. *S* 180, *oratorio; E* fols. 80v–81, *aedicula sua.*

those who wanted to be saints themselves and for those who wanted to represent the saint in a *vita*.[141]

The predictable quality of Foresti's and Garzoni's accounts is just as significant as their innovations. A locality or order trying for a saint faced expensive and time-consuming efforts, which an experimental *vita* put at risk. The Hermits' first *vita* of Elena, written by a theologian, notarized, and approved by the provincial, was no experiment, vernacular though it was. Olmi's lost account was, I have suggested, still more traditional, at least insofar as it was in Latin. Neither are the *vitae* by Jacopo Filippo Foresti and Giovanni Garzoni riskily experimental, whatever their novelties.

❊ ❊ ❊

Nemo est enim tanta praeditus eloquentia, qui ea laudes, ea praeconia, quibus pro sanctitate rigidae vitae digna sit, non dicam scribere, sed nec animo concipere posset. Tulliani flumen siccaretur ingenii.

There is no one so gifted with eloquence who could, I shall not say write, but even conceive in his soul the praises, the celebrations that she deserves for the holiness of her harsh life. The river of Ciceronian eloquence would dry up.

—Giacomo da Udine, *vita Helenae utinensis*[142]

The *vita Helenae utinensis* by Giacomo da Udine most certainly is a generic experiment. It appears, in fact, to be a landmark text, the only saint's life ever written as a convivium or symposium. At any rate, there is no mistaking it for a dialogue. That would have been a less innovative structure, because there were authoritative models—Sulpicius Severus on Martin and Gregory on Benedict—for dialogic *vitae*. But in devising his *vita Helenae,* Giacomo broke completely with the attenuated tradition of dialogic *vitae* and a fortiori with the straightforward narrative model of Foresti and Garzoni. His speakers do not converse, trading facts and opinions, even in the strained manner of Socrates' interlocutors in the Platonic dialogues. Giacomo's personae take turns giving speeches before each other, stepping up to the task (as if up to a podium) with a formal phrase of transition and hardly ever responding to each other's remarks.

Giacomo embraces the rupture wholeheartedly. His account not only breaks with medieval models of saints' lives but also violates the classical requirement that a symposium be verisimilar. It is true that the first prologue, really a dedicatory letter to Paul II, takes up traditional points, even if it does

---

141. Gabor Klaniczay, "Legends as Life-Strategies for Aspirant Saints in the Later Middle Ages," in *The Uses of Supernatural Power: The Transformation of Popular Religion in Medieval and Early-Modern Europe,* trans. S. Singerman, ed. K. Margolis (Princeton, N.J.: Princeton University Press, 1990), 95–110.

142. G fol. 1.

so in sometimes surprising ways. Thus it opens with an avowal of the author's insufficiency, continues with an invocation, protests the worthiness of the *vita* for its illustrious recipient, and explains the importance of commemoration. But the second prologue is a fantastical set of stage directions, proving that the traditional markers of verisimilitude had been rejected.

A new saint has arrived in heaven, where preparations for her welcome are already under way. Almighty God orders the archangel Michael to raise the famous pagans from hell, "ab inferis excitare." The guests include Aristides, Plato, Demosthenes, Lysias, Aeschines, Hyperides, Nestor, Cicero, Varro, Cato, Livy, and Sallust.[143] Then God himself restores the souls ("animas ad eorum corpora reverti") of a group of eloquent early Christians: Basil, John Chrysostom, Gregory Nazianzen, Origen, Cyprian, Ephrem, Jerome, Lactantius, Hermas, John Cassian, and Pope Leo.[144] Five later Christians are brought back to life as well. All are identifiable as friends of the author or of his dedicatee. The first is the Venetian Leonardo Giustinian (lieutenant of the Friuli 1432; d. 1446). Giustinian had been at Guarino's school with Francesco Barbaro and was known to his humanist contemporaries as a composer of popular *laude* and a translator of Plutarch.[145] Anyone in the Venetian orbit, such as Pietro Barbo and Giacomo da Udine, would also know that Giustinian had translated a Greek life of St. Nicholas of Myra. The second near contemporary resurrected (I follow the order given by the manuscript) is the Aretine Leonardo Bruni (d. 1444), chancellor of Florence and much-read translator of Aristotle's *Ethics* and Basil's *On Studies*. Bruni would have been known to Paul II from Paul's own early studies in Florence.[146] The third orator is the Venetian Francesco Barbaro (d. 1454), the learned patron of Giacomo's *De antiquitatibus aquileiensibus libellus*. The fourth, named only as Utinensis, may be Guarnerio d'Artegna (d. 1466), the book collector and Giacomo's fellow canon.[147] Finally, God resurrects the Friulian humanist related by marriage to Guarino Guarini and known to Giacomo and Paul II, Giovanni da Spilimbergo (d. 1454/1457).[148]

---

143. In Giacomo's account, those who are present but do not speak are the Greek orators Demosthenes, Lysias, Aeschines, and Hyperides; Nestor; and the Roman historians Livy and Sallust.

144. Of these, the only silent observer is (prudently) Origen.

145. F. Pignatti, "Giustinian, Leonardo," *DBI* 57 (2001), 249b–255a.

146. Bruni was also admired by Paul's biographer, Gaspare da Verona; see Zippel, *Le vite*, 23 n. 1.

147. See n. 13 above. Guarnerio was originally from Portogruaro. The most obvious Utinensis is Leonardo da Udine, but see n. 8 above.

148. On Giovanni da Spilimbergo (ca. 1380–ca. 1458), see Sabbadini, *Epistolario* 3, letter 444, n. at 232–233; and the entry in Liruti, *Notizie*, 355–365, who gives among his friends a group of Guarino's students: Tobia del Borgo, Leonardo Giustinian, Francesco Barbaro, Cardinal Zabarella, Poggio, Giovanni da Lodi, Mazo dei'Mazi, and Pietro di Monte, as well as a student of Timoteo Maffei's (see below), Sebastiano Borsa.

Once the speakers are gathered, God explains his plan for the event. These men, whom the world considers princes of eloquence ("principes eloquentiae mundus habuit") should instruct each other ("se instruant") about "our Elena."[149] God wants nothing offhand. The orations should be fulsome and well considered, as well as more copious and vehement than is customary: after all, the speakers have been brought back to life to ensure Elena's fame with erudition and sublimity.[150] In the course of these instructions, God quotes by name Dante, Lactantius, and "My Son." Solemnly, the dead orators consider (*matura praemeditatione*) how to depict (*depinxerunt*) Elena.

The fourth-century church father Jerome is the first of the fourteen speech givers. He describes and comments on Elena's obedient childhood, adolescent efforts at asceticism, virtuous courtship, and twenty-two years of happy marriage. Jerome introduces some telling novelties, such as a story that the Virgin appeared with the Child to the seven-year-old Elena, to advise her and prophesy her future. She speaks to the child in the vernacular: "O Elena, be a good girl and fear God, so that a time will come when you will be a great servant of God" ("O Helena, fa che sia bona et temi Iddio, imperoche vegnira tempo che serai grande serva de dio"). In this instance, Giacomo's use of the vernacular appears to be part of his effort at verisimilitude, indeed, a sign of his respect for the reliquary nature of speech in a saint's life. After all, rhetoric requires that the matter (subject, or *res*) be fitted not just to the audience but also to the subject, and the child Elena would not have understood a Latin-speaking Virgin. Similarly, throughout the account, whenever Elena's words are recalled, Giacomo gives the precise vernacular. When Elena does speak in Latin, thanking the speakers at the conclusion of God's symposium in her honor, she is presumably able to do so because of the perfections associated with heaven.[151]

A similar respect for verisimilitude seems to be at work when Jerome laments Elena's decision to marry—"O Elena, you did one thing unwisely, to exchange virginity for chastity" ("O Helena, id solum non sapienter fecisti, mutare virginitatem in castitatem")—and mentions his own *Contra Iovinianum*. But Jerome acknowledges that God permitted her fall from virginity, so that she could make up for it with harsh penance.[152]

149. G fol. 2bisv.

150. G fols. 2bisv–3v.

151. G fols. 4v–8v, corresponding to S 127 = chap. 1: "De la sua nobile progenia." I am preparing an edition of Giacomo da Udine's *vita Helenae* and so keep notes to a minimum in this recapitulation. I am grateful to Caroline Bynum for her comments on all sorts of relics, including reported speech, in Giacomo's account. See also Patrick Henriet's study of the Latin *parole efficace* in monastic hagiography, *La parole et la prière au Moyen Âge* (Brussels: De Boeck and Larcier, 2000).

152. G fol. 7.

Basil speaks next, addressing Elena's widowhood and conversion to a religious life. At the moment of conversion, when she cuts her hair and throws the tresses, along with her jewels, on her husband's grave, Basil, too, recurs to the vernacular, the reliquary word. The speech attributed to Elena at her husband's graveside, renouncing the world, is the very one given by Simone da Roma, which suggests that the author Giacomo understood her words to have legal force not just as relics but also as vows. Basil also, strikingly, addresses a charge not raised in any of the other extant *vitae*: that Elena was insane. He transmutes her extreme behavior into a foolishness for Christ, "inebriata crucifixi amore stulta stultis gerere videbatur." Elena has a new *sponsus*, and Basil turns to the Bible and Dante for words to express her delight.[153]

The longest oration, on Elena's *pia opera* of charity, falls to the Friulian humanist Giovanni da Spilimbergo. He begins with a protestation of inadequacy and obedience and goes on to discuss Elena's gifts of bread and clothing to the poor, delivered with warm words, a kind face, and a loving heart. She cared for the sick but would not visit those who had not confessed; sometimes the sick even rose from their beds to follow her to confession. With sweet persuasion, she settled civic discord, uttering the wise words, "Stade un collautro in carita. Dove e la carita, li e dio." An epideictic passage on *caritas* follows. Giovanni closes his speech by quoting, again in the vernacular, Elena's admonition, "Non credati che l'anima sia morta col corpo" ("Don't believe that the soul dies with the body").[154]

Plato claims this observation as his text for a discourse on the immortality of the soul. He refutes the logic of Epicurus's argument from analogy with animals, that our souls die with our bodies, and proves immortality in support of "sapientissima Helena." Only humans use fire, have virtues, and are rational. No animal makes things, builds cities, takes up books, or cares for posterity. Only man can understand (*intelligere*) God, admire his works, and perceive his virtue and power. And only humans have speech. The remainder of Plato's discourse is a tissue of *auctoritates*: Ovid, Lactantius, Cicero (at length), *imitatores mei* (i.e., Ficinian Neoplatonists?), Pythagoras, Phericides, Augustine, Ecclesiastes, Isaiah, Gregory, Aristotle, Cassiodorus, Cato, Zeno, Empedocles, Democritus, "my teacher Socrates," Virgil, Caesar, Sallust, Seneca, and even Lucretius.[155]

---

153. G fols. 9–13, corresponding to the last part of Simone da Roma's first chapter, "De la sua nobile progenia."

154. G fols. 13–21, corresponding roughly to Simone's brief hints in chap. 3, "De la sua caritate" (S 133). Then Giacomo displaces Simone's chap. 2, "Come entro in la sancta religione," and as a result gives the impression that Elena's chief virtue was charity and that it began to be manifested strongly before she entered the Hermits' Third Order.

155. G fols. 21–26; no equivalent in S. The conspirators against Paul II were accused of Epicureanism; see Pastor, *History* 4:484. Plato's reference to "his imitators" is striking: on a

John Chrysostom speaks about Angelo de Santo Severino's part in Elena's conversion. He identifies Angelo's sermon topic as the indulgences granted to those joining the order of Augustinian Hermits. Angelo officiated when Elena, accompanied by her sisters Profeta and Daniela, took the habit. John Chrysostom declares Elena's value as a model for women (*figura maternarum*), especially for the *vita contemplativa*. The marks of the contemplative, he says, are thinking always of God, seeking peace and quiet, keeping vigils, weeping in prayer, having the crucifix always before one's eyes, meditating on the psalms, and contemplating death.[156]

The sixth orator is Cato the Censor. His speech is the first of two praising Elena's virtues and attacking their sinful opposites. Cato dwells on four pairs of virtues and vices: avarice and generosity, *luxuria* and chastity, anger and peace, and pride and humility.[157]

Varro continues the epideictic on virtues in a negative key, by attacking envy, fraud, bloodshed, perfidy, flattery, astrology, and tyranny. He concludes with praise for Elena's flight from the world.[158]

Ephrem, author of sermons that were much copied in the Quattrocento, speaks in eighth place, returning from these topical considerations to the narrative of Elena's life. He recalls how she dispersed her belongings. She would rather leave her children than neglect Christ, whose sufferings she imitated by having her maid lead her bound hand and neck through the street to her sister Profeta's house. Ephrem concludes with a few words on humility.[159]

Lactantius continues on the subject of penitence. For this speech, Giacomo borrows heavily from Simone da Roma. He modulates Simone's vernacular to show that when Elena's ascetic practices were challenged, she accounted for them all with references to her past married life in comparison with Christ's suffering:

Padre mio, sapiade chomo io porto la corona de spini de ferro in capo per amor de le trezze cum argento et oro et perle ornate che lu mio marito portar in capo mi faceva et altri ornamenti, et per amor

trip to Rome by Marsilio Ficino (1433–1499) during Paul's papacy, see P. O. Kristeller, "Marsilio Ficino and the Roman Curia," in J. IJsewijn, ed., *Roma humanistica: Studia in honorem Iosaei Ruysschaert* (Louvain: University of Louvain, 1985), 85–87, and idem, *Supplementum Ficinianum* (Florence: Olschki, 1937), 2:89.

156. G fols. 26–31v; cf. Simone da Roma's chap. 2, "Come entro in la sancta religione (S 129–131).

157. G fol. 31v–40.

158. G fols. 40–44v.

159. G fols. 45–47; cf. S 133, chap. 3, "De la sua caritate," and 147, chap. 8, "De la sua grande povertade." See especially Tilatti's remarks, *Simone da Roma*, 150 n. 4, pointing out that this penitential reenactment probably predated Elena's entry into the Hermit's Third Order.

de quella corona non doro non dargento non de piere praetiosi, ma de spini pongenti in fin al cervello penetrante che per mio amor misser Iesu nel capo suo porto.

El cerchio de ferro intorno el collo porto per amor delle ornamenti che intorno al collo portava, et per amor di quella corda cum la quale per lo collo fo ligado il mio amor dolce Iesu, al Monte Calvario fo meando alla crudel morte della crose.

Li cerchi che porto nelle braze per amor delle franze che atorno le braza portava et per amor de quell corde co' le quali le man foron legate et conchiavate in croce al mio dolze amor misser Iesu.

Li cerchi nelle gambe porto per amore delle balli a li quali andava et per amor che li piedi del mio dolce Iesu cum chiodi furon foradi.

El cerchio del ferro porto cento per amor delle centure doro et argento che cente cum vanita in el saeculo portava. Et per amor de quellae corde colle quale el mio dolce Iesu alla colomna fo ligato.

My Father, you know how I bore the iron crown of thorns on my head for love of the tresses decorated with silver and gold and pearls that my husband made me wear on my head and other ornaments, and for love of that crown, not of gold, not of silver, not of precious stones, but of sharp spines penetrating all the way to his brain that for love of me Sir Jesus bore on his head.

The circle of iron around my neck I bear for love of the jewelry I wore around my neck and for love of that rope with which my sweet love Jesus was bound by the neck and led to Mount Calvary to the cruel death on the Cross.

The circlets I wear on my arms for love of the fringes that I wore around my arms and for love of those ropes with which the hands of my sweet love Sir Jesus were tied and nailed to the Cross.

The circlets on my legs I wear for love of the dances I used to go to and for love of the feet of my sweet Jesus, which were pierced with nails.

The circlet of iron I wear around my waist for love of the golden and silver belts I wore with vanity in the world. And for love of those ropes with which my sweet Jesus was tied to the column.[160]

In this passage, Giacomo retains the full sense of Simone's account, in which the details of Elena's *imitatio Christi* reveal each of her womanly delights reenacted in penitential mode. Thus the *arma Christi* become systematically feminized: metal bands or chains on her arms, neck, and waist

160. G fols. 48–52v; cf. S 136–137. A similar but less developed transvaluation of the *arma Christi* is found in the life of Clara of Rimini (Dalarun, *Lapsus linguae*, 23).

negate the jewelry and beautiful belts of her married years and affirm the ropes that tied Christ at the Passion. In this instance, too, the vernacular seems to create narrative verisimilitude, legal authority, and reliquary reverence. Indeed, the passage is so powerful that the author Giacomo drops his persona, interrupting Lactantius to declare that he himself has seen and touched the instruments of her penitence, precisely the relics evoked by her words: "I who am writing also saw and touched [these things] and am a willing witness" ("Vidi ego scribens et tetigi et libenter sum testimonio").[161]

Lactantius acknowledges that such extremes of penitential suffering are inexplicable. He considers the objection that Elena ought to have moderated her practice. But, on the authority of Jerome, Seneca, and John, he defends her, noting the sufferings of Isaiah, Daniel, Paul, Peter, and the martyrs and offering the concluding example of Democritus's self-inflicted blindness.

Hermas, author of *The Shepherd*, speaks in tenth place. He picks up Lactantius's quotation of Elena's own explanations for her penitential practice, realigning them to make a Stoic model. He justifies her hair shirt, the thirty-three pebbles in her shoes, and her bed of stones. She lived a harsher life than anyone except John the Baptist, admits Hermas, but her practice was nonetheless consonant with the philosopher's *mediocritas*, because there is no true service to God that transcends the bounds of prudence and reason. Hermas then turns to her diet, describing it in details beyond those given by Simone da Roma; he judges her achievement equal to Hercules' labors, to the penance of Jerome in the desert, and to the fasts of Elias, Daniel, and the apostles. Her reading was entirely devoted to "heavenly histories," *caelestiae historiae*. She read the Marian office and memorized the seven penitential psalms. She had many vernacular books but delighted especially in the *Ten Steps of Humility* and the *Mirror of the Cross*, alternating prayer with reading, as well as singing *laude*. At bedtime, she took up her image of Christ and smothered it with kisses, staring fixedly at the wounds "with the eyes of her soul." Sometimes she would have her maid tie her hands behind her back and lead her through the house, finally removing her hair shirt and tying her to a column, so that she might perceive Christ's sufferings. Hermas (who wrote in Greek) speaks in Latin when he recalls her justificatory speech for these enactments: "She also used to say, 'he suffered such things in order to make me his daughter, his heir'" ("ut me filiam suam, ut heredem faceret, talia passus est").[162]

---

161. G fol. 50–51v; cf. *S* 137; *E* fol. 66v.

162. G fols. 52v–61v; cf. *S* 136, 139, 142–143, and 162. On fasting, cf. *S* chap. 7, "Con quanta devotione receveva il Signore"; and Tilatti, *Simone da Roma*, 145, nn. 1 and 3. Note that chapter 7 of the rule edited by Tilatti, "La regola," does not include special provision for the Virgin's office, but for the offices of Augustine and Monica.

Pope Leo I speaks briefly about Elena's interactions with Church officials: she obtained permission from the provincial for a vow of silence rigorously pursued; she attended church regularly and made a pilgrimage to Rome for the Jubilee, during which she met with Nicholas V and obtained a plenary indulgence.[163]

The twelfth orator is Cyprian. He recalls how the devil tormented Elena, urging her to kill herself by throwing herself out a window or hanging herself, frightening her at home with noises, picking her up and forcefully throwing her down, chasing her through the house, and throwing her into the river as she went to church. At last, the devil broke her leg, leading to her final three bedridden years.[164]

John Cassian gives an *oriatiuncula* on the vision of Christ granted to Elena in this illness, as she described it to Profeta.[165]

The Venetian patrician Leonardo Giustinian is the last of the resurrected orators to join in the symposium. His topic is Elena's final confession and death. Giustinian identifies her confessor at this point as Leonardo da Udine, and he records that the Dominican knew she had predicted her death several days earlier. On her final day, she recited the penitential psalms and asked for extreme unction. The plenary indulgence granted by Nicholas V was read to her before she died. The women who prepared her body were moved by the evidence of her asceticisms. When they placed her crucifix on her chest, Elena's lifeless head rose up half a cubit. A Friar Franciscus spoke at her funeral mass. Everyone wanted to hear and memorize her *vita*. On the following night, as her body lay before the main altar in Santa Lucia, she appeared in splendor and asked that her body be buried in her oratory. All were moved by her memory and by the evidence of her piety revealed in the reliquary instruments of her self-inflicted suffering.[166]

The speakers have finished: the symposium is over. The ceremony returns now to God, who takes Elena's hand, welcoming her to heaven. He gives her a halo and then begins a tour of the "eternal Jerusalem" in that place called by astronomers "the tenth heaven." He points out all the ranks of angels, the blessed dead, and the bosom of Abraham, and his mother, Maria (*dulcissimam matrem meam*). Here, he says, is our household (*domus*), our community (*societas*), our court (*curia*), our city (*civitates*),

163. G fol. 61v–63. Cf. S, chap. 9, "Della sua solitaria uita, silentio et obedientia." On her oratory, see S 163, with Tilatti's n. 1. On her journey to Rome, see G fol. 62v.

164. G fols. 63–68v, based on S 153–159, chap. 10, "Delle tentatione a lei date a percussione dal diavolo," and 161–162, chap. 11, "De la sua patientia grandissima."

165. G fols. 68v–69; cf. S, chap. 12, "On her marvelous visions," in which Simone relates ten numbered visions.

166. G fols. 69v–71v; cf. S 175–178, "Del felice transito de la beata Helena," and 179–180, chap. 15, "Del suo obsequio."

our kingdom (*regia*)—and Elena is now a citizen (*civis effecta es*). She will be happy in this place where everyone is of one heart and soul, loving each other and praising God. There will be no old age, no suffering, and, after the Resurrection, God will return her youth.[167]

The atmosphere darkens, as God goes on to describe in vivid terms the events of the Last Day, when no explanations or justifications will suffice. On that day, shepherds, rustics, and illiterate people will take precedence over philosophers, orators, and the arguments of Cicero. First, God will speak harshly to the damned, condemning their refusal to heed his earlier calls; then, with a peaceful face, he will speak to the saints on his right and invite them to his kingdom.[168]

Finally, God turns back to Elena, remarking how her reputation has spread from Udine throughout Italy and the world. She will resound in letters like a trumpet: "velut tubicen litteris undique personab[is]."[169]

Suddenly, Cicero presses forward, seizing the opportunity of the gathering to appeal to Jerome and Lactantius to be his patrons. Will they intercede on his behalf with God so that his sufferings in hell might be ended or at least lightened? After all, they are his friends, and friendship should trump *patria*. And wasn't he the cause of their virtue and eloquence? What did he do that was so terrible, what sin did he commit? He always cherished ethics and right offices, living in the manner of a Stoic ("Stoyce semper vixi"). He begs them by their friendship, piety, and love, even by the *studia humanitatis* and their religion, to help him.[170]

Aristides seconds Cicero's plea by describing the sufferings of the damned.[171] It is more than they can bear, he complains, quoting Dante, John Scotus, Job, Augustine, Gregory, Virgil, Moses, Habakkuk, Daniel, Dives, and Peter Lombard to make his point. He concludes by begging Jerome for help. Jerome responds charitably, promising Cicero and Aristides that he will do what he can to improve their situations.[172]

Finally Elena speaks in Latin, looking the orators in the eyes, to thank them for their speeches. Giacomo concludes his *vita Helenae* with a brief *peroratio* asking for Paul's corrections.[173]

✳ ✳ ✳

167. G fols. 71v–77v.
168. G fol. 76r–v.
169. G fol. 77.
170. G fols. 77–78.
171. G fols. 78–82v.
172. G fols. 82v–93.
173. G fol. 83r–v.

Vestra vero voluptas, o Celse et Hilari, sint libri.
But let your pleasure, O Celso, O Ilarione, be books.
—Timoteo Maffei, *In sanctum rusticitatem*[174]

Giacomo's *vita Helenae utinensis* is odd on several counts. Its subject represents a model of sainthood that did not typically attract humanist composition. Its dedicatee was uninterested in contemporary sanctity, *tout court*, and favored a group, the Lateran Canons, who were unfriendly to the potential saint's order of Augustinian Hermits. (That Giacomo was concerned about this last problem is obvious: he chose not to include St. Augustine even as a guest, much less as a speaker, at the celestial celebration of Elena.)[175] But if Giacomo's choice of subject and dedicatee are puzzling, his choice of format is even more so. I have suggested that the collection of speeches indicates a desire to present Elena's life as a *convivium* or symposium: no one had ever written a saint's life as a symposium before—and no one would again. But the symposium hypothesis presents two difficulties. In the first place, although the *vita* proper is indeed told as a series of related orations, it is embedded in some more confused narrative: an opening scene of God's instructions, the tacked-on tour of heaven, God's discourse on the Last Judgment, and the histrionic exchange between Cicero and Jerome. Second, the basic rule of the classical symposium is verisimilitude, and Giacomo breaks it.

These two problems—the generic confusion of the vita Helenae and its flagrant inverisimilitude—encourage another interpretation of the account. Could the life be menippean satire?[176] Assigning the *vita* to that genre or antigenre allows many of its odd characteristics to fall into place: Giacomo's palpable delight in his own inventiveness; the plot device of an otherworldly journey; the radical shifts in diction, as exalted orators quote

---

174. De Corso, *Timoteo Maffei*, 183, ll. 1804–1805.

175. In the first preface, after the invocation of the poetic muses, Giacomo says, "Testor insuper te Augustinum et omnes sanctos qui huic religioni [the order remains unnamed] maximi praesident, nec non angelum, qui Helenae datus est custos et comes [a guardian angel not noted by any of the other extant authors or ever mentioned again by Giacomo], uires mea adiuuent mentemque perspiciant. Id negare non poterit Augustinus, cum illud idem a deo ipse expetierit, dum dixit 'Suscepit magnum opus et arduum, sed Deus adiutor noster erit' " (G fol. 1v). Giacomo mentions Augustine nineteen times in his account. Three of these instances are in the preface (fols. 1v–2). Of the remaining instances, only three concern Augustine's importance for the Hermits (fols. 26, 26v). Thus Giacomo's account stands in contrast to Simone da Roma's, which mentions Augustine frequently to the benefit of the Hermits.

176. E. P. Kirk, *Menippean Satire: An Annotated Catalogue of Texts and Criticism* (New York: Garland, 1980), section 5. Seneca's *Apocolocyntosis,* the only (near-) complete Roman example to survive, is the obvious candidate for Giacomo's model. It appears to have been Erasmus's model for the *Encomion moriae* (with which it was published in 1515). See Marcia Colish, "Seneca's *Apocolocyntosis* as a Possible Source for Erasmus' *Julius Exclusus,*" *RQ* 29, no. 3 (1976): 361–368.

Elena in her homely Venetian dialect; the incongruously heaped-up allusions, such as Plato's list of authorities in defense of Elena's opinion on the soul; and the mixture of prose and verse, as almost every orator, pagan as well as Christian, quotes the vernacular of Dante and Petrarch.[177] From this perspective, the *vita Helenae* appears to be a witness to the renewed attention, beginning with William of Malmesbury and continuing right through Erasmus, to Seneca's *Apocolocyntosis*, the apotheosis of Claudius.[178]

Menippean satire plausibly accounts for many aspects of the *vita Helenae* but seriously complicates the task of interpretation, for it raises the question of what Giacomo intended by this semitheatrical *ludus*. Did he come not to praise but to blame the pope's relative? Did Giacomo mock an elderly charismatic's *canonizatio* by recalling the bumbling emperor's *consecratio*?

I suspect that Giacomo did not intend critical satire. On the simplest level, it is hard to square the dedication to Paul II, which foregrounds the pope's kinship to Elena, with mocking intent. Giacomo's delight in his inventiveness is not conclusive proof of satire. The other elements I have noted—the otherworldly journey, the shifts in diction, the breadth of allusion, and the inclusion of verse from Dante and Petrarch—also signified honor and learning in the context of Renaissance culture.

Giacomo's intentions are best described as learned playfulness. Paul II enjoyed theatrical spectacles and even vernacular interruptions of work traditionally done in Latin (and anyone who had spent time in the multilingual Friuli might especially appreciate the complexity of Giacomo's linguistic registers). The pope's love of drama and linguistic sensibilities were held against him by Platina; Giacomo's *vita Helenae* may help us to assess the prejudice in that critique.

Giacomo was aware, however, that readers might well take offense. Halfway through the second preface, he represents a failure of nerve at the immodesty of his invention, interrupting the scene setting to defend himself:

> Neque enim dubito illos quibus Thimoteus librum de sancta rusticitate scripsit non minus impie quam imperite me repraehendere poetice rem sacram scripsisse. Nam si vitiosum esset rem etiam sacram simulare, canones, consuetudines prohibuissent, et expulissent poesim Cypri-

---

177. Giacomo's verse quotations are phrases rather than extensive displays such as occur in the *Apocolocyntosis*. See Peter Dronke, *Verse with Prose from Petronius to Dante: The Art and Scope of the Mixed Form* (Cambridge, Mass.: Harvard University Press, 1994), and Joel Relihan, *Ancient Menippean Satire* (Baltimore: Johns Hopkins University Press, 1994), on the formal requirements.

178. Seneca, *Apocolocyntosis*, ed. P. T. Eden (London: Cambridge University Press, 1984), 19–22. For guidance on menippean satire, I am grateful to my colleague Timothy Moore.

anum, Hieronimum, Lactantium, Hephrem ab aecclesia et eloquentiam. Antedictos introduxi loquentes non ut mentiar, uti poetae solent,
sed ut plenius et magis oratorie [oratoriae *cod.*] de vita sua dicere
liceret, ut maior laudis eius campus aperiretur.

I do not doubt that those to whom Timoteo [Maffei] wrote the book
On Holy Rusticity will reprehend me as both impious and unskilled
for writing up a sacred subject in an artful way [*poetice*]. But if it were
indeed wrong to write imaginatively of sacred material, it would be
prohibited by law and custom, and the poetry [*poesim*] of Cyprian,
Jerome, Lactantius, Ephrem would have to be expelled from the
Church along with their eloquence. I introduced the aforementioned
speakers not in order to lie—as poets are accustomed to do—but so
that it might be possible to speak more fully and oratorically about
her life, so that a greater field for her praise would be opened.[179]

In this staged moment of self-doubt, Giacomo shields his innovation by
referring to *In sanctam rusticitatem* by Timoteo Maffei (ca. 1415–1470).
The reference is a rich one. Timoteo Maffei had studied as a boy with the
humanist pedagogue Guarino Guarini in Verona; his interest in joining
orders was aroused by another student of Guarino's, the Franciscan
Alberto da Sarteano. But Timoteo did not become a Franciscan. Instead,
after postponing his entry into religion for some years, Timoteo was
received into the congregation of Reformed Regular Canons (just beginning to be called Lateran Canons) by a relative, Paolo Maffei. A widely
admired preacher—perhaps the most accomplished of the Lateran Canon
orators during the Quattrocento—Timoteo was also a teacher, helping to
form the Lateran Canons Matteo Bossi (d. 1502), Celso Maffei (d. 1508),
and Severino Calchi (d. 1500).[180] He served as prior of the Lateran Canons

179. G fol. 3v. See De Corso, *Timoteo Maffei*, 100–102, for a manuscript of Timoteo
Maffei's *In sanctam rusticitatem* written by Guarnerio d'Artegna (San Daniele del Friuli, Biblioteca Civica Guarneriana, MS 135). See, further, n. 183 below.

180. On Timoteo as a teacher, see De Corso, *Timoteo Maffei*, 19. On Matteo Bossi, see
C. Mutini, "Bosso, Matteo," *DBI* 13 (1971): 341a–344a, with bibliography. On Celso Maf-
fei, see Scipione Maffei, *Degli scrittori*, 176–181; P. Ghinzoni, "Altre notizie su don Celso
Maffei da Verona," *ASL* 10, no. 1 (1883): 85–97; Sabbadini, *Epistolario* 3:430–431; Lillian
Armstrong, "Opus Petri: Renaissance Miniatures in Venice and Rome," *Viator* 21 (1990),
402 n. 60 (which includes a list of his offices); and eadem, "Nicholas Jenson's Breviarum
Romanum, Venice 1478: Problems of Production and Distribution," *Incunabula: Essays in
Honor of Lotte Hellinga*, ed. Martin Davies (London: British Library Press, 1998, 421–467.
Celso Maffei was not an author of saints' lives; see hand list under Celso delle Falci. On Severino Calchi, see Widloecher, *La congregazione*, 332–333. Although Guarino referred in
some letters to Timoteo as a stellar preacher, he disapproved at length of one of Timoteo's
sermons, accusing the Lateran Canon of moral rigidity; see Sabbadini, *Epistolario*, letter 982
at 3:528–531. Timoteo was defended by Matteo Bosso.

at Rome and, after wisely turning down Nicholas V's offer of an episcopate at Milan, accepted Paul II's offer in Ragusa.[181] In that difficult out-
post, he died. *In sanctam rusticitatem,* his most ambitious extant work, is
dedicated to the humanist pope Nicholas V. Maffei sent a copy to Guarino Guarini, who wrote back with mild praise.[182] Giacomo da Udine himself probably had access to the dialogue through his fellow canon, Guarnerio d'Artegna.[183]

Giacomo may have calculated the value of a reference to *In sanctam
rusticitatem* for his dedicatee Paul II, for the pope admired Timoteo Maffei greatly.[184] But Giacomo may also have hoped that Maffei's message
would ground his own invention. Maffei's dialogue refers to many of the
same authorities named and used in the *vita Helenae.* For Maffei as for
Giacomo, Jerome is the *litterarum parens* whose writings resound with
"the verses of all the poets, with fables, *fabulis,* and with the opinions of
the orators."[185] Lactantius has a "swanlike, even heavenly grace" as he
quotes "from the comics, the poets, the satirists, the orators."[186] Cyprian's
writings show how "secular letters are hardly to be spurned or rejected by
learned and intelligent men and those seeking the blessed life, but rather
embraced, kissed, drunk deeply."[187] Thus Timoteo Maffei's *In sanctam
rusticitatem* allows Giacomo da Udine to claim that the *vita Helenae* safely
encapsulates secular learning into a religious work.[188]

But Giacomo's reference to *In sanctam rusticitatem* deepens the puzzle
of the *vita Helenae* by raising again the problem of religious affiliation. As
a cathedral canon at Aquileia, Giacomo was not a Lateran Canon.[189] Tim-

---

181. On Timoteo's appointments with the Lateran Canons, see Widloecher, *La congregazione,* 317–320 and 418–419; on Milan and Ragusa, see De Corso, *Timoteo Maffei,* 14
and n. 12, and 20.

182. Guarino's letter 828 in Sabbadini, *Epistolario* 2:545 with note in 3:427–431.

183. See n. 179 above. In San Daniele del Friuli, Biblioteca Civica Guarneriana, MS 135,
In sanctem rusticitatem occurs at fols. 79–123v. This codex was bound during Guarnerio's
lifetime; the first few gatherings are in his hand, but there is no note of ownership. On
Guarnerio's library, see n. 13 above. On the date of composition for Maffei's dialogue (c.
1450–1454), see De Corso, *Timoteo Maffei,* 60–62.

184. Pastor, *History* 4:66.

185. De Corso, *Timoteo Maffei,* 176, ll. 1519–1522.

186. Ibid., 177, ll. 1568–1572.

187. Ibid., 177, ll. 1583–1585.

188. Giacomo seems to share the outlook of the Lateran Canon Matteo Bosso, who
sought to fit classical learning to Christianity; see G. Soranzo, *L'umanista canonico regolare
lateranense Matteo Bosso di Verona 1427–1502: Il suoi scritti e il suo epistolario* (Padua:
Libreria Gregoriana, 1965).

189. The status of reform at the cathedral chapter in Quattrocento Aquileia is unclear; no
Udinese church adhered to the Lateran observancy, although a Giovanni da Udine occurs
among the canons resident at the Lateran in the summer of 1451 (Widloecher, *La congregazione,* 375). Camarosano, *Il medioevo,* 177–180, notes that the canons at Aquileia were

oteo Maffei, however, was a Lateran Canon, a member of the *ordinis sancti Augustini,* the order of St. Augustine, which was at odds with Elena's order, that *ordinis sancti Augustini* known as the Augustinian Hermits.[190] Moreover, *In sanctam rusticitatem* presents three interlocutors who are also Regular Canons. Paolo Maffei, the senior and chief speaker, is addressed by two novices, Celso Maffei and an unidentified Ilarione. Paolo and Celso, like the author Timoteo, were from Verona; they would have had no patriotic interest in Elena. And none of the three speakers would have had sympathy for Elena da Udine as a tertiary of the Augustinian Hermits, nor would they have supported the Hermits in an attempt to wrest a canonization from the papacy.

Perhaps that is the point: Giacomo da Udine's *vita Helenae* could be of no use for a canonization process. Indeed, the idea is ludicrous. Not only was the format terribly wrong, but also Elena's case was, in contemporary terms, desperately weak. The problem went beyond the fact that she was an elderly unlearned matron from a part of the peninsula where the Observancy was new. She was not attached to the powerful saint-creating orders of Dominic or Francis. Although she had had many confessors, no confessor wrote up her experience, even in notes. There is no contemporary Latin *vita*—that prime requirement for a serious application—extant today. The author who did write about her in Latin (or mostly Latin) was a cathedral canon who trotted out the writings of a Lateran Canon about a conversation among Lateran Canons to defend his inventive retelling of the life. This cathedral canon did not include St. Augustine among the speakers or the guests in his narrative. The dedicatee was a defender of Lateran Canons, not

---

reformed in the twelfth and thirteenth centuries; the new requirements suggest regular canons. See also letters from Ludovico Foscarini to a "Reverendissimus pater episcopus Friulanensis"—Cardinal Trevisan—and a Regular Canon Fulgentius (Vienna, Österreichisches Nationalbibliothek, MS Lat. 441, fols. 232r and 242v–243v). These are without year, but presumably date from 1439 when Foscarini was lieutenant of the Friuli. In the first, Foscarini claims that the Udinese are often and hotly begging for the "religiosos canonicos sancti Augustini" to stay longer among them. From the second it becomes evident that these Augustinian canons are more likely to go to Venice than stay in the Friuli: "Dulcis est, fateor, Venetiis sanctorum fratrum regularium quies et consuetudo" (242v). Are these canons the group on hardship leave from Aquileia (n. 13 above)? Should we read here any signs of an incipient Augustinian Observancy among the canons of Aquileia?

190. For a contemporary document that refers to Maffei simply as belonging to "the order of St. Augustine," see De Corso, *Timoteo Maffei,* 20 n. 41. As teacher of Celso Maffei and Severino Calchi, and as the man who brought Eusebio Corradi into the Lateran Canons, Timoteo also contributed indirectly to the asperity of the Canons' polemic against the Hermits that began about 1475, as described by Elm, *"Augustinus Canonicus—Augustinus Eremita."*

Hermits. Giacomo may therefore implicitly acknowledge Paul's opposition to contemporary canonizations at the same time he honors the pope's virtuous relative.

Giacomo's concern cannot have been to promote Elena's canonization, although he probably did want to promote wider recognition of an Udinese *santa viva* and, of course, of his own talents. We might even speculate that Giacomo was himself the leading edge of a Lateran Canon reform movement planned for Aquileia. Certainly, his reference to *In sanctam rusticitatem* suggests a focused desire: Giacomo meant to contribute to the education debate. He was, in a sense, promoting the contents of Guarnerio d'Artegna's library. As both humanism and religious reform made headway in the Friuli, he was enacting the program of Basil's *On Studies*. This interpretation suggests that, for all its lack of sophistication, we should see the *vita Helenae* as a real feat: Giacomo makes an *idiota* the first line of defense for the use of classical literature in the training of religious. Elena's exemplarity and historicity are of little interest. Instead, she is the vehicle for a flashy statement of educational propriety.

Giacomo's playful and learned mixture of genres also helps to fill out our image of Paul II. The *vita Helenae* recalls us strongly to Roberto Weiss's project of discerning just how that pope related to the cultural currents around him, especially to the humanist literati. If the dedication is indeed significant, then Paul seems to have been attempting a delicate position that would admit classics, but keep them well within the bounds of early Church usage—that is, the usage of the empire rather than the republic.

The case of Elena thus reveals several important aspects of *vitae et passiones* composed by humanists. First, a humanist might choose a subject in every apparent way his opposite: not a man but a woman; not someone dedicated to the *vita activa* but someone embodying late medieval charism and the *vita contemplativa*; not a product of the *studia humanitatis* but an *illiterata*. But, second, he would do so only in exceptional circumstances. A soft version of those exceptional circumstances can be seen in the accounts of Elena by Jacopo Filippo Foresti (who wrote to support a holy woman of his own order) and Giovanni Garzoni (who wrote, as a learned layman, to please a Hermit friend). Thanks to the survival of Giacomo's experiment, we can also gauge the hard or extreme circumstances. In his willingness to take experimentation to the limit for a member of the pope's family whose ties to the Friuli remain to be fully explored, Giacomo da Udine demonstrates most forcefully that the century preceding the Reformation was a period of wide-ranging experiment that met with exceptional—unprecedented—tolerance. Third, the radical quality of this experiment indicates that traditional representations of the most widely accepted medieval virtues were no longer compelling. In the next chapter, I will examine how, in a series of contexts where less experimentation was possible but the personal import of the text's success was overwhelming, an author might formulate a different response to the need for new representations.

apud Deum sollicitus pia tamen concer
tatione / du; se domino sic obtemperare
suo putat / sanctoq; spiritu pariter instigatur.

Deo gratias.

*Adsit nobis quesumus pne sanctos susti
et Clementis assidua protectio; fi
quorum devote per agimus solem
nitatem, eor precibus subleuemur
P. D. K.*

Hæc officia ut in uniuersali ecclesia dici
possint auctoritate apostolica p breue
Leonis. X. die. y. Nouembris. M. cccc.
xix. concessum. In ecclia uero Volaterrana & tota dioecesi mandatum.

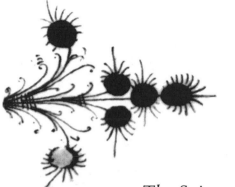

CHAPTER 6

The Saint as Author

Ex eius imitatione pariter ac laude magis proficere valeamus.

Both by imitating and by praising him, we shall become capable of greater things.

—Raffaele Maffei (1455–1522), preface to the life of Jacobus Certaldus[1]

In early 1507 Raffaele Maffei retired from Rome to the family home at Volterra.[2] The small town to the southwest of Florence is still beautiful today; beyond its walls the green hills stretch for miles. For Raffaele, born and educated in Rome, the vista induced a sense

1. *AASS* April II (Paris, 1865): 153, collated with MSS *A* and *B* (see n. 105 below).
2. The date is worked out by John D'Amico, "A Humanist Response to Martin Luther: Raffaele Maffei's Apologeticus," *Sixteenth-Century Journal* 6, no. 2 (1975): 39. On Raffaele, see Angelo Marucci, "Maffei, Raffaele," in L. Lagoro, dir., *Dizionario di Volterra, 3, I personaggi e gli scritti* (Ospedaletto: Pacini, 1997); Pio Paschini, "Teologia umanistica," *RSCI* 11 (1957): 254–256; idem, "Una famiglia di curiali: I Maffei di Volterra," *RSCI* 7 (1953): 337–376; B. L. Ullman, "The Maffei Codices," *Studies in the Renaissance* (Rome: Edizioni di storia e letteratura, 1955): 373–382; B Falconcini, *Vita dal nobil uomo . . . Raffaele Maffei* (Rome, 1722); John D'Amico, "The Raffaele Maffei Monument in Volterra," in J. Hankins, J. Monfasani, and F. Purnell, eds., *Supplementum Festivum: Studies in Honor of Paul Oskar Kristeller* (Binghamton, N.Y.: MRTS, 1987): 468–489; and *Renaissance Humanism in Papal Rome: Humanists and Churchmen on the Eve of the Reformation* (Baltimore: Johns Hopkins University Press, 1983).

of exile.[3] Moving to Volterra, he left behind the papal chancery, where he had served for three decades as *scriptor apostolicus*, shaped by the paradox of a clerical life at once dependent on the venality of office and desirous of reform.[4] He left behind his prestigious confraternity of Santo Spirito in Sasso, the familiar neighborhoods with their classical ruins, and his affectionate male friendships.[5] His clerical brother, Mario (1463–1537), also born in Rome and witty enough to have been recalled in the discussion of *bons mots* in book 2 of Baldassare Castiglione's *Courtier*, stayed in the city.[6] He was to mind family connections, to manage Raffaele's career in print and his own in the Church, and to deal in offices and property. Although Raffaele had chosen to exclude himself from that worldly bustle, he sometimes regretted the decision to leave Rome.

3. In a letter to Adriano Castellesi, Raffaele says "Romam meam in qua et natus et educatus sum revisere cupio" (BAV, MS Ottob. Lat. 2377, fols. 208v–209). The letter is undated but was written at some point after May 31, 1503, to judge from the address to Castellesi as "S. Chysogoni Cardinal." Raffaele recorded in his *Commentariorum Libri*, (Rome: Besicken, 1506) book 26, at fol. 246v, that he had studied with the elderly George of Trebizond and with Domizio Calderini and, at 214v, with Lilius Tifernas. On *exilium*, see Raffaele's marginal note in his own copy of his translation of Xenophon's *Oeconomicus*, held at VBG, and n. 33 below.

4. Thomas Frenz, *Die Kanzlei der Päpste der Hochrenaissance (1471–1527)* (Tübingen: Niemeyer, 1986), 438, entry 2015 (papal scriptor but apparently not abbreviator); D'Amico, *Renaissance Humanism*, 82, dates his entry to 1468; Frenz, to 1469. Raffaele's father and his older brother, Antonio, also held chancery positions. Raffaele continued to draw income from this position until 1514, according to Frenz, that is, long after his retirement to Volterra. He began as a cleric but married to become, as José Ruysschaert, "Recherche de deux bibliothèques romaines Maffei des XVe et XVIe siècles," *La Bibliofilia* 60 (1958): 311, notes, a *clericus coniugatus*; the marriage probably occurred shortly after the death of his sibling Antonio (1478), as Raffaele then became the eldest surviving brother (cf. D'Amico, *Renaissance Humanism*, 83). He worried in a letter of June 8, 1483, to Niccolò Lisci at Avignon, that his wife, Tita, was sterile; see VBG, MS 5377, in a file marked "1473–1521 Raffaello a diversi." The letter helps to date the marriage, usually assigned to some time between 1480 and 1490. Raffaele's concerns were gainsaid by the birth of a daughter, Lucilla, for whom he cared deeply. For her dowry, one thousand gold florins, see VBG, Arch. Maffei, A 05 M2. I am grateful to Angelo Marrucci and Luca Pini of the Biblioteca Guarnacciana for their patient assistance.

5. He had joined the confraternity, which was more honorific than active, on June 3, 1478; see Paschini, "Una famiglia," 345, drawing on P. Egidi, *Necrologi . . . della provincia romana* (Rome, 1908) 2:396, for the date of entry given in the *Liber fraternitatis*. Other important members, some of whom will reappear below, were Jacopo Gherardi (Egidi, *Necrologi*, 139), Agostino Chigi (153), Antonio Zeno (157), Cristoforo Sacromoro (201), and Adriano Castellesi (275). For Raffaele's participation in religious processions in Rome, see Paschini, "Una famiglia," 352; Florio Banfi, "Raffaelo Maffei in Ungheria," *L'Europa orientale*, n.s., 17 (1937): 466 n. 5.

6. On Mario Maffei, whose career included the episcopacies of Aquino (1516–1525) and Cavaillon (1525–1537) but not a cardinalate, see Luigi Pescetti, "Mario Maffei," *Rassegna volterrana* 6, 2, 10 (1932): 65–90; D'Amico, *Renaissance Humanism, ad indicem*; and Angelo Marani, "Maffei, Antonio," in Lagoro, *Dizionario* 3: 1094–1095. Pescetti gives several instances of Mario's wit, e.g., as recorded in Beroaldo's poetry and in Castiglione's *Courtier*. On Mario's witticisms about saints, see below.

Nevertheless, Raffaele left with a plan. In his frequent visits to Volterra before 1507, he had passed the time comfortably with his extended family, often entertaining out-of-town guests.[7] Now, except for the occasional outing to investigate Etruscan archaeology, Raffaele curtailed these pleasures.[8] He turned his patronage to local churches and convents.[9] He restricted his diet and dressed plainly.[10] He lived chastely, spending time apart from his wife and daughter. By feeding Raffaele only bits of mail, the family seems to have shielded him from the more venal aspects of Mario's trafficking in the city.

Raffaele was pursuing sanctity. "Cutting short the course of his previous life," he modeled his new one on the ascetic and scholarly withdrawal of Jerome and on the familial retreats, attentive to relics and chapels and writing, of the Cappadocians Basil of Caesarea, his brother Gregory of Nyssa, and their friend Gregory of Nazianzus.[11] Contemporaries acknowledged the

7. See Banfi, "Raffaelo Maffei," 465, for a list of some guests; D'Amico, "Maffei Monument," 472, with reference.

8. See, e.g., the letter from Raffaele to Piero Soderini, dated "Volterris V Idus Junii [July 11] 1508" (BAV, MS Barb. lat. 2517, fol. 7r–v), describing a rainy day visit to see Etruscan remains, some of which reminded him of martyrs' tombs at Rome.

9. For example, he appears to have arranged funding for a convent of San Lino in Volterra already in 1480; in 1513 it received a rule confirmed by Leo X; in 1517–1518 it was formally enclosed (Falconcini, Vita, 90–98). Raffaele collected holy women from other localities for the foundation (Falconcini, Vita, 100–101). In his will of 1516, Raffaele set aside money for his daughter, Lucilla; it was to go to the convent of Santa Elisabeta if she died without children (Falconcini, Vita, 208–209). But did Raffaele himself join an order? Pescetti, "Mario Maffei," 66 n. 1, states that by 1506 Raffaele had "già da tempo" entered the Augustinian Order (i.e., the Hermits) and was living in Volterra as an anchorite. Pescetti's source is Falconcini, Vita, which mixes scholarship, hagiography, and campanilismo in a way difficult to control. Others have gathered from Raffaele's patronage of San Lino, from his vita of the Franciscan tertiary Umiliana dei Cerchi (discussed below), and from the flanking image of Gherardo at his tomb that he, like that saint, was a Franciscan tertiary. I have found no explicit documentation on either point. Two things, however, seem worthy of consideration: first, that Raffaele intentionally cast himself as the friend of many orders and, second, that the lack of clarity about his affiliation strikingly recalls the situation of religious women in this period (see the discussion in chap. 5 above).

10. On Raffaele's abstinence, see Mario Maffei's letter to Giacomo Giasolario, August 10, 1508, cited by Falconcini, Vita, 161: Raffaele has not died but "valet atque vivit in summa rerum omnium abstinentia." On Raffaele's modestly penitential clothing, see ibid, 154.

11. For the Cappadocian model of conversion and retirement to family estates, see Philip Rousseau, Basil of Caesarea (Berkeley: University of California Press, 1994) and John A. McGuckin, St. Gregory of Nazianzus: An Intellectual Biography (Crestwood, N.Y.: St. Vladimir's Seminary Press, 2001). I adapt the quotation from Basil's De spiritu sancto 15 given in Rousseau, Basil, 17. For the Cappadocian model of the anchoring, memorious women of the family, see ibid., 9–10; it has relevance for Maffei. See also Arnaldo Momigliano, "Life of St. Macrina by Gregory of Nyssa," reprinted in his On Pagans, Jews, and Christians (Middletown, Conn.: Wesleyan University Press, 1987), 206–221, from J. W. Eadie and J. Ober, eds., The Craft of the Ancient Historian: Essays in Honor of Chester G. Starr (Lanham, Md.: University Press of America, 1985), 443–458. For a humanist translation of Macrina's life, see the hand list under "Balbi, Pietro."

change. Raffaele's close friend, the Augustinian Hermit Egidio da Viterbo (1469–1532), admired the holy learning and learned holiness ("sanctissimam doctrinam et doctrinam sanctitatem") of his retirement; Egidio wished to imitate such a consonance of life and rhetoric.[12] Another friend, Cardinal Adriano Castellesi (c. 1458–1521/1522), spoke respectfully about the scholarly aspect of Raffaele's pious withdrawal.[13] Leaving Rome did not, in other words, mean abandoning the *res publica litterarum*, for letters could soften the ascetic's harsh little nest, *nidulus horridus,* in Volterra.[14] Indeed, throughout the last fifteen years of his life, as the new *forma vitae* tested his resolve, Raffaele maintained his correspondence, keeping up with contemporary events in Rome and elsewhere.[15] And he began to write in early Christian forms.

When Raffaele died, contemporaries recognized his *fama sanctitatis,* his reputation for sanctity His brother Mario promoted that reputation, planning a grand tomb that represents an unrealistically emaciated scholar.[16] Reclining on his side, the marble Raffaele lifts the elegantly draped upper half of his body. He rests his weight on his right elbow, turning his severely capped head thoughtfully toward the high altar. Behind him stands his name saint, the Archangel Raphael; at his feet, the family saint Gherardo

12. Egidio's letter of 1513 is in BAV, MS Ottob. lat. 2377, fol. 221v: this letter is not included in the important collections edited by Anna Maria Voci Roth and Clare O'Reilly. Leo X called Raffaele "alter nostri temporis et doctrina et vitae sanctitate Hieronymus," according to Raffaele's son-in-law Paolo Riccobaldo Maffei; see VBG, MS 5376, "Lettere di Paolo Maffei," second letter, undated but after Raffaele's death. Tommaso Inghirami, writing to Raffaele's wife Tita after her husband's death, dwelled especially on his exemplarity: "dovemi sforzarmi con ogni opera d'immitare quella felicissima memoria, ed in le elemosine e in le altre sue cristianissime e lodatissime opere" (Falconcini, *Vita,* 209–210).

13. Castellesi's letter of 1513 is given in Falconcini, *Vita,* 170–171: "urbana fastidia fugiens, ut in patria quietior bonarum artium studio, quae semper a te diligentissime culta sunt, operam dares."

14. The Latin phrase, along with a clear statement of spiritual intent, appears in Raffaele's dedicatory letter to Mario Maffei preceding the translation of several homilies by Basil the Great, *Divi Basilii Magni . . . opera* (Rome: Jacopo Mazzochi, 1515), fol. 58: "in nidulum [h]orridum ac patrium tua et amicorum uenia me conieci, non tam ut eius amorem—sicut Ulyxes immortalitati—quam ut rebus omnibus immortalitatem latitando et aequo tantum comitatus animo praeferrem." Mario probably revised or even wrote this letter (n. 38 below), and so the phrase should be considered part of Mario's promotion of his brother's sanctity.

15. The most striking example of Raffaele's continuing engagement in contemporary debates even during retirement (Jerome, of course, was a good model for that), is his reply to Luther, styled from the *Nasum Romanum.* See Luca D'Ascia, "Martin Lutero e *il genio romano: L'Apologeticus* di Raffaele Maffei: Studi ed edizione," *Rivista di storia e letteratura religiosa* 29 (1993): 107–154. Raffaele considered having the *Apologeticus* printed: see VBG, MS 5376, a collection of loose papers preceding *filze,* a letter from his brother Mario to Raffaele, dated 22 December 1521.

16. Rolf Bagemihl, "Cosini's Bust of Raffaello Maffei and Its Funerary Context," *Metropolitan Museum Journal* 31 (1996): 45–46, describing changes that Cosini made as he moved from the bust to the tomb sculpture. I thank Professor Bagemihl for sending an offprint.

Cagnoli. Below is Mario's epitaph, which makes the claim for Raffaele's saintliness in antique majuscule: "To [the memory of] the servant of Christ Raffaele Maffei, son of Gherardo Maffei, for piety and sanctity worthy to be compared with any of the ancients, as his outstanding miracles bear witness. He lived 70 years. He died in the year of salvation 1513, 7 kalends of February. Mario Maffei Bishop of Cavaillon, peace to his holy brother."[17] In conventional terms, too, Raffaele was perceived as saintly: his body remained uncorrupted for several years, and the nuns at the convent of San Lino, which he had endowed, kept his hairshirt as a relic, recording its miraculous powers.[18] The Bollandists, in the late seventeenth century, spoke of Raffaele as a *beatus*; his eighteenth-century biographer, Benedetto Falconcini, wrote to encourage something more.

Today, Raffaele's ambitions to be a saint are nearly forgotten, as are his handful of *vitae sanctorum*. In the context of this study, both deserve attention. Preceding chapters have shown humanist authors concerned to present sanctity in an effective format, aware that through their own rhetorical training they might change a life or even save the Church. Thus they focused on types of sanctity, such as martyrs and bishops, that mattered to their audiences; they tried out unfamiliar methods of organization, such as new chronologies that underscored parallels between secular and religious heroism; they engaged students in thinking about the literary possibilities of saintly narratives, using novel formats to promote classical education and classical language to promote novel subjects among those who would normally be resistant. Raffaele Maffei was similarly thoughtful about the connections between persuasive speech and exemplary sanctity. His reasons were, however, more intimate than those examined so far: Raffaele thought about *vitae et passiones* as aids to his own ascetic self-fashioning.[19] For a humanist trying to emulate the life of a saint in the last years of his life, what sorts of narratives were most helpful? What would such a person read, and what would he write?

❀ ❀ ❀

17. The Latin is given by D'Amico, "The Raffaele Maffei Monument," 480 n. 44.

18. Falconcini, *Vita*, 97.

19. In "Writing as Devotion: Hagiographical Composition and the Cult of the Saints in Theodoret of Cyrrhus and Cyril of Scythopolis," *Church History* 66 (1997): 707–719; and "Hagiography as an Ascetic Practice in the Early Christian East," *Journal of Religion* 79 (1999): 216–232, Derek Krueger reads humility tropes as ritual acts to argue that they explicitly encourage the writing of saints' lives as ascetic self-fashioning. He discusses not just Cyril and Theodoret but also John Moschus, Leontius of Neapolis, Anthony of Choziba, and Palladius. Most of these authors were available to Renaissance readers of Greek such as Maffei. The Cappadocian model is again relevant; see below.

*Venit in mentem Basilii opere convertere, quum omnibus beate vitae incensis
magnopere profutura.*

I think I will translate the works of Basil, because they will be of great use to all
who burn for the blessed life.

—Raffaele Maffei to Sigismondo de'Conti[20]

When he moved permanently to Volterra, Raffaele chose a new literary
direction to suit his new life. In Rome, he had published the encyclopedic
Commentariorum libri.[21] He had translated Xenophon's *Oeconomicus,*
dedicating it to his wife, Tita.[22] He had written on Aristotle's *Ethics* and
Politics,[23] translated three books of the *Iliad,*[24] and completed a Latin version of Procopius's *Persian Wars.*[25] Now, in Volterra, he turned to Christian doctrinal, polemical, and devotional literature. The change was not
immediate: in the first few years at home, he completed a prose and verse
translation of the *Odyssey,*[26] and helped to edit Paolo Cortesi's *De cardinalatu* after the author's death.[27] Neither, Raffaele let on, was the shift par-

20. VBG, MS 5377, "Raffaello a Diversi," letter 12 (see n. 34 below for the full quotation).

21. Rome: Besicken, 1506. A letter of July 1506 from Piero Soderini praises an "opus
absolutum" (Paschini, "Una famiglia," 353, suggests that the *Commentarii* are meant) and
urges Raffaele to greater things (BAV, MS Barb. Lat. 2517, fol. 7; cf. MS Ottob. lat. 2377,
fol. 222, for a fragment).

22. The imprint was folded into the *Commentarii* (preceding note). There is a contemporary manuscript copy in BAV, MS Ottob. lat. 1649, fols. 1–60 (see Ruysschaert,
"Recherche," 309 n. 3). David Marsh, "Xenophon," *CTC* 7:179–180, notes this manuscript,
as well as the published editions from 1506 to 1559, and edits the letter of dedication (which
is, compared to most humanists' dedicatory letters, so atypically intimate as to name Raffaele's daughter).

23. On the *Ethics* and *Politics,* see Kristeller, *Iter,* 6:308a (not seen). Raffaele recalls his
interest in the *Ethics* in the prefatory letter to Mario in the Basil translation (above, n. 15;
discussed below).

24. On Maffei's Latin hexametrical translation of books 1 and 2 of the *Iliad,* see Renata
Fabbri, ed., *Iliados Libri I, II: A Raphaele Volaterrano Latine Versi* (Padua: Antenore, 1984),
based on the autograph in BAV, MS Capp. 169.

25. Completed by November 1506, the Procopius was seen through the press by Mario
in 1509; see the letter to Mario of November 4, 1506 (MBA, MS S 92 sup., fols. 60v–61v).
On June 7, 1509, Raffaele sent Piero Soderini a copy; cf. Banfi, "Raffaelo Maffei," 468. Falconcini, *Vita,* 119–123, edits the dedicatory letter. Raffaele did not translate Procopius's *Vandal Wars,* but Cristoforo Persona's translation of the *Vandal Wars* is frequently bound with
Raffaele's *Persian Wars.*

26. In 1510 Mario also nursed this translation of the *Odyssey* into print. Raffaele's letter
of dedication to his son-in-law, Paolo Riccobaldi del Bava Maffei, is edited by Fabbri, *Iliados;* see G. N. Knauer's entry, "Homer," forthcoming in *CTC.*

27. Paolo Cortesi was Raffaele's brother-in-law, since Cortesi's sister had been married
to Raffaele's older brother, Antonio. On Raffaele's work editing Cortesi's *De cardinalatu* in
1510, see John D'Amico, "Papal History and Curial Reform in the Renaissance: Raffaele

ticularly smooth: the *sacra volumina* initially excited a certain disgust, *rancidula stomacho*.[28] Contemporaries would have caught his allusion to Augustine's youthful misgivings about the language of the Bible and to Jerome's famous dream of being beaten before the throne of God for his admiration of Cicero.[29] But, in truth, Raffaele's literary conversion was longer in the making than he admitted. Well before leaving Rome, he had decided to initiate a new life by translating the homilies of Basil the Great (d. 397), the Cappadocian father and bishop of Caesarea, himself honored as a learned saint.

There is evidence that, as early as the winter of 1501, Raffaele wanted to borrow Vatican codices for this project. His intention to retire to Volterra was already known, however, and removing manuscripts from the city was discouraged.[30] So he turned to his godfather, Sigismondo de' Conti da Foligno (d. 1512), the papal secretary, for help.[31] "[Basil's homilies] are in the Vatican Library in two separate volumes, half torn and consumed with age," he wrote. "Because you have so much influence with the pope [Alexander VI, 1492–1503], I want you to ask him for them in my name."[32] In a later draft of this letter, anticipating difficulties, Raffaele

---

Maffei's *Brevis Historia* of Julius II and Leo X," *Archivum Historiae Pontificiae* 18 (1980): 163; d'Amico, *Renaissance Humanism*, 73; Giacomo Ferraù, "Politica e cardinalato in un'età di transizione: Il *De cardinalatu* di Paolo Cortesi," in S. Gensini, ed., *Roma capitale (1447–1527)* (Pisa: Pacini, 1994), 519–540; and Ingrid Rowland, *The Culture of the High Renaissance: Ancients and Moderns in Sixteenth-Century Rome* (New York: Cambridge University Press, 1998), 256 and n. 8, and, on Cortesi in general, *ad indicem*.

28. "Ad sacra volumina confugi, quae quam meo prius rancidula stomacho sunt visa, apto quidem pharmaco excussi purgavique," again, from the prefatory letter to the edition of Basil (n. 14 above). For Raffaele's further thoughts on *sermo simplex*, see *Stromata* (discussed below), book 1, chap. 17 (BAV, MS Barb. lat. 753, fol. 23r-v), "Quod diapphonia [simulque] rudiis dicendi modus in eloquio sacro ad fidem faciant."

29. Augustine, *Confessions*, book 3, chap. 5; Jerome, Epistle 22, 30.

30. The lending policy of the library was becoming increasingly strict; see Maria Bertola, "Codici latini di Niccolò V perduti o dispersi," in *Mélanges Eugène Tissérant* VI, i, (Studi e testi 236) (Vatican City, 1964), 129–140, for some good reasons why.

31. On this letter, see D'Amico, *Renaissance Humanism*, 191; and especially Vittore Branca and Manlio Pastore Stocchi, "La seconda centuria dei Miscellanea di Angelo Poliziano," in *Mélanges Eugène Tissérant* 6, 1 (Studi e testi 236), 146–147 and n. 12, working from BAV, MS Barb. lat. 2517, fol. 12r-v (undated).

32. Branca and Stocchi, "La seconda centuria," date the letter to late 1501 on the basis of Conti's retirement as papal secretary to Alexander VI on January 4, 1502. I follow that dating here, but it may be too early. Conti's influence need not have ended with his retirement, and his real influence was not so much with Alexander as with his successor, Julius II; R. Ricciardi, "Conti, Sigismondo," *DBI* 28 (1983): 471a, dates Conti's friendship with Cardinal Giuliano delle Rovere to at least to 1480. In this letter to Conti, Raffaele says that he is *in exilio*. He must therefore have been in Volterra, either on one of his frequent visits or in retirement.

added: "It's not unheard-of [res nova] for books of this sort to travel [peregrinare], if there is good reason. Poliziano had several under [Pope] Innocent [VIII], at Lorenzo de'Medici's request. And," added Raffaele, "you will be praised for your involvement in this matter."[33]

Sigismondo evidently managed to persuade not Alexander but his successor Julius II (1503-1513). The register of the Vatican Library records that Raffaele borrowed two volumes of Basil's homilies in Greek on September 11, 1506, roughly three months before his exodus from Rome.[34] As these manuscripts were not returned until October 10, 1510, more than four years later, Raffaele apparently carried them off in his baggage to Volterra, just as had been feared.[35] Pilgrim volumes came at a cost, however; the conditions of Raffaele's pledge were uniquely severe. In 1506, he signed the register in his own hand, seconded by a guarantor, and he left forty ducats with the librarian as a pledge "in case the book is not returned."[36]

Raffaele claims to have completed the translation of the homilies in less than a year, "non toto vertente anno."[37] That turning year was probably

---

33. Jacopo da Volterra (Gherardi) is named as the person who will see to the transporting of the manuscripts. The letter is extant in an early draft in VBG, MS 5377, "1473-1521 Raffaello a diversi," letter to Sigismundus Fulginatus, lacking signature, place, and date. This Volterra draft finds Raffaele *tristius* and *desidiosius*, lamenting his time in Volterra as *exilium*. I quote from BAV, MS Barb. lat. 2517 (see n. 31 above), regularizing punctuation and capitalization and recording the three major variants between the Vatican and Volterra manuscripts:

> Venit in mentem Basilii opera convertere qum omnibus tum amore beatae vita incensis magnopere profutura. Ea sunt in biblioteca vaticana a duobus sparsa voluminibus semilaceris pre vetustate ac consumptis. Velim [*BAV canc:* ea] meo nomine ex pontifice [*BAV canc.:* potas] [*BAV:* apud quem tua maxime pollet auctoritas] ea petas, munus profecto non tam roganti quam rogato gloriam adlaturum [*Volterra:* ut per diploma bibliothecae custodibus mandet, ea Iacobo Volaterrano tradi, de reddendis infra semestre prius unde accepto]. Res non admodum nova libros huiuscemodi quandoque honesta de causa peregrinari. Politianus sub Innocentio [*BAV:* Laurentio Medice instante] nonnullos habuit. Laudibus etiam tuis adcedet qum causa tam honesti fueris laboris.

See Jeanne Bignami Odier, *La bibliothèque vaticane de Sixte IV à Pie XI: Recherches sur l'histoire des collections manuscrits* (Studi e testi 272) (Vatican City, 1973), 27–30.

34. Maria Bertola, *I due primi registri di prestito della Biblioteca apostolica vaticana, codici vaticani latini 3964, 3966* (Vatican City, 1898; reprint, 1972), reproducing MS Vat. lat. 3966, fol. 84r–v, with transcription at 106–107. Cf. D'Amico, *Renaissance Humanism,* 191.

35. The date of restitution in Bertola, *I due primi registri,* 106–107.

36. Preceding note. For another manuscript, unspecified, that was lent to Raffaele, see the undated entry in Bertola, *I due primi registri,* 107. Bertola proposes that this second codex was returned by 1512.

37. This claim occurs in the dedicatory letter found in the printed edition of Basil's homilies in Maffei's translation (see n. 54 below for the date of publication). But there is no such letter in his dedication manuscript (BAV, MS Ottob. lat. 2377, autograph). I suspect that Mario had a hand in the printed dedication. See Rome, BN, MS Autograf., letter A 92 6/1, dated September 24, 1515: Mario explains to Raffaele that he has made changes in a dedicatory letter, which seems to be this one, and thanks his brother for the dedication.

1507–1508 (1508–1509?), just as he spoke of beginning a translation of Dio Chrysostom.[38] He worked on the homilies quickly because he was excited about the project, "such great desire burned" in him to complete the translation of Basil, and because his friend Piero Soderini was encouraging him. "You above all," Raffaele acknowledged privately, "urged me to this task."[39]

Soderini was, during these early years of the sixteenth century, *gonfaloniere a vita* in Florence, the leader of the republican order established after the fall of the Medici.[40] To fulfill the desire of such a figure for the orations thus promised significant recognition of Raffaele's new *forma vivendi*. The two men also had a more intimate republican connection: Raffaele's oldest brother, Antonio, had been executed for stabbing Lorenzo de'Medici in the Pazzi conspiracy of April 26, 1478.[41] This family tragedy no doubt caused some awkwardness in Rome. It led to Raffaele's marriage, since someone had to continue the family, and it may eventually have contributed to Raffaele's ascetic withdrawal to Volterra and to younger brother Mario's assiduous cultivation of the Medici pope Leo X (1513–1521). But the combination of the personal and the political—

---

38. In BAV, MS Barb. lat. 2517, fols. 8–9v, dated "vii idus iunias [7 June] MDIX," Raffaele tells Pietro Soderini that he is completing the translation of the *Odyssey* and will take up Dio Chrysostom next: "Post hanc Dionem Chrysostemum est in animo persequi." Cf. VBG, MS 6204, fols. 79r–v, two earlier letters mentioning the translation of Dio Chrysostom in progress, one to Jacopo Gherardi, dated September 22, 1507 ("Apud Dionem, quem in latinum converto, multa invenio in Romanorum historiis a nostris non dicta . . . ") and the other from Jacopo, dated October 7, 1507 ("Quae in Dione annotasti et mihi significas placuit Cardinali nostro multum et pluribus viris eruditis . . . "). Raffaele returned to beg from the Vatican, but Inghirami told Maffei firmly that he could not have Vatican manuscripts of "Li tituli di Grisostimo" (VBG, MS 5377, "1491–1521 A Raffaello da diversi," letter 2, dated from Rome, January 11, 1511). No translation of Dio Chrysostom by Raffaele seems to be extant.

39. It was the gonfalonier "qui me ad hanc curam inprimis compulisti" (BAV, MS Barb. lat. 2517, fol. 37r–v), wrote Raffaele to Piero Soderini, in a letter dated only Volterra "V Idus Sep" [September 9]; the letter is quoted further below. By *inprimis*, Raffaele might mean "above all" or "first."

40. His brother Francesco Soderini was bishop of Volterra from 1478 to 1509; see K. J. P. Lowe, *Church and Politics in Renaissance Italy: The Life and Career of Cardinal Francesco Soderini (1453–1524)* (New York: Cambridge University Press, 1993). Francesco, like Raffaele, belonged to the fraternity of Santo Spirito in Sassia in Rome (ibid., 20 and n. 57), was referendary when Raffaele was also working in the curia (ibid., 20, 41), and worked with both Mario and Raffaele Maffei in his capacity as bishop of Volterra.

41. For an introduction to the conspiracy, see P. Clark, "Pazzi Conspiracy," in P. Grendler, ed., *Encyclopedia of the Renaissance* (New York: Scribners, 1999) 4:440–441, with bibliography. In the 1470s Raffaele and Antonio shared a house near Sant'Eustochio where books for curial consumption were printed "Apud Sanctum Marcum" and "In domo Antonii et Raphaelis de vulterris"; see D'Amico, *Renaissance Humanism*, 82; Anna Modigliano, "La tipografia 'Apud sanctum Marcum' " in M. Miglio, ed., *Scrittura, biblioteche e stampa a Roma nel Quattrocento: Atti del 2 seminario, 6–8 maggio 1982* (Vatican City, 1983), 401–420.

which Raffaele nourished with little gifts such as a manuscript of his translation of the *Odyssey*—could be advantageously brought to bear. Now he
importuned Soderini for additional manuscripts of Basil from which to
work. He had learned from trustworthy sources that the "sermons of Basil"
were held "in the Florentine monastery that they call the abbey." If Soderini
would send this codex, Raffaele promised to be quick.[42]

Soderini borrowed the manuscript for his friend. "We're sending you
the book of Basil's sermons that you requested," he wrote. "I want you to
take good care of it and return it with your usual diligence."[43] Raffaele
complied: before the year was out, he returned the manuscript, explaining
to Soderini that he planned to combine homilies from the Florentine manuscript with those from the Vatican codices. The whole, he promised,
would be dedicated to Soderini and printed in time for Basil's feast.[44]

Raffaele apparently missed his deadline. Basil's feast falls on January 2,
but almost two months later, on February 25, 1509 (or 1508, *stilo
fiorentino*), Soderini wrote to say that he was hoping "to have the translation of Basil the Great produced at our press, because we want to enjoy
it this Lent."[45] Soderini's letter suggests that a translation of Basil's homilies was complete and ready to be printed in Florence by the late winter of
1509 (1508). Perhaps it was indeed printed there with exceptional speed
for Lent, as Soderini hoped. Or perhaps the printing proceeded more
slowly, so that the sermons were available for distribution in time for
Basil's next feast, or the next Lent, in 1510 (1509). We cannot know,

42. See Branca and Pastore Stocchi, "La seconda centuria," 148–149 and n. 19, quoting
BAV, MS Barb. lat. 2517, fol. 37, Raffaele to Pietro Soderini (undated): "Adcoepi ex viris
doctis in coenobio Florentino, quod abbatiam vocant, sermones Basilii proculdubio esse.
Eum si mihi miseris . . . morem tibi gerere curabo, cum nihil magis cupiam. Idque brevi spero
me tempore absoluturum." Branca and Pastore Stocchi note that this letter must be dated
after September 22, 1502, on the basis of the address to Soderini as "Vexillifer perpetuus."

43. VBG, MS 5377, "Otto lettere," letter 5, damaged: "Desidero che habiale buona cura,
et expediale con la vestra solita diligentia, et se altro ve occorrebbe possiamo aiudate, et
benevalete. Ex Palatio florentino die xxx Jan MDX." BAV, MS Barb. Lat. 2517, fols. 10v–11,
a letter from Raffaele to Pietro Soderini (undated), is probably the reply to the receipt of the
homilies of Basil. Raffaele explains there why he titled the collection "homilies" rather than
"sermons" and asks Soderini to send anything else by Basil that he may have.

44. BAV, MS Barb. lat. 2517, fol. 37r–v: Raffaele to Piero Soderini, dated Volterra "V
Idus Sep" [September 9]. "Liber coenobii Florentini post esilium semestre ad te revertitur
incolumis quem in hac ferme spatii brevitate . . . converti . . . Deinde ut quaedam alia ipsius
viri sanctissimi praeclara opuscula quae Bibliotheca Vaticana Romae ut describerentur ⟨?⟩
demum agglutinanda convertam ut totum opus tuo foelicissimo nomine dicatum proximis
natalitiis festis, ut remotissimum dicam, ut omnino, existimo, mittam."

45. VBG, MS 5377, "8 Lettere," containing letters of 1508–1511, fourth letter, Pietro
Soderini to Raffaello Maffei at Volterra, dated "ex palatio florentino xxv febr 1509":
"Desideriamo assai havere la traductione facta ad stampa nostra Magni Basilii perche vor-
remo questa quadragesima goderla."

because no Florentine edition is extant.[46] But plans for a Roman printing became urgent with the fall of Soderini in 1512 and the return of the Medici to Florence, and still more so with the accession of Giovanni de'Medici as Pope Leo X on March 11, 1513.

Raffaele seems to have kept on fiddling with the structure of the volume. In December 1511 he pressed friends in Rome to find the panegyrical life of Basil by Gregory of Nazianzen, for he wanted to translate it to serve as the opening piece in his edition.[47] It is unclear whether he knew about the Latin version of Oration 43 that George of Trebizond had made for Nicholas V (1447–1455).[48] Perhaps Raffaele had become familiar with the Greek text during the years he himself had studied with George.[49] But now Tommaso Inghirami's report was discouraging: Gregory's panegyric on Basil "can't be found in the *libreria* [library]," he reported, or "at the *cartolari* [stationers']."[50] Inghirami knew, or assumed, that a translation

46. One may have been printed: Mario told Raffaele that he had found a Milanese printer who wanted to publish new, corrected editions of Raffaele's works. See VBG, MS 5376, which consists of six large bundles, letter 75 of the purple folio of the Archivio Maffei, Mario (in Rome?) to Raffaele in Volterra, dated May 24, 1510, one folio recto: "vole stampare tutte le vostre opere et che le corregate a vostro modo et similiter lopera grande [*Commentarii?*] et fate vostre correctioni et io far notare a nostro Paulo [Riccobaldo Maffei] tutte le anotationi di Fedra su el vostro libro . . . corregete ancor Basilio."

47. Only a reply to this request seems to be extant. See n. 51 below.

48. John Monfasani, *George of Trebizond* (Leiden: Brill, 1976), 73–74, dates George's translation to late 1451/early 1452. For the dedicatory letter to Nicholas V, see John Monfasani, ed., *Collectanea Trapezuntiana* (Binghamton, N.Y., 1985), XCV, 300. The extant manuscripts of George's translation are listed ibid., CLXXIX, 726. For the history of attention to Gregory's Oration 43, see Agnes Clare Way, "Gregory Nazianzenus," in *CTC*, 2: 137; for the text given in *PG* 36, see Jean Bernardi, ed., *Grégoire de Nazianze: Discours 42–43* (Sources chrétiennes 384) (Paris: Cerf, 1992), 116–307, with introduction, 25–45. Two insightful studies that introduce the large bibliography on this discourse are F. W. Norris, "Your Honor, My Reputation: St. Gregory of Nazianzus's Funeral Oration on St. Basil the Great," and David Konstan, "How to Praise a Friend: St. Gregory of Nazianzus's Funeral Oration for St. Basil the Great," in T. Hägg and P. Rousseau, eds., *Greek Biography and Panegyric in Late Antiquity* (Berkeley: University of California Press, 2000), 140–159 and 160–179.

49. See D'Amico, *Renaissance Humanism*, 83 and n. 113, on the study with George, apparently a disappointment to the young man. Monfasani, ed., *Collectanea*, CXLI, 485–489, gives George's scholia on *In laudibus S. Basilii* from the unique manuscript. Elsewhere, in his dedicatory letter to Nicholas V, George had noted Gregory Nazianzenus's intention to present Basil as an imitable exemplar: "Ita pontifex eloquentissimus atque sanctissimus . . . duos pontifices [i.e., both Basil and Athanasius] similiter sanctos atque doctissimos . . . oratione sua posteris imitandos proposuit." In contrast to the imitable saint, the author Gregory is very nearly beyond imitation: "Quis enim illum in dicendo imitabitur, qui, si Demosthenem excipias, nec apud Grecos quidem parem habeat, qui dicendi genera ita rebus accom⟨m⟩odaret ut nunquam a gravitate decedet, quem, etsi usque ad hodiernum diem Greci omnes summopere admirati sunt, nemo tamen recte imitari unquam potuit?" (Monfasani, *Collectanea* XCV, at 301).

50. Silvia Rizzo, *Il lessico filologico degli umanisti* (Rome: Edizioni di storia e letteratura, 1984), discusses *librarius* (*ad indicem*), including at 168 an example of *bibliotheca* and *libraria* (both meaning "library") in the same sentence by Poliziano.

already existed: "You didn't say whether you wanted it in Latin or in Greek. If my J.M. [unidentified] were here, I'd make him look for it." Or if Raffaele could tell him where a copy might be found, Inghirami would see to procuring it.[51]

The project continued to drag. At the end of 1513, a friend asked for a copy of the "sermons of St. Basil that I hear are being printed at Rome."[52] But not until the fall of 1515 was the Mazocchi edition available.[53] In the meantime, the Medici had reentered Florence, so that the plan of a dedication to Soderini had to be discarded. The new dedicatory letter was addressed to Mario. The edition opened with Raffaele's translation of Gregory of Nazianzus's tour de force, his lengthy oration on his friend, fellow student, and fellow bishop Basil, which Raffaele entitled *Monodia Gregorii Nazianzeni in Magnum Basilium*.[54] Then followed fifty-nine orations that Raffaele attributed to Basil, including a new translation of the Greek father's famous letter *On Studies*, well known to educators in its 1403 version by Leonardo Bruni.[55] The success of the Mazzochi edition can be measured in its many sixteenth-century reprints, both in Italy and in the north. In Raffaele's lifetime, the homilies may have found an audience not

51. VBG, MS 5377, "1491–1521. A Raffaello da diversi," letter 1, to Raffaele dated Rome, [December?] 27, 1511: "La vita di Basilio non trovo in libreria, ne a Iac. cartolari. Trovo bene in libraria Basilio de Regula et molti altri opusculi suoi. Voi non dite ne greca ne latina. Se il mio J.M. ci fusse ne darei cura a lui. . . . Avisate se navete notitia alcuna dove [si trova] et non omittam che in qualche modo sarete servito."

52. VBG, MS 5377, "1491–1521. A Raffaello da diversi," ninth letter, from Antonio Zeno to Raffaello Maffei, dated December 5, 1513: "Delli sermoni di s. Basilio intendo a Roma se imprimino. Quando sieno inpresi car(issi)mo mi si poterne havere copia" [sic?]. The same letter inquires about quinterns of Homer. On Antonio Zeno, see Silvano Mori, "Antonio Zeno, I Soderini, ed il restauro della pieve di Santa Maria di Chianni," *Rassegna volterrana* (1994–95): 15–33, giving the date of death, August 7, 1530, at 31, and bibliography in Marucci, "Zeno, Antonio," in Lagorosto, *Dizionario* 3:1241; for Zeno as the instigator of Raffaele's attack on Luther, see D'Ascia, "Martin Lutero," 111 and appendix 1.

53. Mazocchi published two collections of Basil's homilies at Rome in 1515. The first, by Raffaele, bears the colophon date of September 15. The second, bearing the colophon date of December 12, contains Giovanni Argyropoulo's translation of Basil's homilies on the Hexaemeron; see Paschini, "Teologia," 256 and n. 8. Cf. the letter in Rome, BN, MS Autogr., A 96 7/1, dated October 11, 1518, from Mario at Rome to Raffaele: it mentions the printing of "li sermoni," which "tra 8 giorni saranno finiti o prima perche si fa due provi el di. Sara qualche scorrectione nel Greco per non saper costoro nulla et far sempre pegio." Mario probably refers not to Basil's sermons (which Raffaele himself called homilies) but to the Dormition sermons attached to the *Institutes* of 1518.

54. At fols. 58–68 (not to be confused with Gregory's autobiographical *Monodia*). It does not, however, appear in BAV, MS Ottob. Lat. 2377, which opens (fols. 1–5) with Basil on the first psalm (*inc.*: Cum omnia sacra volumina), and neither does it appear in the autograph London, BL, MS Add. 23771. See Agnes Clare Way, "Gregorius Nazianzenus," CTC 2:144.

55. Irene Backus, *Lectures humanistes de Basile de Césarée: Traductions latines (1439–1618)* (Paris: Institut d'Etudes Augustiniennes, 1990), discusses Maffei's translation at 15–28.

just as printed words but also as spoken ones. The dedicatory letter to
Mario closes by asking him to preach the homilies at the Franciscan basilica of Santissimi Apostoli in Rome, where Mario was a canon.[56]

I have traced Raffaele's lengthy engagement with the text of Basil's homilies for two reasons. First, it indicates the depth of commitment involved
in his shift from classical to early Christian literary concerns. Second, it suggests that prolonged attention to Basil not only reflected but also affected
Raffaele's own devotional life and his late writings. In particular, when he
came to translate those homilies that treated saints—Basil's accounts of the
martyrs Iulitta, the Forty Martyrs, and Gordius and, above all, Gregory
Nazianzenus's account of Basil himself[57]—Raffaele's attention was drawn
to a question that had for centuries maintained its immediacy to the men
who wrote and spoke about saints: how best was an audience to be persuaded of the authority, authenticity, and attractiveness of Christian sanctity? In the years that followed the Basil translations, as Raffaele struggled
with his own ascetic life and composed his own *vitae et passiones sanctorum*, finding the answer to this question took on urgency.

❊ ❊ ❊

*Itaque nil magis opportunum est existimavi nec quod magis vestras vires demul-
ceret, animum delectaret, mentem accenderet, quam si sermonis compendio
omnem Christianam rempublicam colligerem et quod pictores qui terrarum situs
pingunt, brevi quasi tabella complecterer.*

And so I thought that nothing was more fitting, and nothing would more entice
your intellects, delight your soul, inflame your mind, than if I should gather in
compendium the whole Christian Republic and, as painters do when they depict
the locations of lands, enfold it briefly as if in a small painting.

—Tommaso Inghirami, Fedra (d. 1516), "In laudem omnium sanctorum oratio,"
delivered *coram papa* in 1497[58]

56. The dedication of the Basil to Mario (cf. n. 38 above) may have been intended to help
him; see the letter of June 26, 1507, from Jacopo Gherardi in Rome to Raffaele in Volterra,
complaining that Mario's colleagues at the basilica "non fraterne, ut deceret, eum tractare"
(VBG, MS 6204, fol. 73v).

57. Raffaele did not translate Basil's homilies on Mamas and Barlaam for the Rome edition. The translations of Basil's homilies on Iulitta, the Forty Martyrs, and Gordius are discussed below.

58. VBG, MS 5885, fol. 39r; see O'Malley, *Praise*, 114, for the date. Basil himself proposed ecphrasis, as Raffaele's translation of Homily 338 on the Forty Martyrs shows: "Igitur in medium eos adducentes ad communem omnium hic adstantium utilitatem constituere
palamque omnibus quemadmodum in pictura fortia illorum facta reddere conabimur. Nam
magnifica in bellis gesta et oratores sepenumero et pictores pulcherrime demonstrant. Hi
oratione, illi tabulis describentes atque ornantes. Amboque plures ad fortitudinem imitan-
dam induxere, que enim sermo historiae per indictionem prebet, eadem et pictura tacens per

The question of effective preaching on saints was a lively one in the latter part of the Quattrocento and early Cinquecento.[59] As John O'Malley has shown, the curial humanists implemented a significant change in the nature of the learned late medieval sermon, replacing the scholastic format of *distinctiones* with the classical model of demonstrative rhetoric.[60] Precisely during the decades that Raffaele spent in the chancery, both lay and clerical humanists were using this new panegyrical model.[61] Raffaele himself was a connoisseur of the style and promoted it.[62] He knew some of the orators and was a close friend of two of the most gifted practitioners,

------

imitationem ostendit. Sic et nos martyrum virtutem commemorantes vos adstantes excitabimus" (this translation, printed in Maffei's *Magni Basilii Opera*, is discussed further below). Basil draws an analogy between narrative and paintings of heroic scenes; in late antique panegyric, the normal, even clichéd analog is portraiture. Inghirami, however, undertakes a landscape (a Thebaid?), or better, a peopled map.

59. O'Malley, *Praise*. See also idem, "Form, Content, and Influence of Works about Preaching Before Trent: The Franciscan Contribution," in *I Frati Minori tra '400 e '500: Atti del XII Convegno Internazionale, Assisi, 18–20 ottobre 1984* (Assisi: Centro di studi francescani, 1986), 27–50. The study of preaching is an area of rapid growth, both for medievalists and early modernists. For a variety of recent approaches, see C. Muessig, ed., *Preacher, Sermon and Audience in the Middle Ages* (Leiden: Brill, 2002); L. Gaffuri and R. Quinto, eds., *Preaching and Society in the Middle Ages: Ethics, Values and Social Behaviour* (Padua: Centro studi Antoniani, 2002); and G. Auzzas, G. Baffetti, and C. Delcorno, eds., *Letteratura in forma di sermone: I rapporti tra predicazione e letteratura nei secoli XIII–XVI* (Florence: Olschki, 2003).

60. O'Malley, *Praise*, 36–76, compares the new and old sermon formats; see esp. 58–60 on structure. As the Quattrocento wore on, preachers evidently worked with a flexible range of tools, picked opportunistically from thematic and demonstrative sermon styles. In an enthusiastic letter, Cardinal Raffaele Riario (1461–1521) described to Raffaele the innovative preaching style—neither typically thematic nor typically classicizing—of Mariano da Genazzano, O.E.S.A. (d. 1498), who "solus enim huic novo concionandi generi [add. in marg. in quo] sive acumine diserendi sive eloquendi facultate magnus clarusque habetur initium dedit. Quippe qui *nihil pristini moris haberet* sed novum quendam modum, novam in sermonibus ad populum introduxerat eloquentiam" (BAV, MS Ottob. lat. 2377, fol. 204, dated Rome, 19 kal. feb., without year, my emphasis). Riario, as cardinal protector of the Hermits, is naturally partial. In this same letter he invites Maffei to write on Mariano as beautifully as he (Maffei) has recently on the Hermit Antonio da Montecchio, da Siena (d. 1497). See n. 62 below for the letter to which this one seems to be a reply.

61. O'Malley, *Praise*, appendix (245–55), lists 161 sermons that were preached *coram papa* circa 1450 and 1521. If Raffaele were an assiduous sermon goer between 1468 and 1507, he might have been present for most of these occasions. Ronald W. Witt, *"In the Footsteps of the Ancients": The Origins of Humanism from Lovato to Bruni* (Leiden: Brill, 2000), at 357 n. 54, acknowledges both O'Malley's *Praise* and John McManamon, *Funeral Oratory and the Cultural Ideals of Italian Humanism* (Chapel Hill: University of North Carolina Press, 1989), but concentrates on secular oratory, although the new homiletic model also supports his thesis.

62. See Maffei's connoisseur's remarks on an oration of more than two hours given by Antonio da Siena, a young Hermit trained in the style of preaching favored by Mariano da Gennazzano (VBG, MS 5377, "1473–1521 Raffaello a diversi," letter 18, to Raffaello

Tommaso Inghirami and Egidio da Viterbo. He could have attended many of their classicizing orations, perhaps even one of the most celebrated, the Good Friday sermon of 1496 preached by his fellow curialist Aurelio Brandolini (ca. 1454–1497). He may also have heard Brandolini's panegyric on Thomas Aquinas.[63]

Brandolini was not just a practitioner but also a theorist of the new classicizing sermon for saints. This fact gives him a claim on the attention of scholars who study *passiones et vitae sanctorum*: Brandolini thought methodically and explicitly about the problem of presenting effective models of sanctity. At some point before 1485, Raffaele's fellow-curialist wrote a treatise, ostensibly on letter writing, entitled *De ratione scribendi*.[64] In book 8, moving beyond instruction on epistles, Brandolini gave careful and original attention to the demonstrative rhetoric of praise and blame.

Riario, cardinal of San Giorgio [undated, unsigned]; cf. BAV, MS Ottob. lat. 2377, fol. 203r–v). Since Raffaele does not name Riario as the cardinal of Santa Sabina, this letter must have been written before 1507, when Riario ascended to that dignity. The *terminus post quem* must be December 10, 1488, when Riario was named to San Giorgio. Raffaele says he is in Volterra. He urges the cardinal to support the Hermits, who

> primis huic seculo novum orandi genus christiano populo ostenderunt, primi eloquentiam cum sacris voluminibus et philosophiam cum theologia coniunxerunt; primi item qui in utramque partem disserendi modum a Socraticis usque illis institutum, deinde ab Aquinate nostro ut ab iniustis possessoribus ad nostrum dogma diligenter traductum, renovaverunt; primi denique qui partes omnis oratoris quantum relligioni fas est, dissimulanter absolvunt. Ita quoque physicis omnia probant distincte atque ornate rationibus ut non minus disputatio subtilis, quam oratio vehemens dici, neque minus docere quam movere possit, ex quo et curiosiorum ingenia pasci et duriorum animi emolliri valent.

For another humanist's appreciation of Mariano da Gennazzano's preaching style, see chap. 4 above.

63. John O'Malley, "The Feast of Thomas Aquinas in Renaissance Rome: A Neglected Document and Its Import," *RSCI* 35, 1 (1981): 10, item 5.; idem, "Some Renaissance Panegyrics of Aquinas," *RQ* 24 (1974): 174–192; and Luciano Cinelli, "I panegirici in onore di s. Tommaso d'Aquino alla Minerva nel XV secolo," *MD* n.s. 30 (1999): 113–120, transcribing the oration on Aquinas and the letter of dedication to Olivero Caraffa. For printed editions of this oration, see H 3716; *GW* 5016, *BMC* 4:1222, *IGI* 2036; Goff B1074; IERS 988 (assigned to Raffaele Brandolini). For Aurelio's oration *De laudibus sancti Joannis Baptiste*, see Kristeller, *Iter*, 4:174a, dedication copy to Innocent VIII. On the phenomenon of printed orations at Rome, see Concetta Bianca, "Le orazioni a stampa," in M. Chiabò, S. Maddalo, M. Miglio, and A. M. Oliva, eds., *Roma di fronte all'Europa al tempo di Alessandro VI: Atti del convegno. Città del Vaticano–Roma. 1–4 dicembre 1999* (Rome: Ministero per i beni e le attività culturale, 2001), 2:441–468.

64. On Brandolini, see A. Rotondo, "Brandolini, Aurelio," *DBI* 14 (1972): 126–128 for earlier bibliography; John McManamon, "Renaissance Preaching: Theory and Practice—A Holy Thursday Sermon of Aurelio Brandolini," *Viator* 10 (1979): 355–373; A. F. Verde, *Lo studio fiorentino* 4, 2 (Florence, 1985), 953–956; and the following notes. On Brandolini's Good Friday sermon, see O'Malley, *Praise*, 50 and n. 34, and on Brandolini's originality, 44–53.

Among the chapters in that innovative section of the treatise was one
devoted to epideictic about saints: *Diis laudandis*.[65]

In *Diis laudandis*, Brandolini presents a Christian revision of classical
advice on panegyric. He draws particularly on Cicero's *De oratore* II, xi,
at 45–46, but also on *De inventione*, the *Rhetorica ad Herennium*, and on
Quintilian's *Institutio oratoria*. These sources, which themselves drew on
earlier Greek ones, were known, at least in part, to educated people in the
Middle Ages. In adapting them for saints' lives, Brandolini both formalized a set of tropes that were widely familiar, and transmuted them into an
ascetic mode. The classical handbooks describe a twofold division of the
topics to be treated in praising anyone: the orator should first treat the gifts
of nature and then the gifts of fortune. Applying this model to the saints,
Brandolini substituted a more appropriate Christian division: gifts human
and divine. This adjustment entailed further changes in the Ciceronian
structure, which Brandolini set out methodically. His first category, the
human aspects of the saint, collapses Cicero's categories of external and
internal goods into one. But Brandolini then re-creates a familiar threefold
division, identifying the human aspects that the orator must address as
natura, fortuna, and *animus*. Still borrowing from Cicero, he develops
three further subdivisions of treatment: as the orator takes up the endow-
ments of nature, fortune, and character, he should explain what gifts each
term encompassed; how to address a saint's possession of these gifts; and
how to address a saint's lack of them. By *natura*, Brandolini means posi-
tive attributes of the body, such as beauty, strength, and health. This much
is standard classical rhetorical procedure. But then, as a Christian praising
ascetic perfection, Brandolini required that these advantages be overturned: the saint must be shown to weaken them through fasting, hide
them in solitude, lessen them with filth, or turn them to God's use. The
saint without these attributes must be shown not to seek them but to scorn
them. A similar pattern, pairing traditional topics of praise with Christian
reversal, follows in the next subdivision. *Fortuna* indicates the attributes
of family, education, *patria*, wealth, and friends. These, too, are to be
depicted as abandoned, hidden, or turned to God's use. If the saint did not
possess them, again they must not be sought but actively avoided. The
third subdivision, *animus*, denotes the four cardinal and three theological
virtues; Brandolini identifies them as *prudentia, iustitia, fortitudo, modes-*

---

65. Brandolini entered the O.E.S.A. house of San Gallo near Florence around 1491, but
was in minor orders when he wrote the instructions presented here. *De ratione scribendi* was
not published until the sixteenth century, after Brandolini's death. O'Malley, *Praise*, 45–46
and nn. 19 and 21, points out that the Basel 1498 edition is a ghost and describes the originality of Brandolini's handbook in comparison to those of the classical rhetoricians and of
his contemporaries.

tia (usually temperance), *fides, spes,* and *charitas.* These virtues, directed to the love of God, must be praised.

Brandolini then speaks much more briefly about his second category, the saint's divine aspects, accomplishments beyond human achievement. He gives three examples: learning without study, knowledge of other languages without experience of other cultures, and cures of illness without training in medicine. These unnatural achievements Brandolini calls *beneficia,* benefits or gifts. He acknowledges the existence of miracles (*non dubitamus*), but, by speaking of the miraculous so cursorily and by avoiding the expected words *miracula* and *prodigia* or even the mild *mirabilia,* he recommends that the orator be circumspect about supernatural phenomena. Miracles occur, but they are not the chief sign or value of sanctity.[66]

Brandolini concludes his advice by describing saintly panegyric as a new fashion in great use at Rome. He was right about its frequency in Rome, but he may have overstated its novelty. Already in the late fourteenth and early fifteenth century, Pierpaolo Vergerio had experimented with a new format in his ten panegyrics for Jerome. Vergerio had emphasized the "human aspects" of Jerome's sanctity, above all, his perseverance in the face of contemporaries' persecution, his difficult penitence in the desert, and his erudition. In some sermons, these accomplishments seem to approximate "divine aspects." But Vergerio did not use the word "miracle" in discussing them. When he does employ the word, he is often vague, evidently more interested in the benefit of Jerome as a model to be imitated. Thus, although almost every sermon mentions miracles, only twice does Vergerio describe miracles at length. In both cases, these miracles occur postmortem and so do not affect the depiction of the "human aspects" of Jerome.[67]

Insofar as Vergerio's early panegyrics on Jerome reject the subdivided scholastic format, they are early models for a humanist or classicizing presentation of saints. But they are not formal statements of method. So

66. Siena, BC, MS H.VII.13, fol. 52v. This manuscript is probably the dedication copy, according to O'Malley, *Praise,* 45 n. 17. For an edition of the relevant section from this manuscript and a fuller description of its sources and instruction, see A. K. Frazier, "The First Instructions on Writing About Saints," *Memoirs of the American Academy of Rome* 48 (2003): 171–202. On the multiple medieval vocabularies of wonder and miracle, see Caroline W. Bynum, *Metamorphosis and Identity* (New York: Zone, 2001).

67. John McManamon, *Pierpaolo Vergerio the Elder and Saint Jerome: An Edition and Translation of Sermones pro sancto Hieronymo* (Tempe, Ariz.: MRTS, 1999), sermon 4, seems to be the only sermon by Vergerio that does not even include the word *miracula,* although this sermon incorporates a long quotation on Jerome's difficulties in the desert. For recounted miracles, see ibid., sermons 6 at 194 (from Pseudo-Eusebius and Pseudo-Augustine) and 7 and 216–218 (from Giovanni Andrea's *Hieronymianum*). In light of the emphasis on martyrdom underlined in chap. 2 above, note Vergerio's presentation of Jerome as a martyr in sermon 7 at 210.

Brandolini was right to claim that his own instructions were novel. Of course, earlier centuries were familiar with the categories of panegyric, thanks to Cicero, Quintilian, and late antique *vitae*. They knew as well a variety of complaints about *vitae*, *miracula*, and *sermones* on saints; such complaints were tropes or commonplaces in the *exordia* (opening remarks) of sermons and in the prefaces of hagiographic narratives and can be found in treatises on quite different subjects as well.[68] These complaints—whatever their validity—may have been taken by prospective authors as hints of advice and instruction. But *Diis laudandis* did not offer implicit instruction. Brandolini's advice to authors and orators was explicit, and it was given in the course of a general guidebook to rhetoric, in a section that focused solely on writing and preaching about saints. Brandolini's *Diis laudandis* thus has the distinction of being the first freestanding set of instructions about writing on saints, the first explicit statement of method to occur outside the context of the hagiographic narrative, its dedicatory letter, and its preface. It therefore deserves notice as part of a long trend in the formulation of method that can be traced from the Victorine didactic program of the twelfth century, through the scholastic *summa*, to Jean Bodin's historical guide in the seventeenth century.

For my purposes here, however, the significance of Brandolini's instructions lies elsewhere. *Diis laudandis* indicates that contemporaries perceived a striking discontinuity: the curial orators were self-consciously attempting something new in their presentation of sanctity. Naturally, scholars have focused on that point. At the same time, however, Brandolini contributes implicitly to a basic continuity. The classicizing format of the orators' encomia shared something with the slightly older format of the scholastic sermon: despite their structural and linguistic dissimilarities, both humanist encomion and scholastic sermon assumed that narratives of sanctity were not about *Bildung* or the gradual, messy, human effort at virtue. The orator's subject, like the preacher's, was the saint's perfections.

The same presumption underlay Basil's homilies on saints, including the three that Raffaele had translated.[69] Basil's answer to the question about the most effective depiction of sanctity is summed up in the phrase

---

68. I am completing an analysis of the humanist hagiographic preface.

69. Recent studies of the Basilian homilies emphasize their novel attention to audience and to imitation. See Averil Cameron, *Christianity and the Rhetoric of Empire: The Development of Christian Discourse*, Sather Classical Lectures 55 (Berkeley: University of California Press, 1991), passim; and the discussion in Rousseau, *Basil*. The difference in my approach stems from the relatively less studied fifteenth-century attention to Basil.

enkomion nomon, the law of panegyric.[70] To honor the saints, one praised them, admitting no fault—not even internal struggle. Basil's model for this sort of praise was the *epitaphios logos*, the classical speech that honored the glorious dead, as described by Menander.[71] But Basil and the other fourth-century church fathers systematically overturned each of the standard categories of praise, just as Brandolini overturned the same categories in Cicero's *De oratore*. They had to do so. As Basil pointed out in his homilies on the Forty Martyrs and on Gordius (both of which Raffaele Maffei translated), the *enkomion nomon* relied for its topics on the goods of the world, such as claims to *patria*.[72] "Those who praise others," Maffei translated from Homily 338 on the Forty Martyrs, "are accustomed to borrow material from the matters of this world. [But] these saints did not share one country; they came from all over. Shall we then say they had no country? Or shall we call them citizens of the world?"[73] Such goods as *patria* were irrelevant to his subjects, whose country was heaven, whose name was "Christian," whose father was God, whose honors were public mutilation and a criminal's death.

70. See Hippolyte Delehaye, *Les passions des martyrs et les genres littéraires* (Brussels: Bollandist Society, 1921), 183–235, which I summarize here; for other views, see Jean Bernardi, *La prédication des pères cappadociens: Le Prédicateur et son auditoire* (Marseilles: Presses Universitaires de France, 1968); and J. M. Campbell, *The Influence of the Second Sophistic on the Style of the Sermons of St. Basil the Great* (Washington, D.C.: Catholic University of America Press, 1922). For a comprehensive survey of technique, see Laurent Pernod, *La Rhétorique de l'éloge dan le monde gréco-romain* (Paris: Études Augustiniennes, 1993).

71. For an introduction to the ancient roots and Second Sophistic transformation of epideictic, see Theodore Burgess, *Epideictic Rhetoric* (Chicago: University of Chicago Press, 1992); Pernod, *Rhétorique*; Joachim Soffel, *Die Regeln Menanders für die Leichenrede* (Meisenheim am Glan: Anton Hain, 1974), especially the overview at 6–105; and Averil Cameron, *Christianity and the Rhetoric of Empire*, 81–84. D. A. Russell and N.G. Wilson, *Menander Rhetor* (Oxford: Clarendon, 1981) is indispensable.

72. For Basil's orations see *PG* 31, 509–510 on the Forty Martyrs; 490–508 on Gordius; and 238–262 on Iulitta. Rousseau, *Basil*, 184–189, esp. 186–187, and Elena Giannarelli, "La biografia cristiana antica: Strutture, problemi," in G. Luongo, ed., *Scrivere di santi: Atti del II Convegno di studio dell'Associazione italiana per lo studio della santità, dei culti e dell'agiografia. Napoli, 22–25 ottobre 1997* (Rome: Viella, 1998), 54 and n. 29, address Basil's observations about *encomion*. It is clear from the stylistic analysis in Campbell, *Influence*, 28, that Homily 334 on Iulitta is a prime instance of pleonasm. Thus it seems possible that the sorts of classroom techniques described in chap. 4 above may have fed Maffei's appreciation of this work. The oration on Iulitta is interesting for another reason that also suggests classroom applications of the text. Basil dispenses with Iulitta's story rather quickly in order to return to his thanksgiving topic of the previous day. Guiniforte Barzizza follows this broken structure closely in his own oration on Iulitta, turning aside after brief remarks to celebrate the recipient. This oration is not included in *Gasparini et Guiniforti Barzizii Opera* (Bologna: Forni, 1969), but see London, BL, MS Add. 15336, fols. 45v–50r.

73. "Qui laudant ceteros ex mundi huius rebus materiam usurpare solent. . . . Non erat his sanctis una patria, alius aliunde venit. Quid, igitur, sine patria dicemus eos? aut orbis cives?" from Raffaele Maffei, *Magni Basilii opera* (Rome: Jacopo Mazzochi, 1517), fol. 145r.

Basil's homily on the Forty Martyrs is thus a far-reaching demonstration of how to erase specificity in search of praise and of why one should erase it. From this form of periphrasis, the avoidance of every earthbound detail, stemmed the paradoxically associated trait of the early Christian panegyrics for the martyrs: hyperbole or exaggeration, achieved by comparison (e.g., of the martyrs to athletes and soldiers) and by ecphrasis or description (e.g., by drawing out the story of the martyr's sufferings).[74] In fact, Basil's homilies on Gordius and the Forty Martyrs are prime examples of his ecphrastic technique.[75] Similarly, the panegyrist was also encouraged to attribute speeches to his characters. Given the judicial situation in which the early Christian martyrs were created, these speeches could be highly dramatic. But the drama was not personalized or localized: Basil demonstrated that the Christian encomiast, unlike the pagan one, was to ignore the specific facts of the matter, the very things that we today consider history. Basil, however, stated frankly that he was proposing *historia* rather than panegyric. And for him, *historia* entailed the possibility of imitation.[76]

The same transcendent nonspecificity attaches to the question of miracle. Basil's panegyrics do not feature miracle to the degree that we associate with later *vitae* and *passiones sanctorum*. No one picks up his severed head and walks to a final resting place; no one survives years of repeated scalding, salting, and starving. The special favor that Basil's subjects found with God is established instead by contrasting the extremes of their suffering with the extremes of their persecutors' cruelty. Basil takes some time, for example, in his homily on the Forty Martyrs, to impress upon his audience the excruciating pain of death by freezing.[77] The tyrant, in contrast, is "that infamous barbarian, swollen with pride" (Maffei's "barbarus ille ac superbia tumidus") who cruelly "consider[s] how he might

74. I rely on Delehaye, *Les passions*, 204–217; see also Tomas Hägg and Philip Rousseau's "Introduction: Biography and Panegyric," in *Greek Biography*, 2–28, although they assume a distinction between primary and secondary rhetoric that may be too sharp. On ecphrasis see Pernod, *Rhétorique* 2:670–674; on hyperbole, idem 1:403–410.

75. Thus Campbell, *Influence*, 141.

76. Delehaye, *Les passions*, 229–233. Because Basil claims *historia* as his object, his encomia fit well into the complexly expanding field of the "biographic" in Late Antiquity, proposed in M. J. Edwards and S. Swain, eds., *Portraits: Biographical Representation in the Greek and Latin Literature of the Roman Empire* (Oxford: Clarendon Press, 1997), although only his letters are even mentioned there.

77. *BHG* 1205; *PG* 31, 513–516, at 5. On this "grisly" passage, strikingly "medical" in its detailed attention to the effects of cold, see Patricia Cox Miller, "'The Little Blue Flower is Red': Relics and the Poetizing of the Body," *Journal of Early Christian Studies* 8, no. 2 (2000): 215–216, where the passage is merely an introductory example. I am grateful to Thomas Head for drawing my attention to this study.

prepare for them the most painful and lengthy death" (in Maffei, "considerare cepit quo mortem eis acerbissimam prolixamque pararet").[78] Such extreme contrasts give rise to a sense of wonder that approaches the miraculous, without the need for either God or the martyrs to produce such miracles as appear in later *vitae et passiones*.[79] Thus, in contrast to late medieval *vitae*, Basil's orations for martyred saints feature no particular drowned child being resuscitated, no broken bowl made whole for a specified neighborhood woman, no local church lamp filled with oil before the eyes of a named priest. In part, this difference has to do with literary kind: a homily is not a *passio*, and a *passio* is not a *vita*. The epideictic rhetoric of Late Antiquity as practiced by Basil was not the legal rhetoric of the late medieval canonization procedure, and so the requirements of proof were outside its purview.[80] The hero represented in early Christian panegyric is not the figure of the historical or legal document.[81] Nonetheless, the extreme contrast of martyr and persecutor cast them both as perfect and perfectly unchanging examples of their respective types. The tyrant was perfectly and forever cruel, and the martyr perfectly and forever abject. And thus, for Quattrocento readers, Basil compounded the tension of panegyrical perfection and historical specificity by calling his panegyric *historia*, seeming thus to demand simultaneously admiration and imitation. Maffei rendered the Greek uncomplicatedly, as *imitari* and *admirari*.[82]

❈ ❈ ❈

Hic est enim martyrum vera laus, alios ad eorum virtutem emulandam invitare.
Here is the true praise of the martyrs: to invite others to emulate their virtue.

—Raffaele Maffei, from the translation of Basil the Great, Homily 338 on the Forty Martyrs of Sebaste[83]

In the course of working among the panegyricizing curial humanists in Rome and as a result of translating Basil during his ascetic retirement to Volterra, Raffaele Maffei came to thorough acquaintance with the structure

---

78. Maffei, *Magni Basilii opera*, fol. 146.

79. Delehaye, *Les passions*, 222.

80. The verbal self-consciousness of late antiquity has been an area of considerable investigation; e.g., Michael Roberts, *The Jewelled Style: Poetry and Poetics in Late Antiquity* (Ithaca, N.Y.: Cornell University Press, 1989); Cameron, *Christianity*; and Patricia Cox Miller, "'Differential Networks': Relics and Other Fragments in Late Antiquity," *Journal of Early Christian Studies* 6, no. 1 (1998): 113–138. The legal rhetoric of late medieval canonization procedure needs similar attention.

81. I translate and lightly paraphrase Delehaye, *Les passions*, 233.

82. See Homily 338 in Maffei's *Magni Basilii Opera*, fols. 144v–147v.

83. Maffei, *Magni Basilii Opera*, fol. 145.

and content of the early Christian model of the panegyric and its development by his contemporaries. He did not approve of that development. Raffaele responded, in fact, with a violent disavowal of the form. Roughly three decades after Brandolini's instructions on saintly panegyric and shortly after he himself had translated Basil's homilies on the martyrs, Raffaele wrote an explicit complaint, *De sanctorum gestis non recte ab omnibus enarratis* (On the lives of the saints, incorrectly told by everyone).[84] The context this time was not a handbook on rhetoric but a guide to Christian life, the *Stromata*.[85] Raffaele spent the last years of his life compiling this ten-book collection of essays, which has been described as a doctrinal complement to the similarly encyclopedic *De institutione Christiana* (a work that Maffei dedicated to Leo X and published in 1518).[86] The *De institutione* was conceived, at least in part, as an aid for preachers: Raffaele noted with approval that two religious visiting Volterra based their sermons on it.[87] In contrast, in its unfinished state, the *Stromata* seems to be a more private document. It consists of reflections on the difficulties of a committed religious life, on the sorts of spiritual problems that Raffaele encountered as he met his own imperfections en route to holiness.[88]

The *Stromata* are also a prime example of the coincidence of moral philosophy and rhetoric, a coincidence that has turned up repeatedly in this study. The collection opens with an essay on the old monastic insight, itself borrowed from a classical source, that no one can persist in the ascetic life unless he knows himself. The text to be elucidated is *Nosce teipsum*.[89]

---

84. For an edition and more detailed discussion of this short essay, see Frazier, "The First Instructions."

85. BAV, MS Barb. lat. 753 (hereafter *Q*) is the autograph draft.

86. D'Amico, *Renaissance Humanism*, 192–198, analyzes the contents of *De institutione*. Leo received his dedicatory copy in a tastefully decorated but carelessly transcribed manuscript, BAV, MS Lat. 1126; cf. the early draft in BAV, MS Ottob. lat. 992, fols. 1–230v. The printing of the *Institutes* was under way by April 1517; see Rome, BN, MS Autograf., A96 6/4 of that date: Mario is planning to send Raffaele some page proofs.

87. After Raffaele's retirement to Volterra, a visiting preacher, Fra Francesco da Pisa, used the *Institutes* to preach "de doctrina scotista et sanctita," much to Raffaele's satisfaction. So did Frate Andrea da Montepulciano, although printer's errors impeded his understanding of the text (VBG, MS 5377, folder entitled "1473–1521 Raffaello a diversi," letter 15, sl, sd, sn).

88. D'Amico, *Renaissance Humanism*, 195, suggests a formal parallel between Raffaele's *Stromata* and Clement of Alexandria's *Stromateis*. The contents of the two collections are not similar, however, and so D'Amico's decision to analyze Maffei's *Stromata* together with his *De institutione christiana* as a two-volume encyclopedia leads him to slight the *Stromata* (196–202). For a published excerpt from the *Stromata*, see D'Ascia, "Martin Lutero," appendix 2.

89. *Stromata*, I, i: "Quomodo ab initio optimam vivendi deliberationem, qua est omnium difficillima nemo in sumpta diu alacriter durare potest nisi qui se cognoscit. Quomodove se nosse valeat" (*S* fols. 10–11). For the classical sources of this saying, see the overview in C. G. Tortzen, "'Know Thyself': A Note on the Success of a Delphic Saying," in B. Amden et al., *Noctes Atticae: Studies Presented to Jorgen Maier on His Sixtieth Birthday, March 18, 2002* (Copenhagen: Museum Tusculanum Press, 2002), 302–314.

Here, for the purpose of knowing oneself, Raffaele proposes the categories *naturalia, fortuita, voluntaria* (the natural, the fortuitous, and the voluntary), explaining that "prima corporis, seconda fortunae sive externa, tertia sunt animi bona malaque" (the first are goods and ills of the body, the second those of fortune or externals, and the third those of the soul). Later in the *Stromata*, which might also be read as an encyclopedia of the virtues and their impediments, Raffaele returns to this utterly traditional threefold division, deriving from demonstrative rhetoric a set of categories by which to evaluate his own struggle toward moral perfection.[90]

The much later chapter *De sanctorum gestis* extends the introductory task of self-definition by analyzing a fatal weakness of the exemplary literature. The Church possessed quantities of holy *vitae* and *passiones*, but what good were all these textual representations of sanctity if they did not actually change people's lives? In thinking through the dilemma of the ineffectual narrative, Raffaele's emotion runs high: *De sanctorum gestis* shows that he was troubled by the contemporary state of *vitae sanctorum*. His own experience told him that the spiritual poverty of these narratives was a measurable reality, but their poverty also struck close to home in another way. When he thought about audience, he had to consider the learned and disabused prelates who were his friends and family.

In late December 1518, the Ferrarese ambassador wrote from Rome about a fireside evening spent at the home of Cardinal Alexander Farnese (later Paul III) with a group of ecclesiastics, among them Mario Maffei, "monsignore San Zorzo," "et molti altri."[91] It was St. Stephen's Eve, and so there was a *lectio sancti Stephani*, a reading about the saint. Whatever the failings of that *lectio*, it set off a spontaneous series of jokes as, provoked by what they heard, members of the group took turns mocking it, *burlando*. The ambassador's letter does not describe the reading or its faults, although the witty, learned, and critical nature of the audience seems clear enough. Their response requires careful evaluation. After all, the object of their facetiousness was not the saints *tout court*. The prelates were not sending up easy targets such as George or Margaret or Sylvester with their dragons—venerable figures but, learned people suspected, ones who stood on shaky historical ground. Stephen was not just any saint. He was the protomartyr, the first human to follow Christ in death. His story, told in Acts 6–7, was a defining moment not just for the early Church but for Christianity's self-image ever after. None other than Augustine had reported eyewitness accounts of the miracles worked by

90. *Stromata*, III, x–xiii (on *natura*), xvi–xx (on *fortuna*), and xxi–xxii (on *virtus animi*); the categories recur in chapters on prayer and ascetic practice.

91. Pescetti, "Mario Maffei," 79; see also Alessandro Ferrajoli, *Il ruolo della corte di Leone X (1514–1516)*, ed. V. De Caprio (Rome: Bulzoni, 1984), 383 n. 5.

Stephen's relics.[92] It seems likely, therefore, that what the Ferrarese ambassador observed was not an atheistic conventicle or a humanist "abolizione della fede," but a kind of professional insiders' amusement, the result—not unfamiliar to preachers—of failed rhetoric, of the inadequate fit between the speaker's expression and the audience's capacity.[93] Whether Stephen's witness was expressed in that *lectio* as a collection of passages from Augustine, as a set of *exempla* and miracles, as a scholastic sermon, or as an emotional and dramatic classicizing oration in the style of Mariano da Gennazzano, we cannot know. But the result was a massive failure of conviction.

In a culture highly attuned to verbal representation, the cure for such a failure was obvious and to hand. Skilled rhetoricians were needed, professional menders of broken speech: the saints could be rescued by rewriting. We have seen, in the case of Giovanni Garzoni, that rewriting could win a humanist some reputation. In the cases of Leon Battista Alberti, Antonio degli Agli, and Francesco da Castiglione, we have seen that there was support at the highest curial levels for such humanist mending. Sometimes, as in the case of Giacomo da Udine's unusual life of his compatriot Elena Valentinelli, even radical rewriting could not save a saint (or could indicate that a saint was past saving). For Raffaele, however, the task went beyond the matters of style that most concerned Garzoni and Giacomo da Udine, to details of content such as troubled those who worked, or who were invited to work, on the martyrology. How could a rhetorician hope to recover the persuasive force of the narrated saint for a learned, witty, and disabused audience made up of men like Raffaele Maffei's own brother Mario and dear friend Raffaele Riario? Humanists knew as well as any mendicant preacher that, as Christ had built the road to salvation and theologians kept the maps up to date, skilled users of words would always be needed to maintain a passable surface.

Although Raffaele Maffei did not have the language to distinguish "hagiographer" clearly from "historian" and "biographer," categories like these distinctions were occurring to him and troubling him. *De sanctorum gestis non recte ab omnibus enarratis* suggests as much, as it first analyzes and then proposes a solution to the impasse of Renaissance *vitae et passiones sanctorum*. Saints' lives have the potential to benefit everyone, especially Christians, Raffaele admits. But nobody who consults these histories, *historiae*, finds benefit there. The problem is that the traditional

---

92. *De civitate dei,* book 22, chap. 8.

93. The quoted phrase is from Raffaele Maffei, *Commentariorum libri,* book 21, fol. 246r, a reference to the Roman Academy's symposium in honor of Romulus; it is repeated by Pastor, *History,* 4:44, note. To help evaluate this phrase, recall that Raffaele owed his appointment to Paul's firing of the abbreviators.

texts depict perfection. The histories, in other words, are not histories at all but "encomia or panegyrics and songs of praise, full of prodigious feats and virtues and good deeds."[94] About "prodigious feats"—miracles—Maffei has nothing to say in this chapter. They are not the problem: presumably a well-documented miracle was, for Maffei, a reliable fact. About the overabundance of "virtues and good deeds," however, he is profoundly concerned. This overabundance of perfections can be mended if authors will turn from the perfections of panegyric to the imperfections of history, which he conceives in Tacitean terms as the impartial "narrat[ion] of all, the good and the bad."[95] The result of attention to *historia* will be a narrative representing a saint who errs but who also recovers. Such an example—a saint who helps readers to self-knowledge by being imperfect as humans are—would offer solace to distressed and frightened consciences, anxious about God's wrath (*ira*). Made strong by such models, the despairing could emerge from the pit of sin (*baratro peccatorum*) and rise to self-knowledge.[96] Clearly we are far from Basil's joining of *encomion* and *historia,* far from the notion that the same text might teach admiration and imitation.[97]

Raffaele Maffei's criticism of the new oratory for the saints is a serious one. If the saints' perfection leads to despair on one hand or to scandalous jokes on the other, then panegyric is not beneficial but harmful. Humanist rhetoricians, by virtue of their participation in the fashion for panegyric, will necessarily undermine the exemplary function of the saints, contributing by their very praises to the decline of faith. Raffaele does not charge that classicizing speeches are pagan or insincere or distracting or damaging to doctrine. The problem is rather one of literary kind. If saints are to be effective models, they cannot be represented according to the law of panegyric. This message is one that Garzoni would not have under-

94. Hyperbole troubles Maffei even in the Bible: see *Stromata book* I, chap. 16 (*Q* fol. 22r–v): "De hyperbolis que in sacris voluminibus reperiuntur." Here he turns to Augustine for help, but admits that even Augustine and Jerome sometimes speak hyperbolically. Cf. *Stromata* book 4, chap. 19, "De historiae utilitate quantum haec inter caetera scripta polleat" (*Q* fols. 114r–v), where Maffei emphasizes reliability (discussed further below). It is followed immediately by a chapter on the virtues and vices of popular preachers.

95. "Historia namque vera omnia bona malaque narrat, et singula hominis describendi ita persequitur ut nec amori neque odio sed iudicio tantum serviat, et censuram morum non encomion facere videatur" (*Q*, fol. 246).

96. The connection of Maffei's concerns to developments in penitential theology are obvious; see Katherine Janson, *The Making of the Magdalene* (Princeton, N.J.: Princeton University Press, 2000), especially chap. 7, "Do Penance," on how the late medieval cult of the quintessential sinning saint fits into these developments. She does not figure in Raffaele's thoughts, however.

97. *Q* fol. 28: "Quod omnia sanctorum admiranda quidem atque laudanda qua laude sunt digna. Imitanda vero non omnia" (Bk 1, chap. 23).

stood, for Maffei appears to have identified a contradiction lodged in the humanists' attempt to apply the *enkomion nomon*. When brought to a certain panegyrical pitch (one that looks like Basil's Second Sophistic), the program of the *studia humanitatis* threatened to create incoherence in an area of pastoral care that it meant to renew, indeed, that practitioners believed themselves uniquely equipped to renew. The perfect saint of panegyric was impossible to imitate and therefore of no use to an audience mired in the merely possible. The ritual saint of the community's liturgy could not help the beset individual. Thus Maffei undid the easy and familiar knot of encomion, history, and moral philosophy that Basil's sermons had so expertly tied.

❈ ❈ ❈

Causae autem scribendi haec mihi potissimum extitere, quod, videlicet, sanctorum vitae gestaque lex quaedam ac disciplina legentibus sint, virtutis certum rursum exemplar ac forma ad quae nos effingere atque componere valeamus. In historia enim quaedam vis est atque potentia qua mirum in modum animus legentis, nisi depravatus penitus sit, afficiatur et ad imitandum que legerit animetur.
These reasons for writing stand out especially strongly, in my opinion: namely, that the lives and deeds of the saints are a kind of law and discipline to readers, and a sure example and model to which we can shape and compose ourselves. For in history there is a certain force and power, by which the soul of the reader (unless he is completely depraved) may be drawn and be stirred to imitate what he reads.

—Antonio degli Agli, from the first preface to *De vitis et gestis sanctorum* (ca. 1450)[98]

Did other humanists, intent on remapping the Christian Republic, share Raffaele Maffei's misgivings about the new panegyric? His misgivings were shared by the Ciceronian theorist of classicizing panegyric for the saints, Aurelio Brandolini. During his stay in Hungary at the close of the Quattrocento, Brandolini had written a dialogue, *De humanae vitae conditione et de toleranda corporis aegritudine* (On the human condition and the necessity of bearing bodily affliction).[99] In it, Brandolini depicts a character named Petrus Ransanus, representing the Dominican humanist

98. Massimo Miglio, *Storiografia pontificia del Quattrocento* (Bologna: Patron, 1975), 177.
99. Aurelius Lippus Brandolinus, *De humanae vitae conditione et de toleranda corporis aegritudine ad Mathiam Corvinum Hungariae et Bohemiae regem et Beatricem reginam dialogus*, ed. Abel Jeno (Budapest, 1890), 10–75. Brandolini was at Corvinus's court only for about a year, from 1489 until the king's death on April 6, 1490; see Rotondo, "Brandolini, Aurelio," 26–28. There is a brief discussion of this work in Charles W. Trinkaus, *In Our Image and Likeness: Humanity and Divinity in Italian Humanist Thought* (Chicago: University of Chicago Press), 1:294–306.

Pietro Ransano of Palermo, who was with Brandolini at the Hungarian court in the 1490s. Ransanus attempts to persuade elderly King Matthias Corvinus to make peace with his approaching death.[100] He offers the consoling example of the saints' virtuous suffering, an offer that is especially affecting since the Dominican Ransano was in fact an accomplished humanist author of *vitae sanctorum*. But Corvinus brusquely dismisses Petrus's offering, finding no use in "those whom we justifiably call gods and saints." Rather, he says, "let us argue about men and those similar to us."[101]

Corvinus's objection to the saints encapsulates Raffaele's, and is all the more impressive because the dying king so badly wants a useful model. Equally striking is the effect of Corvinus's objection, which breaks the flow of Brandolini's dialogue. To respond to Corvinus, Ransanus speaks at length in defense of the exemplary value of sanctity, even modulating his appeal, as such appeals were often modified in the later Quattrocento, to consider virtuous Romans. But the saints cannot be saved: Corvinus's objection wins, for Ransanus ceases to refer to saints in the dialogue. The saints have thus demonstrably lost their power, not because of any crisis of secularization or modernity that could be simply solved by the substitution of exemplary classical heroes, but because of a crisis of imitation forced by the cultural importance of panegyric.

So, despite Brandolini's clear and untroubled instructions on panegyric for the saints in *Diis laudandis*, his *Dialogus* reveals some apprehension of the problem that would torment Raffaele. It is even possible that Brandolini addressed the problem and its solution in his own composition of saints' lives. Unfortunately, although several sources indicate that Brandolini wrote many *historiae sanctorum*, these works appear to be lost.[102]

Raffaele Maffei's saints' lives, however, are extant: we possess not just his complaint about the damage that panegyric does to effective exemplarity but also eight *vitae sanctorum*. All treat locally important saints and all were

100. On Pietro Ransano's stay in Hungary, where he delivered Corvinus's funeral oration, see Ferdinando Attilio Termini, "Ricostruzione cronologica della biografia di Pietro Ransano," *Archivio storico siciliano*, n.s., 41 (1916): 90; A. Barilaro, "Pietro Ranzano, vescovo di Lucera, umanista domenicano in Palermo," *MD*, n.s., 8–9 (1977–78): 88–89. On the verisimilar aspect of Ransano's participation, see Bruno Figliuolo, *La cultura a Napoli nel secondo Quattrocento* (Udine: Forum, 1997), 118–123.

101. "Sed omittamus illos, quos non immerito et deos et sanctos appellamus; de hominibus ac nostri similibus disputemus" (Brandolini, *De humanae vitae conditione*, 22–23), as translated by Trinkaus, *In Our Image*, 1:299.

102. Jacopo Filippo Foresti of Bergamo, O.E.S.A., *Supplementum chronicarum* (Venice, 1503), fol. 437v, asserts that Brandolini "historias multas sanctorum composuit." Later repetitions of this claim appear to derive from Foresti: see Giammaria Mazzuchelli, *Gli scrittori d'Italia* 2, 4 (Brescia, 1753): 2016; and William Cave, *Scriptorum ecclesiasticorum historia literaria* (Oxford, 1740–43), 2:210–211.

written after his withdrawal to Volterra, just after the Roman publication of Basil's homilies and at the same time that Raffaele was working on the *Stromata* (in which his anxious critique of saintly panegyric appears). So we might expect that some tension between *historia* and the *encomion nomon* would be evident in these narratives.[103] Thus the short accounts allow us to test Raffaele's theory (to be generous) against his practice and to measure both the aspirations and the failures of the humanist contribution to the history of writings about the saints.

Raffaele's *vitae sanctorum* have never been discussed as a body of work or in their chronological sequence. So I will address each, at least briefly, before drawing general conclusions. The subject of the first *vita* is the Camaldolese Giacomo Guidi da Certaldo (Jacobus Certaldus, d. 1291), now a *beatus*.[104] This Jacobus had entered the Badia di Santi Giusto e Clemente in Volterra while young (1230) and later served for a short period as its abbot (1268–1274). His virtue lay, however, in the daily evidence of his self-abnegation; he renounced the abbacy to return to the care of souls in an attached parish. He was recognized as a patron both by the Camaldulensians, who honored him in their liturgy, and by the Volterrans.[105] Thinking like a responsible member of a canonization inquiry, that is, recognizing the evidentiary value of continuing *cultus*, Raffaele entertained this double recognition as a proof of Jacobus's sanctity.[106]

---

103. Raffaele chose none of his saintly subjects from Basil (which would have sharpened the tension), for Basil's martyrs were not specially honored at Volterra. It is, however, striking that Raffaele chose not to write on Sebastian, who had been added to the Volterran pantheon on March 23, 1468, by civic decree, according to Umberto Bavoni, *La cattedrale di Volterra* (Florence: Edizione IFI, 1997), 76. See further below.

104. See Magnoaldo Ziegelbauer, *Centifolium* (Venice, 1750; reprint, Farnborough, 1967), 31a; Alberto Pagnani, *Storia dei Benedettini Camaldolesi: Cenobiti, eremiti, monache ed oblati* (Sassoferato: Garofoil, 1949), 97–98, entry 32; C. Somigli, "Giacomo Guidi," *BS* 6 (1965): 352–353.

105. "Et domestici huius apud Deum aduocati precibus uestra imprimis Congregatio, deinde urbs tota Volaterrana tuta perseueret," says Raffaele in his prefatory letter to his brother, ed. D. Papebroek, *AASS* April II (Paris, 1865): 153–154a. The *AASS* edits Maffei's dedicatory letter but presents the *vita* as reworked by Agostino Fortunio. So I will quote the *AASS* for the dedicatory letter (making reference to variants in the manuscripts) but will refer to Raffaele's *vita* on the basis of the two manuscript copies. These are BAV, MS Barb. lat. 2517, fols. 3–4 (= A) and fols. 5–6 (= B).

106. Raffaele also recorded an image in San Giusto that featured Jacobus with a saintly halo: "apud nos in quadam Sancti Iusti ara eius antiqua imago more sanctorum diademata conspicitur" (*AASS* April II [1865]: 154a). See also G. B. Mittarelli and A. Costadoni, *Annales Camaldulenses* 5 (Venice, 1760): 194. Raffaele revised the title of his account to name Jacobus not *sanctus* but *beatus* (see the corrected title in A). Both A and B versions are preceded by Raffaele's pious mark, IE + XC. For some of his thoughts on the power of the sign of the cross, see VBG, MS 5377, "1476–1515 Raffaello a Mon. Mario," letter 3, to Mario in Florence from Raffaele in Volterra, December 8, 1515: "Caeterum sortem deinceps haud in te nescio quomodo coniuratam, crucis signo dum equum conscendis facile temperabis, quo uti scis Constantinus vicit, et nostrorum militum plerique utentes securitatem in periculis auspicantur"; and remarks in Bagemihl, "Cosini's Bust," 47 and 55 n. 21.

The *vita beati Jacobi* was dedicated to Raffaele's brother Mario, perhaps in honor of Mario's appointment as commendatory abbot at the Badia in 1514.[107] Unlike his humble predecessor, Jacobus, Mario Maffei had multiple benefices and lived in Rome. So he had—formally or informally—asked Raffaele to keep an eye on the Badia.[108] This duty led Raffaele to visit the abbey and gave him an opportunity to look over its manuscripts. On one such occasion, he relates in the prefatory letter, while examining neglected codices containing *historiae* of saints, he discovered the life of the blessed Jacobus, "formerly of your guild [i.e., the abbots of Santi Giusto e Clemente]."[109] The manuscript was worn and the writing hard to read. But to preserve the *memoria* of this *vir optimus*, Raffaele derived from it a brief *vita*.[110] His account is extant in two autograph drafts, neither of which is a clean copy, much less a copy meant for presentation. In what is apparently the later draft, the *vita* has been divided after composition into eight *lectiones* or readings (six on the life, followed by two on the miracles).[111]

A *lectio* is a reading honoring a saint; groups of three to twelve *lectiones* were presented for the annual celebratory office of a saint.[112] Such read-

107. Mario, then bishop of Aquino, held the commendatory abbacy from 1514 to 1528. Luigi Consortini, *La Badia dei ss. Giusto e Clemente presso Volterra: Notizie istoriche e guida del tempio e del cenobio* (Lucca: San Paolini, 1915), 25–26, gives the text of Leo X's order passing the commenda to Mario. The *terminus ante quem* for the composition may be 1518, when Mario leased the "goods and movables" of the Badia to Raffaele's son-in-law, Paolo da Riccobaldi. See the "contratto di affitto dei beni e mobili della Badia di Volterra" of October 15, 1518 (VBG, MS 5376, *filza* with that title); it was witnessed by a relative as Paolo was then in Rome.

108. "Nobis [*sci.* Raffaele], quibus absens rerum tuarum curam delegasti," says Raffaele in his dedicatory letter.

109. "Cum nuper apud coenobitas tuos diverterem" (*A*, *B*: coenobitos) "per ocium libros quosdam semilaceros sanctorum continentes historiam evolverem, in vitam beati Iacobi unius a Collegio quondam vestro forte incidi" (*A*). Cf. *AASS* April II (1865): 153, para. 1, relying on *B*.

110. "Praeterquam quod rudi quidem sermone conscripta fuerat, adeo vetustate litteris intercidentibus obscura difficilisque lectu erat ut vix longo post tempore sensum depre[he]ndere potuerim. Ego vero [*A* Inde ego] ne viri optimi ac de nostra regione [*A* de loco isto] bene meriti memoria, posteritatis ingratae negligentia, periret . . . sum conatus eius [*AASS deest* eius] et gesta et vitae cursum brevi quidem oratione . . . seculis renovare" (*AASS* April II [1865]: 153f). Raffaele's account is barely seven hundred words in length.

111. *A* and *B* differ, especially at the end, where *A* has an addition not found in *B*. The drafts of Maffei's *lectiones* show that he wrote each account as a single narrative and then divided it (or it was divided for him) afterward into reasonably equivalent blocks of text. A set of *lectiones* already was in use, as Raffaele remarks, "in officiis item divinis eius solitam coli memoriam ex lectionum ordine digestarum argumento deprehendimus" (*AASS* April II [1865]: 154a).

112. On liturgical offices, see above, 64, n. 60. See also J. Wickham Legg, *The Second Recension of the Quignon Breviary* (Henry Bradshaw Society, 42) (London, 1912) 2:11, a succinct statement of the *desiderata* for *lectiones* under Leo X's reformation, shortly after Raffaele Maffei's death: the offices should be shortened; they should be easy to locate in the larger text of the ceremony; and they should be grammatically correct.

ings represented the most public kind of *vitae sanctorum*. Indeed, to the degree that they were both story- and sermonlike, they constituted one of the most public narrative forms written in Europe before the arrival of print. They therefore raise acutely the question of the intelligibility of Latin for audiences of mixed gender and socioeconomic status. (The question was and is bound to be answered differently in Italy than in, say, England. Moreover, it was a question that the humanists themselves did not answer with one voice.[113]) One part of the audience, and an extremely significant part, was represented by the officiant himself among his peers, fellow priests, monks, and friars, and the canons of the local cathedral. For this discerning audience, *lectiones* might well be the fifteenth-century equivalent of Basil's fourth-century homilies, at once official and artful. Both fourth-century homily and fifteenth-century office were forms of variable length that divided content at will between biographical detail and religious exhortation. Most humanists' offices have nine readings. The slightly unusual number of eight readings in Raffaele's *vita Jacobi* suggests that the account was never completed or that a biblical passage would be added to serve as the ninth.

In its first six readings, Raffaele's *vita beati Jacobi* corresponds not to the author's ideas about *historia* but to Brandolini's instructions for saintly panegyric. The Jacobus presented by Raffaele Maffei is uncomplicatedly perfect, a superior being, unchanged from the beginning of the *vita* to its end. The account begins with the usual threefold human aspects: goods of fortune (family and beauty);[114] goods of nature (virtues such as maturity, silence, delight in reading and meditation); and goods of character (the vow of virginity, fasting, frequent prayer, obedience, modesty, refusal of office, etc.). The final two readings on miracles address Jacobus's divine aspects. In their historical detail, these final readings violate the practice of early Christian oratory noted above, but they do meet the minimal requirements of miracle records for canonization as understood in the fifteenth century, giving vague notices on the names of recipients and indications of place and time. In these last two readings, from among the posthumous *signa immodica* of Jacobus's sanctity, Raffaele

---

113. E.g., Angelo Mazzocco, *Linguistic Theories in Dante and the Humanists: Studies of Language and Intellectual History in Late Medieval and Early Renaissance Italy* (Leiden: Brill, 1993), 14–21, and especially 15–16 and 18–19, quotes comments of both Flavio Biondo and Leonardo Bruni on the ability of untrained contemporaries to understand Latin (at the Mass, at the Curia): Biondo claimed that they could and Bruni that they could not. Later contributors to the debate also disagreed.

114. *A* names the father: "patre Albertino inter suos nobilitate principi equitique admodum strenuo." *B* does not: "patre cuius nomen non traditur milite admodum strenuo laudatoque."

relates five prodigies of healing, which he calls not *miracula* or *mirabilia* or *virtutes* but—as if in perfect concord with Brandolini's instructions—*beneficia*.[115]

Raffaele's explicit aim, announced in the dedicatory letter and repeated at the conclusion of the *vita*, was to encourage imitation.[116] Despite the emphasis on imitation, and despite the fact that the absent Mario might have been an ideal audience for a narrative that represented Raffaele's ideas about the heuristic value of erring sanctity, human imperfection was not broached in the *vita beati Jacobi*. Perhaps local pressures to present the familiar saint were great. Perhaps Raffaele's silence reflects no more than the silence of the historical record. Perhaps Raffaele's uneasiness about the saint's status—actually *sanctus,* or just *beatus*?—made him cautious. Or perhaps the dilemma of *De sanctorum gestis*, that is, Raffaele's apprehension that evidence of human imperfection was needed for the exemplary function of a narrative to achieve its full effect, had not yet dawned in his own mind.

By the time of Raffaele's second foray into *vitae sanctorum*, however, I suspect that it had. In 1518/19 he composed five sets of *lectiones* about saints traditionally honored in Volterra.[117] These figures were the first-century Roman bishop Linus (f.d. September 23), known as the first Latin pope;[118] three martyrs of the Diocletianic persecution, the pair Actinea and Grecimania (f.d. June 16)[119] and Victor Maurus (f.d. May 8/13);[120] and three sixth-century hermits who had emigrated to Italy from North

---

115. *A*, fol. 4, the beginning of *lectio* 7: "Sanctitatis ilico [*sic*] signa immodica apparuerunt, sed quinque tantum memoratu conscribam." Each time the word *beneficium* is used, it is carefully related to God as well as to the saint, for example, "ob tantum beneficium deo ac sancto gratias agens" and "deo tanti beneficii auctori per suum sanctum gratias agens" (*A*, fol. 4, *lectiones* 7 and 8). The final reading in *A* records recent miracles.

116. See the epigraph to this chapter. Maffei's account is for those people, Camaldulensians above all, who will want to imitate Jacobus, "qui eius et ordine et vestigia querunt imitari" (*A*, fol. 3). Presumably this audience can understand spoken Latin.

117. For the date, see Rome, BN, Autografici, Scat. A 96 7/2, quoted below, n. 132.

118. The untitled office of Pope Linus in three lessons that concludes the *Officium* may have been written for the convent of San Lino (above, n. 9). On Linus, see A. Amore, "Lino," in *BS* 8 (1966): 56–57; *ODP*, "Linus"; *AASS* Sept. VI (Paris, 1867): 539–545, especially 542–543. Bavone, *La cattedrale di Volterra*, 95, gives a reproduction of the polychrome terracotta of Linus executed for the cathedral by Giovanni della Robbia or Benedetto Baglioni. For Maffeo Vegio's note on the tomb of Pope Linus at Ostia, see his *De translatione B. Monicae*, quoted in G. A. Consonni, "Intorno alla vita di Maffeo Vegio di Lodi: Notizi inedite," *Archivio Storico Italiano* 5 (1908): 385 n. 3.

119. Raffaele's *officium* for this pair is a recounting of the *inventio* of 1140. See Marucci, *Dizionario* 3:885; M. Japundzic, "Actinea et Grecimana," *BS* 1 (1961): 167; and *AASS* June IV (Paris, 1867): 31–36.

120. See n. 147 below.

Africa: Octavianus (f.d. September 2),[121] and the pair Justus and Clemens (f.d. June 5).[122] All had lengthy associations with Volterra; Justus and Clemens, for instance, are the city's chief patrons. The Duomo still possesses head reliquaries for each.[123]

The five offices were commissioned by the canons of the cathedral at Volterra.[124] Since their instructions are not extant, we must depend on Raffaele's report of what they wanted.[125] His letter intimates that a general reorganization of liturgical practice was under way at Volterra (not surprising, since the canons included Mario Maffei, and Antonio Zeno, and the bishop was Francesco Soderini): this liturgical reform included attention to the celebration of "our patrons."[126] The canons felt that the old accounts were awkwardly and ineptly written, hard to understand and unpleasant to hear.[127] As Raffaele observed to the learned men who had set him the commission, these infelicities were not the fault of the saints themselves but of the illiterate times in which the offices had been composed.[128] The canons asked Raffaele to reshape and develop, *interpolare*, the readings in an appropriate way, *quantum fas fuerit*.[129] Raffaele closed his letter by assuring the canons that his revision would not, for the sake

121. Octavianus is associated with Justus and Clemens, and his feast is celebrated in the octave following theirs. See Marucci, *Dizionario* 3:1138–1139, and *AASS* Sept. I (Paris, 1868): 389–405, for the difficulties with this saint. On the reliquary bust commissioned by Mario around 1534 and made by Angelo Pollaiolo, see D'Amico, "The Maffei Monument," 473–474; Bavoni, *La cattedrale*, 104.

122. On these figures, see Marucci, *Dizionario* 3:1024–1025; S. Ferrali, "Giusto e Clemente," *BS* 6 (1966): 42–47; *AASS* June I (Paris, 1867): 430–444. According to Pescetti, "Mario Maffei," 84, Raffaele's brother Mario—usually taken to be the less conventionally devout of the brothers—arranged for a special inscription of gratitude to Justus after the sack of Rome: "quod duce te, Iuste, hoc anno MDXXVII Volaterrani a bello, peste et fame liberati sint, quibus calamitatibus reliqua Italia vexata fuit."

123. Bavoni, *La cattedrale*, includes good images; see also Ugo Bavoni and F. A. Lessi, *Custodie di santità: Reliquie e reliquiari a Volterra* (Siena: Centrooffset, 1995).

124. The chapter's letter of commission does not seem to be extant. It can be surmised from Raffaele's reply; see the following note. That same reply lists the canons, led by Francesco della Rovere as priest. Of the twenty names given there, Maffei was related by blood, marriage, adoption, or godparenthood to at least six.

125. Raffaele's reply is extant in three drafts: BAV, MS Ottob. lat. 2377, fol. 252 (= L); ibid., fol. 256 (= l); and Ottob. lat. 992, fol. 247 (= O). It is the opening document in the printed *Officium* (to be discussed shortly), from which I quote (sign. lv).

126. "Qum nonnulla in chori dispositione atque ordine minime decenter [l: chori praesertim ordine ac dispositione vetustatis reverentiae gratia hactenus custodita non rite aut decenter] procedere conspexeritis, inter que sunt ea que ad nostros pertinent patronos."

127. "Incongrua et inepta . . . conscripta . . . nec intellectu legentibus facilia, nec denique populo auditu delectabilia sint."

128. "Non hominum illorum quibus maxime debemus, sed temporum vitio [O: litteris iam pene deflorescentibus]."

129. "Negotium mihi dedistis ea quantum fas fuerit interpolandi."

of elegance, deviate from the integrity of history, *historiae integritas*, or from the true authority, *vera auctoritas*, of the traditional text.[130]

These offices were much more successful than the readings that Raffaele had made from the *vita beati Jacobi*. They secured papal approval in 1519 and, apparently by late June of that same year, were published at Florence in a handbook *Officium*, with a colophon to guarantee their legitimacy for the audience of prelates who might want to use them (see plate 6).[131] When Raffaele sent the offices to his brother in Rome, they were read by at least two appreciative and knowledgeable prelates, Mario himself and the bishop of Imola, Dominicus Scribonius (Scrivani, Cerbonio; d. 1533), who was at the time engaged in revising the entire office, *tutto loffitio*.[132]

Most of the accounts in the *Officium* bear the title *historia*. It is a traditional liturgical term for that part of the day's office devoted to readings about a saint. Given Raffaele's opinions about the importance of *historia* for saints as expressed in *De sanctorum gestis* and his assurances to the cathedral chapter regarding the nature of his revisions, it is tempting to make much of this title. But here, too, we must be careful. Whether Raffaele meant something more or hoped that the polysemy of the technical term would increase his contemporaries' appreciation of the office is hard to judge at this distance. We can, however, judge whether Raffaele responded in the *Officium* to the crisis of exemplarity that he had identified in *De sanctorum gestis*. The answer must be that he did not, at least if depicting the saint's human failures—as *De gestis* claims—constitutes the

130. "Sic me adcomodavi ut [*l* ubi sum ita conatus ut] ne ornandi causa ab historiae integritate discederem, nec scripti veteris alioquin [*canc. l* quamquam inepti] veri auctoritati preter stili reconcinnationem ullo [*canc. l* et quorundam ad rerum luculentiorem intelligentiam adiectionem] modo derogarem." The letter does not indicate that Raffaele was provided with a source for this rewriting.

131. The dating is attested by the colophon (plate 6); see also the following note. The only copy I have been able to find is at VBG; it was known to Falconcini, who wrote his name on the title page, but has not been recorded among sixteenth-century publications.

132. Scrivani was named bishop of Imola on February 10, 1511. Nelson Minnich informs me that he was present as apostolic notary at the Fifth Lateran Council (1512–1517) during sessions 3–7, 10, and 12 and at the general congregations before the 11th and 12th sessions (personal communication). See Rome, BN, Autografici, scat. A 96 7/2, from Mario in Rome to Raffaele in Volterra, June 27, 1519:

Ho ricevute tutte le vostre co li offitii da voi novamente facti quali ho lecti et piacemi assai. Credo conociate un certo Scribonio da Cipta di Castello gia secretario del R.mo Pavia [Francesco Alidosi, appointed bishop of Pavia March 30, 1503, and then cardinal December 7, 1505], hora vescovo d'Imola, *quale compone di novo tutto loffitio,* et havendo lui saputo di questi vestri me li ha domandati per vederli. Halli veduti piacerli et molto li lauda et havendo lui desyderio che vediate delli sui mi ha mandate queste due carte che io vele mandi accio le vediate, et se paresse ad voi ci stesse qualcosa male dicte li sara grato lo correggiate.

opposite of panegyric. As in the *vita beati Jacobi*, so in the *Officium*: there is no depiction of a struggling, much less of an erring and recovering saint. None of the martyrs falter toward their goals; none are shown to flinch.

Victor, for example, is a noble youth, brought up as a Christian, possessed of heavenly beauty in body and soul, and so obviously deserving of imperial honors that the persecuting ruler grieves to lose his counsel.[133] Raffaele represents Victor accounting for his faith gravely and coolly with indirect speech: "That intrepid man spoke with great constancy and repeated that it was not a novelty and neither had he been only recently converted, as perhaps might be thought. Rather, he had been educated in Christian discipline from childhood, and nothing gave him more pride than to be called by that name [Christian]. Moreover, if he [the emperor] would try [Christianity], he, too, would follow [the saint's] example so that as a ruler over others he might easily draw all to the same faith."[134] The martyr meets his tortures—beatings, imprisonment, starvation, more beatings, molten lead, more imprisonment—with prayers in direct address.[135] In one instance, an angel intervenes; Raffaele simply states this event, without comment. After each round, Victor recovers his original strength, *vires pristinae*. Before the last torture comes reasoned blandishment, set out in indirect speech just as cool as Victor's earlier declaration of faith: "they urged upon him that he had been punished enough, lest he experience more of Maximianus's anger, lest he incur further cruelties for himself, lest he allow his youth and dignity to be wasted. It would take just a moment to fulfill the command. Let him just sacrifice to the gods, and

133. Raffaele's account of Victor follows in outline *BHL* 8580, although he does not mention Ambrose, Nazarius, or Celsus, all of whom are associated with Victor. Victor's reliability is claimed in *lectio* 1 in the *Officium*, sign. 4v: "Nobili ortus prosapia . . . in lege ac timore domini diligenter educatus ad exercendus animi corporisque dotes que coelitus ei obvenerant . . . in equestrem ordinem cooptari locumque honoratissimum in aula meruit." From *lectio* 3, sign. 5v: "Maximianus vero quod ilum magnopere diligeret ne tanto viro qui ornamento sibi aulaeque foret privatione doleret." In *lectio* 4, further honors are offered. Such offerings are, of course, a *topos* of panegyric for martyrs.

134. *Officium, lectio* 2, sign. b: "Ille intrepidus magnaque constantia fatetur ac dictitat non rem esse novam nec paulo ante persuasam quemadmodum forte putaret. Verum ab ineunte aetate in Christi disciplina nutritum fuisse gloriarique se nulla magis re quam tali nomini censeri. Praeterea si sapiat ipse quoque suum sequatur exemplum ut qui ceteris imperaret ad eandem fidem omnis facile invitaret. Unde et Romanae rei publicae et orbi universo meliora succederent secula."

135. *Officium, lectiones* 4, 5, and 7 include prayers in direct address. At one point in these tortures, the martyr quotes David (*Officium, lectio* 4, sign. b3r–v: "Ego vero, respondebat, nunquam sacrificabo ac cum David potius dicam, 'Omnes dii gentium daemonia'"). Cf. the version given in Mombrizio's *Sanctuarium* (*BHL* 8580), which is filled with dialogue, including this quotation from David. Mombrizio also includes a similar prayer in direct address mentioning the three children in the fiery furnace. I have been unable to discover if Maffei had access to the *Sanctuarium*.

not show disdain for the gods who had made the Roman republic beloved throughout the world."[136] Again, Victor does not hesitate: "It was useless. Indeed, it more and more confirmed him in this stubborn faith of his."[137] After the final torments and execution, the emperor learns of a prodigy, *prodigium*: the martyr's unburied body is being guarded by lions.[138] Led by God to retrieve the body for burial, the Milanese priest Maternus is struck with wonder, *admiratus*, to discover the lions.[139] Here, as throughout, the troublesome word *miracula* is avoided, even when Victor escapes from prison; Raffaele does not revert to *beneficia* but otherwise seems closer to Brandolini's promotion of panegyric than to his own strictures against it. The Latin is set out in short, simple phrases.

Nevertheless, the *sancti Victoris historia* also shows that Raffaele did—as he urged in *De sanctorum gestis*—attend to history in these writings about saints. Contrary to the *encomion nomon* that required periphrasis, Raffaele included factual details whenever he could. His nine *lectiones* for Victor are an interesting example, since the early account on which he seems to have relied (scholars suppose this account to be no earlier than the eighth century, and it is widely diffused in later manuscripts) closed with a subscription claiming authorship by a fourth-century Christian Maximianus, notary and eyewitness.[140] Raffaele might, therefore, have

---

136. *Officium*, *lectio* 5, sign. b4: "Rationibus omnibus adhortatur ne maximianum iratum magis experiatur satis poenarum dedisse. Ne sibi amplius crudelis existat. Ne aetatem pariter et dignitatem suam perditum iri permittat. Breviter fieri posse quod illi iubet. Tantum diis thurificet, Deo patrios quos Romana respublica per orbem coli iusit ne despiciat." The speaker is Maximianus's counselor Anolinus.

137. Ibid.: "Qumque nihil proficeret et hoc magis ac magis eum in obstinato fidei proposito confirmarent."

138. *Officium*, *lectio* 7, sign. b5v: "Ubi vero sensit a duobus leonibus custoditum incolumemque servatum prodigio perterritus tumulari concessit."

139. *Officium*, *lectio* 8, sign. b5v–c: "Aderat autem eo tempore Maternus praesul mediolanensis vir sanctitate conspicuus. Is a Deo monitus locum adiit ubi ille iacebat. Conspectisque leonibus qui ei venienti veneratione quadam loco cesserant, admiratus Deo gratias egit."

140. For diffusion of the Victor legend, see Jean-Charles Picard, *Le souvenir des évêques: Sépoltures, listes épiscopales et culte des évêques en Italie du Nord des origiines au Xe siècle* (Rome: BEFR, 1988), 37–40, 445–446, 622–623. See also n. 147 below. The subscription is included in Mombrizio's *Sanctuarium* (Paris, 1910), 2:632: "ego Maximianus notarius imperatoris christianus ab infantia iuravi per paganissimum eorum : et tamen per noctem cum luminaribus in hippodromo circi scripsi prout memoria potui retinere : quia ibi manebam : et adiuravi omnes : ut si quis inveniret scripturam hanc : christiano viro non negaret haec omnia oculis meis vidi deo teste et sancta trinitate." Cf. Raffaele's *Officium*, *lectio* 8, sign. c:

Et haec quidem de Victoris vita morteque ex monumentis maiorum nobis relictis deprendimus praesertim Maximii [*sic*]. Is in principis aula scriba christianusque fuit interque sacrilegos homines virtute patientiae Christi Deique sui sine querela legem servabat. Dumque haec fierent apud Hippodromum habitans omnibus interfuit. Huius veritatem historiae testatur : insuper obtestans omnis qui hanc habere scireque contingat ne celent cateros Christi fideles. Ut tanti martyris gesta in honorem Iesu Christi verso innotescerent ac ipsius memoria posteritati perpetuo celebranda comendaretur.

considered any factual detail particularly authentic. So, as he winnowed the traditional account, he carefully kept the notice of Victor's birth in Mauritania ("opposite Spain") and of his arrival in Milan (specifying first a journey *in Italiam*).[141] He named the emperor and then went further, with an eye on his audience, to explain who this emperor was: "Maximianus was then the ruler. It was he who administered the empire together with Diocletian and had such great hatred for the faithful," adding an authority, "as Eusebius bears witness."[142] Victor's most appalling tortures take place *pro tribunali*, before the tribune in the Hippodrome: "Now the Hippodrome," Raffaele explains with disarmingly direct concern for the audience's comprehension, "was a space where horse races were held."[143] Likewise, all the Milanese locations are specified: the first prison is at the Ticino Gate, near the circus; the second, at the Roman Gate; Victor awaits sentencing at the Vercelli Gate; and he is executed in a copse of oaks, the Viridarium, outside the city.[144] The concluding reading is not given over to miracles, unlike the *vita beati Jacobi*, where Raffaele may have been intent on posthumous miracles in order to substantiate the sanctity of the *beatus*. Rather, Raffaele devotes the final *lectio* of the office for Victor to a clear explanation of the twelfth-century events that had caused a Spaniard martyred in Milan to become patron of Volterra.[145] His main concern, in other words, is to give a credible account.

In an early chapter of the *Stromata*, Raffaele had argued that those who wrote about church matters especially needed to be good historians. *De historiae utilitate quantum haec inter caetera scripta polleat* commends an early pope for requiring his notaries to collect factual notices about the martyrs.[146] It is impossible, Raffaele remarks, to write about such events without recourse to secular history, the emperors, kings, and peoples under whom the martyrs suffered. Every kind of writing, from biblical commentary to poetry to astrology, had recourse to history because of its reliability. That reliability was what he attempted to offer in his office for Victor.

There was, however, a serious problem with Raffaele's recourse to history as factual detail: the seven saints of the *Officium* were more distantly in the past than the Camaldolese abbot Jacobus. Raffaele had chosen, or

141. *Officium, lectio* 1, sign. 4v: "Victor in Mauritania tingitana contra Hispaniam sita, . . . in Italiam transfretavit, Mediolanumque venit."

142. *Officium, lectio* 1, sign. 4v: "Tunc Maximianus princeps agebat. Is est qui cum Diocletiano pariter imperium administravit tantoque infideles odio Eusebio teste."

143. *Officium, lectio* 3, sign. bv: "Erat enim Hippodromus spatium ubi equorum cursus exercebatur."

144. *Officium, lectio* 3, sign. bv: lectio 4., sign. b3v; lectio 6, sign. b4v and b5r.

145. *Officium, lectio* 9, sign. cv–c2.

146. *Q*, book 1, chap. 18, fol. 113v: the pope named is Telesphorus, so the notice is not factually correct. Cf. Kelly, *ODP* 9. No notice of the martyred Telesphorus as a collector of martyrs' *acta* occurs in the *Liber pontificalis*. Cf. chap. 2 above.

the canons had handed him, obscure saints, figures burdened with untrustworthy dossiers. He probably misjudged, for example, the head relic of Victor that was held at Volterra, mistaking it for Victor Maurus of Milan.[147] If
the Victor of his *Officium* is not the Volterran Victor, then no amount of
factual detail can authenticate the account. Similar sorts of problems dog
the other narratives. Of the first pope, Linus, for example, almost nothing
was known. In his *Liber de vita Christi ac omnium pontificum*, Bartolomeo
Platina (1421–1481) had managed to make a short entry on Linus into a
long one by padding the account first with a discussion of Galba, Otto, and
Vitellius and then with notices on Philo and Josephus drawn Jerome's *De
viris illustribus*.[148] Raffaele did well in the circumstances; the Bollandists
complimented the historical accuracy of the office by editing it in part.[149]
He drew on his own *Commentariorum libri* to make the first *lectio*;[150] he
used Platina's entry in the *Vitae pontificum* for notices of Linus's papal
achievements.[151] He was original in mentioning the witness of Hegesippus
(d. 180) and Damasus (d. 384), based on Eusebius.[152] But Raffaele could
only manage three *lectiones* for Linus and had to spin the third out of the
sententia that honor was owed to local gods.[153]

Even when he had more information with which to work, Raffaele did

147. Raffaele seems to have thought that he was writing about the Milanese Victor Maurus, on whom see A. Rimoldi, "Vittore," *BS* 12 (1969):1274–1275; C. Pasini, *Dizionario dei
santi della chiesa di Milano* (Milan, 1995): 53–56; and M. Forlin Patruccio, "Vittore di
Milano," *GLS* 1967a–1968b. But *AASS* May II (Paris, 1866): 201, conjectures that the Victor
in Volterra is probably Victor M. Polentiae. See also *AASS* May II (Paris, 1866): 284, para. 4.

148. Bartolomeo Sacchi, il Platina, *Liber de vita Christi ac omnium pontificum*, ed. G.
Gaida, in *RRIISS* 3, 1 (Città di Castello: Lapi, 1913), entry 2, at 13–15.

149. *AASS* Sept. VI (Paris, 1867): 542, paras. 14–15, mentioning the office for Linus
"quod pro civitate et dioecesi Volaterrana compositum fuit et approbatum a Leone Papa X
anno 1519" and noting, without naming the author, that "referuntur ea, quae visa sunt prob-
abiliora ceteris S. Lini gesta."

150. *Officium, lectio* 1, sign. f5, is very close in wording to *Commentariorum libri*, book 22.
That entry draws on a discovery that Raffaele had made at Volterra. It allowed him to go beyond
the entry Antonio degli Agli had made in his preliminary revision of the martyrology, which had
included the comment, "De vita vero eius ac gestis nihil ultra reperi. Cum tamen et discipulus et
successor Petri extitisset, non nisi magnum quid existimari fast est. Gesta rursus huius sic oblivione obruta sunt, ut de eo non nisi quae ex precepto beati Petri xv presbiteros ordina⟨v⟩it reperi"
(Florence, BN, MS Nuovi acq. 399, fol. h; BAV, MS Lat. 3742, fols. 15v–16).

151. From Platina, Raffaele seems to draw the notice that Linus first required women to
cover their heads before entering church, wrote the "res gestas Petri," and created fifteen
bishops and eighteen presbyters; see Platina, *Liber,* 14, ll. 23–25.

152. *Officium, lectio* 2, sign. f5v: "Cuius item Aegesippus vicinus apostolis mentionem
faciens ex eodem mutuatus videtur. A Neronis anno ultimo ad Domitiani tempora pervenit
sub quo martyr fuit, ut ait Damasus."

153. *Officium, lectio* 3, sign. f5v–f6v: "Quod si alienigenas rerum nostrarum apud Deum
eligimus promotores : Quanto magis nostri generis homine in maxima superni regis digna-
tione constitutos nobis usui ornamentoque in Christo futuros sperare debemus." The importance of Moses to the Hebrews is given as an example, as is the biblical fact that the angel of
Persia fought the angel of Israel, "Quisque pro suis apud Deum sollicitus."

not always make convincing use of it. In these instances, his conservative response to the chronological and factual problems thrown up by the dossiers dismayed even the Bollandists, who wanted to think well of Raffaele as a *beatus*.[154] Daniel Papebroek, for example, wished to subtract from Raffaele's account at least the office of Justus and Clemens because of its chronological inaccuracy.[155] The office for Octavian showed the same disregard for chronology that had marred the office for Justus and Clemens, and Papebroek complained, "turpissime contra chronologiam errat lectionum auctor," the author has erred most basely against chronology.[156]

Raffaele, in short, was caught between his desires for persuasive exemplarity and for convincing factual accuracy. What he found by way of historical evidence did not serve what he believed his audience needed from these saints. At times, the historical record was so faulty that Maffei decided to acknowledge the lacunae in the course of the office. The three drafts of his *legendum* for the invention of Actinia and Grecimania, for example, reveal him grappling with the best ways to state many uncertainties. Already in an early draft, Maffei toyed with having the priest announce that research on the question of the martyrs' *forma vitae* (were they virgins or widows?) was still incomplete, "not well ascertained."[157] Maffei also wanted the priest to explain in the course of the office that the *inventio* was ascribed to Innocent III on the basis of conjecture.[158] This approach leads Maffei to tread the boundaries of the genre in the office for Justus and Clemens.[159] By the last reading, Maffei has abandoned

154. Raffaele is described as "nobilitate vitae austeritate, pietate, longe clarissimus, ac post mortem in magna apud moltos habitus veneratione, corpore ad annos plures incorrupto" in *AASS* Feb. I (1658): 330, para. 9.

155. *AASS* June I (1867): 431, 4; further complaints in 6–7, and on 432, 8, and 10–12.

156. Repetition helped memory, Raffaele said, directing that the office for Octavian should begin with the same readings as that for Justus and Clemens. Having condemned the anachronism in the entry for Justus and Clemens, the Bollandists could only condemn it in the entry for Octavian. See *AASS* Sept. I (1868): 391, para. 7; the editor goes on to discuss those errors committed by the unnamed author on the basis of the *Commentariorum libri*, book 5, fol. 51, by Raffaele Maffei. Raffaele's difficulties with these saints are understandable; see Ovidio Lari, *I santi Giusto e Clemente patroni di Volterra: Ricostruzione storica* (Volterra, 1962), 5–10.

157. "Hae itaque Voltaerranae sub Diocletiano et Maximiano principibus martyres fuere virginesne an matronae [*canc.* seu viduae] non satis exploratum" (*virgines . . . viduae* add. in marg. dextr.), given in BAV, MS, Ottob. Lat. 2377, fol. 255. The first draft, BAV, MS Ottob. Lat. 992, fols. 254–255, also includes the announcement of the lacuna (fol. 254). The statement remains in the printed *Officium*.

158. Raffaele Maffei, third draft of the *legendum* for the office of the *inventio* of Actinea and Grecimania (untitled), in MS Ottob. Lat. 2377, fol. 261v: "ut ex coniecturis deprendere valui hunc tertium fuisse putaverim." See Marko Japundzic, in *BS* I (1961): 167.

159. Raffaele Maffei, "Historia sanctorum Justi et Clementis," in MS Ottob. Lat. 992, fol. 253r–v.

Volterra's patron saints altogether and resorted to emending the local martyrology. The priest is to direct that the city name "Antonia" be expunged from the martyrology and replaced with "Otonia," the name given to Volterra by Emperor Otto, who refounded the city after its devastation by barbarians.[160] The office concludes, in other words, with the priest reciting a simple history lesson. Raffaele thus gave the priest an explicit new role: to mediate not just between God and the faithful but also between the devotional present and the historical past. Not only can philology be *about* the sacred, it can be *sacralized*, folded into the commemorative exposition of the liturgy.

Raffaele's penultimate effort brought him back to the thirteenth century and a subject more fully documented: the Florentine widow and Franciscan tertiary Umiliana dei Cerchi (1219–1246).[161] It also brought him a new sort of problem. Shortly after the publication of the *Officium*, Raffaele accepted an invitation from the Observant Franciscans of San Salvatore in Florence to compose a more "suitable" (*comodior*) life of the Beata Umiliana.[162] The Franciscans may have hoped to have Umiliana canonized, estimating her chances favorably under a Florentine pope. Raffaele completed this *vita* by June 6, 1521, the date of the letter of thanks that he received from the Observants' vicar general Illarione Sachetti.[163]

Sachetti praised Raffaele as another Jerome, perhaps intimating a parallel not just between the two authors in their scholarly retreats but also

160. *O*, fol. 253v.

161. Umiliana has become a popular subject. See Bernard Schlager, "Foundresses of the Franciscan Life: Umiliana Cerchi and Margaret of Cortona," *Viator* 29 (1998): 141–166; Anne M. Schuchman, "The Lives of Umiliana de'Cerchi: Representations of Female Sainthood in Thirteenth Century Florence," *Essays in Medieval Studies* 14 (1998): 15–28; Monica Cristina Storini, "Umiliana ed il suo biografo: Costruzione di un'agiografia femminile fra XIII e XIV secolo," *Annali d'Italianistica* 13 (1995): 19–39; Carol Lansing, *Florentine Magnates: Lineage and Faction in a Medieval Commune* (Princeton, N.J.: Princeton University Press, 1991), 109–124; and, still valuable, Anna Benvenuti Papi, "Umiliana dei Cerchi: Nascità di un culto nella Firenze del Dugento," *Studi francescani* 77 (1980): 87–117, reprinted in eadem, *In castro poenitentiae: Santità e società femminile nell'Italia medievale* (Rome, 1990), 59–98; and eadem, "Cerchi, Umiliana de'," *DBI* 23 (1979): 692b–696a, giving a copious earlier bibliography. I thank Anne Schuchman for notice of her doctoral dissertation on Umiliana's cult from her death in 1246 to her canonization in 1694, directed by Maria Luisa Ardizzone at New York University.

162. *Comodior* might mean "extensive" or "fully developed," but since Raffaele produced an epitome (see below), the word must mean "appropriate" or "suitable" here. The initial invitation came from Frater Andreas of Florence; see Raffaele's first prefatory letter, to Andreas (*L*, fol. 1; *O*, fol. 242r), mentioning the friar "rogans ut lectione comodiore quantum fas esset interpolarem" (a phrase found also in Raffaele's letter to the Volterran canons).

163. Sachetti's letter is edited in *AASS* May IV (Paris, 1866): 412b. Leo X died on December 1, 1521, before a formal case for the canonization could be presented, and the new pope, Adrian VI (January 9, 1522–September 14, 1523), was neither Florentine nor Franciscan.

between Raffaele's Umiliana and Jerome's Paula. The comparison flatters both Raffaele and Umiliana, but, at least in the case of the author, it will barely hold. Raffaele's drafts, as well as his finished account, suggest that he felt much less warmly toward his subject—whom, of course, he had not known—than Jerome had felt toward his dear friend, the mother of his spiritual daughters Eustochium and Blesilla.[164] The problem seems to have lain in the nature of Umiliana's spirituality, as least as that was transmitted by his source. This source was the earliest life, by Umiliana's contemporary, Fra Vito da Cortona; Raffaele says in his prefatory letter that Frater Andrea had sent this source in the form of a booklet (*libellus*).[165] The booklet may also have included her postmortem miracles, collected by Fra Ippolito.[166]

In the final draft of his prefatory letter, Raffaele says that he read through the *libellus* twice and composed a short *vita* of three pages for readers' convenience.[167] But in an earlier draft, he admits to some trepidation after the initial two readings: "I was so alarmed [*territus*]," he added there, "that I reread the first book; then, quickly rereading [he cancels "by divining"] again and again, after a long time I gathered from it all [literally, "from many things"] this account [*sensum*], which [gathers the things that] I thought most necessary."[168] Now Raffaele was willing, at other points in the letter, to be frank with his patrons about the shortcomings of the *libellus*. He did not fear to tell them, for example, that the old *vita* had a "graceless style" and said many "other vacuous and pointlessly repetitive things," which it would be "better to omit."[169] So his decision to delete his initial sentences of dismay with the source deserves some reflection. If the Franciscans desired Umiliana's canonization, then all these documents (or notarized copies of them) would go off to Rome. At the most,

164. Raffaele's account is edited by D. Papebroek in *AASS* May IV (1866): 409a–412b (= P). It is difficult to say which of the two extant manuscripts Papebroek used: the presentation copy in Florence, BN MS Landau Finaly 243 (= F, a codex mostly in Italian; cf. Rome, BNC, Sess. 412) or the early draft in BAV, MS Ottob. lat. 992 (= O, a codex containing drafts of many of Raffaele's writings).

165. This information comes from Raffaele's prefatory letter (F, fol. 1; cf. O). Vito's account is edited in P, 385b–400b.

166. Thus Papebroek, who edits Ippolito's miracles as well: P, 400b–407b.

167. "Libellum eius continentem gesta semel atque iterum percurri ad eam redigere brevitatem sum conatus quam necessariam et ad rem magis facere dixi ut omnis eius vite cursus tribus explicatae chartis legentibus facile patere posset" (F, fol. 1).

168. Following the word *conatus*, Raffaele's first draft reads: "Ita sum territus ut primum quidem [*canc.* rem] libellum relegerim mox vero iterum atque iterum vix [*canc.* divinando] lectitari. Longo post tempore sensum hunc ex multis ⟨h⟩ausi quam potissimam magis necessaria⟨m⟩ [*canc.* ex consilibus] duxi [*canc.* adnotarique]" (O).

169. "Cetera vero preter stili inconcinnitatem ut admodum supervacuam et ab [P abs] re sepe repetita consulte preterii" (F, O).

his condensed account would serve as a sort of cover letter to the graceless but legally impeccable eyewitness testimony provided by Vito.[170] Moreover, whatever Raffaele thought of miracles, there was no gainsaying their value for canonization. Thus Raffaele responsibly referred to Ippolito's collection of Umiliana's miracles, emphasizing its authenticity and official nature.[171] In short, when he wrote about Umiliana, the author Raffaele had very little room to maneuver.

The *vita Humilianae* by Raffaele Maffei reduces Vito's more-than-12,000-word account of the life and a few postmortem miracles and Ipplito's almost-4,000-word relation of further postmortem miracles to not quite 3,000 words. (There is no preface or exordium; these would have been superfluous for a canonization submission.) Raffaele excises Vito's enthusiastic rhetorical questions, which had served to underline Umiliana's extremes of virtue, as well as Vito's heartfelt first-person exclamations to the saint herself. But otherwise, with the single exception of presenting Umiliana as drawn to the spiritual life as a child, Maffei faithfully preserves the outline and emphases of Vito's account: an obedient daughter and wife but always spiritually alert, Umiliana engages in charity until her means to do so are curtailed. After her husband's death, she becomes a Franciscan tertiary, withdrawing to a *cellula* in a family tower in search of hermitical solitude. There, she exhibits the gifts of prophecy, of visions, and of ecstatic rapture. She is sustained by a special devotion to a *tabula* of the Virgin and Child. Although she is close to her confessor and to a female relative by marriage and although she has visitors, she longs for the solitude of the desert. She wishes as well for martyrdom and receives in compensation the gift of agonizing stomach pains. Her life of frequent prayer, little sleep, and less food ends at twenty-six. Umiliana's struggles toward sanctity do not seem to elicit sympathy from Raffaele, despite his own aspirations. Not all saints are to be imitated.

Raffaele's final hagiographic work was an office for the Florentine archbishop Zenobius (d. ca. 420). It was commissioned by the canons of the Florentine cathedral, who had been impressed by the handbook *Officium* of Volterran saints.[172] Clearly, then, whatever our misgivings about the

170. Vito's preface, for example, lists the witnesses, *testes vitae*, to Umiliana's life. He almost certainly wrote with an eye to canonization himself: *P*, 385–386, para. 1.

171. *P*, 411b, para. 8.

172. On Zenobius, see G. D. Gordini and M. C. Celletti, "Zanobi," *BS* 12 (1969): 1467–1470; *AASS* May VI (Paris, 1866): 46–69. Lowe, *Church and Politics*, 167–168, describes the interest that the former bishop of Volterra, Cardinal Francesco Soderini, protector of the Camaldulensians, showed in the *translatio* of the relics of Saint Apollinaris to Classe in 1511. She notes that, at about that same time, Piero Soderini seems to have proposed a *translatio* of Zenobius to a similar underground chapel. Soderini would not, of course, have participated in the 1520 request for a set of *lectiones* on Zenobius. But Raffaele might have been mindful of his old friend's attention to the saint.

spiritual utility of those accounts, they were not shared by Raffaele's ecclesiastical contemporaries. In the letter of commission, dated September 5, 1521, the Florentine canons referred approvingly to "the offices of Victor and Octavian and others that have been printed here" ("Victoris Octavianique aliorumque officia quae hic typis cuduntur").[173] To celebrate Florence's own Zenobius, they requested a *duplex officium* suitable for the traditional feast of May 25, that is, the day of Zenobius's death, and for the commemoration of Zenobius's translation in 1439 from San Lorenzo to the Duomo on April 26. They also asked Raffaele to devise some fitting hymns.[174]

The canons were specific about the sorts of improvements they wanted. The traditional office they were using disagreed in places ("non satis . . . congruere") with still older accounts they consulted.[175] Their phrasing suggests that they had factual concerns about the historicity of the presentation. But the canons also wanted the style of their *lectiones* improved, asking for "other, more suitable forms" ("alia concinniora forma").[176] Would Raffaele apply the same zeal (*studium*) evident in the printed *Officium* to renewing and reforming (*innovare, reformare*) their texts? If he did, they pointed out, he would win for himself an influential heavenly patron.[177]

Zenobius's historical existence is not in doubt. Nevertheless, contemporary documentation is sparse: birth and death dates are disputed; he himself left no writings; and there are no contemporary *vitae*.[178] By the

---

173. The canons' letter is extant in BAV, MS Barb. lat. 2517, fol. 17r–v (= B).

174. "Hymnis insuper, quos duxeris vitae congruere, si convenerat cum ea que in pontificibus et confessoribus habentur . . . non adcedant ingrati" (B, fol. 17v).

175. The canons' letter opens, "Cum habuerimus iampridem divi Zenobii officium nobis a maioribus nostris traditum, idque non satis cum priscis (ut in antiquis codicibus continetur) nobis congruere videretur" (B, fol. 17r).

176. The canons resort to a variety of words to describe the rewriting: "renovandi . . . redigendi . . . innovata . . . reformandi . . . amplectereris . . . innovares ac reformares . . . redigi" (B, fol. 17r–v).

177. "Quamobrem oramus omnes obsecramusque animo lubenti nobis benignus adsis, et quae nos tantopere cupere videris, praestar minime dedigneris, ad Dei Optimi Maximi ac tanti sancti honorem, quem sis habiturus in coelis, apud Deum pro te perpetuo patronum non vulgarem" (B, fol. 17r).

178. Analysis of the date of death by Papebroek, *AASS* May VI (Paris, 1866), 50, para. 4. As for the birth date, Pseudo-Simplicianus (*BHL* 9015), Laurentius of Amalfi (*BHL* 9014), and the monk Blasius (*BHL* 9016) are all silent (see following note). The humanist Giovanni Tortelli is apparently the first to calculate a birth date (6 kal. feb. 335 = January 27); neither Antonio degli Agli nor Antonino Pierozzi follow him in this innovation, although Clemente Mazza (imprint, in the vernacular) tries (January 17, 335). Naldo Naldi offers the same variant (16 kal. feb. = January 17). Raffaele Maffei repeats Tortelli's calculation (6 kal. feb. 335). Among the many authors of *vitae Zenobii*, Antonino Pierozzi alone observes that the saint left no writings: *Chronicon*, tertia pars historialis, tit. X, cap. 12, fol. 42v, col. b (I used the edition of Basel, 1491).

time Raffaele wrote, however, the handful of medieval accounts had been increased by a whole series of fifteenth-century revisions, including versions by Giovanni Tortelli, Antonio degli Agli, Antonino Pierozzi, Clemens Mazza, and Naldo Naldi.[179] Raffaele seems to have known at least some of these Quattrocento versions, although it appears that the canons provided him with only one source: the *vita* composed in the fourteenth century by the Florentine Vallumbrosan Blasius.[180] This assertion may be mildly gainsaid by noting that Raffaele gave, for example, the birth date first found in Giovanni Tortelli's account; that, following Antonino, he recorded the saint's pagan upbringing; and that, similar to Naldo Naldi, he began by stating the saint's connection to the Girolami family. But his office is a half-hearted effort, its prose dull and lifeless. I do not know that it was ever used.

❊ ❊ ❊

179. The medieval accounts included (1) a sermon by Lorenzo of Amalfi (written shortly after 1030), whose intellectual attainments are discussed in W. Holtzmann, "Laurentius von Amalfi, ein Lehrer Hildebrands," in G. Borini, ed., *Studi gregoriani* (Rome, 1947), 1:206–236; (2) an account claiming to be by Simplicianus, eyewitness to the fifth-century translation of Zenobius, but composed in the twelfth or thirteenth century according to Anna Benvenuti Papi, "La memoria e il santo. San Zanobi: memoria episcopale, tradizioni civiche, e dignità familiare," in *Pastori di popolo: Storie e leggende di vescovi nell'Italia medievale* (Florence: Arnaud, 1988), 128–129; (3) a fourteenth-century account by the Florentine monk Blasius; and (4) shorter fourteenth-century accounts in the compilations by Petrus Calo and Petrus de Natalibus. See also the list in Carlo Nardi, "Un volgarizzamento quattrocentesco della vita di San Zanobi di Lorenzo di Amalfi (sec. X)," in *La cattedrale e la città: Saggi sul Duomo di Firenze. Atti del Convegno internazionale di studi. Firenze 16–21 giugno 1997* (Florence: Edifil, 2001), 149–153, noting Maffei's contribution at 153. Sally Cornelison, "A French King and a Magic Ring: The Girolami and a Relic of St. Zenobius in Renaissance Florence," *RQ* 55 (2002): 343–469, and Blake Wilson, "Music, Art, and Devotion: The Cult of St. Zenobius at the Florentine Cathedral during the Early Renaissance," in P. Gargiulo, G. Giacomelli, and C. Gianturco, eds., *Cantate Domino: Musica nei secoli per il Duomo di Firenze* (Florence, 2001), 17–36, describe other aspects of Zenobius's cult.

180. Raffaele indicates only one: "Verum quo magis faciliusque quod cupimus praestare valeas, eius sancti vitam cum his mittimus, [ut] totum [poteris] officium continue componi, et in condignam formam rediti" (*B*, fol. 17v). Raffaele's office for Zenobius depends on Blasius, according to Papebroek in *AASS* May VI (Paris, 1866), 50, para. 4. Cf. A. K. Frazier, "Italian Humanists as Authors of *vitae sanctorum*, 1417–1521" (PhD thesis, Columbia University, 1997), appendix D, part 3 (a comparative survey of the miracles *in vita* from all the sources), which shows that, at least in the cases of several miracles, Raffaele's sources are less obvious than Papebroek implies. For example, in the miracle of the two sons cursed by a Florentine woman, Maffei's dependence on Blasius is not complete. Although, in comparison with other accounts, both Maffei and Blasius give the miracle out of order (as does Antonino), Maffei does not follow Blasius in the number of sons (but Antonino does follow Blasius). Likewise, in the case of the miracle that Zenobius, as he prayed, could see Ambrose with his spiritual eyes, Raffaele misleadingly names Simplicianus as a source (but the account is not in Simplicianus and not in Blasius).

Puto enim sanctissimum hominem fuisse Hieronymum, sed hominem tamen, et
quid didicerit, et qui erraverit, et qui correxerit, et qui mutaverit, ut caeteri solent.
I do think that Jerome was a very holy man, but a man nevertheless, who learned,
and erred, and corrected, and changed, as others are accustomed to do.

—Pier Candido Decembrio to Francesco Pizzolpasso, October 1438[181]

As Raffaele Maffei knew, rhetoric must persuade, or it fails in its defining
task. His perception of the moral inadequacy of *vitae sanctorum* in his
own day, coupled with the fact that he himself could not embody his proposed corrections effectively in revised accounts, bespeak a profound failure of sacred rhetoric. Perhaps this failure was inevitable. Christ's status as
God and man is an item of faith, but the saints do not have that luxury.
Vitae sanctorum, throughout the Middle Ages, seem designed to discover,
or even to test, the extent of an audience's compliancy before claims of
extravagant achievement. At times, one has the feeling that by exercising
the will to believe or even by encouraging a delight in compliancy of will,
its expansive qualities could be increased. If Raffaele had ever delighted in
such compliancy, his ascetic retreat at Volterra seems to have required
more pragmatic exercises.

Several humanists, even early in the Quattrocento, believed that rhetoric could persuade only when it had a subject who was recognizably
human. It would fail if the subject was impossibly perfect. But not until the
early sixteenth century was the case made in a widely available Latin
saint's life that exemplary figures capable of remorse might be more persuasive than those who led blameless lives. This brave author was not
Maffei but Erasmus, in his life of Jerome.[182] In the *vita Hieronymi*, first
published in 1516, Erasmus pointed out to prospective authors the greater
persuasiveness of erring sanctity, claiming that "nothing is better than to
portray the saints just as they actually were, and if even a fault is discovered in their lives this very imperfection turns into an example of piety for
us." Arguing that Jerome was no virgin, Erasmus encouraged authors "to
acknowledge in the saints some blemish like a scar," for, he urged, "greater

---

181. Quoted in E. F. Rice Jr., *St. Jerome in the Renaissance* (Baltimore: Johns Hopkins,
1985), at 248 n. 80.

182. Rice, *St. Jerome*, 116–136. Erasmus criticizes Raffaele Maffei for using the
"Plerosque nimium" life of Jerome in the *Commentariorum libri*—the same account included
in Bonino Mombrizio's *Sanctuarium*. See James F. Brady and John C. Olin, "Life of St.
Jerome," in *Collected Works of Erasmus*, vol. 61, *Patristic Scholarship: The Edition of St.
Jerome* (Toronto: University of Toronto Press, 1992), 23. The scholarship on Erasmus's
Jerome is large. In addition to Rice, *Saint Jerome*, see David J. Collins, "A Life Reconstituted:
Jacobus de Voragine, Erasmus of Rotterdam, and Their Lives of St. Jerome," *Medievalia et
Humanistica*, n.s., 25 (1998): 31–51; Irene Backus, "Erasmus and the Spirituality of the Early
Church" in H. Pabel, ed., *Erasmus' Vision of the Church* (Kirksville, Mo., 1995): 95–114;
and John C. Olin, "Erasmus and Saint Jerome: The Close Bond and its Significance," *Eras-
mus Society Yearbook* 7 (1987): 33–53.

influence is exerted on us by the example of those whose lot it has been to experience a conversion to holiness from a life of sin."[183] Such figures do not need miracles.[184] Neither do they need the panegyrical excess that supporters felt was their due. Indeed, Erasmus, like Raffaele Maffei, thought that the utility of a holy life lay more in the story of a struggle for virtue than in its uncomplicated and unchallenged presence: Mary Magdalene was of more use to sinners than the virginal Thecla.

Erasmus's energetic attack on earlier accounts of Jerome was multifaceted. Pointing out the ethical uselessness of panegyric was only a small part of his undertaking: he also defended truth against fable and rhetoric against "sophists." He pitted the "free" monasticism of the first centuries against the weak and "ceremonial" practice of his own day; made a case for studying Hebrew; championed male and female friendship; explained the nature of Rufinus's attacks on Jerome; and belittled the scholarship of Lorenzo Valla, Francesco Filelfo, and Filippo Beroaldo.[185] One thing that Erasmus did not do was to set *historia* in stark opposition to *panegyricus*. That was Maffei's particular anxiety, one particularly suited to his curial background and to his eremitical retreat.

Gathered together under the banner of rhetoric, *historia* and *panegyricus* for the saints had not been entirely peaceful in the Middle Ages. In rewriting the lives of the saints, the Quattrocento humanists found themselves forcing the issue of a real divorce. I have pointed out repeatedly aspects of their growing tension: from Agli's and Manetti's efforts to locate the saints in secular time as the surest way to guarantee their authority, virtue, and reality to Giovanni Garzoni's stepped rewritings that encouraged classicizing vocabulary and syntax as the surest way to guarantee the efficacy of a panegyrical account. The Renaissance is a well-known site of historiographical change: the ambiguities of *historia* were ballooning almost uncontrollably. Since the thirteenth century, the success of the mendicants had certified the preacher's *exemplum* as *historia*. In the early Quattrocento, Leon Battista Alberti had extended this usage by describing the preferred subject of painting as a good *historia*. In liturgical terms, a *lectio* was a *historia*. Maffei originally thought, following Basil, that *historia* was

183. Erasmus, "Life," at 22 and 49, naming Mary Magdalene. See Janson, *The Making of the Magdalene*, especially chap. 9, "Responses to the Legendary Saint," which includes some attention to fifteenth-century responses.

184. Erasmus, "Life," 47; cf. 24: Jerome's own writings contain "almost as many miracles as . . . opinions."

185. Truth vs. fable, ibid., 22; see also 36 (Jerome not a cardinal) and 37 (Jerome did not put on women's clothes to escape Rome). Rhetoric: ibid., 26; see also 52 against "theological jargon." Early monasticism: 29; cf. 28, for Jerome's attention to *Nosce teipsum*, as attributed by Erasmus. Hebrew: 34. Friendship: 35–36, cf. 37 on the Origenists' abuse of friendship. Rufinus: 43–45. Italian humanists: Filelfo at 49–50; Theodore Gaza at 54–55; Crinito at 55–56; Beroaldo at 59–61; Valla at 59; taking up Battista Pio at 61.

panegyric and later felt that notion should be castigated by his concept of *historia*, subordinated to developments in penitential theology but expressed in the Tacitean phrases of disabused impartiality. His theoretical solution was to make *historia* into ethical biography, to rewrite the cult of the perfect saints as the cult of struggling humans. But because the saints' past was imperfectly recoverable, this high ethical aim required that even saintly histories must include *historia* as didactic philology. In some instances, Raffaele was compelled to be a hagiographer in our modern sense of the term. His accounts of Giacomo Guidi and Umiliana de'Cerchi show that he understood the requirements of unalloyed praise. But when he had room to maneuver, as in his handbook *Officium* entries on local, traditional, and early saints, Raffaele Maffei stumbled onto another solution to the problem of persuasive exemplars. He rewrote the cult of the perfect saints as the cult of the textual *lacuna*, the cult of our anxious ignorance about the past.

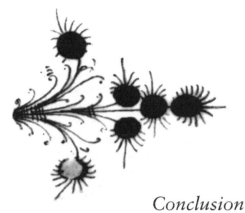

CHAPTER 7

Conclusion

Non enim Crispos aut Xenophontas aut ex illa cohorte quenquam vitae facino-
rumque suorum interpretem habuere.

But the saints have not yet found their Sallusts or Xenophons, or anyone of that
sort, to interpret their life and deeds.

—Leonardo Giustinian, preface, *Beati Nicolai Myrensis vita*[1]

Possible Lives has explored some of the ways that the
humanists participated in the cult of the saints through
narrative. Should we describe this textual participation as success or failure? Perhaps it is a bittersweet
mixture. I have, it is true, presented a sheaf of failures.
Every chapter introduces material that is little known

---

1. *BHL* 6128, quoted from *Poetae christiani*, ed. Aldus Manutius (Venice, 1502), sign.
H1r; cf. BAV, MS Vat. Lat. 7751, fols. 3v–4r. My loose translation attempts to catch the
thrust of the sentence in its context. Giustinian, lamenting his contemporaries' interest in
pagans (*gentiles*), has just named several subjects made memorable by Plutarch's efforts
(none of them figures whose lives he himself had translated). Here he seems to have in mind
Xenophon's *Cyropaedeia* and Sallust's *Bellum Catalini*, both of which explored character in
a manner that was morally didactic and historically stirring. Both also represented the work
of contemporary eyewitnesses.

even to Renaissance specialists: surely that demonstrates the humanists' inability to create an impact. The labors of Antonio degli Agli and Giannozzo Manetti to account for the historical martyrs did not save the martyrology; the variety of textual manipulations practiced by Aurispa or Lorenzo Valla, even the handbook and exemplary death of Tommaso d'Arezzo, could not construct a viable social good out of martyrdom. The first task was left to Cesare Baronio, the second to the bodies disciplined by the Reformations. Bonino Mombrizio's *Sanctuarium* is such a rich exhibit for the history of politics and printing that its contribution to philology looks increasingly insecure. Even if we set politics and printing aside, we must admit that what Mombrizio intended for the collection is hardly clear; almost two centuries later Jean Bolland was still trying to sort out (and defend) a philological approach to similar accounts. As for Giovanni Garzoni, his Ciceronian rewriting excluded him from the *Acta sanctorum* by definition and won him no sustained attention from hagiologists. Historians of education may yet find value in his efforts. More research on the humanist classroom, and especially on lay humanists teaching for religious orders, may render his example less eccentric. Giacomo da Udine and his subject Elena are known to hardly anyone, even in Udine, while his experiment in literary form remains nearly beyond assimilation into the history of any genre. Raffaele Maffei died without fulfilling his literary-ethical aim of providing texts of pastoral care in honest narratives that represented imperfect factuality and imperfect sanctity; his own sanctity, or rather, beatitude, was secured as much by his brother's efforts as by his own private struggles. What is the point of resurrecting so much failure?

The chief defense of this project lies in the quantity and variety of the evidence. As the hand list shows, the chapters of this book could be multiplied many times; in case after case, humanist authors grappled energetically with the representation of sanctity. Indeed, the hand list does not begin to address the actual number of surviving and reported accounts. An area of production that I have not systematically investigated, for example, is the contribution of a host of minor, local teachers and clerics who promoted civic virtue and civic religion—and presumably the value of a humanist education—by rewriting the lives of city patron saints in a variety of formats. An argument might also be made that humanist funeral oratory significantly extended the reach of contemporary hagiography; perhaps this study lays the conceptual groundwork for such a claim. And I have not considered one of the most prolific and contested forms of hagiographic production around 1500—namely, lives of Savonarola.

Faced with this quantity and variety of evidence, a historian is bound to acknowledge the fundamental optimism that underlies it. Perhaps the obvious point needs stating: the humanists did not write *vitae et passiones* expecting to fail. There is also a less obvious point: the quantity, variety, innovations, and above all, the self-consciousness of these *vitae et pas-*

siones together suggest that the classicizing Renaissance was also a literary Renaissance for the saints. I hope to have demonstrated the reasonableness of this hypothesis in quantitative terms, at least. It matters to know that there were many of these texts around, and that they were known more widely and for more various reasons than we have suspected, for that is a kind of success. Such quantity may, in turn, contribute to a qualitative appraisal of the hagiographic Renaissance.

It is true that many of the narratives had a poor *fortuna*. More seriously, others turned out, at the moment of composition, to be impossible to write, or even to conceive. Nevertheless, to ignore the scope and personal significance of the authors' efforts among their contemporaries is to neglect a part of our own humanity. In various ways—by winning patrons, students, eloquence, miracles, fame, security, cash—humanists sought through these writings to make their own lives possible. How then can we have overlooked this literature?

The answer is complicated. Certain notions of the Renaissance and of humanism encourage a polite blindness. The field has traditionally focused on the reception of the classics. That focus leads us to seek hagiographic equivalents in humanist accounts of Socrates, Plato, or Seneca—subjects that suit our period concept—while ignoring the saints themselves. The elite intellectual traditions of Renaissance studies (as opposed to the populism of Early Modern studies) underwrite the dismissal of vacuous accounts such as Garzoni's *vitae et passiones*; thus we do not see how they bear witness to a practice that helped secure the success of the *studia humanitatis* among its strongest critics. Pursuing the topic of religion in the Renaissance or Early Modern period, we turn almost single-mindedly to contemporary saints and canonizations; thus we may find ourselves "bobbing for data" in the engaging contemporary *vitae* and sermons without recognizing the broader literary context (creating the lay academic complement, perhaps, to the Bollandist project). Or we dismiss Latin composition of *vitae* for the undeniably more successful vernacular, diminishing the context through which to approach the explanandum.[2] By defining humanism as secular ethics or as rhetorical eloquence (to name just two poles of its contested definition), we justify our rejection of texts that, with ideological élan, proclaim themselves neither secular nor eloquent. By reducing hagiography to mere propaganda, we deny ourselves the opportunity to investigate its multitudinous functions, the vast extent of its epidemiology.[3] We have overlooked this literature because our categories have told us that it ought not to be there.

---

2. Essential now is J. Dalarun et al., *Bibliogiofia agiografica italiana* (Florence: Galluzzo, 2003)

3. The model of cultural transmission as "epidemiology" is strongly identified with the work of anthropologist Dan Sperber. See especially his *Explaining Culture: A Naturalistic Approach* (London: Blackwell, 1996).

That is not the whole story of the failure, however; the responsibility is not ours alone. A certain amount of failure was handed to the humanists by contemporary events. The *deus ex machina* of the Reformations ended the experiment fairly abruptly. To maintain the focus of this study, I will restrict my remarks to Catholic Europe. First, confessional persecutions substituted actual for textual martyrdom; the old words in the old texts suddenly vibrated with new implications. Second, lay authors seem to have been quickly excluded from recounting *vitae et passiones*, an exclusion that needs more investigation. And third, the violence of the period so narrowed the scope of this literature that experiment became more difficult. Perhaps, by 1520 or so, the *studia humanitatis* was sufficiently firmly implanted in the educational system of Europe that Counterreformation hagiology continued parts of the Quattrocento project, as the Quattrocento had continued projects undertaken by earlier centuries; that exploration, too, is for another book.[4]

In the middle range, the humanists' narratives failed because they were suspicious to early modern scholars. As Europe developed its characteristic historiographical stance in the polemical atmosphere of Reformation and Counterreformation, derivative and ornamental rewritings had precise uses for internal audiences, but were useless and embarrassing as history. A few *vitae et passiones* written about contemporaries by eyewitnesses were lauded: Francesco da Castiglione's life of Antonino Pierozzi, for example, or Pietro Ransano's passion of Anthony of Rivalto. But for a world that experienced heroic confessional deaths, it was important to secure the reality of earlier witnesses. The kinds of truths and persuasions known to the Quattrocento rhetorician were suspect, as the contrasting receptions of Bonino Mombrizio and Giacomo da Udine indicate.

Responsibility for the humanists' failure in the long term may be attributed to the labyrinth called secularization (and its Minotaur, modernity). If the catalog demonstrates that many humanists undertook *vitae et passiones*, it also shows that many more did not. It is reasonable to ask why they did not. We are considering here such figures as Poggio Bracciolini (1380–1459) and Angelo Poliziano (1460–1494). The former wrote funeral orations praising contemporaries, including a cardinal, Niccolò Albergati, who was eventually canonized. Poggio also had some interest in relics, to judge from his commission of a reliquary. But Poggio failed to

---

4. For a strong start in this direction, see Simon Ditchfield, *Liturgy, Sanctity and History in Tridentine Italy: Pietro Maria Campi and the Preservation of the Particular* (New York: Cambridge University Press, 1995), and forthcoming work by David Collins and Anne Schuchman that links late medieval and Counterreformation developments.

write saints' lives.[5] Poliziano seems still more alienated from the saints, to judge from his complaint that he had once lost a good day's work by reading the Bible. Nevertheless, he had some interest in patristics and explicitly promoted biography as an encouragement to *imitatio*.[6] Such authors found the subjects unattractive or the institutional entanglements of a commission unwelcome. Regarding the evidence from their perspective, we would have to say that humanist *vitae et passiones* were cultural sports, evolutionary dead ends. They flourished among the hothouse elites of urban Italy, but with demonstrable brevity. Allied with traditional and authoritarian institutions, they stood in opposition to whatever tendrils of "individualism" scholars might hope to identify. How could such texts hope to succeed anyway, being largely in Latin, and so by definition exclusionary? Thus they can have no significance for the social history of the cult of the saints at the end of the Middle Ages (largely about women and the vernacular), or for our understanding of civic religion and the crucial state-building tasks of Early Modern Italy (largely about men and the vernacular). The history of the secular state in the West proves that these accounts did not and do not have any real significance.

5. On Poggio, see M. Davies in P. Grendler, dir., *Encyclopedia of the Renaissance* (New York: Scribners, 1999), 1:274–276, E. Bigi and A. Petrucci in *DBI* 13 (1971): 640b–646b; and the portrait that emerges in Riccardo Fubini, "Intendimenti umanistici e riferimenti patristici dal Petrarca al Valla," *Umanesimo e secolarizzazione da Petrarca a Valla* (Rome: Bulzoni, 1990), 137–181. Poggio's funeral oration on Niccolò Albergati (*BHL* 6097) is discussed in John McManamon, *Funeral Oratory and the Cultural Ideals of Italian Humanism* (Chapel Hill: University of North Carolina Press, 1989). On Poggio's container for relics of St. Laurence, see J. J. Rorimer, "A Reliquary Bust made for Poggio Bracciolini," *Bulletin of the Metropolitan Museum of Art* 14 (1955–56): 246–251. Poggio's estimate of St. Bernardino of Siena is addressed by Riccardo Fubini, "Poggio Bracciolini e S. Bernardino: Temi e motivi di una polemica," in D. Maffei and P. Nardi, eds., *Atti del simposio internazionale cateriniano-bernardiniano. Siena, 17–20 aprile 1980* (Siena, 1982), 509–540; repr. in Fubini's *Umanesimo*, 183–219. See also R. Guidi, "Vecchi e nuovi veleni contro S. Bernardino da Siena," *AFH* 93, nos. 1–4 (2000): 261–340. R. N. Watkins, "The Death of Jerome of Prague" *Speculum* 42 (1967): 104–120, is crucial.

6. On Poliziano, see P. Colilli in Grendler, *Encyclopedia*, 5:114a–116b, for introductory bibliography, and V. Fera and M. Martelli, eds., *Agnolo Poliziano Poeta Scrittore Filologo. Atti del convegno internazionale di studi, Montepulciano, 3–6 novembre 1990* (Florence: Le Lettere, 1998) for specialized studies. Poliziano's deprecatory comment on Bible-reading is attributed to Melanchthon by A. Desguine, ed., Fantino [Vallaresso], *Compendium catholicae fidei* (Paris: Vrin, 1968), 255. Poliziano's interest in early Christian literature is suggested by his notes in Florence, Bibl. Laurenziana, MS S. Marco 695, a fourteenth-century manuscript of Athanasian excerpts; see E. Rostagno and N. Festa, *Catalogus codicum manuscriptorum Bibliothecae Mediceae Laurentianae* (Leipzig, 1893), 193–194. See also Poliziano's notes in Munich, Bayerische Staatsbib., MS CLM 766, described by I. Maier, *Les manuscrits d'Ange Politien* (Geneva, 1965), 204–205 (recording, *inter alia*, several folios of notes on Philo's life of Moses). For Poliziano's promotion of biography, see the "praefatio in Suetoniii expositionem" in his *Opera omnia* (Venice: Aldus Manutius, 1502), at sign. 2a8v.

Although it seems, for better or worse, early to decide about secularism in the West, I do think that the failure of many important humanists to compose *vitae et passiones* is a serious challenge to my proposal of significance. Secularization had a hand in that silence and in the participating authors' long-term failure. I want to approach the matter indirectly—secularization is an ambiguous and polemical word. I would not, for example, argue that the failure of humanist hagiography can be attributed to the fact of Latin. Indeed, if we consider the Latin of these *vitae et passiones* some of the complexities of the secularization thesis begin to emerge.

Consider two starkly different examples. Both Alberti's life of Potitus and Garzoni's life of Augustine were solicited by powerful patrons who wanted authoritative and long-lasting texts.[7] Latin was not, in either instance, frivolously imposed by two authors beset with classicizing tics. Rather, Latin was a defining aspect of both ecclesiastical commissions. One came from the curia, and the other from a religious order, and so, unsurprisingly, the language requested was liturgical.[8] The power of that Latin can be measured in the fact that it was the language of the Mass until 1969.

How, though, should we appraise the use of Latin in these Quattrocento cases? True, some authors were linguistic purists. For example, the simultaneous arrival of barbarians and Christians was a hypothesis of cultural decline for Benedetto Accolti (1415–1466) as for Edward Gibbon, and the printer of the *editio princeps* of Ammianus Marcellinus felt the need of a vehement dedicatory letter to justify a fourth-century publication that was not patristic. But looking at the overall picture, we would have to say that the Renaissance did not just congratulate itself on recovering the Latin of Cicero; the Latin of Cyprian, Lactantius, Jerome, and Augustine was also part of its plan.[9] That patristic Latin guaranteed the historical authenticity of the saints (which is not quite the same as their doctri-

---

7. Alberti's *Potitus* (*BHL* 6910) is addressed in chap. 2 above. Garzoni's life of Augustine (*BHL* 798f/g) is edited and placed in context—the quarrel between the Augustinian Canons and Augustinian Hermits—in a forthcoming article.

8. This fact reinforced humanist attention to patristics, on which see M. Cortesi and C. Leonardi, eds., *Tradizioni patristiche nell'umanesimo* (Florence: Galluzzo, 2000).

9. See Neil Adkin, "The Preamble to Book V of Lactantius' *Divinae Institutiones* and Jerome" *Rivista di storia e letteratura religiosa* 39 (2003): 101–108, and Philip Rousseau, "Christian Culture and the Swine's Husks: Jerome, Augustine, and Paulinus," in W. E. Klingshirn and M. Vessey, eds., *The Limits of Ancient Christianity: Essays on Late Antique Thought and Culture in Honor of R. A. Markus* (Ann Arbor: University of Michigan Press, 1999), 172–187, on the dense exegetical webs of patristic Latinity, giving earlier bibliography on the fourth century as a tense locus of cultural change acted out in a common language. A similar acting-out occurs in humanists' saints' lives in the fifteenth century.

nal authenticity). It especially fortified the *passiones* that I have argued were so important to the Quattrocento Church's self-image. Thus, when we consider the humanists' Latin *vitae et passiones*, we miss the point if we see only a shallowly classicizing vocabulary and tropes applied to saints' lives in a naive or cynical effort to win patronage from a corrupt and unresponsive institution. Classicizing Latin was the most profound contribution to liturgical renovation that this Catholic Reformation could offer.

In the case of liturgical texts, such an interpretation might be relatively uncontroversial. The significance of the humanists' classicizing Latin deserves, however, to be considered across the board, as an aspect of all the *vitae et passiones* considered here. A counterintuitive example may help to make my point. Luther's claim, "I thank God that I hear and find my God in the German tongue, whereas I, and they with me, previously did not find him either in the Latin, the Greek or the Hebrew tongue,"[10] is taken by most readers today as a statement of the obvious. His vernacular represents success in just the areas where the late medieval Catholic Church represents most serious failure. The Protestant Reformations were conducted not in exclusive but in inclusive languages, mother tongues. This linguistic change was, moreover, allied to a theology that removed priestly intercession to make the claim, at least, of each individual's unmediated access to God. Europe, according to some interpreters, had been languishing in wait for such liberation.

There are many reasons to query that formulation, not least the continued emphasis in present-day Judaism and Islam on the mastery, respectively, of Biblical Hebrew and Qur'anic Arabic. One reason especially deserving thought is that such a formulation might not hold in quite the same way for highly urbanized and literate Italy. On the peninsula, Latin and most vernaculars were largely cognate, and the possibility that Latin was the original of the emerging Italian was widely discussed.[11] In fact, the humanist resurrection of classical Latin as a liturgical language could be interpreted as just as optimistic and potentially revolutionary a move as

---

10. Martin Luther, preface to *The German Theology*, in *Works*, ed. J. Pelikan (Philadelphia: Fortress Press, 1954), 31:75.

11. See J. IJsewijn, *Companion to Neo-Latin Studies* (Louvain: University Press, 1990), 41–49, esp. 46 and 48. On Latin and the Tuscan vernacular, see Angelo Mazzocco, *Linguistic Theories in Dante and the Humanists: Studies of Language and Intellectual History in Late Medieval and Early Renaissance Italy* (Leiden: Brill, 1993). On the continuing vivacity of Latin, see F. Waquet, *Latin, or the Empire of the Sign*, tr. J. Howe (New York: Verso, 2001), and most provocatively, R. Wright, *A Sociophilological Study of Late Latin* (Turnhout: Brepols 2002).

Luther's claims for German. After all, classicizing Latin was in the hands of a mostly lay educating class. These laymen were, at least in the fifteenth century, increasingly involved in forming boys who would enter orders or in finishing novices already in-house. The Latin in which they wrote their saints' lives is often quite elementary, suggesting an effort to be accessible to even a vernacular-educated urban middling class. That audience was thereby invited to experience in its linguistic, grammatical, and rhetorical "original"—which is to say in its moral force—the pre-Constantinian Church or the Church of the fourth century.[12] The promise of a transhistorical connection embedded in the humanists' Latin is analogous to the Reformers' promise of a similar connection to the uncorrupted primitive Christianity of the apostles. And for adherents at both poles of the analogy, the whole point was to establish a historical authenticity that might secure virtuous imitation. Thus it is a central achievement that the humanists studied here provided an entrée into that world by proposing some of its most dramatically appealing figures, the saints. As one young humanist observed hopefully to his patron, "Lots of people like to read about saints."[13]

Neither the fact of saints nor the fact of Latin fully accounts for the poor *fortuna* of the humanists *vitae et passiones*. But secularization did have a part, secularization in Riccardo Fubini's sense that it had become possible, thanks to the development of a highly articulate lay culture, to say "no" in all sorts of complex ways to institutions or social structures perceived to be coercive.[14] Or, to put it schematically, the revised and newly composed narratives failed because of the effects of certain sociopolitical structures on discursive environments. Whatever saints meant, narratives about saints were the province of traditional institutions. To produce *vitae et passiones* was to risk implication in the authority (the treacherously factionalized authority) of the Church or a religious order. We can see a whole range of response to this situation. Antonio degli Agli was delighted to be implicated; Mombrizio may have hoped to use the institution to save himself; Alberti thumbed his nose at it. Garzoni, at least in the case of his Augustine, accepted the invitation with aplomb and then had

12. For an argument that emphasizes the increasing theological competency of the laity in the fifteenth century, see I. Gagliardi, "Dibattiti teologici e acculturazione laicale nel tardo medioevo," *Rivista di storia e letteratura religiosa* 39 (2003): 23–64.

13. Celso delle Falci, preface to the *vita Euphrosynae* in Coimbra, BU, MS 2581, fol. 23v, going on to complain that few like to imitate the saints.

14. Fubini, *Umanesimo*, introduction. Throughout his work, Fubini is careful not to reduce this oppositional stance to a quarrel about scholasticism. Nevertheless, it is ever more apparent that we need to approach stylistic and generic developments in late scholasticism with more subtlety. Daniel Hobbins's essay "The Schoolman as Public Intellectual: Jean Gerson and the Late Medieval Tract," *American Historical Review* 108, no. 5 (2003): 1308–1337, arrived too late for me to take into account, but it suggests many commonalities between scholastics and humanists that might be usefully applied to saints' lives and canonizations.

to back down when he realized that he had entered a debate beyond his competence. Valla shifted institutions, writing *passiones* not for the Church but for the anti-papal State. Giacomo da Udine rewrote the rules, rendering the genre useless to the institution. Raffaele Maffei served the institution with discrete revisions whose surface placidity is betrayed by his tumultuous disappointment with the traditional narratives.

Similarly, the fact that few of the humanists' accounts were printed in the authors' lifetimes does not mean that these texts failed for their Latin or for their subjects. Rather, it is to acknowledge that the narratives were densely polysemous, and that some part of their meaning always derived from their origins in the complexities of order politics, or humanist polemic, or city-state animosities. Those that were published were often successful thanks to their resolutely, even blandly functional qualities. They were, for instance, intercessory texts such as Francesco Diedo's prose life of Rocco; classroom texts such as Leonardo Giustinian's life of Nicholas; promotional texts for religious orders, such as the encyclopedic *De viris illustribus ordinis praedicatorum* by Leandro Alberti and Giovanni Antonio Flamini; major patristic biographies, such as Giovanni Tortelli's life of Athanasius. Diedo's *Rocco* and Giustinian's *Nicholas* were frequently reproduced; the Dominican collection of great men served as a reference tool for centuries; Tortelli's *Athanasius* continued for several decades to preface collections of that father's *Opera*.

When Leonardo Giustinian complained that the saints had not yet found their Sallusts or Xenophons—had not found, that is to say, the proper narrative form through which moral philosophy teaching by example might also be history—he actually meant to offer a solution. The problem was clear: because *vitae* were badly written, no one took the saints' virtue seriously and worse, no one wanted to revise old accounts or compose new lives. Indeed, this literary failure caused people to think that there were no more saints around. But that was a mistake, countered Giustinian. To correct it, he did a little advertising or social engineering in the best classroom tradition. In the lengthy preface to his life of Nicholas of Myra, he called on authors to step forward, proposing to them that there was fame to be won as a hagiographer. "Who does not know that to make a name famous, to commend it to posterity for a long time, what matters is not so much the telling of how each [saint] excelled in character, virtue, and deeds. What matters most is whom that saint has as the trumpeter of his deeds and praise."[15] Lysippus's art ensured Alexander's immortality,

---

15. The argument follows the quotation given in the epigraph to this conclusion: "Nam ad nominis celebritatem, posteritati diutissime commendandam, quis nesciat non tam referre quibus quisque moribus, qua virtute, quibus rebus gestis antecellat, sed multo maxime quem factorum et laudum suorum praeconem sit habiturus" (Giustinian in *Poetae christiani*, sign. H1r–v; cf. BAV, MS Vat. lat. 7751, fol. 4r).

Giustinian points out, while the heroes who lived before Homer lie nameless. "It is not so much the subject that makes the writer famous," he advised young readers, "but the writer who makes the subject famous and long lived."[16] The obedience of the anonymous monk is of no value here, and the saint whose virtues are known only to God suffers, in the eyes of the humanists, the hell of oblivion.

Giustinian's reversal of the established hierarchy between author and saint is breathtaking. True, the superior importance of the author over his subject is a humanist commonplace. But we should not make the mistake of thinking that one repetition of this commonplace has the same meaning as any other. What makes this particular repetition unusual is the context of *vitae et passiones*. No other author, so far as I know, dared explicitly to remove the saint from the center of attention and fill the gap with the author, whose monastic humility had been more or less thoughtlessly assumed for centuries.[17] To compare the saint and an illustrious dedicatee was accepted procedure: Giovanni Tortelli compared Athanasius and Eugene IV in the preface to the life of Athanasius, for example, and Andrea Biglia (c. 1395–1435), speaking before Sigismund in August 1432, fashioned an introduction out of his dilemma: "how to eulogize a saint in the presence of a king without slighting either."[18] But to set aside the saint, and a fortiori illustrious recipients, and then to fill the void with the author, as Giustinian did, would seem to realize the deepest suspicions of the monastic opponents of the *studia humanitatis*. It might also, however, win the saints just the kinds of articulate trumpeters, both lay and clerical, that they needed. And those authors would make the lives of saints into the personally and socially reforming literature that the humanists desired.

As the case studies and hand list set out in this study indicate, Giustinian's hopeful approach to lives of the saints was not unique, even if it was uniquely phrased. The sad *fortuna* of humanist *vitae et passiones* is belied by successes that may amount to much more, quantitatively and even

---

16. Continuing from the previous note: "Unde lirycum illud est, 'vixere fortes ante Agamemnona multi ignotique longa nocte carentque vate sacro' . . . Scite igitur, Alexander diuturnitatis cupidine incensus statuas suas ab alio quoque fieri quam a Lisippo vetuit quia illius opera ob incomparabilem artis praestantiam immortalia fore putabat. Ita non tam res ipsae scriptorem quam scriptor illas celebras atque longaevas facit" (ibid.).

17. Jerome's preface to the life of Hilarion is Giustinian's probable source or at least his inspiration: "Eorum enim, qui fecere, virtus, ut ait Crispus, tanta habetur quantum eam verbis potuere extollere praeclara ingenia." Then Jerome tells the story of Alexander at the tomb of Achilles, which Giustinian would also have known from Plutarch's Alexander. The reference to Sallust comes from *Cat.* 8, 4. Humanist use of Jerome's *vitae* in their classrooms is proposed in chap. 4 above.

18. J. C. Schnaubelt, "Andrea Biglia (c. 1394–1435), Augustinian Friar and Humanist: A Critical Edition with Introduction, Translations, Commentary, and Appendices" (PhD thesis, Catholic University of America, 1976), 258.

qualitatively, than has been perceived. Giustinian made plain to students that the lives of the saints offered unparalleled opportunities to win fame while practicing virtue and good Latin. The lives of the saints could be historically true, stylistically beautiful, and profoundly transformative. They could be, in all senses, possible.

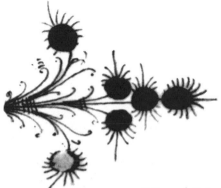

Hand List: An Annotated List of Authors and Their *Vitae, Passiones,* and Liturgical *Historiae* About Saints (Manuscript and Print, ca. 1420–1521)

Ego autem, cum non viderim etiam quos alii vidisse potuere absque frontis rubore confitear multos omissos fore et non nullos forsan ob labilis memoric culpam non enim sufficit visis. Et idcirco indulgeant, queso, memores, et quod ignorantia seu oblivione facta est, nolint equiperare malitie.

—Giovanni Boccaccio, *Genealogie deorum gentilium,* Book XV, chap. iv, 1

This appendix, arranged in alphabetical order by author's name, is a preliminary hand list of Italian humanists' Latin prose *vitae et passiones sanctorum* from about 1420 to 1520. It provides the basis for figure 1.1 and tables 1.1 and 2.1 and contextualizes the arguments presented in the preceding chapters. In each case, I have sought to provide:

a. author's name and birth and death dates

b. *BHL* or *BHG* numbers for each narrative; when these are absent, I note simply "*BHL* —" or "*BHG* —"; or I note the format, e.g., "collection"; or I note the loss of the account

c. contemporary titles; titles in brackets are those conjectured by the *BHL* or by myself, or are titles suggested by phrasing in the body of the source text (see below under "Titles")

    d. date of death for each subject saint (see below under "Dating Saints")

    e. date of composition for each narrative

    f. names of dedicatees, patrons, or those who encouraged the composition

    g. notice of dedicatory letters and prefaces that accompany each narrative, with *incipits*

    h. *incipit* and *desinit* of each narrative, with identification of the source for these

    i. present-day locations of manuscripts and notice of printed editions to 1521 (I include post-1521 editions only when they serve as source texts for the *incipit* and *desinit*); Roman numerals following shelfmarks indicate an approximate date for undated manuscripts (e.g. XV for fifteenth-century manuscripts) Manuscripts are listed in alphabetical order by city of current location; imprints, as far as possible, by ascending date.

Dating saints. Each saint is assigned to a century on the basis of date of death. This assignment is given in Roman numerals in parentheses directly following the title; an exact year of death is given only if the saint died in the fifteenth or sixteenth century. In such cases, the precision is necessary to determine if the author and the saint were, in fact, contemporaries. As far as possible, all dates are taken from the authors' explicit references to the year of death or to datable contemporaries such as emperors. Thus, caveat lector, the dates may not be correct according to the standards of today's scholarship. When the author provides no dating but offers a conservative text, I rely on dating suggested by the *BHL* or other reference works. If dating is impossible, I record "n.d." and explain.

Prefatory material. Few authors distinguish sharply between dedicatory letters and prefaces, but the distinction is worth noting because authors who use both forms may be invoking Late Antique precedents such as Sulpicius Severus's life of St. Martin. I include some *exordia* from *orationes*. Occasionally, I indicate that a work has no formal prefatory material but opens with introductory remarks not formally separated from the narrative.

Dedications. If the author states explicitly—in his text or elsewhere—that the dedicatee commissioned or encouraged the work, then the dedicatee's name is italicized. If there is evidence that other people also encouraged the work, they, too, are named in the brief description under the title.

Titles. To understand contemporary ideas about genre and usage requires strict attention to contemporary titling. The titles are taken from the best sources available, preferably autograph manuscripts. In cases where manuscripts do not provide titles and printed editions do not exist, I give conjectural titles based on the author's references to his composition in the work itself or elsewhere, or on later editions, in brackets.

Incipits and desinits. Whether manuscript or imprint, the source text for incipits and desinits is indicated under each title. In the interest of saving space, when a manuscript is included in P. O. Kristeller's *Iter Italicum*, I usually give that reference alone and do not repeat Kristeller's references to earlier catalogs. Similarly, when a *BHL* reference to printed works exists, I note only those up to 1521 and my source texts.

Caveat lector. This hand list is far from exhaustive. In the manner of the humanists, I leave margins wide to encourage annotations and additions. Readers are invited to use the list to supplement, not to supplant, the *BHL* listings of humanist *vitae et passiones sanctorum*. I do not follow the *BHL* in consistently recording sources that give only extracts of a work available in complete form elsewhere. Most important, the reader should recall that, because of constraints of space, oratory, historiographical entries, epic poetry, and hymns—four areas of considerable humanist production—are not registered here. To estimate the loss, consider that Lorenzo Valla's translations of accounts of the Forty Martyrs of Sebaste are included below but not his oration on Thomas Aquinas; that Baptista Mantuanus's epics, Ugolino Verino's *Silvae*, and Teofilo Folengo's massive *Hagiomachia* (its nineteen entries apparently based on Mombrizio's *Sanctuarium*) are not listed; that Pietro Ransano's many entries on saints in his immense *Annales omnium temporum* are unrecorded; and that none of Andrea Biglia's orations on saints, carefully cataloged by Joseph Schnaubelt, are given. Neither are vernacular accounts included, even when these are by authors whose Latin prose production is important (as, for example, Bonino Mombrizio on Katherine of Alexandria). The hand list aims to incite further scholarship, not to give the final word.

The following accounts have been excluded for reasons of date, definition, or access:

1. Anelli, Giuseppe, di Mazzara (d. 1520). According to Mazzucchelli I, ii, 729, Anelli wrote an account of the local patrons and martyrs Vitus, Modestus, and Crescentius. I have not been able to confirm this reference and so do not include this author or his narrative in the figures or tables.

2. Flamini, Giovanni Antonio (1464–1536). Flamini's collection *Vitae patrum inclyti ordinis praedicatorum,* printed at Bologna by Hieronymus

de Benedictis in 1529, includes several accounts that are too late for this study. Nonetheless, Flamini's importance for the field is such that I note those contents here:

Vita s. Antonini (d. 1459), fols. 185–189. The life records the canonization of 1523.

Vita s. Dominici (XIII), fols. 1–93, a life in three books followed by miracles. The sole manuscript known to me includes the date 1524 (Florence, BN, MS. Conv. soppr. D 3 501; Kristeller, *Iter* 1:150a).

Vita et res gestas diui Petri Martyris (XIII), fols. 93v–106. Prefatory letter to Gaspar Elephantutius (Fantuzzi).

Beati Thomae Aquinatis vita (XIII), fols. 123–158, a preface, life, *translatio,* and miracles. Dedicatory preface to Leandro Alberti as provincial of the Holy Land, an appointment that Alberti received on May 4, 1525.

Flamini's translation of the life of the Franciscan tertiary Catherina Bononiensis (de Vigri) from the vernacular of Giovanni Sabadino degli Arienti (itself adapted and published by Dionisio Paleotti, O.F.M. obs. in 1502) falls after the date of this study. See Flamini's *Epistolae familiares,* at 341–342, to Gaspar Elephantutius (Fantuzzi); and at 342–344 to the nuns of Corpus Christi, dated "VII Kal. Oct. MDXXII."

3. Isolani, Isidoro, O.P., of Milan (1477–1528). *Inexplicabilis mysterii gesta beatae Veronicae [Negroni] virginis, praeclarissimi monasterii S. Marthae urbis Mediolani, sub observatione regulae divi Augustini.* Dedicated to Francis and Claudia of France. The work was published in 1518 to seal the canonization. So far as I can tell, Isolani had a scholastic education, and that is why I exclude him from the catalog. Remo Guidi, "Gli *studia humanitatis" Studi francescani* 88 (1991): 93–95, argues that the sanctity described by Isolani is of a type "agli antipodi di quelli promossi dagli umanisti," both because Veronica surrendered her autonomy and because she was profoundly illiterate. For my delineation of the field, neither of those shortcomings is relevant. See also J.-M. Matz, "La *Vie* en français de la bienheureuse Veronique de Binasco (d. 1497): Sainteté, politique et dévotion au temps des guerres d'Italie" *MEFR, Moyen Age* 109, no. 2 (1997): 603–611.

4. Jacobus Egidius, O.P. *De martyrio baptiste Johannis*, with a dedication to Enea Silvio Piccolomini. Rome, Bibl. Casanatense, MS 974. XV. Kristeller, *Iter* 2:100a. Not seen.

5. Simone de Zanacchi de Parma, O. Carth. In *AASS* April II (Paris, 1866): 721–735, the Bollandists provide a Latin translation of the 1615 Italian edition made from Simone's now lost Latin life of the laywoman Beata Ursulina de Parma (d. 1408/1410). They state that the Latin must have been in a simple style.

ACCIAIUOLI, Donato (1429–1478)[1]

BHL 1617. *Vita Caroli Magni* (IX)[2]

Dedicatory preface to Louis XII. The life, written in 1461 in both Latin and vernacular, is a "hagiographic" improvement of Einhard's *vita Caroli*. Only Latin copies are noted below.

inc. proem.: Cum oratores omnium Christianorum privatique etiam homines

des. proem: vehementer commendat.

inc.: Carolo Francorum Regi, cui postea ex magnitudine rerum gestarum Magno fuit cognomen

des.: post Caroli mortem diligentissime sanctissimeque servavit.

MSS

1. Berlin, Deutsche Staatsbibliothek, MS Phillipps 1905. XV. Kristeller, *Iter* 3:368b. Not seen.

2. Florence, BN, MS Conv. soppr. 544, fols. 128–146. XV. Kristeller, *Iter* 1:75b. Not seen.

3. Florence, BN, MS Prin. II, II, 10. Autograph. See item 1 under Editions.

4. Florence, BN, MS Strozz. XXIV 157. misc. XV. Not seen. Kristeller, *Iter* 1:126b (both Latin and vernacular). Not seen.

5. Genoa, Bibl. della Congregazione di RR Missionari Urbani, MS 79, misc. (1511). Kristeller, *Iter* 1:241a. Not seen.

6. Genoa, BU, Fondo Gaslini, MS 47. Now MS A IX 28, fols. 62–79v (vern.), 81–100v Latin), with the date March 25, 1462. Kristeller, *Iter* 1:244b. Not seen.

7. Milan, Bibl. Ambrosiana, MS T 76 sup. XV. Kristeller, *Iter* 1:315a. Not seen.

8. Palermo, BN, MS I B 6, fols. 95–132, misc. XV (at 132v the date 1531). Kristeller, *Iter* 2:29a. Not seen.

9. Vatican City, BAV, MS Reg. Lat. 768, fols. 158–159v (preface) and 159v–172 (life). XV. Kristeller, *Iter* 2:405b. Not seen.

Editions

1. Daniella Gatti, *La vita Caroli di Donato Acciaioli* (Bologna: Patron, 1981), transcriptions of the vernacular and the Latin texts from Florence, BNC, MSS II, II, 325 and II, II, 10. Source text.

---

1. A. D'Addario, in *DBI* 1 (1960), 80–82; Vespasiano da Bisticci, *Le vite*, ed. Aulo Greco (Florence, 1976), 2:21–50.
2. On Carolus Magnus, see G. Mathon in *BS* 3 (1963): 853–861.

2. A. Campanus, [*Plutarchi vitae parallelae*] Ulrich Han. [Rome, 1470], 2, fols. 297–304. HC 13125*; *IGI* 7920; Goff P830; *BMC*, 4:21; *IERS* 39 ISTC ip00830000.

3. id., s.l.a. [Strasbourg, Adolf Rusch, after 1470–1471], 2, fols. 231v–238. H 13124*; *BMC* 1:62; *IGI* 7921 Goff P831; ISTC ip00831000.

4. *Virorum illustrium vitae ex Plutarcho*. Venice: Nicholas Jenson, 2 Jan. 1478, at sign. **5–9v (lacking prologue). H 13127*; Goff P832; *BMC* 5:178; *IGI* 7922 ISTC ip00832000.

5. [*Plutarchi vitae parallelae*]. Venice: Giovanni Ragazzo, ed. Lucantonio Giunta. December 7, 1491. HCR 13129; *BMC* 5:501; *IGI* 7923 ISTC ip00833000.

6. [*Plutarchi vitae parallelae*]. Venice: Bartolomeo Zani, June 8, 1496. HC 13130* ; *BMC* 5: 432; *IGI* 7924 ISTC ip00834000.

7. [*Plutarchi vitae parallelae*]. Brescia: Jacopo de'Britannici, August 9–13, 1499. HC Add. 13131*, BMC 7: 983, *IGI* 7925 ISTC ip00835000.

8. *Vite Plutarchi Cheronei . . .* [Paris]: Josse Badius and Jean Petit, 1514. Renouard 3, 175–178.

ADIMARI, Taddeo, O.S.M. and then O.Vallumbr. (d. August 27, 1517)[3]

BHL 6822a. *De origine ordinis servorum libellum* (XIII)[4]

Preface to Cristoforo Tornielli, newly elected general of the Servites. The treatise and life of Filippo Benizi were written in 1461, during Adimari's early schooldays, according to Soulier.[5] According to A.-M. Serra, Adimari draws on the *vita* by the layman Niccolò Borghesi (*q.v.*). Counted in figure 1.1 for Filippo Benizi.

inc. *proem.*: Quum nullam dicendi periciam in me nullum sermonis[6]
des. *proem*: quem colam observaboque dum vita fruar
inc.: Laudes Ordinis nostri scripturus sum et quorundam fratrum
des.: Hocque brevissimum de laudibus tui Ordinis regendi trado com-

3. Not in Kristeller, "Contribution"; not in *DBI*. Mazzucchelli, *Scrittori* vol. I, fasc. i, 145; Aristide M. Serra, "Memoria di fra Paolo Attavanti (1440 ca.–1499)," *Studi storici dell'Ordine dei Servi di Maria* 21 (1971): 47–87. See also Schutte, *PIVRB*, 192; and Kristeller, *Iter* 1:108a, for Adimari's vernacular account of Giovanni Gualberto; Adimari collected Gualberto's miracles, e.g., in Florence, AS, Vallombrosa, MS 244, fols. 67–107.

4. A.-M. Serra in *BS* 5 (1964): 736–752; F. A. Dal Pino in *GLS* 678a–681b. Although the manuscript title does not indicate it, the narrative includes *vita* and miracles of Filippo Benizi.

5. P. Soulier, "Fratris Thaddaei Adamarii," *MOSSM* 14, no. 1 (1913): 7; see ibid., 11, for a plate of the first folio, from which I take the author's title.

6. Cf. *BHL* 6822a: Soulier's edition opens with a reproduction of the first leaf of the dedication copy, from which it becomes clear that Soulier has adjusted the incipit, at least.

pendium, obsecrando ut ipsum vultu facieque serena suscipias, meque tibi
in dies et maiora et pulchriora de me labore ostensurum scias. Vale.

MSS

1. Florence, BN, MS Conv. soppr. C 8, 1250, fols. 1–43v, followed by
poems on Filippo and Joachim. XV. Kristeller, *Iter* 5:588b. Not seen.

Editions

1. P. Soulier, "Fratris Thaddaei Adamarii *De origine Ordinis Servorum
libellus et Mores Beati Philippi in ordinem digesti*, 1461," *MOSSM* 14, no.
1 (1913): 11–50. Soulier corrects orthography and numbers paragraphs.
Source text.

ADRIA, Giovanni Giacomo (ca. 1485–1560)[7]

*BHL —. De vita sanctorum martyrum mazariensium Viti, Modesti et
Crescentiae* (IV)[8]

The poet and historian Adria studied first in his hometown of Mazara with
Tommaso Schifaldo (*q.v.*) and then in Naples with Agostino Nifo. This
work, published in Palermo in 1523, celebrates the martyred patrons of
Mazara. No manuscripts known to me; imprint not seen. Not included in
fig. 1.1 or table 2.1.[9]

AGLI, Antonio degli (ca. 1400–1477)[10]

Collection. *De vitis et gestis sanctorum* (I–VII)

Dedicatory preface to *Nicholas V* (d. March 24, 1455). Its ten books contain 228 entries. A preface precedes each book; in the first, Agli notes that
the initial impulse for the collection came from *Ambrogio Traversari*. See
chap. 2 above.

inc. proem. 1: Sanctorum vitas gestaque scribere ac iuxta temporum ali-

7. R. Zapperi, in *DBI* 1 (1960): 307b.

8. On these saints, see A. Amore in *BS* 12 (1969): 1244–1246; M. Forlin Patrucco in *GLS*
1961b–1963a.

9. See Gianvito Resta, "La stampa in Sicilia nel Cinquecento," in M. Santoro, ed., *La
stampa in Italia nel Cinquecento: Atti del convegno, Roma, 17–21 ottobre 1989* (Rome: Bulzoni, 1992), 2:825, item 5, recording a copy at the Biblioteca Alexandrina.

10. Nelson Minnich, "The Autobiography of Antonio degl Agli (ca. 1400–1477)," in
Renaissance Studies in Honour of Craig Hugh Smyth, ed. C. Morrogh (Florence: Giunti Bar-
bera, 1985), 177–191. For Agli's panegyric on Francis, dedicated to Sixtus IV, see Kristeller,
Iter 2:322b.

quam rationem ordinare digerereque adortus et desperatione inveniendi quae certa

inc. proem. 2: Visum mihi est, Beatissime Pater, in huius secundi libri exordio, ante sanctorum martyrum gesta aggrediar, paululum inquirere cur tam acriter

inc. proem. 3: Huius tertii libri scripta eadem que superiora continentur omnia.

inc. proem. 4: In parte operis huius scribuntur gesta sanctorum quae sub Dioclitiano Maximianoque agnita sunt, quorum Dioclitianus multa molitus est ut Deus haberetur.

inc. proem. 5: Hic rursus quintus liber Dioclitiani Maximianique temporibus assignatur

inc. proem. 6: Liber hic sextus Dioclitiani rursum ac Maximiani temporibus persequutionem in Christianos exercitam continet

inc. proem. 7: Siquis quae et quanta uirtus sit patientia nosse desiderat, legat martyrum sanctorumque reliquorum inuicta certamina

inc. proem. 8: Liber octauus continet et quaedam sub Juliano ac Valente principibus gesta

inc. proem. 9: Nonus liber haud pauca Vuandalicae persecutionis continet martiria

inc. proem. 10: Decimus liber multorum sanctorum cum martyrum tum alias Christi dogmatis

MSS

1. Florence, BN, MS Nuovi acq. 399, autograph draft. XV. Kristeller, *Iter* 1:172a. Source text.

2. Vatican City, BAV, MS Lat. 3742, a ca. 1530 reconstitution of a manuscript damaged in the 1527 sack of Rome. Kristeller, *Iter* 2:323a. Seen.

Editions

The preface to the first book is edited from BAV, MS Lat. 3742, in M. Miglio, *Storiografia pontificia del quattrocento* (Bologna: Patron, 1975), 177–180. All the prefaces are edited from both manuscripts in A. K. Frazier, "Italian Humanists as Authors of *vitae sanctorum*, 1417–1521" (PhD dissertation, Columbia University, 1997), 551–579.

BHL —. ⟨Cosmae et Damiani Vita⟩ (IV)[11]

Dedicatory preface to Cosimo de'Medici (d. 1464). Riccardo Fubini first called attention to this account in "Papato e storiografia nel Quattrocento," *Studi medievali*, ser. 3, 18, no. 1 (1977): 339 n. 39. In the 1430s

---

11. On Cosmas and Damian, see E. Caraffa in *BS* 4 (1964): 223–225; M. Forlin Patrucco in *GLS* 491a–492b.

Ambrogio Traversari (*q.v.*) had wanted to make a translation of Simeon Metaphrast's narrative on these saints; see Charles Stinger, *Humanism and the Church Fathers: Ambrogio Traversari (1396–1439) and Christian Antiquity in the Italian Renaissance* (Albany, N.Y., 1977), 128.

inc. proem.: Cosmae et Damiani uitam gestaque breve adorsus vix prosequi audeam, tam magna enim sunt tamque obstupenda ut fictis scribere ratus.

des. proem: et imitari conemur.

inc.: Ea igitur tempestate qua Dioclitianus Maximianusque imperium orbis habebant, Cosmas ac Damianus Arabia

des.: Legi litteras a quodam fratre minorum ordinis qui dum Iohannes de Capistrano ad archiepiscopum Florentinum ex Boemia missus ubi ad octingenta uariorum generum miracula factam inter quae et mortuos suscitatos affirmat. Sed de his alias. Ego quidem nulla tam magna tamque obstupenda dici de fortissimis his martiribus Cosma videlicet et Damiano audire ualeam quin maiora quinque miraculo digniora existimem. Vale.

MSS

1. Florence, BN, MS Nuovi acq. 399, lower left foliation: fols. 280v–281 (preface) and 281–286v (*vita* and *miracula*). Autograph. XV. Kristeller, *Iter* 1:172a. Source text.

Editions

None. The preface is edited in Frazier, "Italian Humanists," 589–592.

ALBERTI, Leandro, O.P. (1479–1553)[12]

Collection. *De viris illustribus ordinis praedicatorum libri sex.*

Dedicatory prefaces precede each of the six books. The anthology was compiled by Alberti and his friend Giovanni Antonio Flamini in the space of about a year, 1516–1517. A woodcut depicting a triumph stands at the head of each book.[13]

inc. proem. 1 (fol. 5r): Plinius iunior ille litterarum optimus excultor (to Cardinal Nicolaus Fliscus)

inc. proem. 2 (fol. 51v): Post primum ordinis nostri de uiris (to Eustachius Platesius, O.P. of Bologna)

---

12. Kristeller, "Contribution," 126; A. L. Redigonda, in *DBI* 1 (1960), 699–702.

13. The first preface is preceded by three testimonial letters that touch on the aim and utility of Alberti's collection. See especially fol. 3, by Franciscus Ferrariensis, O.P., a student of Giovanni Garzoni's (*q.v.*) who had died by 1504 (Lind, *Letters*, letter 182 and n. to letter 200); and fol. 3v, by Bartholomaeus Mortarius, O.P.

inc. proem. 3 (fol. 63v): Quantis laudibus quantis preconiis (to Laurentius Fliscus)

inc. proem. 4 (fol. 129v): Aueroes ille Aristotelis aemulus (to Philippus Saulus)

inc. proem. 5 (fol. 155v): Salomon ille hebraeorum sapientissimum (to Joannes de Lasko)

inc. proem 6 (fol. 253v): Posteaquam Salomon totius terrarum orbis (to Andreas Novellus)

MSS
None known to me.

Editions
1. The collection has been published once, "Bononiae 1516" (1517). Source text.

BHL —. *Iordani Saxoni ord. praed. generalis magistri secundi vita* (XIII)

Prefatory letters to and from Giovanni Antonio Flamini, dated 1516 (fol. 23r–v). In the first, Alberti says he has completed this *Liber primus*, treating all the masters general of the Dominicans, in just twenty-two days.

inc. epist.: Mitto ad te Iordani uiri sanctissimi ac caeterorum nostrae religionis dictatorum

inc. epist.: Legi tuum libenter et magna cum uoluptate

inc.: Iordanes vir sanctissimus oppido Botergae provinciae Saxoniae originem duxit, quibus parentibus non produnt scriptores

des.: scripsit praeterea libellum de ordinis nostri initio.

MSS
None known to me.

Editions
1. L. Alberti, ed. *De viris illustribus ordinis praedicatorum* (Bologna 1516 [1517]), 23v–35v. Source text.

BHL —. *B. Iacynthi Poloni ord. praed. vita* (XIII)

Prefatory letter to Giovanni Antonio Flamini dated 1516 (fol. 175). A formal canonization process for Hyacinthus did not open until 1521; it was completed in 1594.[14]

---

14. See V. Koudelka, *BS* 6 (1964): 326–331; *AASS* Aug. III (Anvers, 1737): 309–379; R. J. Loenertz, "La vie de S. Hyacinthe du Lecteur Stanislaus," *AFP* 27 (1957): 5–37.

inc. epist.: Hicynthi [*sic*] uitam scripsimus uiri sanctitate
inc.: Hiacynthus ex oppido Poloniae saxo nobili stemmate
des.: Longum esse si uellem cuncta complecti. Sed haec ad testandam uiri clarissimi sanctitatem sufficere possunt.

MSS
None known to me.

Editions
1. Alberti, *De viris illustribus ordinis praedicatorum* (Bologna 1516 [1517]), fols. 175–178v. Source text.

BHL —. [*Vita*] *Raimundus de Penaforti Cathalanus* (XIII)

No preface. Alberti explicitly acknowledges that the canonist Raymond (c.d. 1604) is not officially a saint but, finding the oversight inexplicable, attributes miracles and saintly qualities to him.
inc.: Raimundus de penaforti Cathalanus originem
des.: Rex autem Arragonum uisis miraculis . . . instetit ut inter diuos connumeratur, sed nescio quo accidente tam egregium opus ommissum est . . . de tanto uiro peruenere.

MSS
None known to me.

Editions
1. Alberti, *De viris illustribus ordinis praedicatorum* (Bologna 1516 [1517]), fols. 35v–36v. Source text.

ALBERTI, Leon Battista (1404–1472)[15]

BHL 6912d. *Vita s. Potiti* (II)[16]

Prefatory letter to *Biagio Molin*, who had set Alberti the subject. The life and martyrdom were written between late 1432 and March 1434. See chap. 2 above.
inc. epist.: Blasi pater et domine . . . pax tibi
des. epist.: quid agendum censeas imperabis.
inc.: Potiti adolescentis uitam non iniuria primam esse
des.: non longe a Calabrio fluuio adolescentem decapitarunt.

---

15. C. Grayson, in *DBI* 1 (1960), 702–709; idem, *Studi su Leon Battista Alberti* (Florence: Olschki, 1998); A. Grafton, *Leon Battista Alberti* (New York: Hill and Wang, 2000), 64–70.
16. On Potitus, see N. Del Re in *BS* 10 (1968): 1072–1074.

MSS

1. Florence, Bibl. Riccardiana, MS 767, fols. 34–40, with dedicatory letter on fol. 41 and other letters at fol. 42r–v. XV. Kristeller, *Iter* 1:200a. Seen.

Editions

1. Cecil Grayson, ed., *Opusculi inediti* (Florence: Olschki, 1954), 63–88. Source text.

AMBROGIO Da Cora, Massarius, O.E.S.A. (d. May 17, 1485)[17]

BHL 797. Vita s. Augustini (V)

Preface, no dedicatee. The text suggests an oral delivery. Ambrogio also addresses Augustine's life in the course of his *Defensorium* (ISTC ic00877000) and commentary on the rules.

inc. proem: Saepenumero cum in maioribus perorandi generibus tempus meum haud inane ducerem

des. proem: ac etiam ut breuior fiam, allegandi contestandique frequentiam aliis meis in orationibus facere consueui, hoc tempore omittam

inc.: Augustinus itaque, ut dicere incipiam, genere quidem Afer

des.: Sanctaque anima illa corporis soluta domicilio ad suum rediit creatorem. Amen.

MSS

Manuscripts of Ambrogio's orations on Augustine are extant, but I know of no manuscripts of the life of Augustine.

Editions

1. *Vita S. Augustini: Commentarii super Regula S. Augustini*. Rome: Georgius Herolt, December 8, 1481. H 5683*; Goff C881; *BMC* 4:126; *IGI* 439; *IERS* 673; ISTC ic00881000. Source text.

2. *Canones Aurelii Augustini iuxta triplicem . . . regulam*. Strassburg: Martin Schott, 1490. Goff A 1229. H 2076*; *IGI* 965; *BMC* 1:95; *GW* 2937.

---

17. Kristeller, "Contribution," 146; J. de Guibert, in *DS* 1:429–430; Johannes Felix Ossinger, *Bibliotheca Augustiniania Historica, Critica, et Chronologica* (Ingolstadt, 1768), 260–264. For Ambrogio da Cora's orations on Augustine and John the Baptist, see O'Malley, *Praise*, 251.

BHL 1736. ⟨*Vita et miracula beatae Christinae de Vicecomitibus*⟩
O.E.S.A. tert. (d. 1458)[18]

No preface. Agostina Camozzi, *ad saec.*, was born at Lago di Lugano but is associated with Calvisano as well. She was promoted for canonization by Milan but denied.[19]

inc.: Priori ac ceteris fratribus spoletani conuentus. . . . Gaudeo ac uehementer laetor

des.: Haec breuiter, me patres optimi, ingeniolo meo oblata sunt . . . ualeamus imitari. Amen.

MSS
   1. Modena, Bib. Estense, MS Est. lat. 894 (Alpha Q 6, 13), fols. 58–71, with a preface to Aurelius sublacensis at 57v–58. Kristeller, *Iter* 1:383a. Not seen.
   2. Paris, BN, MS Lat. 5621, fols. 1–11. XV. *Catalogus codicum hagiographicorum latinorum antiquarium saeculo XVI qui asseruantur in Bibliotheca nationali parisiensi* (Brussels: Bollandist Society, 1889–93), 2:526. Not seen.

Editions
   1. *AASS* Feb. II (Paris, 1864): 799, para. 3. Source text.

AMERINO
See GERALDINI, Alessandro.

ANTONINUS
See PIEROZZI, Antonino.

---

18. N. Del Re in *BS* 4 (1964): 341. She is called Cristina Visconti in the *Breviarium Augustinianum* but Cristina Semenzi da Calvisano in the *Breviarium Brixianum*. See also *AASS* Feb. II (Antwerp, 1658): 799–802.

19. T. Herrera, *Alphabetum Augustinianum* (Madrid, 1644; repr. 1990) 1:137–138, gives a birthdate of 1435/36. See *BHL* 1739, the "responsio" by Francesco Sforza. Cf. G. Brunati, *Leggendario o vite di santi bresciani* (Brescia: Gilberti, 1834), 4 and n. 21; P. Guerrini, "Intorno alla beata Christina di Spoleto, erroneamente chiamata beata Christina Semenzi di Calvisano," *Brixia sacra* 7 (1916): 140–168; N. Concetti, "De beata Christina a Spoleto Ord. F.F. Erem. S.P. Aug. tertiaria," *AA* 5 (1914): 457–465; Emilio Motta, "La beata Christina da Spoleto era del Lago di Lugano," *Bollettino storico della svizzera italiana* 15 (1893): 84–93.

ANTONIUS Bargensis, O.S.B. (d. 1452)[20]

BHL 1250n. ⟨*Vita Bernardi Ptolomaei*⟩ (XIV)[21]

Dedication to *Giovanni da Marca Nova*, O.S.B., teacher of philosophy at Padua, who had, along with a professor of civil law, *Giovanni da Prato*, O.S.B., requested the work after approving Antonio's earlier composition on Tuscan geography, history, customs, and ceremonies (lost). Antonio planned to write a second part of the *Chronicon* to address famous Montolivetans, their miracles, and their writings.

inc. epist.: In preterito quidem anno, dum una cum abbate nostro in partes Venetorum uisendi causa uenissem

des. epist.: quos sagaciter ediderunt. Vale feliciter.

inc.: Igitur in Tuscie prouincia, ciuitate Senensi, quidam fuit uir, Bernardus nomine

des.: Propterea si quid in hac normula apostolice uite et religionis, dispensatione, correctione, uel mutatione indiget, episcopo nostro . . . dispenset, mutet et corrigat. Cuius nos gratia fulciti, seruire ualeamus . . . per omnia secula. Amen.

MSS

1. Monte Oliveto Maggiore, Archivio dell'Abbazia, s.n. XV. See P. M. Lugano, ed., *Chronicon . . . Montolivitensis* (Florence: Cocchi and Chiti, 1901), li, n. 1 and Kristeller, *Iter* 2:543b–544a. Not seen.

Editions

1. P. M. Lugano, ed. *Chronicon . . . Montolivitensis* (Florence: Cocchi and Chiti, 1901), 3–28. Source text.

BHL Epitome. ⟨*Vita Bernardi Ptolomaei*⟩ (XIV)

No preface. The epitome, based on the *Chronicon* account, is included in Antonio's accompanying chronological list of abbots general.

inc.: Quartus abbas fuit frater Bernardus de Tholomeis de Senis.

des.: Et sepultus est Senis, in monasterio Sancti Benedicti.

MSS

1. See preceding entry.

---

20. Kristeller, "Contribution," 127. All biographical information taken from P. M. Lugano, *Chronicon . . . Montolivitensis* (Florence: Cocchi and Chiti, 1901), xxv–li.

21. G. Picasso in *BS* 12 (1969): 518–525; idem in *GLS* 313b–315a; R. Grégoire, "L'agiografia del beato Bernardo Tolomei (d. 1348)," in R. Donghi and G. Picasso, eds., *Alla riscoperta di un carisma: Saggi di spiritualità e storia olivetana* (Monte Oliveto Maggiore, 1995), 83–118.

Editions

1. P. M. Lugano, ed., *Chronicon . . . Montolivitensis* (Florence: Cocchi and Chiti, 1901), 31–33. Source text.

ARIOSTO, Alessandro, O.F.M. Obs. (d. after July 16, 1485)[22]

Lost. ⟨*Vita s. Bonaventurae in lectiones divisa*⟩ (XIII)[23]

BHL —. ⟨*Vita Marci Bononiensis* [Fantuzzi/Elefantuzzi, O.F.M. Obs.]⟩ (d. 1479)[24]

inc.: Scripturus admiranda vite opera et iam dormientis in Christo preclarissima signa beatissimi patris . . . Beatus autem hic pater ex Bartholomeo Lisiaque civibus Bononiensibus progenitus

des.: Quam ob rem sciant ex quam plurimis me per pauca sumpsisse [miracula] . . . pene defunctos, quoniam sunt eum bona merita subnixa Dei virtute, qui est benedictus in secula. Amen.

MSS

The earliest manuscript, lost in WWII, is described in C. Mesini, "La più antica biografia del b. Marco da Bologna," *Il Carobbio* 7 (1981): 278b–279a. Mesini records that there was both a life (fols. 1–11v) and miracles (fols. 11v–26v).

Editions

1. Mesini, "La più antica biografia," 281–286, apparently from Santa Maria di Campagna in Piacenza, made from a Quattrocento exemplar in

---

22. Not in Kristeller, "Contribution"; R. Pratesi, in *DBI* 4 (1962): 166b–168a.

23. See Geroldus Fussenegger, "De vita et scriptis Fr. Alexandri Ariosti (ob. ca 1486)," *AFH* 49 (1956): 164–165.

24. On Marco da Bologna, see G. D. Gordini in *BS* 8 (1966): 707–708; C. Piana, "Per la biografia del beato Marco da Bologna (d. 1479) e per la storia del suo convento di S. Paolo in Monte nel '400," *Deputazione di storia patria per le province di Romagna, Atti e memorie* n.s. 22 (1971): 179–189. On this account, see Fussenegger, "De vita et scriptis Fr. Alexandri Ariosti," 144–145. See also *BHL* 5300m–q, where item 3, "Vita et miracula," not assigned a *BHL* number, is the life that Fussenegger describes as a "sermo panegyricus stilo ingenioque humanistico" and attributes to Ariosto. Benvenuto Bughetti, "De obitu et miraculis B. Marci Fantutii de Bononia, vicarii gen. observantiae ord. Fr. Min. (d. 1479) cum appendice de vicariis generalibus cismontanis observantium (1430–1488)," *AFH* 27 (1934): 100, assigns this account the siglum V and cites it occasionally in his edition of *BHL* 5300m–5300q. See also idem, "Quo anno et die B. Marcus Fantutius de Bononia obierit," *AFH* 2 (1909): 539 and n. 1.

1779, according to the notary's *additamentum* (286, cols. b–c). Mesini (274a), follows the notary in giving 1479 as the date of composition, that is, immediately following the death of the *beatus*. No shelfmark given.

ATTAVANTI, Paolo, Florentinus, O.S.M. (ca. 1440–May 16, 1499)[25]

BHL 6824. *Vita Philippi Benitii* (XIII)

Dedicatory preface to Cristoforo Tornielli, general of the Servites from May 1461.[26] Paolo, dedicated by his mother to Filippo Benizi at his birth, was not quite sixteen when he began his novitiate and seems to have written this account at the end of it.[27]

inc. epist.: Tametsi in studiis humanitatis, ut appellant, parum mihi profecisse uidear, et ad ornate grauiter appositeque dicendum aetas mea nequaquam sufficiat, tua tamen humanitate fretus atque clementia, nihil est quod dubitum hunc libellum tibi gratum fore. Non sane ut officiorum, quae quidem in me contulisti, tibi gratiam referam . . . uerum enimuero cupiens ob animi magnitudinem te studiorum meorum participem reddere, hunc ad te transcripsi libellum.

inc.: Philippo parens fuit Iacobus, ciuis Florentinus, genere nobilis, qui tametsi non pari splendore auctoritateque in republica fuerit, perhumanus tamen habitus est imprimisque liberalis.

des.: Viuet enim semper illius fama, ibitque per ciuitates, illustrabit prouincias, peruagabitur regiones, donec terrarum orbem suo splendore ac sanctitate compleuerit.

inc. mir.: At Deus immortalis et aeternus non modo eius sanctitatem in uita ostendere, uerum post mortem multis atque praeclaris miraculis omnibus palam esse uoluit. Principio itaque quaedam erat mulier . . .

des. mir.: eum ad sanctissimum Philippi corpus tulerunt. Cuius se meritis in pedes erexit.

---

25. Kristeller, "Contribution," 149 (*s.u.* "Paulus Florentinus"); G. M. Besutti, "Paul Attavanti de Florence," *DS* 12 (1983): 536–40; Aristide Serra, "Memoria di fra Paolo Attavanti (1440–ca. 1499)," *Studi storici dell'Ordini dei Servi di Maria* 21 (1971): 47–87. On dating, Besutti, "Paul Attavanti," and Serra, "Memoria," 49–50 n. 9, supersede [R. Capasso] in *DBI* 4 (1962): 531a–b, who follows Soulier. Kristeller, *Iter* 6:552b, gives 1439–1499. Attavanti's lost *Sermones de sanctis* are cited by Serra, "Memoria," 79–80. See also Schutte, *PIVRB*, 55, for a vernacular life of Rocco attributed to Attavanti and for Attavanti's *Legenda de la nativita de Christo* and a *Legenda et oratione che fu trovata alli piedi de santa Maria da Loreto, con il prego al Crucifixo*. See also *BHL* 4520d.
26. Dating from Serra, "Memoria," 53 and 71; Capasso, in *DBI* 4 (1962): 531a.
27. Serra, "Memoria," 49–50. On Filippo Benizi, see F. A. dal Pino in *GLS* 678a–681b.

inc. transl. cum alia mir.: Ceterum, postquam in dies omnibus in rebus sua uisa est augeri sanctitas ...

des.: Magna nimirum sunt haec et admiratu dignissima. Talis est igitur Philippus, ut qui eius sanctitatem fuerit imitatus, mirabiles ex ea fructus referat ... Optimus vero maximusque Deus, qui te pium ac dignissimum pastorem nostro ordini praecipuum dare uoluit, ipse nobis partem et hereditatem tribuat inuenire ... in saecula saeculorum. Amen.

MSS

1. Paris, BN, MS CCCLIV (5374), *Cat. cod. hag. lat. B.N. Parisiensi* 2:438. Not seen.

Editions

1. P. Soulier, "Vita Beati Philippi," *MOSSM* 3.1 (1899), 99–112 and 3.2 (1899), 113–123. Source text.

BHL 4287. Beati Ioachimi vita (XIV)

Dedicatory preface to Cristoforo Tornielli, general of the Servites. The life was written shortly after May 1461.[28]

inc. proem.: Operae pretium est Ioachini uitam, lectu iucundam et imitatione dignissimam, enarrare

inc. vita: Is a teneris igitur annis ingenue a parentibus educatus

des. vita: Sed quum infinitae sapientiae Deo uisum est, pauca de eo in hominum memoriam redacta sunt, nam ubi singula Ioachini gesta quisque describere uellet, maximam sibi prouinciam imponeret.

inc. mir.: Postquam vero ex mundi laqueis euanuit, exaltari usque ad nouissimum iudicii diem dignus euasit.

des. mir.: Quae flagitiorum dolens, moribus operam dedissse fertur.

peroratio: Is ergo, ut exordium finemque iuxta faciam, felicissime uixit, qui Ioachinum imitans, eius morem agit eritque particeps illius diuini ac sempiterni gaudii. Et is qui uniuersum terrarum orbem nutu quodam summa ratione gubernat, in eadem quoque patria colendum dabit, in qua quidem electi mortalium Sancti permanent, gloriam Trinitati reddentes in saecula saeculorum.

MSS

1. Florence, BN, MS Conv. sopp. G 8 1467, fols. 2–3v (prologue), 3v–33 (*vita*), 33–45v (miracles), 45v–46 (*peroratio*). Copied from the autograph, according to Soulier in *MOSSM* 5 (1902), 47. Kristeller, *Iter* 1:150b. Seen.

---

28. Dating from Serra, "Memoria," 72; and Capasso, in *DBI* 4 (1962): 532a. On Gioacchino da Siena, see P.-M. Suarez in *BS* 6 (1964): 476–478.

2. Rome, Bibl. Alexandrina, MS 92, fols. 630–647v. On this incomplete copy, see Soulier in *MOSSM* 5 (1902), 74. Not seen.

Editions

1. P. M. Soulier, "Beati Ioachimi uita per fratrem Paulum digesta," *MOSSM* 5 (1902): 49–72. Source text.

BHL 2484m. *Vita Elisabettae* (d. 1468)[29]

Attavanti based this account, which he placed in his history of Mantua, on one written between 1468 and 1472.[30] *Incipit* and *desinit* from BHL. Not recorded in figure 1.1.

inc.: Elisabeth, patre Leonardo Cremone nata 1428
des.: Quedam puella, in lacum mantuanum cadens

MSS

1. Casale Monferrato, Seminario Vescovile, MS II b 2. Cart., misc., XVI. Kristeller, *Iter* 1:41b. Not seen.

2. Mantua, Bibl. Comm., MS A IV 27. Kristeller, *Iter* 1:272a. Not seen.

3. Mantua, Bibl. Comm., MS A IV 18. Kristeller, *Iter* 1:272a; Kristeller, *Supplementum Ficinianum* (Florence, 1937), 2:117. Not seen.

4. Rome, Bibl. Angelica, MS 1420 (T 7 7), fols. 1–173v XV. Kristeller, *Supplementum Ficinianum*, 2:17. Not seen.

5. Turin, Accademia delle Scienze, MS 0289. Kristeller *Iter* 2:174. Not seen.

6. Venice, BN Marciana, MS Lat. X 17 (3324). Kristeller, *Iter* 2:230a. Not seen.

Editions

1. D. M. Montagna, "Nuove ricerche sulla beata Elisabetta Picenardi," *Moniales ordinis servorum* 1 (1963): 29–32. Not seen.

Lost. ⟨*Vita Francisci* [*Patritii*] *Senensis, O.S.M.*⟩ (XIV)

Only the preface to Pius II (d. August 15, 1464) is extant. The account is mentioned by Soulier in *MOSSM* 4, no. 1 (1900–1901): 35; again in *MOSSM* 5 (1902): 49; and by Aristide Serra, "Memoria di fra Paolo Attavanti (1440–ca. 1499)," *Studi storici dell'Ordine dei Servi di Maria* 21 (1971): 79.

---

29. On Elisabetta Picenardi see D.-M. Montagna in *BS* 10 (1968): 550–552.
30. Friar Servants of Mary, *Origins and Early Saints of the Order of Servants of Mary: Writings of the Fourteenth and Fifteenth Century* (Chicago: University of Chicago Press, 1984), 124, citing Montagna, "Nuove ricerche," 23.

BHL —. Dialogus de origine ordinis servorum[31]

Dedicated to Piero di Cosimo de' Medici. The dialogue between Piero de' Medici and Mariano Salvini was written about 1465 according to Serra, "Memoria," 53–54 and n. 25. D. Montagna, "I nomi dei sette santi," *Studi storici dell'Ordine dei Servi di Maria* 38 (1988): 24, observes that it had no diffusion in the Quattrocento. Not included in figure 1.1.

inc. proem.: Cum ad Petrum Cosmae, uirum quippe adspectu iocundum et multarum rerum periculo grauem, Marianus Antistes [Salvinus], fama et gloria celebris, aliquando uenisset

des. proem.: Rem igitur dilucidam ante oculos ponere festino . . . iterum iterumque legendum.

inc.: MARIANUS: Efflagitasti ex me saepe numero, Petre,

des.: MARIANUS: Ego uero . . . diuae Virginis uoluntatem in hoc ducem crederem. Riccius scripsit. FINIS.

MSS

1. Florence, BN, MS Conv. soppr. G 8 1468. XVI. Serra, *"Memoria,"* 72–74; Kristeller, *Iter* 1:150b. Not seen.

Editions

1. P. Soulier, ed., *MOSSM* 11, no. 1 (1910): 88–112. Source text.

AUGUSTINUS Ticinensis de Novis, Can. Lat. (fl. 1500)[32]

BHL 798b. Vita s. Augustini et b. matris Monicae (V)[33]

Prologue. These accounts (listed separately here because each is counted in figure 1.1) were part of the Hermits' and the Canons' polemic (see above, chap. 5). Cf. this author's earlier *De antiquitate et dignitate ordinis canonicorum regularium s. Augustini,* published in Milan in 1503. The *Elucidarium,* in which these texts occur, also includes entries on Gelasius, Bernardus, Albinus, Herculanus, Patricius, Ubaldus, Figdrianus, Johannes, and Anianus. ISTC ia01373450 may derive from it.

---

31. On this account, see Anonymous, in *DBI* 4 (1962): 532a; Kristeller, *Supplementum Ficinianum,* 2:117. On the Sette Santi Fondatori, see F. A. Dal Pino in *GLS* 1777b–1782a.

32. Not in Kristeller, "Contribution"; not in *DBI*; not to be confused with the Hermit Augustinus Novellus de Padua recorded by Adolar Zumkeller, *Manuskripte von Werken der autoren des Augustiner-Eremitenordens in mitteleuropäischen Bibliotheken* (Würzburg: Augustinus, 1966), 81.

33. On Augustine, see A. Trapé in *BS* 1 (1961): 428–596; V. Grossi in *GLS* 43a–55b. On Monica, see A. Trapé in *BS* 9 (1967): 548–558; B. Jimenez Duque in *GLS* 1459–1460.

inc. prol.: Priscorum fuit trita satis et probata sententia
inc.: Creator omnium Deus
des.: sic aperietur. Amen.

MSS
None known to me.

Editions
1. Augustinus Ticinensis, *Elucidarium christianarum religionum*. Brescia: Angelus Britannicus, 1511, signs. A–E3.

BHL 6004g. *Vita s. Augustini et b. matris Monicae* (IV)

See the life of Augustine, above; this account of Monica is divided into eleven *lectiones* for the office.

inc. argumentum: Pia igitur et uenerabilis diui patris Augustini mater
. . . qui in libro confessionarum suarum eius uitam describit quam et nos non more falsographorum, non corrupto, non denique deprauato, sed fideli stilo ac sincero ordine sententiarum prosequimur
des. argumentum: in orando mira charitate flagrauerit.
inc. lectio 1: Accipe, inquit, Domine Deus, confessiones meas et gratiarum actiones
des.: Et ciuium meorum in eterna hierusalem cui suspirate peregrinatio nostra. Haec diuus Augustinus ex lib. ii, v, vi, ix et x libro confessionum suarum.

MSS
None known to me.

Editions
1. Augustinus Ticinensis, *Elucidarium christianarum religionum* (Brescia: Angelus Britannicus, 1511), signs. 2E3–E7. Source text.

BHL 8816. ⟨*Vita Warini*⟩ bp. of Praeneste (XII)[34]

This account, divided into five *lectiones* for the office, epitomizes the text of the twelfth-century life of St. Guarinus, Augustinian canon and cardinal from Bologna, that was presented to Guarino Guarini (*q.v.*) by Timoteo Maffei.

inc. lectio 1: B. Guarinus Christi confessor genere praeclarus Bononie oriundus

---

34. G. D. Gordini in *BS* 7 (1966): 435–436.

des.: cernentibus omnibus, luminaria accenderetur, praestante domino nostro Jesu Christo cui est honor et gloria in secula seculorum. Amen.

MSS

1. BAV, MS Barb Lat 2375, fols. 75–80v. XVII. Poncelet 1910, 480. Seen.

2. BAV, MS Barb. Lat. 2363, fols. 31–35. XVIII. Poncelet 1910, 185. Seen. Both late mss include a marginal note referring to an "exemplar unicus" that I cannot identify.

Editions

1. Augustinus Ticinensis, *Elucidarium christianarum religionum*. Brescia: Angelus Britannicus, 1511, signs. E.7–E.8. Source text.

AURISPA, Giovanni (1376–1459)[35]

BHL —. *Vita s. Mamantis* (III)[36]

Preface to Janus, king of Cyprus from 1432 to 1458. His patron saint was Mamas. The life is dated to 1438 by R. Sabbadini, *Carteggio di Giovanni Aurispa* (Rome: Tipografia del Senato, 1931), 176. Aurispa was an ordained priest at the time of writing, but mostly nonresident.

inc. proem.: Cum grecorum regis societati uenetiis peregrinarer
des. proem: Mamantis uitam inspice
inc.: Mamas hic magnus et famosus patriam habuit Paflagoniam
des.: Multa quidem deus miracula per sanctum mamantem et fecit et facit . . . ad gloriam patris . . . in secula seculorum Amen. Telos.

MSS

1. Camaldoli, Archivio del sacro eremo, MS 1112. XVIII. Kristeller, *Iter* 5:521a. Not seen.

2. Venice, BN Marciana, MS Lat. XIV 68 (4735), fols. 39v–6. XV. Kristeller, *Iter* 2:264a–b. Seen.

3. Venice, BN Marciana, MS Lat. XIV 244 (4681). XV. Kristeller, *Iter* 2:249a and 6:263. With preface. Seen.

4. Vicenza, Bib Bertoliana, MS 93 (formerly 3, 7, 12). Mazzatinti, 2 (Forlì: Bordandini, 1892), 59–60, no. 298. Seen.

---

35. E. Bigi, in *DBI* 4 (1962): 593a–595b, with earlier bibliography; Adriano Franceschini, *Giovanni Aurispa e la sua biblioteca: Notizie e documenti* (Padua, 1976), esp. 10–11 on the question of whether Aurispa was an Augustinian Canon; Diana Robin, *Filelfo in Milan* (Princeton, N.J.: Princeton University Press, 1991), 30–34.
36. F. Scorza Barcellona, "Mama di Cesarea," *GLS* 1283b–1284b.

Editions
All late; see *BHL*.

BAGNATORIUS, Nicolaus, O.P. (fl. 1520)[37]

cf. *BHL* 1916 (unattributed). *Vita Conradini brixiensis*, O.P. (1429)[38]

Dedicatory preface to Agostino Comotta, O.P., dated 1516. The author mentions *Leandro Alberti*'s encouragement; he hopes to write more for Comotta than this "brief life." Cf. Cristoforo Barzizza, below.

    inc. epist.: Tanta est erga te fidei meae obseruantia amorisque synceritas

    inc.: Beatus Conradinus non ficta uirtutum effigies ex antiqua praeclaraque familia

    des.: totum attitudini sapientiae et scientiae Dei relinquendum censeo.

MSS
None known to me.

Editions
    1. Alberti, *De viris illustribus,* fols. 249–251. Cf. *AASS* Nov. I (Paris, 1889): 410–413, with a brief discussion of the problem of authorship at 402, para. 2.

BALBI, Pietro (1399–September 9, 1479)[39]

Lost. cf. *BHG* 1012. *De vita s. Macrinae* (IV)[40]

This account, a translation from the Greek of Gregory of Nyssa, may have been written between 1471 and 1473. The manuscript was once in the library of the Cathedral of Capua.[41]

---

37. Not in Kristeller, "Contribution"; not in *DBI*; J. Quétif and J. Echard, *Scriptores ordinis praedicatorum recensiti notisque historicis et criticis illustrati* (Turin: Bottega d'Erasmo, 1959, from 1719–1721 edition), 1:34a–b, sub 1516; Alfonso D'Amato, *I Domenicani a Bologna* (Bologna: Edizioni Studio Domenicano, 1988), 1:474–475. He is included here as a humanist solely on the basis of Leandro Alberti's request that he contribute to the *De viris illustribus ordinis praedicatorum.*

38. On Corradino da Brescia, see S. M. Bertucci in *BS* 3 (1963): 362–363.

39. A. Pratesi, in *DBI* 5 (1963): 378–379.

40. On Macrina, see J-M. Sauget in *BS* 8 (1966): 456–458.

41. Helen Brown Wicher, "Gregorius Nyssensus," *Catalogus translationum et commentariorum* 5, ed. F. E. Cranz and P. O. Kristeller (Washington, D.C.: Catholic University of America, 1984), 65–66 and 181.

BARBARO, Ermolao, senior, bp. (ca. 1410–1471)[42]

BHL 732b. *Vita Athanasii* (IV)[43]

Preface to the *Sisters of Santa Croce di Giudecca*, whose abbess had been, since 1444, the strict Eufemia (d. 1487), a relative of the patriarch Lorenzo Giustinian.[44] It is said that the original Barbaro translated is lost, but it is more likely that his narrative should be appreciated as a paraphrase of common Latin sources. Barbaro states in his prefatory letter that he has no Greek sources to hand. It is striking that he did not set his secretary, Antonio Beccaria, to work acquiring them, for Beccaria had translated several works by Athanasius for a former patron, Duke Humphrey of Gloucester.[45] Barbaro's account was probably written after May 11, 1455, when Giustinian's investigation into the authenticity of the relics, begun on April 10, was successfully completed.[46] Barbaro also wrote a homily for the third nocturn of Athanasius's feast for the sisters and translated their vernacular account of the *translatio* into Latin.

inc. proem.: Petiistis a me, sorores ac filiae in Christo

des. proem: quae semper cultrices extiterint eius uiri continentiae et integritatis.

inc.: Athanasius Alexandrinus episcopus cum parentes ex ea ciuitate

des.: uniuersum orbem ob miraculorum magnitudinem in sui admirationem conuertit.

MSS

1. Camaldoli, Archivio del sacro eremo, MS 1201, fols. 230–243. XVII. Kristeller, *Iter* 5:522b–523b at 523b. Not seen.

2. Padua, BU, MS 346, fols. 2v–16. XIX. Kristeller, *Iter* 6:126a. Not seen.

3. Udine, Bibl. Com., MS Manin 1333 (174), fols. 166–177. XVIII. Kristeller, *Iter* 2:207a and 6:242b. Not seen.

---

42. E. Bigi, in *DBI* 6 (1964), 95b–99b; Margaret L. King, *Venetian Humanism in an Age of Patrician Dominance* (Princeton, N.J.: Princeton University Press, 1986), 320–322; cf. Luigi Pesce, *La chiesa di Treviso nel primo Quattrocento* (Rome: Herder, 1987), 329–373, giving the dates 1407–1471.

43. On Athanasius, see D. Stiernon in *BS* 2 (1962): 522–540; A. A. R. Bastiaensen in *GLS* 216b–221a.

44. On Eufemia, see A. Niero, *BS* 6 (1964): 1349–1350.

45. C. Vasoli, in *DBI* 7 (1965): 448a; BL, MS Royal 5 F II, described by G. F. Warner and J. P. Gilson, *British Museum Catalogue of Western Manuscripts in the Old Royal and King's Collections*, vol. 1, *Royal Mansucripts I A I to II E XI* (British Museum, 1921), 120, cols. a–b. Pesce, *La chiesa di Treviso*, 367 n. 823, intimates that Beccaria also translated a life of Athanasius, but such a work does not appear in the description of the relevant manuscripts or in B. L. Ullman, *Studies in the Italian Renaissance* (Rome, 1973), 353–354.

46. On the translation of 1455, see G. Musolino, A. Niero, and S. Tramontin, *Culto dei santi a Venezia* (Venice, 1965), 202–203.

4. Vatican City, BAV, MS Barb. Lat. 422 (XI 65). XV. Kristeller, *Iter* 2:444b–445a. According to Ronconi, *Ermolao Barbaro* (see "Imprints"), 76, this is the best manuscript, "uscito dallo scrittoio del Barbaro."[47] Source text microfilm SLU 8456.3.

5. Venice, BN Marciana, MS Lat. IX 40 (3497). XVI. Kristeller, *Iter* 2:229a. Not seen.

6. Venice, BN Marciana, MS Lat. II 123 (10383). XV. Kristeller, *Iter* 2:251a. Ronconi, *Ermolao Barbaro,* considers this a second-best manuscript.

7. Venice, Bibl. Correr, MS Cicogna 1143 (854), fols. 3v–9v. XV–XVI. Kristeller, *Iter* 2:284b. Ronconi, *Ermolao Barbaro,* considers this a second-best manuscript. Not seen.

8. Venice, Bibl. Correr, MS Cicogna 2978 (2903), fasc. 5. XVIII–IX. Kristeller, *Iter* 6:267b. Not seen.

Editions

1. G. Ronconi, ed., *Ermolao Barbaro il vecchio: Orationes contra poetas. Epistolae.* (Florence: Sansoni, 1972), 157–159 (preface only).

BARNABA di Nanni di Barna (fl. 1445)[48]

BHL 1188. *Vita Bernardini* [*senensis*] (1444)[49]

Dedication to Alfonso of Aragon dated "Kal. Aprilis 1445." Alfonso was promoting Bernardino's canonization.

inc. proem.: Vetusta sane ac laudabilis antiquorum omnium, serenissime Princeps, adhuc consuetudo uiget

des. proem: faustum, felix, fortunatum perficiat. Vale.

inc.: Bernardinus, qui ob res eius sanctissime gestas in omni uita sua beatus habitus est

des.: et in postera saecula et qui uenturi sunt etiam ipsi intellegant.

MSS

1. Vatican City, BAV, MS Ottob. lat. 2227 (XXXII 18). XV. Presentation manuscript with contemporary corrections in other hands. Kristeller, *Iter* 2:450b. Source text.

---

47. On the manuscripts, see G. Ronconi, ed., *Ermolao Barbaro il vecchio: Orationes contra poetas/Epistolae* (Florence: Sansoni, 1972), 74–76.

48. See G. Ferrau, ed., *Barnabà Senese: Epistolario* (Palermo: Università degli studi di Messina, 1979). Diana Webb, "Eloquence and Education: A Humanist Approach to Hagiography," *Journal of Ecclesiastical History* 31 (1980): 319–339, judges Barnabà only marginally connected to the humanists; cf. G. Fioravanti, "Maestri di grammatica a Siena nella seconda metà del '400," *Rinascimento,* ser. 2, no. 33 (1993): 193–207.

49. On Bernardino, see B. Korosak in *BS* 2 (1962): 1294–1316; S. Spanò in *GLS* 297a–300a.

Editions
All are late; see *BHL*.

BAROZZI, Pietro (1441–1507)[50]

BHL 1024f.; cf. *BHG* —. ⟨*Vita s. Basilii magni*⟩ (IV)[51]

Dedicatory letter to an unnamed *praesul reverendissimus* who gave Barozzi the Greek text.

inc. epist.: Accipe, Reverendissime ac singularissime praesule, quod indigno tradidisti homunculo de Basilii magni uita opusculum

inc.: Apud Capadociam prouintiam nobilem et non magis equorum quam hominum bonorum faecundam

des.: Quem ut pro merito laudare difficillimum sic ad unguem imitari omnino impossibile arbitramur.

MSS
    1. Venice, BN Marciana, MS Lat. IX 79 (3051), fols. 1–81. XVII. Kristeller, *Iter* 2:229b. Seen.
    2. Padua, BU, MS Provv. 206. XVI in. Anon. *Vita S. Basilii*, trans. Petr. Barocius, with preface facing 1r; subscription fol. 27: "Magni Basilii vita e graeco diligentissime in Latinum versa per R.m.d. Petrum Barocium ep. Paduanum quam ego Blasius eiusdem ecclesiae presbiter ad sui honorem et gloriam ex suo proprio originali emendate et fideliter in hoc exemplario transcripsi anno domini MDIII." Kristeller, *Iter* 2:19–20. Seen.

Editions
None.

Lost. ⟨*Vita Bernardini feltrensis*⟩ (1494)[52]

See F. Gaeta, in *DBI* 6 (1964): 512a, who also records a lost *Vita Christi versibus exarata*.

Lost? *Libellus de vita et laudibus beati Eustochii* (d. 1469)[53]

Exordium of one sentence in the Padua manuscript only. Presumably written during Barozzi's episcopacy, 1487–1507. Barozzi's life of Eustochium of Padua, O.S.B., may be lost; cf. notes in manuscripts 1 and 3 below,

---

    50. F. Gaeta, in *DBI* 6 (1964): 510–512; King, *Venetian Humanism*, 333–335. It is not clear to me that Barozzi is indeed the translator rather than the recipient of a translation. For his poem on St. Martin, see Kristeller, *Iter* 2:496a.
    51. On Basil, see D. Stiernon in *BS* 2 (1962): 910–937; M. Simonetti in *GLS* 249b–255a.
    52. On Bernardino da Feltre, see S. Spanò in *GLS* 295a–297b.
    53. I. Daniele in *BS* (1964): 305–306.

which suggest that Barozzi's account of Eustochium remains only in the vernacular translation by Daniele Villa.

inc.: Ex multis causis partim occultis partim manifestis

des.: Joannes Marius papiensis monacus diui Benedicti ex conuentu Montis Oliueti in laudem eius sermonem eleganter scripsit et aliis alia praecipue uersus et himnos singulos referre non permitit. Amen.[54]

MSS

1. Padua, Museo Civico, Fondo B.P., vol. 1, MS 1273, fols. 9v–15 (Latin; a vernacular translation precedes it on fols. 1–9). Kristeller, *Iter* 2:22b. Seen. A note on fol. 46r–v records: "Extat enim libellus de eius vita et laudibus a Petro Barocio ep. pat. . . . " Source text.

2. Padua, Museo Civico, Fondo B.P., vol. 1, MS 1274. Kristeller, *Iter* 2:22b. Seen.

3. Milan, Bibl. Ambrosiana, MS D 514 inf.. XVI (1547) *vita B. Eustachiae*, volg. by Danielle Villa. Kristeller, *Iter* 1:289a. According to M. Bolzonella, *Pietro Barocio, vescovo di Padova, 1487–1507* (Padua, 1941), 40 n. 1, this is Villa's autograph. Not seen.

Editions
None known to me.

BARTOLOMEO da Palazzuolo, O.E.S.A. obs. (1426–Oct. 3, 1502)[55]

Collection. Usuard, *Martylogium* [sic].

Fra Bartolomeo's edition of Usuard's martyrology was printed in Pavia by Giovan'Antonio de Birretis and Francesco de Ghirardenghis in 1487 (*IGI* 6253; Goff U80; ISTC iu00080000). Cf. Giorgio Antonio Vespucci, below.

BARZIZZA, Cristoforo (fl. 1475)[56]

BHL 1914. *Vita Conradini brixiensis*, O.P. (d. 1429)[57]

Dedicatory letter to *Martino Trivella*, nephew of the saint. Cf. entry under "Bagnatorius" above..

---

54. This concluding note ends with the date "1469 id. feb.," that is, almost immediately after Eustochium's death on February 13 and well before Barozzi's assumption of the episcopate.

55. Not in Kristeller, "Contribution"; A. Alecci in *DBI* 6 (1964): 742a–b.

56. Not to be confused with the homonymous physician; see P. Sambin, in *DBI* 7 (1965): 33b; John Monfasani, "Episodes of Anti-Quintilianism in the Italian Renaissance: Quarrels on the Orator as a *vir bonus* and Rhetoric as the *scientia bene dicendi*," *Rhetorica* 10, no. 2 (1992): 119–138.

57. See n. 38 above.

inc. epist.: Diui Corradini auunculi tui, Martine Triuellae, uitam hortatu tuo adorsus sum scribere

des. epist.: utriusuis etenim auctor diceris.

inc.: Corradinus, ciuis Brixianus, Virgilio patre, Bornada stirpe et antiqua et imprimis spectata fuit

des.: Cum annos duos ac triginta in terris egisset, quorum duos et uiginti pie in saeculo, decem autem in religione piissime consumauit. Sic annuente summo maximo et omnipotenti deo, cui honor sit et gloria in saecula saeculorum. Amen.

MSS

1. Brescia, Bibl. Queriniana, MS C.VII.9, fifth item in the codex. XV. Kristeller, *Iter* 1:35b. Seen.

Editions

1. *AASS* Nov. I (Paris, 1887): 403a–407b. Source text.

BESSARION (January 2, 1408–November 18, 1472)[58]

BHG 2063; *BHL* —. *Oratio de laudibus Bessarionis* (IV)[59]

Exordium. Bessarion presumably wrote this biographical *oratio*, which is a *vita* in format, in Greek about the time he took his religious name on January 30, 1423. Niccolò Perotti (1429/30–1489) made a Latin translation between 1469 and 1471.[60]

inc. exord.: Omnibus certe qui secundum deum vixerunt

des.: Fac me dignum ex indigno et merita salutis meae ab eo accipies, cum convenit . . . in saecula saeculorum. Amen.

MSS

1. Milan, Bibl. Ambrosiana, MS R 4 sup., fols. 253–268. XV. Kristeller, *Iter* 1:309a. Seen.

---

58. John Monfasani, "Platina, Capranica, and Perotti: Bessarion's Latin Eulogists and the Date of His Birth," in *Bartolomeo Sacchi il Platina (Piadena 1421–Roma 1481): Atti del convegno internazionale di studi per il V centenario (Cremona, 14–15 novembre 1981)*, ed. P. Medioli Masotti (Padua: Antenore, 1986), 97–136; cf. S. Caprioli, in *DBI* 9 (1967): 686–696. For Bessarion's sermon for the translation to Rome of the head of St. Andrew (1462), see MBA, MS I 30 sup., fols. 116–119; Manchester, John Rylands Library, MS Lat. 347, fols. 15–17v; and the tiny fragment in BAV, MS Barb. Lat. 17, fol. 38r. For his Greek poem on St. Pantaleymon, see VBM, MS Gr. 533, fols. 39–41v.

59. J. M. Sauget in *BS* 3 (1963): 140–141.

60. L. Labowsky, in *DBI* 9 (1967): 686a and 694; P. Joannou, "Un opuscule inédit du Cardinal Bessarion: Le Panégyrique de Saint Bessarion, anachorète égyptien," *AB* (1947): 115. On the date of this translation, see John Monfasani, "Bessarion Latinus," *Rinascimento*, ser. 2, 21 (1981): 175–177.

2. Venice, BN Marciana, MS Zan. Lat. 133 (1693), fols. 227v–241. XV. Kristeller, *Iter* 2:211a. Source text.

3. Venice, BN Marciana, MS Zan. Lat. 134 (1519), fols. 178–187v. XV. Kristeller, *Iter* 2:211a. Source text.

Editions

The Latin version has not been edited. For the Greek, see P. Joannou, "Un opuscule inédit du Cardinal Bessarion: Le Panégyrique de Saint Bessarion, anachorète égyptien," *AB* (1947): 116–138, based on VBM, MS Marc. gr. 533, fols. 3–12.[61]

BETTINI, Antonio, Gesuate, bp., *beatus* (1396—after November 20, 1486)[62]

BHL 4385. ⟨*Vita Iohanne de Columbinis*⟩ (XIV)[63]

No dedication or preface. The translation was made at Milan, where Bettini had helped to reform several institutions. *Incipit* and *desinit* from *BHL*. Not included in figure 1.1.

inc.: Antiqua et famosa civitas Senarum
des.: quem portavit per annum.

MSS

1. Milan, Bibl. Ambrosiana, MS H 26 sup., dated at the end "MCCC-CXLVI die XVIIII Julii," according to Kristeller, *Iter* 1:332a (cf. the date of 1467 from Prunai's entry in the *DBI*). R. M. Guidi, "Questioni di storiografia agiografica nel quattrocento," *Benedictina* 34 (1987): 189 n. 49. Not seen.

Editions
None.

---

61. A. Rigo, in Gianfranco Fiaccadori, ed., *Bessarione e l'umanesimo: Catalogo della mostra, Venezia, Biblioteca nazionale Marciana* (Naples: Vivarium, 1994), 394–397, describes the manuscript fully.

62. G. Nardini in *BS* 3 (1963): 145–147; G. Prunai, in *DBI* 9 (1967): 746a–747b. Guidi, "Questioni di storiografia," 196, observes that "il Bettini stesso non ha nessun entusiasmo per la retorica," and, at 195, describes his translation as "pedissequa e insolita." Frati, "Indice," 82, notes his translations from Pliny the Younger and Josephus.

63. G. B. Proja in *BS* 4 (1964): 122–123; A. Benvenuti in *GLS* 880a–883b.

BIGLIA, Andrea, O.E.S.A. (ca. 1395–1435)[64]

BHL 1187m. *De institutis, discipulis, et doctrina fratris Bernardini* [*senensis*], *O.F.M.*[65]

A critical dialogue, and consequently not treated here.

BORGHESI, Niccolò (1432–1501)[66]

BHL 1706a. *Diui Catherinae Senensis uita.* (XIV)[67]

Dedicatory preface to Agostino Barbarigo, dated "pridie idus Iulias. MD." The miracle that led to the writing of the life occurred in 1499.[68]

inc. proem.: Catharinae Senensis uitam litteris mandaturus . . . quam susceperim prouincium non sum nescius

des. proem.: beatitudinem ad quam mortales nos omnes procreati sumus . . . deditissimus extiti. Bene uale.

inc.: Catharina Senensis parentes habuit ex ordine populari

des.: ad aeternam perducunt hereditatem. Laus Deo. Finis.

MS
None known to me.

Editions

1. *Diui Catharinae Senensis uita.* Venice: Iohannes de Tridino, alias Tacuinum, April 16, 1501. Source text.

BHL 3141. *Divi Francisci* [*Patritii*] *Senensis Ordinis Servorum Sancte Marie Vita* (XIV)

No preface.

inc.: Franciscus, patria Senensis, Arrigo non humillimae sortis patre natus

des.: et alios vita defunctos, veluti sollemnia monumenta testantur.

---

64. Kristeller, "Contribution," 131; Joseph C. Schnaubelt, "Andrea Biglia (c. 1394–1435): His Life and Writings," *Augustiniana* 43, nos. 1–2 (1993): 103–159, giving earlier bibliography; and idem, "Prolegomena to the Edition of the Extant Works by Andrea Biglia, O.S.A. (d. 1435)," *AA* 40 (1977): 141–184, for Biglia's orations on saints.
65. Schnaubelt, "Andrea Biglia," 211; see also idem, "Prolegomena," no. 9; Kristeller, *Iter* 1:293a and 2:42b; Daniel Arasse, "Andrea Biglia contre Saint Bernardin de Sienne: L'humanisme et la fonction de l'image religieuse," *Acta conventus neo-latini turonensis* (Paris: Vrin, 1980), 1:417–437.
66. Anon., in *DBI* 12 (1970): 605–609.
67. A. C. Oddasso in *BS* 3 (1963): 996–1044; S. Boesch Gajano in *GLS* 397b–405a.
68. Ludovico Zdekauer, *Lo studio di Siena nel Rinascimento* (Milan: Hoepli, 1895; repr. Bologna: Forlì, 1977), 201, item 290.

MS

1. Rome, Collegio Sant'Alessio Falconieri, Archivio Generale dell'Ordine dei Servi di Maria, MS 9, fols. 15–23. XV. Kristeller, *Iter* 6:194a. Not seen.

Editions

1. P. Soulier, in *MOSSM* 4, no.1 (1900–1901): 50–57. Source text.

BHL 4104. *Beati Iacobi Philippi [Bertoni] Faventini Vita*, O.S.M. (d. 1483)

Dedicatory letter to *Thaddeus Aretinus* (da Anghiari), prior at Faenza, who encouraged Borghesi to write the life in 1483/1484.[69]

inc. epist.: Profecti Sena patriis sedibus, reuerende patre et prior, confrater tuus Dominicus, plebanus Bergamensis, et ego

des. epist.: Accipies pariter meam animi uoluntatem, quam tuis studiis obsequentem semper inuenies. Bene uale, et cetera.

inc.: Iacobus Philippus ex bonis mediocris fortunae parentibus Fauentiae nascitur

des.: quibus beatus Iacobus Philippus cuius inculte uitam scripsimus, potissimum excelluit.

MSS

1. Rome, Collegio Sant'Alessio Falconieri, Archivio Generale dell'Ordine dei Servi di Maria, MS 9, fols. 31–32 (preface) and 32–36 (life). With a date on fol. 36: "MCCCCLXXXIII VIII Kl Junii." Kristeller, *Iter* 6:194a. Not seen.

Editions

1. P. Soulier, in *MOSSM* 4, no. 1 (1900–1901): 63–64 (preface), 64–67 (vita), 68–80 (miracles).[70] Source text.

BHL 4288. *Vidualis Dive Virginis Servi Ioachini Senensis Vita Institutaque Morum* (XIV)

No preface.

---

69. D. Montagna, "La *legenda* beniziana arcaica e la *vita* scritta da Nicolo Borghese," *Studi storici dell'Ordine dei Servi di Maria* 36 (1988): 22 and n. 6; Aristide M. Serra, "Niccolò Borghese (1432–1400) e i suoi scritti agiografici servitani," *Studi storici dell'Ordine dei Servi di Maria* 14 (1964): 72–230. The Rome 1966 reprint of Serra's study includes documents and bibliography.

70. A. Morini and P. Soulier, eds., "Quinque beatorum ex ordine servorum B.M.V. vitae per Nicolaum Burgensium circa 1488 editae," *Studi storici dell'Ordine dei Servi di Maria* 4, 1 (1900–1901): 34; Friar Servants of Mary, *Origins*, 128.

inc.: Ioachinus a matre non minus quam a patre generosus fuit. Patria ei Sena

des.: iustas egit gratias, ibique gratiae monumenta reliquit.

MSS

1. Rome, Collegio Sant'Alessio Falconieri, Archivio Generale dell'Ordine dei Servi di Maria, MS 9, fols. 10v–14v. XV. Kristeller, *Iter* 6:194a. Not seen.

Editions

1. P. Soulier, in *MOSSM* 4, no.1 (1900–1901) 45–49. Source text.

BHL 6629. *Vita Beati Peregrini Foroliviensis ordinis Servorum Sanctae Mariae* (XIV)

No preface.

inc.: Beato Peregrino patria fuit oppidum Romandiolae non ignobile Forum Liuii

des.: gratiae memor, debitas egit gratias.

MSS

1. Rome, Collegio Sant'Alessio Falconieri, Archivio Generale dell'Ordine dei Servi di Maria, MS 9, fols. 24–30. XV. Kristeller, *Iter* 6:194a. Not seen.

Editions

1. P. Soulier, in *MOSSM* 4, no. 1 (1900–1901): 58–62. Source text.

BHL 6824a. *Philippi Florentini Servi Marie Virginis Vita.* (XIII)

No preface. All Borghesi's Servite hagiography is connected to pilgrimage visits he made to the Servite convent in the Romagna, probably at Faenza, in 1483/1484.[71]

inc.: Philippus, patria Florentinus, ex clara gente Bonitia natus

des.: Deo Philippoque gratias uotaque cumulate satisfacit.

MSS

1. Rome, Collegio Sant'Alessio Falconieri, Archivio Generale dell'Ordine dei Servi di Maria, MS 9, mbr. XV. 78 fols. (formerly Florence, Annunziata MS 369), fols. 5–10. XV. Kristeller, *Iter* 6:194a. Not seen.

Editions

1. P. Soulier, in *MOSSM* 4, no.1 (1900–1901): 40–44. Source text.

---

71. Soulier and Morini, "Quinque beatorum," 36, for other editions.

BRUNI, Ludovico (attrib.) (1434–1508)[72]

BHL 8874. *Breuis translatio ⟨Vita Guidi episcopi Aquensis⟩* (XI)

No preface. A *terminus post quem* may be provided by the date of Bruni's accession to the bishopric of Acqui: February 6, 1499.

inc.: In prouincia Lombardiae, ineunte principatum Rodulfo
des.: Corpore autem ipsius . . . recondito, meritissime ueneratur.

MSS
  1. Acqui, Archivio vescovile, s.n. unattributed.

Editions
  1. G. Castelli, *Il santo vescovo Guido d'Acqui* (Genoa, 2001), 129–132 with remarks at 50–60.

CALEPINO (Calepio), Ambrogio, O.E.S.A. (ca. 1435–1509/10)[73]

BHL 4353. *Vita Johanne Boni, O.E.S.A.* (XIII)[74]

No preface. This life was written after February 1484. It is not mentioned by G. Soldi-Rondinini and T. de Mauro in *DBI* 16 (1973): 669–70, or by G. Lucchesi, "Giovanni Bono," in *BS* 6 (1965): 629–631. Cf. Johannes Felix Ossinger, *Bibliotheca Augustiniania Historica, Critica, et Chronologica* (Ingolstadt, 1768), 180, citing the *Encomiasticon augustinianum* (Brussel, 1654), 44 (not seen); and *AASS* Oct. IX (Paris, 1869): 745–746, paras. 204–206. The *AASS* does not edit or mention a preface. I follow para. 204 for the dating of the life. Calepino's version depends on that by Agostino Cazzuli (*q.v.*); Antonino Pierozzi's version in the *Chronicon* (*BHL* 4352) may as well.[75]

inc.: Janbonus ex patre Joanne et matre Bona
des.: ab ullo comprehendi queant.

----

72. G. Rill, in *DBI* 14 (1972): 669–671, does not mention this *vita*. On Wido of Acqui, see F. Caraffa in *BS* 7 (1966): 496.

73. Kristeller, "Contribution," 133; G. Soldi-Rondinini and T. de Mauro, in *DBI* 16 (1973): 669–670.

74. L. Canetti, in *DBI* 55 (2000): 731b–734b; Vauchez, *La sainteté*, refers frequently to the Augustinian hermit Johannes Bonus but does not mention this life. The subject is not to be confused with the homonymous seventh-century bishop of Milan, on whom see V. La Salvia, "Giovanni," in *DBI* 55 (2000): 512b–514a.

75. Cf. J. B. Walker, *The Chronicles of St. Antoninus: A Study in Historiography* (Washington, D.C.: Catholic University of America, 1933), 97 and n. 157, proposing that Antonino Pierozzi relied on the proceedings.

MSS

None known to me.

Editions

1. *AASS* Oct. IX (Paris, 1869): 748–767. Source text.

CAROLI (di Carlo dei Berlinghieri), Giovanni, O.P. (1428–1503)[76]

Collection. *Vitae fratrum sanctae Mariae Novellae.*

Dedicatory letter to Cristoforo Landino at the head of the collection, followed by a *Laus domus*. See Salvatore Camporeale, "Giovanni Caroli e le *Vitae fratrum S.M. Novellae*: Umanesimo e crisi religiosa (1460–1480)," *MD* 12 (1981): 176–178. The contents are given below in the order of the Santa Maria Novella manuscript, identified by Camporeale as the most reliable. He dates the composition to 1475–1480 (ibid., 166–168).[77]

BHL 4434. *Vita Johannis Salernitensis*, OP (XIII)

Preface; no dedicatee named.

inc. epist.: Paucis ante diebus cum plurimorum *rogatu quorundam fratrum* nostrorum illustrium uitas scripsissem

inc. laus: O fortunati quorum iam menia surgunt, Eneas ait

inc. proem.: Ego si nulla alia ratione

inc.: Johannes salernitanus uir profecto uenerabilis atque iustissimus

des.: potest utilius inuenire, qui cum Spiritu sancto . . .

MSS

1. Florence, Bibl. Laurenziana, MS Plut. 89 inf. 21. Autograph. Seen.

---

76. Kristeller, "Contribution," 142 (s.v. "Johannes Caroli"), whose dating I follow; V. Marchetti, *DBI* 20 (1977): 523–526; Stefano Orlandi, ed., *Necrologia di Santa Maria Novella* (Florence: Olschki, 1955), 2:353–380; Salvatore Camporeale, "Giovanni Caroli e le *vitae fratrum S. M. Novellae*: Umanesimo e crisi religiosa (1460–1480)," *MD* 12 (1981): 141–267, and *idem*, "Umanesimo, Riforma e le origini della Controriforma. Alla ricerca di interrelazioni e differenze," *MD*, n.s., 20 (1989): 301–307; Guidi, "Questioni di storiografia," 222–225. I do not count all the lives contained in *Vitae nonnullorum fratrum beate Mariae Novellae* toward the tables and figures because in most cases I have not studied the full versions found in the manuscripts but only the abbreviated versions edited by Leandro Alberti (*q.v.*). Only Giovanni Dominici and Johannes Salernitensis (whom I do count) have been beatified; none of the other figures are officially recognized as saints. See Orlandi, *Necrologia*, 364–368; and Camporeale, "Giovanni Caroli."

77. Camporeale, "Giovanni Caroli," 165–167, describes the two main manuscripts, one—the sole complete version—in Santa Maria Novella, the other, autograph but lacking the lives of Giovanni Dominici and Angelo Acciaioli, in Florence, BNC.

2. Florence, Archivio del Convento di Santa Maria Novella, MS B 28, fols. 15–19 (preface), 19–52 (*vita*). XVI inc. Kristeller, *Iter* 5:541a–b. Not seen.

Editions

1. Alberti (*q.v.*), *De viris illustribus*, fols. 198v–204v (incomplete). Source text.

2. The letter, the *laus domus*, and the preface to the life of Johannes Salernitanus are edited by Camporeale, "Giovanni Caroli," 237–247, who gives references to the edition by A. M. Bandini, *Catalogus codicorum latinorum Bibliothecae Mediceae Laurentianae* (Florence, 1774), 3:371–378. Source text.

BHL —. *Vita Aldobrandini Cavalcanti* (XIII)

Preface; no dedicatee named. Not included in figure 1.1.

inc. proem.: Perspectum satis cognitumque mihi est in describendis precipuorum quorumdam fratrum nostrorum gestis

inc.: Maiores nostros in eo libro, in quo posteritati fratrum nostrorum nomina reliquere conscripta nimia constat breuitate usos fuisse

des.: dignissimum extitisse.

MSS

1. Florence, Bibl. Laurenziana, MS Plut. 89 inf. 21. XV. Seen.

2. Florence, Archivio del Convento di Santa Maria Novella, MS B 28, fols. 53–56 (preface) and 56–95 (*vita*). XVI inc. Kristeller, *Iter* 5:541a–b. Not seen.

3. Brussels, Société des Bollandistes, MS 421, fols. 4–23v. Dated *Ex nostro conventu S.M. Novelle 1512 die 16 Maii*. Kristeller, *Iter* 3:126a. Not seen.

Editions

1. Alberti (*q.v.*), *De viris illustribus*, fols. 116v–119v (incomplete). Source text.

2. The preface is edited by Camporeale, "Giovanni Caroli," 247–249. Source text.

BHL —. *Vita Simonis* [*Saltarelli*] (XIV)

Dedicatory preface to Giorgio Antonio Vespucci (*q.v.*). Written in 1477, according to Caroli's note in the manuscript. It includes notice of Saltarelli's presiding over the January 1330 translation of Zenobius. Not included in figure 1.1.

inc. proem.: Memoria teneo, me Georgi Antoni, me cum superioribus annis non nulla mea tibi scripta ostenderem *inc.*: Simoni pisano quondam presuli paternum genus a Guidone Salterello fuit

des.: indicatum est.

MSS

1. Florence, Archivio del Convento di Santa Maria Novella, MS B 28, fols. 96–99 (preface) and 99–128 (*vita*). XVI inc. Kristeller, *Iter* 5:541a–b. Not seen.

2. Florence, Bibl. Laurenziana, MS Plut. 89 inf. 21. XV. Seen.

Editions

1. Alberti (*q.v.*), *De viris illustribus*, fols. 86v–94 (incomplete). Source text.

2. The preface is edited by Camporeale, "Giovanni Caroli," 249–251. Source text.

BHL —. Vita Angeli Acciaioli (XIV)

Dedicatory preface to Donato Acciaioli (*q.v.*), 1477.[78] Not included in figure 1.1.

inc. proem.: Cum proximis diebus fratris Simonis Salterelli quondam pisani antistitis uitam edidissem subit in mentem ut Angeli quoque Acciaioli presulis florentini in nostra familia uiri prestantissimi gesta describerem

inc.: Acciaiolorum familia preter eam quam ex nomine ipso consequitur dignitatem nobilissima Florentie fuit et uirorum magnitudine et copia diuitiarum

des.: celebratum est.

MSS

1. Florence, Archivio del Convento di Santa Maria Novella, MS B 28, fols. 129–135 (preface) and 135–208 (*vita*). XVI inc. Kristeller, *Iter* 5:541a–b. Not seen.

2. Vatican City, BAV, MS Vat. Lat. 8808. XV. Not seen.

Editions

1. Alberti (*q.v.*), *De viris illustribus*, fols. 121–123v (incomplete). Source text.

2. The preface has been edited by Camporeale, "Giovanni Caroli," 251–255. Source text.

---

78. Orlandi, *Necrologia*, 366; Camporeale, "Giovanni Caroli," 166.

BHL —. Vita Fratris Alexii Stroze (XIV)

Preface, dated October 28, 1478.[79] Not included in figure 1.1.

inc. proem.: Inter hanc nostram et superiorem etatem distare plurimum apertissime constat, cum uirtute atque prudentia tum uiribus corporis

inc.: Stroza familia antiqua sane ac nobilis per multa hominum et diuitiarum gloria floruit, et superiori etate et nostra

MSS

1. Florence, Archivio del Convento di Santa Maria Novella, MS B 28, fols. 209–214 (preface) and 214–249 (*vita*). XVI inc. Kristeller, *Iter* 5:541a–b. Not seen.

2. Florence, Bibl. Laurenziana, MS Plut. 89, inf. 21. XV. Seen.

Editions

1. The preface has been edited by Camporeale, "Giovanni Caroli," 255–258. Source text.

BHL —. Vita Fratris Guidonis Regiolani (XIV)

Dedicatory preface to Roberto Boninsegni and his son. The life was written in 1479.[80] Not included in figure 1.1.

inc. proem.: Admirari non numquam soleo, mi Roberte, cum eorum hominum uitam qui supra LXXXm claruere annum considero

inc.: Reggiolum oppidum casentinatis agri. Guidoni uiro Deo et hominibus acceptissimo originem satis honestam dedit.

MSS

1. Florence, Bibl. Laurenziana, MS Plut. 89, inf. 21. XV. Seen.

2. Florence, Archivio del Convento di Santa Maria Novella, MS B 28, fols. 249v–252v (preface) and 252v–268v (*vita*). XVI inc. Kristeller, *Iter* 5:541a–b. Not seen.

Editions

1. The preface is edited by Camporeale, "Giovanni Caroli," 258–262. Source text.

BHL 4387. Vita Johanne Dominicae (d. 1419)

Dedicatory preface to Francesco Berlinghieri. The account was written in 1477 (see manuscript 2 below).[81]

---

79. Camporeale, "Giovanni Caroli" 166.
80. Ibid.
81. Ibid.

inc. proem.: Cogitanti mihi sepenumero, Francesce frater, quid pro maximis in me beneficiis tuis efficere possem

inc.: Varias admodum et diuersas homines nominandi causas hactenus extitisse qui ignoret est nemo

des.: annus supra M.CCCC.XX. beato fine conclusit.

MSS

1. Florence, Archivio del Convento di Santa Maria Novella, MS B 28. fols. 269–272 (preface), and 272–299v (*vita*). XVI in. Kristeller, *Iter* 5:541a–b. Not seen.

2. Vatican City, BAV, MS Vat. Lat. 6329, fols. 283v–317r. XVI; the preface in this manuscript (fols. 280–283v) is dated 1477. Kristeller, *Iter* 2:340a. Seen SLU microfilm 895. Source text.

Editions

1. Alberti (*q.v.*), *De viris illustribus*, fols. 70–82 (incomplete).

inc.: Ioannes Dominici Florentinus romanae prouinciae patrem habuit Dominicum

2. The preface is edited by Camporeale, "Giovanni Caroli," 262–267. Source text.

BHL 8615. *Vita Villanae Bottiae,* O.P. tert. (XIV)[82]

According to the Bollandist editors in *AASS* Aug. V (Paris, 1867): 864 and note b, Giovanni Caroli wrote the life based on notes provided by Girolamo di Giovanni. Aviad Kleinberg suggests the reverse: that Girolamo wrote the life based on notes from Caroli.[83] According to Stefano Orlandi, Caroli was only the scribe (in 1452) of the sole manuscript of a life that was actually composed by Girolamo di Giovanni, O.P. (ca. 1389–August 30, 1454).[84] That Girolamo composed the preface is undisputed. The issue of who composed the life must be decided on the basis of the meaning of Caroli's note at the end of the life: "Explicit Vita Villanae de Florentia, scripta per me Fr. Joannem Caroli."[85] The participle *scripta* is ambiguous but probably means transcribed, as Orlandi sup-

---

82. G. Di Agresti in *BS* 3 (1963): 369–370.

83. Aviad M. Kleinberg, *Prophets in Their Own Country: Living Saints and the Making of Sainthood in the Later Middle Ages* (Chicago: University of Chicago Press, 1992), 173.

84. Stefano Orlandi, *La Beata Villana: Terziaria Domenicana Fiorentina del sec. XIV* (Florence: "Il Rosario," 1955), 33–37. See also Orlandi, *Necrologia,* 224–225. The Bollandists apparently approve of Orlandi's thinking on this issue, since they cite his study of 1955 in the *BHL* supplement of 1986, although they still give Johannes Carolus's name with *BHL* 8615 in the index to that volume.

85. *AASS* Aug. V (Paris, 1867): 869, para. 23.

poses.[86] His opinion appears to be shared by Camporeale, who did not, so far as I know, discuss this life in any of his studies of Caroli.

Vernacular. Italian translation of P. Ransano (*q.v.*), *Vita Vincentii (Ferrer)* (d. 1419)

Vernacular preface by Giovanni Caroli, dated 1490, followed by Caroli's translation of Pietro Ransano's preface and *vita*.[87] Not counted toward figure 1.1.

MSS

1. Florence, BN, MS Magl. XXXVIII 10, 124, fols. 1–59v. XVI. Kristeller, *Iter* I:142b–143a. Seen.

Editions

1. There is a partial transcription (in modern Italian) of Caroli's prologue in Stefano Orlandi, ed., *Necrologia di Santa Maria Novella* (Florence: Olschki, 1955), 2:369.

CARRARA, Giovanni A. M. (1438–October 26, 1490)[88]

BHL —. Vita Clarae Montefalcensis, O.E.S.A. (XIV)[89]

Dedication to the city of Spoleto. Carrara wrote this account in 1480, basing it on Berengar's *vita Clarae* (*BHL* 1818), which had been lent to him by a Franciscan patient, P. Bautista de Montefalco.[90] He first heard about Clara in Brescia from the preacher Paolo Olmi, O.E.S.A. (*q.v.*).[91] In his list of Carrara's writings, *Supplementum chronicarum* (Venice: Benaliis, 1483), book 15, fol. 176, Jacopo Filippo Foresti, O.E.S.A., neglects this *vita*.

inc. proem.: Spoletum uetustissima ciuitas est in Togata Gallia, quantum Plinio placuit

---

86. Silvia Rizzo, *Il lessico filologico degli umanisti* (Rome: Edizioni di storia e letteratura, 1973/1985) does not discuss precisely this word. But see her remarks on *scrivere* (94–95) and *scriptor* (199–205). The familiar Quattrocento usage suggests that the English word "transcribe" is a fair equivalent. Rizzo points out, however, that Angelo Decembrio followed Guarino in disapproving of this meaning as unclassical. That is to say, some sense of ambiguity about the meaning of Caroli's closing remark was possible even in the Quattrocento.

87. See Orlandi, *Necrologia* 2:368–369.

88. G. Ineichen, in *DBI* 20 (1977): 684–686; Carlo Alonso, "La biografia inedita de Santa Clara de Montefalco por el humanista Giovanni Michele Alberto Carrara (s. XV)," *AA* 54 (1991): 7–11.

89. N. Del Re in *BS* 3 (1963): 1217–1222; G. Barone in *GLS* 428a–431a.

90. According to Alonso, "La biografia inedita," 9.

91. Alonso, "La biografia inedita," 58.

des. proem.: ut christianus moriar, tecumque [in] perpetuum Iesu Christo fruar.

inc., book 1: Oppidum est Mons Falchus in agro Spoletano moenibus nobile

des., book 3: Non dubito . . . plurima et maxima a Deo Clarae concessa, quae mihi ignota sunt.

inc. peroratio: In agro Brixiano agenti, in quo uix cognitum eius nomen, magna cum infamia praedicatorum qui notam eam nostris populis non fecere, mihi uero a Reuerendo Patre Paulo Lulmo . . . primum de ea uerba facta sunt .

des. peroratio: conterat Turcos aliosque hostes Ecclesiae . . . et regnat cum Deo . . . saecula saeculorum. Amen.

MSS

1. Milan, Bibl. Ambrosiana, MS Pinelli N 131 sup.. XV. Kristeller, *Iter* 1:302a. Seen.

Editions

1. C. Alonso, "La biografia inedita de Santa Clara de Montefalco por el humanista Giovanni Michele Alberto Carrara (s. XV)," *AA* 54 (1991): 12–60, giving a *Hymnus sapphicus* and *Carmen ad pedes imaginis eius* at 60–61. Source text.

CASCIOTTI, Bartolomeo (early 1400s–late 1470s)[92]

Oration. BHL 798d. ⟨*Elogium sancti Augustini*⟩

This oration is termed a *vita* by the editors of the *BHL*. Title as attributed by Sesto Prete (below) in his edition. I do not count the oration toward figure 1.1.

inc.: Si in me tantum ingenii uel aliquid disciplinae
des.: sine ullo peccatorum impedimento consequi ualeamus.

MSS

1. Ferrara, Bibl. Ariostea, MS II, 110, at 118v, with the title *laudatiuncula*. Kristeller, *Iter* 1:57a–b, at 57b, unidentified. Not seen.

---

92. G. Schizzerotto, in *DBI* 21 (1978): 289a, notes that Casciotti had been a student of Guarino. But his relations with Guarino deteriorated to such an extent that Casciotti taught at Verona in competition with his master. See also Sesto Prete, *Two Humanistic Anthologies* (Studi e testi 230) (Vatican City: BAV, 1964), 75–77; and idem, "An Unknown Humanistic *Elogium sancti Augustini*," *Revue des études augustiniennes* 11 (1965): 270, for Casciotti's oration on St. James and hymn for St. Benedict.

Editions

1. S. Prete, "An unknown humanistic *Elogium sancti Augustini*," *Revue des études augustiniennes* 11 (1965): 273–276. Source text.

CASSETTA, Salvo, O.P. (ca. 1413–September 15, 1483)[93]

BHL —. [Canonization process of Vincent Ferrer] (d. 1419)[94]

In his *De viris illustribus ordinis praedicatorum* (Bologna, 1516), fol. 46, in an entry on the thirty-second master general, Leandro Alberti (*q.v.*) recorded that Cassetta "uitam diui Vincentii Confessoris edidit." As in the case of Giovanni Caroli's account of Villana Bottia (*q.v.*), the verb is a problem, for it need not indicate an original composition. A.A. Strnad argues that this *vita* was probably a copy of the canonization process made for the Bolognese convent.[95] If he is right, then the process must have included a *vita*, because it would be unlikely for a Dominican theologian and humanist such as Alberti to refer to a canonization process as a *vita*. Like A. Foa, in *DBI* 21 (1978): 462a, I think that Alberti reports a composition by Cassetta based on the canonization process and that the piece has been lost or not yet identified. Not counted toward figure 1.1.

CASTIGLIONE, Francesco da

See FRANCESCO Catellini da Castiglione.

CAZZULI, Agostino, da Crema, O.E.S.A. (ca. 1423–1495)[96]

BHL —. *Diui Ioannisboni Mantuani* (XIII)[97]

Dedicatory preface to Federico Gonzaga. After failing to interest the Franciscan Sixtus IV in the canonization of Zanbono (although Sixtus issued a

---

93. A. Foa, in *DBI* 21 (1978): 460a–462a, esp. 461b, for Cassetta's part in the translation of Matteo Carreri in Mantua in 1482 and of Albertus Magnus in Cologne in 1483.

94. J. M. Sauget in *BS* 12 (1969): 1168–1176; S. Spanò in *GLS* 1936b–1939a.

95. A. A. Strnad, "Salvo Cassetta Verfasser einer Vita des hl. Vinzenz Ferrer?" in R. Creytens and P. Künzle, eds., *Xenia medii aevi historiam illustrantia oblata Thomae Kaeppeli, O.P.* (Rome, 1978), 2:519–545. In this article, Strnad misidentifies G. A. Flamini (*q.v.*) as a Spaniard.

96. Not in Kristeller, "Contribution." See K. Walsh, in *DBI* 23 (1979): 182a–184a.

97. On Johannes Bonus, see n. 74 above. Cazzuli's account is not mentioned by L. Canetti, in *DBI* 55 (2000): 731b–734a, or by Vauchez, *La sainteté*, who knows the process in the Mantua *busta*. Cf. Rome, Archivio Agostiniano, MS C c 37, a miscellany of notes, well

bull, "Licet sedes apostolica," allowing limited *cultus*), Agostino wrote this life, based on the thirteenth-century process, for Federico. The dedication is dated "Ex aedibus Diuae Agnetis Mantuae in kal. Febr. MCC-CLXXXIIII."[98]

inc. pref.: Tuam ingenui animi magnitudinem, Federice Princeps,

des. pref.: Quod si feceris, et divini cultus augmentum et tuam rempublicam est propagaturum . . . Cui me iterum atque iterum commendam

inc.: Ioannesbonus binomius est. Ex duobus enim nominibus componitur. Ioannes bonus Mantua ortus fuit, habuit patrem Ioannem

des.: et uobis pro tanto desiderio gratiam indulgeat. Amen.

des. mir.: (95) stupendum uidetur quod ipsa die ut honorificentior etc. [*sic*]

MSS

1. Mantua, AS, Archivio Gonzaga, *libellus* in *busta* 3305. Dedication copy. Source text.

Editions
None known to me.

BHL 6446. *Historia s. Pantaleonis* (IV)[99]

Dedicatory preface to the city of Crema (not Cremona). The account was completed in 1492.[100]

inc. prol.: Nec dum ego ex ephebis excesseram, o uiri magnifici, hanc sacram diui Augustini religionem . . . ingressus sum.

inc.: Nicomedia urbs Asiae a Nicomede [Nicomedia cita nobile de Asia]

des.: Passus est autem gloriosus christi martir post annum gratie quartum supra ducentos octuaginta vi calendas Augu. Finis Historie.

MSS
None known to me.

---

known thanks to the fact that some are by Egidio da Viterbo and Girolamo Seripando. At fols. 99–104 is a life of Johannes Bonus, *inc*: Beatus Iohannes Bonus fuit de Mantua oriundus eius pater uocabatur Iohannes Mater uero Bona.

98. *AASS* Oct. IX (Paris, 1869): 745, para. 204, is a description of Augustinus Cremensis's charge from Federico Gonzaga to pursue the institution of canonization proceedings and of his confection of a life from thirteenth-century canonization proceedings. Lucchesi, in *BS* 6 (1965), cols. 629–631, mentions this *vita* only in his bibliography and gives the date of composition as 1483. Cf. K. Walsh, in *DBI* 23 (1979): 183b.

99. J.-M. Sauget in *BS* 10 (1968): 108–117; G. Luongo in *GLS* 1549a–1553a.

100. Walsh, in *DBI* 23 (1979): 183b, notes that it is based on a Greek account (unspecified).

Editions

1. Cremonae, August 8, 1493. C 2:774; *IGI* 1066; *BMC* 7:957; *GW* 3055; Goff A1368; ISTC ia01368000. See A. Davoli, "Della duplice e rarissima edizione del sec. XV de *La historia del martyrio del glorioso sancto Pantaleleymone,*" *La Bibliofiia* 30 (1928): 276–292; W. Terni de Gregory, *Frater Agostino da Crema agente sforzesco* (Crema: Vinci, 1950), 49–50 and 59 n. 25. See also *BHL* 6448 for an oration on the saint bound with this and the following edition.

2. [Italian] Cremona: Bernardinus de Misintis and Caesar Parmensis, August 18, 1493. R 1455; Goff A1369 *IGI* 1067; *GW* 3056. With the preface to Crema.

BHL 6447. ⟨Translatio brachii Cremam⟩

Printed and bound with the preceding. Not included in figure 1.1.

inc.: Annus erat a salutifero immaculatae virginis partu III ac XXX super annum CCCC ad M, cum Mahumetes

des.: apud Cremonam in sacello eiusdem veneratur os brachii, quod folcinum appellant.

inc. transl. brachii vulg.: Era lo anno dopo che la immaculate viergini parturite il salutifero parto Millesimo quadragentesimo trigesimo tertio quando Mahumete Otomano principe de li Turchi mosto de una grandissima cupidita de signoreggiare . . .

des. transl. brachii vulg.: Anchora in la chiesia soa di Cremona e uno osso duno bracio che si chiama folcino, le quale sanctissime reliquie sono coruscenti de grandissimi miracoli e questo a laude e gloria . . . de seculi. Amen.

CELSO delle Falci, O.S.B. (fl. 1475)[101]

BHL —. *Vita Euphrosynae* (1427–January 16, 1476), canoness, obs. Aug. at Vicenza[102]

Preface to Bishop Pietro Dandolo (Vicenza, 1501–1507), extremely lengthy, and a second, shorter preface to the *sorores* of San Tommaso in Vicenza. Ziegelbauer contends that the narrative was written in 1505; it

---

101. Not in Kristeller, "Contribution." Not to be confused with Celso Maffei (*q.v.*), also of Verona. For the little known about our Celso, professed at the reformed monastery of San Nazario and Celso (where Ambrogio, the eldest son of Pietro Donato Avvogario [*q.v.*] was also professed), see Magnoaldo Ziegelbauer, *Historia rei literariae ordinis s. Benedicti* (Augsburg, 1754), 4:410a.

102. Death date from Coimbra, BU, MS 2581, fol. 78. According to this *vita*, Euphrosyna was one of six girls, three of whom became nuns: "Euphrosynam Augustini, Agatem et Brigidam Francisci" (fols. 51v and 60 for the name of the monastery, San Tommaso; see also 52, for Celso's avowal of conversations with Euphrosyna's saintly father, following her death; and 53, for conversations with her sister nuns).

seems to have been begun much earlier, although not during the saint's life-time. Ludovico Barbo (d. 1443) had been the reformer of Santa Croce in Coimbra, which is where the manuscript finally resided.[103]

inc. proem. 1: Theophrastum, uir amplissime, hominem in eloquentia tantum

des.: Ego enim ratum habebo, quicquid ratum habendum iudicabis. Vale.

inc. proem. 2: Accipite, o uirgines, Euphrosynam uirginem ad fores pul-santem

des.: quamquam nihil latere uos arbitrar, ex me tamen aliter quam uel dedicistis vel meministis accipite.

inc.: Euphrosinam Vicentia Venetiae Civitate Parentibus quanquam haud illustribus, nec tamen uulgaribus honestis alioquin atque catholicis, M.cccc.vii et xx salutis anno exortam accaepimus. Pater eius Franciscus dictus est, Iulia mater; ille ex Aurificibus, haec e Togis originem duxit.

des.: toto cordis affectu commendauit, in gradum pristinum restituta conualuit.

peroratio: Haec habui de te, Euphrosyna, quae scriberem, quanquam pro rerum uirtutumque tuarum magnitudine, minus faciunt tuis laudibus satis. Sed memento siquis in nos satuiret unquam, suppetias ferre supplici tuo. Lectorem hortabor interim, non hic verborum exornationem quaerat, praeclaras uirtutes tuas, quod et conducibilius sit et praestabilius, imitetur.

MSS

1. Coimbra, Biblioteca Geral da Universidade, MS 2581. XV. *Vita* fols. 51–94v, prefaces fols. 1–44v and fols. 45–50v. Kristeller, *Iter* 4:449a. Source text.

2. In A. Desguine, ed., F. Dandolo [*recte* F. Vallaresso], *Compendium catholicae fidae* (Paris: Vrin, 1964), 274, reference is made to a manuscript of this work in Venice, at the library of Sts. John and Paul. Cf. Kristeller, *Iter* 3:197b, noting a copy sold from Dublin, Chester Beatty Library, in 1968, MS W 163, mbr. XV. Decorated. Probably dedication copy. Written in Italy. 34 fols. Caelsus monachus, vita S. Euphrosynae.

Editions
I am preparing an edition.

BHL 8348. *Vita* [al. *historia*] *Tuscanae* (XIV)[104]

Preface; no dedicatee. According to Scipione Maffei, *Verona illustrata* (Verona, 1731), 2:175, the life was completed August 21, 1474. Maffei defends the attribution to Celso delle Falci; see the *desinit*

---

103. J. Mattoso, *DS* 12 (1986): 1955.
104. G. D. Gordini, *BS* 12 (1969): 719.

below. Toscana was a widow affiliated with the order of St. John of Jerusalem.

inc. proem.: Historiam diuae Tuscanae Veronensis quae non tam dolo quam incuria maiorum relicta iam et pene obliterata fuerat

inc.: Tuscana igitur Iebeto antiquissimo ac celeberrimo quondam oppido oriunda

des.: lector possit et multa et miranda colligere. CVM. MCCCCLXXI-III, x cal. aug.

MSS

1. Florence, Laurenziana, MS Ashb. 193 (269–201), fols. 25v–33v. XV. Marginal notations in Greek and Latin. Kristeller, *Iter* 1:82b. Not seen.

2. Vatican City, BAV, Fondo Patetta, MS 1015, fols. 18–38v. XV; the manuscript includes two letters dated 1467. Kristeller, *Iter* 6:405. Not seen.

Editions

1. A. Valier [R. Bagatta and B. Peretti], *SS Episcoporum Veronensium Antiqua Monumenta* (Venice, 1576), fols. 71r–v (prologue), fols. 71v–76 *(historia)*, misattributing the narrative to Celso Maffei. Source text.

CORA, Ambrogio de

See AMBROGIO da Cora, Massarius.

CORRADI, Eusebio, Can. Lat. (1447–1500)[105]

BHL —. De vita et moribus divi Augustini hiponensis epi. tractatus (V)[106]

No preface or dedication to the *vita*, which is part of a classroom collection of Augustine's *Opuscula*.[107] The *vita* is declared anonymous in the title ("viri cuiusdam religiosi"), and the author is not announced in the editor's prefatory letter to the collection, but Corradi identifies himself toward the end of the account. The *vita* is largely based on Possidius and the *Confessions*, but Corradi also acknowledges using Antoninus's *Chronicon*. He wrote the life between 1487 and 1491, when it was pub-

---

105. Kristeller, "Contribution," 136 (s.v. "Corradus"); K. Walsh, in *DBI* 29 (1983): 412–413.

106. See n. 33 above.

107. The prefatory letter to the *Opuscula*, by the Lateran Canon Severino Calchi, prior of Santa Croce in Mortara, describes the plan of the book, which offers something of Augustine for every age.

lished.[108] Corradi aims to support the Canons against the Hermits. See chap. 5 above.

inc.: ⟨I⟩n Africae oppido quod Tagastum appellatur : Idibus nouembris annus gratiae salutaris . . . usus sum ita periodis, comatibus et uocibus eius ut compendiosius scribens eum imitare magis quam mutare sim oblectus, in caeteris sanctae et antiquae simplicitatis stilo magisquam uerborum fuco, ut qui breuitatem amant et totam Augustini uitam habere & legere uoluerint

des.: Natum autem indubitata fide atque certissima anno salutatis nostrae trecentesimo quinquegesimo octauo. Hac summa quid rectius ueriusque supputari possit non intelligimus.

MSS

None known to me. Cf. Mazzatinti 6 (1896): 64–70, no. 4 on Novara, Biblioteca del seminario, "Eusebii Conradi Mediolanensis Canonici regularis . . . ," dated at the end: Piacenza, December 25, 1466 (73 fols.). Not seen.

Editions

1. Augustine, *Opuscula*. Parma: Angelus Ugoletus, March 31, 1491, signs. Rv–D6v. HC 1952; Goff A1220; *IGI* 1018; *BMC* 7:944; *GW* 2867; ISTC 01220000.[109] Source text.

COSIMO da Firenze, O.S.M. (d. ca. January 1526)[110]

BHL —. *De origine ordinis servorum et vita beati Philippi* (XIII)[111]

No preface or dedication. Cosimo may have completed this prose narrative, which combines order origins, founder's *vita* and *translationes*, origin

---

108. In the course of the life, Corradi claims that in 1487 he discovered Augustine's lost *De grammatica*.

109. On this edition, see the entry for Guarini.

110. Not in Kristeller, "Contribution"; not in Giuseppe M. Besutti, *Ricerche di Bibliografia Servitana sulle edizioni del secolo XV* (Vicenza: Convento dei Servi di Monte Berico, 1971). But see the entries about Cosimo from M. Poccianti's *Catalogus scriptorum Florentinorum* (1589) and L. G. Cerracchini's *Fasti teologali* (1738), quoted and discussed in Peregrino Soulier, "Frater Cosmas Favilla, *De origine ordinis servorum et vita beati Philippi* (1512)," *MOSSM* 14, no. 1 (1913): 96–100 (I depend heavily on Soulier's introduction); F. A. Dal Pino, *I Frati servi di Maria* (Louvain, 1972), ad indicem, and G. M. Besutti, ed., *Cosimo da Firenze O.S.M.: Operetta novamente composta a consolatione delli devoti religiosi frati de servi della vergine Maria (Verona 1521)* (Rome: Marianum, 1993), at 7 and n. 2. For a much later work by Cosimo, see Stefano dall'Aglio, "Il Flagellum pseudoprophetarum di Cosimo Favilla: Nota su un'opera antisavonaroliana del primo cinquecento," *MD* 29 (1998), esp. 442; a brief English summary of the 1526 treatise is provided in Lorenzo Polizzotto, *The Elect Nation: The Savonarolan Movement in Florence 1494–1545* (Oxford: Clarendon Press, 1994), 332–333.

111. Cosimo also wrote an Italian life and account of the miracles of Filippo Benizi (Soulier, "Fratris Thaddaei Adamarii," 99); on Benizi, see n. 27 above.

and miracles of his convent's image of the Virgin, and a list of Servite generals (to 1512) and *beati* (to 1506), by September 25, 1512.[112] The narrative concludes with two poems: the first treats the *significatio* of the work; the second is a couplet from the scribe begging readers' prayers. The sole manuscript is untitled. The only indications of authorship are the "M.C." (*magistri Cosmae,* according to the conjecture of Peregrino Soulier) at the head of the first poem; the later restoration of the damaged name "Cosmus" (?) in the second; Filippo Tozzi's later note in the manuscript; and traditions of authorship given in order histories.

inc.: Antequam Florentina urbs ad eam in qua nunc est magnitudinem peruenisset

des.: oratione soluta nos prosecuti sumus

inc. poesia I: Alma Parens Christi, nos rapti numine sacro

inc. poesia II: [Cosmus] ut haec scripsi, sic qui mea scripta uidebis

MSS

1. Florence, BN, MS Conv. soppr. C 1, 1458. XVI in. Kristeller, *Iter* 1:152a and 5:588b. Not seen.

Editions

1. P. Soulier, "Pater Cosmas Favilla: *De origine ordinis servorum et vita beati Philippi,*" MOSSM 14, fasc. 1 (1913): 101–112 and 14, no. 2 (1913): 96–135. Note well p. 133 n. 1, concluding with two poems. The subdivisions in the text are Soulier's. He provides a plate (101). Source text.

DATI, Agostino (1420–1478)[113]

BHL 1197. ⟨lectiones⟩ de Bernardino senensis[114]

No preface. Dati's *Opera omnia* includes orations on several saints. This one is closest to the contents of a *vita*. I do not count this oration toward figure 1.1.

---

112. Soulier, "Frater Cosmas," 99, provides this date, rejecting Filippo Tozzi's assignment of 1485, first because Cosimo was not yet a novice in 1485, and second because the list of Servite generals in the last part of the work runs to 1512. The first argument is inconclusive because this sort of Latin rewriting of order origins is typically a young man's work. Moreover, Cosimo's later writings are vernacular and polemical. The second is inconclusive because the scribe of the manuscript is not identified (despite the restored name "Cosmas" in the final poem; see the *incipit* above).

113. P. Viti, in *DBI* 33 (1987): 15–21.

114. See n. 49 above.

inc. orat. preced. lect.: Velim hodie dari mihi maiorem dicendi potestatem
inc.: Bernardinus patria Senensis bonis progenitus parentibus
des.: et caelesti secum gaudio frui per infinita saeculorum saecula.

MSS
None known to me.

Editions
  1. *Augustini Dati Senensis Opera* (Siena, 1503), fols. 61v–62. Source text.
  2. *Augustini Dati Senensis Opera* (Venice, 1516), fol. 49.
  3. *Augustini Dati Senensis Opera* (Paris, 1516, fol. 12r–v.

Office. *Oratio ac laudes panegyricae divorum Augustini, Nicolai, Margaritae, Theodorae*

Dati composed an *antiphon* and prayer for a single office that invoked the
name saint of each member of his immediate family. See his *Opera* (Siena,
1503), fol. 58. I do not count this entry toward the figures or tables.

DECEMBRIO, Pier Candido (October 24, 1399–November 12, 1477)[115]

Lost. ⟨*Vita Sancti Ambrosii*⟩ (IV)[116]

No dedication or preface known. Decembrio was working on this life,
which was meant to put Guarino's account (*q.v.*) to shame, in 1468. Its
existence is attested in three letters from Decembrio. The first was written
to the *primacerius* of the Milanese Duomo, Francesco della Croce, in
November 1466 and is quoted in part by F. Argelati, *Biblioteca Scriptorum
Mediolanensium* (Milan, 1745), 1:149. The second was written to
Francesco Marescalchi, dated Ferrara 1468, and is quoted in part by Carlo
de'Rosmini, *Vita e disciplina di Guarino Veronese* (Brescia, 1806),
2:186–188, n. 304; see especially 187, col. b, where Decembrio says he has
taken three years to write the *vita*. This is letter A253 according to Vittorio Zaccaria, "L'Epistolario di Pier Candido Decembrio," *Rinascimento* 7
(1956): 57, no. 31. The third was written to Bonino Mombrizio (*q.v.*) and
is quoted in part by Argelati, *Biblioteca*, 1:148. Neither Jacopo Filippo
Foresti (*q.v.*), in his *Supplementum chronicarum*, nor Pietro Ransano (*q.v.*),
in book 8 of his *Annales*, chap. 41, fol. 224, mention the *vita Ambrosii*
among the works by Decembrio that they know. See chap. 3 above.

115. P. Viti in *DBI* 33 (1987): 488–498.
116. G. D. Gordini, *BS* 1 (1961): 945–965; L. T. Pizzolatto in *GLS* 105b–112b.

DELPHINUS, Petrus, O.Cam. (November 24/25, 1444–January 15, 1525)[117]

BHL 3915. Epistola de translatione Hilarii (VI)[118]

Letter directed to the cardinal-protector of the Camaldulensians, Francesco Piccolomini. The translation took place in 1495. Because the letter describes the *translatio* and is not a narrative of the saint's life, I do not count it toward the material in the tables and figures.

inc.: Quoniam religionis successibus gaudes, Domine Colendissime, referam tuae Amplitudini, quae per hos dies in Coenobio quodam nostri Ordinis contigerunt.

des.: Hoc agit major quam pro meritis de tua erga me humanitate fiducia. . . . Vale Domine . . . Ex Fonte Bono die XX mai MCCCXCVI.[119]

MSS
    1. Florence, BN, MS Conv. soppr. E 3 405 (a four volume collection of Delfino's letters). XV–XVI. Kristeller, *Iter* 1:158b. Not seen.
    2. Venice, BN Marciana, MS Lat. XI 92 (3828) (a collection of Delfino's letters). XVI. Kristeller, *Iter* 2:255a. Not seen.

Editions
    1. Petrus Delphinus, *Epistolae* (Venice, 1524), signs. r2v–r3.
    2. *AASS* May III (Paris, 1866): 470. Source text.

DIEDO, Francesco (ca. 1433–March 25, 1484)[120]

BHL 7273. Vita s. Rochi (XIV)[121]

Dedicatory preface to Brescia, dated "Brixiae, Kalendis Iuniis M.CCCC.LXXVIIII." To avert the plague from the city, Diedo propitiated the saint by promising a new church and this *vita*. Some editions conclude with a letter to Diedo from Ludovico Maldura.

117. Kristeller, "Contribution," 136; King, *Venetian Humanism*, 362–363; R. Zaccaria, in *DBI* 40 (1991): 565b–571a.
    118. G. Lucchesi, *BS* 4 (1964): 1140–1141.
    119. See *AASS* May III (Paris, 1866): 457 note d.
    120. Gilbert Tournoy, "Francisco Diedo: Venetian Humanist and Politician of the Quattrocento," *Humanistica Lovaniensia* 19 (1970): 201–234; King, *Venetian Humanism*, 361–363.
    121. A. Vauchez, *BS* 11 (1968): 264–273; idem in *GLS* 1724a–1727b.

inc. proem.: Etsi de Rocho, cuius uitam scripturi sumus, certi nihil . . . compertum habemus

inc.: Rochum patre Joanne, matre uero Libera nomine genitum constat.

des.: diuinae clementiae munera consequamur.

inc. epist. ad auctorem: Quamquam bonorum operum est proprium ut externo commendatore non egeant

MSS

1. Leuven, Bibl. Faculteit Godgeleerdheit KUL, Fonds Groot Seminarie Mechelen MS 22, 62–63. XVI. Kristeller, *Iter* 3:134a. Not seen.

2. London, Robinson Trust, MS Phillipps 11547. XVI. Damaged. Kristeller, *Iter* 4:234b. Not seen.

3. Padua, BU, MS 239, fols. 34v–56v. XV. Kristeller, *Iter* 2:18a. Seen.

4. Udine, Bibl. Com. MS Manin 1335 (176). XVIII. Kristeller, *Iter* 2:207b. Not seen.

5. Verona, Bib. Capitolare, MS 113. Cranz, reel 326. Not seen.

6. Vicenza, Bibl. Comunale Bertoliana, Fondo Principale, MS 3.9.20. XV. Kristeller, *Iter* 2:302a. Seen.

Editions

1. *Vita S. Rochi* [Milan: Simon Magniagus, after June 1, 1479]. Goff D188; *IGI* 3425; *BMC* VI 760; *GW* 8329; ISTC id00188000.

2. *Vita S. Rochi* [Venice: Bernardinus Benalius, 1483–84]. H6159*; *IGI* 3426; *GW* 8330; ISTC id00188300.

3. *Vita S. Rochi* [Nuremberg: Peter Wagner, about 1483–1486]. *GW* 8331; ISTC id00188500.

4. *Vita s. Rochi* [Paris: Jean Du Pré, 1493–1494]; *GW* 8333 [Jean Tréperel, about 1495]; ISTC id00189100.

5. *Vita s. Rochi* [Mainz: Peter von Friedberg, 1494–1495]. Goff D189; HC 10546*; *IGI* 3427; *BMC* I 49; *GW* 8332; ISTC id00189000.

6. *Vita s. Rochi*. Milan: [Johannes Antonius de Honate, about 1484], vernacular. *IGI* 3428; *GW* 8335; ISTC id00189600.

7. For numerous late imprints, see *BHL*.

Collection. ⟨*vitae sanctorum veronensis?*⟩

According to Cochrane, *Historians*, 51 and 514 n. 78, Diedo "rewrote the lives of the saints of Verona in a form that was still considered definitive by the reforming bishop Agostino Valier in the sixteenth century and by the Bollandists in the seventeenth." I have been unable to trace this work. Perhaps it results from a misreading of Zeno, *Dissertazioni*, 2:60.

Lost? ⟨*vita Rosae viterbiensis*⟩

According to David Herlihy's posthumously published *The Black Death and the Transformation of the West* (Cambridge, Mass.: Harvard University Press, 1997), Diedo wrote a life of Rose of Viterbo. The account appears to be attributed to Diedo in error.

DONATO Avogaro, Pietro, veronensis (1446/1451–after January 10, 1517)[122]

BHL —. *De sanctissimorum presulum Veronensium Euprepii, Cricini, Agapii, Proculique inventione et vita* (I–IV)[123]

Autograph letter to Hieronymus Bernardinus, podestà in 1494; preface to provisors Jacobus Maffeus and Christophorus Sacramosius. Pietro Donato Avogaro completed this work in 1494, when he added the notes to be found in the Laurenziana manuscript, which also includes a slightly reworked prologue. The translation of the bishops' relics that Donato describes took place either on March 23 or February 21, 1492.[124] In 1503 the list of thirty-six holy bishops of Verona was codified by synodal constitution.[125] Included as one entry in figure 1.1 for the fourth century.

inc. epist.: Quemadmodum pollicitus sum, ita libellum hunc

des. epist.: Studium ac uoluntatem declarisse. Vale.

inc. proem. 1: Veronae urbis nobilissime et italicarum uetustissime quis fuerit conditor

inc.: Philippus domini nostri Iesu Christi discipulus

des.: Haec sunt patres quae de sanctorum praesulum inuentione uita & rebus gestis in unum redigere potui . . . atque in ordine digestam celebriorem posteris reddiderim.

MSS

1. Florence, Bibl. Laurenziana, MS Ashb. 1396 (1320), with both autograph letter and preface. XV. Kristeller, *Iter* 1:86b. Source text.

2. Vatican City, BAV, MS Vat. Lat. 9202, fol. 405r–v. XIX. Preface only. Not seen.

---

122. Date from Rino Avesani and B. M. Peebles, "Studies in Pietro Donato Avogaro of Verona," *IMH* 5 (1962): 9 and 11.

123. See respectively S. Tonoldi in *BS* 5 (1964): 236–237; idem in *BS* 1 (1961): 296–298; G. D. Gordini in *BS* 10 (1968): 1152–1154.

124. See B. M. Peebles, in Avesani and Peebles, "Studies in Pietro Donato Avogaro," 39 and n. 3. In 1493 two other bishops, Verecundus and Volens, were translated (*AASS*, Oct. IX [Paris, 1869], *chronologia*).

125. *AASS* Oct. IX (Paris, 1869): 586c.

3. Verona, Bibl. Com., MS 56, incomplete. G. Biadego, *Catalogo descrittivo dei manoscritti della Biblioteca Communale di Verona* (Verona, 1892), 1014. Not seen.

Editions
No complete edition.

ENRICHETTI, Zaccaria (ca. 1423–1509 or soon thereafter)[126]

BHL 6642. ⟨*Vita Petronii ep. Bononiensis*⟩ (V)[127]

Incipits and *desinit* taken from *BHL*.
   inc. prol. De imperiali origine . . . Hanc precor ut primum
   inc.: Petronius Bononiensis episcopus, ut in antiquis historiis legimus
   des.: Hactenus, at finem tempora longa manent.

MSS
   1. Bologna, BU MS 52, i, fasc. 1. Frati, "Indice," 122–123, no. 61. Not seen.
   2. Bologna, BU, MS 686, a miscellany; item 22B: [Zaccaria Righetti] *Della nobiltà del casato o sia stirpe di s. Petronio*. Mazzatinti, 19 (1912/1975): 19–22, no. 524. Vernacular. Not seen.
   3. Bologna, BU, MS 3875, vi. Copied in 1711, according to Gherardo Ortalli, "Notariato e storiografia in Bologna nei secoli XIII–XVI," in *Notariato medievale Bolognese: Atti di un convegno (febbraio 1976)* (Rome, 1977), 2:173 n. 46. Not seen.
   4. Lost? Archivio della Fabbrica di San Petronio, and used by G. Melloni for his partial edition (see below), according to Ortalli, "Notariato"; Frati, "Indice," 102 and n. 3, gives the shelfmark as 11.

Editions
   1. Partial edition in G. Melloni, *Atti, o memorie degli uomini illustri in santità nati, o morti in Bologna* I, i (Bologna, 1786), 532–534, with a misattribution to Zaccaria Enrichetti's homonymous father, corrected by F. Lanzoni, *S. Petronio vescovo di Bologna nella storia e nella leggenda* (Rome, 1907), 45. References from Ortalli, "Notariato," 173 n. 46. Not seen.

---

126. P. Cherubini, in *DBI* 42 (1993): 703a–705a.
127. G. D. Gordini, *BS* 10 (1968): 521–530. Title and dates taken from Cherubini (preceding note), who describes the incipit of the *vita* in such a way as to suggest two works by Enrichetti on Petronius.

FABIANUS Cretensis, O.S.B. Congr. S. Giustina (fl. 1490)[128]

BHL 2790. ⟨*Vita Eustachii* [recte *Eutychii patriarchae Constantinopolitanensis*]⟩ (VI)[129]

Dedication to Gregorio Beaqua, abbot in Milan and Venice. A translation from the Greek made with Hilarion Veronensis *(q.v.)*.[130]

inc. prol.: Omnium quidem praeclara gesta sanctorum, fratres, nihil aliud esse probantur quam quaedam humanae uitae praesidia

inc.: Sanctus itaque pater magnusque Eustachius, cuius hodie festa

des.: a monachis deuotissime colitur.

MSS

1. Venice, Bibl. Marciana, MS Zan. lat. 360 (1809). Kristeller, *Iter* 2:213a. Source text.

Editions
All are late; see *BHL*.

FAIELLI (FAIELLA, FAVELLA, FAVILLA, FAVILLAS), Cosimo

See COSIMO DA FIRENZE.

FERRERI, Zaccaria, O.S.B. Congr. di Santa Giustina, then O.Carth., then lay (1479–August 1524)[131]

BHL —. Vita beati Casimiri confessoris (d. 1484)[132]

No preface, no dedication. Life in four books.

---

128. Not in Kristeller, "Contribution."

129. R. Janin in *BS* 6 (1964): 323–324.

130. Barry Collett, *Italian Benedictine Scholars and the Reformation* (Oxford: Oxford University Press, 1985), 44 and n. 55, for note of Fabianus's profession in 1488, of the confusion in the title of the *vita* between Eutychius and Eustachius, and of the fact that Fabianus worked on the translation with Hilarion of Verona, "professed in 1464."

131. Not in Kristeller, "Contribution"; see A. Ferrajoli, *Il ruolo della corte di Leone X (1514–1516)*, ed. V. De Caprio (Rome: Bulzoni, 1984), 531–544; Paolo Rabikauskas, in *BS* 3 (1963): 895–906. Ferreri wrote metric offices on St. Casimir and on Hugh of Lincoln, as well as a lengthy metric life of Benedict, not treated here because verse. See B. Morsolin, *Zaccaria Ferreri: Episodio biografico del secolo decimosesto* (Vicenza: Burato, 1877), 14 and 39; and C. L. Stinger, *The Renaissance in Rome* (Bloomington: Indiana University Press, 1985), 47–48 and n. 120. On his metric *De Carthusiae origine Heroicon*, which includes a narrative of the founder Bruno, see M. Calabrese, in *BS* 3 (1963): 561–569; and Morsolin, *Zaccaria Ferreri*, 37–38.

132. G. Platania in *GLS* 337a–379a. The saint's death date is from Rabikauskas (pre-

inc.: Zacharias, Dei et apostolicae Sedis gratia, Episcopus Gardiensis Immensa et incomprehensibilis Dei sapientia. . . Quum enim Lituania, seu potius Litaliania, Sarmatiae ampla et nobilis apud Bastarnas prouincia[133]
des.: quae singularia . . . descripserimus, annotauerimus.

MSS

    1. Venice, Bibl. Giustiniani Reccanati, MS VI 12 (865), fols. 34r–v. Kristeller, *Iter* 6:287a–b. Not seen.

Editions

    1. *Vita beati Casimiri confessoris ex serenissimi Poloniae regibus et magnis Lithuaniae ducibus . . . ex fide dignorum tertium depositionibus scripta aedibus.* Thorun, 1521.
    2. *AASS* March I (Antwerp, 1663): 347–351. Source text.

FLAMINI, Giovanni Antonio (1464–1536)[134]

Collection. *De uitis quattuor protectorum fauentiae* (1526–1534)[135]

Letter to the cathedral canons and magistracy of Faenza; this letter accompanied a copy of the *uitae* that Flamini had made for the city of Faenza. Flamini's accounts of Terentius, Savinus, Aemilianus, and Petrus Damianus are listed below in alphabetical order among his other saints' lives.

---

ceding note), who observes that canonization proceedings started under Leo X have been lost, so that it is not known when or if Casimir was ever declared a saint; see also *AASS* March I (Anvers, 1663): 337–357, with comm. praev. on 334–345. For Ferreri's commission from Leo X on September 15, 1519, to begin inquiries prefatory to canonization, see Henricus Damianus Wojtyska, ed., *Zacharias Ferreri (1519–1521) et nuntii minores (1522–1553)* (Rome: Institutum Historicum Polonicum, 1992), vi and letter 3, 9–10; also relevant are letter 9, 14–17; an oration, 37–44, at 38; Sigismund's response, 68–70, at 69; and the *relatio* of ⟨March 1521⟩, 98–104.

    133. According to Wojtyska, *Zacharias Ferreri*, viii, the life was written in Vilna in July 1520, following the canonization inquiry that Ferreri held there.

    134. F. Lanzoni, "Le *uitae* dei quattro santi protettori della città di Faenza," *RRIISS* 28, no. 3 (Bologna: Zanichelli, 1921), 296–301. V. De Matthes, in *DBI* 48 (1997): 278b–281a. See also Pieter F. J. Obbema, "A Flaminius Manuscript in Leiden: Autograph and Printer's Copy," *Quaestiones Leidenses: Twelve Studies on Leiden University and Its Holdings* (Leiden, 1975), 211, noting the fact that "the university world of Bologna seems to have almost totally ignored this devout and skillful teacher and his writing."

    135. For the date of composition, see Lanzoni, "Le *uitae*," 297. On Flamini's lost autograph, see ibid., 297–298. Note the disagreement between Lanzoni and H. Delehaye on the status of the 1512 (?) epitome of these saints' lives (ibid., 301); cf. chap. 4 above on the possibility that humanists used saints' lives for writing and speaking exercises.

Due to their late date of composition, they are not included in Figure 1.1, but are noted here because of the importance of the author in the field.

inc. epist.: Cum proxima aetate uobiscum familiarissime uersatus fuerim[136]

MSS

1. P. Beltrami in G. Mazzatinti and A. Sorbelli, eds., *Inventari dei manoscritti delle biblioteche d'Italia* XXVI (1918–20; repr. 1967): 74–75, on two late manuscripts: Faenza, Bibl. Com. MSS 185 and 188. Not seen.

2. See F. Lanzoni, "Le *uitae* dei quattro santi protettori della città di Faenza," *RRIISS* (Bologna: Zanichelli, 1921), 298–299, for a sixteenth-century parchment manuscript with illuminated letters once owned by G. Magnani and then by Annibale Ferniani (who allowed Lanzoni to consult it). Current location not known.[137]

Editions

1. G. B. Mittarelli, ed., *Ad scriptores rerum italicarum . . . accessiones Fauentinae* (Venice, 1771).

2. F. Lanzoni, ed., "Le *uitae*" (above under MSS), 337–384, col. a.

BHL 104d, e. *Beatus Aemilianus*[138]

Introductory remarks. One of Flamini's lives of the four protectors of Faenza.

inc. proem.: Diuina prouidentia, quae nihil unquam omisit

des.: apud sancti Clementis ecclesiam sepeliuit . . . et usque in hodiernum diem illustrem facere non desinit

inc. mir.: Erat tunc extra urbis muros sancti Clementis aedes

des. mir.: quorum nos similiter uitam scripsimus, publico sibi uoto colendum statuit

MSS

1. See above under *De uitis quattor protectorum*.

Editions

1. Mittarelli, *Ad scriptores*, 816–819.

2. F. Lanzoni, "Le *uitae*," 360–367. Source text.

---

136. Edited in Lanzoni, "Le *uitae*," 385, appendix 1.

137. Neither V. De Matteis in *DBI* 48 (1997): 280b, nor Webb, *Patrons,* indicates any manuscripts.

138. Date of composition for Aemilianus and the other three protectors given by G. Lucchesi, *BS* 4 (1965): 1184–1185, from Lanzoni.

BHL —. *Magni Alberti vita* (XIII)[139]

Prefatory letter to Leandro Alberti. Written by 1516–1517 for inclusion in Alberti's collection.

inc. epist.: Solent plerique, mi Leander, eruditi uiri

inc.: Sueui Germaniae sunt populi ii quidem toti regioni

des.: Quae facile declarant diuino hominem ingenio proculdubio diuinitus adiutum documento esse mortalibus . . . atque confirmant.

MSS
None known to me.

Editions

1. Alberti (*q.v.*), *De viris illustribus*, fols. 105r–v (preface), 105v–114v (*vita et opera*). Source text.

Lost. ⟨*Vita Benedicti XI*⟩[140] (XIV)

Lost. ⟨*Vita Catherinae Senensis, O.P. tert.*⟩ (XIV)

See Flamini, *Epistolae familiares*, xxix, and letters on 341–344. Flamini also left notice of this account in his life of Dominic, saying "Cujus [*sci.* Dominici] eximiam sanctitatem illa quoque Diuae Catherinae Senensis uisio mirifice indicat. Quod tametsi ejus uita, quam nuper scripsimus, silentio non praeteriuimus, hic tamen etiam non tacendam putauimus."

Lost. ⟨*Vita s. Columbae, O.P. tert.*⟩[141]

See Flamini, *Epistolae familiares*, xxix. In 1521, Flamini's friend and collaborator Leandro Alberti (*q.v.*) made a vernacular translation of Sebastiano Bontempi's life of this saint. Not included in figure 1.1.

BHL —. *Beati Iacobi alemani Vita* (d. 1491)

Dedicatory preface to Thomas Cospio, O.P., dated at the end "Calen. Augusti, MDXVI."

inc. epist.: Scripsi iam multorum uitam uirorum inter praedicatores tuos

inc.: Ulma Germaniae ciuitas est. Hanc Beati Iacobi

---

139. A. Walz in *BS* 1 (1961): 700–716; F. Santi in *GLS* 66a–72a.

140. Alberti, *De viris illustribus*, fols. 64–65v, edits an unattributed *Vita Benedicti XI* that he may have written or revised himself. It follows the prefatory letter to Lorenzo Fieschi that introduces book 3; cf. book 1, fols. 39–40, on the future pope's work as ninth master general of the Dominicans. G. Capponi, the editor of Flamini's familiar letters, notes that Flamini wrote a life of Benedict IX (*sic*, for XI?), O.P., that was praised by Leandro Alberti in his *Descrittione*; see G. A. Flamini, *Epistolae familiares* (1744), xxix.

141. S. Mostaccio in *DBI* 60 (2003): 84a–87b; G. Zarri in *GLS* 467b–470a.

des.: Sed haec (ni fallor) satis esse uideri possunt, quae uiri tanti apud deum merita et sanctitatem eximiam abunde testari queant.

MSS
None known to me.

Editions
1. Alberti (*q.v.*), *De viris illustribus*, fol. 262r–v (preface) and 262v–267v (*vita*). Source text.

BHL —. *Beati Iacobi veneti vita* (XIV)

Dedicatory preface to Matteo Bandello, O.P., dated at the end "Pridie Calen. apriles MDXVI."
   inc. epist.: Magna proculdubio uirtuti est uis
   inc.: Natus est Beatus Iacobus in urbe clarissima Venetiarum
   des.: et mortuo ut inuocent etiam atque etiam rogo, quicunque haec legerint.

MSS
None known to me.

Editions
1. Alberti (*q.v.*), *De viris illustribus*, fols. 205 (prefatory letter) and 205–217 (*vita*). Source text.

Lost. ⟨*Vita Hosannae Andreasi, O.P. tert.*⟩ (d. 1505)[142]

See Flamini, *Epistolae familiares*, xxix.

BHL —. ⟨*Vita Petri Damiani*⟩ (XI)[143]

Dedicatory preface to the citizens of Faenza. Not included in figure 1.1.
   inc. proem.: Magna soleo uoluptate affici, uiri Fauentini, quoties repeto
   inc.: Initia uitae uiri clarissimi atque sanctissimi
   des.: magnus fauentinae urbis protector et custos

MSS
1. See above under *De uitis quattor protectorum*.

Editions
1. Mittarelli, *Ad scriptores* 820–831.
2. Lanzoni, "Le *uitae*," 367–384. Source text.

---

142. G. Cappelletti in *BS* 1 (1961): 1170–1174; G. Zarri in *GLS* 1528a–1530a.
143. P. Palazzini in *BS* 10 (1968): 554–574; G. Fornasari in *GLS* 1620a–1625a.

BHL —. *Vita et gesta inclyti martyris et episcopi Sabini* (IV)[144]

The preface does not name a dedicatee; it was not written before 1526–1534.[145]

inc. proem.: Sanctorum martyrum, quorum sanguine in testimonia
inc.: Alto diuinae prouidentiae consilio permissum fuisse credimus
des.: Martyrii autem coronam beatus Sabinus septimo idus decembris adeptus est . . . relatus
inc. translatio prima: Beatus Sabinus quo tempore ex patria discessit
des. translatio secunda: quiescit et miraculis claret.

MSS

1. See above under *De uitis quattuor protectorum.*

Editions

1. Mittarelli, *Ad scriptores,* 816–819. Source text.
2. Lanzoni, "Le *uitae,*" 345–360. Source text.

BHL —. *Beati levitae Terentii vita*[146]

The preface does not name a dedicatee. The life was written about 1530.[147] Not included in figure 1.1.

inc. proem.: Magna quidem ac caelesti dono factum cernimus
inc.: Beatus Terentius Imolensis fuit non obscuris natus parentibus
des.: Annum, mensem et diem obdormitionis suae in Domino ac translationem sanctissimi sui cadueris in praedicta ecclesia Sancte Crucis . . . nunquam in alioquo loco potui inuenire.
des. oratio: quem nobis te instante protectorem eligimus in terris . . .

MSS

1. See above under *De uitis quattuor protectorum.*

Editions

1. Mittarelli, *Ad scriptores,* 798–805. Source text.
2. Lanzoni, "Le *uitae,*" 338–344. Source text.

144. G. Lucchesi in *BS* 11 (1968): 705–716; Webb, *Patrons,* 171-173. For identification of source *BHL* 7455, see Lanzoni, *Storia ecclesiastica,* 118. The incipit and desinit given for *BHL* 7455, however, are "Saeviente adhuc tyrannorum rabie" and "ubi in sepulcro ex candido marmore facto quiescit et miraculis claret. Deo gratias," respectively. Cf. the incipit and desinit above, taken from Mittarelli's edition. Lanzoni's brief discussion does not account for differences of this magnitude between the version edited by Mittarelli and the version edited from the Venetian manuscript by Cappelletti (e.g., minor spelling variants noted by Lanzoni at 119).
145. According to Lanzoni, *Storia ecclesiastica,* 118.
146. On the problem of dating this saint, see G. Lucchesi, *BS* 12 (1969): 372–374.
147. See Lucchesi (preceding note) on dating and documentation.

Lost. ⟨*Vita Theodori*⟩ (III–IV)

Flamini mentions having written this *vita* in the preface to his life of Sabinus; see Mittarelli, *Ad scriptores*, 806:

> Scripsi ego superioribus annis, et adhuc scribere non cesso, sanctorum quidem non paucorum uitam, et res memoratu dignas, sed omnes illi ex eorum fuere numero, qui more Christiano confessores appellantur, uno excepta Beato Theodoro insigni martyre, quem clarissima Venetiarum ciuitas, antequam Sancti Euangelistae Marci corpus in eam adueheretur, praecipuum sibi, ac tutelarum diuum habuit, ac diu venerata est, cujus marmorea cum dracone quem interemit effigies in altera ex duabus ingentibus columnis in ipso Beati Marci foro conspicitur. Venerabile autem illius corpus in eadem urbe in templo Saluatoris, quod ibi celeberrimum est, requiescit, cujus nos *vitam*, et praeclara facinora, rogatu patrum qui ibidem commorantur, hac ipsa aetate a nobis descripta Venetias misimus.

BHL —. *Beati Venturini Bergomensis* (XIV)[148]

Dedicatory preface to Vincentinus Vicentii, O.P., dated "xii Cal. Iul. MDXVI."
inc. epist.: Nosti me, Vincenti, iandiu clarissimo
inc.: Galliae Cisalpinae quam iuniores Lombardiam dixere urbes
des.: Cuius opem ut mihi uiuo et mortuo inuocent quicunque haec legerit etiam atque etiam rogo.

MSS
None known to me.

Editions
1. Alberti (*q.v.*), *De viris illustribus*, fols. 238r–v (prefatory letter) and 238v–247 (*vita*). Source text.

BHL —. *Divi Vincentii Valentini* [Ferrer] (d. 1419)[149]

Prefatory letters to Francesco Bentivoglio and to Gaspar Elephantutius (Fantuzzi).
inc. epist. 1: Quantum me tibi ac toti familiae tuae[150]
inc. epist. 2: Scripsi iam multorum utriusque sexus[151]
inc.: Habuit unaquaeque aetas magnum aliquid ac memorabile

---

148. P. Bertocchi in *BS* 12 (1969): 1013–1016.
149. On Vincent Ferrer, see n. 94 above.
150. Flamini in Alberti, *De viris illustribus*, fol. 156.
151. Ibid., fols. 93v–95.

des.: Tertio demum die sepultus fuit. . . . Clarus hodieque plurimis et eximiis in toto orbe miraculis.

MSS
None known to me.

Editions
1. Alberti (*q.v.*), *De viris illustribus*, fols. 156 (preface to Francesco Bentivoglio) and 156v–174v (*vita*). Source text.
2. Flamini, *Vitae patrum inclytum ordinis praedicatorum* (Bologna: Hieronymus de Benedictis, 1529), fols. 93v–95 (letter to Gaspar Elephantutius) and 95–122v (*vita*).

FLAMINI, Marcantonio (1498–1550)[152]

BHL —. Vita Beati Mauritii Pannonii (XIV)[153]

Prefatory letter from Giovanni Antonio Flamini (*q.v.*), the author's father, to Leandro Alberti (*q.v.*), followed by another from Marcantonio himself to Andrea Bentivoglio. The life was written by 1516/17 for Alberti's anthology. See Albano Sorbelli, "Una raccolta poco nota d'antiche vite di santi e religiosi domenicani," *Rendiconti della R. Accademia dell'Istituto di Bologna, Classe di scienze morali*, ser. 2, 6 (1922): 93–94, for Flamini's source, the order chronicle by the Dominican Girolamo Albertucci de'Borselli.
inc. epist. 1: Misit ad me filius meus Iunior Flaminius
inc. epist. 2: Non sum nescius, Andrea Bentiuole
inc.: Regium Beati Mauritii genus est
des.: et cum omnium stupore uisum continuo recuperauit . . . et sanctitatem abunde testari possunt.

MSS
None known to me.

Editions
1. Alberti (*q.v.*), *De viris illustribus*, fols. 217r–v (Giovanni Antonio Flamini to Leandro Alberti), 217v (Marcantonio Flamini to Andrea Bentivoglio), and 217v–220v (*vita*). Source text.

---

152. A. Pastore in *DBI* 48 (1997): 282a–288a.
153. E. Pasztór in *BS* 9 (1967): 207–208.

FLAMINI, Sebastiano (fl. 1500)[154]

BHL —. B. Ambrosii Senensis Ord. Praedic. Vita (XIII)[155]

Prefatory letter to Alberto Albergati. It does not name the year, but 1516/17 is the likely date of composition. The preface also declares that this *vita* is simply a Latin translation (i.e., paraphrase) from the Italian: "Accipe igitur beati Ambrosii uitam, quam Leandri Alberti praedicatorum sectae uiri celeberrimi nutu latinam fecimus."

inc. epist.: Mos fuit antiquitus omnium quos impraesentia
inc.: Sicuti alta miraque dicenti materia offertur
des.: Tu quicunque hanc beati leges uitam siquid in ea minus quam deceret bene dictum reperies, non mihi sed temporis breuitati ascribito. Non enim nobis licuit Horatianum praeceptum seruare.

MSS
None known to me.

Editions
   1. Alberti (*q.v.*), *De viris illustribus*, fols. 230 (prefatory letter) and 230–237v (*vita*).

FORESTI, Jacopo Filippo, of Bergamo (1434–1520) O.E.S.A.[156]

Collection. *De claris sceletisque [sic] mulieribus.*

Foresti's anthology, published in Ferrara by Laurentius de Rubeis on April 29, 1497 [H 2813], treats 191 noteworthy women, good and bad, pagan and Christian, of whom 43 are martyrs.[157]

Lost? ⟨*Vita Rochi*⟩

Kristeller, *Iter* 4:234b, London, Robinson Trust, MS Phillipps 11547, includes "Jac. Phil. Bergomas, vita di San Rocco, volg. Bapt. Mantuanus." There is, to my knowledge, no other record that Foresti wrote a life of Rocco or that Baptista Mantuanus translated such a life. Cf. below, under Sabellico, Marcantonio Coccio. Not included in figure 1.1.

---

154. Among the Flamini treated in the *DBI*, there is no Sebastiano.
155. S. M. Bertucci in *BS* 11 (1968): 629–633.
156. Kristeller, "Contribution," 139; L. Megli Frattini, in *DBI* 48 (1997): 801b–803a.
157. V. Zaccaria, "La fortuna del *De mulieribus claris* del Boccaccio nel secolo XV: Giovanni Sabbadini degli Arienti, Jacopo Filippo Foresti e le loro biografie femminile (1490–1497)," in F. Mazzoni, ed., *Il Boccaccio nelle culture e letterature nazionale* (Florence, 1978), 519–545, counts 191 entries.

FOSCARINI, Ludovico (1409–August 17, 1480)[158]

BHL —. *Gesta Victoris et Coronae ⟨in Sicilia⟩* (II)[159]

Dedicatory letter to *Jacopo Foscaro*, undated, and prologue. The account was written in 1439, when Foscarini was serving as *praetor* in Feltre, where Victor and Corona were city patrons.[160] Foscarini apparently continued to promote these civic patrons. In 1448 (*sic?*), there was a translation of the relics to a new marble tomb, with a dated Latin inscription naming Foscarini.[161] According to A. Pertusi, "L'umanesimo greco dalla fine del secolo XIV agli inizi del secolo XVI," *Storia della cultura veneta* 3, 1 (Vicenza: Pozza, 1980): 202–203, the *vita* was translated from the Greek; see also G. Moro, in *DBI* 49 (1997): 383b.

inc. epist.: Dubitaui persepe mecum, uir insignis, an tuis litteris, quibus hec mea scripta tantopere expostulabas, facerem. . . . Tu uero, pro suma tua in me beniuolentia, lege, corige, emenda. Et si quid dignum iudicaueris, id pietati in superbos et tue inposuerim. Vale.

inc. prol.: Permulti sunt non solum comunes sed graues etiam atque in omni uirtutum genere illustres uiri, quo partim nostra hec etas sua cum laude genuit, partim maiorum dignitas suma gloria excepit, qui cum cristianam religionem profiteantur a teneris usque annis, ut aiunt, necessitatis causa poetarum figmentis summo studio summis uigilijs elaborauerunt. Inter quos fuisse me negare non ualeo.

inc.: Imperante Antonio dedit editum Sebastiano eius exercitum in cicilia gubernanti quilibet aut nostris diis sacrificet aut crudelissimis penis afflictus mala morte moriatur

des.: Nec unquam aliquid praeter ea quae tibi grata sunt aut cupiamus aut perficiamus. Laus Deo.

MSS

1. Baltimore, Walters Art Gallery, MS W393, fols. 65–66 (letter), 66–68 (preface), 68v–94v (*vita*). XV. Kristeller, *Iter* 5:214b. Source text.

2. Camaldoli, Archivio del sacro eremo, MS 1112. XVIII. Kristeller, *Iter* 5:521a; cf. Pertusi, "L'umanesimo greco," 203 n. 99. Not seen.

---

158. King, *Venetian Humanism*, 374–377. For a note on his preuniversity education, see G. Moro, in *DBI* 49 (1997): 383a.

159. G. Lucchesi in *BS* 12 (1969): 1290–1292.

160. G. Moro in *DBI* 49 (1997): 383b; degli Agostini, *Notizie*, 1:49 and 103. According to King, *Venetian Humanism*, 374, he was *podestà* and *capitano* in Feltre; later in 1439 he was appointed *luogotenente* in the Friuli.

161. *AASS* May III (Paris, 1866): 269, para. 5, but the date of 1448 is impossible to square with what is known of Foscarini's career.

Editions

I am preparing an edition from the Baltimore manuscript.

FRANCESCO Catellini da Castiglione, cathedral canon (ca. 1420–May 29, 1484)[162]

BHL 577. Divi Antonii archiantistitis florentini vita (d. 1459; c.d. 1523)

Dedicatory letter to the convent of St. Dominic in Bologna and preface. Francesco had served as the archbishop's secretary. For vernacular translations, see Kristeller, *Iter* 1:143a and 2:467a.

inc. epist.: Cum uitam reuerendissimi patris fratris Antonii [*sic*] archiepiscopi Florentini nuper conscripsissem

inc. proem.: Nonnullis rebus saepe numero annexa est quaedam, ut ita dixerim uis officii

inc.: Antonius Florentina urbe oriundus honestissimis parentibus

des.: Haec de signis . . . pro tempore dicta sufficiant.

inc. epil.: Non possum autem huius tanti uiri mortem

des.: incertum est, utinam bene uortat. Amen.

MSS

1. Bologna, BU, MS 1999, fols. 208–214. According to Sorbelli, "Una raccolta poco nota," 100–101, the Dominican chronicler Girolamo Albertucci de'Borselli copied the account into his *Cronica magistrorum generalium ordinis fratrum praedicatorum*. Not seen.

2. Florence, Bibl. Laurenziana, MS S. Marco 408 (123), fols. 1 (letter, fragmentary), 1v (preface), and 2v–27v. XV. Kristeller, *Iter* 1:76b–77a; Paolo Cherubini, ed., *Iacopo Ammannati Piccolomini Lettere (1444–1479)* (Rome, 1997), 41–42. Source text.

3. Florence, BN, MS Conv. soppr. J VII 30 (411), fols. 56–57 (letter), 57–58 (preface), 58–81 (*vita*). XV. Kristeller, *Iter* 1:163b–164a. Source text.

4. Florence, BN, MS Magl. XXXVIII 142, fols. 24–48. XV. Kristeller, *Iter* 1:143a. Bausi, "Francesco da Castiglione fra umanesimo," 130 n. 53, gives a date at the end of the manuscript: September 28, 1461. Source text. Seen.

5. Milan, Bibl. Ambrosiana, MS Cimelli F 4 sup., fols. 1 (preface), 2v–44 (*vita*). XV. Kristeller, *Iter* 1:330b; A. Poncelet, *AB* 11 (1892):

162. Francesco Bausi, "Francesco da Castiglione fra umanesimo e teologia," *Interpres* 11 (1991): 112–181; idem, in *DBI* 49 (1997): 713a–715b. On Antonino Pierozzi, Francesco's most important subject, see at least A. D'Addario in *DBI* 3 (1961): 524a–532b.

320–321, no. 27. Includes epitaphs of Antoninus and Vittorino da Feltre. An early ownership note reads "Est conventus S. Mariae Gratiarum M⟨ilano⟩," that is, the Milanese house of the Observant Augustinian Hermits. Seen.

6. Prague, former Statni Knihovna Ceske Socialisticke Republiky, MS XLVII C 1 a/I. XVI. Kristeller, *Iter* 6:464b. Not seen.

7. Ravenna, Bibl. classense, MS 278 (?), fols. 1–19. Mazzatinti, 4 (1894): 207, no. 278, with the subscription, "Gundissalvus de Heredia hispanus scripsit" and lengthy ownership note. Not seen.

8. Siena, Bibl. Comunale, MS E IV 16, fols. 52–82v. XV. Kristeller, *Iter* 2:162a. In this manuscript the life of Antoninus is followed by that of Vittorino da Feltre. Not seen.

9. Siena, Bibl. Comunale, MS T III 1. XV. Kristeller, *Iter* 2:170a. In this manuscript, the life of Antoninus is followed by that of Vittorino da Feltre. Not seen.

Editions

1. Alberti (*q.v.*), *De viris illustribus*, fols. 94r–v (letter), 94v–95 (preface), 95–104 (*vita*). Alberti omits Francesco's bleak concluding paragraph about contemporary moral decline.

2. *Jesus. In hoc volumine continentur*. Venice: Johann Emerich de Spira, 1495, signs. h.4–i10. *IGI* 702. Goff A883; H1274.

3. For many late editions, see *BHL*.

BHL 607. *Antonii de Ripolis ex pedemontium vita* (d. 1460)[163]

Dedicatory letter to Cardinal Jacopo Ammannati. The life, written by the end of 1468 or the first days of 1469,[164] includes several accompanying pieces: besides the dedicatory letter, there is also a prefatory letter from Cardinal Jacopo Ammannati, a response to Ammannati, and a letter from Girolamo Aliotti, abbot of Santa Flora (Arezzo), to Francesco.[165] Francesco may have known this young man who entered the Dominican order under Antonino Pierozzi at San Marco. His account may have contributed to the translation of the martyr's body from Tunis to his hometown of Rivoli (east of Turin) on August 29, 1469.

inc. epist. Francisci ad Jacobum: Cum pro tua singulari virtute summaque in me benivolentia

163. G. L. Masetti Zannini in *BS* 9 (1967): 841–843.

164. The date 1469 occurs twice in material supplementary to the life, found in Florence, Magl. XXXVIII 142: see the letter to Jacopo Ammannati, at fol. 65v; and the letter from Girolamo Aliotti, at fol. 76. Ammannati's response (following note) is dated January 25, 1469, so Francesco may have been writing his work in late 1468.

165. See Paolo Cherubini, *Iacopo Ammannati Piccolomini Lettere (1444–1479)* (Rome, 1997), esp. 109 and 1227.

inc. epist. Jacobi ad Franciscum: Antonianum martyrium quod misisti ad me magna dulcedine sensus omnes compleuit

inc. epist. Francisci ad Jacobum: Humanissimas ac disertissimas litteras manuque propria conscriptas ab te, Reuerendissime domine, nuper accepi

inc. epist. Hieronymi ad Franciscum: Noui martyris Antonii uirtus apud barbaros sepulta et christianis ferme omnibus iacuisset incognita nisi eam praeclarum ingeniam tuum extulisset

inc.: Eo tempore quo sanctissimus uir Antoninus, qui postea fuit archiepiscopus Florentinus

des.: et sapientum iudicio dicendum erit. Amen.

MSS

1. Bologna, BU, MS 1999, fols. 215–216. According to Sorbelli, "Una raccolta," 101–102, Girolamo Albertucci de'Borselli copied this account into his *Cronica magistrorum generalium ordinis fratrum praedicatorum*. Not seen.

2. Florence, Bibl. Laurenziana, MS San Marco 408, 2v–27v, with Leonardo Ser Uberti's additions, 28–50v. XV. Kristeller, *Iter* 1:76b–77a. Source text.

3. Florence, BN, MS Conv. soppr. J VII 30, fols. 108–112, with the preface to Jacopo Ammannati on fols. 106–108, the letter from Jacopo on fols. 112v–113, and Francesco's reply on fols. 113v–116. XV. Kristeller, *Iter* 1:163b. Source text.

4. Florence, BN, MS Magl. XXXVIII 142, fols. 58v–65 (*vita*), 65–68v (prologue). XV. Kristeller, *Iter* 1:143a. Source text.

5. Florence, BN, MS Magl. XXXVIII 138, fols. 55–63v (Italian translation). Kristeller, *Iter* 1:143a. Seen.

Editions

1. Alberti (*q.v.*), *De viris illustribus*, fols. 59v–61v, lacking letters.

2. For later editions, see *BHL*.

BHL —. *Vita sancti Dominici* (**XIII**)[166]

Preface, no dedicatee. The text is drawn, on Francesco's own word, from Antonino Pierozzi's *Chronicon*.

inc. proem.: Prospera rerum initia ut plurimum foelices exitus

inc.: Beatus Dominicus praedicatorum dux et pater

des.: Rogatum autem uolo ipsum ante omnes beatum dominicum patriarcham ac omnes electos domini . . . deinde pium lectorem ut suis nos precibus adiuuare et per uenia peccatorum simul et gratia promerenda apud altissimum suffragari dignetur. Cui est honor et regnum in perpetuam aeternitatem. Telos.

---

166. V. J. Koudelka in *BS* 4 (1964): 692–727; E. Montari in *GLS* 539b–550b.

MSS

1. Florence, BN, MS Magl. XXXVIII 142, fols. 1–2 (preface), 3–40v (*vita*). XV. Kristeller, *Iter* 1:143a. With an ownership note from the Congregation of Santa Giustina. Source text.

Editions
None.

Lost. ⟨*Vita Marci papae*⟩ (IV)[167]

On this and the following entry, see Bausi, "Francesco da Castiglione fra teologia," 160–161 and n. 123. Both were derived from a *historia* that Francesco found at San Lorenzo: see the letter from Francesco to Jacopo Ammannati, edited in A. Orsi, *Francisci Castilionensis Martyrium Antonianum* (Florence, 1728), 28–29.

Office. *Lectiones matutinales* ⟨de Marco papa⟩ (IV)[168]

The text matches that of the *Sermo . . . de vita Marci* that Francesco delivered March 19, 1464 (see Bausi, "Francesco da Castiglione," 136 n. 62). But in one manuscript this sermon has marginal *notae* indicating nine readings. Not included in figure 1.1.

MSS

1. Florence, BN, MS Conv. soppr. J VII 30, fols. 117v–121. XV. Kristeller, *Iter* 1:163b. Seen.

Editions

1. D. Moreni, *Continuazione delle Memorie dell'Ambrosiana Imperial Basilica di s. Lorenzo di Firenze* (Florence: Daddi, 1816), 2:350–55, edits the sermon. Source text.

BHL 6726. *Vita sancti Petri martyris* (XIII)[169]

Dedicatory letter to Bartolomeo Roverella, cardinal of Ravenna. This life, based on Antonino Pierozzi's *Chronicon*, titulus 23, chap. 6, was written by late April 1471.[170]

inc. epist.: Veterem, Reuerendissime Patre, familiae nostrae laudem reuocare

---

167. G. D. Gordini in *BS* 8 (1966): 699–700; Kelly, *ODP* 28b–29b.

168. See Francesco's letter to his patron, Cardinal Jacopo Ammannati, written shortly after January 25, 1469: I. A. Orsi, ed., *Francisci castilionensis martyrium Antonianum* (Florence, 1728), 29; Cherubini, *Iacopo Ammannati*, 2:1227–1229, edits Ammannati's response.

169. V. J. Koudelka in *BS* 10 (1968): 746–754; P. Golinelli in *GLS* 1630a–1631a.

170. The date "Florentiae xxii aprilis 1471" is found in Florence, BNC, MS Conv. soppr. J VII 30, at fol. 18v. For Antonino's sources, see Walker, *The Chronicles*, 93–94 n. 155.

des. epist.: eos in patria collocatos esse arbitramur. Vale.

inc.: Petrus martyr et praedicator ueritatis Verona uetustissima Italiae urbe oriundus

des.: ad laudem nominis eius per quo passus est qui est benedictus in secula. Telos.

MSS

1. Florence, BN, MS Conv. soppr. J VII 30, fols. 4–5v (preface) and 5v–18v (*vita*). XV. Kristeller, *Iter* 1:163b. Source text.

2. Florence, BN, MS Magl. XXXVIII 142, fols. 87–88 (preface) and 88–100 (*vita*). XV. Kristeller, *Iter* 1:143. Source text.

Editions

All are late; see *BHL*.

BHL —. *Vita beati Thomae Aquinatis* (XIII)[171]

Dedicatory letter shared with the preceding account. This account was written by the end of 1472.[172] It is based on Antoninus's *Chronicon*, titulus 18, chap. 7, 4–9.[173]

inc.: Beatus Thomas cuius doctrinae ac pietatis gloria

des.: pontificatus eius anno septimo Saluatoris autem anno ccc.lxviiii. Quis est benedictus in saecula. Telos.

MSS

1. Florence, BN, MS Magl. XXXVIII 142, fols. 100v–116. XV. Kristeller, *Iter* 1:143. Source text.

2. Florence, BN, MS Conv. soppr. J VII 30 (411), fols. 19–35v, dated 1472. Kristeller, *Iter* 1:163b. Source text.

Editions

None known to me.

BHL 8664. *Vita beati Vincentii* [*Ferrer*] (d. 1419)

Dedicatory letter to Cardinal Jacopo Ammannati, 1470.[174] In the letter, Francesco claims to have ordered material he found in the canonization

---

171. F. Santi in *GLS* 1869b–1876b.

172. The life may have been written by late April 1471, since it shares the same prologue with the life of Peter Martyr. However, the desinit in Florence, BNC, MS Conv. soppr. J VII 30, at fol. 32v, states that the life was "nuper de anno salutis MCCCCLXXII edita."

173. See Walker, *The Chronicles,* 94 n. 155, for notice that Antoninus himself drew on Bernard Gui.

174. This date is indicated in Florence, BNC, MS Conv. soppr. J VII 30 (411), fol. 36v, and is accepted by Bausi, "Francesco da Castiglione," 121, as the date of dedication.

records. Walker, *The Chronicles*, 94, claims that Antonino Pierozzi drew on Francesco's account for the *Chronicon* entry on Vincent Ferrer. So the archbishop's death in May 1459 may be a *terminus ante quem* for Francesco's composition. Sorbelli, "Una raccolta," 100, notes that Girolamo Albertucci de'Borselli, O.P., of Bologna, seems to have drawn on Francesco's account to make his own entry for Vincent Ferrer in the *Cronica*.

inc. epist.: Protulit ut nosti, R.P., diuersis etatibus egregios hispania uiros

des. epist.: et quid in posterum nobis hoc scribendi genus prosequendum censeas. Vale.

inc.: Beatus Vincentius ex Valentia, ciuitate Hispanie

des.: sit pro nobis perpetuus intercessor. Amen.[175]

MSS

1. Florence, BN, MS Conv. soppr. J VII 30 (411), fols. 36r–v (preface) and 36v–48v (*vita*). XV. Kristeller, *Iter* 1:163b. Source text.

2. Florence, BN, MS Magl. XXXVIII 142, fols. 41–42 (preface) and 42–58 (*vita*). XV. Kristeller, *Iter* 1:143a. Source text.

Editions

1. *Sermones Sancti Vincentii Fratris Ordinis Praedicatorum de Tempore*, in 3 parts, *pars hyemalis*. Venice: Jacobus Pentius, de Leuco, 1496. Facing sign. a2 (preface) and signs. a2–a5, with some deviations from the manuscripts. Goff F137; HC 7010*; *IGI* 10292, 10303, 10282; BMC 5:564; GW 9843.

GABRIELE da Crema, O.E.S.A.[176]

Lost. ⟨*Dialogus de vita Clarae Montefalcensis*⟩, O.E.S.A. (XIV)[177]

Evidence of this Latin composition, a dialogue between mother and son, remains only in the vernacular version by Gabriele, which was printed at Milan in 1504 and at Venice in 1515 (Schutte, PIVRB 134–135); for an example, see M. L. Gatti Perer, *Codici e incunaboli miniati della Biblioteca*

---

175. Cf. Girolamo Albertucci de'Borselli, *Cronica magistrorum generalium ordinis fratrum praedicatorum*, in Bologna, BU, MS 1999, fols. 155–160v, *inc.*: Hoc anno, scilicet 1418, beatus Vincentius de Valentia; *des.*: Satis suffitiant illa que narrata sunt et scripta que gessit in vita.

176. Not in Kristeller, "Contribution."

177. See n. 89 above.

Civica di Bergamo (Bergamo, 1989), no. 108: Bergamo, Bibl. Angelo Mai, MS MA 471 (Sigma 4.48). 1504 edition seen.

GADOLO, Bernardino, O. Cam. (1463–1499)[178]

BHL —. *De vita sanctissimi patris nostri Romualdi, de initio item successu et nobilitate ordinis nostri.* (XI)

No preface; letter in the form of historical report, written by Gadolo on August 30, 1496 to Jacopo Filippo Foresti, O.E.S.A. *(q.v.)*. This *vita* was the source of Foresti's entry on the history of the Camaldulensians, inserted into the revised Venice 1503 edition of his *Supplementum chronicarum,* at fols. 383v–384.[179]

inc. epistola: Scripsi hortatu tuo pater uenerande de uita sanctissimi patris nostri

des. epistola: mihi certum est. Vale, pater obseruandissime . . .

inc. vita: Romualdus abbas, pater et dux atque institutor ordinis camaldulensis

des. vita: magna incolarum frequentia ac celebritate deuotissime ueneratur.

inc. narratio de ordine: Eremus Camaldulensis que nunc tocius ordinis caput est

des. narratio (i.e., de vita Ambrosii Traversarii): Quae autem predictus scripsit haec. . . . Cronica Cassinensis quam latinam fecit. Finis.

MSS

1. Camaldoli, Archivio del Sacro Eremo, MS 734. XVIII. Kristeller, *Iter* 5:519b. Caby, "Bernardino Gadolo," 253. Not seen.

2. Camaldoli, Archivio del Sacro Eremo, MS 735, fols. 1–41. XV. Kristeller, *Iter* 5:519b. Cecile Caby, "Bernardino Gadolo ou les debuts de l'historiographie camaldule," *Memoirs de l'Ecole française de Rome, Moyen Age* 109, no. 1 (1997): 240 n. 40. Not seen.

Editions

1. Caby, "Bernardino Gadolo," 253–266. Source text.

---

178. G. Moro in *DBI* 41 (1998): 182b–184a; C. Caby, "Bernardino Gadolo ou les débuts de l'historiographie camaldule," *Mémoires de l'Ecole française de Rome* 109, no. 1 (1997): 240 n. 39 and 241. Caby's study, from which I take the title of Gadolo's historical report, is the source of this entry.

179. The insertion is edited in Caby, "Bernardino Gadolo," at 268. A similar report appears to have been used by Marc'Antonio Sabellico for the relevant entry in the *Enneades* (ed. in ibid., 267–268). On Romuald, see G. Fornasari, in *GLS* 1732a–1737a.

GARATONE, Cristoforo, of Treviso, bp. (ca. 1397–1449)[180]

In a letter to Giovanni Aurispa from Francesco Pizolpasso, dated Basel, May 15, 1435, mention is made of the apostolic secretary Garatone, asked by the pope to transcribe a multivolume Greek work on saints. This collection may have been a menology.[181]

GARZONI, Giovanni (ca. 1428–1506)[182]

BHL 138f. *Vita Agathae* (III)[183]

Preface, no dedicatee. The composition cannot be dated from internal evidence.

inc. proem.: Quanti aestimanda sint animi bona ab historiarum scriptoribus satis superque explicatum arbitror.

des. proem.: insolens est et omni egens consilio.

inc.: Decium secundo ducentesimae et septimae

des.: nec ultra progressa est.

MSS

1. Bologna, BU, MS 1622 III, fols. 229v–232. XV–XVI. Kristeller, *Iter* 1:24a; Poncelet 1924, 347, no. 17. Seen.

2. Bologna, BU, MS 1676, fols. 29–38. Poncelet 1924, 348, no. 3; G. Manfré, "La biblioteca dell'umanista bolognese Giovanni Garzone," *Accademie e biblioteche d'Italia* 27, no. 4 (1959): 249–278 and 28, nos. 1 3 (1960): 17 69, at 62. Source text.

Editions
None.

BHL 292d. *Vita beati Alexii* (V)[184]

Preface, no dedicatee. The composition cannot be dated from internal evidence.

---

180. Luigi Pesce, *Cristoforo Garatone, trevigiano, nunzio di Eugenio IV* (Rome: Herder, 1975); G. Moro, in *DBI* 52 (1998): 234b–238b.

181. See Giovanni Mercati, *Scritti di Isidoro il cardinale ruteno* (Rome, 1926), 106–116; and esp. Agostino Sottili, "Ambrosio Traversari, Francesco Pizolpasso, Giovanni Aursipa: Traduzioni e lettere," *Romanische Forschungen* 78 (1966): 58 and n. 90.

182. On Garzoni, see chap. 4 above.

183. G. D. Gordini in *BS* 1 (1961): 320–335; C. Crimi in *GLS* 29a–30b. Garzoni sets the narrative in the Decian persecution (Bologna, BU, MS 1676, fol. 30).

184. L. Leonardi in *GLS* 91a–92b.

inc. proem.: Quanto immortali deo simus beneficio deuincti hac coniectura facile consequi possumus

des. proem.: uitam sancte pie honestque actam ac decursam scribere. Finis prohemii.

inc.: Cum igitur Alexius primos illos annos in eorum[185]

des.: laudibus atque honoribus absumerentur.

MSS

1. Bologna BU MS 738, fols. 23–24 (preface) and 24–31v (*vita*). XV. Poncelet 1924, 327, no. 3; Manfré, "La biblioteca," 34; Frati, "Indice," 257, no. 430. Source text.

2. Bologna, BU, MS 1622 III, fols. 192v (preface), 193–196 (*vita*). XV–XVI. Kristeller, *Iter* 1:24a; Poncelet 1924, 347, no. 9. Source text.

Editions
None.

BHL 611b. *Vita divi Antonii* (IV)[186]

Preface to Johannes Blanchfeldus Berliniensis, a former student. Written by 1503, when it was first printed. See Lind, *Letters*, letter 54 and letter 77, for Garzoni's response to an attack on the *vita*.

inc. proem.: Saepe ac diu mecum cogitaui, uir eloquentissime

des. proem.: Cognosces profecto quanto fuerit Antonius uirtutibus ornatus.

des. proem. (MS 741): et quid sequendum sit, illi ante oculos ponere.

des. proem. (1503 edition): Cognosces profecto quantis fuerit Antonius uirtutibus ornatus.

inc.: Parente ortus est Antonius homine et nobili et severo

des.: uenia detur et impunitas.

MSS

1. Bologna, BU, MS 741, fols. 2–18v. Poncelet 1924, 236, no. 10, and 328, no. 1; Manfré, "La biblioteca," 36. Source text.

2. Bologna, BU, MS 1896, fols. 1–9v. XVI in. Kristeller, *Iter* 1:24b; Poncelet 1924, 352, no. 1. Source text.

Editions

1. Lind, *Letters*, 386–387, letter 452, preface only, taken from the 1503

---

185. The exemplar in Bologna, BU MS 1622 III (a late hand), has a different incipit: "Ut Gratianus excessit e vita, in eius locum Theodosius senior suffectus est." I have not collated these two lives.

186. A. A. R. Bastiaensen in *GLS* 176a–182a.

edition bound into Bol. BU MS 424 (732). See Poncelet 1924, 326, no. 10; and Manfré, "La biblioteca," 32.

2. *Vita Divi Antonii* (Bologna, 1503), signs. A–B4v. Seen.

BHL 798f/g. *Vita Augustini hipponensis* (V)

Preface, no dedicatee, although at one time Garzoni thought of making a dedication to a *Joannes*, evidently an Augustinian Hermit, whom the author compliments for his learning.[187] This account must have been written by about 1500, since Garzoni mentions the life to Leandro Alberti in a letter of that date.[188]

inc. proem.: Si illius caelestis ac diuinae domus felicitatem cum animis nostris consideraremus

des. proem.: quam pauci philosophorum doctrina praeceptisque instituti consequi potuerunt.

inc.: Tagastum ciuitas admodum nobilis

des.: Papiam delatum est.

MSS

1. Bologna, BU, MS 737, fols. 1–54v. XV. Poncelet 1924, 326, no. 1; Manfré, "La biblioteca," 33. The first part of this manuscript is heavily corrected. Source text.

2. Bologna, BU, MS 1622 III, fols. 267v (preface) and 267–280v (*vita*). XV–XVI in Kristeller, *Iter* I:24a; Poncelet 1924, 348, no. 24. Source text.

Editions
I am preparing an edition.

Lost. ⟨*Historia Blasii ep. et m.*⟩ (n.d.)[189]

Prefatory material, addressed to Giovanni Torfanino, seems to be lost. See Lind, *Letters*, letter 173, at 152: "Historiam de Blasio nuper a me scriptum quam tibi dicavi te lecturum puto." I take the title for the work from the author's reference to it as a *historia*. Garzoni dedicated several of his compositions to the Dominican Torfanino; see below. Included in figure 1.1 and table 2.1 (fourth century).

---

187. In Bologna, BU, MS 737, fol. 1, the deleted name "Joannes" can be made out. This could be Johannes Paxius Ripanus, who encouraged Garzoni to write about Augustine and helped Garzoni with the life. See Lind, *Letters*, 267–268, letter 334. Another letter (ibid., 208, letter 249) suggests that this life was dedicated to Cardinal Tamás Bakócz, protector of the Hermits.

188. Lind, *Letters*, 208, letter 249; cf. 310–311, letter 387.

189. A Bishop Blasius was martyred in Spain on February 2 under Nero (second century); another Blasius, bishop of Sebaste, was martyred under Licinius (fourth century), along

BHL 1496d. *Passio Caeciliae* (III)[190]

Preface, no dedicatee. Not able to be dated from internal evidence.

inc. proem.: Cum multorum martyrum confessorumque uitas, cruciatus, mortes, litteris prodiderim

des. proem.: precibus fatigabunt.

inc.: Cecilia ciuis Romana nobili genere nata sese ab ineunte aetate Christo dicauit.

des.: beatae uitae domicilium ingressa est.

MSS

1. Bologna, BU, MS 741, fols. 49v–50 (preface) and 50–56v (*vita*). Poncelet 1924, 329, no. 4; Manfré, "La biblioteca," 36. Source text.

2. Bologna, BU, MS 1896, fol. 25 (preface) and fols. 25–28v (*vita*). XVI in. Kristeller, *Iter* 1:24b; Poncelet 1924, 352, no. 4. Source text.

Editions
None.

BHL 1678d. *Vita gloriosissimae virginis Catharinae aegyptiacae* (IV)[191]

Preface, no dedicatee. Not able to be dated from internal evidence.

inc. proem.: Quoniam fatu fieri dixerim ut cum nostra et maiorum nostrorum memoria

des. proem.: scribere incipiam.

inc.: Alexandrum eum qui magnus appellatus est

des.: In haec uerba pons corruit, ipse a flumine absorptus est.

MSS

1. Bologna, BU, MS 738, fols. 4 (with acephalous preface) and 4v–17v (*vita*). Poncelet 1924, 326–327, no. 1; Manfré, "La biblioteca," 34. Source text.

2. Bologna, BU, MS 1622 III, fols. 184r–v (full preface), 184v–90 (*vita*). Kristeller, *Iter* 1:24; Poncelet 1924, 346, no. 7. Source text.

---

with nine women and children, on February 3. See *AASS* Feb. I (Paris, 1866): 324 on Blasius of Oretanus and 334 on Blasius of Sebaste. On the latter, probably Garzoni's subject, see G. D. Gordini in *BS* 3 (1963): 157–160, and P. Chiesa in *GLS* 316b–318b.

190. E. Josi in *BS* 3 (1963): 1064–1081; E. Giannarelli in GLS 409a–412b. Garzoni gives her date of death as 225 (BBU, MS 741, fol. 56v).

191. D. Balboni in *BS* 3 (1963): 954–963; M. Donnini in *GLS* 381b–383a. The title is from Bologna, BU, MS 1622 III, fol. 184r (a late copy). Garzoni sets the story of Katherine of Alexandria during the Diocletianic persecution; see Bologna, BU, MS 738, fol. 5v.

Editions
None.

BHL 1759f. *De cruciatibus et nece ⟨Christinae⟩ libellum* (III)[192]

Preface, no dedicatee. Garzoni mentions that he has already written the lives of many martyrs and confessors.[193]

inc. proem.: Qui Romanam historiam litteris prodiderunt
des. proem.: me omnibus contemnendum despiciendum praeberem.
inc.: Tirus admodum nobile fuit Ethrurie opidum
des.: plerique autumant.

MSS

1. Bologna, BU, MS 739, fols. 60v (preface) and 60v–71v (*vita*). Poncelet 1924, 328 (cf. 346); Manfré, "La biblioteca," 35. Source text.

2. Bologna, BU, MS 1622 III, fols. 207 (preface) and 207–212v (*vita*). Kristeller, *Iter* 1:24a; Poncelet 1924, 346, no. 3. Seen.

3. Bologna, BU, MS 2648, fols. 101r–v (preface) and 101–106v (*vita*). Poncelet 1924, 346, no. 3. Source text.

Editions
None known to me.

BHL 1779b. *Gloriosissimi martyris Christophori cananei vita* (III)[194]

Dedicatory preface to Johannes Blanchfeldus, a former student (see Garzoni's life of Anthony, above). This life was written by 1500.[195]

inc. proem.: Multis, et his quidem clarissimis uiris, id uite genus perbeatum uideri solet[196]
des. proem.: Suscipienda erit excusatio mea
inc.: Qui martyrum cruciatus mortesque memorie prodiderunt
des.: ad Christi fidem aduolaverit.

---

192. A. Amore in *BS* 4 (1964): 330–332. Garzoni dates Christina's death "a natali domini saluatoris anni agebantur duceni ottogeni septenii cum Diocleciano imperante" (Bologna, BU, MS 2648, fol. 106).

193. Bologna, BU, MS 2648, fol. 1v.

194. G. D. Gordini in *BS* 4 (1964): 349–353; G. Cremascoli in *GLS* 496a–499b. No references in the narrative allow me to date this martyr's death; he is traditionally taken to be a third-century saint.

195. See Lind, *Letters*, 167, letter 193, to Giovanni Torfanino, dated 1500: "Christophori mei tibi legendi copiam feci."

196. From the Leipzig 1510 edition of this work, which also includes a preface from Mathias Fromuth to Christophorus Cupenerius, dated at the end, "Lips. 16 calend. Aug. anno M.D.X." (sign. A1v–A2).

MSS
None are given by Poncelet, Manfré, or Frati.

Editions
1. *Vita Gloriosissimi Martyris Christophori Cananei*. Bologna: Benedetto Ettore, 1503. Not seen.
2. *Gloriosissimi Martyris Christophori Cananei Vita*, ed. M. Fromuth. Leipzig: Martinus Herbipolensis, 1510. Source text.

BHL 1976d. *Vita Cosmi et Damiani* (IV)[197]

Preface, no dedicatee. The composition cannot be dated from internal evidence.

inc. proem.: Vereor equidem ne Cosmi ac Damiani iram mihi concitauerim

des. proem.: Nullam profecto scientiae genus inueniunt in quo tot sanctissimi uiri floruerint.

inc.: Quo tempore ad Dioclitianum et Maximianum delatum

des.: nec cruciatus nec mortis eorum animos terruit.

MSS
1. Bologna, BU, MS 1622 III, fols. 242–244. Kristeller, *Iter* 1:24a; Poncelet 1924, 348, no. 20. Source text.
2. Bologna, BU, MS 1676, fols. 75–76v (preface) and 76v–83 (*vita*). Poncelet 1924, 349, no. 6; Manfré, "La biblioteca," 62. Source text.

Editions
None.

BHL 2236. *Vita divi Dominici*[198] (XIII)

Preface to Vincenzo Bandello, O.P. This account may have existed as early as the 1470s; Garzoni speaks of it again in the 1490s.[199] A secure *terminus ante quem* of 1494 is provided by Girolamo Albertucci de' Borselli's *Cronica magistrorum generalium ordinis fratrum Praedicatorum* (Bologna, BU, MS 1999).[200]

---

197. See n. 11 above. Garzoni set the narrative in the Diocletianic persecution (Bologna, BU, MS 1676, fol. 76v).

198. See n. 166 above. The title is given thus in Alberti, *De viris illlustribus*, fol. 7. In Bologna, BU, MS 1622 III, fol. 147, the title is *Vita Sancti Dominici*. See also Garzoni's *Laus Beati Dominici*, edited in Lind, *Letters*, letter 181, and the *Oratio de laudibus Sancti Dominici* in Bologna, BU, MS 732, fols. 107v–115v (Poncelet 1924, 325, no. 4; Manfré, "La biblioteca," 31).

199. See Lind, *Letters*, letter 67, to Vincenzo Malmignati, dated by Lind to the 1470s; letter 68, from Pomponius Laetus, dated by Lind 1493–1496; letter 180, to Leandro Alberti, dated by Lind to 1499.

200. See Sorbelli, "Una raccolta poco nota," 83, for the passage from this unedited chronicle.

inc. proem.: Quantum utilitatis et emolumenti consequantur

des. proem.: Nam si Aristoteles cum deposito philosophiae studio dicere cepisset et adolescentes docere summa erat in gloria, haud ipse, si cura historiarum scribendarum posthabita tam officiosam prouinciam mihi deposco, dedecore sum afficiendus.

inc.: Adriano Quarto pontifici maximo successit

des.: seque ab illorum oculis eripuerunt.

MSS

1. Bologna, BU, MS 744, fols. 1–29v. Poncelet 1924, 329, no. 1; Manfré, "La biblioteca," 41. Source text.

2. Bologna, BU, MS 1622 III, fols. 146v–171. Kristeller, *Iter* 1:24a; Poncelet 1924, 346, no. 5. Source text.

Editions

1. Alberti (*q.v.*), *De viris illustribus*, fols. 7–22v. Source text.

BHL 2763d. *Vita Eustachii* [*Placidii*] (II)[201]

Dedicatory preface, although the dedicatee, Johannes, is indicated only in the margins of one manuscript (BBU, MS 738, at fol. 33). The composition cannot be dated from internal evidence.

inc. proem.: Otioso mihi ac Eustachii historiam scribere, [*add. in marg.* humanissime Iohannes], uenit ad manus meas libellus quidam

des. proem.: Cum igitur libellum semel, iterum, tertio legeris, haud grauaberis eius legendi aliis copiam facere

inc.: Placitum eum is qui Eustachius appellatus est

des.: atque Eustachio dedicatum.

MSS

1. Bologna, BU, MS 738, fols. 33–34 (preface), 34–48 (*vita*). Poncelet 1924, 327, no. 4; Manfré, "La biblioteca," 34. Source text.

2. Bologna, BU, MS 1622 III, fols. 196v–203. Kristeller, *Iter* 1:24a; Poncelet 1924, 347, no. 10. Source text.

Editions
None known to me.

BHL 2850d and 6922e. *Historia Feliciani ⟨et Primi⟩* (IV)[202]

Dedicatory preface to Garzoni's friend and frequent correspondent "Trofanine pater" (the Dominican Giovanni Torfanino), only in *BHL* 2850d.

---

201. I. Daniele in *BS* 4 (1964): 281–289. Garzoni sets the narrative in the time of Trajan (Bologna, BU, MS 738, fol. 33v).

202. A. Amore in *BS* 10 (1968: 1104–1105. Garzoni sets the narrative in the Diocletianic persecution (Bologna, BU, MS 732, fol. 159v, and Bologna, BU, MS 738, fol. 48v).

The two *BHL* numbers assigned to this work, 2850d and 6922e, suggest that it consists of separate accounts, one treating Felicianus and the other Primus. But that is not the case. There are two drafts of a single *passio*; each draft treats both Felicianus and Primus. *BHL* 6922e seems to represent the author's final intentions. Torfanino appears to have taken orders recently, which might help to date the composition.

inc. proem. 2850d: Quam hii, cum quibus male agitur, uoluptatem, quae diuturna esse non potest, consequantur, haud scio[203]

des. proem.: Cognosces quanto hii gloriosissimi martyres fuerunt constantia praediti

inc.: Cum Diocletianus atque Maximianus a diis suis auxilia implorarent

des.: illis iusta magnifice fecerunt.

inc. proem 6922e: Quanta laude digne censeri debeant, qui pro sancta Christi religione sanguinem efuderunt, nullis possum uerbis consequi.[204]

des. proem.: ad ueram idest Christianum religionem euolerunt

inc.: Dioclicianus cum probitate polleret et prudentia

des.: ad christianam rempublicam aduolarunt.

MSS

1. Bologna, BU, MS 732, fols. 159r–v (preface) and 159v–160v (*vita*). Poncelet 1924, 325, no. 8; Manfré, "La biblioteca," 32 = *BHL* 2850d. Source text.

2. Bologna, BU, MS 738, fols. 48–51v. Poncelet 1924, 327, no. 5; Manfré, "La biblioteca," 34; Frati,"Indice," 257, no. 430 = *BHL* 6922e. Source text.

3. Bologna, BU, MS 1622 III, fols. 203v (preface), 203v–205 (*vita*). XV–XVI in. Kristeller, *Iter,* 1:24a; Poncelet 1924, 347, no. 11 = *BHL* 6922e. Source text.

Editions
None.

BHL 2884m. *Vita Felicis et Felicis [Adaucti]* (IV)[205]

Preface, no dedicatee. The composition cannot be dated from internal evidence.

inc. proem.: Quanto in Christianos Dioclitianus princeps exarserit odio

des. proem.: ac diuinae domus premium consecuti sunt

---

203. This preface is found in Bologna, BU, MS 732, at fol. 159.
204. This preface is found in Bologna, BU, MS 738, fol. 48, and MS 1622 III, fol. 203v. It apparently represents the author's final intentions.
205. V. Monachino in *BS* 7 (1966): 222–278; G. Leonardi in *GLS* 1022a–1028a.

inc.: Foelices duos et eos quidem ciues Romanos
des.: sempiternum cum Christo aeuum acturi.

MSS

1. Bologna, BU, MS 741, fols. 45–49. Poncelet 1924, 328, no. 3; Manfré, "La biblioteca," 36. Source text.

2. Bologna, BU, MS 1896 I, fols. 23–25. XVI in. Kristeller, *Iter* 1:24b; Poncelet 1924, 352, no. 3. Seen.

Editions
None.

BHL 3406g. *De cruciatibus atque obitu Georgii* (IV)[206]

Preface, no dedicatee. The composition cannot be dated from internal evidence.

inc. proem.: Semper ea fui sententia, ut martyribus Christianis, qui ut diuinam illam celestemque domum consequerentur

des. proem.: que suo loco explicabuntur a nobis.

inc.: Silena urbs est Lybis admodum nobilis

des.: Quae animo intendent ea perficient.

MSS

1. Bologna, BU, MS 738, fols. 52–61. Poncelet 1924, 327 no. 6; Manfré, "La biblioteca," 34. Source text.

2. Bologna, BU, MS 1622 III, fols. 205v–209. XVI in. Kristeller, *Iter* 1:24a; Poncelet 1924, 347, no. 12. Seen.

Editions
None.

BHL 3519f. *Vita Gervasii et Protasii* (III)[207]

Preface, no dedicatee. The composition cannot be dated from internal evidence. The preface declares the source: Ambrose.

inc. proem.: Quanta sit eorum, cum quibus bene actum est, futura felicitas

des. proem.: sic historiae fides accedit.

inc.: Cum Ambrosium plurimis curis confectum

des.: illis aedem aedificandam curauit.

---

206. D. Balboni in *BS* 6 (1964): 512–525; A. Labate in *GLS* 823b–825b. Garzoni sets the narrative in the time of the Diocletianic persecution (Bologna, BU, MS 738, fol. 57v).

207. A. Rimoldi in *BS* 6 (1964): 298–302; C. Pasini in *GLS* 794a–795b. Garzoni sets the time as the war of Diocletian and Maximian against the Marcomanni; see Bologna, BU, MS 1676, fol. 42.

MSS

    1. Bologna, BU, MS 1622 III, fols. 232v–234. XVI in. Kristeller, *Iter* 1:24a; Poncelet 1924, 347, no. 18. Source text.

    2. Bologna, BU, MS 1676, fols. 39–44v. Poncelet 1924, 349, no. 4; Manfré, "La biblioteca," 62. Source text.

Editions
None.

BHL 3645e. *Vita Gregorii papae* (VII)[208]

The preface does not name a dedicatee.[209] The *terminus post quem* is 1478.[210]

    inc. proem.: Vereor equidem ne sint qui me impudentissimum existiment

    des. proem.: quid sequendum sit ante oculos ponit.

    inc.: Gregorio ciui Romano parentes fuerunt

    des.: in sepulchro constitutum.

MSS

    1. Bologna, BU, MS 737, fols. 57–76. Poncelet 1924, 326, no. 2; Manfré, "La biblioteca," 33. Source text.

    2. Bologna, BU, MS 1622 III, fols. 282–289v. XVI in. Kristeller, *Iter* 1:24a; Poncelet 1924, 348, no. 25. Source text.

Editions
None.

BHL 3794d. *Vita b. Helenae utinensis*, O.E.S.A. (d. 1458)[211]

Preface to Johannes Paxius Ripanus, O.E.S.A., who provided Garzoni's source. The *terminus post quem* appears to be 1497–April 17, 1501; these dates are assigned to the exchange of letters between the author and his patron by Lind, *Letters*, letters 457–458.

    inc. proem.: Summum illum opificem edificatoremque mundi Deum

    des. proem.: magna ex eo sis uoluptate precepturus. Vale.

    inc.: Iapedia regio est Italiae

    des.: in aedicula sepeliendi consilium fuerit.

    inc. epist. Ioannis Paxii: Venit ad manus meas

    inc. responsio Garzonii: Alexander nepos tuus

---

    208. V. Monachino in *BS* 7 (1966): 222–278; G. Leonardi in *GLS* 1022a–1028a.

    209. But in Bologna, BU, MS 737, at fols. 57 and 58, Garzoni writes and then cancels "prestantissime doctor."

    210. See Bologna, BU, MS 737, fol. 57r–v.

    211. See chap. 5 above for a discussion of this saint and this account.

MSS

    1. Bologna, BU, MS 752, iv, fols. 56–81. Not in Poncelet; Manfré, "La biblioteca," 49. With letters.

    2. Bologna, BU, MS 1622 III, fols. 244v–252v. XVI in. Kristeller, *Iter* 1:24a; Poncelet 1924, 348, no. 21.

Editions

None. For the exchange of letters, see Lind, *Letters.*

BHL 3877d. Oration. *Amplissima laus beati Hieronymi*[212]

Garzoni may have written this oration in the 1470s.[213] The *BHL* editors identify it as a *vita*, but I do not count it among the *vitae* in figure 1.1.

    inc.: Vereor equidem, praestantissimi uiri

    des.: in huius doctissimi ac sanctissimi uiri laudationem conferam.

MSS

    1. Bologna, BU, MS 742, fols. 116v–119v. Poncelet 1924, 329; Manfré, "La biblioteca," 39. Source text.

    2. Bologna, BU, MS 1622 III, fols. 69–71. XVI in. Kristeller, *Iter* 1:24a; Poncelet 1924, 346, no. 1. Source text.

    3. Bologna, BU, MS 2648, fols. 218–219. Poncelet 1924, 358, no. 4. Seen.

Editions
None.

BHL 3967d. *De cruciatibus et morte Hippoliti* (IV)[214]

Dedicatory preface to Garzoni's Dominican friend and frequent correspondent Giovanni Torfanino. It mentions slightingly Garzoni's source, Jacobus de Voragine.

    inc. proem.: Non gravabor, Trofanine pater, Hyppoliti gloriosissimi martyris cruciatum mortemque litteris mandare

    des. proem.: sed relinquendus cum ignorantia sua.

    inc.: Hyppolitus cum Laurentii de quo alio loco

    des.: res minime obscura erit.

---

212. A. Penna in *BS* 6 (1964): 1109–1132; V. Grossi in *GLS* 947a–958a.

213. See Lind, *Letters*, letter 70, to Johannes Paxius Ripanus, O.E.S.A., and letter 71, to Vincenzo Malmignati of Ferrara, both dated by Lind to the 1470s.

214. Garzoni sets the narrative in the time of the Diocletianic persecution (Bologna, BU, MS 732, fol. 146). For Hippolytus's companion, Vitus, see below.

MSS

   1. Bologna, BU, MS 732, fols. 144–157v. Poncelet 1924, 347, no. 15;
Manfré, "La biblioteca," 32; Frati, "Indice," 256, no. 424 (Frati does not
mention Vitus). Source text.

Editions
None.

BHL 4323cb. *Vita Johannis apostoli* (I)[215]

Preface, no dedicatee. This composition cannot be dated from internal
evidence.

   inc. proem.: Etsi multa existunt quae cum dignitate litteris mandare
poteram

   des. proem.: neque oratores, ut uerbis utar M. Tullii, quicquam magna
laude digna sine usu et exercitatione consequi possunt

   inc.: Domicianus is qui post Neronem in Christianos

   des.: ut quisque uolet, accipiat.

MSS

   1. Bologna, BU, MS 1622 III, fols. 221v–226v. XVI in. Kristeller, *Iter*
1:24a; Poncelet 1924, 347, no. 15. Source text.

   2. Bologna, BU, MS 1676, fols. 1–20v. Poncelet 1924, 348, no. 1; Manfré, "La biblioteca," 62. Seen.

Editions
None.

BHL 4772d. *Vita Laurentii* (III)[216]

Brief introductory remarks. This composition cannot be dated from internal evidence.

   inc.: Quod in praesenti nactus sum otii

   des.: ubi ab eis in sepulchro constitutum est.

MSS

   1. Bologna, BU, MS 1622 III, fols. 227–229 (fragmentary). XVI in.
Kristeller, *Iter* 1:24a; Poncelet 1924, 346, no. 16. Source text.

   2. Bologna, BU, MS 1676, fols. 21–28. Poncelet 1924, 348 no. 2.
Source text.

---

215. T. Stramare in *BS* 6 (1964): 599–616; E. Lupieri in *GLS* 858a–861b.

216. S. Carletti in *BS* 8 (1966): 108–121; E. Susi in *GLS* 1213b–1215a. Garzoni correctly
sets the narrative under Decian and Valerianus (Bologna, BU, MS 1676, fol. 21r–v).

Editions
None.

BHL 4996d. *Vita Luciae* (IV)[217]

Dedicatory preface to a Bonifacio, probably Garzoni's former student
Bonifacio da Casale, O.P., praising his entry into orders. See Lind, *Letters*,
454–455, letters 15–17.

inc. proem.: Quid praestantius efficere poteris, Bonifaci pater optime,
cum te religione dicasti, non facile dixerim.

des. proem.: Nec paruam tibi uoluptatem afferet libelli lectio cum quam
intelliges in tribuendis deo laudibus, in reddendo deo officio, in adolescentibus
ad bonam frugam deducendis, constantium memoratu esse dignissimam.

inc.: Urbem Syracusanam incolebat Euricia matrona
des.: proclium secundum fecerunt.

MSS
1. Bologna, BU, MS 741, fols. 121–133. Poncelet 1924, 329, no. 5;
Manfré, "La biblioteca," 36. Source text.
2. Bologna, BU, MS 1896, fols. 70–77v (fragmentary). XVI in. Kristeller, *Iter* 1:24b; Poncelet 1924, 352, no. 5. Source text.

Editions
None.

BHL 5309d. *De suppliciis Margaritae* (IV)[218]

No preface, no dedicatee, undatable.
inc.: Anthiochia nobilis admodum est Syrie civitas
des.: securi percussa est.

MSS
1. Bologna, BU, MS 738, fols. 82–86v. Poncelet 1924, 327, no. 8; Manfré, "La biblioteca," 34. Source text.
2. Bologna, BU, MS 1622 III, fols. 219v–221. XVI in. Kristeller, *Iter*
1:24a; Poncelet 1924, 347, no. 14. Source text.

Editions
None.

---

217. A. Amore in *BS* 8 (1966): 241–252; T. Sardella in *GLS* 1228a–1231a.
218. J.-M. Sauget in *BS* 8 (1966): 1150–1160; M. Arnoldi in *GLS* 1371a–1373a. Garzoni mentions the usual prefect of Antioch named Olimbrius (*recte* Olybrius); see Bologna,
BU, MS 738, fol. 82. Although Margaret is apocryphal, she is traditionally assigned a death
date in the Diocletian persecution. I take Garzoni's mention of Olimbrius to indicate that he
follows this ascription.

Lost? ⟨*Vita Mauritii*⟩

Garzoni mentions this account in a letter to Leandro Alberti, addressing him as *frater* and therefore writing after November 1493, when Alberti joined the Dominicans. Garzoni knows that Alberti takes great pleasure in saints' lives, and Alberti has evidently asked specifically for this one. See Lind, *Letters*, letter 4, and above, under Marcantonio Flamini, for the life of a Mauritius Panonius, O.P., considered a *beatus* from 1494.[219] Not included in figure 1.1.

BHL 6067d. *Nerei et Achillei sanctissimos martires* (I)[220]

Preface, no dedicatee. The composition cannot be dated from internal evidence

inc. proem.: Domicianus et qui apud ipsum auctoritate poterant et uoluntate

des. proem.: quod ad praesens planum faciam. Finus prohemii.

inc.: Domiciano Caesari frater fuit quidem

des.: de uita exierunt.

MSS

1. Bologna, BU, MS 738, fols. 17v–21v. Poncelet 1924, 327, no. 2; Manfré, "La biblioteca," 34. Source text.

2. Bologna, BU, MS 1622 III, fols. 190v–192. XVI in. Kristeller, *Iter* 1:24a; Poncelet 1924, 347, no. 8. Source text.

Editions
None.

BHL —. *Vita Nicholai* (IV)[221]

Incipit mutilated, so no prefatory material. The composition cannot be dated from internal evidence.

---

219. I have not collated Lind's letter 4 against the sole copy, in Bologna, BU, MS 842 (1896, i), but it is possible that rather than *Mauritii* one should read here *Maurit<an>ii*, so that instead of a reference to a missing saint's life, this is a reference to Garzoni's lost *De Dioclitiani crudelitate, qua in Mauritanis usus est libellus* (cf. Vincenzo Fassini [pseud. Dionysius Sandellius], *De vita et scriptis Joannis Garzonis Bononiensis . . .* [Brescia: Petrus Vescovus, 1781], no. 28). See Lind, *Letters*, letter 153, dedicating that *libellus* to Leandro Alberti and comparing Diocletian's cruelty in Nicomedia to that in Mauretania.

220. U. M. Fasola in *BS* 9 (1967): 813–820; E. Susi in *GLS* 1470a–1471a. The title is from Bologna, BU, MS 1622 III, fol. 190v. Garzoni sets the narrative in the time of Domitian (Bologna, BU, MS 738, fol. 17v).

221. N. Del Re in *BS* 9 (1967): 923–939; G. Cioffari and N. Del Re in *BS* suppl. (1987): 972–976; O. Limone in *GLS* 1483b–1488a. According to Garzoni, Nicholas died in 343; see Bologna, BU, MS 732, fol. 17v.

inc.: . . . ⟨ma⟩trona nulla egens virtute matrimonio coniungebatur
des.: Difficile est in tantis mundi illecebris nullo errore labi.

MSS
1. Bologna, BU, MS 732, fols. 57–78. Poncelet 1924, 325, no. 1; Manfré, "La biblioteca," 31. Source text.

Editions
None.

BHL 6578d. Epistola. *De laudibus b. Pauli apostoli*[222]

Not a *vita* but a letter to Johannes Paxius Ripanus, edited by Lind, *Letters*, letter 417, from two manuscript exemplars: Bologna, BU, MS 1896 I and MS 1622 II. For additional manuscripts, see Poncelet 1924, 329 and no. 2, on MS 742, at fols. 125v–127. Cf. Manfré, "La biblioteca," 32; not given in Frati, "Indice." Poncelet 1924, 326, no. 9, records yet another copy in MS 732, fols. 164v–167. Cf. Manfré, "La biblioteca," 32; Frati, "Indice," 260, no. 434. Garzoni expressed his intention to write a *vita* of Paul; see Lind, *Letters*, letters 417, 111, and 174. Not included in figure 1.1.

Lost. ⟨*Vita Petronii*⟩ (IV)[223]

See Niccolo Burzio, *Bononia illustrata*, published in Bologna in 1494 by Plato de Benedictis, at sign. b5v, recording that Garzoni, an "orator facundissimus," wrote a "hystoria[] diui Petronii luculentissime descripta[]." See also Poncelet 1924, 329, on Bologna, BU, MS 746, missing fols. 1–28, which once held a life of Petronius.

BHL 6725. *Vita Petri Martyris* (XIII)[224]

Dedicatory preface to Vincenzo [Malmignati].[225] Possibly written well after the *terminus post quem* of 1478.[226]

inc. proem.: Qui pro patria mortem occubuissent
des. proem.: necte ullum simulationis genus delectat.

---

222. A. Penna and D. Balboni in *BS* 10 (1968): 164–212; R. Penna in *GLS* 1567b–1578a
223. G. Gordini in *BS* 10 (1968): 521–530; P. Golinelli in *GLS* 1599a–1600a.
224. See n. 169 above.
225. Bologna, BU, MS 741, fol. 140r–v.
226. Garzoni's earliest traceable contacts with Vincenzo Malmignati date to the 1470s; see Lind, *Letters*, e.g., letter 67; I follow Lind's dating. In a letter to Vincenzo da Piacenza, Garzoni mentions having written lives of Dominic, Augustine, Gregory, Peter Martyr, and Thomas Aquinas. The order of this list is strange, and if it indicates the chronological order in which the lives were written, then the date mentioned in the life of Gregory (1478) provides a *terminus post quem* for the lives of Peter Martyr and Thomas Aquinas and a *terminus ante quem* for the lives of Dominic and Augustine.

inc.: Quibus Petrus ortus sit parentibus

des.: hunc non mediocri uerborum honore prosequar.

MSS

1. Bologna, BU, MS 736, fols. 31–43. Poncelet 1924, 326; Manfré, "La biblioteca," 33; Frati, "Indice," 256, no. 428. Seen.

2. Bologna, BU, MS 741, fols. 146–156v. Poncelet 1924, 329, no. 6; Manfré, "La biblioteca," 36; Frati, "Indice," 259, no. 433, twenty-third item in codex. Seen.

3. Bologna, BU, MS 1622 III, fols. 132–140v. XVI in. Kristeller, *Iter* 1:24a; Poncelet 1924, 346, no. 4. Seen.

4. Bologna, BU, MS 1896, fols. 85–91v. XVI in. Kristeller, *Iter* 1:24b; Poncelet 1924, 352, no. 6. Not given in Frati. Seen.

Editions

1. Alberti (*q.v.*), *De viris illustribus*, fols. 52–55v. Source text.

BHL 6922e. *De obitu Primi et Feliciani*

See above under Felicianus.

BHL 6957d [unattributed]. *Exitus Proculi* (VI)[227]

Dedicatory preface to Lodovico, apparently a former student who had been a good reader of the orators and poets.[228] The composition cannot be dated from internal evidence.

inc. proem.: Cum prioribus annis plurium martyrum cruciatus mortesque litteris mandauerim

des. proem.: omnia enim quae a sapientissimus uiris ad bene uiuendum tradita sint, summo studio curaque didicisti.

inc.: A natali Domini Saluatoris anni agebantur

des.: ubi a christianis in sepulchro constitutum est, iter direxerit.

MSS

1. Bologna, BU, MS 732, fols. 93v–100. Poncelet 1924, 325, no. 3; Manfré, "La biblioteca," 31; Frati, "Indice," 255, no. 424, fifth item in codex. Source text.

---

227. G. D. Gordini in *BS* 10 (1968): 1152–1154; P. Golinelli in *GLS* 1673b–1674. Garzoni dates the passion "a natali Domini Salvatoris anni agebantur quincenti et vigeni [520], cum a Iustino imperatore Anastasio successum est," under the prefect Marinus (Bologna, BU, MS 732, fol. 94v).

228. For two possibilities, Lodovico Orlandini, prior of the Dominicans at Santo Spirito, and the theologian Lodovico Campana of Verona, see Lind, *Letters*, letter 459; Lind's notes, 559–60; and the poem edited by Lind, xiii.

Editions
None.

BHL —. *Vita sancti Sebastiani* (IV)[229]

Preface, no dedicatee. The composition cannot be dated from internal evidence.

inc. proem.: Urbs Romana, quantum ex historiarum fontibus haurire potui

des. proem.: Nunquam Diocletianus ipsum ut deos falsos coleret, in eam sententiam adduxit.

inc.: Sebastianus quibus ortus sit parentibus nobilibusne

des.: Paucis post annis est a christianorum persecutione cessatum. Finis.

MSS

1. Bologna, BU, MS 1622 III, fols. 234v–235 (preface) and 235–241v (*vita*). XVI in. Kristeller, *Iter* 1:24a; Poncelet 1924, 347, no. 19. Source text.

2. Bologna, BU, MS 1676, fols. 49–73v. Poncelet 1924, 349, no. 5; Manfré, "La biblioteca," 62; Frati "Indice," 375, no. 866. Source text.

Editions
None.

BHL 7767d. *De obitu Simonis* (d. 1475)[230]

Preface, no dedicatee. Simon's death provides a *terminus post quem*.[231]

inc. proem.: Quam pertinaciter innanis erroribus inhereant iudei

des. proem.: diuina iustitia sic instituente.

inc.: Tridentum ciuitas est admodum nobilis

des.: mea uersabitur oratio.

MSS

1. Bologna, BU, MS 732, fols. 132–142. Poncelet 1924, 324, no. 6; Manfré, "La biblioteca," 32; Frati, "Indice," 256, no. 424, twelfth item in codex. Source text.

---

229. G. D. Gordini in *BS* 11 (1968): 775–789; F. Scorza Barcellona in *GLS* 1768a–1769b. Garzoni sets the martyrdom in the time of Diocletian and Maximian.

230. I. Rogger in *BS* 11 (1968): 1184–1187; for notice of this account see P. O. Kristeller, "The Alleged Ritual Murder of Simon of Trent (1475) and Its Literary Repercussions: A Bibliographical Study," *Proceedings of the American Academy for Jewish Research* 59 (1993): 113.

231. See Lind, *Letters*, letter 19, in which Garzoni praises an account of Simon by Rodericus of Bohemia, his student.

Editions
None.

Lost. *Sancti Symphoriani libellum* (n.d.)[232]

Only the letters of dedication are extant. Garzoni dedicated the composition at least twice: to a *Iurisconsultus* and in 1500 to Cardinal Tamás Bakócz. See Lind, *Letters*, letters 188 and 154. Lind mistakenly says that the paired narratives of Hippolytus and Symphorianus are extant in Bologna, BU, MS 732, fols. 144–157v (that account pairs Vitus and Hippolytus). Since the *passio* of Symphorianus undoubtedly existed, Garzoni may have substituted Vitus for Symphorianus as the figure paired with Hippolytus. Included in figure 1.1 (fourth century).

> *inc. epist. ad iuriscon.*: Quanti uirtus aestimanda sit
> *inc. epist. ad card.*: Egregia excellensque uirtus tua

BHL 8086d. *Vita sancti Theodori* (III–IV)[233]

Dedicatory preface to "Frater Io. Ma.m Venetum," whom Garzoni describes as general of the Augustinian Canons Regular at San Salvator in Venice.[234] None of the manuscripts bears a date.

> *inc. proem.*: Semper mea sententia fuit, praestantissime pater, ut qui martyrio
> *des. proem.*: ut qui se religioni addixerint te imitari possint ac debeant.
> *inc.*: Quibus parentibus natus sit Theodorus
> *des.*: quae, ne longior essem, praetereunda duxi.

MSS

1. Bologna, BU, MS 740, fols. 55–75. Poncelet 1924, 328, no. 2; Manfré, "La biblioteca," 35; Frati, "Indice," 257, no. 432, fifth item in codex. Source text.

2. Bologna, BU, MS 1622 III, fols. 253r (preface), 253v–258 (*vita*). XVI in. Kristeller, *Iter* 1:24a; Poncelet 1924, 348, no. 22. Source text.

3. Bologna, BU, MS 2648, fols. 24v–31. Poncelet 1924, 358, no. 2; Frati, "Indice," 78, no. 1391. Source text.

Editions
None.

---

232. M.-O. Garrigues in *BS* 11 (1968): 1216–1217. Symphorian's martyrdom is traditionally assigned to the second or third centuries.

233. A. Amore in *BS* 12 (1969): 238–241. Garzoni sets the martyrdom in the time of Emperor Maximianus (285–306), under a Licinius; see Bologna, BU, MS 2648, fol. 25.

234. Cf. Lind, *Letters*, letter 330 and letter 411, for Garzoni's acquaintance with Giovanni Mariano's preaching ability; Giovanni Mariano da Gennazzano was an Augustinian Hermit.

BHL 8160d. *Vita Thomae Aquinatis* (XIII)[235]

Preface to Leandro Alberti. It does not seem possible to date this life.[236]
inc. proem.: Hercules, ut apud Xenophontem scribitur
des. proem.: quae hominem in pernitiem ducere solent.
inc.: Aquinum Latinorum admodum nobilis est ciuitas
des.: opportet uerum etiam necesse est.

MSS

1. Bologna, BU, MS 738, fols. 61v–80v. Poncelet 1924, 327, no. 7; Manfré, "La biblioteca," 34; Frati, "Indice," 257, no. 430. Seen.

2. Bologna, BU, MS 741, fols. 19v–33v. Poncelet 1924, 328, no. 2; Manfré, "La biblioteca," 36; Frati, "Indice," 358, no. 433, second item in codex. Seen.

3. Bologna, BU, MS 744, fols. 31–39. Poncelet 1924, 329, no. 2; Manfré, "La biblioteca," 41; Frati, "Indice," 261, no. 436. Seen.

4. Bologna, BU, MS 1622 III, fols. 172 (preface), 172v–179 (*vita*). XVI in. Kristeller, *Iter* 1:24a; Poncelet 1924, 346, no. 6. Seen.

5. Bologna, BU, MS 1622 III, fols. 209v–210 (preface), 210–219 (*vita*). XVI in. Kristeller, *Iter* 1:24a; Poncelet 1924, 347, no. 13. Seen.

6. Bologna, BU, MS 1896, fols. 10–17v. XVI in. Kristeller, *Iter* 1:24b; Poncelet 1924, 352, no. 2; not given in Frati, "Indice."[237] Seen.

Editions

1. Alberti (*q.v.*), *De viris illustribus*, fols. 130–135. Source text.

Lost. ⟨*Vita sancti Vincentii Ferreri*⟩ (d. 1419)[238]

For this account of the theologian and thaumaturge Vincent Ferrer, see Lind, *Letters*, 500, in a note to letter 274. Garzoni's letters touching on the Dominican *vitae* do not, however, mention such a life. Cf. Sandellius, *De vita et scriptis Joannis Garzonis*, 20, no. 1, recording the publication of a miscellaneous group of Garzoni's *vitae* in Bologna, first by Hector in 1505 and then again by an unnamed printer in 1515, among which appears a "Vincentius," not further specified. I have not been able to trace either of these printings.

---

235. See n. 171 above.

236. Lind was unable to date the letters that mention the life. See Lind, *Letters*, letters 36, 254, 284, and 387.

237. According to Poncelet, all these manuscripts provide the same text, which corresponds to the printed version. My collation of BBU MS 738 with Alberti's edition suggests some revision.

238. See n. 94 above.

BHL 8715b. *De cruciatibus et morte Viti* (IV)

Dedicatory preface to Johannes Torfaninus. See under Hippolytus above.
   inc. proem.: Immortale ac diuinum apostolis ac martyribus
   des. proem.: non uerebor in posterum aggredi maiora.
   inc.: Vitus qui deos falsos contemneret
   des.: dum spiritum duxero.

MSS
   1. Bologna, BU, MS 732, fols. 145–155. Poncelet 1924, 325, no. 7.
Source text.

Editions
None known to me.

GEORGE of Trebizond (1395–1472/73)[239]

BHL 444. cf. *BHG* 2024d. *De beato Andrea Chio* (d. 1465)[240]

Introductory remarks. George wrote his life of Andrea, who was martyred
by the Turks on May 29, 1465, St. George's day, two years after making a
vow for safety during a storm at sea. The account was begun on April 23,
1468, "and finished soon after."[241]
   inc.: Quando iam Tirennio e Creta Constantinopolim nauigassem
   des.: sic insurgentes in Italia Platonicos intercessione tua reprime.

MSS
John Monfasani, ed., *Collectanea Trapezuntiana* (Binghamton, N.Y.:
MRTS, 1984), 597: "I have not found a single manuscript."

Editions
All are late. See Monfasani, *Collectanea*, 598.

BHL —. *BHG* 186. Oratio. ⟨translation of Gregory of Nazianzen, *Oratio
in laudem sancti Athanasii funebris*⟩[242]

A single dedicatory preface to Nicholas V serves this *oratio* and the following one on Basil, both translated from the Greek. Monfasani dates

---

239. P. Viti, in *DBI* 55 (2000): 373b–382b. See also George's sermon to Paul II, "Quod
Ioannes evangelista non sit adhuc mortuus," written in 1450–1451; John Monfasani, *George
of Trebizond* (Leiden: Brill, 1976), 90ff., and idem, ed., *Collectanea Trapezuntiana* (Binghamton, N.Y.: MRTS, 1984), 574–576, no. CXLVI, with 30, 65, and 67.
   240. N. di Grigoli in *BS* 1 (1961): 1126–1127.
   241. See Monfasani, *George of Trebizond*, 189; Viti, in *DBI* 55 (2000): 378a.
   242. D. Stiernon in *BS* 2 (1962): 522–544; A. A. R. Bastiaensen in *GLS* 216b–221a.

both to "some time between late December 1451 and the end of April 1452."[243] Not included in figure 1.1.

inc. proem.: Gregorius ille Nazazenus, cui cognomen theologia dedit

des. proem.: Nunc ipsi Latine dicenti aures suas tua sanctitas prebeat.

inc.: Cum laudandi Athanasii munus susceperim, uirtutem ipsam mihi opus est laudare.

des.: sin uero bella imminent, reducas ad te atque assumas et tecum atque cum tuis colloces, quamuis magna petitio sit in ipso Christo, deo nostro, cui gloria in secula seculorum.

MSS

1. Padua, Bibl. Cap., MS D 44, fols. 277v–287v. XV. Monfasani, *Collectanea*, 40; cf. Kristeller, *Iter* 2:6b. Not seen.

2. St. Petersburg, former Library of the Roman Catholic Academy, no shelfmark, fols. 329–353 (both Basil and Athanasius). XV. Lost: see Monfasani, *Collectanea*, 24.

3. Valencia, Bibl. de la Catedral, MS 231, fols. 157v–170v. XV. Monfasani, *Collectanea*, 54. Not seen.

4. Vatican City, BAV, MS lat. 4249, fols. 65v–92r. XV. Kristeller, *Iter* 2:326a; Monfasani, *Collectanea*, 68 and 727, "with autograph corrections." Source text.

5. Venice, BN Marciana, MS Lat. X 83 (3302), fol. 146, incomplete. XV. Kristeller, *Iter* 2:231a; Monfasani, *Collectanea*, 72. Not seen.

6. Warsaw, Bibl. Narodowa, MS Baworowski 74, fols. 36–50. XV. Kristeller, *Iter* 4:419b–420a; Monfasani, *Collectanea*, 75. Not seen.

Editions

1. Monfasani, *Collectanea*, 300–301, preface only. Source text.

BHL—. BHG 245. ⟨**translation of Gregory of Nazianzen, *Oratio in laudem Basilii Magni funebris*⟩**[244]

Preface to Nicholas V, shared with the preceding oration for Athanasius. All information from Monfasani, *Collectanea*. Not included in figure 1.1.

inc.: Cum multas nobis dicendi causas magnus Basilius semper proponeret

des.: Nos autem, si quicquam laude orationeque dignum fecerimus, quis laudabit post te nature cessuros?

---

243. Monfasani, *George of Trebizond*, 73–74; Viti, in *DBI* 55 (2000): 376a–b.
244. See n. 51 above.

MSS

1. Padua, Bib. cap., MS D 44, fols. 262–277v. XV. Kristeller, *Iter* 2:6b; Monfasani, *Collectanea*, 40. Not seen.

2. Rieti, BC, Fondo di Sant'Antonio del monte, MS O I 21, excerpts (lacking the oration on Athanasius). XV. Kristeller, *Iter* 2:86b; Monfasani, *Collectanea*, 46 and 726. Not seen.

3. St. Petersburg, former Library of the Roman Catholic Academy, no shelfmark, fols. 392–353 (both Athanasius and Basil). XV. Lost; see Monfasani, *Collectanea*, 24.

4. Valencia, Bibl. de la Catedral, MS 231, 126v–157v. XV. Kristeller, *Iter* 4:650a; Monfasani, *Collectanea*, 54 and 726. Not seen.

5. Vatican City, BAV, MS lat. 4249, fols. 3–65. XV. Kristeller, *Iter* 2:326a; Monfasani, *Collectanea*, 68 and 727, "with autograph corrections." Source text.

6. Venice, BN Marciana, MS Lat. X 83 (3302),fols. 101–146. XV. Kristeller, *Iter* 2:231a; Monfasani, *Collectanea*, 72. Not seen.

7. Warsaw, Bibl. Narodowa, MS Baworowski 74, fols. 1–36. XV. Kristeller, *Iter* 4:419b–420a; Monfasani, *Collectanea*, 75. Not seen.

Editions

1. For the preface, see the preceding entry.

BHL — . BHG 2278. *De vita Moysis* (translation of Gregory of Nyssa, *De perfecta hominis vita*). (Bibl.)

Dedicatory preface to Cardinal Lodovico Trevisan. Probably written in 1446.[245]

inc. proem.: Nuper, Reuerendissime pater, beati Gregorii Nyseni de uita Moysi

des. proem.: qua sola, meo iudicio, uita hominis perficitur.

inc.: Quemadmodum qui certamen equorum non sine magna delectatione animi spectant, etsi nihil ad cursum diligentie illi pretermittant quos uincere optant, oculis tamen cursum ipsorum soliciti perspicientes clamant atque hortantur

des.: Id enim certe perfectio es ut non timore penarum sicuti mancip-

---

245. See Helen Brown Wicher, "Gregorius Nyssenus," *CTC* V (Washington, D.C.: Catholic University of America, 1984), 182–185; Monfasani, *George of Trebizond*, 57 and *ad indicem*; idem, *Collectanea*, 727–729. From this last, which should be consulted especially for the evaluation of George's translation, I take my list of manuscripts.

ium a vitiis declines nec uirtutem spe premiorum quasi mercator amplectaris, sed unum tantummodo terribile arbitreris ab amicitia dei repelli, unum expectibile solum amicitiam dei qua solo meo iudicio uita hominis perficitur.

MSS

1. Bologna, BU, MS 2682, not after 1495, fols. 4v–100, with preface; owned by Peter Váradi. Monfasani, *Collectanea*, 8, 728. Not seen.

2. Florence, Bibl. Laurenziana, MS Fiesol. 45, fols. 243–267v; with preface. Monfasani, *Collectanea*, 18 and 728. Manuscript given by Cosimo de'Medici to the Regular Canons. Not seen.

3. Kraków, BU Jagiellonska, MS 1286, fols. 147v–191, with preface. XV. Kristeller, *Iter* 4:405b; Monfasani, *Collectanea*, 22. Not seen.

4. Vatican City, BAV, MS Urb. Lat. 399, fols. 201–239, with preface. 1482. Monfasani, *Collectanea*, 58. Not seen.

5. Vatican City, BAV, MS Vat. Lat. 255, fols. 3–60, with preface. XV. Monfasani, *Collectanea*, 61. Not seen.

6. Vatican City, BAV, MS Vat. Lat. 4534, fols. 152–188v, autograph draft without preface. XV. Monfasani, *Collectanea* 69 and 728. Seen SLU reel 7330.

7. Vienna, Österreichische NB, MS Lat. 3457, fols. 1–91, with preface. XV. Monfasani, *Collectanea*, 76 and 728. Not seen.

Editions

1. *Gregorii episcopi nyseni viri et vitae sanctitate et ingenii magnitudine inter graecos christianae professionis assertores praecipui de vitae perfectione sive vita Moysi liber utilissimus per Georgium Trapezuntium e graeco in latino conversus* (Vienna: Hieronymus Victor for Leonardus and Luca Alantseae, December 1517).

2. *Gregorii nyseni vetustissimi theologi mystica mosaecae vitae enarratio perfectam formulam vivendi cuilibet christiano praescribens Georgio Trapezuntio interprete* (Basel: Andreas Cratander, May 1521).

3. For later editions, see Monfasani, *Collectanea*, 728.

Lost? *Liber collectarius in sacra pagina*

Giovanni Mercati, *Codici latini Pico Grimani Pio* . . . (Studi e testi 75) (Vatican City, 1938), at 4, item 28, and n. 3, hypothesizes that this autograph *liber*, found among Cardinal Marco Grimani's books, might have been either a synaxary or the *Methodus et ratio, ad quam reperiri possint anni totius festa quae celebrantur in Ecclesia Graecorum*, a rationalized list of Greek saints and their feasts attributed to George by Zeno, *Dissertazioni vossiane* vol. 2, 15, no. 24.

GERALDINI, Alessandro (1444–1525)[246]

BHL 231. *Vita Alberti ep. Montis Corvini in Apulia* (XII)[247]

Brief preface, no dedicatee. Alessandro, who came from an influential ecclesiastical family, is best known as the first bishop in the Americas, at Santo Domingo (1519–1524). His *vitae sanctorum,* which include a metric life of Benedict, a life of Katherine of Alexandria, and several liturgical offices, remain virtually unstudied.[248] Alessandro also wrote lives of the popes through Paul II (MBA, MS H 38 inf.; Kristeller, *Iter* 1:292b). The life of Albert is a revised version of an earlier account and was written after Alessandro became bishop of Volturara and Montecorvino in 1496, perhaps as late as 1499.[249]

    inc. proem.: Ego Alexander Gerardus episcopus . . . cum diocesim meam peragrarem

    des. proem.: lucudiori eam stylo conscribere constitui.

    inc.: 463 anno a tempore nostro cum illustris ciuitatis

    des.: studebis igitur, Alberte, . . . haec animo et opere adimplere.

MSS
None known to me.

Editions
    1. *AASS* April I (Paris, 1865): 433–435. Source text.

GIACOMO da Udine, canon of Aquileia (d. 1482)[250]

BHL 3794b. *Vita Helenae Utinensis,* O.E.S.A. (d. 1458)

Dedicatory preface to Paul II (1464–1471), followed by a scene-setting preface. The life concludes with a brief *peroratio* to the pope.

246. F. D'Esposito, in *DBI* 53 (1999): 312a–316b; *DHGE,* 1:1436. On the presence of Quintilian in Geraldini's early education, see Mauro Donnini, "Alla scuola di Grifone di Amelia maestro di Alessandro Geraldini," in Enrico Menestò, ed., *Alessandro Geraldini e il suo tempo: Atti del Convegno storico internazionale. Amelia, 19–20–21 novembre 1992* (Spoleto, 1993), 125–156.

247. G. Musca in *DBI* 1 (1960): 737–738; G. Carata in *BS* 1 (1961): 693.

248. The proceedings of a recent congress on him, in Menestò, *Alessandro Geraldini,* do not mention the saints' lives. They are listed among works known by title only in D'Esposito (n. 246 above) at 315b.

249. Dating of the composition from *AASS* April I (Paris, 1865): 432, para. 3; repeated by G. Musca, in *DBI* 1 (1960): 737.

250. See chap. 5 above for both author and saint.

inc. prol. 1: B. Helenae uitam sentio quidem
inc. prol. 2: Omnipotens Deus Michaeli iussit
inc.: Hieronymus, qui ceteris anteibat
des.: Dominum exorare.
peroratio: Scripsi hanc uitam . . . dignum esse certum habeo.

MSS

    1. Vatican City, BAV, MS Lat. 1223. Poncelet 1910, 84–85; Kristeller, *Iter* 2:311a. Source text.

Editions
I am preparing an edition.

GIROLAMO da Raggiolo of Chioggia (Razzuolo; Hieronymus Radiolensis), O. Vall. Umbr. (1435/40–1515)[251]

Collection. *Chronicon beatorum patrum ordine Vallumbrosae*[252]

Dedication to Lorenzo de'Medici (1449–1492), who had encouraged the author's early studies; written about 1480 in five parts. Its contents include *BHL* 4373, 4406, and 8306. Not included in figure 1.1. The miracles of Johannes Gualbertus (*BHL* 4406) are extant in two Florentine manuscripts (Kristeller *Iter* 1: 110b and 128a) and were edited by P. Soulier in *MOSSM* 14, no. 1 (1913); see *BHL* for late editions. *BHL* 4406, although not a *vita*, is counted in figure 1.1. Its preface, given in *AASS* July III (Paris, 1867): 363–364, states the author's intention in presenting the miracles: first, Lorenzo, having heard them related "in our garden," asked Girolamo to write them up; second, Girolamo felt compelled to set down what he himself had seen and heard; third, Girolamo wanted to correct the bad Latin of the jurisconsults who had first recorded them.

---

251. Not in Kristeller, "Contribution"; G. Cremascoli, "*Vitae* latine di Giovanni Gualberto: Analisi dell'*ars scribendi*," in G. Monzio Compagnoni, ed., *I Vallombrosani nella società italiana dei secoli XI e XII. Vallombrosa, 3–4 settembre 1993* (Vallombrosa: Edizioni Vallombrosa, 1995), 160–161 and 170–173; A.-M. Voci, *Petrarca e la vita religiosa: il mito umanista della vita eremitica* (Rome, 1983), 138, quoting from Girolamo's *De vita solitaria*, "possedendo la santa rusticità si vive più sicuri che possedendo la fallace eloquenza."

252. Anna Benvenuti-Papi, *Pastori di populo: Storie e leggende di vescovi nell'Italia medievale* (Florence: Arnaud, 1988), 155 and 176 n. 133. For the early tradition of Vallombrosan *vitae*, see A. Ravasi, "Vite parallele di santi medievali (sec. XI)," *Poliorama* 1 (1982): 62–61 (addressing Girolamo at 147–148); Sofia Boesch Gajano, "Storie e tradizione vallombrosane," *Bollettino dell'Istituto storico italiano per il medioevo e archivio muratoriano* 76 (1964): 99–215; and Monzi Compagnoni, *I Vallumbrosani*.

GIROLAMO da Udine, O.F.M. obs. (XV)

BHL 4362. ⟨*Vita Iohannis de Capestrano, O.F.M. obs.*⟩ (d. 1456)[253]

Letters from and to *Pietro Morosini*. Girolamo da Udine, a close companion of Giovanni da Capestrano, wrote in 1457. Incipits and desinit from *BHL*.

> *inc. epist. Petri ad auctorem*: Cupienti mihi, immo sitienti
> *inc. epist.*: Rogarunt me suauues litterae tuae
> *inc.*: Est in primis satis probata ueritas
> *des.*: dicendique facilitate restaurata. Vale. Ex conuentu . . . XV kal. iul. MCCCCLVII.

MSS
See F. Banfi, "Le fonti per la storia di S. Giovanni da Capestrano" *Studi francescani* 53 (1956): 315.

Editions
All are late; see *BHL*.

GIUSTINIAN, Bernardo (January 6, 1408–March 10, 1489)[254]

BHL 4749. *Vita Laurentii Justiniani, O. Carth.* (d. 1456)[255]

Dedicatory preface to the Carthusian monks. Bernardo was the subject's nephew. The account was written in the early 1470s as the Venetian senate began a campaign for Lorenzo's canonization.[256]

> *inc. proem.*: Etsi non dubito, uenerandi patres, quin Patriarcha Laurentius
> *des. proem.*: et uoluptatem in legendo et fructum in imitando percipere possitis.
> *inc. cap. 1*: Natus est igitur Laurentius
> *des. cap. 12*: iacere diutius in tenebris patiatur.

---

253. H. Angiolini in *DBI* 55 (2000): 744a–759a.
254. G. Pistilli in *DBI* 57 (2001): 216a–224b; King, *Venetian Humanism*, 381–383.
255. G. Di Agresti in *BS* 8 (1966): 150–156; A. Bianci in *GLS* 1218a–1220b. See also the anonymous life, uniquely organized as a bibliographical list, edited in A. Derolez, "Un bio-bibliographie de saint Laurent Justinien edité d'après le manuscrit New York Public Library 82," *Latomus* 55, no. 4 (1996): 786–805, and two studies of the politics of his cult: P. Labalme, "Religious Devotion and Civic Division in Renaissance Venice," in A. Vauchez, ed., *La religion civique à l'epoque mediévale et moderne* (Rome: BEFR, 1995), 297–308; and A. Niero, "Pietà popolare e interessi politici nel culto di s. Lorenzo Giustiniani," *Archivio veneto* 117 (1961): 197–224.
256. See Pistilli in *DBI* 60 (2003): 357a–369b.

MSS

1. Modena, Bibl. Estense, MS 1036 (Alpha o 7 13) XVI. Kristeller, *Iter* 1:373b. Not seen.

2. Venice, BN Marciana, MS Lat. IX 46 (3050). XVI. J. Valentinelli, *Bibliotheca manuscripta ad S. Marci Venetiarum, Codices mss latini* (Venice, 1868–1873), 5:329; Kristeller, *Iter* 2:229a. Seen.

3. Venice, Bibl. Giustiniani Recanati, MS V 7 (992). XV. Kristeller, *Iter* 6:287a. Not seen.

Editions

1. Bernardus Justinianus, *De vita beati Laurentii Justiniani*. Venice: Jacobus Rubeus, May 10, 1475. Goff J611a (the copy at Yale has the author's corrections). *IGI* 5548; *BMC* 5: 215; C 3383; ISTC ij00611500; cf. Kristeller, *Iter* 1:250a. Source text.

2. *Laurentii Iustiniani opera*. Brescia: Angelus Britannicus, 1506, I, signs. ii.y–6.Zv.

3. See *BHL* for later editions.

BHL 4750. *Narratio de ultimis diebus et obitu Laurentii Justiniani*

Preface, no dedicatee. After the author's death, this last part of the *vita* was printed separately and thus received its own *BHL* number. I do not count it toward the charts and figures.

inc. prol.: Perfunctus maiori parte desiderii uel officii mei

inc.: Annum IV supra LXX agebat

des.: donec a Turonensibus furto sublatus propriae ecclesiae redderetur.

MSS

See preceding entry.

Editions

All are late; see *BHL*.

BHL 5292. *Divi Marci Evangelistae Vita* (I)[257]

Introductory remarks. The life follows Giustinian's history of Venice and is followed in turn by a narrative of the *translatio* and of the relics.[258]

inc.: Cum Venetiae urbis originem scribere constituissem

inc. de translatione: Descripta Beatissimi evangelistae uita

inc. de reliquiis: Vita igitur Euangelistae translatioque

des.: summo cum assensu atque fide suscipiat.

---

257. B. Maggioni in *GLS* 1289a–1291a.
258. I count these three parts as one whole in composing the charts.

MSS

1. Venice, Bibl. Correr, MS Cicogna 1809. XV. Kristeller, *Iter* 2:281a. Not seen.

Editions

1. Bernardus Justinianus, *De origine urbis Venetiarum . . . adiecta insuper divi Marci evangelistae vita*. Venice: Bernardinus Benalius, [not before 31 Jan. 1492/93]. Goff J 605; HC 9638*; *IGI* 5547; *BMC* V: 374; ISTC ij00605000. Source text.

2. See *BHL* for later editions.

GIUSTINIAN, Leonardo (ca. 1389–November 10, 1446)[259]

BHL 6128. *Vita Nicolai myrensis ep.* (IV)[260]

Dedicatory preface to *Lorenzo Giustinian* (d. 1456). The life is a loosely paraphrasing translation from Greek sources,[261] and may be linked to the series of miracles performed in Venice by Nicholas's relics in 1443.[262]

inc. proem.: Cum aetatis nostrae ingenia mecum considero
des. proem.: quam uiuens quisque in terris prodesse.
inc.: Patarum rerum scriptores tradunt urbem fuisse
des.: triumphares cum Christo in gloria . . . Amen.

MSS

1. Cesena, Bibl. Malatestiana, Bibl. Piana, MS Piana 3.169. XV. Kristeller, *Iter* 1:46b. Not seen.

2. Florence, Bibl. Laurenziana, MS Ashb. 916 (847), fols. 3v–5v (preface); 6–36v (*vita*). XV. Kristeller, *Iter* 1:91b. Seen.

3. Florence, Bibl. Riccardiana, MS 334 (K V 6), fols. 6–61v (*vita*); fols. 61v–62, with the title *Oratio in b. Nicolai laudem*. XV. Kristeller, *Iter* 1:190b. Seen.

4. Florence, Bibl. Riccardiana, MS 452 (K IV 21) , fols. 71v–98. XV. Kristeller, *Iter* 1:192b. Seen.

5. Milan, Bibl. Ambrosiana, MS J 119 sup. XVI in. Kristeller, *Iter* 1:300b. Seen.

---

259. King, *Venetian Humanism*, 383–385; F. Pignatti in *DBI* 57 (2001): 249b–255a. For Leonardo's part in pressing for the canonization of Lorenzo Giustiniani, see Labalme, "Religious Devotion," 299.

260. On Nicholas of Myra, see O. Limone in *GLS* 1483b–1488a.

261. A. Pertusi, "L'umanesimo greco dalla fine del secolo XIV agli inizi del secolo XVI," in *Storia della cultura veneta* 3, no. 1 (1980): 208.

262. See BAV, MS Reg. Lat. 536, fol. 14.

6. Naples, BN, MS Fondo Principale V G 43, fols. 89v–109v. XV. Kristeller, *Iter* 1:421a. Seen.

7. Naples, BN, MS Fondo Principale VI D 29. XV. Kristeller, *Iter* 1:402b. Seen.

8. Naples, BN, MS Fondo Principale VIII B 39. XV. Kristeller, *Iter* 1:403b. Seen.

9. Subiaco, Bibl. del Monumento Nazionale Santa Scolastica, MS 222 (CCXIX), fols. 77–81 (preface), fols. 81–124v (*vita*). XV. Kristeller, *Iter* 6:219b. Not seen.

10. Treviso, BC, MS 313. XVIII, copied from Urb. Lat. 389. Kristeller, *Iter* 2:195b. Not seen.

11. Udine, BC., MS Fondo Manin 1334 (175), fols. 198–199 (preface); fols. 199v–211v (*vita*). XVII. Kristeller, *Iter* 6:243a; cf. 2:207. Seen.

12. Vatican City, BAV, MS Urb. Lat. 389, fols. 228–249. Poncelet 1910, 296. Not seen.

13. Vatican City, BAV, MS Vat. lat. 411, fols. 75–76v (prologue), fols. 77–97 (*vita*). Poncelet 1910, 19. Seen; also SLU reel 1351.

14. Vatican City, BAV, MS Vat. Lat. 2945, fols. 38–63. Poncelet 1910, 97–98; Kristeller, *Iter* 2:315a. Seen; also SLU reel 876.

15. Vatican City, BAV, MS Vat. Lat. 7751. Poncelet 1910, 217; Kristeller, *Iter* 2:343a and 6:323b; cf. 6:304b. Seen; also SLU reel 870.

16. Warsaw, BU, MS 720. XVI. Kristeller, *Iter* 4:434b. Not seen.

Editions

1. *Poetae christiani*, vol. 2 (Venice: Aldus Manutius, 1502), signs. H–K4v. H 15168. Source text.

2. *Vita Nicolai Myrensis* (Deventer: Theodore de Borne, 1513). Not seen.

3. *Simeon Metaphrastus* (Paris: Simon Colline, 1521), fols. 3–19v, without prologue. Seen.

4. For later editions, see the *BHL*.

GUARINO Guarini (1370/1–1459/60)[263]

BHL 379. **Vita et actus beati Ambrosii, ep. Mediolanensis (IV)**[264]

Dedicatory letter to Alberto da Sarteano, O.F.M. Obs., a former student; Sabbadini dates the letter to 1434. The *vita* is a translation from the Greek.

---

263. G. Pistilli, in *DBI* 60 (2003): 357a–369b. See Sabbadini, *Epistolario*, 2:680–682, with notes at 3:515 (letter 932), for a partial edition of Guarino's oration on behalf of the Servites to Francesco Sforza, delivered to encourage the duke's attention to the canonization of Filippo Benizi, as well as ibid., 2:646–648, for an edition of the letter in which Guarino refuses to rewrite the life of St. Guarinus (discussed above, chap. 3).

264. On Ambrose, see n. 116 above.

inc. epist.: Vetus mos, Alberte pater, cum apud maiores

des. epist.: deleat obliuio.

inc.: Valentinianus post Jouiani obitum

des.: Quorum imitatores et nos euadere utinam digni efficiamur pari-
aque illi praemia et coronas assequi gratia & humanitate domini nostri . . .
In secula amen. FINIT.

MSS

1. Ferrara, Bibl. Comm. Ariostea, MS II 90, fols. 2v–7. XV (2 copies).
Kristeller, *Iter* 1:57a–b. Not seen.

2. Naples, BN, MS VII G 15, fols. 2v–7. XV. Kristeller, *Iter* 5:112b; cf.
1:423. Seen.

3. Vatican City, BAV, MS Reg. Lat. 1612, fols. 24–39 (autograph?).
Kristeller, *Iter* 2:409b. Seen.

4. Warsaw, BU, MS 720. XVI. Kristeller, *Iter* 4:434b. Not seen.

Editions

1. Sabbadini, *Epistolario* 2:192–194 (dedication only).

BHL —. Commentarium in Timothei vitam apostoli sancti dei (I)[265]

Dedicatory letter to *Timoteo Maffei*, a former student who had requested
the translation from a Greek text that he himself provided. Sabbadini tentatively dates the letter to 1455.

inc. epist.: Timotheum, quem tuum ad me misisti, nostrum tandem ad
te remitto

des. epist.: et pro me communem Dominum proque meis depreceris.
Vale.

inc.: Lycaonia quidem magnum produxit Timotheum

MSS

1. Paris, BN, MS Lat. 12116, fols. 84–87v. XVII. Kristeller, *Iter* 2:252b.
Not seen.

2. Rome, Bibl. Vallicelliana, MS C 90, fols. 13v–21. XV. Kristeller, *Iter*
2:132a. Not seen.

Editions

1. Sabbadini, *Epistolario,* 2:649 (dedication only).

265. G. Lucchese in *BS* 12 (1969): 482–488; R. Penna in *GLS* 1861b–1863b.

HILARION [Lantieri], Mediolanensis, O.S.B. obs. (d. 1511)[266]

BHL 9044. Legendarium ... Supplementum Varaginis secundum calendarium monastichum

Published in Milan by Jacopo Sannazzaro on April 16, 1494 (H8661; *IGI* 4776; Rogledi Manni 501; ISTC ih00266500), as listed below on the basis of the MBA copy. Hilarion suggests the title *supplementum* in his letter to the chapter general, indicating that he is supplementing the *Legenda aurea*. The entries below are not included in figure 1.1 or table 2.1.

inc. versus ad lectorem: Multorum uitas, mortes, et nomina, lector, / Sanctorum: nostri cerne laboris ope/Non musas, non falsa deum uocabula canto / Nec uanas latebras hic heliconis habes / Nil ficti inseritur, tantum obscruatio facti / Panditur ut ueterum pagina certa docet. / Laus deo.

inc. praef. ad capitulum generalem: Cum plerasque, obseruandissimi patres, sanctorum uitas, quorum in calendario nostro quotannis propriis diebus felix memoria recensetur lectoribus nostris mensalibus deesse perspicerem, et propterea non paruam deuotionis accesionem que nobis ex eorum imitatione ingenue contingeret aufferri, nacto aliquantis per otio ab iniuncto (et oneroso quidem) seruitutis mee munere easdem compendiose colligere pro uirili animum institui . . . (verso facing fol. 1)

BHL 602d. De sancto Antonio confessore ordinis minorum (XIII)[267]

inc.: Beatus Antonius, confessor Christi et Ordinis Minorum, generis hispanus a parentibus suis in baptismo Ferdinandus est appellatus

des.: Ibi denique optat fidelibus beneficia quinque prestantur salutaremque suc petitionis effectum ex diuersis mundi partibus uenientes uiri feminaeque consequuntur. Imperante domino . . . in secula seculorum. Amen. (fols. 48ra–49rb)

BHL epitome. De sancta Apolonia virgine et mar. (III)[268]

inc.: Beata virgo Christi et martir Apolonia, tempore Decii imperatoris apud Alexandriam passa est. Nam ut beatus Dionisius Alexandrinus episcopus ad Anthiochenum episcopum scribens attestatur, sicuti Eusebius libro quinto historie ecclesiastice refert

des.: ut dentium dolore affectis suum fideliter patrocinium exposcentibus, illico subueniat et succurrat. Prestante eodem domino nostro . . . in secula. Amen. (fol. 20va–b)

---

266. Not in Kristeller, "Contribution"; see F. Argelati, *Scriptores mediolanenses* (Milan, 1735), 1, 2, cols. 784–786 (ch. 968).

267. G. Spanò in *BS* 2 (1962): 156–179; S. Brufani in *GLS* 182a–189b.

268. G. D. Gordini in *BS* 2 (1962): 256–262; D. Frioli in *GLS* 200b–201b.

BHL epitome. *De sancta Clara virgine* (XIII)[269]

inc.: Venerabilis Christi sponsa deoque dicata Clara de ciuitate Assisii preclaris exorta parentibus post acceptam superne gratie claritatem in toto terrarum orbe refulsit

des.: Beata itaque Clara diues meritis miraculorum prodigiis coruscans luce clarius manifestat quod qui paupertatis obedientie castitatis uotum perfecte seruauerint introducentur superne glorie claritatem perpetuo possidendam. . . . in eterna secula. Amen. (fols. 72rb–72va)

BHL epitome. *De sanctis martiribus Cyro et Iohanne* (IV)[270]

inc.: Beati martires Christi Cyrus et Ioannes tempore Dioclitiani imperatoris extiterunt

des.: Post multum uero temporis beate memorie Cyrillus eiusdem Alexandrie urbis episcopus predictis sanctis martiribus in loco qui dicitur monofides gloriosam extruxit ecclesiam, in qua ipsorum beatorum corpora . . . collocauit . . . in secula seculorum. Amen. (fols. 114rb–vb)

BHL epitome. *De sancto Damaso papa et confessore* (IV)[271]

inc.: Beatus Damasus natione hispanus, post Liberium electus in sumum pontificem fuit. Hic uoce publica damnauit predictum Liberium hereticum

des.: Demum expletis annis decem et octo mensibus duobus ac diebus decem pontificatus sui . . . quieuit . . . qui uiuit benedictus in secula. Amen. (fols. 6va–7ra)

BHL epitome. *De sancto Dionisio episcopo mediolanensi et confessore* (IV)[272]

inc.: Beatus Dionisius mediolanensis episcopus tempore Constantii imperatoris fuit. Hic beatus pontifex uirtute signorum et fama sacre religionis insignitus per diuersa terrarum spacia celebre diffamatus emicuit

des.: Perductum itaque mediolanensium corpus illud sanctissimum, beatus Ambrosius cum magna reuerentia ac solemnitate, nam tredecim ex eius suffraganeis episcopi interfuerunt in ecclesia confessorum . . . in omnium seculorum secula. Amen. (fols. 38va–39rb)

BHL epitome. *De sancto Ludovico confessore* (XIII)[273]

inc.: Beatus confessor Christi Ludovicus francorum rex extitit genere nobilissimus sublimis potentia facultatibus opuletus precelsus uirtutibus moribus elegans honestate conspicuus

---

269. A. Blasucci in *BS* 3 (1963): 1201–1208; S. Brufani in *GLS* 420a–428b.
270. F. Caraffa in *BS* 4 (1964): 2–4.
271. L. Galones in *GLS* 508a–509b; Kelly, *ODP* 32b–34a.
272. A. Amore in *BS* 4 (1964): 642.
273. H. Platelle in *BS* 8 (1966): 320–338; A. Vauchez in *GLS* 1244b–1248b.

des.: Cuius admirandis papa Bonifacius preconiis auditis curiosa diligentia ut ipse testatur plenarum actorum illius obtinens certitudinem ipsum de consensu fratrum suorum aliorumque prelatorum in curia existentium sanctorum cathalogo letanter ascripsit. Prestante domino . . . in secula seculorum. Amen. (fols. 76va–78rb)

BHL epitome. *De sanctis martiribus Marcellino et Petro* (III)[274]

inc.: Beati martires Christi Marcellinus presbiter et Petrus exorcista tempore Dioclitiani imperatoris extiterunt

des.: Anno autem dominice incarnationis octingentisimo uigesimosexto imperante Ludovico pio Karoli magni filio, predictorum sanctorum martirum corpora de urbe Roma sublata sunt et in Franciam translata ibique multis signis domino cooperante clarificata . . . in secula. Amen. (fols. 45rb–46ra)

BHL epitome. *De sanctis Christi martiribus Marco et Marcelliano* (IV)[275]

inc.: Beati martires Christi Marcellianus et Marcus gemini fratres filii fuerunt Tranquillini romani ciuis preclarissimi

des.: Tali ergo martirio coronati, migrauerunt ad dominum, sepultique sunt Via Appia secundo ab urbe miliario in loco qui uocatur ad arenas, quia cripte arcnarum ibi erant ex quibus urbis menia construebantur. Passi sunt autem sub Dioclitiano imperatore . . . in secula. Amen. (fols. 49rb–vb)

BHL epitome. *De sancto Marco papa et confessore* (IV)[276]

inc.: Beatus Marcus natione Romanus post beatum Siluestrum primus papa fuit.

des.: Cumque per annos duos menses octo et dies uiginti digne pretuisset ecclesie feliciter in pace quieuit circa annum domini trecentesimum uigesimum octauum qui est deus benedictus in secula Amen. (fol. 93va)

BHL epitome. *De sancto Petro celestino confessore* (XIII)[277]

inc.: Beatus petrus confessor domini gloriosus de castello sancti Angeli quod est in prouincia terre laboris extitit oriundus ex honestis catholicis et deuotis parentibus procreatus. Hic cum ex matris utero exiit quodam monachiali habitu uestitus apparuit

des.: Ad cuius tumulum crebra facta sunt prodigia, sicque et in uita et post mortem plurimis claruit miraculis. . . . Cuius admirandis summus pontifex Clemens quintus preconiis auditis . . . ipsum sanctorum confes-

---

274. A. Amore in *BS* 8 (1966): 657–658.
275. J.-M. Sauget in *BS* 8 (1966): 744–745.
276. See n. 167 above.
277. G. M. Longhi in *BS* 3 (1963): 1100–1107; A. M. Piazzoni in *GLS* 1631a–1634b.

sorum cathalogo duxit adscribendum. . . . Prestante eodem domino . . . in secula. Amen. (fols. 34rb–38ra)

BHL 6863.[278] De sancto Placido abbate et martire (VI)[279]

inc.: Beatissimus Placidus Christi martir egregius Tertulii patricii filius sanctissimo Benedicto omnipotenti deo sub regulari institutione nutriendus ab eodem patre suo septennis traditus est

des.: Ex die uero qua sepulta sunt corpora sanctorum martirum Placidi ac sociorum suorum in ecclesia sancti Ioannis Baptiste ultra iam basilica illa sancti Ioannis uocata non est sed in honore sanctorum qui intus erant sepulti sancti Placidi ecclesia uocabatur usque ad tempora illa quando Romani Siciliam amiserunt. Omnibus etiam temporibus quibus Sarraceni Sicilie dominati sunt ecclesia ipsa ex beati martiris Placidi nomine uocabatur. Regnante domino . . . secula seculorum. Amen. (fols. 86va–90va)

BHL epitome. De sanctis Processo et Martiniano (I)[280]

inc.: Beati martires Christi Processus et Martinianus fuerunt tempore Neronis imperatoris. Qui Nero post mortem Simonis Magi beatos apostolos Christi Petrus et Paulum in manus Paulini uiri clarissimi tradidit

des.: Tunc sancti eiecti de custodia in uiam aureliam perducuntur ibique capite cesi Christi martires consecrantur. Quorum corpora canibus deuoranda derelicta. . . . Regnante domino nostro . . . in secula. Amen. (fols. 56va–57ra)

BHL 7954. De sancto Simeone monacho et confessore (XI)[281]

inc.: Beatus confessor Christi Symeon in Armeniae partibus clara ex tirpe [*sic*] nobilium progenitus magistri militum filius extitit

des.: Puer etiam quidam ex Cremonensium finibus graui langore correptus ad sanctum corpus nauigo adductus . . . et ante eius tumulum depositius, post aliquantum temporis sospitati redditus ad propria cum gaudio remeauit . . . Imperante domino . . . in secula. Amen. (fols. 61va–64vb)

BHL epitome. De sancto Simpliciano episcopo et confessore (V)[282]

inc.: Beatus confessor Christi Simplicianus tam moribus quam genere clarissimus in pago Betuatensi extitit oriundus. Traditus autem a parentibus liberalibus studiis

---

278. According to *BHL* new supplement; cf. *BHL 6864*.
279. On Placidus, see V. Cattana in *GLS* 1663b–1664b.
280. A. Amore in *BS* 10 (1968): 1138–1140.
281. F. Caroffa in *BS* 11 (1968): 1114–1115. See also Mantua, BC, MS B.IV.17 (Kristeller, *Iter* 1:237a), and BAV, MS de Marinis 7, 10v–15v, an oration with verse to Pius II (Kristeller, *Iter* 6:414b).
282. A. Rinaldi in *BS* 11 (1968): 1194–1197; L. Crevelli in *GLS* 1807a–1808b.

des.: Suscepto ergo beatus Simplicianus episcopatus officio mediola-
nensem ecclesiam solicite gubernavit demumque bonis operibus plenus et
meritis sancto fine quievit . . . in secula seculorum. Amen. (fols.
74vb–76ra)

BHL epitome. *De sancto Sothere papa et martire* (II)[283]

inc.: Beatus Sother campanie natus tertius decimus papa fuit. Hic beatus pontifex sanctitate insignis licet in multis periculis constitutus fuerit
des.: Apparuit namque stella quedam crinita et celum totum ardere
uidebatur. Aues quoque dire domos incendebant portantes carbones, circa
annum domini centesimum septuagessimumtertium. Cui est honor . . .
Amen. (fols. 28rb–28va)

BHL epitome. *De sancta Susanna virgine et martire* (IV)[284]

inc.: Beata Susanna uirgo Christi ac martir Gauinii presbiteri fratris
uterini beati pape Gaii filia fuit qui erant de genere Dioclitiani imperatoris.
Gauinianus autem cum in diuinis esset libris mundialibusque litteris doctissimus, filiam suam unicam Susannam pulcherrimam in eruditione litterarum mundane artis et libris diuinis optime imbuit
des.: Beatus autem Gaius episcopus domum in qua Christi uirgo
Susanna percussa fuerat celeriter introiuit sacrificium offerens deo . . . in
secula seculorum. Amen. (fols. 71rb–72rb)

BHL epitome. *De sanctis martiribus Symphorosa et septem filiis suis* (II)[285]

inc.: Beata martir Christi Symphorosa uxor quondam Gettulii tribuni
pro Christo capite plexi sub Adriano principe cum septem filiis suis apud
urbem Tyburtinam passa est
des.: Tunc factus est timor Christi super paganos et quieuit persecutio
aliquo tempore in quo omnium martirum honorata sunt corpora . . . in
secula seculorum. Amen. (fols. 61ra–va)

BHL epitome. *De sancto Syro episcopo et confessore* (IV)[286]

inc.: Beatus Syrus urbis papie episcopus, discipulus primo fuit beati
Hermagore
des.: Sepultusque est in basilica quam ipse construxerat beatorum martirum Geruasii et Prothasii. . . . Cui successit beatus Pompeius diaconus
eius . . . ad dominus cui est honor et gloria . . . Amen. (fols. 4vb–6rb)

---

283. Kelly, *ODP* 11.
284. A. Amore in *BS* 12 (1969): 78–80; R. Cavedo in *GLS* 1831a–b.
285. B. Cignitti in *BS* 11 (1968): 1217–1229.
286. A. M. Raggi in *BS* 11 (1968): 1241–1244.

BHL epitome. *De sancta Tecla virgine et martire* (I)[287]

inc.: Beata uirgo Christi Tecla ciuitatis Iconii nobilissima beati Pauli apostoli predicatione ad fidem Christi conuersa

des.: Ob hoc et principatu martirii et uirginitatis triumpho sublimis choris circumcincta uirgineis agni sequitur immaculati uestigia. Hec b. Ambrosius prestante domino . . . in secula seculorum. Amen. (fols. 85ra–86va)

BHL epitome. *De sancto Tiburtio martire* (II)[288]

inc.: Beatus martir Christi Tiburtius iuuenis sapientissimus et nobilissimus Aggrestini Cromatii prefecti urbis Rome filius fuit. Qui ambo baptizati sunt a beato Policarp presbitero

des.: Tunc Fabianus iratus iussit eum decolari. Ductus igitur in Via Lauicana tertio ab urbe miliario oratione ad dominum fusa ictu una percussus migrauit ad deum . . . in secula seculorum. Amen. (fols. 70va–71rb)

BHL epitome. *De sancto Triphone* [al.: *Trophime*] *martire* (III)[289]

inc.: Beatus martir domini Triphon tempore Decii imperatoris extitit. Hic ab infantia sua multis claruit miraculis in Sansaducome ciuitate caste a matre sua instructus

des.: Tandem iusit eum prefectus gladio interimi sicque consumatus adeptus est palmam martirii. Utrum tamen hic Triphon sit ille qui hodie recolitur a nobis pro constanti non habetur. Passus est autem circa annum domini ducentesimum quinquagesimum quartum. Cui est . . . in eterna secula. Amen. (fols. 105vb–106v)

BHL epitome. *De sanctis martiribus Tyburtio Valeriano et Maximo* (III)[290]

inc.: Beati martires Christi Tyburtius et Valerianus Romani ciues illustres carnis quoque fratres ac spiritus, tempore Alexandri imperatoris extiterunt, quorum unus scilicet Valerianus beate uirginis et martiris Cecilie sponsus fuit

des.: Cuius corpus beata Cecilia iuxta beatos Christi martires Tybur-

---

287. U. M. Fasola in *BS* 12 (1969): 174–175.

288. Not the Tibertius associated with Cecilia, but one sometimes grouped with Sebastian, on whom see n. 229 above.

289. J.-M. Sauget in *BS* 12 (1969): 673–674. Hilarion probably draws on Bonino Mombrizio's *Sanctuarium* (Paris, 1910) 2:564–565.

290. See under Cecilia, n. 190 above and A. Amore in *BS* 12 (1969): 466–469.

tium et Valerianum in novo sarcofago sepeliuit circa annum domini ducentesimum uigessimum tertium. Cui est honor . . . Amen. (fols. 26rb–27ra)

BHL epitome. *De sancto Victore martire* (IV)[291]

inc.: Beatus Victor Maurus genere apud Mediolanum Maximiani imperatoris miles egregius fuit

des.: Hec tua est domine uirtute et gloria. Hec b. Ambrosius. Prestante domino . . . in secula. Amen. (fol. 31ra)

BHL epitome. *De sanctis martiribus Vitali et Agricola* (IV)[292]

inc.: Beati martires Christi Vitalis et Agricola passi sunt in ciuitate Bononiensi sub Dioclitiano et Maximiano. Beatus autem Vitalis seruus fuit sancti Agricole

des.: Et multi qui diuersis egretudinibus affligebantur contingentes sanctorum sudaria sanabantur. Sed et alia multa mirabilia per sanctos suos. . . . Hec beatus Ambrosius. Prestante domino . . . in secula. Amen. (fols. 104rb–104va)

BHL epitome. *De sancto Zenone episcopo e confessore* (IV)[293]

inc.: Beatus confessor Christi Zeno episcopus Veronensis fuit

des.: Quo uiso miraculo populus in admirationem conuertitur. . . . Prestante domino nostro . . . benedictus in secula. Amen. (fols. 41b–vb)

BHL epitome. *De sancto Zeferino papa et martire* (III)[294]

inc.: Beatus Zeferinus natione romanus papa sextusdecimus fuit. Hic gloriosus pontifex deuotione et sanctitate precipuus statuit ut Christiani omnes annorum duodecim in die sancto pasce uenerandum eucharistie sacramentum in publico accipiant

des.: et martirio coronatus in cimiterio Calixti sepultus est circa annum domini ducentesimum uigesimum quintum . . . in secula seculorum. Amen. (fol. 78va)

291. A. M. Rinaldi in *BS* 12 (1969): 1274–1275; C. Pasini in *Dizionario dei santi della chiesa in Milano* (Milan, 1995), 53–56; M. Forlin Patrucco in *GLS* 1967a–1968b.

292. G. D. Gordini in *BS* 12 (1969): 1225–1228; G. Malaguti in GLS 1959a–1960b.

293. A. Amore in *BS* 12 (1969): 1477–1479; P. Golinelli in *GLS* 1980b–1982a.

294. Kelly, *ODP* 12.

HILARION Veronensis, O.S.B. Congr. S. Georgii in Alga, *in saeculo* Niccolò Fontanelli (ca. 1440–September 30, 1485)[295]

BHL 1380d. *Passio Blasii ep. Sebastenus* (IV)[296]

Preface, no dedicatee. Written (*conscriptus*) by Hilarion on the strength of a relic held at Verona, at the reformed Benedictine monastery of Sts. Nazarius and Celsus, where he professed in 1464.

inc. proem.: Debueram ab exordio lectori morem gerere et quam ueritas historiae poposcisset, fidem astruere

inc.: Blasius igitur Sebasta Cappadociae urbe exortus, quum per totum fere orbem

des.: Ades igitur, faue ciuibus tuis, et quae nunc usque sancta tua ossa custodit, Veronam semper tuere.

MSS

1. Rome, Bibl. Alessandrina, MS 199, fols. 39–48v. XV. Poncelet 1909, 198. One of three narratives about saints by Hilarion in this manuscript. Not seen.

Editions
None known to me.

BHL 3396. *Martyrium gloriosi militis Georgii* (IV)[297]

Preface, no dedicatee. The Hilarion named in the manuscript as author of the pieces on St. George seems to be Fontanelli: the manuscript opens with the translation by Fabianus Cretensis (*q.v.*) of "Eustachius" (i.e., Eutychius) that was made with Hilarion.[298] On Hilarion Mediolanensis (Lantieri), see above.

inc. proem.: Historiam diui Georgii, licet inter apocryphas, patrum decreto sancta Romana Ecclesia connumerandum acceperit

des. proem.: ueram ad historiam potius conuertamur

inc.: Georgius Melitina Cappadociae urbe exortus, ex eo pugnatorum

---

295. Not in Kristeller, "Contribution." See Collet, *Italian Benedictine Scholars*, *ad indicem*; and especially Lucia Gualdo Rosa's introduction to her edition of Hilarion's *Copia Idruntine expugnationis* in L. Gualdo Rosa, I. Nuovo, and D. Defilippis, eds., *Gli umanisti e la guerra otrantina: Testi dei secoli XV e XVI* (Bari, 1982), 21–41, giving earlier bibliography; at 21 and 25, she gives the date of death as September 30, 1485, by shipwreck. Cf. Collett, *Italian Benedictine Scholars*, 44, giving the date 1521.

296. See n. 189 above.

297. On George, see n. 206 above. Title taken from *BHL*. F. Argelati, *Bibliotheca Scriptorum Mediolanensium* (Milan, 1745), col. 785, no. 9, ascribes this account to Hilarion Lantieri of Milan.

298. R. Janin in *BS* 3 (1964): 323–324.

illustrium numero fuisse traditur quod Graeci —[*sic*] Latini "inuincibiles" uocant

des.: et meritis optimis et precibus saluberrimis tuearis. Amen.

MSS

1. Rome, Bibl. Alessandrina, MS 199, fols. 39–48v. XV. Poncelet 1909, 198. Not seen.

2. Venice, BN Marciana, MS Zan. Lat. 360 (1809), fols. 3 (preface) and 3–8v (*vita*). XV. Kristeller, *Iter* 2:213. Source text.

Editions
None known to me.

BHL 3402–3403. *Translatio capitis Divi Georgii ab Aeginae insula Venetias* (with miracles)[299]

Dedicatory preface to *Teofilo Beaqua*. The manuscript is dated 1462. Not included in figure 1.1.

inc. proem.: Cogis me, Pater Theophile, id ipsum quod datur otii

inc.: Aegina insula, quam ita aeacus

des.: cuius auxilio haec omnia feliciter gesserant anno Domini MCCC-CLXII, id. dec., Pio II pontifice maximo, duce uero Venetiarum Christophoro Mauro. . . . Amen.

inc. mir.: Non erit autem abs re duo martyris ipsius miracula

des. mir.: cultoribus suis praesto esse.

MSS

1. Venice, BN Marciana, MS Zan. Lat. 360 (1809), fols. 8v–9 (preface) and 8v–10 *(translatio)* and 10r–v (miracles). XVI. Kristeller, *Iter* 2:212b. Seen.

Editions
None known to me.

BHL 3404. *Translatio brachii Venetias an. 1296* (cf. *BHL* 3405)

Not included in figure 1.1.

inc.: Nunc unde et a quo hominum, quoue ordine, quibus auspiciis prodigisque translatum . . . In ea ora Italiae, quae Calabria nuncupatur

des.: orationum brachio . . . tuetur et protegat, cui est honor . . .

---

299. See also *BHL* 3405–3406, an account of the translation by another monk of San Giorgio, Johannes Antonius. For Hilarion's thirteenth-century source, see *AASS* April III (Paris, 1866): 105, n. 14.

MSS

1. Venice, BN Marciana, MS Zan Lat. 360 (1809), fols. 10v–11v.
XVI. Kristeller, *Iter* 2:213a. Seen.

Editions
See *BHL* for editions, all late, and F. Corner, *Ecclesiae venetae antiquis monumentis* (1749), 2:161–163, interpolated.

BHL 6049b. *Historia divorum martyrum Nazarii et Caelsi* (I)[300]

Preface, no dedicatee. Here, too, Hilarion seems to have paraphrased an earlier text, adding his own preface.

inc. proem.: Quum diuorum Nazarii et Celsi martyres historiam rusticitate sua et uerborum ac sententarium inconcinnitate mendosam meliorem facere peroptarem

inc.: Nazarius patrem habuit Aphricanum, genere (ut aiunt) et patria Aphrum

des.: signa vero scribere et referre miracula, quia longum et haec innumerabilia sunt, aliis, e toto terrarum orbe et qualia et quanta fuerint, colligenda et scribenda reseruo.

MSS

1. Rome, Bibl. Alexandrina, MS 199, fols. 61–69. XV. Poncelet 1909, 198. Not seen.

Editions
All late; see *BHL*.

LAPIUS, Maurus, O. Cam. (1399–November 7, 1478)[301]

BHL —. *Vita Petri Sardiniensis*[302] (d. 1453)

Preface, no dedicatee. Lapi arrived at San Michele from nearby San Mattia only in 1476, long after the priest and monk Pietro Massaleni of Ottana,

---

300. A. Amore in *BS* 9 (1967): 780–784; C. Pasini in *GLS* 1468b–1469b.

301. Kristeller, "Contribution," 144. The Florentine Lapi was first a Carmelite, but his hagiography belongs to his Camaldolese period; see Magnoaldo Ziegelbauer, *Centifolium Camaldulense* (Venice, 1750; reprint Farnborough, 1967), 39a–b. V. Meneghin, *S. Michele in Isola di Venezia* (Venice, 1962), 1:136–138, is dismissive of Lapi's learning, but in light of the respect accorded his Tuscan in the Venetian convent and of his correspondence with the learned, I propose him as a humanist.

302. See *BHL* 1:978, where the work is listed under this author but no number is assigned.

Sardinia had died. The author's preface explains his procedure in detail; he appears to have been gathering material to promote canonization.

inc. proem.: Pater meus usquemodo operatur et ego operar, ait Joannes euangelista

MSS

1. Venice, BN Marciana, MS Lat. XIV 112 (4383), 50 (title), 51–52v (prologue); 52v–82v (*vita*). There is a date on fol. 82: "in die beati Matthiae apostoli 1455." The prologue recurs on fols. 84–85; the *vita* recommences on 85 and ends incomplete on 87v. Kristeller, *Iter* 2:265a and 6:261b. Seen.

2. Venice, BN Marciana, MS Lat. XIV 295 (4348). XV. Kristeller, *Iter* 2:270b. Seen.

Editions

1. A. Fortunio, *Historiarum Camaldulensium libri tres* (Florence, 1575), edits a reworked version that is reproduced in F. Corner, *Ecclesiae Torcellanae antiquis monumentis* (Venice: Pasquali, 1749), 3:24–26 and extracted by G. B. Mittarelli and A. Costadoni, *Annales Camaldulenses* (Venice, 1755–1773), 7:205–206 and 237–238. None of these editions includes the preface.

BHL 7327. *De miraculis sancti Romualdi* (XI)[303]

Brief prefatory remarks by Lapi, no dedication. Although the composition of this list of 15 miracles is sometimes ascribed to Lapi, he is only the scribe: he names the author, or rather, the notary, in the desinit. The miracles occurred following the *inventio of* 1466 in Valdicastro. Not included in figure 1.1.

inc. praef.: Hic erunt inferius miracula sanctissimi patris nostri Romualdi . . . Ista erunt ipsa miracula per notarium supradicti domini generalis scripta, ut uidebatur.

inc.: Placuit in his scriptis pauca de multis breuissime referre

des.: a periculo euadens gratiam recipere impetrauit. Finis. . . . Ego Johannes Juliani a Laterino notarius et scriba reu. Domni Mariotti generalis praefati praedictis omnibus una interfui, eaque rogatus componere composui. Et ego domnus Maurus ipsa copiaui ex suo proprio originali.

303. On Romuald, see n. 179 above; see G. Fornari in *GLS* 1732a–1737a; C. Caby, "Du monastère à la cité: Le culte de saint Romuald au Moyen Age," *Revue Mabillon* n.s. 6 (1996): 137–158.

MSS

    1. Venice, BN Marciana, MS Marc. lat. XIV 112 (4283), 35r–43r. Kristeller, *Iter* 2:265a and 6:261b. Seen.

Editions

    1. Mittarelli, *Annales Camaldulenses* 7:175–185. A further 110 miracles from 1467 are listed following this entry.

Lost. *De dormitione Ambrosii* [*Traversarii, q.v.*] *generalis* [*Camaldulensis*] *(d. 1439)*

Letter to Eugene IV (1431–1447), an encomion with an epitaph. The manuscript described by Fortunio, *Historiarum Libri*, is lost. The composition is not recorded among Lapi's works by V. Meneghin, *S. Michele in Isola di Venezia* (Venice, 1962), 136–138. For the context of its writing, see Cécile Caby, "Culte monastique et fortune humaniste: Ambrogio Traversari, *vir illustre* de l'ordre camaldule," *MEFRM* 108 (1996), mentioning Lapi at 324–325.

Lost. ⟨*Vita Laurentii Justiniani*⟩ (d. 1456)

Mittarelli, *Annales Camaldulenses,* 7:300, citing Fortunio, *Historiarum libri,* records Lapi's composition of a life of the patriarch of Venice; cf. Meneghin, *S. Michele in Isola,* 136–138.

Lost. ⟨*De reliquiis venetiis*⟩

Cécile Caby, *De l'éremetisme rural au monachisme urbain: Les Camaldules in Italie à la fin du Moyen Age* (Rome: BEFR, 1999), 633, drawing on Fortunio, *Historiarum libri*, records Lapi's composition "d'un traité sur les reliques de Venise"; cf. Meneghin, *S. Michele in Isola,* 136–138. Not included in figure 1.1.

LAPO da Castiglionchio (ca. 1406–1438)[304]

BHL 5111a. *Iosepi Macabeicorum liber* (Biblical)[305]

The prefatory letter is directed to a Johannes, cardinal of San Lorenzo in Lucerna; it may have been written by March 1437.[306] Incipits and desinit from *BHL*.

---

    304. Christopher S. Celenza, *Renaissance Humanism and the Papal Curia: Lapo da Castiglionchio the Younger's De curiae commodis* (Ann Arbor: University of Michigan Press, 1999), 1–29.

    305. Title from Poncelet 1910, 96–97; incipits and desinit from *BHL*. F. Spadafora, *BS* 8 (1966): 434–437.

    306. F. P. Luiso, "Studi sull'epistolario e le traduzione di Lapo di Castiglionchio," *SIFC* 7 (1899): 291–292 n. 3, suggests that Cardinal Johannes of St. Laurence is Rochtaillée (d. March 24, 1437) rather than Vitelleschi (who acceded to the cardinalate on August 9, 1437).

inc. proem.: Permagnam mihi uidetur, clementissime pater

inc. proem. auctoris: Cum de rebus in media philosophia additis nunc omnis mihi disputatio futura sit

inc.: Cum patribus nostris, optime stabilita re publica, diuturnitas pacis ocium confirmasset

des.: atque immortales a Deo consecuti, cui sit gloria . . . Amen.

MSS

1. Paris, BN, MS Lat. 1616, fols. 1–16, two prefaces only. XV. Kristeller, *Iter* 3:215b. Not seen.

2. Vatican City, BAV, MS Lat. 1989 (olim 910), fols. 1–25. XV. Poncelet 1910, 96–97. Not seen.

Editions
None known to me.

LILIUS, Zacharias, Can. Reg. (fl. 1500)[307]

BHL 1618a. *Caroli magni viri illustris . . . vita* (IX)[308]

Dedicatory letter to Gabriel Vincentinus, described as an "orator" and as Lilius's (Gigli's) "concanonicus." Although this narrative has been assigned a *BHL* number, I do not count it among *vitae sanctorum* in figure 1.1. The author is quite clear that he does not understand himself to be writing about a saint or saintlike figure; he is trying to correct chivalric romance into history.

inc. epist.: Cum frequenter imperitum uulgus lyricis

des. epist.: enitar diuinarum rerum studii consectari. Vale.

inc.: Carolus Francorum Rex, cui ob magnitudinem

des.: christianae salutis XV super DCCC.

MSS
None known to me.

Editions

1. *Zacharii Lilii Opuscula.* Florence: Francesco Bonacorsi for Piero Pacini, 1496, item five. H10103. Goff L 221; *BMC* 6: 675 ISTC il00221000. Source text.

---

307. Not in Kristeller, "Contribution"; not in *DBI*. But on the family, see *DBI* 54 (2000): 674–676 and 690–693.

308. See n. 2 above.

LITIANUS, Stephanus, Celestine[309]

BHL —. *Beatissimi patris nostri Petri [de Murrone] confessoris vita* (**XIII**)[310]

Dedicatory preface to the professor of theology and Celestine abbot Petrus and to the Celestine brothers.

inc. proem.: Consuetudo ueterum coenobitarum iam usitata et probata fuit, Abba pater caeterique in Christo fratres, nonnulla et memoriam quidem digna litteris mandare posterisque relinquere quae uel laudem uel uitam simul et gesta sancti alicuius explicarent seu moralia quibus homines et potissimum religiosi uirtuti se dedant pariter et contemplationi, qua fari cum immortali Deo possint. Id plane et Iohannes Cassianus, id Cassiodorus, id Ciprianus, id Gregorius, id et doctus Hieronymus effecere. Et ut de graecis aliquem unum enumerem fecit et magnus ille theophanator Basilius

des proem.: Munusculun itaque hoc est libellum . . . deum orate

inc.: Petrus de Castello Santi Angeli comitatus Molisii prope Limosanum ex optimis ortus parentibus Maria et Angelo, seu corrupto ut reor vocabulo Angelerio, effectus est Christi servus et monachus

des.: Atque et nos quoque laetamur omnes . . . continuis suis precibus et intercessionibus . . . in secula seculorum. Amen.

MSS

1. Vatican City, BAV, MS Vat. lat. 14517. XV. Kristeller, *Iter* 1:474a, cf. *Iter* 6:353a. Source text.

Editions
None known to me.

LOLLIUS, Antonius (d. 1486)[311]

BHL —. *Vita Eugeniae* (IV)[312]

Dedicatory preface to Cardinal Francesco Todeschini Piccolomini and so to be dated after 1460. Lollius, alleging recent study of Cicero, revises the

---

309. Not in Kristeller, "Contribution." On the eremitical Celestines, see J. Duhr in *DS* 2, no. 1 (1953): 379–384.

310. On Celestine's sanctity, see n. 283 above, and George Ferzoco, "Church and Sanctity: The Hagiographical Dossier of Peter of Morrone," in M. C. Deprez-Masson, ed., *Normes et pouvoir à la fin du Moyen Ages; Actes du colloque "La recherche en études médiévales au Québec et en Ontario"* (Montreal: Ceres, 1990), 53–69, with references.

311. On this lawyer, employed by Francesco Piccolomini, see Cosenza, *Dictionary*, 3:2003c–2004a; Maria Graziosi, ed., *Paolo Cortesi, De hominibus doctis* (Rome: Bonacci, 1973), 107 n. 140; O'Malley, *Praise*, 117 n. 158.

account of Eugenia that Ambrogio Traversari (*q.v.*) had mildly touched up.

inc. proem.: Saepenumero me plures interrogarunt, observandissime domine, et ingenti quadam admiratione nostra tempora deplorantes, quid in causa sit cur sacrae litterae et historiae martyrum apud doctos et elegantes viros nullius pretii habeantur et cur potius quam ad sanctorum vitam ad poeticas fabulas mira quadam celeritate cecurrant

des proem.: Amor tamen . . . fecit ut . . . ignorantiae meae detegere non curarim.

inc.: Commodus imperator generosa prosapia Phylippum in septimo suo consulatu Alexandriae regie Aegyptorum urbi praefecit

des.: Et cum his sermonibus euanescens . . . angeli . . . concanebant sine fine dicentes Gloria patri et filio et spiritui . . . in saecula saeculorum. Amen.

MSS
1. Vatican City, BAV, MS Chis. F IV 83. XV. Kristeller, *Iter* 2:474a. Source text.

Editions
None known to me.

MAFFEI, Raffaello (1455–1522)[313]

BHL —. *Historia Actineae et Grecimaniae* (IV)[314]

Lacking prologue. The printed edition provides a *terminus ante quem* of 1519. The account is a retelling of the *inventio* of 1140 and has been divided into *lectiones* for the office.

inc. (lectio 1): Actiniae et Graecimanae hodierna die memoriam

des. (lectio 6): ut earum imitandi exemplum posteris occasio daretur.

MSS
1. Vatican City, BAV, MS Ottob. Lat. 992, fols. 254–255. XVI in. Autograph. Kristeller, *Iter* 2:426b. Seen.

---

312. G. D. Gordini in *BS* 5 (1964): 181–183.
313. On Maffei, see chap. 6 above. For his attention to the 1484 translation of Benedict, see Paul Meyvaert, "Peter the Deacon and the Tomb of St. Benedict," *Revue bénédictine* 65 (1955): 53–55.
314. M. Japundzic in *BS* 1 (1961): 167; A. Marucci in *Dizionario biografico e bibliografico di Volterra* (Ospedaletto: Pacini, 1997), 3:885a–b.

2. Vatican City, BAV, MS Ottob. lat. 2377, fols. 255–255v. XVI in. Autograph. Kristeller, *Iter* 2:437a. Seen.

3. Vatican City, BAV, MS Ottob. lat. 2377, fols. 261v–262, untitled. XVI in. Autograph. Kristeller, *Iter* 2:437a. Seen.

Editions

1. *Officium S. Victoris, S. Octaviani, S. Iusti & Clementis, S. Actiniae & Grecinianae, S. Lini* [Florence, 1519], signs. fv–f4, an office in six readings. Source text.

BHL —. cf. BHG 245. *Monodia Gregorii Nazianzeni in magnum Basilium* (IV)[315]

Maffei translated Gregory of Nazianzen's panegyrical account of the life as the introduction to his edition of selected homilies by Basil.

inc.: Cum Magni Basilii, uiri sanctissimi, preconiis mea pene omnia scripta sint referta

des.: Tu ob iter e coelo nos respice et datam mihi renum debilitatem ac articulorum dolorem uel iube discedere, uel adiuua & hortare ita me aequo fere animo ut hinc demum descedentem me in eterna tabernacula recipias, et beatam Trinitatem eo quo est modo tecum pariter contemplari ualeam. Finit Monodia Gregorii Nazianzeni.

MSS
None known to me.

Editions

1. *Magni Basilii Opera*, tr. Raffaele Maffei. Rome: Jacopo Mazzochi, 1515, fols. 3–20. Source text.

BHL —. *Vita b. Humilianae*, O.F.M. tert. (XIII)[316]

Preface mentioning Andrea Florentinus, O.F.M. The account was commissioned by the Florentine Franciscans, perhaps as part of a renewed effort to have Humiliana canonized.

inc. proem.: Humiliane uidue uita a fratre Vito Cortonese uiro quodam inter beati Francisci commilitones

des. proem.: et hereditas glorie pertinere uidebatur.

inc.: Igitur Humiliana uirgo Florentina patre Oliuerio e familia Circorum

---

315. See n. 51 above.
316. R. Sciamannini in *BS* 3 (1963): 1132–1134; A. Benvenuti Papi in *DBI* 23 (1979): 692–697; *eadem* in *GLS* 1903b–1905a.

des.: tot patentie uirtutumque omnis generis exempla pre se tulerit, unde ob uite labores pro domino toleratos iure possit cum martyribus comparari . . . in secula seculorum. Amen.

MSS

1. Florence, AS, Carte Cerchi 155 bis, fols. 1–5. No epistle. Not seen. Reference from Anne M. Schuchman.

2. Florence, AS, Carte Cerchi 155. No epistle. Not seen. Reference from Anne M. Schuchman, who identifies Alessandro de'Cerchi's hand.

3. Florence, BN, MS Landau Finaly 243, fols. 1–10v. XVI in. Kristeller, *Iter* 1:170a. Seen.

4. Rome, BN Vittorio Emmanuale II, MS Sessoriano 412 (2063), vernacular. XVI in. Kristeller, *Iter* 2:119a. Cf. contents of Landau Finaly 243. Seen.

5. Vatican City, BAV, MS Ottob. Lat. 992, fols. 242–246. XVI in. Autograph. Kristeller, *Iter* 2:426b. Seen.

Editions
All are late; see *BHL*.

BHL —. *Vita b. Jacobi Guidii ex Comitibus* [de Certaldo] (XIII)[317]

Dedicatory epistle to Mario Maffei. The *terminus ante quem* is Raffaele's death date, 1522.

inc. epist.: Qum nuper apud coenobitas tuos diuerterem

inc.: Jacobus is e castro Certaldi proximo fuit patre Albertino[318]

des.: eos presertim qui eius et ordine et uestigia querunt imitari.

MSS

1. Vatican City, BAV, MS Barb. Lat. 2517, fols. 3–4. XVI in. Autograph. Kristeller, *Iter* 2:463a. With a different *des.*: "Ante uero mortem non multos annos Ingheramis eques frater ipsius exemplum imitatus eidem se loco uno tantum sibi famulo ob tenuem valitudinem reservato de mare moriendo addixit. Possessionem quoque que in Elsae nunc Valle pulcherima adspicient, ut una cum religione patrimonio, quod omnium suorum superstes esset, perturris donauit, ut apud eiusdem archiuium coenobii testamenti tabula testatur." Source text.

2. Vatican City, BAV, MS Barb. Lat. 2517, fols. 5–6. XVI in. Autograph. Kristeller, *Iter* 2:463a. Source text.

---

317. C. Somigli in *BS* 6 (1965): 352–353.

318. Thus the incipit on fol. 3; cf. the incipit to the version found later in the same manuscript, fol. 5: "Jacobus is e castro Certaldi proximo fuit patre cuius nomen non traditur."

Editions
All are late; see *BHL*.

BHL —. Historia sanctorum Justi et Clementis (VI)[319]

No preface. Composed after Raffaele's withdrawal to Volterra (1507).
 inc. (*lectio* 1): Imperante siquidem in oriente[320]
 inc. (*lectio* 4): Iustus autem et Clemens Volaterras petierunt
 des. (*lectio* 9): Quae post modo Saxonum imperii maiestate paulatim dificiente [*sic*] pristinum nomen recuperauere.

MSS
 1. Vatican City, BAV, MS Ottob. Lat. 992, fols. 253–253v. XVI in. Autograph. Kristeller, *Iter* 2:426b. Seen.
 2. Vatican City, BAV, MS Ottob. Lat. 2377, fols. 259–260. XVI in. Autograph. Kristeller, *Iter* 2:437a. Seen.

Editions
 1. *Officium S. Victoris, S. Octaviani, S. Iusti & Clementis, S. Actiniae & Grecinianae, S. Lini* [Florence, 1519], signs. c2v–f, an office in nine readings. Source text.

BHL —. Historia s. Lini (primae papae) (I)[321]

No preface. A *terminus ante quem* may be provided by the founding of a church dedicated to Linus in Volterra in 1513; the *terminus post quem* may be 1480, when Raffaello funded construction at San Lino, the convent of the Poor Clares.[322]
 inc. (*lectio* 1): De Lini genere quod de regione Tusciae fuerit tantum antiquis scriptum reperitur.
 des. (*lectio* 3): sic obtemperare suo putat sanctoque spiritu pariter instigatur. Deo Gratias.

MSS
 1. Vatican City, BAV, Ottob. Lat. 992, fols. 255v–256. XVI in. Autograph. Kristeller, *Iter* II, 426b. Seen.

---

319. Marucci, *Dizionario biografico* 3:1024–1025; S. Ferrali in *BS* 7 (1966): 42–47. Maffei dates these figures to 520 (Ottob. Lat. 2377, fol. 258).
 320. For the incipit of *lectio* 1, see Octavianus below: Maffei directs that the first three *lectiones* for Justus and Clemens be repeated from the office for Octavianus. The two offices also share hymns and antiphons.
 321. Kelly, *ODP* 6.

Editions

　1. *Officium S. Victoris, S. Octaviani, S. Iusti & Clementis, S. Actiniae & Grecinianae, S. Lini* [Florence, 1519], signs. f5–f6v, an office in three readings. Source text.

BHL —. Historia b. Octaviani (VI)[323]

No preface.

　inc. (*lectio* 1): Imperante siquidem in oriente

　des. (*lectio* 9): ac laeti in domino uiuere ualeamus ipsiusque fidei exemplo . . . ac benignitate domini nostri Iesu Christi . . . in secula seculorum.

MSS

　1. Vatican City, BAV, MS Ottob. Lat. 992, fols. 250v (*inc.*: Imperante in oriente)–252v. XVI in. Autograph. Kristeller, *Iter* 2:426b. Seen.

　2. Vatican City, BAV, MS Ottob. lat. 2377, fols. 258–259. XVI in. Autograph. Kristeller, *Iter* 2:437a. Seen.

Editions

　1. *Officium S. Victoris, S. Octaviani, S. Iusti & Clementis, S. Actiniae & Grecinianae, S. Lini* [Florence, 1519], signs. c4–cr, an office in nine readings. Source text.

BHL —. S. Victoris historia (IV)[324]

Prefatory letter to the cathedral chapter of Volterra. In Ottob. Lat. 992, fol. 247 (lower right foliation), there is a notice of approval, dated "Anno salutis millesimo quingentesimo decimonono quinto idus intercalares" (1519).

　inc. epist.: Caritate in res diuinas admoniti

　inc. (*lectio* 1): Victor genere Mauritanus

　des. (*lectio* 9): Huius insuper martyris caput uenerandum singularis loco muneris Volaterranis donauit. . . . de hac urbe meriti nobis in benedictione memoria foret.

MSS

　1. Vatican City, BAV, MS Ottob. Lat. 992, fols. 248–250 (lacking the letter). XVI in. Autograph. Kristeller, *Iter* 2:426b. Seen.

---

322. On the 1513 founding, see A. Amore, *BS* 8 (1966): 56–57; on the 1480 foundation, see John F. D'Amico, "The Raffaeli Maffei Monument in Volterra," in J. Hankins, J. Monfasani, and F. Purnell, eds., *Supplementum Festivum: Studies in Honor of Paul Oskar Kristeller* (Binghamton, N.Y.: MRTS, 1987), 472.

323. Marucci, *Dizionario biografico* 3:1138–1139. Octavianus's dates are uncertain, but Maffei considers the hermit a contemporary of Justus and Clemens, since he allows the two offices to share the introductory readings.

324. Umberto Bavoni, *La cattedrale di Volterra* (Florence, 1997), 93, 97–100.

2. Vatican City, BAV, MS Ottob. Lat. 2377, fols. 252–253v, with a letter to the cathedral chapter of Volterra. XVI in. Autograph. Kristeller, *Iter* 2:437a. Seen.

3. Vatican City, BAV, MS Ottob. Lat. 2377, fols. 256–257v. *Inc. epist.*: Caritas vestri, Patres Reverendi; *inc.*: [*del.* Voscei tempore Basilicam Volterranam] constructam fuisse. XVI in. Autograph. Kristeller, *Iter* 2:437a. Seen.

Editions

1. *Officium S. Victoris, S. Octaviani, S. Iusti & Clementis, S. Actiniae & Grecinianae, S. Lini* [Florence, 1519], signs. a–c2, an office in nine readings. Source text.

BHL —. *Historia beati Zenobii* (V)[325]

Prefatory letter to the *cathedral chapter* at Florence, which had requested the work. There is also a letter preceding the version of the life written for reading outside the confines of the office. The letter of commission is BAV MS Barb. Lat. 2517, fol. 17r–v, from the cathedral chapter at Florence, dated "nonas sept. 1521."

inc. epist.: Vestra epistola, Patres uenerandissimi, me parumper in deliberanda

inc. epist.: Salute uir doctissime. Cum habuerimus iampridem Diui Zenobii officium nobis a memoribus nostris traditum

inc.: Zenobius patria Florentinus ex uetusta et nobili Hieronymorum prosapia natus est, parentibus qunquam infidelibus attamen honestissimis Luciano et Sophia

des.: Quo ferme duce felicitate in domino perpetua floreant et nullas hostium metuant impugnationes . . . in secula seculorum.

MSS

1. Vatican City, BAV, MS Ottob. Lat. 992, fols. 264v–267 (bottom right foliation), without letters. XVI in. Autograph. Kristeller, *Iter* 2:426b. Source text.

2. Vatican City, BAV, MS Ottob. Lat. 2377, fols. 262–266, with a letter to the cathedral chapter of Florence. XVI in. Autograph. Kristeller, *Iter* 2:437a. Source text.

3. Vatican City, BAV Barb Lat 2517, fol. 19, with letters from and to the cathedral chapter at Florence on fols. 17–18v. XVI in. Autograph. The letter to the cathedral chapter differs from that in Ottob. Lat. 2377. Kristeller, *Iter* 2:463a. Source text.

325. On Zenobius, see G. D. Gordini in *BS* 12 (1969): 1467–1468, and A. Benvenuti in *GLS* 1978a–1979b.

Editions

None known to me.

BHL —. BHG 703. *In Gordium martyrem* (trans. from Basil)

Not included in figure 1.1.

inc.: Naturae lex apibus innata, fratres dilectissimi, ut nisi rex prius agmen praecedat, ab aluearibus nusquam discedant

des.: Sic et huius uiri sanctissimi memoria quo maiori eam temporis spatio retinemus eo recentior in nostris animis floret, in memoria enim aeterna erit iustus. In terris quidem dum terra durabit, in coelis uero apud aequem et altissimum iudicem dominum nostrum . . . in aeterna secula. Amen.

MSS

    1. BAV, Ott. Lat. 2377, fols. 267–271v. XVI in. Autograph. Kristeller, *Iter* 2:437a. Seen.

Editions

    1. *Opera Magni Basilii*, Rome: Jacopo Mazzochi, 1515, fols. 147v–151. In the letter of dedication that opens this volume, Raffaele confesses his reliance on an earlier translation by "Gaspare Volterrano."

BHL —. BHG 972. *In martyrum Iulittam* (trans. from Basil)

Not included in figure 1.1.

inc.: Commonis [*impr.* concionis] hodiernae causa in hoc sacro templo, fratres dilectissimi, Beatae Iulittae martyris praeconium

des.: Postremo quomodo in omnibus deo gratias agas, et demum quemadmodum adflictos consolari debeas, ut ex omni parte integer ac perfectus existas auxilio sancti spiritus et gratia domini nostri . . . in aeterna secula. Amen.

MSS

    1. BAV, Ottob. Lat. 2377, fols. 230–235v. XVI in. Autograph. Kristeller, *Iter* 2:437a. Seen.

Editions

    1. *Opera Magni Basilii*, Rome: Jacopo Mazzochi, 1515, fols. 118v–123. Source text.

BHL —. BHG 1205b. *In laudem XL martyrum* (trans. from Basil)

Not included in figure 1.1.

inc.: Quis modus aut que satietas martyrum memoriam prosequendi erit

des.: uno omnino pro pietate omnes tropaeum erigentes una iustitiae corona ornati fuere in Christo. . . . in aeterna secula. Amen.

MSS

 1. BAV, Ottob. Lat. 2377, fols. 263–267. XVI in. Autograph. Kristeller, *Iter* 2:437a Seen.

Editions

 1. *Opera Magni Basilii,* Rome: Jacopo Mazzochi, 1515, fol. 144v–147v. Source text.

MANETTI, Giannozzo (1396–October 26, 1459)[326]

Collection. *Adversus Judaeos et Gentes*, books VII–IX

The incomplete treatise, which was dedicated to Alfonso of Aragon (d.1458), concludes with three books that list hundreds of saints, in many cases giving brief narratives such as might be found in a historical martyrology. See chap. 2 above.[327]

BHL 1192b. [untitled epitome of the life of Bernardino of Siena] (d. 1444)

Not included in figure 1.1.

 inc.: Bernardinus Masse natus, que quidem est urbs Etrurie Senis finitima

 des.: et quattor Maffei Vegii laudensis . . . libris breuitatis causa excerpsimus, quos ille de uita et obitu atque officio . . . prosecutis est.

MSS

 1. *Adversus Judaeos et Gentes,* Vatican City, BAV, MS Urb. Lat. 154, fols. 152–154. XV. Autograph. Seen.

Editions

 1. Dionisio Pacetti, in *Bollettino di Studi Bernardiniani* 1 (1935): 186–190. Source text.

BHL 3133m. [untitled epitome of the life of Francis of Assisi] (XIII)

Not included in figure 1.1.

---

326. On Manetti see S. U. Baldessari and R. Bagemiho, eds., *Giannozzo Manetti: Biographical Writings* (Cambridge, Mass.: Harvard University Press, 2003), viii–xi, with further bibliography.

327. A. De Petris, "Le teorie umanistiche del tradurre e l'*Apologeticus* del Giannozzo Manetti," *Bibliothèque d'humanisme et renaissance* 37 (1976): 15–32; and G. Fioravanti, "L'Apologetica anti-giudaica di Giannozzo Manetti," *Rinascimento*, ser. 2, 23 (1983): 3–32, address the logic of the collection. Delorme (see below) edits other excerpts from book 5, "De scriptoribus sacris," book 7, "De confessoribus sanctis," and book 10, "De mulieribus, virginibus ac martiribus," from *Adversus Judaeos.*

inc.: Franciscus in opido Asisii natus, Be[r]nardonis cuiusdam mercatoris ac Ioanne uxoris sue filius

des.: nouis quibusdum examinationibus diligentissima habitis, eum non immerito in catalogo sanctorum collocauit et posuit.

MSS

1. *Adversus Judaeos et Gentes*, Vatican City, BAV, MS Urb. Lat. 154, fols. 148–151v. XV. Autograph. Seen.

Editions

1. Ferdinand-Marie Delorme, in *AFH* 31 (1938): 213–218. Source text.

MARULUS, Marcus (August 18, 1450–January 6, 1524)[328]

BHL 415. Passio sancti Anastasii [de Aquilegia] martyris Salernitani (IV)[329]

Preface, no dedicatee, undated.

inc. proem: In Salomonis ede ad diuersorum necessitatem

inc.: Diocletiano igitur Romani Imperii iniquissime moderante

des.: Aquileienses confusi ad propria rediere. Immenso igitur gaudio laetare, Salona . . .

BHL 2270 (not attributed). Passio sancti Domni Martyris Archiepiscopi Salernitani (III)[330]

inc.: Post gloriosam ascensionem

des.: in honorem s. Dei genetricis u. Mariae paulo ante construxerat. Ubi dominus . . .

---

328. Since I began this study, secondary literature on Marulus has become voluminous. As it is conducted in a language in which I am not competent, I note here only titles for the passions of Anastasius and Domnus, because I have adduced them in chap. 2 above and have counted them toward figure 1.1 (Venice, Bibl. Marciana, MS Lat. XIV 181 [4668]). Marulus also wrote important Latin verse accounts of David (a Turin manuscript was rediscovered by Carlo Dionisotti in 1952); of Jerome, in Latin prose and verse, dedicated to Pope Leo X; and of Judith, in the vernacular, a poem held to mark the birth of Croatian literature. He wrote short poems on the passions of the twelve apostles and on the four doctors of the Church. Also important is Marulus's *De bene vivendi instituta*, a treatise on the saintly virtues arranged in the alphabetical order of the virtues, which had great success in the sixteenth and seventeenth centuries.

329. E. Giannarelli in *GLS* 115b–118b.

330. A. Amore in *BS* 4 (1964): 764–767.

MOMBRIZIO, Bonino (ca. 1424–ca. 1480)[331]

Collection. *Sanctuarium*

Verse dedications to Cicco Simonetta and to the reader. In penultimate position is a second poem to Simonetta. The two volume collection may have been published in the spring of 1477. See chap. 3 above.

MSS

1. F. Argelati (1685–1755) described a fifteenth-century manuscript, perhaps autograph, but it has been lost. Other manuscript fragments, for example, the late vernacular excerpts at Brescia noted by Kristeller, *Iter* 1:32a, appear to derive from the incunable.

Editions

1. [Milan, ca. 1477]. Goff M810; HC 11544*; *IGI* 6690; *BMC* VI, 736. Source text. Paul Needham kindly provides this collation of the Morgan Library copy:

vol. I: π⁴; a¹⁰ 2a-7a⁸ 8a¹⁰; b-10b⁸; c-8c⁸ 9c⁶ (6 + 1: *amori Christi*); d-4d⁸; e-3e⁸ 4e²; f⁸; 2f⁶; F-2F⁸; 3F⁶; g-4g⁸. 349 leaves: fos. 1 (π1), 5(a1), 255 (4d8), 281 (4e2), 349 (4g8) blank.

vol. II: π²; h¹⁰ 2h⁸; I-4I⁸; L⁸ 2L¹⁰; m-10m⁸ 11m¹⁰; n-3n⁸ 4n⁸ (3+1: *uertitis*); p-5p⁸ q⁸ r⁶ 2r⁴; s-8s⁸; T¹²; t⁸ 2t-3t⁶; V⁸ 2V¹⁰: 365 leaves: fos. 3 (h1), 347 (3t6), 365v (2V10) blank.

2. Paris, 1910, reprints the fifteenth-century edition, adding an introduction and source studies for most accounts. Reprinted Paris, 1978.

NALDI, Naldo (1436—ca. 1513)[332]

BHL —. Vita Zenobii Urbi Florentiae Antistitis (V)[333]

Dedicatory preface to Raffaello Girolami, in which his family's descent from Zenobius's *stirps* is mentioned. The Baltimore manuscript is dated at the end 1499, with the scribe's name, Andreas Verazanus.

---

331. Consult chapter 3 for other saints' lives by Mombrizio.

332. Kristeller, *Supplementum Ficinianum*, 328; W. Leonard Grant, "Naldo Naldi and Cod. Urb. lat. 1198," *Manuscripta* 6 (1962): 67–75; idem, "The Major Poems of Naldo Naldi," *Manuscripta* 6 (1962): 131–154; idem, "Naldo Naldi and the Volaterrais," *Rassegna Volaterrana* 32 (1965): 3–21; M. Martelli, "Le *Elegie* di Naldo Naldi," in R. Cardini, ed., *Tradizione classica e letteratura umanistica: Per Alessandro Perosa* (Rome: Bulzoni, 1985), 1:307–322.

333. On Zenobius, see n. 325 above.

inc. proem.: Cum ea sit et gratia et gloria familiae uestrae, Raphael Hieronyme, ut non modo in terris

des. proem.: auxilium operaque allatur.

inc.: Cum in Florentina urbe Hieronymorum domus a priscis usque deducta temporibus

des.: ita semper in posterum speret atque confidat ab illo pariter se fore consecuturum.

MSS

1. Baltimore, Walters Art Gallery, MS W 406. XV. Kristeller, *Iter* 5:215a. Source text.

2. Florence, Bib. Marucelliana, MS A CXXXV. XVII–XVIII, fragm. Kristeller, *Iter* 1:106b. Not seen.

3. Florence, BN, MS Magl. XXXVIII 106. XVI. Kristeller, *Iter* 1:128a. Not seen.

Editions
None known to me.

NEGRI, Francesco (April 17, 1452–after November 19, 1523)[334]

BHL —. Felicissimum Theodosiae virginis de tyranno tropheum (IV)

In 1513, Negri, a grammar teacher, dedicated this lengthy three-part work—he describes it as life, martyrdom, and miracles—to Vittoria Colonna. Among the miracles, he recorded his own earlier appeal to the virgin martyr, and his promise to write her history and office if she helped him. See *AASS* April I (Paris, 1865): 66, para. 12: "Ego enim historiam passionis tuae hinc inde dispersam, in pulcherrimum stylum to juvante colligere voveo celeberrimumque officium praeparare." Does that statement support the attribution to Negri of the anonymous office and *vitae* in the incunable (below)? Giovanni Mercati, *Ultimi contributi alla storia degli umanisti, 1. Traversariana* (Studi e testi 90) (Vatican City: BAV, 1939), 93–94, believes that Negri composed the anonymous office, but not the *vitae* also found there.

---

334. See King, *Venetian Humanism*, 413–415; Giovanni Mercati, *Ultimi contributi alla storia degli umanisti, 1. Traversariana* (Studi e testi 90) (Vatican City: BAV, 1939), 93–94 and 107–109. See also the commentary by J. Henschenius, in *AASS* April I (Paris, 1860): 63, paras. 10–11.

MSS

1. In the seventeenth century, the Bollandists had access to the 1513 autograph; see *AASS* April I (Paris, 1865): 63a–b, para. 10. I do not know if it still exists.

Editions

1. An edition of the miracles, that is, the third part of the *Tropheum* dedicated to Vittoria Colonna, is in *AASS* April I (Paris, 1865): 64a–66b.

2. Cf. *Martyrium sanctae Theodosiae. Miracula sanctae Theodosiae. Officium sanctae Theodosiae.* Venice: Antonio de Zanchi, December 22, 1498. *IGI* 9503; ISTC it00147500. Not seen.

NOVIS, Augustinus de, Ticinensis

See AUGUSTINUS Ticinensis.

OLMI, Paolo, O.E.S.A. (1414–1484)[335]

BHL 6004d. *Hystoria s. Monicae matris s. Augustini (et miracula)* (IV)[336]

Prefatory letter to Johannes Senensis, confessor to Sixtus IV and priest at Massa, dated 1479. See also Olmi's *Apologia religionis fratrum eremitarum ordinis sancti Augustini*, dedicated to Johannes Senensis and complimenting the Hermits' cardinal protector, Guillaume d'Estouteville (1403–1483).[337] Incipits and desinits from *BHL*.

inc. epist.: Inter caetera que uiris eruditis sacrarumque literarum studiosis

inc.: Domine quia ego seruus tuus, ego seruus tuus et filius ancille tuae accipe confessiones meas. . . . Non enim preteribo quicquid mihi anima mea

---

335. Not in Kristeller, "Contribution." See Maria Luisa Gatti Perrer, *Umanesimo a Milano: L'Osservanza agostiniana all'Incoronata* (Milan: Arte Lombarda, 1980), 73 and 207–208; Girolamo Tiraboschi, *Storia della letteratura italiana* (Rome: Salvioni, 1783), vol. 6, part. 1, 176, notes that Olmi was a canon at Bergamo before joining the Lombard Congregation of Hermits; see also Ossinger, *Bibliotheca Augustiniania*, 522–524. For Olmi and Clara of Montefalco, see under G. M. A. Carrara, above.

336. See n. 33 above.

337. See Pietro Ransano, O.P., *Annales omnium temporum* (Palermo, BC, MS 3 Q q C, fasc. 59, fols. 348–350v) on Monica (*inc.*: Migrasse ipsam ad dominum apud Ostiam) that mentions a "vir quidam religiosus ordinis heremitarum sancti Augustini Bergomensis Paulus nomine prolixioribus eius vitam descripsit omnia fere ex sancti filii eius libris excerpta . . . Ad cuius vitae lectionem curiosos lectores remittimus."

des.: Neque enim respondebit illa se nihil debere. . . . Sit ergo in pace cum uiro ante quem nulli et post quem nulli nupta est cui seruiuit fructum tibi asserens cum tollerantia ut eum quoque lucraretur tibi.

inc. mir.: Quae uero

des. mir.: carmine salutauit dicens.

MSS

    1. Bergamo, Bibl. Civica, MS Delta IV 47. XV. Kristeller, *Iter* 1:10b. Seen.

Editions

    1. *Hystoria S. Monicae Matris S. Augustini. Libellus de Apologia Religionis Fratrum Heremitarum.* [Rome, F. da Cinquines, 1479]. H10328; Goff P162(1). *IGI* 10021; ISTC ip00162500. Source text.

Lost? *Vita et miracula b. Helenae de Utino*

See chap. 5 above.

Lost? *Vita et miracula b. Mariae de Genoa*

See chap. 5 above.

BHL 5132. *Vita et miracula b. Maddalena Alberici da Como*, abb. **Brunatensis, O.E.S.A. (d. 1465)**[338]

    inc.: Miro religionis et sanctitatis odore floruit B. Magdalena de Albricis de Como . . . in somniis a S.P.N. Augustino admonita, solitudinem quamdam extra ciuitatis moenia adiit

    des.: Mitto beneficia . . . ne uitae limites excedere uidear. Sciant tamen historiarum cultores, ea omnia, quae hic prae oculis ponuntur, a probatis piisque Magdalenae familiaribus fuisse collecta, et potissimum a Philosopho de Sala, qui de ejus prudentia qua in infantia praelucebat metrum uulgauit; a Nicolao Zaffarone, S. Antonino Rectore et coenobio s. Andreae ante receptos fratres ordinis nostri confessario; ac a Fr. Augustino de Perlaschis, Nicolai in eodem munere successore.

MSS
None known to me.

Editions

    1. *Pauli Ulmi Bergomensis vita et miracula B. Mariae de Albericis* [Rome, 1484?]. H 16087. Cf. *IERS* p. 252. Not seen.

    2. *AASS* May III (Paris, 1866): 252–254. Source text.

---

338. See Ossinger, *Bibliotheca Augustiniana*, 522–524; N. Del Re in *BS* 1 (1961): 728–729.

PETRUS de Natalibus (Nadal), O.P.

Collection. *Catalogus sanctorum et gestorum eorum diversis voluminibus collectus*

Compiled between 1369–1372, mainly from the *Legenda aurea* and the hagiographic encyclopedia of Petrus Calo.[339] Included here because of the frequent early editions.

Editions

1. Vicenza: Henricus de Sancto Ursio, Zenus, 1493. With hendecasyllables from Antonius Verlus Vicentinus to the reader, *inc.*: "Quam tot heroum legeres olympi / Gesta, millenis reserata chartis." Appending twenty-five new saints at the end. HC 11676*; *IGI* 6769; *BMC* 7:1047; Goff N6. Seen.

2. Venice: Bartolomeo de Zanis with Lucantonio Giunta,1506. The edition by Antonio Verlo. Seen.

3. Lyon: Claude Davost with Stephan Gueynard, 1508. With the 1493 preface by Antonio Verlo. Not seen.

4. Strasbourg: Martin Flach, 1513. Not seen.

5. Lyon: Jacob Saccon, 1514. With the 1493 preface by Antonio Verlo. Not seen.

6. Lyon: Johannes Thomas, 1514. Not seen.

7. Venice: Nicholas of Frankfurt, 1516. Ed. Alberto Catellano, O.P. Incorporates the twenty-five new saints of the Venice 1493 edition, with the exception of Rocco. Seen.

8. Lyon: Jacob Saccon, 1519. Not seen.

9. [Strasbourg: Johann Knobloch], 1521. Not seen.

PETRUS Rodulphius, de Viglevano (fl. XV)[340]

Officium. *Officium s. Bernardini Senensis* (d. 1444; c.d. 1450; f.d. May 20)

Dedication to the Sienese general of the Franciscans. Petrus wrote three extensive offices for Bernardino, each consisting of nine readings. I record only the first here and in figure 1.1.

inc. praef.: Existimo nequaquam ex tua memoria decidisse, generalis reuerendis/sime pater, te mihi sepenumero precipisse

des. praef.: Quod si forte probes, crescet tua gloria, sancti / crescet

---

339. G. Musolino, A. Niero, and S. Tramontin, *Culto dei santi a Venezia* (Venice: Studium Cattolico Veneziano, 1965), 21–22.

340. Not in Kristeller, "Contribution"; Petrus appears to be a layman or in minor orders.

honor, cultus crescet amorque dei, / at Bernardini meritis precibusque beati / ecclesia et regnum crescet in orbe tuum.

inc.: Apparuit gratia dei saluatoris nostri diebus istis nouissimis

des.: Ut ciues tam docti quam imperiti eum audientes uehementem admirationem assumerent

MSS
None known to me.

Editions

1. Untitled. Rome: Johannes Bulle, ca. 1479. C70; IGI 7803 *IERS* 587; ISTC ip00678000. See Wouter Bracke, *Fare la epistola nella Roma del Quattrocento* (Rome, 1992), 26, item five. The three offices are bound into BAV, MS Ottob. lat. 1982, fols. 163–170v. Cf. Kristeller, *Iter* 2:434b–435a. Seen. SLU reel 8554.

PIZAMANO, Antonio, O.P., bp., *beatus* (1462–1512)[341]

BHL 8160. *Vita Thome Aquinatis* (XIII)[342]

Dedicatory preface to Agostino Barbarigo (doge 1486–1501). The life of Aquinas precedes a collection of seventy-three works by the saint.

inc. proem.: Quamquam sine magno labore in optime quoque uirtutes ipsae, quae uera bona sunt, emicare nequeant atque hominum genus ab ardua et recta semita in pronam et deteriorem partem potius uergat, optimis tamen rationibus humanae uitae magistris et magnorum uirorum claris exemplis ad proprium et felicem locum bene beateque uiuendi ducitur.

des. proem.: sed iam ad opus promissum deueniamus.

inc.: Diuus Thomas Landulpho patre Aquini comite Campaniae urbis celeberrime ac multorum oppidorum principe natus, Theodoram matrem et genere et sanctissimis uite moribus insignem sortitus est

des.: nostri temporis homines uix latinum sapiunt . . . Amen.

MSS
None known to me.

---

341. Degli Agostini, *Notizie* 2:189–199; Cosenza, *Dictionary* 4:2830–2831 and 5:1431–1432; A. Niero in *BS* 10 (1968): 939–941; Musolino, Niero, and Tramontin, *Santi e beati veneziani*, 243–250. For Pizamano's vernacular account of Ludovico Rizzi, see Kristeller, *Iter* 2:206b.

342. See n. 171 above.

Editions
    1. *Opuscula divi Thome Aquinatis,* Venice: Hermann Liechtenstein, September 7, 1490, fols. 2–7. *IGI* 9552; H 1541;* *BMC* 5:358; Goff T258; ISTC itoo258000. Source text.
    2. *Opuscula s. Thome,* Venice: Boneto Locatello for Ottaviano Scoto, December 22 or 31, 1498, fols. 2–6. *IGI* 9553; H 1542;* *BMC* 5:452; Goff T257; ISTC itoo257000.

POLENTON, Sicco (ca. 1375–ca. 1447)[343]

BHL 598–599. *Sancti Antonii Confessoris de Padua Vita,* O.F.M. (XIII)[344]

Dedicatory preface to his son *Modesto.* The presentation manuscript includes the date, 1437. *Michele Savonarola* requested that Sicco write the *vita.*
    inc. proem.: Desideranti mihi perdiu a saepenumero perquirenti aliquid scribere ad te Modeste
    inc.: Antonio igitur uenerabili confessori et sancto patri nostro
    des.: constituti quoque annuatim quatuor uiri . . . oblata dispensent.
    inc. mir.: Auriema infans, sex mense supra annum nata
    des. mir.: quod in caponem talis bestia sit conuersa, ac tute quisque uesci potuerunt. Laus deo et sancto.

MSS
    1. Chicago, Newberry Library, MS It. 1437. *Vita et miracula s. Antonii de Padua,* followed by *Beatorum Antonii Peregrini ac Elene Monialis vitae.* P. Saenger, *A Catalogue of the Pre-1500 Western Manuscript Books at the Newberry Library* (Chicago: University of Chicago Press, 1989), 193a–b. Vernacular. Seen.
    2. Padua, Biblioteca Antoniana, MS 559, fols. 1–25v. On the scribe, see Vergilio Gamboso, "Sancti Antonii confessoris de Padua vita," *Il Santo* 11, nos. 2–3 (1971): 215. Not seen.
    3. Pesaro, Bibl. Oliveriana, MS 48. Gamboso, "Sancti Antonii . . . vita," 218. Not seen.
    4. Ravenna, Bibl. di San Francesco. See Gamboso, "Sancti Antonii . . . vita," 218. Lost.

    343. For an overview of his major works, see A. Dalmaso, "Note sull'attività letteraria dell'umanista Sicco Polenton," *Studi trentini di scienze storiche* 34 (1955): 3–27 and 236–264 and 35 (1956): 22–48.
    344. G. Grossato in *DBI* 3 (1961): 561b–566b; J. Toussaert, *Antoninus von Padua* (Cologne, 1967); G. Staro in *BS* 2 (1962): 156–179; *S. Antonino 1231–1981: Il suo tempo, il suo culto, e la sua città* (Padua: Signum, 1981); S. Blake Melton, "The Cult of St. Anthony in Padua," in S. Sticca, ed., *Saints: Studies in Hagiography* (Binghamton, N.Y.: MRTS, 1996), 215–232.

5. Venice, BN Marciana, MS Lat. IX 182 (3293), fols. 1–52v. 1464. Kristeller, *Iter* 2:229b. On the scribe, see Gamboso, "Sancti Antonii . . . vita," 217. Not seen.

Editions

1. *S. Antonii conf. de Padua vita* [Padua: Bartholomaeus de Valdezocco 1476]. Goff P883; *IGI* 7949; H 13212; *BMC* 7:907. Not seen.
2. Vergilio Gamboso, *Fonti agiografiche antoniane* 5: 586–785. Source text.

BHL 605. *Vita beati Antonii peregrini, O. Cam.* (XIII)[345]

Preface shared with life of Helena (below). The presentation manuscript includes the date, 1437.
inc.: Manziorum familia quae Paduae honesta cum opibus
des.: quam perdiu ac ipsa a natiuitate passus erat.

MSS

1. Chicago, Newberry Library, MS It. 1437. Saenger, *A Catalogue*, 193a–b. Vernacular. Seen.
2. Padua, Bibl. Antoniana, MS 559, fols. 26–27 (preface shared with life of Helena, *q.v.*) and 27–32v (*vita*); the presentation copy. XV.[346]
3. Padua, BU, MS 1683. XIX. Kristeller, *Iter* 2:17b. Not seen.
4. Venice, BN Marciana, MS Lat. IX 182 (3293), fols. 61–62v (preface shared with life of Helena), 62v–71r (*vita*). Kristeller, *Iter* 2:229b.

Editions

1. *AB* 13 (1894): 417–425, with variant readings in *AB* 14 (1895): 109. Source text.

BHL 3791–3792. *Vita Beati Helenae (Enselminiae)*, vid. Ord. S. Clarae Patavii (XIII)[347]

The dedicatory preface to his son *Lazaro* is shared with the life of Anthony pilgrim.
inc. proem.: Sollicitare me soles precibus, Lazare filii,
inc.: Helena uirgo beata Paduae oriunda civis fuit nobili
des.: futura calamitas. Haec sunt, mi Lazare

---

345. C. Somigli in *BS* 2 (1962): 188–189; A. Rigon, "Devotion et patriotisme dans la genère et diffusion d'un culte: Le bienheureux Antoine de Padoue surnomé Il Pellegrino (1267)," in *Faire croire: Modalités de la diffusion et de la reception des messages religieux du XII au XVe siècle* (Rome: BEFR, 1981): 259–278; Webb, *Patrons*, 139.

346. Vergilio Gamboso, *Fonti agiografiche antoniane* (Padua, 1997), 5: 543–585.

347. I. Daniele in *BS* 4 (1964): 1247–1248; L. Paolini, in *DBI* 42 (1993): 802–804; and Ada Gonzato Debiasi, "Elena Enselmini clarissa padovana: Le fonti agiografiche e il processo di canonizzazione," *Il Santo* 34, no. 1 (1994): 35–69.

MSS

1. Chicago, Newberry Library, MS It. 1437. Saenger, *Catalogue,* 193a–b. Vernacular. Seen.

2. Padua, Biblioteca Antoniana, MS 559, fols. 33–39v. Not seen.

3. Padua, Museo Civico, MS BP, I, 93. Kristeller, *Iter* 2:22a. Not seen.

4. Rome, Bibl. Vallicelliana, MS H 80, fols. 280–293. XVI–XVII. Kristeller, *Iter* 2:129b. Not seen.

5. Venice, BN Marciana, MS Lat. IX 182 (3293). XV. Kristeller, *Iter* 2:229b. Not seen.

Editions

1. *AASS* Nov. II (Paris, 1894): 512–517. Source text.

POLUCIIS, Johannes Maria de, O. Carm. (d.c. 1505?)

BHL 229a. *Vita s. Alberti de Abbatibus de Drepano . . . et aliqua eius miracula* (XIV)

No preface, no dedication. See C. de Villiers, *Bibliotheca carmelitana* (Rome, 1927; orig. 1752), 2: 50–51.

inc.: Albertus animi ordinis fratrum et sororum
des.: anno salutis MCCXXII septimo idus augusti
inc. mir.: Cum esset ille vir dei senex
des. mir.: apud altarem magnam apparet. Finis. Laus deo.

MSS
None known to me.

Editions

1. [Venice, after April 1499]. C4809; *BMC* 5:591; *IGI* 7977; Goff P906; IGI 7977, BMC 5:591; ISTC ip0090600. Seen.

RANSANO, Pietro, O.P. (1427–1492)[348]

BHL 608b. *Martyrium beati Antonii Lombardi Ordinis Praedicatorum* (d. April 10, 1460)[349]

Verse preface. Introductory remarks. The account, in the form of a letter to Pius II, was written in 1461. It ends abruptly, the *peroratio* incomplete.

---

348. Kristeller, "Contribution," 150; Cochrane, *Historians,* 153–154.
349. On Anthony of Rivoli, see n. 163 above.

Ransano names his source, the Dominican Constantius, who had also been a captive in North Africa and a close friend to Anthony.

inc. proem.: Munus ob exiguum me insulsum forte putabis / cum deceant summum munera magna uirum.

inc.: Dignum esse existimaui Beatitudini tuae rem quandam nouam et a multis iam saeculis inauditam significare

des.: Tandem locello, cui Christi crucifixi imago collocata supereminebat quem ipse uiuens sibi elegerat, sepultum est quarto idus aprilis.

inc. peroratio: Haec erant, pater beatissime, quae Celsitudini Tuae significare institueram.

des. peroratio: Singula fere haec, quae ego per epistolam ad Tuam Beatitudinem scripsi, ipse prior licet rudi oratione narrauit. Asse/

MSS
   1. Rome, Bibl. Casanatense, MS 112, fols. 82–94v. XV. Kristeller, *Iter* 2:93b. Cf. BAV, MS Chigi J VII 260 (XV), fols. 123v–124v (carmen). Kristeller, *Iter* 2:485a. Seen.

Editions
   1. E. Hocedez, "Lettre de Pierre Ranzano au Pape Pie II sur le martyre du B. Antoine de Rivoli," *AB* 24 (1906): 357–374. Source text.
   2. Bruno Figliuolo, *La cultura a Napoli nel secondo Quattrocento: Ritratti di protagonisti* (Udine: Forum, 1997), 275–276, edits the poem of dedication from BAV Chigi I.VII. 260, fols. 123v–124v, and Bib. Casinense, MS 112, fols. 81–82.

BHL 9171. *Vita Barbarae* (IV)[350]

Prefatory letter to *Filippo Perdicario*, mentioning that Barbara had been the patron of both Pietro Ransano and Filippo Perdicario since their infancies. The life is dated at the end "Neapoli sexto idus Novembres M.CCCC.LXVIIII." It is presented as a compilation of translations from the Greek and adaptations of Latin sources.

inc. epist.: Annui tandem, Philippe Perdicarie iure consulte clarissime, piis efflagitationibus tuis, quibus me aliquando adhortatus es, ut diuae Barbarae uirginis et martyris Christi uitam martiriumque perscriberem

inc.: Beatam Barbaram constat fuisse natam Nicomediae, quae urbs in Bitinia est

---

350. Barbara's passion is set sometimes in the third, sometimes in the fourth century; see Gian Domenico Gordini, in *BS* 2 (1962): 759–765, and M. Donnini in *GLS* 239a–240b. Ransano sets it in the fourth. See the reference in his *Annales omnium temporum*, Palermo, BC, MS 3 Q q C 54, fol. 213r–v (in the course of a discussion of Nicomedia). See also B. Figliuolo, *La cultura a Napoli nel secondo Quattrocento* (Udine: Forum, 1997), 151–153.

des.: Illud itaque ante omnia te nosse uelim, Philippe optime, beatam Barbaram a nationibus pene omnibus quae germaniam galliamque incolunt in maxima ueneratione haberi . . . composuere. Vale. Neapoli VI id nov. 1469.

MSS

1. Madrid, BN, MS 17890, fols. 456–494v. Acephalous. XVIII. Kristeller, *Iter* 5:575a. Not seen
2. Rome, Bibl. Casanatense, MS 112, fols. 1–35v. XV. Kristeller, *Iter* 2:93b. Source text.

Editions

1. F. A. Termini, "Ricostruzione cronologica della biografia di Pietro Ransano," *Archivio storico siciliano,* n.s., 41 (1916): 92–93 (preface only).
2. Figliuolo, *La cultura a Napoli,* 245–272, life and passion. Source text.

Officium. ⟨Office for Barbara⟩ (IV)

Dedicatory letter to *Filippo Perdicario.*
  inc. epist.: Efflagitasti federice Perdicare ciuilis pontificiique consulte
  inc. epist.: uelis emendare diligentius. Vale. Neapoli idibus Novembriabus M.CCC.LXVIII.
  inc.: Beata Barbara ex clarissimo genere Nicomediae, quae urbs in Bitinia est, patre Dioscoro, matre Laodomia nata fuit
  des.: quo tempore beata Barbara uix quartum dedimum aetatis annum compleuerat.

MSS

1. Rome, Bibl. Casanatense, MS 112, fols. 37v–38v. Nine readings. XV. Kristeller, *Iter* 2:93b. Source text.

Editions

1. Termini, "Ricostruzione," 94–95, edits the dedicatory letter and 97–100, the hymns.

BHL 5333. ⟨*Vita Margaritae Hungaricae, O.P.*⟩ (XIII)[351]

Excerpted from Ransano's *Epitome rerum hungaricarum*; see Péter Kulcsár, *Epithome rerum Hungarum id est annalium omnium temporum liber*

---

351. E. Pasztór in *BS* 8 (1966): 796–800; G. Klaniczay in *GLS* 1300a–1302a.

primus et sexagesimus in *Bibliotheca scriptorum medis recentisque aevorum*, dir. L. Juhász (Budapest, 1977), 368–373. Not included in figure 1.1.

inc.: Huius [Belae] filia fuit, beata illa Christi uirgo

des.: excessisse a narratione rerum, quas perstringere decreueram.

BHL —. ⟨*Vita Stephani Hungaricae*⟩ (XI)[352]

Excerpted from Ransano's *Epitome rerum hungaricarum*;[353] see Kulcsár, *Bibliotheca*, 354–356. Not included in figure 1.1.

inc.: Hic est beatus ille Stephanus, de quo mentionem hoc loco me facturum, paulo ante pollicitus sum

des.: deque uitae sanctitate et obitu scripserim

BHL 8656–8657. *Vita Vincentii de Valencia* [Ferrer] (d. 1419; c.d. 1455)[354]

Dedicatory epistle to *Marziale Auribelli*, O.P., dated from Palermo, 1455. In three books; some manuscripts have part of a fourth.

inc. epist.: Si maiorum nostrorum qui post nostrum inclitum ducem Dominicum ordinis praedicatorum gubernationem habuerunt

des. epist.: ea quae narrabuntur facile intelligi possint. Vale. Ex panormio anno domini nostri Jesu Christi M.CCCC.LV.

inc. 1: Vincentius a uincendo quodam diuino praesagio nomen sortitus est

inc. 2: Postquam autem de diui Vincentii uita narrata sunt ea quae de puericia deque adolescentia

inc. 3: Ennumeratis quam pluribus ex miraculis quae beati Vincentii merita apud deum . . . ostenderunt

des. lib. 3: ut uidelicet unus idemque esset huius libri et uitae eius terminus, quo . . . migrauit cum Christo uicturus. . . . Amen.

MSS

1. Basel, BU, MS E III 12 , fols. 59–99 (lib. 1–3). XV. Not seen.
2. Deventer, Athenaeum-Bibl., MS 32 (XV–XVI), n. 2. Not seen.

---

352. E. Pasztór in *BS* 12 (1969): 18; G. Klaniczay in *GLS* 1825a–1829b.

353. I have not seen L. Blazovich, "Ransanus és a *legrégibb Istvàn-legenda,*" *Irodalmtörtèneti Közlemènyek* 79 (1975): 186–188, mentioned by Figliuolo, *La cultura a Napoli*, 154 n. 20. See also Ransano's entries on Ladislaus (Kulcsar, *Biblioteca*, 360–362) and on the deaths of Mattias Corvinius and John Capistrano (ibid., 368–369).

354. On Vincent, see n. 94 above. *BHL* 8657 is listed in Kaeppeli, *Scriptores*, 3319; cf. *BHL* 865b, the same text with an incomplete fourth book. The Bollandists record a copy in Vienna, NB, MS s.n. 12708, fols. 339v–346v. I have not examined it; cf. Kristeller, *Iter* 3:67b.

3. Edinburgh, Nat. Library, MS 18.2.3, fols. 102–118v (corrected foliation provided by K. Dunn, National Library of Scotland). XV. Not seen.

4. Eichstätt, Staats- und Seminarbibliothek, MS 708, fols. 180–218. Kristeller, *Iter* 3:524a. Not seen.

5. Florence, BN, MS Conv. soppr. F 7. 378, third item. XV. Kristeller, *Iter* 5:589a–b. Seen.

6. Florence, BN, MS Magl. XXXVIII 10, 124, fols. 1–59v. XV. Vernacular translation, with a vernacular preface dated 1490, by Giovanni Caroli (*q.v.*, partially edited in Orlandi, *Necrologia*, 2:369). Kristeller, *Iter* 1:142b–143a. Seen.

7. Kraków, Bibl. Jagiellonska, MS 5467, fragm. XV. Kristeller, *Iter* 4:407a. Not seen.

8. Munich, Kirchenhist. Seminar der Universität, MS, fols. 58–106. XV. Not seen.

9. Nuremberg, Stadtbibliothek, Cent. IV, MS 75, fols. 1–32. XV. Kristeller, *Iter* 3:663a. Not seen.

10. Paris, BN, Réserve des imprimés, MS D 1740, fols. 87–125. XV. Kristeller, *Iter* 3:331b. Not seen.

11. Seville, Bibl. Colombina, MS 5–6, fols. 1–32. XV. Not seen.

12. Toulouse, Bibl. municipale, MS 486, in four books, "parait autographe." XV. C. Samaran and R. Marichal, *Catalogue des manuscrits datés* (Paris 1965), 6:501. Not seen.

13. Vatican City, BAV, MS Chigi F IV 91, fols. 1–23v, in three books. XV. Seen.

14. Venice, BN Marciana, MS Lat. IX 61 (3287). XV. This codex belonged to the Bolognese Dominicans; Ransaro's preface announces four books, but no fourth book appears here. Kristeller, *Iter* 2:229a. Source text.

15. Warsaw, BU, MS I.Q. 330, fols. 166–208v. XV. Kristeller, *Iter* 2:423a ("in four books, copied in 1465"). Not seen.

Editions

All are late; see *BHL*.

BHL 8659. ⟨*Acta pro canonizatione Vincentii*⟩[355]

Prefatory letter to Martiale Auribelli, O.P., stating that the *vita* (above) has four books.

inc. proem.: Nemo est qui ambigat, pater reuerendissime, opera tua magna ex parte

inc.: Mortuus est autem beatus Vincentius, ut alias scripsimus

---

355. Title from *BHL*; Kaeppeli, *Scriptores*, 3319.

des. mutil.: nihil aliud nisi de beati Vincentii canonizatione esse cogitandum.

MSS
None known to me.

Editions
1. *AASS* April I (Paris, 1865): 521–522. Source text.

BHL 8660. *Epitome Vita Vincentii Ferreri* (based on Ransano's *Annales omnium temporum*)[356]

Dedicatory letter to a Dominican correspondent, *Giovanni da Pistoia* of Messina, who had requested the life.

inc. epist.: Perlegi literas tuas, uir optime, quibus petis
des. epist.: miro quodam ardore affectauerint. Vale. Panhormi. Kalendis sextilibus, MCCCC. LXIII.
inc.: Nicolao V Pontifice maximo defuncto
des.: uulgaui quam diligentissime.

MSS
1. Rome, Bibl. Casanatense, MS 112, fols. 51–70v. XV. Kristeller, *Iter* 2:93b; Poncelet 1909, 216–217. Source text.
2. Madrid, BN, MS 17890, fos. 439–457. XVIII. Not seen.
3. Nuremberg, Stadtbibliothek, MS Cent. I. 75. XV. Not seen.
4. Paris, BN, Réserve des imprimés, D 1740, fos. 87–125. XV. Not seen.

Editions
All are late; see *BHL*.

BHL 8660b. ⟨*Officium Vincentii O.P.*⟩ (d. 1419)

inc.: Beatus Vincentius Valentiae ex honestis probisque parentibus
des.: iunctasque extendens manus ad caelestia regna feliciter evolavit.

MSS
1. Rome, Bibl. Casanatense, MS 112, fols. 71–80v, with nine readings at fols. 73–79v. XV. Kristeller, *Iter* 2:93b; Poncelet 1909, 216–217. Source text.

Editions
None known to me.

356. Kaeppeli, *Scriptores*, 3320; see also 3321.

Collection. *Annales omnium temporum*

Palermo, BC, MS 3 Qq C, fasc. 54–60 includes accounts, some quite lengthy, of many saints, omitted here for lack of space.

RONTO, Matteo, Olivetan (d. 1442)[357]

BHL 5728n, p. *Vita et inventio Maurelii,* bishop of Ferrara (VII)[358]

This account is extant only in a fragmentary state; it has been partially reconstructed by M. Tagliabue, "L'anonima *vita* latina di San Maurelio martire vescovo di Ferrara e il *De inventione* di Matteo Ronto," *Studi monastici: Analecta Pomposiana* 6 (1981): 221–263. Although the *inventio* itself occurred in 1419, the account was probably written later, either in 1431 or between 1439 and October 14, 1442.[359]

SABELLICO, Marcantonio Coccio, detto (ca. 1436–May 20, 1506)[360]

Lost. ⟨*Vita S. Rochi*⟩ (XIV)[361]

In the 1503 edition of Jacopo Foresti's *Supplementum chronicarum,* at fol. 436v, under the year 1490, Foresti includes a notice on his contemporary, reporting that Sabellico wrote a life of Rocco. The life, if it existed, was written around 1490–1503.[362] It is possible that the life of Rocco attributed to Foresti in MS Phillipps 11547, held by the Robinson Trust, and described by Kristeller, *Iter* 4:234b, is Sabellico's (not seen). Not included in figure 1.1.

---

357. Kristeller, "Contribution," 151; G. Picasso, "Il monachesimo alla fine del Medio Evo: Tra umanesimo e *devotio,*" in G. Penco, ed., *Cultura e spiritualità nella tradizione monastica* (Rome, 1990), 134–135.

358. The *BHL* gives Maurelius's era as the seventh century, with a query. On Maurelius, see also *AASS* May II (Paris, 1866): 153–160; Dante Balboni in *BS* 9 (1967): 172–182; and Webb, *Patrons,* 231.

359. M. Tagliabue, "L'anonima *vita* latina di San Maurelio martire vescovo di Ferrara e il *De inventione* di Matteo Ronto," *Studi monastici: Analecta Pomposiana* 6 (1981): 235–236, pointing out that Ronto was in Bologna when the translation occurred and did not move to Ferrara until 1431. Tagliabue prefers the later dating.

360. F. Tateo in *DBI* 26 (1982): 510b–515a.

361. See n. 121 above.

362. See Giovanni Mercati, *Ultimi contributi,* fasc. II, *Note sopra A. Bonfini, M. A. Sabellico, A. Sabino, Pescennio Francesco Negro, Pietro Summonte e altri* (Studi e testi 91) (Vatican City, 1939), 11–13, on a letter of 1486 from Sabellico to a certain Foresi, identified by Mercati as Jacopo Foresti of Bergamo, O.E.S.A. The identification is accepted by Tateo, *DBI* 26, 510b, who does not, however, record the *vita Rochi* among Sabellico's works.

SALANDI, Pietro Antonio, of Reggio (ca. 1460–ca. 1540)[363]

BHL 4519b. *Legenda sancte Juliane vidue de Bancis de Bononia* (IV)[364]

No preface, no dedication. Salandi appears to have been only the scribe; no author is indicated.

inc.: Fuit olim praeclarissima in ciuitate Bononiae Italiae quaedam puella nomine Iuliana ex honesta satis domo genita, patre uidelicet Iulio de Bancis, matre uero iucunda nuncupatis, qui Iesu christi prae cunctis diligentes

des.: ibique multitudine orphanorum, pupillorum ac pauperum grauiter gementibus, maximo cum honore ad intra sepulchrum marmoreum collocatum fuit quinto idus februarii, hoc est die septima februarii, regnante Theodosio romano imperatore ac Iesu Christo domino nostro, qui vivit. . . . Amen.

MSS

1. Vatican City, BAV, MS Lat. 3708, fols. 1–20. XVI. Kristeller, *Iter* 2:365a–b; Poncelet 1910, 102. At fol. 28, "scriptum per me Petrum antonium Salandum Regiensem die vigesimo quinto mensis martii millesimo quingentesimo secundo." Seen SLU reel 580.

Editions

1. Cf. Schutte, *PIVRB*, 193, a vernacular Bolognese imprint.

(?)SALUTATI, Coluccio (1331–1406)[365]

Lost? ⟨*Vita Andreae Corsini*⟩[366]

According to Anna Benvenuti-Papi, *Pastori di Populo: Storie e leggende di vescovi nell'Italia medievale* (Florence: Arnaud, 1988), 152–153 and 175 n. 123, Salutati may have written a life of Andrea Corsini. She refers to it as "una ipotetica *vita*" (152) and proposes that it was composed around 1450. It would then have served as the basis for the life of Corsini once attributed to the Florentine Carmelite Andrea del Castegno (d. 1459). See

---

363. See James Wardrop, "Pierantonio Sallando and Girolamo Pagliarolo, Scribes to Giovanni II Bentivoglio: A Study in the Later Development of Humanistic Script," *Signature*, n.s., 2 (1946): 9, with bibliography.

364. J.-M. Sauget in *BS* 6 (1964): 1176–1177.

365. For an introduction to the large bibliography on this important figure, see R. Witt in P. Grendler, ed., *Encyclopedia of the Renaissance* (New York: Scribners, 1999), 389–392.

366. S. Spanò in *GLS* 129b–131a.

G. Ciappelli, "A Trecento Bishop as Seen by Quattrocento Florentines: Sant'Andrea Corsini, His 'Life,' and the Battle of Anghiari," in S. K. Cohn, Jr., and S. A. Epstein, eds., *Portraits of Medieval and Renaissance Living: Essays in Memory of David Herlihy* (Ann Arbor: University of Michigan Press, 1996), 283–300, which dismisses the attribution to Salutati at 286–287, on the basis of "tone and style." M. Miglio, "Un nome per tre epitaffi: Coluccio Salutati e gli elogi funebri dei Corsini," *IMU* 26 (1983): 361–374, suggests that Salutati may have written the tombstone inscription. Not included in figure 1.1.

SCHIFALDO, Tommaso, O.P. (1430–1500)[367]

Collection. *De viris illustribus ordinis praedicatorum*

Dedicatory preface and peroration to Cardinal Olivero Caraffa; the work consists of forty-one chapters on Sicilian Dominicans and their houses.

    inc. proem.: Caius Iulius Caesar dictator, Oliveri excellentissime, a quo familia et appellatio Caesarum

    inc.: (De conventu Messanensi): Lucubraciuncula nostra non ab re quidem efferri inchoarique poterit

    des.: *(peroratio)*: majora quaedam concipiam, quae propediem litteris mundare decrevi . . . non immemor

MSS

    1. Bologna, BU, MS 868 (1678). XV. Frati, "Indice," 375–376. Not seen.

    2. Chicago, Newberry Library, New acq. MS 71.5, fasc. 4. XV. Kristeller, *Iter* 5:244a Panella, *Scriptores* no. 3858. Seen.

Editions

    1. Ed. G. Cozzucli, *Tommaso Schifaldo, umanista siciliano del sec. XV (notizie e scritti inediti)* (Palermo, 1897), 59–94. Source text.

Office. *Officium Catharinae senensis*, O.P. tert. (XIV; c.d. 1461)

The *peroratio* of Schifaldo's *De viris illustribus* claims that he, not Pius II, wrote the office for Catherine of Siena.[368] Not included in figure 1.1.

---

367. Kristeller, "Contribution," 152; Panella, *Scriptores* 4: 385–390. Francesco Giunta, "Documenti sugli umanisti Tommaso Schifaldo e Cataldo Parisio," *L'Ultimo medio evo* (Rome, 1981), 118–125.

368. G. Cozzucli, ed., *Tommaso Schifaldo, umanista siciliano del sec. XV (notizie e scritti inediti)* (Palermo, 1897), 93. Panella, *Scriptores* no. 3848.

Lost? ⟨*vita Petri Hieremias, O.P.*⟩ (d. 1452)[369]

The anonymous life of Pietro Geremia, *BHL* 6713, presented in an emended form in *AASS*, March I, is not by Schifaldo, says Cozzucli, *Tommaso Schifaldo*, 33–35, because its style is too unlike the entry in Schifaldo's *De viris illustribus* entry on the saint. No manuscripts known. Editions are interpolated and late. See *BHL*. Not included in figure 1.1.

SECUNDINUS, Nicolaus (d. 1463)[370]

BHL —. Epitome *Vita Gregorii Nazianzenus* (IV)

> *inc.*: Oppidi cui Nazianzus nomen in prouincia Cappadocia
> *des.*: in pace suum spiritum Deo Optimo Maximo reddidit.

MSS
　　1. Venice, Bibl. Marciana, Marc. Lat. XIII 62 (4418), fols. 159–160v. Kristeller, *Iter* 2:262b; P. D. Mastrodimitis, *Nikolaus Sekundinos (1402–1464): Bios kai ergon* (Athens, 1970), 118–120. Seen.

Editions
None known to me.

BHL —; *BHG* 723. [*translation of Gregory Presbyter's oration on Gregory of Nazianzus*] (IV)

The *peroratio* mentions but does not name a patron. Franz Babinger in 1940 observed that BAV, MS Ottob. 1732, was "dello stesso contenuto" as the Marciana manuscript (above) containing an epitome of Gregory's life. But in BAV, MS Ottob. Lat. 1732, a codex containing works by Sagundino, the only candidate for a piece about Gregory Nazianzen is clearly not the epitome. It seems to be a version of that same work by Gregory "the Presbyter" translated by Traversari (*q.v.*) (*BHG* 723; *BHL* 3668). Not included in figure 1.1.

　　inc.: Inuitat nos hodie a spirituale conuiuium Magnus Gregorius atque semet ipsum nobis ueluti epulas

---

369. On Geremia, see G. Cappelluti, in *DS* 12 (1986): 1601–1602; Pietro Ransano, *Annales omnium temporum*, Palermo, BC, MS 3 Q q C, fasc. 54, fol. 347r–v; cf. *AASS* Feb. I (Paris, 1866): 652–657b, paras. 21–22.

370. On Niccolò Sagantino, see Zeno 1:333–343; P. D. Mastrodimitis, *Nikolaus Sekundinos (1402–1464): Bios kai ergon* (Athens, 1970).

des.: eterne frueris tranquillitatem perenium. Explicit deo gratias Amen.

MSS

   1. Vatican City, BAV, MS Ottob. lat. 1732, fols. 142v–156v. XV ex.
Kristeller, *Iter* 2:432a–b. Unattributed. Source text. SLU reel 2255.

Editions
None known to me.

SERICO (della Seta), Sebastiano (fl. 1500)[371]

BHL —. ⟨*Vita divi Amati de Ronconiis*⟩ (XII)[372]

Dedicatory letter to Bishop Simon Bonadies of Rimini (1511–1518) and
prologue. After the earliest documents had been destroyed in a fire, Serico
was asked to write the life from oral testimony; the original plan, for
heroic verse, was not carried out.

   inc. epist.: Singularis tua, praestantissime Pater, in omnes humanitas
amorque in patriam nostrum
   des. epist.: quam deinceps posteris innotescere. Vale, Saleduciensesque
tuos, qua solitus es humanitate persequere
   inc. proem.: Cum litterarum usus inter mortales nondum esset repertus
   inc.: Saludeciensem natione fuisse B. Amatum, inter omnes
   des.: Tandem ad auxilium B. Amati cum se conuertisset, cruciatibus
maximis in urina emittenda fuisse liberatum
   epilogus: Haec sunt quae de B. Amati uita deque eius miraculis expli-
canda litterisque mandanda existimaui . . . quae ad cultum seruandamque
beatissimi uiri memoriam pertinent hactenus neglexere.

MSS
None known to me.

Editions

   1. *AASS* May II (Venice, 1738): 345–351. See esp. 350b–351a for
Serico's letter to his patron Francesco Modesti on further plans for the
account. Source text.

---

   371. I have not been able to see G. Bordoni, *Sebastiano Serico di Saludecio* (Rimini,
1886).
   372. Giovanni Lucchese, in *BS* 11 (1968): 394–395.

SIMONETTA, Bonifacio, O.Cist. (fl. 1460–1490)[373]

Collection. *Historia persecutionum christianorum*

Prefatory letter from Stefano Dolcini to Giovanni Battista Ferro and a concluding poem from Giovanni Biffi to the author. See chap. 2 above.

MSS

None known to me.

Editions

1. *Historia persecutionum christianorum*. Milan: Antonio Zarotto, January [not before 11], 1492. H 14750; *BMC* 6:722; *IGI* 9011; Goff S530; Rogledi Manni 919; Ganda, *I primordi*, 174. Source text.

2. *De Christiane fidei et romanorum pontificum persecutionibus opus* . . . Basel: Nicolaus Kesler, 1509.

TAVELLI, Giovanni, da Tossignano O.F.M., *beatus* (1386–1446)[374]

BHL 4384. *Brevis annotata compendio vitae Iohannis de Columbinis* (XIV)[375]

The account was written at the request of Cardinal *Niccolò Albergati* (d. 1444); it is best known in the vernacular translation of Feo Belcari.[376] Giovanni Colombini was founder of the Gesuates.

inc.: Italica regione Tusculanis oris fuit uir quidam in urbe senarum nomine dei gratia Iohannes

des.: Rursus et post illum caeteri Romani pontifices sedi apostolici presidentes huic eidem fraternitati beneficia ac priuilegia nonnulla gratis indulgentes, proppitios super ac favorabiles se, operante Dco, prestiterunt ad laudem et gloriam redemptoris nostri Iesu Christi, qui omnium . . . in saeculorum saecula. Amen. Explicit origo Iesuatorum.

MSS

1. Florence, Bibl. Riccardiana, MS 290. XV. Kristeller, *Iter* 1:190. Not seen.

---

373. A. Redaelli, "Della vita di Cicco Simonetta," *Annali universali di statistica* 22 (1829): 198–200.

374. On Tavelli, see D. Balboni, "Il beato Giovanni Tavelli," *Atti e memorie della Deputazione ferrarese di storia patria*, n.s. 4 (1946–1949): 147–152, who edits Guarino's oration for Tavelli's accession to the episcopate.

375. G. B. Proja in *BS* 4 (1964): 122–123; A. Benvenuti in *GLS* 880a–883b.

376. For Belcari's innovations, cf. *BHL* 4385; and R. Guidi, "Uomini e simulacri" in *Il dibatito sull' uomo nel '400* (Rome: Tielle Media, 1999), 969–1002.

2. London, BL, MS Harl. 2508, fols. 212–217v. XV. Kristeller, *Iter* 4:160b. Source text.

3. Siena, BC, MS K VII 27. Not seen.

Editions
   1. All late; see *BHL*.

TIBERINO, Giovan Mattia (fl. 1475)

BHL 7762, 7765, 7766. *Passio beati Simonis puer Tridentini* (1475)

Preface; dedicatory letters to Brescia, or Johannes Hinderbach, or Raffaele Zovenzoni, depending on the manuscript or printed edition. Because the medical doctor and orator Tiberino was personal physician to the bishop of Trent Hinderbach, who aggressively promoted the cause of Simon pseudo-martyr, it is likely that episcopal patronage as well as regional politics and humanist self-promotion played a role in these compositions.[377] The complex printing history of Tiberino's narrative, which began as an oration or letter to the city of Brescia, is not well served by the *BHL* descriptions. As I have not seen all the editions, much less collated them, I rely on F. Hamster's survey in "Primärliteratur zu Simon von Trient: Drucke and Handschriften vom 1475 bis 1500 mit Standortnachweisen," in *Frumenzio Ghetta O.F.M.: Scritti di storia* (Trent, 1991), 311–319, with reference to P. O. Kristeller, "The Alleged Ritual Murder of Simon of Trent (1475) and Its Literary Repercussions: A Bibliographical Study," *Proceedings of the American Academy for Jewish Research* 59 (1993): 129–133. Despite these two studies, there is more analytical work to be done. Humanist verse on Simon is a large field in itself.

inc. prol.: Rem maximam qualem a passione domini ad hec usque tempora nulla unquam etas audiuit[378]

---

377. Hinderbach's role is explored in I. Rogger and M. Bellabarba, *Il principe vescovo Johannes Hinderbach (1465–1486) fra tardo medioevo e umanesimo* (Bologna: Dehoniane, 1992). The bishop's publicity campaign was, unfortunately, successful. See, for example, evidence of testaments from the Quattrocento that required heirs to visit Simon's relics, noted by G. Mantese, *Memorie storiche della chiesa vicentina*, vol. 3, part 2 (Vicenza: Neri Pozza, 1964), 481 n. 90 and 573 n. 24; see also the documentary list assembled in P. O. Kristeller, "The Alleged Ritual Murder of Simon of Trent (1475) and Its Literary Repercussions: A Bibliographical Study," *Proceedings of the American Academy for Jewish Research* 59 (1993): 103–135. For a complementary approach to the spate of composition, cf. Miri Rubin, *Gentile Tales: The Narrative Assault on Late Medieval Jews* (New Haven: Yale University Press, 1999).

378. This prologue may be preceded by a letter to the Brescians, or to Raffaele Zovenzoni [H 8668], who wrote verse on Simon, or to Bishop Hinderbach (*inc.*: Hortaris me saepe, reverende praesul, ut imperfectum quam nuperrime edidi). It may be followed by a poem on the miracles (*inc.*: Sayth iudeorum) [*BHL* 7763]. Note as well that Kristeller, "Alleged Ritual Murder," includes references to J.-C. Brunet, *Manuel du Libraire et de l'amateur de Livres* (Paris, 1860–1880) and J. G. T. Graesse, *Trésors de livres rares et precieux* (Dresden, 1859–1869), that are not addressed by Hamster.

inc.: Nuper in ciuitate Tridentina, quae uersus Aquilonem
des.: prius quam debitas poenas luant[379]

MSS

1. Brescia, Bib. Queriniana, MS N E 1527 (two copies). See Hamster,
"Primärliteratur," 311 and 322. (Cf. Kristeller, *Iter* 1:36a on MS D VIII
34, not listed in Kristeller, "Alleged Ritual Murder." Cf. MS G IV 10, likewise a letter on Simon of Trent, in Kristeller, *Iter* 1, 31a and 32b, but not
idem, "Alleged Ritual Murder.") Not seen.

2. Rovereto, Bib. Civica, MS 22, fols. 2–4, with the title *De obitu Beati
Simonis Tridentini ad Rectores et Ciues Brixianos,* incipit and desinit as
above, followed by miracles. See Kristeller, *Iter* 6:205b and idem, "Alleged
Ritual Murder," 124, noting two accounts of Jewish atrocities, one dated
1476 and the other 1481. Not seen.

3. St. Petersburg, Biblioteka Publichnaja, MS Lat. Q. 177, fols.
225v–230v, incipit as above. Kristeller, *Iter* 5:186a; idem, "Alleged Ritual
Murder," 124. Not seen.

Editions

1. [Cologne: Printer of the *Dialogus Salomonis et Marcolphi,* after April
4, 1475]. H 15648*; Goff T482; *BMC* 1: 260; *IGI* 9645 ISTC it0048200;
Hamster, "Primärliteratur," 312; Kristeller, "Alleged Ritual Murder," 130.

2. [Augsburg: Cloister of Sts. Ulrich and Afra, after 4 April 1475]. H
15649*; Goff T483; ISTC it00483000; Hamster, "Primärliteratur," 312;
Kristeller, "Alleged Ritual Murder," 130; Kristeller, *Iter* 3:332a.

3. [Rome: Bartolomeo Guldinbeck, 1475 1476], with the title *Passio
beati Simonis pueri tridentini.* H 15650; *IGI* 9648; Goff T488; ISTC
it00488000, Hamster, "Primärliteratur," 312–313; Kristeller, "Alleged
Ritual Murder," 130; Marco Santoro, *La Stampa a Napoli nel Quattrocento* (Naples: Istituto nazionale di studi sul rinascimento meridionale
1984), 166, items 345–346.

4. Mantua: [Johannes Schall, after 4 April 1475]. H 15651, *IGI* 9646,
ISTC it00482500; Hamster, "Primärliteratur," 313, Kristeller, "Alleged
Ritual Murder," 130.

5. Santorso: Hans vom Rin [after 4 April 1475]. H 15652; *BMC* 7,
1027, *IGI* 9649; Goff T484; ISTC it00484000, Hamster "Primärliteratur," 313; Kristeller, "Alleged Ritual Murder," 130.

6. Treviso: Gerardus de Lisa (of Flanders), June 20, 1475, H 15653; *IGI*
9650; ISTC it00488500; Hamster "Primärliteratur," 313–314; Kristeller,
"Alleged Ritual Murder," 131, 133.

7. [Nüremberg]: Friedrich Creussner [after April 4, 1475], with the title

---

379. Cf. *BHL* 1766: those editions that open with the letter to Hinderbach end with a different *des.*: tuoque nomini feliciter consecraui.

De Simone puero ad Brixianos. H 15654*; IGI 9647; Goff T485; *BMC* 2, 447; ISTC it00485000; Hamster, "Primärliteratur," 314, Kristeller, "Alleged Ritual Murder," 131.

8. Rome: Bartolomeo Guldinbeck, June 19, 1475, H 15656; *IGI* 9653; *BMC* 4, 67; Goff T486; ISTC it00486000 Hamster, "Primärliteratur," 315; Kristeller, "Alleged Ritual Murder," 131.

9. Rome: Bartolomeo Guldinbeck, July 24, 1475. H 15655*; Goff T487; ISTC it00487000 Hamster "Primärliteratur," 314; Kristeller, "Alleged Ritual Murder," 131.

10. [Naples: Arnold of Brussels, after June 22 1475]. See Hamster, "Primärliteratur," 315, suggesting a publication date of early 1476. Not in Kristeller, "Alleged Ritual Murder." Cf. item 3 immediately above: Santoro, *La Stampa a Napoli*, 165–166, rejects the possibility that Tiberino's work was printed at Naples. Cf ISTC it00488500.

11. [Venice]: Nicolas Jenson, [after April 30, 1475]. *IGI* 9652. Hamster, "Primärliteratur," 317; Kristeller, "Alleged Ritual Murder," 129.

12. [Venice: Gabriele di Pietro of Treviso, after April 30, 1475]. H 15639; *IGI* 9651; *BMC* 5: 201; GoffT480; ISTC it00484500;; Hamster, "Primärliteratur," 317; Kristeller, "Alleged Ritual Murder," 132.

13. Trent: [Albrecht Kunne], 9 Feb. 1476, with the title *Historia completa . . . de passione et obitu beati pueri Simonis* [includes *BHL* 7767 *Miracula*]. H 15661*; *BMC* 3: 805; Goff T481; ISTC it00481000; Hamster, "Primärliteratur," 319; Kristeller, "Alleged Ritual Murder," 131.

14. Trent: [Leonardus Longus], August 8, 1482, with the title *In heatum Symoneyn noum . . . martirem . . . epigrammata.* H 15660; *IGI* 9644; *BMC* 3, 806; Goff T479; Hamster, "Primärliteratur," 318; Kristeller, "Alleged Ritual Murder," 132.

TICINENSIS, AUGUSTINUS de Novis
See AUGUSTINUS Ticinensis.

TORTELLI, Giovanni (ca. 1400–ca. 1466)[380]

BHL 732. *Vita Athanasii ex Graecis in Latinum Deducta* (IV)[381]

Dedicatory letter to Eugene IV; one manuscript copy has an alternative letter of dedication to Bishop Johannes de Mela; preface. This translation

---

380. G. Mancini, "Giovanni Tortelli, cooperatore di Nicolao V nel fondare la biblioteca Vaticana," *ASI* 78 (1920): 161–268; O. Besomi and M. Regoliosi, "Nuove ricerche intorno a Giovanni Tortelli," *IMU* 9 (1966): 123–189; 12 (1969): 129–196; 13 (1970): 95–137; L. Chines, *La paroli degli antichi* (Rome: Carocci, 1998), 84–112.

381. D. Stiernon in *BS* 2 (1962): 522–540; A. A. R. Bastiaensen in *GLS* 216b–221a. I take the title from BAV, MS Vat. lat. 1216, fo. 4; cf. the copy with Tortelli's autograph corrections, BAV, MS Vat. lat. 1215, fo. 2v: *vita sancti atanasii episcopi alexandrini.*

was drawn, as Tortelli remarks, from Eusebius (Rufinus), Sozomen, and Theodoret; it was written about 1439.[382] Nicholas V later commissioned a translation of Gregory of Nyssa's life of Athanasius from Tortelli.[383]

inc. epist. 1: Non ab re futurum arbitror, Eugeni pater

des. epist. 1: et consolatio tibi et amor ingens atque deuotio in sanctissimum Athanasium augeatur.

inc. epist. 2: Ego quidem, pater humanissime et episcoporum omnium doctissime, optabam

des. epist. 2: et in conciliis antiquis suo ordine referuntur intelligas. Vale . . . uir omnium doctissime.

inc. proem. de traductione: Cum post persecutionem Diocliciani et Maximiani

des. proem.: que apud latinos approbatissimos auctores legendo didicimus.

inc.: Atque in primis quae nam fuerit pueri indoles

des.: Romam ad Damasum pontificem maximum profugit qui sua uirtute et sapientia pacem ecclesie reddi producauit donante domino nostro Jesu Christo . . . in secula seculorum. Amen.

MSS

1. Dresden, Sachsische Bibl., MS * A 69. XV. Heavily damaged. Kristeller, *Iter* 3:374a. Not seen.

2. Florence, Bibl. Laurenziana, MS Fies. XLV, fols. 155–179. G. Mancini, "Giovanni Tortelli, cooperatore di Nicolao V nel fondare la biblioteca Vaticana" *ASI* 78 (1920): 183. Not seen.

3. Florence, BN, MS Nuovi acq. 1003. XV. Kristeller, *Iter* 1:175a, noting at fol. 66 the date "MCCCCLXXVI quinta febr." Seen.

4. Florence, BN, Fondo princ. II, IX, 117. Mazzatinti, vol. 12 (1902/1987), 9. Seen.

5. London, BL, MS Add. 21063. XV. Kristeller, *Iter* 4:76a. Seen.

6. Pistoia, Bibl. Forteguerriana, MS D 277. XV. Kristeller, *Iter* 2:79b. Not seen.

7. Rome, Collegio di S. Antonio, MS 15. XV. Kristeller, *Iter* 2:134a. Not seen.

8. Vatican City, BAV, MS Chis. G IV 97. XV. Poncelet 1910, 275; Kristeller, *Iter* 2:481a. Seen; also SLU reel 6292.

382. See M. Cortesi, "Tecnica versoria e composizione agiografica nella *Vita Athanasii* di Giovanni Tortelli," in C. Moreschini and G. Menestrina, eds., *La traduzione dei testi religiosi: Atti del convegno tenuto a Trento il 10–11 febbraio 1993* (Brescia: Morcelliana, 1994), 197–223. She notes thirteen manuscripts but does not list them (199).

383. See Cesare Vasoli, *La dialettica e la retorica dell'umanesimo: "Invenzione" e "metodo" nella cultura del XV secolo* (Milan, 1968), 106; R. Fubini, "Papato e storiografia nel Quattrocento," *Studi medievali*, ser. 3, 18, no. 1 (1977): 336 n. 31; Pesce, *La chiesa di Treviso*, 367–368.

9. Vatican City, BAV, MS Urb Lat. 46, fols. 1–39v. XV. Poncelet 1910, 288. Not seen.

10. Vatican City, BAV, MS Urb Lat. 389, fols. 50–103v. XV. Poncelet 1910, 296. Not seen.

11. Vatican City, BAV, MS Vat. Lat. 1215, with some marginal additions in Tortelli's hand, mostly *notabilia* and corrections, but, at fol. 52v, describing Athanasius's reception into Alexandria, Tortelli records in the margin "Legi postquam scripseram ista, in quodam sermone Gregorii naçançeni: quem de laudibus ipsius beati athanasii compilavit, similem honorem et pompam, non praesidi, non consuli, non imperatori unquam factam fuisset." XV. Kristeller, *Iter* 2:311a. Poncelet 1910, 80. Seen; also SLU reel 9178.

12. Vatican City, BAV, MS Vat. Lat. 1216, fols. 2–83. XV. The sole manuscript containing the prefatory letter to Johannes de Mela in addition to the letter to Eugene IV. Kristeller, *Iter* 2:311a. Poncelet 1910, 80. Seen; also SLU reel 7181. Source text.

13. Vatican City, BAV, MS Vat. Lat. 5101, fols. 1–53. XV. Poncelet 1910, 128; Kristeller, *Iter* 2:330b. Seen.

Editions

1. Athanasius, *Sanctissima eloquentissimaque opera*, [ed. Nicolaus Beraldus] (Paris: Jean le Petit, 1520).

2. For later editions, see *BHL*.

BHL 9018. *Vita sancti Zenobii* (V)[384]

Dedicatory preface to Giovanni di Paolo, presbyter of San Michele, Florence. Written around 1439.[385]

inc. proem.: Cum non solum ecclesiae tuae administrationem

des. proem.: imitari conaberis. Vale pater optime et deum pro me rogabis.

inc.: Claram b. Zenobii exstitisse progeniem siue paternam seu maternam

des.: et, me praesente, transtulerunt.

MSS

1. Florence, Bibl. Laurenziana, MS Plut. XIX, 29, fols. 268–291. Mancini, "Giovanni Tortelli," 185. Seen.

---

384. See n. 325 above.

385. See Francesca Violoni, "La *Vita sancti Zenobii* di Giovanni Tortelli: L'architettura delle fonti," *Aevum* 2, no. 68 (1994): 407–424; Violoni announces that she is preparing a critical edition of the life and of Tortelli's short poem on Zenobius from BAV, MS Lat. 3908.

2. Florence, Bibl. Moreniana, MS Palagi 197, fols. 1v–20v. XVI. With a preface "ad presbiterum ecclesiae Sancti Michaelis vicedominorum." Kristeller, *Iter* 1:111b. Not seen.

3. Florence, BN, MS Conv. soppr. A 9 2832. Bound with Ambrogio Traversari's translation of Palladius on Chrysostom. Kristeller, *Iter* 1:153b. Seen.

4. Florence, BN, MS Conv. soppr. B 3 1138, fol. 1v (preface), fol. 2v. Unattributed, at the end of the *vita*, a date (1447) and a few more folios on Zenobius. XV. Kristeller, *Iter* 1:155b. Seen.

5. Florence, BN, MS Magl. XXXVIII 134. XV. Kristeller, *Iter* 1:128a; M. Regoliosi, "Nuove ricerche intorno a Giovanni Tortelli," *IMU* 12 (1969): 159, on this copy made for the dedicatee (it includes his ownership note) in Tortelli's hand. Seen.

6. Vatican City, BAV, MS Chis. F IV 84. XV or XVI in., with preface to Johannes presbyter. Poncelet 1909, 272; Kristeller, *Iter* 2:481a. Seen.

7. Venice, BN Marciana, MS Lat. IX 26 (3719). XVI. No preface; Kristeller, *Iter* 2:229a. Seen.

Editions
All are late; see *BHL*.

TRAVERSARI, Ambrogio, O. Cam., *beatus* (1386–October 19, 1439)[386]

Lost? ⟨*vita s. Athanasii*⟩

See R. Blum, *La Biblioteca della Badia fiorentina e i codici di Antonio Corbinelli* (Vatican City, 1951), 22 and n. 36, on a letter dated October 27, 1449, in which Nicholas V asks Abbot Gomez of Portugal to send him a copy of the life of Athanasius, "composta da Ambrogio Traversari" (Fubini, "Papato e storiografia," 336 n. 31). Not included in figure 1.1.

BHL —. *Dialogus de miraculis s. Benedicti* (VI)

No dedication, no preface. See Virgina Brown, "Ambrogio Traversari's Revision of the *Chronicon Casinense* and the *Dialogus de Miraculis s. Benedicti*: The Oldest Manuscript Rediscovered," *Medieval Studies* 58 (1996): 327–338. Traversari worked on this mild revision of Desiderius's account between June 1424 and November 1433, using manuscripts procured with the help of Cosimo de'Medici and Niccolò Niccoli.

---

386. Kristeller, "Contribution," 155–156; Charles L. Stinger, *Humanism and the Church Fathers: Ambrogio Traversari (1396–1439) and Christian Antiquity in the Italian Renaissance* (Albany: SUNY Press, 1977).

MSS

1. Moscow, Rossiiskaia Gosudarstvennaia Biblioteka, Fond 218, N 389, fos. 172^R–195^R. Formerly S. Michele in Murano, MS 727 (Kristeller, *Iter 5*: 199b–200a). Not seen.

Editions

1. For a collation indicating Traversari's revisions, see Brown, "Ambrogio Traversari's Revision," 335–337.

BHL 2088d. BHG 490. *Vita Danielis Stylite* (V)[387]

Preface; no dedication. Traversari began this translation from Simeon Metaphrastus about 1431 but left it incomplete; see Stinger, *Humanism and the Church Fathers*, 128.

inc. proem.: Quemadmodum uiris fortibus, cum quis de praeliis
inc.: Fuit igitur uiro sancto patria quidem ea

MSS

1. Florence, Bibl. Laurenziana, MS Med.-Fies. LXII. Bandini, *Biblioteca* 3, 6; Mioni, "Le *vitae patrum*," 325. Not seen.

2. Florence, BN, MS Conv. soppr. G 4 844, fols. 107v–111. XV. Autograph, incomplete. From Santa Maria degli Angeli. Kristeller, *Iter* 1:160a. Seen.

3. Florence, Bibl. Riccardiana, MS 245, fols. 145v–151. XV. Kristeller, *Iter* 189b–190a. Not seen.

4. Vatican City, BAV, MS Vat. Lat. 1212, fols. 131–136. 1436. Poncelet 1910, 78; Kristeller, *Iter* 2:311a. Seen. SLU reel 9172.

5. Vatican City, BAV, MS Vat. Lat. 1213, fols. 123–128. XV. Poncelet 1910, 79; Kristeller, *Iter* 2:311a. Not seen.

Editions
None known to me.

BHL 2666m. *Passio sanctorum Prothi et Hyacinthi et Eugenie*[388] (IV?)

No dedication; no preface. The relation of Traversari's mild revision (or transcription?) of pseudo-Rufinus's version of the Eugenia *passio* to the *translatio* of the relics of Protus, Hyacinthus, and Nemesius is unclear. The *translatio*, at the Camaldolese convent of Santa Maria degli Angeli, had

---

387. J. Becquet in *BS* 4 (1964): 470–471; *PG* 116, cols. 969–1033. See also Elpidio Mioni, "Le *vitae patrum* nella traduzione di Ambrogio Traversari," *Aevum* 24 (1950): 323.
388. G. D. Gordini in *GLS* 627a–629a. According to the *BHL*, Traversari has slightly adapted *BHL* 2666.

been planned for several years in connection with Ghiberti's production of a reliquary. It occurred on January 7, perhaps as early as 1422 or as late as 1428 or even 1430. Only Traversari reports the last-minute addition of Eugenia to the famous urn; the inscription on the reliquary does not include her name. (Leonardo Bruni is said to have been responsible for the text of the inscription.) The priest Antonio degli Agli (q.v.), who records the *translatio* in *De vitis et gestis sanctorum* in his entry for Nemesius and Lucilla, does not mention Eugenia; neither does he include an account of Eugenia elsewhere in his draft of *De vitis*, which suggests that he found her story factually suspicious.[389] Moreover, Traversari's passion of Eugenia relates poorly to the *translatio* because it does not mention Nemesius, and given the participation of Cosimo de'Medici in financing the reliquary, one might expect a dedication to the Medici if the *vita* were associated with the translation. For the hypothesis that Traversari wrote the account of Eugenia perhaps as late as 1430, see Elpidio Mioni, "Le *vitae patrum* nella traduzione di Ambrogio Traversaro," *Aevum* 24 (1950): 321 and 323–324, disagreeing with Casimiro Stolfi, *Leggende di alcune santi e beati venerati in S. Maria degli Angeli di Firenze: Testi di buon secolo* (Bologna, 1864), 21–22; Stolfi himself draws on Agostino Fortunio, *Historiarum Camaldulensium libri tres* (Venice, 1579). Benvenuti-Papi, *Pastori*, 174–175 and n. 115, follows Stolfi without reference to Mioni or Richard Krautheimer, *Lorenzo Ghiberti* (Princeton, N.J.: Princeton University Press, 1956/1982).[390]

inc.: Septimo consulatu suo Commodus imperator

des.: Plures autem annos postea uiserunt in timore Dei, et ipsi ad aeternam uitam migrarunt . . . Amen.

389. Agli mentions the translation in his entry on Nemesius and Lucilla, BAV, MS Vat lat. 3742, fol. 187: "Sed a beato postmodum Xisto romano episcopo inde sublatus, postremo vero hac aetate nostra Florentiam advectus et in monasterio (quod dicitur Angelorum) magna processionum pompa atque honoribus una cum Prothi et Jacinthi corporibus collocatus est." Note that Agli does not refer to Eugenia in this report, and neither does he say that he himself was present at the translation (as he does, for example, in recalling the translation of Zenobius). Given that Agli did not become "primo rettore" at San Lorenzo under Medici sponsorship until 1428, his silence here supports the notion of a pre-1428 *translatio*. In MS Vat Lat. 3742, the early-sixteenth-century version of Agli's *De vitis et gestis sanctorum*, Traversari's account of Eugenia is added at the end without attribution (see below under manuscripts).

390. Richard Krautheimer, *Lorenzo Ghiberti* (Princeton, N.J.: Princeton University Press, 1956/1982), 139 n. 4, dates the translation to 1421–22; he is followed by Stinger, *Humanism and the Church Fathers*, 128. Whatever the confusion in the dating of the letter that mentions Cosimo de'Medici's provision for the reliquary, it is worth noting that Traversari nowhere mentions working on this *passio* and that he was, during the years 1428–1430, regularly meeting Antonio degli Agli (q.v.) at Santa Maria degli Angeli.

MSS

1. Florence, BN, MS Conv. soppr. D 3 34, fols. 225–231. XV. Kristeller, *Iter* 1:157b. Not seen.

2. Florence, BN, MS Conv. soppr. G 4 844, fol. 112r, fragm. XV. Autograph from Santa Maria degli Angeli according to Mioni, "Le vitae patrum," 321. Cf. Kristeller, Iter 1:160a. Not seen.

3. Florence, Bibl. Laurenziana, MS Med.-Fies. LXII. A.M. Bandini, Bibliotheca Leopoldina Laurentiana (Florence, 1791–1793), vol. 3, 6; Mioni, "Le vitae patrum," 325. Not seen.

4. Florence, Bibl. Riccardiana, MS 245, fols. 151–166. Kristeller, *Iter* 1:189b–190a. Not seen.

5. Vatican City, BAV, MS Urb. Lat. 389, fols. 249v–164v. XV. Poncelet 1910, 296. Not seen.

6. Vatican City, BAV, MS Vat. Lat. 274, fols. 41v–55v. XV. Poncelet 1910, 2. Not seen.

7. Vatican City, BAV, MS Vat Lat. 404, fols. 154v–174. XV. Poncelet 1910, 19. Seen.

8. Vatican City, BAV, MS Vat Lat. 1212, fols. 136v–151v. 1436. Poncelet 1910, 78; Kristeller, *Iter* 2:311a. Seen.

9. Vatican City, BAV, MS Vat. Lat. 3623, fols. 1–30. XV. Unattributed. Mioni, "Le vitae patrum," 324 n. 3, Poncelet 1910, 101. Seen.

10. Vatican City, BAV, MS Vat. Lat. 3742, fols. 198v–207 (unattributed). XVI in. See above under Agli. Not in Poncelet 1910. Kristeller, *Iter* 2:323a. Seen.

Editions

All are late; see BHL.

BHL 4381. BHG 882. *Vita Johannis Scholastici* (i.e., of Johannes Climax, author of the *Scala Paradisi*; translated from the Greek of Daniel Monachus) (VII)[391]

Preface to Pater Mattheus. Traversari finished translating the *Scala paradisi* (also known as the *Paradisus animae*) on September 26, 1423; the translation of the author's life must have been completed around this same time.[392]

inc. proem.: Hortatus es, domine amantissime

inc.: Quaenam hunc uirum diuinum ciuitas tulerit

des.: intrinsecus uero contemplatiuae doctrinas continentes.

---

391. G. Zannoni in *BS* 6 (1964): 664–666. The life of the author was usually given along with the *Scala paradisi*. See now P. Varalda, "Prime indagini" *Rivista di storia e letteratura religiosa* 37 (2003): 107–144.

392. Date from Mioni, "Le *vitae patrum*," 321.

MSS

1. Budapest, National Library, MS Clmae 344. Dated at the end "26 Septembris 1470 Jo." (Vitez). Kristeller, *Iter* 4:294a. Not seen.

2. Copenhagen, Kongelige Bibliothek, MS Ny Kgl. S 2926. XV. Kristeller, *Iter* 3:178b. Not seen.

3. Florence, BN, MS Conv. soppr. F 7 1387. XV. Kristeller, *Iter* 1:159a. Not seen.

4. Florence, BN, MS Conv. soppr. G 4 844, fols. 107v–111. XV. Autograph, incomplete. From Santa Maria degli Angeli. Kristeller, *Iter* 1:160a. Not seen.

5. Oxford, Bodleian Library, MS Lyell 62. Copied in Venice, 1455. Kristeller, *Iter* 3:33a. Not seen.

6. Vatican City, BAV, MS Urb. Lat. 47. XV. Poncelet 1910, 288. Not seen.

7. Vatican City, BAV, MS Vat. Lat. 522, fols. 2–4v, with the date 1436 at fol. 125. Poncelet 1910, 19. Not seen. Varalda, "Prime indagini" 113.

8. Vatican City, BAV, MS Vat. Lat. 523, fols. 2v–6. XV. Poncelet 1910, 20. Not seen.

9. Venice, Bibl. Correr, MS 905, fols. 1–3v. XV. From San Mattia di Murano. The colophon at the end of the sixty-one folios of this manuscript says that Traversari was the translator and that it was copied in Venice in 1450. Kristeller, *Iter* 6:272a. Not seen.

Editions

1. Johannes Scholastici, *Scala paradisi* (Toledo: Successor of Pedro Hagenbach, 1505), signs. a2–a5v.

2. Johannes Scholastici, *Climax seu scala paradisi* (Milan: J. M. de Ferrariis, 1506), signs. a2v–a7.

3. Varalda, "Prime indagini" 135–140.

BHL 4374. BHG 870. *Vita s. Johannis Chrysostomi* (translation of Palladius's dialogue life of Johanne Chrysostomi) (V)[393]

Dedicatory preface to Eugene IV. Traversari translated the life in 1432.
inc. epist.: Conuerti nuper ex graeco uitam sanctissimi uiri Iohannis
des. epist.: Christus dominus noster seruare dignetur incolumem domine . . . pater.
inc.: Cum uenisset aliquando Romam Palladius
des.: Ipse nobis partem et hereditatem tribuat inuenire cum illo in terri-

---

393. D. Stiernon in *BS* 6 (1964): 669–700; M. Simonetti in *GLS* 883a–889a; Singer, *Humanism and the Church Fathers*, 148–150. Walker, *The Chronicles*, 74–75, says that Archbishop Antoninus put Traversari's translation of the life of Palladius in his *Chronicon*, tit. 10, chap. 9, introduction and sections 1–7. I have not confirmed this claim.

bilis iustique iudicii die cui est gloria honor maiestas et magnificentia patri
et filio et spiritu sancto nunc et semper et in secula seculorum. Amen.

MSS

1. Faenza, BC. See Mazzatinti, vol. 26 (1967): 243, no. 40, at fols.
74v–82v. Not seen.

2. Ferrara, Bib. Comm. Ariostea, MS II 334, 42v. XV. Kristeller, *Iter*
1:60a. Not seen.

3. Florence, BN, MS Conv. soppr. A 9 2832, bound with Tortelli's life
of Athanasius (*q.v.*). XV. Kristeller, *Iter* 1:153b. Seen.

4. Rome, Bibl. Vallicelliana, MS A 13 (2). Kristeller, *Iter* 2:128a; Poncelet 1909, 374–375. Not seen.

5. Salamanca, BU, MS 526. XV. Kristeller, *Iter* 4:604b. Not seen.

6. Salzburg, Stiftsbibliothek St. Peter, MS A VIII 19, fols. 67–142v. XV.
Kristeller, *Iter* 3:39b. Not seen.

7. Vatican City, BAV, MS Ottob. Lat. 11, fols. 1–100. XV. Poncelet
1910, 413. Not seen.

8. Vatican City, BAV, MS Urb. Lat. 389, fols. 124v–190. XV. Poncelet
1910, 296. Not seen.

9. Vatican City, BAV, MS Vat. Lat. 1217. XV. Poncelet 1910, 80; Kristeller, *Iter* 2:311a. Seen.

10. Venice, BN Marciana, MS Zan. Lat. 76 (1716). XV. Kristeller, *Iter*
2:210b. Not seen.

Editions
All are late; see *BHL*.

BHL 6536a—m. *Vitas patrum* (IV)

Preface, no dedicatee. Though Traversari was working on this collection
in 1424, he did not complete it until 1431. He sent it to Eugenius IV.
Mioni, "Le vitae patrum," 321–322, lists the contents of the autograph
manuscript and observes that Traversari referred to his translation of
John Moschus's *Pratum Spirituale* as the *Vitas patrum*. The titles I give
to each of the entries below come from Mioni's description of the manuscript; they differ slightly from those given in the *BHL*. Mioni does not,
however, give the incipits; these I take from the *BHL*. I have checked
them against one manuscript, from which I also take the desinits: BAV,
MS Vat. Lat. 1212. Included as one mixed group in figure 1.1 (fourth
century).

BHL 6536a. *De sanctis patribus in Raithu*

> *inc. proem.*: Profectus est monachus quidam de Raithu
> *inc.*: Moyses quidam a puero solitariam sectatus uitam

des.: et deposuimus eum cum sanctis qui ante illum obdormierant patribus.

BHL 6536b. *De Beato Marco Salo*

inc.: Erat in Sciti senex quidam, nomine Daniel habebatque

des.: Cunctaque cum ramis et cerpis afferebant reliquias . . . et semper per infinita secula seculorum.

BHL 6536c. *De S. Daniele*

inc.: Abbas uero ipse Daniel a puero renuntiauit saeculo

des.: Pro his autem omnibus gratias referamus christo domino et deo nostro.

BHL 6536d. *De S. Eulogio Latomo*

inc.: Aduenit abbas Daniel presbyter ex Sciti in Thebaidem

des.: sanctae dei genitricis semperque virginis Mariae et omnium sanctorum. Amen.

BHL 6536e. *De Patricia Anastasia*[394]

inc.: Eunuchus quidam morabatur in interiore heremo scitiae

des.: coram terribili illo tribunali domini nostri . . . et gloria in secula seculorum. Amen.

BHL 6536f. *De Senatrice Eremita*

inc.: Quidam sanctorum ac spiritualium patrum, Silas nomine genere arabe

des.: qui miseretur diligentibus se et ex toto animo seruiunt ipsi. Amen.

BHL 6536g. *De Canonica Sancta Muliere*

inc.: Anachorita quidam narrauit fratribus, dicens, die quadam

des.: omnes simul glorificauimus deum qui talia habet occulta uasa . . . in secula seculorum. Amen.

BHL 6536h. *Septem capita quae misit Abbas Moyses Abbati Pemeni*

inc.: Debet monachus a proximo suo mortuus esse[395]

des.: utinam digni efficiamur gratia et misericordia dei . . . in secula seculorum. Amen.

---

394. Mioni, "Le *vitae patrum*," 320 notes that in the autograph the incipit to this entry is lacking because a folio has been lost.

395. According to Mioni, "Le *vitae patrum*," 320, this is an abbreviated version of *PL* 73, cols. 1014–1015, cols. 1–7.

BHL 6536i. *Item alia eiusdem de virtutibus capitula*

inc.: Timor Dei persequitur omnem accidiam
des.: et habere mortem ante oculos.

BHL 6536k. *Abbatis Zosimae dicta*

inc.: Beatus Zosimus dicebat sic, cum primum sibi signum crucis fecisset
des.: omni studio curemus uestigia sanctorum et uenerabilium senum imitari . . . in secula seculorum. Amen.

BHL 6536m. *Incipit Abbatis Ammonis capitula utilia numero decem et novem*

inc.: Serua te ipsum diligenter dilectissime utpote confidens
des.: hic enim opinione celebri omnes trahit ad se.

MSS

1. Florence, BN, MS G 4 844, fols. 83–104.[396] XV. Autograph. Kristeller, *Iter* 1:160a. Seen.

2. Florence, Bibl. Riccardiana, MS 245. XV. Kristeller, *Iter* 1:189–190. Not seen.

3. Vatican City, BAV, MS Vat. Lat. 1212. Copied from the Florentine autograph by Johannes Andreas de Colonia, *vi idus maii anno domini 1436,* according to a note, fol. 148. Poncelet 1910, 76–78, gives a complete description with references to the *BHG.* Kristeller, *Iter* 2:311a. Seen. SLU reel 9172.

4. Vatican City, BAV, MS Vat. Lat. 1213, perhaps made from the Florentine autograph.[397] XV. Poncelet 1910, 79; Kristeller, *Iter* 2:311a. Not seen.

5. Vatican City, BAV, MS Vat. Lat. 1214, with the concluding note "absolutum die beati Jeronimi 1435. Complevi revidendum librum hunc totum 12 decembris 1443" (fol. 145v). This copy was made for Biagio Molin by Andreas Senensis. The marginalia are Molin's, as is the note of review.[398] Kristeller, *Iter* 2:311a. Seen.

---

396. Foliation taken from Mioni, "Le *vitae patrum,*" 320, although he does not indicate that fols. 105–107 are blank. Mioni does note that fol. 104 concludes: "Explicit liber sanctorum ac venerabilium Patrum qui dicitur Spiritale pratum." According to ibid., 324, this is the very manuscript Traversari sent to Eugene IV for review on August 6, 1431, before the incomplete life of Daniel Stylite and the life of Eugenia were written into it. If MS Conv. soppr. G 4 844 is as much a working copy as Mioni says, then Traversari's relations with Eugenius IV, at least on the subject of recovering and propagating early Christian hagiography, would seem to have been very close indeed.

397. Ibid., 326.

398. Ibid., 325. This is the same Biagio Molin who shortly before commissioned Leon Battista Alberti's life of Potitus. See chap. 2 above.

Editions
All are late; see BHL.

BHL 3668. BHG 723. *Vita Gregorii Nazianzeni* (translation of Gregory presbyter's *vita Gregorii Nazianzeni*)[399] (IV)

Dedicatory letter to Giuliano Cesarini, on the occasion of his elevation to the cardinalate in November 1430.[400] Also preface.

inc. epist.: Vetus consuetudo est ut amicorum secundis successibus amici gratulentur

des. epist.: Christi domini nostri clementia seruare dignetur domine . . . pater.

inc. proem.: Inuitat nos quidem

des. proem.: unde maxime conuenit.

inc.: Patria illi secunda Cappadocia fuit religione et probitate

des.: Deo gratum esse quo illi iuxta uires offertur.

MSS

1. Cortona, Bibl. Comm. et Accad. Etrusca, MS 39, fols. 104–105. XV. Mazzatinti, vol. 18 (1912/1965), 21–22. Not seen.

2. Florence, Bibl. Laurenziana, MS Ashb. 992 (921), fols. 1–35v. XV. Kristeller, *Iter* 1:92. Not seen.

3. Florence, Bibl. Laurenziana, MS Fies. 45. XV. Bandini, *Catalogus codicum latinorum Bibl. Med. Laur.* (1774, 1778), 2, 816. Not seen.

4. Florence, Bibl. Laurenziana, MS Plut. 67 4, fols. 1–32. XV. Not seen.

5. London, BM, MS Harl. 4923, fols. 459–472v. XV. Kristeller, *Iter* 4:182a–b. Not seen.

6. Milan, Bibl. Ambrosiana, MS F 18 Sup. XVI. Kristeller, *Iter* 1:298b. Not seen.

7. Oxford, Magdalen College, MS LXXVI, fols. 1–21. XV. Not seen.

8. Paris, BN, MS Lat. 5578, fols. 112v–129v. XV. *Cat. cod. Lag. lat. bib. Par.*, 2:486. Not seen.

9. Vatican City, BAV, MS Ross. Lat. 50 (VII, 50), fols. 112–152v. XV. Kristeller, *Iter* 2:468b. A pedagogical collection. Source text.

---

399. On Gregory Nazianzen, see M. Simonetti in *GLS* 1053a-1059b. Other translations of lives of Gregory Nazianzen relevant to this study are those by Niccolò Sagundino (*q.v.*) and by the monk Matthias of Santa Giustina. The latter was sent to Pietro Barozzi (*q.v.*)—further evidence of bishops seeking information about early, model bishops. On the translation by Matthias Monachus, see Agnes Clare Way, "Gregorius Nazianzenus," in *CTC* (Washington DC: Catholic University of America, 1971) 2:175; and Kristeller, *Iter* 2:284a–b (Venice, Museo Correr, MS Cicogna 949 [851]).

400. Stinger, *Humanism*, 146. See also Lorenzo Mehus, *Ambrosii Traversari generalis camaldalensium aliorumque ad ipsum et ad alios de eodem Ambrosio latinae epistolae a domino Petro Canneto . . . in libros XXV triubatae* (Florence, 1759; repr., Bologna: Forlì, 1968), book 8, letter 26, cols. 394–397, and book 2, letter 30, cols. 100–101.

10. Vatican City, BAV, MS Urb. Lat. 389, fols. 103v–123. XV. Poncelet 1910, 98. Not seen.

11. Vatican City, BAV, MS Vat. Lat. 2950, fols. 1–31v. XV. Kristeller, *Iter* 2:358. Not seen.

12. Vatican City, BAV, MS Vat. Lat. 4279, fols. 7–31. XV. Kristeller, *Iter* 2:326.[401] Source text.

Editions
All are late; see *BHL*.

TUBERINO, Giovan Mattia

See TIBERINO.

VALLA, Lorenzo (1407–Aug. 1, 1457)[402]

Lost. cf. *BHG* 1205. ⟨Translation, Basil the Great, *Laudatio* on the Forty Martyrs of Sebaste⟩ (II)

BHL —. cf. *BHG* 1201. *Martirum sanctorum et gloriosorum victoriam consecutorum qui in Sebastia interfecti sunt numero quadraginta* (II)[403]

Dedicatory letter to Matthias Pugiades; the translation can be dated to spring of 1446.[404]

inc. epist.: Beatissimorum quadraginta martirum quam proxime e greco translati

des. epist.: ex fortibus fortissimis reddes magnaque pars ob id uictorie debebitur.

inc.: circa Licinii tempora nefandi imperatoris ingens extitit persecutio

des.: nunc tamen peruertam corda principum.

MSS

1. Salamanca, BU, MS 1530, fasc. 3, fols. 1–4. XV. Kristeller, *Iter* 4:604b. Unpublished transcription by Martin Davies.

---

401. From Way, "Gregorius Nazianzenus," 174–175.

402. For an introduction to the extensive bibliography, see C. Trinkaus in Grendler, ed., *Encyclopedia of the Renaissance* 6:207–212.

403. A. Amore in *BS* 11 (1968): 768–771.

404. See Valla's *Epistolae*, ed. O. Besomi and M. Regoliosi (Padua: Antenore, 1984), 286, letter 32, with notes at 272–273. Besomi and Regoliosi follow Sabbadini's suggestion for dating the letter.

Editions

1. Mariarosa Cortesi, "*Sanctissimum militum exemplum*: I martiri di Sebastia e Lorenzo Valla," *Bollettino della Badia greca di Grottaferrata*, n.s., 54 (2000): 319–336, edits the prefatory letter to Pugiades and the incomplete narrative. Source text.

VALLORI, Santi, O. Vallumbr. (fl. XV)[405]

BHL 4404. ⟨*Vita Iohannis Gualberti*⟩ (XI)

Prologue with dedication to *Tommaso Salvetta* who had encouraged the composition, and mentioning the interest of *Niccolò Vallori*, Santi's father, who had died. Valori was part of Lorenzo de'Medici's circle and abbot of S. Reparata di Marradi at the time of writing. The *vita* was subsequently translated into the vernacular by Taddeo Adimari and published at Venice in 1510. Incipits below from *BHL*. Explicit from A. Ravasi, "Vite parallele di santi medievali (sec. XI)," *Poliorama* 1 (1982): 70, from Florence, AS, MS Conv. soppr. 260, fol. 163v. Ravasi describes the account as stylistically "more like literature than hagiography" (146).

inc. proem.: Minime probandam audaciam illam

inc.: Ex Gualberto equestris ordinis clarissimo uiro

des.: et sanctum corpus ea fide qua seruandum decreuerat in ipso ardente caolore (mirabile dictu) potius odore conditum quam putredinis feto corruptum uenerabili sepolturae tradiderunt. Finis.

MSS

1. Florence, AS, MS Conv. soppr. 260, 243, fos. 148r–163v. Not seen.

2. Florence, BN, MS Conv. soppr. B 8 1895. Citation from A. degl'Innocenti, "L'agiografia su Giovanni Gualberto fino al secolo XV," in G. Monzio Compagnoni, *I Vallombrosani nella societa italiana dei secoli XI e XII. Vallombrosa, 3–4 settembre 1993* (Vallombrosa: Edizioni Vallombrosa, 1995), 155 n. 85, without foliation. Not seen.

Editions
None.

---

405. T. Sala, *Dizionario storico biografico di scrittori, letterati ed artisti dell'ordine di Vallombrosa* (Florence: Sordomuti, 1929), 2:299–300.

VEGIO, Maffeo, O.E.S.A. (1407–1458)[406]

BHL —. *De vita et officio beati Augustini liber. In vigilia beati Augustini ad vesperas* (V)[407]

Vegio's *liber . . . Augustini* contains two offices, both excerpted from the *Confessions*. Here is described the first, for the vigil, 27 September. The office, with the usual complement of versicles and responses, is preceded by two hymns and a prayer and followed by another hymn. The earliest dated manuscript (see below) includes a notice of place, "Fabrianum." Vegio went with Eugenius IV to Fabriano in 1450 to escape the plague: see Luigi Raffaele, *Maffeo Vegio* (Bologna, 1909), 43–44.

    inc. (*lectio* 1): Imbecilla ego tunc aetate discebam libros eloquentiae in qua eminere cupiebam

    des. (*lectio* 9): prima doctrina est uidere bonum; secunda autem audire.[408]

MSS
    1. Vatican City, BAV, MS Ottob. Lat. 1253, fols. 53–56v. Dated 1453. Poncelet 1910, 436. Source text.

Editions
None known to me.

BHL —. *De vita et officio beati Augustini. In conversione beati Augustini* (V)

The second part of the *liber Augustini* celebrates the conversion (5 May). Vegio instructs that "omnia dicuntur ut supra in natali praeter lectiones et responsoria ut infra."

    inc. (*lectio* 1): Miserum ergo me quis liberabit

    des. (*lectio* 9): mater defuncta est.

MSS
    1. Vatican City, BAV, MS Ottob. Lat. 1253, fols. 56v–61v. Dated 1453. Poncelet 1910, 436. Source text.

---

406. Kristeller, "Contribution," 157. For Vegio's extremely popular metric Latin account of Anthony Hermit in the Thebaide (*BHL* 600) see the critical edition by M. Putnam and J. Hankins in Vegio, *Short Epics* (Cambridge: Harvard University, 2004). For his metric *Laudatio s. Monicae* (*BHL* 6003d), dedicated to Eugene IV and possibly the source of the miracles collected in Paolo Olmi's *Apologia* (q.v.), see Kristeller, *Iter* 2:562a.

    407. On Augustine, see n. 33 above.

    408. See Luigi Raffaele, *Maffeo Vegio* (Bologna, 1909), 86. The place of the seventh *lectio* is taken by an excerpt from a homily by Johannes Chrysostom (BAV, MS Ottob. Lat. 1253, fol. 56).

Editions
None known to me.

BHL 1189. *De vita et obitu atque officio beati Bernardini liber* (d. 1444)[409]

The narrative in four books was written by 1453. The first part of book 1 has been made into two offices. The first is to be said at vespers and includes versicles and responses, a hymn for vespers, a prayer, and a hymn for matins before the first *lectio* and a hymn following the ninth *lectio* (cf. Celestine V, below). The second office, for the vigil one week later, is in six readings; it includes no versicles or responses. Not included in figure 1.1.

inc. (*liber* 1 et *lectio* 1): Bernardinus ex senis clarissima etruriae ciuitate

des. (*lectio* 9): quantam assecutus est gratiam adiuuerunt.

inc. (*lectio* 1 per ebdomadam): Iam vero earum exemplo

des. (*lectio* 6 per ebdomadam): donec sanatus est discesserunt.

des. (*liber* 1): spiritus eum ducebat se accinxit.

inc. (*liber* 2): Et nunc maiora longe atque illustriora eius monimenta attingimus.

inc. (*liber* 3): Nec vero quamuis talis ac tantus habitus fuerit, statim tamen ac primum publice

inc. (*liber* 4): Cum exequiae pro more ei sollemnes exhibitae sunt, ad quem uidendum

des. (*liber* 4): Anno autem christi M.cccc.l atque anno quidem Iubilei : ut nihil quod ad uenerandam sanctamque laetitiam pertineret omnino deesset.

epitaphium: Quod vero restabat epitaphium . . . edidimus huiuscemodi. Hic Bernardinus aquilana conditus urbe est

MSS

1. Bamberg, Staatliche Bibl. MS Hist., 145, fols. 25–56v. XV. Kristeller, *Iter* 3:463a. Not seen.

2. Berlin, Kunstbibliothek, MS Gris. 10. XV. Kristeller, *Iter* 3:465a. Not seen.

3. Vatican City, BAV, MS Ottob. Lat. 903, fols. 20–33v. XV. Poncelet 1910, 433; Kristeller, *Iter* 2:415b. Seen.

4. Vatican City, BAV, MS Ottob. Lat. 1253; *liber* 1, fols. 141–154v (the six *lectiones* for the vigil have not been labeled by the rubricator); *liber* 2, fols. 155–164v; *liber* 2, fols. 165–172v; *liber* 4, fols. 173–181v. At 181v, there is a subscriptio: "Romae apud sanctum Petrum kl. Iunii MccccLiii. Finit." Below that, the scribe has signed his name: "B. Castaneo exscripsit." Poncelet 1910, 437; Kristeller, *Iter* 2:417a. Source text; also SLU reel 2237.

---

409. On Bernardino of Siena, see n. 49 above.

5. Vatican City, BAV, MS Vat. Lat. 2110, fols. 124–128. B. Nogara, "I codici di Maffeo Vegio nella Biblioteca Vaticana e un inno di lui in onore di Sant'Ambrogio" *ASL* s. 3 19 (1903): 7–10; Kristeller, *Iter* 2:312a. Not seen.

Editions
All are late; see BHL.

BHL—. *De vita et obitu beati Bernardini*

Text of the four books as above, but without the offices.

MSS
1. Vatican City, BAV, MS Vat. Lat. 3492, fols. 30v–84v, with the subscription "Finis. Romae apud sanctum Petrum Kl. Iunii 1454." From the library of Antonio Caraffa. Poncelet, 1910, 99; Kristeller, *Iter* 2:320a–b. Seen; also SLU reel 489.

Editions
None known to me.

BHL— (cf. *BHL* 6752 below). *De vita et obitu Caelestini Quinti liber* (XIII)[410]

Dedicatory letter to *Eugene IV*, who may have commissioned the work. Although Vegio does not title this work an office, the first book of the narrative is divided into nine *lectiones* (a tenth reading, of significantly greater length than the others, may indicate that the *lectio* was to be continued in refectory). The subsequent books are not divided into readings. Vegio suggests that the pope may recognize some of his own difficulties in Celestine's grand tragedy ("gradisonisque tragoediarum coturnis").

inc. epist.: Laudo animum tuum, beatissime pater, qui Caelestini quinti uitam inepte hactenus discerptam magisquam descriptam aptius ornatiusque explicari cupis.

des. epist.: consolari possis

inc. (*liber* 1 et *lectio* 1): Caelestinus quintus qui et petrus

inc. (*liber* 2): Hactenus quae de se ipsemet scripta reliquit exposuimus, caetera nunc

inc. (*liber* 3): Haec dum ita aguntur decesserat interea Nicolaus quartus

des. (*liber* 3): nunc fruitur pacis et gloriae sempiternae.

---

410. On Celestine, see n. 283 above.

MSS
1. Rome, Bibl. Vallicelliana, MS J 36, fols. 150–174. XVI–XVII. Poncelet 1909, 459; Kristeller, *Iter* 2:129b. Not seen.

2. BAV, MS Ottob. lat. 1253, fols. 120–141, with a subscription, "Romae apud sanctum Petrum IIII non. Maii Mccccxlv. FINIT" at 141. The dedicatory letter to Eugene IV is at fol. 119v. Poncelet 1910, 437; Kristeller, *Iter* 2:417a. Source text.

3. Vatican City, BAV, MS Vat. Lat. 12110. XVI. Kristeller, *Iter* 2:348a, 6:326a. Seen.

Editions
All late; see *BHL.*

BHL 6752. *Celestini Quinti vita*

Dedicatory letter to Eugene IV (see above). Text in three books, but this version of the life has not been divided into offices. Thus, although the incipit and desinit match the preceding work, the internal organization differs.

inc.: Celestinus quintus qui et Petrus primo a parentibus

des.: nunc fruitur pacis et gloriae sempiternae. Finis.

MSS
1. Vatican City, BAV, MS Barb. Lat. 2278 (xxxii 69). Letter to Eugene at fol. 1. Not divided into books. Scribe's subscription at fol. 24. Poncelet 1910, 474; Kristeller, *Iter* 2:450b. Seen; also SLU reel 3991.

2. Vatican City, BAV, MS Barb. Lat. 2601, fols. 149–177v. XVII. Poncelet 1910, 484. Not seen.

3. Vatican City, BAV, MS Ross. Lat. 1128, fols. 83r–v. Kristeller, *Iter* 2:468a. The miscellaneous codex includes only a fragment of Vegio's *vita Celestini*: the letter to Eugene is followed by twenty-six lines of text. Seen.

4. Vatican City, BAV, MS Vat. Lat. 3492, fols. 1 (letter to Eugene IV)–30. Divided into three books, but without the offices. With the subscription at the end: "Romae apud sanctum Petrum quarto Nonas Maii M.cccxlv. Finit." From the library of Antonio Caraffa, dated by Kristeller, *Iter* 2:320a–b, to XVI. Seen; also SLU reel 489.

5. Vatican City, BAV, MS Vat lat 12110 (stamped foliation lower right), fols. 70 (title), 714–v (letter to Eugene IV), 72–99. With dated subscription. Kristeller, *Iter* 2:348a. Seen; also SLU reel 1030.

6. Vatican City, BAV, MS Vat. lat. 12110 (stamped foliation lower right), fol. 104 (letter to Eugene IV), 104–120v, a second copy. Seen; also SLU reel 1030.

BHL 6003b. *De vita et obitu beatae Monicae ex verbis sancti Augustini liber* (IV)[411]

No preface; no dedication. Vegio's interest in the translation of Monica to Rome in 1430 is well known. In 1449 he had a reliquary made for the head; it is one of the treasures of Sant'Agostino in Rome.[412] This narrative in three books (with further subdivision into chapters) is taken from the *Confessions* and from letters attributed to Augustine. It appears to be the origin of the two offices included in the *De vita et officio beatae Monicae liber* described further below.

inc. (*liber* 1): Non praeteribo quicquid mihi anima parturit

inc. (*liber* 2): Iam uenerat ad me mater pietate fortis

inc. (*liber* 3): Iam liber erat animus meus a curis

des. (*liber* 3): deus exaudiret in suis petitionibus.

MSS

1. Vatican City, BAV MS Ottob. lat. 1253, fols. 86–119, with a subscription, "Romae apud sanctum Petrum" at 119. XV. Poncelet 1910, 437; Kristeller, *Iter* 2:417a. Seen.

2. Vatican City, BAV MS Vat. lat. 5860, fols. 24–52, with a subscription and what appears to be the scribe's mark below. XV. Poncelet 1910, 155; Kristeller, Iter 2:336a. Seen; also SLU reel 9131.

Editions

None known to me.

BHL —. *De vita et officio beatae Monicae liber. In vigilia Beatae Monicae ad vesperum* (IV)

No preface; no dedication. The two offices contained in this *liber*, composed between 1453 and 1458, are taken largely from Augustine's *Confessions*. This one for the vigil is preceded by two hymns and four prayers and followed by a third hymn.

inc. lectio 1: Ubi eram et quam longe exulabam

des. lectio 9: caelis uero maiorem illustrioremque reddidit.

MSS

1. Vatican City, BAV, MS Ottob. Lat. 1253, fols. 63v–70. 1453. Poncelet 1910, 437; Kristeller, *Iter* 2:417a. The fourth *lectio* is not labeled. The sixth *lectio* is followed by a homily on Luke. Seen.

---

411. On Monica, see n. 33 above.

412. See Meredith J. Gill, "'Remember Me at the Altar of the Lord': Saint Monica's Gift to Rome," in J. C. Schnaubelt and F. Van Fleteren, eds., *Augustine in Iconography: History and Legend* (New York: Lang, 1999), 554 and n. 39.

2. Vatican City, BAV, MS Vat. Lat. 5860, fol. 13 (*lectio* 1)–18v. The homily (16r–v) is here attributed explicitly to Maffeo Vegio. XV. Poncelet 1910, 155; Kristeller, *Iter* 2:336a. Seen.

Editions
I know of no complete edition.

BHL 6004c. *De vita et officio beati Monicae liber. In translatione* (V)

No preface; no dedication. Here, as in the paired offices for Augustine, Vegio instructs that "caetera dicuntur ut supra," that is, the *lectiones* are the only material that is to change. Readings seven, eight, and nine are not taken from the *Confessions* but are a narrative of the translations, first from Ostia under Martin V and then within Rome under Nicholas V and Callixtus III.

   inc.. (*lectio* 1): Accipe confessiones meas et gratiarum actiones
   des. (*lectio* 9): tamque sanctae foeminae honor exhiberetur.
   subscriptio: Qui uero haec legis . . . et fabricandi operis illius auctor fuit. Romae apud sanctum Petrum. Finit.

MSS
   1. Vatican City, BAV, MS Ottob. lat. 1253, fols. 71–76v, with a subscription at 76v. XV. Poncelet 1910, 436; Kristeller, *Iter* 2:417a. Seen.
   2. Vatican City, BAV, MS Vat. lat. 5860, fols. 19–23v. At 23v are four marginal notes identifying Cardinal Estouteville and Maffeo Vegio as patrons of the cult of Monica at Rome. XV. Poncelet 1910, 155; Kristeller, *Iter* 2:336a. Seen; also SLU reel 9131.

Editions
I know of no complete edition.

BHL —. *De vita et obitu atque officio beati Nicolai Tollentinatis liber . . . In vigilia . . . ad vesperas, O.E.S.A.* (XIII, c.d. 1446)[413]

No preface; no dedication. This *liber* opens with an office for the vigil, taken, as Vegio notes in the label for *lectio* 1, from the "historia sancti Nicolai." Written in Rome between 1454 and 1458.[414]
   inc. (*lectio* 1): Nicolaus ex piceno ortus fuit
   des. (*lectio* 9): etiam oculorum priuatus erat.

---

413. On Nicolaus Tolentinas, see D. Gentili in *BS* 9 (1967): 953–966; N. Raponi in *GLS* 1489a–1493b.
414. Raffaele, *Maffeo Vegio*, 84.

MSS

1. Vatican City, BAV, Ottob. Lat. 1253, fols. 77–82v. 1453. Poncelet 1910, 436; Kristeller, *Iter* 2:417a. Source text.

Editions
I know of no complete edition.

BHL —. *De vita et obitu atque officio beati Nicolai Tollentinatis liber . . . lectiones per ebdomadam* (XIII)

Vegio offers no instructions for the versicles and responses in this instance. All the readings are about miracles.

inc. (lectio 1): Sed et memorabilis est liberatio illius mulieris quae propter nimius fletum

des. (lectio 6): magnus et potens et admirabilis per omnia saecula saeculorum.

MSS

1. Vatican City, Ottob. Lat. 1253, fols. 83v–86v, with subscription at 86v. XV. Poncelet 1910, 436; Kristeller, *Iter* 2:417a. Source text.

Editions
I know of no complete edition.

VESPUCCI, Giorgio Antonio, cathedral canon, then O.P. (ca. 1434–1514)[415]

COLLECTION. Usuard, *Martylogium* [sic].

The colophon names Vespucci as emender and corrector of this edition, which was published in Florence by Francesco Bonaccorsi with the colophon date November 6, 1486 (*IGI* 6252; Goff U79; HCR 16110; BMC 6:670; ISTC iu00079000). D. Moreni, *Continuazione delle memorie dell'Ambrosiana imperial basilica di S. Lorenzo in Firenze*, vol. 2 (Florence: Daddi, 1817), 448, describes the work as Usuard "accomodato all'uso della Chiesa Fiorentina colla enumerazione dei nostri santi" and

---

415. Arnaldo Della Torre, *Storia dell'Accademia Platonica* (Florence: Carnesecchi, 1902), 772–774. Among his students were Piero Soderini, Lorenzo di Pier Francesco de'Medici, and apparently the nephew of Johannes Reuchlin. On his library, see F. Gallori, "Un inventario inedito dei libri di Giorgio Antonio Vespucci," *Medioevo e Rinascimento*, n.s., 6 (1995): 215–231; along with F. Gallori and S. Nencioni, "I libri greci e latini dello scrittoio e della biblioteca di Giorgio Antonio Vespucci," *MD* 28 (1997): 155–359. Karl Schlebusch is preparing a biography; see *MD* 28 (1997): 152–154.

reports Lami's opinion that "Vespucci ha fitti que'Santi, che voleva, e come voleva, interpolando e guastando tutto Usuardo."

VOLPE, Niccolò (ca. 1410?–1460?)[416]

BHL 6642c. *Vita sancti Petronii episcopi et confessoris* (V)[417]

The account, composed in 1442 for the Lateran Canons of San Giovanni in Monte in Bologna, is attributed to Volpe on the basis of his statement in BHL 6643d (following entry): "eo libello quem de uita beatissimi Petronii non penitus oratorio, non ecclesiastico sed medio quodam stilo conscribsimus."

inc. prol.: Petronius dicitur a Petro qui interpretatur agnoscens et omnia quasi agnoscens

des. prol.: vel Petronius dictus a petra et tenens : quasi petra tenens in Christum cui inseparabiliter adhaesit.

inc.: Beatissimus Petronius natione Grecus ex patre Petrunio imperialis praetorii praefecto, urbis Bononiae Ytaliae episcopus

des.: Sepultusque est in basilica sancti Stephani quam ipse a fundamentis construxit debito honore ac summa diligentia. Cuius festa celebrantur quarto nonas octubris. Complete est a. 1442.

MSS

1. Bologna, BU, MS 1473 bis, fols. 84v–86v. *SIFC* 16 (1908): 364, item 42; A. Teste-Rasponi, "Note marginale al *Liber pontificalis*," *Atti e memorie delle Reale diputazione di Storia patria per le provincie di Romagna* ser. 4, no. 2 (1912): 232–234, item 42. Source text.

Editions
None.

BHL 6643d. *Narratio seu descriptio eiusdem [Petronii] sancte reliquie* (V)

In the manuscript belonging to the Lateran Canons of San Giovanni in Monte in Bologna, Volpe's account follows a description of the translation of Petronius's relics by the rector of San Leonardo, Benedict of Bologna;

---

416. Chines, *La parola degli antichi,* 89 n. 76 and 90–94. L. Quaquarelli, "Umanesimo e letteratura dei classici alla scuola di Niccolò Volpe," *Schede umanistiche* n.s. 9 (1999): 97–120; Davide Canfora, "L'elegia di Niccolò Volpe ad Albert Enoch Zancari," *Rinascimento* 2, no. 39 (1999): 129–155.

417. G. D. Gordini in *BS* 10 (1968): 521–530; P. Golinelli in *GLS* 1599a–1600a.

the translation was conducted under the auspices of Niccolò Albergati, cardinal bishop of Bologna.

inc.: Si maiores res populi romani terra marique gestas accuratissime descripserunt

des.: hominesque ad maiorem deuotionem et peccatorum contritionem inflammarent. Solent enim sanctorum patrum reliquie et integra uita religiosorum gloriam sempiternam ecclesiis afferre. Deo gratias.

MSS

1. Bologna, BU, MS 1473 bis, fols. 87–90. See *SIFC* 16 (1908): 364, item 43; Teste-Rasponi 1912, 232–234, item 43. Seen (microfilm).

Editions

1. A. Teste-Rasponi 1912, 232–234, item 43. Source text.

ZACCHIA, Laudivio, (ca. 1435–after 1478)[418]

BHL 3877. *Vita beati Hieronymi* (IV)

Dedicatory preface to *Francinus Beltrandus.*
  inc. proem.: Iam tuo sepe hortatu, Francine, Hieronimi uitam
  des. proem.: sed re quoque ipsa imitaris.
  inc.: Hieronymo pater fuit Eusebius qui nobili genere natus
  des.: ut plura fortasse ac meliora deinceps afferamus.

MSS

1. Bamberg, Staatliche Bibliothek, MS Patr. 90, fols. 100v–111. XV. Kristeller, *Iter* 3:461. Not seen.

2. Florence, BN, Fondo Princ. II, I, 201, fols. 100–110. Mazzatinti, vol. 8 (1898), 64. Seen.

3. Florence, BN, Fondo princ. II, VIII, 129, fols. 190–199. XV. Mazzatinti, vol. 11 (1902/1962), 247–248. Seen.

4. Heidelberg, Universitätsbibliothek, MS Salem 9, 71, last item. XV. Kristeller, *Iter* 3:574b. Not seen.

5. Melk, Stiftsbibliothek, MS 824 (40) (B, 4). XV. Kristeller, *Iter* 3:29a. Not seen.

6. Melk, Stiftsbibliothek, MS 1398 (650) (L 80), first item. XV. Kristeller, *Iter* 3:31b. Not seen.

---

418. See Eugene F. Rice Jr., *Saint Jerome in the Renaissance* (Baltimore: Johns Hopkins University Press, 1985), 102–104.

7. Oxford, Bodleian, MS Canon. Pat. Lat. 223, fols. 272–282v. Not seen.

Editions

1. *Vita beati Hieronymi.* Naples: [Sixtus Riessinger], June 14, 1473. Goff L84. HR 9944; ISTC il00084000.

2. *Laudivius Eques Hyerosolimitanus ad Franciscanum Beltrandum bachinonesem de vita beati Hieronimi.* [Rome: Johannes Gensberg, about 1474]. H 9943; *BMC* 4:50; Goff L85; *IGI* 5700; *IERS* 243; ISTC il00085000.

3. *Vita beati Hieronymi.* Rome: [Ulrich Han], November 22, 1475. H 9945; *IGI* 5701; *IERS* 366; ISTC il00085500.

4. *Vita beati Hieronymi.* [In Hungaria: typogr. Confessionalis. (H 1180), ca. 1478–1479]. G. Sajo and E. Soltèsz, *Catalogus incunabulum quae in bibliothecis publicis Hungariae asservantur* (Budapest, 1970), no. 2041; see also Elizabeth Soltèsz, facsimile reprint (Budapest 1975) with an introduction.

5. *Vita beati Hieronymi.* Rome, [Johannes Besicken], July 11, 1495. HC 9946*; *BMC* 4:140; Goff L86; *IGI* 5702; *IERS* 1442; ISTC il00086000.

ZENO, Jacopo (ca. 1417–1481)[419]

BHL 6096. *De vita et moribus Nicolai (Albergati)* (d. 1433)[420]

Dedicatory preface to Pietro Barbo (who became Paul II in 1464). Albergati was beatified in 1744. Not counted toward figure 1.1 or tables.

inc. proem.: Quantum uim uel uirtus vel opinio fidesque uirtutis apud potissimum bene institutum animum

des. proem.: et incessabili deprecatione deposco. Vale felix.

inc.: Inter reliquas Bononiae urbis familias prestans satis et clara

des.: inde ut recte iudicandum est superis gloriosa felicitate beata.

MSS

1. Vatican City, BAV, MS Vat. Lat. 3703, fols. 1–36. XV. Presentation copy. Kristeller, *Iter* 2:322a and 583a. Source text.

2. Paris, BN, MS Dupuy 662, misc. XV–XVII. Kristeller, *Iter* 3:320b. Not seen.

---

419. Zeno 2:126–183.

420. C. D. Fonseca in *BS* 1 (1961): 662–668; S. Spanò in *GLS* 1475a–1476b. See also the funeral oration by Poggio Bracciolini, *BHL* 6097.

Editions
    All editions are late; see *BHL*.

ZORZI, Francesco, O.F.M. (1460–1540)[421]

Lost. [draft life of Chiara Bugni, O.F.M. tert.] (d. 1514)[422]

Zorzi, a Cabbalist theologian, was Chiara's spiritual director. He drafted
a Latin *vita*, highly attentive to miracle and prophecy. A vernacular translation by the Florentine friar Andrea Pilolini, completed in the late sixteenth century, is extant and appears to be faithful to Zorzi's draft.[423]

    421. Kristeller, "Contribution," 140, s.v. "Georgius."
    422. On Chiara, see I. Daniele, in *BS* 3 (1964): 590–591.
    423. See Gabriella Zarri, "Living Saints: A Typology of Female Sanctity in the Early Six-
teenth Century," in Bornstein and Rusconi, *Women and Religion*, 265 and n. 28, with further bibliography.

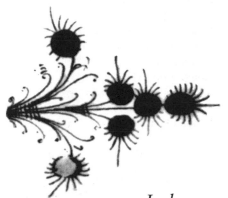

Index:
Manuscripts Consulted

Page numbers in italics refer to the hand list.

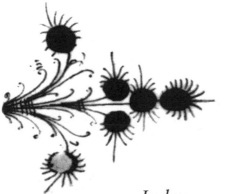

Index:
People and Places

Italicized page numbers refer to the hand list. Italicized Latin names indicate primary entries for saints and beati, according to the usage of the BHL. Other personal names are given in Latin or vernaculars according to accepted usage or that of Kristeller's Iter Italicum.